NEWCOMER'S®

HANDBOOK

FOR MOVING TO AND LIVING IN

PORTLAND

Including Vancouver, Gresham, Hillsboro,
Beaverton, Tigard, and Wilsonville

BRYAN GEON

3rd Edition

503-968-6777
www.firstbooks.com

3rd Edition

Newcomer's Handbook® and First Books® are registered trademarks of First Books.

Author: Bryan Geon
Editor: Linda Franklin
Cover design and layout: Emily Coats
Cover images: Erin Johnson Design, Jillian Gregg, and Nicholas Winchester, Masha Shubin
Cover: Portland City Scape © 2010 4x6. Illustration from iStockPhoto.com
Interior design: Erin Johnson Design and Masha Shubin
Interior layout and composition: Emily Coats
Interior photos by Bryan Geon
Maps provided by Jim Miller/fennana design
TriMet Rail System map courtesy of TriMet

Paperback
ISBN-13: 978-1-937090-56-2   ISBN-10: 1-937090-56-6

Kindle eBook
ISBN-13: 978-1-937090-57-9   ISBN-10: 1-937090-57-4

ePub eBook
ISBN-13: 978-1-937090-58-6   ISBN-10: 1-937090-58-2

Published by First Books®, 503-968-6777, www.firstbooks.com.

What readers are saying about Newcomer's Handbooks:

I recently got a copy of your Newcomer's Handbook for Chicago, and wanted to let you know how invaluable it was for my move. I must have consulted it a dozen times a day preparing for my move. It helped me find my way around town, find a place to live, and so many other things. Thanks.

– Mike L.
Chicago, Illinois

Excellent reading (Newcomer's Handbook for San Francisco and the Bay Area) ... balanced and trustworthy. One of the very best guides if you are considering moving/relocation. Way above the usual tourist crap.

– Gunnar E.
Stockholm, Sweden

I was very impressed with the latest edition of the Newcomer's Handbook for Los Angeles. It is well organized, concise and up to date. I would recommend this book to anyone considering a move to Los Angeles.

– Jannette L.
Attorney Recruiting Administrator for a large Los Angeles law firm

An exceptional book for relocators. However, even non-relocators will find it very enjoyable. It features great coverage of the city of Portland, including the very desirable West Hills and Bridlemile sections, as well as its incorporated suburbs, yet it also covers unincorporated areas...as well as the often-overlooked towns of Wilsonville and Happy Valley, and Vancouver, Washington and its suburbs. Many great ideas for education, dining, house-hunting, shopping, health/fitness, and recreation are included in this book. DON'T PASS THIS BOOK UP UNDER ANY CIRCUMSTANCES!!!!!!!!!!

– "The Footpath Cowboy"
(on amazon.com)

In looking to move to the Boston area, a potential employer in that area gave me a copy of the Newcomer's Handbook for Boston. It's a great book that's very comprehensive, outlining good and bad points about each neighborhood in the Boston area. Very helpful in helping me decide where to move.

– no name given (online submit form)

We were considering moving to Portland, Oregon and recently took a scouting mission there to see whether that was an idea worth pursuing. This book proved invaluable and I would highly recommend it to anyone considering the same thing. Its neighborhood descriptions were spot on and helped us focus our search.

– L. Gillespie
New York, New York (on amazon.com)

TABLE OF CONTENTS

CONTENTS

215 **Finding a Place to Live**
Getting to know the neighborhood, crime/safety, renting vs. buying, finding a place, checking it out/staking a claim, tenant/landlord relations, renter's insurance; buying, financial matters, house hunting, purchase agreements/ closing, insurance, contractors; building your own home

235 **Moving and Storage**
Truck rental, movers, packing, loading/unloading, storage, consumer complaints, tax deductions, children, pets, resources

247 **Money Matters**
Bank accounts/services, consumer protection, taxes, starting a business

257 **Getting Settled**
Utilities, trash/recycling, automobiles, bicycles, voter registration, public libraries, passports, print and broadcast media

CONTENTS

INTRODUCTION

WELCOME TO PORTLAND, ONE OF THE MOST LIVABLE URBAN AREAS in America! Call it Stumptown, Rose City, Rip City, Beervana, Bridgetown, Puddletown, Portlandia, or PDX, it's your town now. (Just don't call it Portland, or-eh-GONE. The state name is pronounced OR-uh-gun. Practice before you arrive.) Portland is located at the northern end of the fertile Willamette Valley, just over an hour east of the coast—it's called the coast here, not the shore or the beach—and an equal distance west of the crest of the Cascade Mountains. The high desert is a two-hour drive to the east, and world-class wineries are 45 minutes to the southwest. Abundant recreational opportunities make the city a favorite of outdoor enthusiasts, and from the city's West Hills, and even from some downtown office buildings, it's possible to see the Columbia River Gorge and five snowcapped volcanoes: Mounts Hood, St. Helens, Adams, Rainier, and Jefferson. Top that, Topeka!

Of course, Portland's appeal transcends its spectacular setting. The city is known for its vibrant neighborhoods, activist urban planning, environmental awareness, progressive politics, coffeehouse and brewpub culture, and, yes, for its rain. So what's it really like here? Well, though Portland enjoys more than its fair share of pleasant, well-preserved urban neighborhoods, connected to one another by bike lanes and transit, and benefits from a state law limiting the extent of urban sprawl, it is also afflicted with strip malls, traffic congestion, ill-conceived development, and other assorted maladies of the modern American metropolis. A key difference is that in Portland you can arrange your life so that you don't *have* to deal with those problems. If you want to live in a close-in neighborhood, within walking distance of cafés and food markets, and ride your bike to work every day, you can. (You won't necessarily be able to afford to buy a house in such a neighborhood, however.) If you prefer to live in a suburban community and move around by car, you can do that, too.

A word on politics: it is true that Portlanders on average are more liberal than the citizens of the typical American burg—when *Money* magazine rated Portland the country's best place to live in 2000, it warned conservatives to stay away, and the views of most residents have not lurched to the right since then—but it is not the solidly left-wing monolith it is often portrayed to be. The city and its surrounding region boast a surprising diversity of political opinion, ranging from a vocal community of socially conservative evangelicals to proud anarchists, and from a strong libertarian contingent to a small community of Trotskyites. (The latter get nervous around ice picks.) In general, suburban communities tend to be more conservative than city neighborhoods, and inner Southeast Portland is more liberal than other parts of the city, but as a whole the region is probably no more liberal (or conservative) than any other large coastal metropolitan area.

When it comes to craft beer and coffee, most Portlanders sensibly put ideology aside. There are 74 breweries in the Portland metro area. Of these, 54 operate within city limits, giving Portland reportedly more breweries than any other city in the world. Oregonians spend more on craft beer than on Anheuser-Busch and MillerCoors beers combined. And Portland's coffee scene is every bit the equal of Seattle's, with local roasters like Stumptown Coffee Roasters (www.stumptowncoffee.com) winning awards for both quality and sustainable business practices. Don't miss the burgeoning tea scene, either, based on well-established local tea manufacturers as well as an increasing number of unique tea houses. Many Portlanders consider coffee (or tea) essential for coping with the rain.

Ah, the rain. While it's true that Portland has its share of rainy days, much of the city's precipitation falls in the form of a fine mist or drizzle. Often a day that starts out cloudy becomes bright and sunny by afternoon (or vice versa). Many locals will tell you that the rain is easier to cope with than the seemingly interminable parade of cloudy days we endure in late autumn and winter. Spring and fall have their share of bright days, however, and summers are reliably warm and sunny.

Whatever you think about the weather, it certainly doesn't seem to be deterring new residents. Lured by Portland's reputation, by job opportunities in certain industries, and even by the results of online relocation quiz sites like www.findyourspot.com and Find Your Own Best Place (www.bestplaces.net/fybp/), it seems like everyone knows someone who's moving to Portland (or thinking about it). Portland's regional government, Metro, estimates that at least 725,000 newcomers, and possibly many more, will arrive in the area by 2035.

Despite (and to some extent because of) the population influx, not everything is rosy in the Rose City. The region's economy never fully recovered from a sharp recession in the early 2000s, and the Great Recession hit Oregon early and hard. The Portland metro area has subsequently seen strong job growth, but the state as a whole (and Clark County in southwest Washington) still has an unemployment rate above the national average. At the same time, Portland's median income is comparatively low, at least compared to other large coastal cities.

Perhaps low incomes wouldn't be a problem if you could still buy a home for $100,000, but those days are gone. Home prices in many areas have rebounded and median prices now match or exceed prices at the peak of the pre-crash housing bubble (which in Portland was roughly summer 2007). And good luck finding a stand-alone house in a desirable close-in neighborhood for anything close to the median price. The pre-2007 boom in housing prices produced a corresponding explosion in residential construction, with new infill development and condo towers changing the faces of many neighborhoods; with the recovery of the housing market, this process seems to have restarted and may even be accelerating.

The faces of Oregon's residents are changing as well. Portland has had a vibrant African-American community since the First World War, and substantial Chinese and Japanese communities have been present since the nineteenth century, but the city is still, by some measures, the whitest major city in the country. Nonetheless, the metropolitan area is becoming more ethnically and racially diverse. The Hispanic population is fast-growing, and the area has also experienced substantial immigration from East and South Asia (especially Southeast Asia), Eastern Europe, and East and West Africa. Moreover, much of the growth in the nonwhite population has taken place in the suburbs, so the demographics of the entire region are changing. Still, while we are definitely becoming more diverse, the region has a long way to go before it mirrors the population mix in the United States as a whole.

LOCAL QUIRKS

You'll see plenty of bumper stickers proclaiming a desire to "Keep Portland Weird!" (Never mind that this exhortation was lifted from a similar campaign in Austin, Texas.) Indeed, quirkiness (along with environmentalism) is the closest thing the city has to an official religion. The following are a few local quirks you should know about in advance:

- You can't pump your own gas in Oregon. It's against the law. (The only other state with this restriction is New Jersey.)
- There's a nickel deposit on soft drink, beer, and water cans and bottles. Oregon was the first state in the country to pass a bottle bill.
- Despite the rainy winter climate, most Portlanders don't carry umbrellas, and some don't even own one.
- Voters in both Oregon and Washington have approved initiatives legalizing recreational marijuana use. Oregon is in the process of setting up a regulatory regime for sale and distribution, which should be finalized in 2016 (although possession of small quantities for personal use is legal as of mid-2015). Washington has already set up its system, and a number of stores are operating across the Columbia River. Local governments can regulate or choose to completely prohibit marijuana sales, and of course pot possession or sale (or transport

across state lines, for Oregonians who just can't wait) is still technically illegal under federal law.

- The Oregon Supreme Court has interpreted the Oregon Constitution to protect nude dancing as expressive speech. As a result, Portland supposedly has more strip clubs per capita than any other city in the country. There is also an annual naked bike ride, attracting thousands of participants.
- Many intersections in Eastside residential neighborhoods lack stop signs, resulting in trepidation for motorists, bicyclists, and pedestrians alike.

LOCAL LINGO

Portland lacks a distinctive local dialect, and most Oregonians do not have a discernible regional accent (unless they've brought one from somewhere else). Most slang is age-based, rather than regional—who knows what teenagers are talking about half the time?—but some localisms can throw off the newcomer. Here's a handy guide to a few potentially confusing expressions and pronunciations:

Back East: Anywhere east of Denver.

Ban Roll-On Building: The 1000 Broadway office tower downtown, so called because of its distinctive white dome (most noticeable from a distance).

Big Pink: The US Bancorp Tower at Southwest Oak Street and Fifth Avenue downtown; this decidedly pinkish 42-story skyscraper is the second tallest building in Oregon.

Car Prowl: Theft from an automobile.

Civic Stadium: The old name for the stadium in Goose Hollow, now called Providence Park, where the Timbers soccer team plays; formerly, it was the home of the Portland Beavers minor-league baseball team, and was known over the years as Civic Stadium, PGE Park, and Jeld-Wen Field.

Civil War: The annual football game between in-state rivals University of Oregon (the Ducks) and Oregon State University (the Beavers).

Couch Street: It's pronounced "cooch," not like a sofa.

CRC: The Columbia River Crossing project, a multi-billion dollar plan to replace the current Interstate 5 bridge over the Columbia River. After hundreds of millions were spent on planning, the project was abandoned for lack of funding.

Doug Fir: The Douglas fir (*Pseudotsuga menziesii*), Oregon's state tree. Also the name of a trendy bar and live music venue on East Burnside.

Freddy's: The Fred Meyer one-stop-shopping chain, now owned by Ohio-based Kroger. Fred Meyer was an actual person, and long-time residents still refer to the market as "Freddy's."

Front Avenue: The old name for Naito Parkway, which runs along the Willamette River downtown.

Glisan Street: Almost universally pronounced "GLEE-son," although a few purists insist that it should be pronounced "glisten."

The Gorge: The Columbia River Gorge east of the city, where the Columbia cuts through the Cascade Mountains.

Gorge Winds: The strong east winds that sometimes blow through the Gorge and into the metropolitan area.

The Kicker: The somewhat controversial Oregon tax refund that is distributed during biennial budget cycles in which actual state revenues exceed projected revenues.

Macadam: The name for Highway 43 between downtown Portland and Lake Oswego. Pronounced "mac-AD-um."

MAX: Metropolitan Area Express, Portland's light rail system.

McLoughlin: The name of a major thoroughfare in Southeast Portland and the adjacent suburbs. Pronounced "McLofflin."

NoPo: Hipster name for North Portland

The Pearl: The Pearl District, a hot neighborhood of high-end condos, restaurants, and boutiques, a few blocks northwest of downtown Portland.

Pill Hill: Marquam Hill, just south of downtown Portland, home to Oregon Health & Science University and its associated hospitals and clinics, along with the Portland Veterans Administration Hospital.

***Portlandia*:** Popular IFC sketch-comedy show starring Fred Armisen and Carrie Brownstein that pokes fun at the city's quirks and foibles; some people refer to it, only half-jokingly, as a documentary.

Put a Bird On It!: Catchphrase from a *Portlandia* sketch in which a pair of designers "improved" various products by slapping an image of a bird onto them; used to connote a shallow, facile approach to addressing a perceived flaw.

Right 2 Dream Too: Homeless advocacy organization that sponsors a semi-permanent homeless camp at the corner of West Burnside and Northwest Fourth Avenue; the organization has been looking for a new, permanent location.

Rip City: Term coined in 1970 by Trail Blazers announcer Bill Schonely, apparently completely spontaneously, to describe an impressive jump shot; has since come to be used as a slogan for the team and as a nickname for Portland.

Rose Garden: In addition to the actual garden of rose bushes in Washington Park, this is what most people call the arena where the Trail Blazers play, now officially known as Moda Center.

Spendy: Expensive.

Webfoot: A native or thoroughly naturalized Oregonian.

Willamette: The river that flows through the city, and everything named after it, should be pronounced "will-AM-it," *not* "will-um-ETTE." If you forget, locals will remind you that it rhymes with "dammit."

You might also glance through the **Transportation** chapter to get a feel for the nicknames of major highways.

LOCAL BLOGS

It's easy to get the official line on Portland, but what do people who live here really think? One way to find out: check out some local blogs. Keep in mind that some bloggers are complete nutcases, and blog commenters can be even worse, so, as always, take what you read on the web with a grain of salt. More importantly, don't take the raving and kvetching as representative of Portlanders in general. **IgnOregon** (www.ignoregon.com), an aggregator of Oregon blogs, is a good place to start. While it's not a blog, the **"For Portlanders Only"** site (www.platypuscomix.net/fpo/) offers an interesting grab bag of Portland cultural history.

USEFUL APPS

A smartphone or tablet can be a very helpful tool for getting oriented, finding your new home, and settling in. Few things in the modern world are more idiosyncratic than one's choice of apps, but here are a few general categories of apps that might make your life easier when you arrive in Portland.

Map Apps: Any GPS-enabled map app will be a big help, but apps that offer turn-by-turn directions (or phones with this capability) can be invaluable in an unfamiliar environment.

Househunting Apps: If you're looking to rent, consider an app that can identify listings either in a defined geographic area or near your actual location. There are dozens of apps in this niche; *Lovely* and *PadMapper Apartment Search* are two of the most popular. If you're seeking a property to buy, try *Real Estate by Redfin*, or the *Trulia*, *Zillow*, or *Realtor.com* apps.

Traffic and Road Condition Apps: While you're getting your bearings, it's hard to predict bottlenecks and traffic jams. Local television station KGW's *Portland Traffic* app shows real-time traffic conditions across the metro area. The Oregon Department of Transportation doesn't yet offer an app, but the mobile version of its TripCheck website (m.tripcheck.com) includes traffic advisories and live traffic cam data.

Transit Apps: If you plan to use public transit, you would be well-advised to install one of the two-dozen-odd apps that use TriMet's open-source data to provide bus and train arrival times, plan routes, warn of delays, and find nearby transit stations. Every app is a bit different; to peruse the selection, visit TriMet's app center at www.trimet.org/apps. You can also use your smartphone as your ticket with mobile ticketing from the *TriMet Tickets* app.

Weather Apps: Even on rainy days (yeah, it rains here occasionally) you can find dry windows of opportunity, but you'll need to know when the next wave of showers is coming through. Even most barebones weather apps now have hourly forecasts, but an app that includes radar is a must-have to optimize your outdoor time. Several apps fit the bill, but the *Portland Weather* app (another KGW product) is a good basic app with Doppler radar, live cams, and ski conditions.

Entertainment, Shopping, and Dining Apps: The number of choices in this category is truly dazzling, and personal preference plays a large part in which apps will suit you best. *Portland Insider* and *Portland Essentials* are two popular, if fairly basic, Portland-focused apps.

Settling-In Apps: Once you start settling in, you'll want to take advantage of, for example: apps that help find hikes and bike routes; mobile banking apps; local walking tours and museum guide apps or the *Multnomah County Library* app. Here again, you'll be faced with a dizzying range of options, depending on your interests and situation.

URBAN PLANNING

Entire books have been written, bureaucracies built, and legal careers made on interpreting Oregon's arcane land use planning laws. Anything more than a brief overview is way beyond the scope of this book, but as a newcomer you should have a general understanding of the region's urban planning arrangement.

Under the leadership of Governor Tom McCall, the Oregon legislature enacted a state land use planning system in 1973. The purpose was to curb urban sprawl and protect rich farmland, forestland, rangeland, and scenic vistas from development. The law required each local government to create a comprehensive land use plan for its region. In making planning decisions, local governments are required to adhere to a set of 19 statewide goals—energy conservation, preservation of farmland, discouraging development on land subject to natural disasters, and more. The law also requires every city or metropolitan area to establish an Urban Growth Boundary (UGB), outside of which large-scale residential development (among other things) is generally prohibited. Several outlying communities in the Portland area, such as Sandy, North Plains, and Estacada, are outside the main Portland UGB, and have established UGBs of their own.

In the Portland area, the regional government, Metro, is responsible for maintaining the metropolitan area's UGB. (Its predecessor agency created the original boundary.) By law, the UGB must include enough land to meet the projected need for residential development for 20 years. Every few years, Metro expands the Portland UGB accordingly. An expansion in 2005 added a large chunk of rural land in Clackamas County (the southeastern part of the metro area) to the urban growth area. In 2007, a new law allowed the Portland region to establish urban reserves—areas that are suitable for urban development over a 50-year period—and rural reserves, which are protected from urban development for 50 years. In the subsequent years, an often acrimonious process led to the designation of various urban and rural reserves on the fringes of the UGB. The plan for Washington County's reserves (perhaps the most contentious process) was finalized in 2014. At press time, the reserve issue has not been finalized in Multnomah or Clackamas counties.

It is important to understand what the land use laws generally, and the UGB in particular, do not do. For one thing, they do not prohibit all residential use of rural land. The so-called rural exception lands, already subdivided lands outside the UGBs, are available for rural, non-farm uses. (Areas such as Stafford, the area between Wilsonville and West Linn, fall within this category.) Furthermore, they do not directly mandate dense development inside the UGB, as a drive down one of the area's many suburban strip mall–lined highways will demonstrate. The UGB may indirectly increase density, however, by artificially restricting the supply of buildable land in the metropolitan area. Local governments may also set density requirements, and generally permit or even encourage infill development, such as tall, narrow houses on small urban lots or houses built on "flag lots" that have become common (and controversial) in outer Southeast Portland and some suburban communities. Perhaps most importantly, Oregon's land use laws have no effect in Clark County, Washington, just across the Columbia River. (Washington state recently enacted its own urban growth management laws, and Clark County communities now have their own urban growth boundaries.)

In 2004, Oregon voters passed Measure 37, a sweeping and somewhat poorly drafted property-rights measure that essentially said: when a land use or zoning rule prohibits a use that might once have been permitted, under certain circumstances the government agency responsible for the rule (generally city or county governments) must pay compensation to the landowner or permit the requested use. Since the law did not provide funds for compensation, in practice Measure 37 meant the use must be allowed. More than 7,500 applications for compensation or to allow a prohibited use were submitted to local governments by the filing deadline, these claims covering three-quarters of a million acres. In the city of Portland alone, claims for compensation totaled more than $250 million. Many of the applications around the state were for massive proposed development projects (in contrast to the impression conveyed by poster-little-old-lady for Measure 37 during the election, nonagenarian Dorothy English, who just wanted to build a house for her children on the property behind her house). In 2007, voters approved Measure 49, which limited, clarified, and partially repealed Measure 37's provisions; crucially, the new law limits large subdivisions on prime farm and forestland while still allowing some small-scale rural development. In short, Oregon's land use laws are complex and evolving.

WHAT TO BRING

- **A detailed map**; although most of Portland proper is on a straightforward grid, parts of western Portland and many of the suburbs don't follow the rules. Don't plan to rely on a smartphone map app; the small screen size won't give you the big picture of how different areas relate to one another, and data coverage in the hills can be spotty.
- **Rain gear**; unless you move during the summer, there's a good chance it will be raining when you arrive. A water-resistant (often hooded) coat and rain hat are the most common forms of rain gear. Bring an umbrella if you like, but be aware

that you may be alone in using one. (See "Local Quirks" above.) No adult wears galoshes in Portland.

- **A cell phone**; a cell phone is convenient for contacting potential landlords from the road, setting up utilities, and generally staying in touch during your transition.
- **A car or bike**; public transportation is perfectly adequate in many neighborhoods, but it can be difficult to househunt or otherwise explore the area quickly without your own transport. Once you settle down, unless you're in a close-in neighborhood, you'll need a bike or car; in the suburbs and in much of the Westside, a car is almost essential. If you want to blend in, consider a Subaru or a Toyota Prius. If you don't own a car yet but plan on buying one, wait until after you move; you won't pay any sales tax in Oregon.
- **Tolerance**; no matter how narrow- or broad-minded you are (or think you are), something or someone in Portland is bound to annoy you, or to try to do so. Bring a good attitude and a smile, and you'll get along just fine.

ADDRESS LOCATOR

Since the city was founded, Portland's street layout has followed the so-called Philadelphia pattern, with a grid comprised of named east-west streets intersecting numbered avenues, which run north-south parallel to the riverfront. The grid pattern largely vanishes in the West Hills and other high-relief parts of the city, and all bets are off in the suburbs, but the basic framework remains.

The Willamette River naturally divides the city into east and west halves. Burnside Street serves as the dividing line between north and south. The city is thus quartered into **Northwest** (west of the river and north of Burnside), **Southwest** (west of the river and south of Burnside), **Northeast** (east of the river and north of Burnside), and **Southeast** (east of the river and south of Burnside). The Columbia River forms the city's (and state's) northern limit. North of downtown, the Willamette veers northwest before flowing into the Columbia; the resulting peninsula, to the west of Northeast Portland, is designated as **North Portland**. North Williams Avenue serves as the boundary between North and Northeast Portland.

The numbered avenues begin on each side of the river; the numbers increase with distance from it. Southwest 10th Avenue, for example, is roughly 11 blocks west of the Willamette (Naito Parkway runs along the west bank, and 1st Avenue is one block west), while Southeast 10th Avenue is 11 blocks east of the river (with Water Street the closest street to the river on the inner Eastside). Numbered avenues are used throughout the city, with a few exceptions. On the Eastside, Martin Luther King Jr. Boulevard (or MLK) takes the place of 4th Avenue and Grand Avenue takes the place of 5th; in a controversial move, the City Council voted in 2009 to rename 39th Avenue César E. Chávez Boulevard. On the Westside, Broadway substitutes for 7th Avenue and Park for 8th Avenue.

Named streets run from east to west. Except in the "Alphabet District" of North-west Portland, where the street names are in alphabetical order from B (Burnside) through W (Wilson), there is no special system in place for street names.

There are 100 street numbers per block (although, obviously, few if any blocks contain 100 addresses). Thus, once you learn the system, it is fairly easy to find a specific address. For example, the 4300 block of Southeast Hawthorne Boulevard would begin at Southeast 43rd Avenue and end at 44th, while the 3000 block of Northeast 33rd Avenue would begin 30 blocks north of Burnside. (By the way, even numbers are on the south and east sides of the street, odd numbers on the north and west sides.) There are two significant wrinkles to this pattern. In North Portland, east-west streets are numbered according to their distance west from Williams Avenue. In the Johns Landing and South Waterfront areas of South Portland, certain addresses, while west of the Willamette, are actually east of the downtown riverfront; these addresses are prefaced by a "0," making 0715 SW Ban-croft Street a valid address and not a typo.

Some suburbs, like Beaverton, Tigard, and Gresham, number their streets and addresses according to the Portland street grid. Others, including Vancouver, Lake Oswego, West Linn, and Hillsboro, use their own grids, usually centered on a city hall or some other local landmark. The bottom line: don't expect addresses in Portland and the 'burbs to match up.

A (VERY) BRIEF PORTLAND HISTORY

The first Native American inhabitants of the Portland region are thought to have arrived about 10,000 years ago. By the 18th century, various tribes and bands of the Chinook people occupied the land. The Chinook had a salmon-based economy, and the resource was sufficiently abundant to allow them to live settled lives in large plank houses, and to develop social classes and rules of property ownership and inheritance. Like indigenous people throughout North America, their lives would change radically following European contact.

While Spanish, English, and other European ships sailed along the Oregon coastline as early as the 16th century, the first European ships to sail upstream past the mouth of the Columbia River arrived in the 1790s. The Lewis and Clark expedition reached the area from the other direction, passing the current site of Portland on its outbound journey in 1805 and again upon its return in 1806. In 1811, the American Fur Company, owned by John Jacob Astor, founded Astoria as its Pacific headquarters. The following year Robert Stuart traveled overland from Astoria to St. Louis, marking the first traverse of the route that would ultimately become the Oregon Trail. Shortly after its founding, Astoria was abandoned to the British Hudson Bay Company. In 1825, the Company founded Fort Vancouver, the first European settlement in what is now the Portland metropolitan area. Both the British and the Americans, who each claimed and jointly occupied what had become known as the Oregon Country, conducted official and unofficial explorations of the Pacific Northwest region.

A few early pioneers began to settle in the area around modern Portland in the 1830s. Beginning in 1840, an increasing flow of American emigrants began to make the trek from Missouri to Oregon (although the California gold rush diverted the stream of migrants in 1848 and 1849). After crossing the Great Plains, the Rocky Mountains, and the arid inland Northwest, early emigrants had to float down the Columbia River from The Dalles to Fort Vancouver; the Barlow Road, a toll road alternative over the shoulder of Mount Hood, opened in 1843 and terminated at Oregon City. Also in 1843, a group of pioneers gathered at Champoeg, in the Willamette Valley between present-day Portland and Salem, to establish a provisional territorial government with its seat at Oregon City. (The Oregon Territory did not formally come into being until 1848, and originally included all land north of California and south of Canada between the Pacific Ocean and the Continental Divide.) The Oregon Treaty of 1846 set the 49th parallel as the boundary between British and American territory, and the Washington Territory was carved out of the northern half of the Oregon Territory in 1853. Oregon became a state in 1859.

In the meantime, successive epidemics of smallpox, measles, and other infectious diseases in the first half of the 19th century, combined with the arrival of malaria in about 1830, took a devastating toll on the native population. Outright warfare, however, was mainly confined to eastern and southern Oregon. In the 1850s, ratified and unratified treaties dispossessed the tribes of their Willamette Valley lands, and the surviving Indians were removed to reservations.

Portland itself began as a river city, which of course it remains to this day. Downtown Portland lies at the effective head of navigation on the Willamette River for oceangoing ships, and in 1843 William Overton recognized the potential of the site and filed a land claim there. (The story goes that he could not afford the 25-cent filing fee, so he got a quarter from fellow pioneer Asa Lovejoy in exchange for half the 640-acre claim.) In 1845, Overton sold his half of the claim to Francis Pettygrove and moved on. Lovejoy and Pettygrove—who had perhaps the least rugged names of any pioneers in the history of the American West—could not agree on a name for their new settlement. Lovejoy, a Massachusetts native, wished to name the place Boston; Pettygrove was from Maine, and preferred the name Portland. They agreed to flip a coin—now known as the Portland penny—for the right to name the town. Pettygrove won best two out of three.

Having finished the hard work of choosing a name, Lovejoy and Pettygrove platted a 16-block grid the same year. The city grew rapidly, and at the time of its incorporation in 1851 covered just over two square miles. Portland had a series of early rivals, including Oregon City, Sellwood, and Linnton, but it eventually emerged as the center of trade for the Willamette Valley and the largest city in the Northwest. The first of three transcontinental railroads to serve the area reached Portland in 1883, and this crucial connection cemented the city's status as a major trading center. The population of Portland and its surrounding areas nearly tripled during the 1880s, and the first streetcar lines reached the Eastside during that decade.

A series of annexations beginning in the 1880s extended the city's size and population dramatically. In 1891, Portland consolidated with the cities of East Portland (incorporated in 1870) and Albina (incorporated in 1887). Despite an economic slowdown in the 1890s, Portland remained the largest city in the Northwest until the early 20th century, when Seattle (spurred in part by growth during the Klondike Gold Rush) surpassed it. By 1900, Portland had a population of nearly 100,000.

The Lewis and Clark Centennial Exposition of 1905 had 1.5 million visitors and marked the beginning of Portland's greatest wave of growth and prosperity. In 1906, the Eastside population surpassed that of the Westside, and by 1910, the city's population had more than doubled, to 207,000. In 1915, Portland absorbed the cities of St. Johns (incorporated 1903) and Linnton (incorporated 1910), and the shipbuilding industry attracted more workers during the First World War. The twenties saw another wave of growth on the Eastside, and even the Depression, which spawned Hoovervilles in locations like Sullivan's Gulch and under the Ross Island Bridge, did not halt the city's expansion. By the eve of the Second World War, the city had a population of more than 300,000.

The war kicked Portland's growth into overdrive. The Kaiser shipyards built more than 1,000 ships during the war, and the demand for labor was intense and not confined to Portland proper: 38,000 people worked at the Kaiser shipyard in Vancouver, Washington, and the population of the metropolitan area increased by one-third during the war years. Housing was in short supply; a few small houses were built on vacant lots in the old Eastside neighborhoods during the war, but most workers were placed in huge housing projects like Vanport, located in North Portland at the present site of Delta Park. Vanport was the largest public housing project ever built in the United States, with some 40,000 inhabitants. A massive flood in 1948 destroyed Vanport, and its residents, many of whom were African-American, were relocated to other parts of the city.

After the war, the pent-up demand for housing drove a wave of suburban expansion that has lasted for more than half a century. Portland's population actually declined slightly during the 1950s. The Interstate Highway System encouraged development in areas that were formerly well outside the metropolitan area. In 1950, the three largest suburbs on the Oregon side of the river—Gresham, Hillsboro, and Beaverton—had a combined population of less than 11,000; today, more than a quarter-million people live in these three cities. Clark County also experienced rapid population growth in the postwar years. The population of the city of Portland has continued to grow since the 1960s, but much of this growth is due to annexation of unincorporated areas of Multnomah County east of Portland.

In the early 1970s, state land use laws mandated the creation of an urban growth boundary (see "Urban Planning," above), which helped channel and restrain suburban growth. At about the same time, a grassroots effort by local community activists killed the Mount Hood Freeway project, which would have bulldozed large sections of Southeast Portland to make way for a freeway to Gresham. The transportation dollars that had been earmarked for the freeway instead went to several smaller-scale road projects and to the development of Portland's first light-rail line. The decisions made in the 1970s and 1980s have literally shaped Portland and earned it a worldwide reputation as a leader in land use and transportation planning. It remains to be seen whether Portland can maintain that reputation in the face of financial constraints and continued growth.

For Portland keeps growing. New residents, often drawn by the region's beauty and vaunted high quality of life, continue to arrive. Presumably you are one of them. Welcome to Portland. Please help us keep the character and livability of this special part of the world intact.

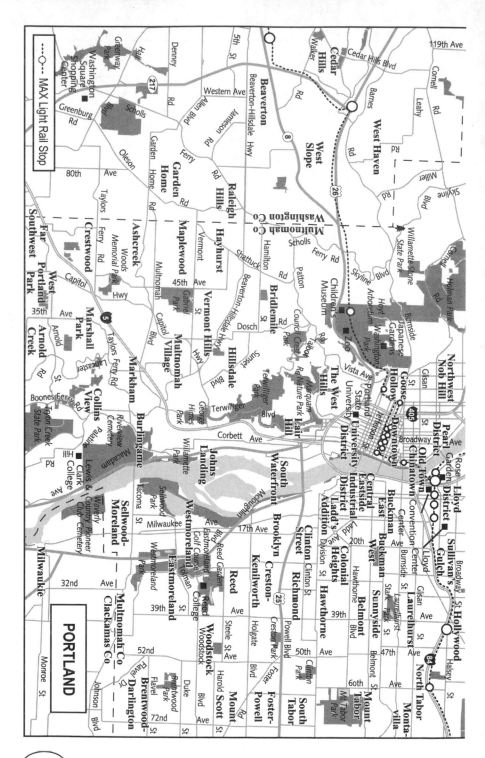

PORTLAND

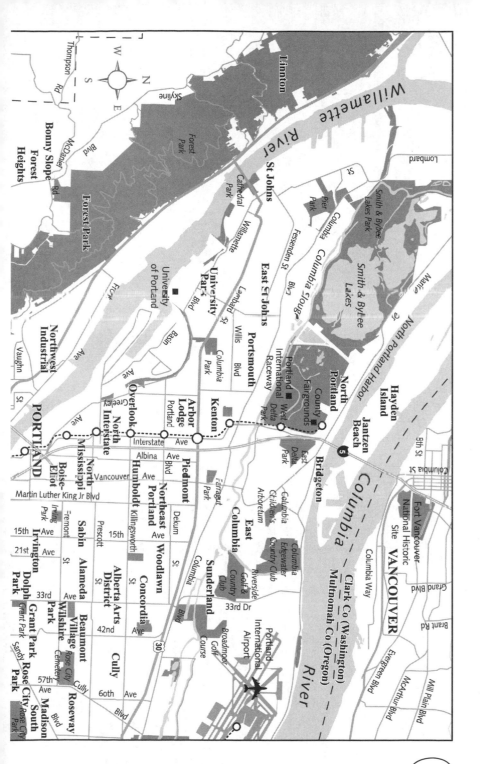

THE NEIGHBORHOOD AND COMMUNITY PROFILES BELOW ARE INTENDED to help you get a feel for the character of each Portland neighborhood or suburban community. There is no substitute for scouting out a neighborhood in person or meeting face-to-face with a knowledgeable local real estate agent, but these introductions will let you know what to expect.

CITY OF PORTLAND

Boundaries: North: Columbia River; **West**: Beaverton; Cedar Mill, West Haven, West Slope, Raleigh Hills, Garden Home (unincorporated Washington County); Tigard; **South**: Lake Oswego; Dunthorpe (unincorporated Multnomah and Clackamas counties); Milwaukie; Clackamas (unincorporated Clackamas County); Happy Valley; **East**: Gresham; Unincorporated Multnomah County; **Area**: 145 square miles; **Population**: 610,000

Oregon's largest city is, above all, a city of neighborhoods. Portland's Office of Neighborhood Involvement (http://www.portlandoregon.gov/oni/) officially recognizes more than 90 neighborhood associations, although the names and boundaries of the "official" neighborhoods don't necessarily correspond to commonly used neighborhood designations. Every one of these neighborhoods is unique. Many Portland neighborhoods began as small communities located outside the city limits, while others sprang into being along new electric streetcar lines in the early 20th century (just as new developments today sometimes follow freeways), and these older neighborhoods tend to have a distinct and cohesive feel. Neighborhoods developed in the postwar, automobile-oriented era are generally more homogeneous, but they are not nearly as interchangeable as their detractors would have you believe.

The Willamette River cleaves Portland into two very different realms, the Westside and the Eastside, and many Portlanders swear that never the twain shall meet. Some people consider it a minor sport to mock the denizens of the opposite side of the river with crude stereotypes—Westsiders are rich, conceited, materialistic, and car-bound, Eastsiders are methhead yokels, flag-burning communists, or bike Nazis—that in most cases are simply false. In fact, wealth and poverty, crime and security, liberals and conservatives, are found in every quadrant of the city (albeit in varying concentrations), and the two halves of Portland have much more in common with one another than either half does with, say, Houston. In short, don't let mean-spirited stereotypes cause you to write off entire sections of the city; explore without preconceptions, and determine for yourself what neighborhood feels like the best fit.

A final note on Portland neighborhoods: East Burnside Street forms the official boundary between Northeast and Southeast Portland, but most people (including the Office of Neighborhood Involvement) consider the less surmountable Banfield Freeway (Interstate 84) to be the informal boundary between them. This chapter follows the unofficial convention.

THE WEST SIDE

DOWNTOWN PORTLAND AND ENVIRONS

Boundaries: North: Interstate 405; Burnside Street (west of 405); **West**: Interstate 405 (north of Burnside); Washington Park; **South**: Interstate 405, Sunset Highway (US 26); **East**: Willamette River

DOWNTOWN PORTLAND
Neighborhood Association: Downtown Portland

Downtown Portland is generally understood to encompass the city's central business district and the immediately surrounding area within the Interstate 405 loop and south of Burnside Street. Downtown occupies the west bank of the Willamette River, on the site where the city was founded in 1845. This former riverside clearcut—the original Stumptown—has been the commercial and cultural heart of the city and of Oregon as a whole for more than 150 years.

Today, downtown is a mix of new and old buildings on sites with evolving uses: Pioneer Courthouse Square, the city's innovative "living room," was by turns a school, the opulent Portland Hotel, and a parking lot. Most downtown structures are commercial or civic in nature—office buildings, retail stores, courthouses,

Downtown Portland

etc.—and while the area remains reasonably vibrant even after business hours, relatively few people have chosen to live here. Until very recently, the few housing units in the heart of downtown tended to fall into the "transitional" or residential hotel category, with a few notable exceptions (such as the luxury condominiums on the upper floors of the KOIN Center [Tower]). A few new market-rent apartment and condominium towers have been built or are under construction in the core area, however, especially in or near the so-called **Cultural District** along Broadway and the South Park Blocks, home of the Portland Center for the Performing Arts, the Portland Art Museum, and the Oregon Historical Society. For its few residents,

Cultural District

this neighborhood offers not only the eponymous cultural offerings—art, theatre, movies, and more—just footsteps away, but also some of the city's best restaurants, such as local stalwart Higgins (www.higginsportland.com).

The Cultural District overlaps the once-forlorn **West End**, a region located roughly between Park Avenue and Interstate 405, which is now perhaps the hottest, hippest part of downtown. Traditionally, somewhat shabby subsidized housing has been the residential norm in this area, which also features several historic churches, some low-rent office and retail buildings, and various bars and parking lots. In the past few years, this area has undergone rapid redevelopment, spurred in part by the dramatic evolution of the Pearl District just across Burnside. Apartments are being spiffed up, new condominiums are rising, and trendy boutiques, restaurants, bakeries, food cart pods, and other interesting businesses like Living Room Theaters (www. livingroomtheaters.com) on 10th Avenue have colonized the area. Also on 10th, the Safeway supermarket, once locally known as the "scary Safeway" because of its many mentally ill or drug-addled customers (who have not entirely gone away), has been reconstructed as the centerpiece of the mixed-use Museum Place complex; the spiffy Eliot Tower condominium building is just across the street. The beautifully restored Central Library, unquestionably one of the finest historic library buildings on the West Coast, stands proudly down the street. Wind turbines sprout improbably (and largely symbolically, given Portland's low average wind speeds) from the roof of the ultra-modern Indigo@TwelveWest apartment tower. The Portland Streetcar, which trundles along 10th and 11th Avenues, arguably has helped spur investment in the area.

The edgy, quirky Ace Hotel (www.acehotel.com) on Stark Street has become an unexpected darling of the travel press, and anchors the northern portion of the West End, which includes the "Burnside Triangle," one of the less salacious names for the triangular wedge between West Burnside Street and Southwest Alder Street. (The Burnside Triangle has long been a center of the Portland gay community.) Despite the rise in the West End's fortunes, the area still features a dwindling number of surface parking lots, a few derelict buildings, and more than a few panhandlers, but the physical structure of the neighborhood, at least, is rapidly changing.

Portland State University dominates the south end of downtown, which has accordingly been dubbed the **University District**. Much of the housing in this end of downtown is intended for and occupied by students, with all that implies for the condition of, and noise level in, buildings. The extension of the Portland Streetcar through the PSU campus to the South Waterfront district, the new MAX lines along the transit mall, and the growth of PSU's physical plant have all encouraged the construction of new condominiums, apartment buildings, and academic buildings in the area, and some of the more dilapidated structures are being demolished.

Between PSU and the Willamette River, the southern end of downtown was a vibrant residential zone until the early 1970s, when it was razed in the name of urban renewal. This area includes the Keller Auditorium, a few small parks, various nondescript office buildings, and several semi-upscale residential towers, some with magnificent river and mountain views. Along the riverfront, adjacent to the RiverPlace hotel and a small marina, are several condominium complexes; these include both low-rise traditional condos and newer condo towers with views of the river, the city skyline, and the Marquam Bridge looming just to the south.

Downtown Portland is possibly the only part of the city in which having a car is not merely optional but a positive liability. Ongoing construction projects periodically wreak havoc with automobile traffic; moreover, because downtown Portland was platted before the rest of the city, the streets are not oriented to true north, but instead to magnetic north. (The reason for this is unclear, although presumably early planners tried to plat numbered streets to run parallel to the waterfront along the Willamette.) As a result, the corners where east-west downtown streets intersect Burnside are acute angles; a number of interesting wedge-shaped, mini-Flatiron-style buildings occupy the resulting oddly shaped lots. These corners may be picturesque, but they can be difficult to navigate. Fortunately, downtown Portland is pedestrian-friendly; assuming you can endure the ubiquitous and often creative panhandlers, the poorly timed lights, and the confused suburbanite drivers trying to focus on navigating instead of looking out for pedestrians;

University District

new aluminum directional signs help orient touristic foot travelers. Downtown is also the hub of the region's transit system, with frequent bus, light rail, and streetcar service within downtown and to other parts of the city. Downtown Portland has an abundance of retail shops of all kinds, but they are scattered throughout the city core rather than concentrated in one small area, although the West End is starting to generate a critical mass of boutiques. In addition, other than the Safeway there are no large supermarkets in the downtown core; you may need to drive or hop on a bus or the streetcar to buy groceries. If you're looking for a densely urban environment with plenty of residential options and amenities, high end boutiques galore, and hip restaurants on every corner, you might be happier in the Pearl.

No one moves to downtown Portland for its wide open spaces, but several parks nonetheless provide opportunities to stretch your legs, get some fresh air, and maybe witness a drug deal or two. Waterfront Park and the leafy South Park Blocks are downtown's prime parklands, but smaller parks like the Plaza Blocks, between 3rd and 4th Avenues near the county and federal courthouses, provide additional oases of green in the heart of the city. The parks also provide a home for several farmers' markets. (See www.portlandfarmersmarket.org for details.)

Goose Hollow

GOOSE HOLLOW

Neighborhood Association: Goose Hollow

Goose Hollow is a social and topographical transition zone between relatively flat downtown Portland and the loftier and more genteel precincts of the West Hills. The neighborhood was once dotted with grand Victorian- and Edwardian-era homes, many of which are still standing; most of these structures have been divided into condos or professional offices, but a few remain in use as very impressive single-family homes. (Most of these older homes have enough historical or architectural significance to warrant a formal name, e.g., The McMaster House on SW Vista.) At the south end of the neighborhood, Gander Ridge and Vista Ridge, which form the rims of the "hollow" for which Goose Hollow is named, contain an abundance of older homes and winding streets that are more reminiscent of Portland Heights. Lower down, a wave of building in the 1920s left a legacy of attractive old-fashioned apartments, especially near Southwest Vista Avenue, while later apartment construction resulted in a crop of high-rises, some with magnificent views.

Many of the neighborhood's historic buildings were lost to the wrecking ball in the 1960s, especially in the lower part of the neighborhood, which is now largely devoted to non-residential uses, including the Providence Park stadium, Lincoln High School, a few manufacturing facilities and auto-related businesses, and the exclusive Multnomah Athletic Club (if you want in, make friends with a member and take a lottery number). As proximity to the Pearl District and downtown has become more desirable in recent years, some new condominium projects have sprung up, especially in the vicinity of Providence Park and along Southwest Jefferson Street.

With a few exceptions, most notably the Goose Hollow Inn (www.goosehollowinn.com) owned by former Portland mayor Bud Clark (who gained minor celebrity as the flasher in the popular "Expose Yourself to Art" poster), the neighborhood lacks much in the way of dining or shopping except along the fringes, close to Interstate 405 or along Burnside. Nonetheless, it is a quick stroll from almost any point in Goose Hollow to the tantalizing offerings of downtown Portland or Northwest 23rd Avenue. (Keep in mind that your walk home will invariably be uphill.) Moreover, transit service is very good: several bus lines pass through or along the edges of the neighborhood, and the Westside MAX light rail line passes right through Goose Hollow, with stops at Providence Park, Kings Hill/SW Salmon, and Goose Hollow/SW Jefferson.

Goose Hollow's central location and semi-urban ambiance have made it popular with a diverse set of residents—PSU students near Columbia and Jefferson streets, empty nesters, retirees, young professionals, twenty-something hipsters, and even some families who are happy to take advantage of the well-regarded public schools that serve the neighborhood (Chapman Elementary, West Sylvan Middle, and Lincoln High). At the same time, these characteristics have made Goose Hollow a relatively expensive neighborhood in which to rent or buy housing; this is especially if you're looking for a single-family home rather than a condo or apartment. While Goose Hollow itself is densely populated, the upper (western) end of the neighborhood lies on the doorstep of 130-acre Washington Park. Note that, while on-street parking is generally free (if not necessarily easy to find) in the neighborhood, a resident parking permit is required for long-term and overnight parking.

OLD TOWN AND THE PEARL DISTRICT

Neighborhood Associations: Old Town–Chinatown, Pearl

It was the best of times; it was the worst of times. These two adjacent neighborhoods that lie just north of West Burnside Street tell, if not a tale of two cities, at least a tale of two districts with very different fortunes. Just to the northwest of the downtown skyscrapers luxuriates Portland's urban Cinderella, the **Pearl District**. The Pearl is Portland's closest analogue to New York's SoHo. Like SoHo, it was once a warehouse district where real artists lived and worked; also like SoHo, it has been redeveloped and gentrified to such a degree that most working artists have been priced out and have moved elsewhere. As for the name, the story goes that the neighborhood's old warehouses, like crusty oyster shells, contained hidden "pearls" in the form of galleries and lofts. Most of the warehouses have been wholly renovated (or just torn down) and while there are still plenty of galleries, the Pearl is now positively packed with trendy boutiques, creative workspaces, and some of the city's best and most expensive restaurants. Thanks to its proximity to downtown and the laziness of some travel writers, the Pearl has been the focus of many recent articles, including features in the travel sections of the *Los Angeles Times* and *The New York Times*, and is now Portland's go-to zone for whatever subset of the jet set drops into PDX.

Pearl District

While most neighborhoods contain discrete commercial districts, the Pearl is unique in Portland in that the entire neighborhood is basically a mixed-use quasi-commercial district. The modern furniture stores, fancy eateries, and offices (including some corporate headquarters) coexist with, and in many cases actually are part of, the neighborhood's residential buildings. The area is awash in a sea of mostly new, mostly high-end lofts and condominiums, with a smattering of urban row houses in the idealized Brooklyn mode. Per-square-foot prices for residential real estate are probably the highest in the state, and are double, triple, or even quadruple the per-square-foot average in other neighborhoods. The median price is likewise high, but because most Pearl units are relatively compact—a small condo in a tower instead of a three-bedroom standalone house, for example—the price of an average housing unit is comparable to the cost in other desirable parts of the city. That said, rents are not quite as stratospheric as sale prices, and there are even a few affordable housing units scattered around. The Pearl's wave of redevelopment started in the southern part of the neighborhood, near Powell's Books, then quickly spread north (along with the streetcar line) a dozen blocks to Northrup Street and beyond. The newest developments are generally in the northern part of the Pearl; some stand along the riverfront.

In part because of its high profile (and high prices), the Pearl District and its generally affluent inhabitants get hit with a lot of verbal vitriol. Part of this resentment is pure envy, but part of it is the perception that the Pearl is somehow antithetical to Portland values: unaffordable, unfriendly, sanitized, *faux* New York, increasingly dominated by out-of-state chains, and definitely not egalitarian. Residents who complain about the train whistles from railroad tracks that run along the edge of the neighborhood, and which long predated the construction of their gleaming lofts, do not help to erase this perception. (The tax abatements that were given to condo developers didn't do much to alleviate resentment, either.) Still, the Pearl is a great place to wander around, on foot or by streetcar, and it exerts a strong pull for both affluent young professionals and empty nesters.

A few businesses, like Powell's Books (www.powells.com), the Pearl Bakery (www.pearlbakery.com), and greasy spoon Fuller's Coffee Shop (possibly the only Pearl business with no website) are holdovers from the days before the district's virtually wholesale transformation into Trend Central. Another holdover is First Thursday—the first Thursday evening of each month—when gallery owners and other businesses throw open their doors to the public. (Of late, First Thursday is more about the scene—and being seen—than about art, but it can still be a lot of fun.) Some of the more architecturally interesting buildings in the Pearl are the mixed-use Brewery Blocks, on the site of the old Henry Weinhard brewery; the old Portland Armory, which has undergone a "green" makeover into the Gerding Theater, home of Portland Center Stage; and the Ecotrust building, a repurposed warehouse that is a model of sustainable design. (It even has an eco-roof.) For several years, until a new Safeway opened in 2008, the only supermarket in the Pearl was a Whole Foods; this fact may tell you everything you need to know about the neighborhood's demographics.

Some families with children live in the Pearl, in part because the area is so walkable and because the schools that serve it are excellent. Besides the high cost of even a two-bedroom pad, a possible drawback for families is the complete absence of yards and the relative dearth of parks. There are only three parks in the neighborhood—Jamison Square Park (popular for its fountains on summer days), Tanner Springs Park, and the North Park Blocks—and only the last of these is a "real" park with grass and a play structure. Highly regarded Emerson School, a public K–5 charter school, is conveniently located on the North Park Blocks, but has a long waitlist for enrollment.

Just across Northwest Broadway, yet worlds away, **Old Town** glowers blearily at its fortunate stepsister. Old Town is indeed filled with many old brick and masonry buildings, some of which date back to the 1870s and 1880s, and which in many cases still retain their original cast iron facades. The neighborhood is honeycombed with underground tunnels—the so-called Shanghai tunnels through which hapless, drunken saloon patrons were purportedly carried off to ships that needed crew members in the 19th and early 20th centuries.

A reputation as a haven for drug-dealing and a high concentration of homeless shelters, soup kitchens, and other social service providers has until recently limited Old Town's appeal. Old Town has traditionally had few market-rent apartments or condos—most residential units were either subsidized or of the short-stay, transitional variety, and only about 20% of the neighborhood's housing units are owner-occupied. The neighborhood also has a high concentration of paroled sex offenders, in part because few children live here (although, ironically, the area is served by some of the best public schools in the city).

Despite these grim facts, Old Town is undergoing a modest renaissance. Several apartment buildings and luxury loft-type condominiums have risen along the river and near Union Station, Portland's quasi-Romanesque train station. (Union Station, built in 1896, is recognizable by the neon "Go By Train" sign on the station's

Chinatown

clock tower and is still an active passenger station, with trains heading north to Seattle and Vancouver, British Columbia, south to Eugene and California, and east to Spokane, St. Paul, and Chicago.) Although they are subject to train-related noise, these housing units offer central location with enviable transit access and, in some cases, gorgeous city views. A number of historic buildings are being renovated, and restaurants and shops have opened to serve employees of businesses that have moved their offices here to take advantage of relatively cheap rents. Tens of millions of dollars of new investment are planned for Old Town over the next few years, and it is likely that this cash infusion, combined with bubble-over effects from the Pearl, will create dramatic changes in the neighborhood in the near future.

Old Town has a couple of notable sub-neighborhoods. **Skidmore Historic District**, which extends south under the Burnside Bridge along the waterfront, is home to the long-running Portland Saturday Market (www.portlandsaturdaymarket.com), as well as a host of nightclubs. **Chinatown**, easily identified by the Chinatown Gate that looms over Fourth Avenue at West Burnside and by a cluster of Chinese restaurants, is a shadow of its former self: most of the area's Chinese residents and some of its businesses have long since decamped to other city or suburban neighborhoods, notably the area around 82nd Avenue in the outer Eastside. Nonetheless, Chinatown is home to the lovely Lan Su Chinese Garden (www. lansugarden.org). Near the Chinatown Gate, on a private lot at the corner of West Burnside and Northwest Fourth Avenue, the Right 2 Dream Too semi-permanent homeless camp is adorned by a series of painted and decorated doors that form a sort of palisade around the camp. The camp, which is operated by a local nonprofit, is searching for a new home. After reading this section, you may not be surprised to learn that plans to move to the Pearl District were not met with open arms.

Both Old Town and the Pearl District are unusually well served by transit. The downtown Portland transit mall with bus and MAX light rail service extends along 5th and 6th Avenues to Union Station; the MAX lines continue over the Steel Bridge at the north end of Old Town. A separate MAX line runs along 1st Avenue, with stops at Skidmore Fountain (under the Burnside Bridge) and Old Town/Chinatown. The NS Portland Streetcar route runs north-south along 10th and 11th Avenues to Lovejoy and Northrup Streets, at which point the line turns and runs east-west as far as Northwest 23rd. The CL streetcar line shares the NS route to as far as Lovejoy, then branches off and crosses the Broadway Bridge near Union Station.

DOWNTOWN AND ENVIRONS NEIGHBORHOOD INFORMATION
ZIP Codes: 97201, 97204, 97205, 97209
Post Offices: Central Post Office, 204 SW 5th Ave; Portland Post Office, 715 NW
    Hoyt St; Waterfront Station, 101 SW Madison St
Police Station: Portland Police Bureau, Central Precinct, 1111 SW 2nd Ave, 503-
    823-3333 (non-emergency)
Emergency Hospitals: Legacy Emanuel Medical Center, 2801 N Gantenbein Ave,
    503-413-2200, www.legacyhealth.org; Legacy Good Samaritan Medical Center,
    1015 NW 22nd Ave, 503-413-7711, www.legacyhealth.org; OHSU Hospital, 3181
    SW Sam Jackson Park Rd, 503-494-8311, www.ohsu.edu/xd/health/
Library: Central Library, 801 SW 10th Ave, 503-988-5123
Parks: Major parks include Washington Park, Waterfront Park, and the Park Blocks
    (north and south); www.portlandparks.org
Community Publication: *Northwest Examiner*, www.nwexaminer.com
Public Transportation: TriMet, 503-238-RIDE, www.trimet.org; comprehensive
    bus, light rail, and streetcar service.

THE WEST HILLS

Boundaries: North: Forest Park; Northwest Industrial District; **West**: Forest Heights; unincorporated Multnomah County; unincorporated Washington County; **South**: Hillsdale; Bridlemile; **East**: Downtown; Goose Hollow; Northwest Portland/Nob Hill; South Portland

Neighborhood Associations: Arlington Heights, Healy Heights, Hillside, Homestead, Northwest District, Southwest Hills, Sylvan-Highlands

When Art Alexakis, frontman of the Portland band Everclear, promises, "I will buy you a big house way up in the West Hills" (in the song "I Will Buy You a New Life"), he is channeling the aspirations of generations of Portlanders. Not every house in the West Hills is big—some are tiny, in fact—and not everyone who lives here is rich or even upper-middle class. But ever since the late 19th century, when timber barons, successful merchants, and other members of the city's incipient upper crust began to literally look down on flatlanders from their lofty palaces, the West

Portland Heights

Hills have been the destination of choice for many socially and financially successful Portlanders.

It's not hard to see why. The West Hills is the colloquial name for the portion of the Tualatin Mountains that parallels the Willamette River to the west and forms the backdrop to downtown Portland. The hills rise to more than 1,000 feet above sea level in places, and the often fog-shrouded slopes and canyons are forested with mature conifers. Many homes here have incomparable views—a few choice homes offer expansive vistas of virtually the entire city, along with several snow-capped volcanoes—and others feel as if they are well-appointed cabins in the woods. The icing on the West Hills cake is the incredible proximity of these woodsy neighborhoods to downtown Portland—some West Hills homes are a five-minute drive (and perhaps a 30-minute walk) from the center of the city.

Many less fortunate (or simply hipper) Portlanders mock denizens of the West Hills, sometimes out of envy, and sometimes—well, in any city (except perhaps Los Angeles), tanned, well-coifed people zipping to their Botox appointments in luxury SUVs will be a target of derision. While the stereotype of the mansion-dwelling executive certainly applies to some residents, the reality is that the neighborhoods of the West Hills feature residents with a mix of ages, professions, educational backgrounds, and incomes, and many of these supposed snobs are actually quite unassuming people. West Hills houses are equally heterogeneous, and the area encompasses several distinct neighborhoods with different characteristics. Yes, there are ridiculously huge mansions that look as if they were brought over lock, stock, and barrel from Sussex, but there are also small, wisteria-shrouded cottages, charming bungalows, unrenovated 1950s ranches, and the city's highest concentration of custom-designed homes; many of the latter are sleekly modern and decidedly not fuddy-duddy. To cope with steep slopes, quite a few houses are built on piers or stilts: the structures jut out over the hillside, with a gulf underneath. From the street, only a garage (or garages) and a front door are visible, and sometimes passers-by see only a wall with a gate. These houses usually have decks, but yards are clearly impossible.

Not every block in the West Hills is actually hilly, but the entire area is laced with narrow, winding, steep streets that utterly abandon the city's grid pattern and that make traveling through these neighborhoods a bit of an adventure (especially without a map, or during rare snow or ice storms). Virtually the entire West Hills region is at risk from landslides, wildfire, and earthquake damage. An additional hazard is the acrimonious disputes that erupt when a tree in one person's yard grows tall enough to block a neighbor's mountain view. If you can live with these dangers, and have the money and desire to buy into the West Hills, read on.

Just southwest of (but high above) downtown Portland, **Portland Heights** centers on a tiny commercial district, located around Southwest Vista Avenue and Spring Street (home of the aptly named Vista Spring Café, which serves up surpris inqly qood pizza), and unlike most other parts of the West Hills, the immediately surrounding area is on a plateau of sorts, so is *relatively* level and mostly adheres to a grid pattern. (Lamb's at Stroheckers—just Strohecker's to most people—an upscale supermarket, is just up the hill on Southwest Patton Road.) Ainsworth Elementary School, one of the top elementary schools in the city, is also at the intersection of Vista and Spring; the surrounding area has a strong attraction for affluent families with young children. The remainder of the neighborhood is a warren of narrow, winding streets carved into hillsides or tucked into shady dells; some homes have jaw-dropping views over the city, and many of the streets have a relatively European/English village feel (an impression that is deliberately accentuated by street names such as Georgian Place and English Court).

Portland Heights was largely developed in the 'teens and 1920s, and most homes here are in traditional styles—foursquares, bungalows, English Tudors, and colonials—and generally range in size from large to palatial. Many of the grandest old houses line Vista Avenue, south of the high bridge over Jefferson Street; a streetcar line once ran along Vista, and captains of industry in the late 19th century built to impress. Some newer contemporary and custom homes perch on the hillsides, particularly on slopes too steep for prewar engineering to manage. The sinuous streets leading up to Portland Heights from downtown feature an interesting cross-section of structures, from virtual mansions to condo complexes and even a few mossy, tumbledown shanties in the woods.

Uphill to the south, **Healy Heights** and **Council Crest** occupy the loftiest real estate in Portland, and homes with a view feature similarly lofty prices. (Tiny Healy Heights has by far the highest average and median home prices of any neighborhood in the city, but the sample size is tiny.) These neighborhoods are draped across a saddle on the very pinnacle of the West Hills, between Council Crest Park (the highest point in the city, with a nearly 360-degree panorama) and the giant red-and-white KGON radio tower (officially now called Stonehenge tower, as it is owned by the Stonehenge Towers company) atop Healy Heights to the southeast.

Healy Heights

The Vista streetcar line once served Council Crest, which was home to an amusement park, complete with roller coaster, lookout tower, and, absurdly, a giant paddleboat in an artificial channel. Some homes, particularly on the north and northeast slopes of Council Crest, survive from this era—the park closed in 1929, just before the stock market crash of that year—but the majority of houses here date from the post–World War II period. The neighborhood includes some surprisingly modest 1950s ranch-style houses, as well as a large number of spacious, architect-designed dwellings; the latter are especially common on lots with prime views, especially those coveted eastward views taking in the city and the mountains. Level Fairmount Boulevard, a favorite walking and biking loop, encircles these high points; the downhill side of the street is lined with architecturally interesting "stilt" homes and other structures built to cope with steep slopes, including modified geodesic domes and other quirky dwellings. Council Crest's labyrinthine street layout and confusing access routes tend to discourage nonresidents from driving through, except to visit the park (which closes to cars at 9 p.m. in summer and 7 p.m. in winter), and this neighborhood typically enjoys one of the lowest crime rates in the city. Despite its lofty perch, the neighborhood has some sidewalks and even a bus line, the modern descendant of the old streetcar line. This area is also a center of the Southwest Trails system, which threads through the hills and fans out into surrounding residential neighborhoods.

On the eastern slope of Council Crest, Oregon Health & Science University (OHSU) is a sprawling complex of clinics, labs, classrooms, and hospitals that stands prominently atop Marquam Hill, a.k.a. "Pill Hill." The compact **Homestead** neighborhood is tucked into the hills around and just above OHSU. While there are plenty of interesting single-family homes here, this area also features a large crop of apartment and condominium buildings, which primarily serve the population of medical students and residents at the university and its hospitals; unusually for the West Hills, the neighborhood population is evenly split between renters and owners. Many houses and apartments here have amazing Mount

Hood views, while others back onto greenspaces like Marquam Nature Park. On-street parking is at a premium in and around OHSU, and resident parking permits are required for long-term parking. Terwilliger Boulevard connects the neighborhood to downtown and Hillsdale, while steep, windy Marquam Hill Road leads up to Fairmount Boulevard. Because of OHSU's huge employee and patient base, the neighborhood is well served by bus transit, and is at the upper terminus of the Portland Aerial Tram.

Arlington Heights, a small neighborhood south of Burnside, tucked in between Washington Park and Hoyt Arboretum, has experienced blistering growth in home prices in the last decade, and it is now one of the most expensive neighborhoods in the city on both an absolute and per-square-foot basis. It's not hard to see the appeal of the neighborhood: residents enjoy practically backyard access to walking trails in the Arboretum and around Washington Park, yet are only minutes away from downtown and Northwest Portland. The majority of the homes here

Homestead

are of prewar vintage—grand English Tudor–style homes, shingled cottages, and the like—but some ranch houses were built in the 1950s, and some large custom homes have been built in recent years. The neighborhood has few through streets, and is very quiet—except on Sunday nights, when the Zoobombers tear down Fairview Boulevard. The Zoobombing phenomenon involves a group of grownups who modify kids' bikes, tall bikes, and other two-wheeled vehicles (often removing brakes and other critical components in the process), take them on the MAX line to the Oregon Zoo, then blast downhill to Goose Hollow, where they hop back on the MAX and repeat the process. The Zoobombers maintain a "pile" of minibikes at Southwest 13th and Burnside. The Zoobombers are largely self-regulating, and police calls are infrequent, but some Arlington Heights residents are not enamored of this group.

Arlington Heights

Across Burnside Road to the north, **Kings Heights**, also known as the Hillside neighborhood, spreads across the hillside (hence the nickname) above the bustle of Northwest 23rd Avenue and below the grandest West Hills palace of them all, Pittock Mansion (www.pittockmansion.org). Most of the homes on the steep, switchbacking streets are gracious older homes, in a variety of styles but typically a jumbo variation on the bungalow, foursquare, or half-timbered theme. Many of these homes are truly grand, multilevel affairs, while others are more modest but still charming. Given the slope, many of these homes lack much of a yard but have fantastic city, river, and/or mountain views. Some condominium complexes have been built in the lower reaches of the neighborhood. Tiny Hillside Park, with its small community center, indeed perches on the hillside in the middle of the neighborhood. The street layout can be highly confusing to the uninitiated; a network of stairways and shortcuts (also potentially confusing to the uninitiated) connects the various levels of the neighborhood and provides pedestrian access

Kings Heights

to the shops and restaurants of Northwest. This layout is also confusing to crooks, apparently; the Hillside neighborhood has one of the lowest crime rates in the city. Predictably, Kings Heights is one of the most expensive neighborhoods in Portland.

A bit further north, across Cornell Road, **Willamette Heights** lies at the doorstep of the foggy fastness of Forest Park; some homes are literally a stone's throw from a trailhead, and the neighborhood's main thoroughfare, Northwest Thurman Street, dead-ends at Leif Erikson Drive, the main mountain bike route into the park. Willamette Heights is full of grand early-20th-century homes, some of which stand high above the street with only a steep staircase for access. Most

Willamette Heights

views here are northward, over the industrial district and Willamette River toward Mount St. Helens, although many homes are tucked into woodsy ravines with no views at all. One of the neighborhood's significant advantages is its proximity not only to Forest Park and the Northwest 23rd district, but also to the commercial zone along Thurman Street itself west of 23rd; neighborhood fixtures include St. Honoré Boulangerie (www.sthonorebakery.com); Kenny & Zuke's Bagelworks (www.kennyandzukes.com), where the bagels are properly boiled; and Food Front Cooperative Grocery (www.foodfront.coop). The Northwest branch library is also located here. The lower end of Thurman Street has seen the construction of several small-scale modern apartment buildings and condos in recent years, which mingle with the remaining old homes, but most residences in this area are single-family structures or duplexes. For a literary perspective on the thorough-fare, you might want to grab a copy of Thurman Street resident Ursula K. LeGuin's *Blue Moon Over Thurman Street.* (For information about Forest Heights, Linnton, and other neighborhoods near Forest Park, see "Forest Park and Environs" below.)

West of the main ridge of the West Hills—in the neighborhoods along Skyline Boulevard near **Sylvan**, where the Sunset Highway crests the hills on its congested way to Beaverton—development is far less dense and generally newer, with homes dating anywhere from the 1950s to last week. The area just north of the Sylvan exit has a concentration of small office buildings, restaurants, and apartment complexes, but outside this zone many homes are on large lots, giving parts of the neighborhood a semi-rural feel. There is no typical home style here: houses run the gamut from nondescript boxes to thoughtfully designed, architecturally noteworthy structures tucked away in the woods. Some homes offer westward views over Washington County to the Coast Range. In addition to easy access to the Sunset Highway, Sylvan is close to Burnside, which provides an alternate commuting route to either downtown Portland or Beaverton/Hillsboro.

The neighborhoods south of the Sunset Highway, between Humphrey Boulevard and Patton Road, sometimes known as the **Southwest Hills**, share affinities with both Sylvan and Portland Heights. As in Sylvan, most homes date from the postwar period, and many are on large lots, but socio-economically the area has more in common with Portland Heights (with which it shares a neighborhood association, the Southwest Hills Residential League). Many homes are quite large and impressively landscaped, quite a few are set back from the road (in some cases, behind walls), and some offer expansive vistas to the northeast, west, or

Sylvan

southwest. A gas station at the corner of Patton and Dosch, where the Southwest Hills, Portland Heights, and Council Crest meet, is the only commercial establishment in the area. This area, like Sylvan, is relatively close to downtown Portland and the Northwest District, but also offers easy access to the Sunset Highway for commuters to Washington County. It is often overlooked by newcomers who focus on more "name-brand" neighborhoods.

Given the terrain and the low population density, the West Hills enjoy surprisingly good bus service. Bus lines serve Portland Heights, Council Crest and Healy Heights, Willamette Heights, Kings Heights, the Homestead/OHSU neighborhood,

Southwest Hills

Sylvan, and the area around Washington Park. In some areas, residents who live more than a few blocks from a bus line may have difficulty safely reaching the nearest bus stop.

WEST HILLS NEIGHBORHOOD INFORMATION

ZIP Codes: 97201, 97210, 97221, 97239

Post Office: Forest Park Post Office, 1706 NW 24th Ave; also see "Downtown and Environs"

Police Station: Portland Police Bureau, Central Precinct, 1111 SW 2nd Ave, 503-823-3333 (non-emergency)

Emergency Hospitals: Legacy Good Samaritan Medical Center, 1015 NW 22nd Ave, 503-413-7711, www.legacyhealth.org; OHSU Hospital, 3181 SW Sam Jackson Park Rd, 503-494-8311, www.ohsu.edu/xd/health/; Providence St. Vincent Medical Center, 9205 SW Barnes Rd, 503-216-1234, www.providence.org

Libraries: Central Library, 801 SW 10th Ave, 503-988-5123; Hillsdale Library, 1525 SW Sunset Blvd, 503-988-5388; Northwest Library, 2300 NW Thurman St, 503-988-5560

Parks: Several major parks, including Washington Park, Hoyt Arboretum, Council Crest Park, Macleay Park, Marquam Nature Park, Forest Park, and Keller Woodland; www.portlandparks.org

Community Publications: *Northwest Examiner*, www.nwexaminer.com; *Southwest Community Connection*, www.swcommconnection.com; *Southwest Portland Post*, www.swportlandpost.com; *SW News*, 503-823-4592, www.swni.org

Public Transportation: TriMet, 503-238-RIDE, www.trimet.org; bus service on several routes, MAX light rail service available at Washington Park; Portland Aerial Tram (www.gobytram.org) serves the Homestead neighborhood

SOUTHWEST PORTLAND

Boundaries: North: Burnside Street (official); West Hills (unofficial); **West:** Beaverton; West Slope, Raleigh Hills, Garden Home (unincorporated Washington County); Tigard; **South:** Lake Oswego; East: Willamette River

With a few notable exceptions like Lair Hill, the South Waterfront district, and Multnomah Village, Southwest Portland as a whole feels more suburban than any other quadrant of the city. Many Portlanders from other parts of the city either dismiss the neighborhoods here as insufficiently interesting and too "white bread" or ignore them entirely. At the same time, many parts of Southwest Portland are closer to downtown, in terms of both distance and travel time, than some "urban" Eastside neighborhoods are, and no bridge crossing is required to get there. Southwest Portland is also one of the more family-friendly parts of the city, with generally good-to-excellent schools, relatively low crime rates, and plenty of open space; if you take the time to look, there are some decent restaurants and quirky shops, too.

That said, Southwest's nightlife and cultural scene is admittedly inferior to the hot spots of the Pearl, Northwest Portland, and the Eastside, and the area also lacks some of the attributes that many newcomers to Portland seek. Most houses in this part of the city are postwar or newer structures, not the cute bungalows or English Tudor cottages of the older streetcar neighborhoods of the Eastside. An increasing interest in mid-century design, however, means that many Southwest neighborhoods are getting a second or third glance from newcomers who might once have sought out a century-old bungalow. The general lack of sidewalks discourages casual strolling, and the hilly terrain can make cycling a challenge, although the Southwest Trails network offers off-street and low-traffic routes for hikers. Some parts of Southwest Portland feel almost rural, with rutted, potholed, unpaved streets (a characteristic that disconcerts some people). Keep in mind that Southwest Portland, like all parts of the city, is comprised of a diverse set of neighborhoods; chances are that *somewhere* in Southwest may have the specific attributes you're looking for.

SOUTH PORTLAND

Neighborhood Association: South Portland (formerly Corbett–Terwilliger–Lair Hill)

The neighborhoods that border the west bank of the Willamette River south of downtown are among the oldest residential areas in Portland, yet also include some of the most rapidly changing parts of the city. The area offers a diverse range of housing and a quick commute to OHSU or to downtown Portland via various transit options, bicycle path, and a network of major roads: Barbur Boulevard, Interstate 5, Macadam Avenue, and Corbett Avenue. This easy access to highways

Lair Hill

is also a curse, however; the roads chop up entire neighborhoods, and many parts of South Portland are never free of the distant roar of traffic.

The **Lair Hill** neighborhood occupies the lower slopes of Marquam Hill just south of Interstate 405 and downtown Portland. This compact area harbors the oldest largely intact residential development in the city, with a relative abundance of Victorian houses, including Queen Anne and Italianate styles, which are otherwise rare in Portland. These homes were built for workers, not captains of industry, so they are generally small. Many of these old homes have been beautifully renovated since the 1960s, when the then-blighted area was slated for demolition and "urban renewal." The neighborhood is by no means pristine: some houses remain in poor or even dilapidated condition, several major thoroughfares cut through the area, and various more modern and not necessarily attractive buildings—small commercial buildings, apartments, and townhouses—have mixed in with the old homes. New condo and apartment buildings have been built in the vicinity of Duniway Park, primarily to serve the Portland State and OHSU populations. At the same time, the "bones" of the old neighborhood remain, and the close-in location is a significant draw for some newcomers.

The shiny metallic pods of the Portland Aerial Tram soar over the south end of the neighborhood as they shuttle between OHSU atop the hill and the South Waterfront district on the east side of Interstate 5. Major controversy erupted when the tram was first proposed; most Lair Hill residents opposed the project, pointing out quite reasonably that it would not directly serve the neighborhood and that tram riders would be able to peer down directly into residents' back yards. Despite these concerns, the tram was built and began operation in 2007. Local attitudes toward the tram are currently mixed; many residents still object to the invasion of privacy, but others embrace the tram as a new, distinctive neighborhood symbol.

Meanwhile, in the **South Waterfront** district (which the tram directly serves, www.southwaterfront.com), the advent of this novel form of transportation (along with major financial incentives from the city) helped fuel a major construction boom. Once the province of shipbuilders and scrapyards, the district that sarcastic, syllable-challenged hipsters call SoWa now bristles with several new high-rises. OHSU's Wellness Center, one of the greenest buildings in the country (the toilets use harvested rainwater), stands just off the freeway at the lower terminus of the tram. OHSU, which has run out of space on Pill Hill, claims to be planning a major expansion in this area. Meanwhile, several gleaming high-end condo towers rose here—just in time for the real estate bust and the resulting collapse in demand for units in gleaming high-end condo towers. The circular John Ross tower auctioned off many of its unsold units at (relative) fire-sale prices, and the developers of the Ardea scrapped the condo idea entirely and turned the place into a luxury apartment building. With the recovery of the real estate market, construction of several more buildings is planned or under way, and the semi-ghost-town vibe has

South Waterfront

largely vanished. The Portland Streetcar was extended to serve the South Waterfront in 2007, and a new MAX light-rail line will serve the neighborhood beginning in 2015, but the pace and extent of residential development in this area will likely depend on unpredictable economic factors, particularly on the state of the real estate market.

The city hopes that South Waterfront will have 5,000 residents by 2020, and planners and developers seem to be envisioning a sort of mini-Manhattan (or at least mini–Vancouver, BC)—or a Pearl District South—on the banks of the Willamette. These visions may be optimistic. Until recently, shops, restaurants, and other amenities that most people associate with dense urban living have been thin on the ground. Restaurants that have opened in the area, in particular, seem to have been cursed. South Waterfront may finally be getting some traction in this department, with new restaurants, a pub, a wine bar, and a bakery opening their doors in 2014. At the center of the neighborhood, Elizabeth Caruthers Park hosts occasional movies in the park and other community events, including a farmers' market on Thursday afternoons and evenings from June through October. While South Waterfront still has detractors, it also has admirers, and many of its residents appreciate the close-in location along the river, the views, and the relative quietness of the neighborhood (barring traffic noise from nearby Interstate 5).

The neighborhoods south of Lair Hill and the South Waterfront are a mix of commercial, residential, and light industrial uses. Terwilliger Boulevard was one of four city parkways that famed park planner John C. Olmsted envisioned for Portland at the beginning of the 20th century; it was the only one actually built, and today it winds along the slopes of Marquam Hill high above the rest of the city, passing just below OHSU. (If the boulevard's name seems oddly familiar, it may be because *The Simpsons* creator Matt Groening appropriated "Terwilliger" as the surname for the show's Sideshow Bob character.) A broad pedestrian path parallels the road, and the adjacent corridor is almost entirely semi-natural woodland. A small enclave of prewar single-family homes downhill from this parkway, along and off of Hamilton between Terwilliger and Barbur Boulevard, is within strolling distance of OHSU, and offers a rare combination of expansive views and sidewalks. This small, steep neighborhood is popular with doctors and others who work or study on Pill Hill.

A cluster of apartment buildings, some of which are not visible from the street and which offer great views, perch on the slope downhill from Barbur Boulevard and uphill from Interstate 5. East of the freeway, newer offices, townhomes, and condos mix with bungalows and the occasional ranch-style or even modernist home. The **Johns Landing** area along Macadam Avenue is largely devoted to suburban-style office buildings, retail uses, and townhomes, condominium complexes, and apartment buildings, with some restaurants and bars thrown in for spice. Many of the residences have views of the Willamette River and Mount Hood. Johns Landing is also home to a community of houseboats floating in the Willamette. Further south, single-family homes reappear, mixed with townhomes and apartments, in the blocks west of Macadam Avenue and popular Willamette

South Portland

Park on the riverfront. A Zupan's supermarket anchors the south end of the neighborhood at the lower end of Taylors Ferry Road. Uphill from Macadam, along the Corbett Street corridor, mostly older homes in various styles and various sizes have tremendous views over the river and out to Mount Hood.

The neighborhoods of South Portland in general have a more transient population than some other parts of the city; more than half the residents are renters. Because of its abundant supply of rental housing and its close-in location, this area is a popular place for newcomers to settle, at least initially.

HILLSDALE AND MULTNOMAH VILLAGE
Neighborhood Associations: Hillsdale, Multnomah

Hillsdale (not to be confused with Hillsboro, a western suburb) combines a pleasant small-town/suburban ambiance with proximity and easy access to downtown Portland and OHSU. As its name suggests, the neighborhood straddles the lower slopes and dales of the West Hills, between Barbur Boulevard and Dosch Road/Bertha Boulevard. The heart of the neighborhood is Hillsdale Town Center, a 1950s-era business district along SW Capitol Highway that boasts boutiques, several popular restaurants and cafés such as Baker & Spice (www.bakerandspice-bakery.com), a Food Front co-op supermarket, various service providers, and a green-built branch library. The Hillsdale Town Center area also encompasses the full range of K–12 public schools: Wilson High School, Robert Gray Middle School, and the highly regarded Mary Rieke Elementary School. The popular open-air Hillsdale Farmers' Market (www.hillsdalefarmersmarket.com) takes place every Sunday during summer and twice per month in winter.

Hillsdale's amenities and convenient location appeal to young families, and the neighborhood is slowly turning over generationally as the original or second

Johns Landing

Hillsdale

homeowners age. A fairly dramatic rise in home prices in the first decade of this century made the area prohibitively expensive for many entry-level buyers, however. Housing here is largely a mix of postwar single-family styles—Cape Cods, ranches, split-levels, and contemporary homes, many of them extensively remodeled—with daylight ranches (ranch homes built into the side of a hill, with a basement opening to ground level on the downhill side) perhaps the dominant type. A few older bungalows, English-style cottages, and farmhouses survive. (The latter are reminders of the old orchard and dairy farms that dominated the neighborhood until after the Second World War.) Some apartments and townhouses line the major thoroughfares. The Wilson Park neighborhood south of Wilson High School is a 1950s-era subdivision, with sidewalks; in the hilly terrain north of Capitol Highway, the sidewalks vanish, and many homes occupy steep, forested lots with expansive westward or southward views. Some of these homes are fairly ordinary (but not inexpensive) daylight ranches, notable mainly for their hillside perches, but others are dramatic modern structures, custom-designed for their sites. These hillside neighborhoods share many of the wildfire and landslide hazards of the West Hills (which, geographically if not necessarily socially, they are part of). The eastern part of the neighborhood has a heavy concentration of Cape Cods and colonials of various kinds; this area was once part of Burlingame until Interstate 5 was built and sundered this northern portion from the rest of Burlingame. Some of these homes, which are built on the east slope of the West Hills, have terrific views of Mount Hood and the Cascades.

If you're in the vicinity of Seasons and Regions (www.seasonsandregions.com), a popular seafood restaurant in the 6600 block of Capitol Highway, you may notice, especially on Friday through Saturday evenings, a large number of folks walking by in traditional Orthodox Jewish attire. This block is home to the synagogue, day school, and more run by the Chabad Lubavitch of Portland group, and consequently the area is home to a large number of primarily Orthodox Jews.

Multnomah Village

The Mittleman Jewish Community Center and attached Portland Jewish Academy, more or less across the street, serve a much more diverse group of both Jews and non-Jews.

Down Capitol Highway to the southwest, **Multnomah Village** bills itself as "the village in the heart of Portland." This moniker, while not strictly true—it lies a full five miles from downtown—effectively conveys the neighborhood's urban village vibe. (Built around an electric railway station, Multnomah *was* a village until Portland annexed it in the mid-20th century.) Like Hillsdale, Multnomah Village centers on a thriving business district (www.multnomahvillage.org), which encompasses several short blocks of antique stores, restaurants, bars, and quirky specialty shops; local favorites include Marco's Café (www.marcoscafe.com), Thinker Toys (www.thinkertoysoregon.com), and independent bookstore Annie Bloom's Books (www.annieblooms.com). The historic Multnomah Arts Center (a former school) hosts music and theater classes, exercise programs, and community events.

Multnomah Village was built out over a long period of time, and as a result has one of the city's most diverse housing mixes. Although there are plenty of mid-century ranches and funky contemporary homes in the neighborhood, Multnomah has a larger stock of prewar bungalows and cottages than most other parts of Southwest Portland; recent infill development has also brought an onslaught of row houses, new custom homes, and even lofts. Some homes situated on the higher ridges have views of the Cascades or the Coast Range. Home prices here tend to be slightly lower than in Hillsdale, and there are a few truly dilapidated shacks on some streets. There are also an inordinate number of dead-end streets, some of which are rutted and unpaved, and the layout can be confusing to outsiders. Thanks in part to its older urban fabric and unorthodox street grid, the core of Multnomah Village is relatively pedestrian-friendly, and the area accordingly attracts lots of families with small children. The entire neighborhood is within walking distance of 90-acre Gabriel Park, and some streets dead-end into the park.

Thousands of residents and visitors turn out each August for Multnomah Days, a two-day community celebration complete with street fair and parade. Multnomah Village is popular enough, and unusual enough in the context of Southwest Portland, that some real estate listings describe homes that are actually one or two miles away as being in or "close to" Multnomah Village.

Busy Barbur Boulevard, which parallels Interstate 5 and borders both Hillsdale and Multnomah on the south and east, is lined with supermarkets, fast-food restaurants, auto repair stores, and other services (some of a less than savory nature). Multnomah Village and the southern half of Hillsdale, including the Town Center, have frequent bus service to downtown Portland, Beaverton, and Tigard.

BRIDLEMILE AND VERMONT HILLS

Neighborhood Associations: Bridlemile, Hayhurst, Maplewood

As its unimaginative name suggests, Beaverton-Hillsdale Highway runs from the edge of Hillsdale west to Beaverton. Lined for miles by apartment complexes, restaurants, small businesses, supermarkets and strip malls, this thoroughfare is not especially inviting, but the pleasant neighborhoods on either side of the highway are popular with families and with others who are looking for a quiet lifestyle. These areas have many happy long-time residents, however, and there is typically a low inventory of houses for sale.

To the north of the highway, **Bridlemile** is the sort of neighborhood that real estate agents describe as "coveted." Not quite in (or of) the West Hills, Bridlemile nonetheless shares some of the characteristics of that area (including hills). Indeed, the boundary between these regions is indistinct: the neighborhood's northeast corner Is disputed territory claimed by both the Bridlemile Neighborhood Association and the Southwest Hills Residential League. Turf wars aside, Bridlemile is generally quiet and almost wholly residential. Lower Bridlemile, south of Hamilton Street, is largely comprised of relatively small, but by no means inexpensive, one-level ranch homes in tidy subdivisions like Brookford. North of Hamilton, houses are generally larger, and offer better views. Homes in the eastern end of the neighborhood generally date from the 1950s and 1960s; the median home age progressively declines as one travels west, and the western end of the neighborhood has some newer houses, including a few small gated communities that wall themselves off from the essentially nonexistent crime of the surrounding neighborhood. This western part of the neighborhood also includes Wilcox Manor, a former mansion that has been turned into a condo complex.

Bridlemile Elementary School on Hamilton Street, one of the best public elementary schools in the city, feeds into the city's most sought-after middle and high schools; school quality is one of the area's biggest draws. A number of small streams flow through the neighborhood, and some backyards abut these waterways. (The stream corridors are also used by coyotes; keep pet cats indoors.) One

Bridlemile

of the neighborhood's drawbacks is the almost complete absence of sidewalks, or even reasonably wide shoulders, on the main thoroughfares; residents are dependent on vehicles to travel even a few blocks along Shattuck or Dosch Road (for example) without some risk to life and limb. A feature that is either a drawback or an attraction, depending on one's point of view, is the almost complete lack of shops or other commercial activity except along Beaverton-Hillsdale Highway. Barring the neighborhoods of the West Hills proper, the average home price in Bridlemile is the highest Southwest Portland; the crime rate is one of the lowest,

Vermont Hills is the generic name given to the Hayhurst and Maplewood neighborhoods south of Beaverton-Hillsdale Highway. The terrain is indeed somewhat hilly; the main east-west thoroughfare is Vermont Street, which passes along the northern edge of 90-acre **Gabriel Park**, one of the city's best neighborhood parks. (Some people colloquially apply the name Gabriel Park to the entire surrounding area.) Gabriel Park is home to the Southwest Community Center complex, which includes a popular pair of indoor pools. Like Bridlemile, Vermont Hills is mostly residential, but a small shopping center across the street from the Southwest Community Center contains several businesses, including the child-friendly Laughing Planet Café (www.laughingplanetcafe.com). These neighborhoods are also reasonably close to Multnomah Village: Maplewood homes are routinely identified in real estate listings as being "in" Multnomah Village despite actually being up to two miles away.

Vermont Hills was developed mostly in the decades after the Second World War, and daylight ranches and other styles of the 1950s and 1960s dominate here, along with a smattering of Cape Cods, bungalows, and other older home types. However, since many homes originally had large lots, the neighborhood is experiencing substantial infill development, with quite a few large new homes rising in former side yards. There are also pockets of 1970s- and 1980s-vintage contemporary homes scattered on culs-de-sac throughout the area and on some of the steeper slopes, particularly on the ridge south of Beaverton-Hillsdale Highway.

The western part of Maplewood, near April Hill Park, has a number of small new housing developments, generally with large, Craftsman-inspired homes. Wooded stream corridors lace the neighborhood; these corridors provide habitat for wildlife that you might be surprised to see in Portland city limits, including deer and even cougar. A unique feature of the Hayhurst neighborhood is Alpenrose Dairy on Southwest Shattuck Road (www.alpenrose.com), an actual working dairy with an attached little league stadium, velodrome, and child-sized replica of an old western town.

TriMet buses serve both Bridlemile and Vermont Hills along the main thoroughfares, with particularly frequent service along Beaverton-Hillsdale Highway; some routes operate only at peak hours.

Vermont Hills

BURLINGAME AND THE TRYON CREEK AREA

Neighborhood Associations: Arnold Creek, Collins View, Marshall Park, South Burlingame

The neighborhoods south of Interstate 5's Terwilliger curves in Southwest Portland are among the city's hidden delights. These leafy precincts offer generally good schools, low crime rates, and abundant recreational opportunities, but are just minutes away from downtown Portland and from the antique stores and restaurants of Sellwood. These neighborhoods lie between the West Hills to the north and Dunthorpe and Lake Oswego to the south, and some residents feel that the area offers many of the benefits of those areas without the stratospheric real estate prices or perceived snobbery. That's not to say these neighborhoods are cheap—home prices in all these neighborhoods are well above the city average—but they are certainly less expensive than more "established" parts of the city.

The **Burlingame** neighborhood on either side of Southwest Terwilliger Boulevard was largely developed from the 1930s through the 1960s, although some houses in the area date to the 1920s or earlier. Home styles tend toward gracious Cape Cods and ranches, with quite a few English Tudor–style houses and small cottages in the mix. Unfortunately, the construction of Interstate 5 in the 1960s split Burlingame in two; the northern half of the neighborhood became part of Hillsdale (including the "Burlingame" Fred Meyer on Barbur Boulevard), while the southern half became South Burlingame. The most coveted houses stand high on a ridge above Terwilliger and offer excellent views of Mount Hood and Mount St. Helens; more modest homes are tucked into the valleys on either side or in the blocks adjacent to the freeway, although even some of these lower homes have impressive views. (Traffic noise can be troublesome in the areas closest to Interstate 5.) A small commercial district at the intersection of Terwilliger and Southwest Taylors Ferry Road includes a high-end Market of Choice supermarket, a Eugene-based competitor of New Seasons and Whole Foods.

Burlingame

To the south, the **Collins View** neighborhood occupies the slopes above Riverview Cemetery near Lewis and Clark College. The area is popular with professors and others who enjoy living in close proximity to a collegiate environment and to the college's campus and athletic fields; the area also is popular with students, and some residents have complained about recurring problems with noise and litter from off-campus parties. The neighborhood mix is also reflected in the housing stock, which is a blend of well-kept homes, primarily in various post-war styles, many of which sit on large lots with tree cover and abundant greenery, and smaller, sometimes somewhat ramshackle rental houses occupied by students. The neighborhood's grandest homes cluster at its southern end, where Collins View borders, and merges rather seamlessly with, the unincorporated Dunthorpe neighborhood; Dunthorpe's high school, Riverdale High, is actually in Collins View (although it does not serve students in the neighborhood).

Tryon Creek State Natural Area comprises nearly 650 acres of forested hills and canyons between Terwilliger Boulevard and Southwest Boones Ferry Road. The **Marshall Park** and **Arnold Creek** neighborhoods lie just to the west of this unique and eminently hikeable urban park. Both neighborhoods are overwhelmingly residential, with streets winding through hilly terrain cut by numerous creeks, and are characterized mainly by homes built from the 1960s to the present, in many cases on large wooded lots. A few old homes from the early 20th century stand moldering in the dense shade, while some brand-new small-scale developments (of large homes) are being built in the neighborhood's vacant parcels. A few large properties that have not been subdivided are still farmed or otherwise used for traditionally rural purposes. In addition to the State Natural Area, to which some homes have essentially direct backyard access, these neighborhoods include several other natural areas, such as Marshall Park, which lies along Tryon Creek upstream of the state park. The nearest commercial area is actually in Lake Oswego, on Boones Ferry Road. Stephenson Elementary, in the southern part of the Arnold Creek neighborhood, is considered one of the best elementary schools in the city.

OUTER SOUTHWEST NEIGHBORHOODS

Neighborhood Associations: Ashcreek, Crestwood, Far Southwest, Markham, West Portland Park

The neighborhoods in Portland's far southwest—including the neighborhood aptly named Far Southwest—are often overlooked by newcomers and long-time Portlanders alike. While they lack any real commercial districts (excepting the strip mall of Barbur Boulevard), they offer relative convenience. The quiet **Ashcreek** neighborhood, between Multnomah Village and the Washington County border, has consistently enjoyed one of the lowest crime rates in the city. Most homes date from the 1950s to the present, with some older homes along Garden Home Road. Infill development has resulted in a crop of new homes mixed in with existing houses, including entire streets of new subdivisions—a rarity in Portland proper. Overall, Ashcreek is one of the city's woodsier neighborhoods, and some streets have an almost rural feel—a feel enhanced by the absence of pavement on some streets. Nearby, **Crestwood** is something of a southwestern extension of Multnomah Village (and is usually identified as Multnomah Village in real estate listings). The crime rate is nearly as low as Ashcreek's. Homes here are generally well-kept, and the neighborhood has excellent access to Interstate 5; it's also fairly close, via back routes, to the Washington Square mall area. In the heart of the neighborhood, the vegetation in 32-acre Woods Memorial Natural Area is almost entirely native, and the park occasionally attracts elk.

South of Interstate 5, the gently hilly, mostly residential **Markham** neighborhood has a mix of housing, with plenty of daylight ranches, split-levels, contemporary homes and small, nondescript cottages, along with some large, relatively new homes, particularly on the curving streets in the southern part of the neighborhood; 17-acre Maricara Natural Area provides the only significant open space. Freeway noise can be a problem in the northern part of the neighborhood. The hilly **Far Southwest** and **West Portland Park** neighborhoods border Portland Community College's Sylvania campus. The area around the campus features some apartment complexes, but most residential areas are comprised of fairly large, well-kept contemporary and ranch-style single-family homes. In West Portland Park, the area around Jackson Middle School and south to Lake Oswego has some large, newer homes, as well as pre-existing homes that have been subject to high-end remodels. These neighborhoods border the Mountain Park neighborhood of Lake Oswego, and are very convenient to that city's Kruse Way business district. Some homes have good views south over the northern Willamette Valley and west to the Coast Range. Freeway noise is a potential problem near Interstate 5.

Bus service in most parts of outer Southwest Portland is spotty to adequate, with frequent service along Barbur Boulevard and to the Portland Community College campus.

SOUTHWEST PORTLAND NEIGHBORHOOD INFORMATION

ZIP Codes: 97219, 97221, 97239

Post Office: Multnomah Post Office, 7805 SW 40th Ave

Police Station: Portland Police Bureau, Central Precinct, 1111 SW 2nd Ave, 503-823-3333 (non-emergency)

Emergency Hospitals: OHSU Hospital, 3181 SW Sam Jackson Park Rd, 503-494-8311, www.ohsu.org/xd/health/; Providence St. Vincent Medical Center, 9205 SW Barnes Rd, 503-216-1234, www.providence.org

Libraries: Capitol Hill Library, 10723 SW Capitol Hwy, 503-988-5385; Hillsdale Library, 1525 SW Sunset Blvd, 503-988-5388

Parks: Parks throughout area; major parks include Gabriel Park, George Himes Park, and Woods Memorial Park, www.portlandparks.org, and Tryon Creek State Natural Area

Community Publications: *Southwest Portland Post*, www.swportlandpost.com; *Southwest Community Connection*, www.swcommconnection.com; *SW News*, 503-823-4592, www.swni.org

Public Transportation: TriMet, 503-238-RIDE, www.trimet.org; frequent bus service along Barbur Boulevard and Beaverton-Hillsdale Highway between downtown Portland, Beaverton, and Tigard. Additional bus lines with standard or peak hour–only service serve most neighborhoods. Portland Streetcar, Portland Aerial Tram, and MAX light-rail (beginning in fall 2015) serve the South Waterfront district.

NORTHWEST PORTLAND

Boundaries: North: Unincorporated Multnomah County; **West**: Unincorporated Multnomah County; Unincorporated Washington County; **South**: Burnside Street (official); West Hills (unofficial); **East**: Willamette River

It's a bit of an understatement to call Northwest Portland geographically diverse. This part of the city includes the state's most densely populated residential neighborhood, a major industrial complex with port facilities for oceangoing freighters, and a 5,000-acre expanse of virtual wilderness—all within a few minutes of one another. The close-in Northwest neighborhoods are among the city's most desirable and dynamic areas; at the same time, much of Northwest Portland is effectively uninhabited, and large tracts of unincorporated rural land lie just to the west, while historic Linnton on the lower Willamette River was an early rival to Portland. On the west slope of the Tualatin Mountains, the relatively new Forest Heights neighborhood attracts professionals to a master-planned slice of suburbia. Whatever you're looking for in a neighborhood, someplace in Northwest Portland is likely to have it.

NORTHWEST–NOB HILL
Neighborhood Association: Northwest

When Portlanders refer to "Northwest Portland" they generally mean the busy commercial and residential district centered on Northwest 21st and 23rd (or "trendy-third," in ironic hipster parlance) Avenues, north of Burnside Street at the foot of the West Hills. The area is sometimes known as **Nob Hill**, after the San Francisco neighborhood, and rarely as the "Alphabet District," the semi-official name that appears on street signs. This neighborhood is one of the oldest in the city: Captain John Couch claimed the land just north of the incipient settlement of

Nob Hill

Portland in 1845, and platted the area in 1865, with the east-west streets designated by letters of the alphabet in ascending order (i.e., A Street, B Street, and so on) moving north from downtown; for this reason, the area came to be known as the Alphabet District. In 1891, the streets were given names—Captain Couch's name now graces his original C Street—but the alphabetical street order remained. (*Simpsons* fans may notice that Flanders, Lovejoy, and Quimby Streets—formerly F, L, and Q Streets—have lent their names to prominent characters on the show.)

Although it is small, the Northwest district is arguably the most architecturally diverse and interesting part of the city. The early industrialists' grand Victorian houses—some of which have been turned into offices, while others are still used for residential purposes—stand amid modernist residences and offices, uninspired 1960s commercial buildings, apartment buildings and condominiums that span a century of styles, grand 19th-century churches and cathedrals, and the imposing 1928 temple of the Beth Israel congregation. The neighborhood has a particular abundance of vintage apartment buildings, many of which are quite ornate and retain their period features; they are found throughout the district, and the concentration of apartments is such that Nob Hill has long had the state's highest population density. The blocks west of 23rd, and especially west of 25th near Wallace Park, have more houses than apartments; east of 23rd, apartments dominate. Some of these apartments have been converted to condos in recent years, and rents have increased dramatically, but the area still exerts a powerful draw for newcomers, especially young singles and couples, both gay and straight. In general, homes are pricy here compared to homes in much of the city, but are less expensive than in the West Hills or the Pearl, or some of the most sought-after Eastside neighborhoods.

A large part of the district's appeal lies in its stunning variety of shops, bars, and restaurants. For years, before the Eastside commercial districts became the hotspots they are today, and before the Pearl District was even a gleam in a condo developer's eye, Northwest Portland was *the* place to go for nontraditional shopping and dining. (The late lamented Zefiro, which opened in 1990 on Northwest 21st Avenue and closed 10 years later, is widely credited with starting Portland's foodie revolution.) Now that other parts of the city have found their commercial legs, Northwest Portland is still going strong. It would be pointless to try to pick out highlights—Northwest 23rd, and to a lesser extent 21st, are lined with temptations all the way from Burnside to Thurman Street. (Remember, that's B Street to T Street, or 18 blocks.) Just wander down the street and see what strikes your fancy. If you need some visual entertainment, Cinema 21 (www.cinema21.com) on 21st Avenue screens art house films, foreign films, classic films, edgy documentaries, and animation festivals, while the Mission Theatre on Glisan Street shows second-run Hollywood movies accompanied by pizza and beer; CoHo Productions (www.cohoproductions.org) puts on plays at its performance space on Raleigh Street.

It is possible—desirable, even—to live in Northwest without a car. Because so many old apartments lack off-street parking, on-street parking is hard to find.

Even though resident parking permits are required in some parts of Northwest, you might have to park several blocks away from your apartment, which is probably not a big deal if you've moved from New York City but may be a shock if you're coming from, say, Fargo. On the other hand, public transit is frequent and comprehensive; in addition to several bus routes along the main streets, the Portland Streetcar serves the northern end of the neighborhood. It is also quite feasible to walk to downtown Portland. Moreover, unlike many neighborhoods, Northwest Portland has a full crop of markets within walking distance: Fred Meyer and Zupan's supermarkets are on Burnside, the upscale City Market is on 21st (just down the street from Ken's Artisan Bakery, www.kensartisan.com), and a Trader Joe's occupies the site of the old Thriftway supermarket, at 21st and NW Glisan (long known to many neighborhood residents as "Theftway" for its perceived high prices). If a craving for expensive organic products strikes you, the Whole Foods supermarket in the Pearl District is just a few blocks away. Need to get out of town or run a far-flung errand? Zipcar and Car2Go station vehicles in the neighborhood. In short, if you want to live an urban, car-free lifestyle without paying Pearl District rents, Northwest Portland might be for you—if you can afford it. Northwest Portland seems about as developed as it can possibly be, but the district has a last frontier in charmingly named Slabtown, generally east of 21st Avenue and north of Lovejoy Street (or NoLo, as some would have it, tongue not entirely in cheek). This zone of formerly (or currently) dilapidated warehouses and commercial structures, much of it owned by Conway Freight Company, is slowly being redeveloped into a dense urban neighborhood, with scattered condos and apartment buildings already rising. A New Seasons supermarket, frequently a harbinger of revitalization/gentrification, is slated to open at NW 21st and Raleigh in 2015. Stay tuned for new development(s).

Northwest is perhaps most attractive to the young and stylish, but it also appeals to families; Chapman Elementary School, on Northwest Pettygrove, is one of the best public elementary schools in the city, and Northwest feeds into equally high-quality middle and high schools. The entire area is walkable, although you'll have to dodge the occasional junkie or homeless person, especially east of 21st Avenue. A potential downside of the neighborhood for families, besides the traffic congestion, is the relative dearth of parks: the area's two city parks, Couch Park and Wallace Park (next to Chapman Elementary), both have playgrounds, but they can seem painfully far away on a rainy day when junior is melting down in your third-floor, two-bedroom walkup apartment.

Forest Heights

FOREST PARK AND ENVIRONS

Neighborhood Associations: Forest Park, Linnton, Northwest Heights, Northwest Industrial

Most of the land west of Forest Park, along Skyline Boulevard and Thompson Road, is rural, hilly, wooded terrain that is lightly populated and generally outside city limits; the homes that do exist here tend to be mid-century outposts, relict farmhouses, or large, custom-designed houses, often with spectacular views. The exception to the area's sparse development is **Forest Heights**, a vast newer neighborhood created from scratch in the 1990s. Forest Heights spreads across the western slopes of the West Hills, west of Skyline and north of Cornell Road. While Forest Heights could have become a standard suburban cookie-cutter development, an attempt was made to create a community with varied architectural styles and with such neighborhood amenities as walking paths, common areas, and open spaces. The result won't fool you into thinking you're in a traditional urban neighborhood, and the newness of it all creeps some people out, but Forest Heights is arguably one of the better-executed suburban developments in the Portland area.

Home styles in Forest Park range from townhomes and single-family structures built in quasi-traditional "Craftsman" or English Tudor styles to bold contemporary houses and custom-built luxury homes (with not a few McMansions thrown in). The entire neighborhood is part of one homeowners association (www.fhhoa. com) and an architectural review committee must approve all building plans and color schemes, so the neighborhood may not be the best place to try out that nautical crow's nest addition you've always wanted; townhouse and condominium owners also belong to homeowners associations of their own, with monthly association fees. Home prices range from quite a bit above average to *way* above average; median rents are among the very highest in the metro area. Many homes have outstanding views to the south and west, over the Tualatin

Valley to the Coast Range. While the neighborhood is almost entirely residential, there is a small commercial zone that features a small grocery, a Starbucks, a bakery, a wine shop, a day spa, and other essential community services. Forest Park Elementary School, a new school in the middle of the neighborhood, has an excellent academic reputation but suffers from enrollment levels that substantially exceed its design capacity: several classes camp out in portable classrooms.

Forest Heights is not especially close to anything (other than a few other suburban developments), and it feels less like an integral part of Portland than perhaps any other neighborhood in the city. Still, it is a reasonable commute from downtown Portland via Cornell Road or to the employers of Washington County's Sunset Corridor. (The neighborhood seems to be a particular favorite of Intel employees, who can live here with a Portland address but still avoid a grueling commute on the Sunset Highway.) There is no public transit, but the homeowners association operates a private shuttle between Forest Heights and the MAX stop at the Sunset Transit Center.

On the other side of Forest Park, and in sharp contrast to Forest Heights, **Linnton** is an old, mainly industrial neighborhood. Founded about the same time as Portland, Linnton and Portland were originally rivals; the larger city, having won the battle for pre-eminence, absorbed the smaller one in 1915. Most of the houses here perch on the hills or are tucked into wooded canyons west of Highway 30 on the edge of Forest Park, high above the tank farms and other industrial facilities that line the Willamette riverfront. Many homes overlook the river, which is a busy maritime thoroughfare at this point. The bulk of Linnton houses are old, and many have been lovingly restored, but there are also some ranch homes, some newer contemporary or custom homes, and even a few condos. A small commercial district along the highway has a few taverns, convenience stores, gas stations, and a community center. (The district used to be larger; the state bulldozed half of it to make way for extra highway lanes in the 1960s.)

Forest Heights

Linnton

Although Linnton no longer has the job base it once had, it is centrally located for commuting to downtown Portland, zipping across the St. Johns Bridge (which connects Linnton directly to North Portland), or even for winding over the hills to Washington County. Despite the industrial character of the lower parts of the neighborhood, Linnton has a strong community spirit. A decade ago, Linnton residents proposed a rezoning and redevelopment plan that envisioned a mixed-use development—shops, a park, offices, and row house condos—in place of a derelict lumber mill on the waterfront. The City Council put the kibosh on that plan in 2006, citing multiple dangers from earthquakes, landslides, explosions, and other industrial accidents. Some community leaders, bitter over the rejection of their efforts, called for Linnton to secede from the city, but that particular brouhaha seems to have died down.

South of Linnton, the **Northwest Industrial** neighborhood is, as the name indicates, a predominantly industrial neighborhood. A few houses huddle forlornly under the eaves of the forest west of Highway 30, overlooking the area's industrial facilities, but these dwellings are really only appropriate for trainspotters and fans of industrial chic.

NORTHWEST PORTLAND NEIGHBORHOOD INFORMATION

ZIP Codes: 97210, 97229, 97231

Post Office: Forest Park Post Office, 1706 NW 24th Ave; Portland Post Office, 715 NW Hoyt St

Police Stations: Portland Police Bureau, Central Precinct, 1111 SW 2nd Ave, 503-823-3333 (non-emergency); North Precinct (for Linnton), 449 NE Emerson St, 503-823-5700 (non-emergency)

Emergency Hospitals: Legacy Good Samaritan Medical Center, 1015 NW 22nd Ave, 503-413-7711, www.legacyhealth.org; Providence St. Vincent Medical Center, 9205 SW Barnes Rd, 503-216-1234, www.providence.org
Library: Northwest Library, 2300 NW Thurman St, 503-988-5560
Parks: Major parks include 5,000-acre Forest Park and Linnton Park; see www.portlandparks.org
Community Publication: *Northwest Examiner*, www.nwexaminer.com
Public Transportation: TriMet, 503-238-RIDE, www.trimet.org; frequent bus and streetcar service to Northwest Portland–Nob Hill and vicinity; standard bus service along Burnside/Barnes Road to Beaverton and to Linnton, St. Johns, and Sauvie Island via St. Helens Road. Forest Heights neighborhood has a private shuttle to Sunset Transit Center (bus and MAX).

THE EAST SIDE

NORTHEAST PORTLAND

Boundaries: North: Columbia River; **West**: North Williams Avenue; **South**: East Burnside Street (official); Interstate 84 (unofficial); **East**: 82nd Avenue (unofficial)

Northeast Portland offers some of the city's most distinctive and desirable neighborhoods, ranging from the grand homes of Irvington and Alameda Ridge to the family-friendly Grant Park neighborhood and the quirky, self-consciously hip Alberta Arts District. Most neighborhoods in this part of the city have tree-lined, walkable and bikeable streets, attractive parks, and easy access to vibrant commercial districts. The southern half of Northeast Portland is only a few minutes away from downtown or the Pearl District. All these advantages come at a price— median home prices in the most desirable neighborhoods are much higher than the citywide median, and rents are no bargain, although there are still a few pockets of (relatively) affordable houses—but many newcomers who can afford to live here fall in love with this part of the city.

IRVINGTON, SABIN, AND THE LLOYD DISTRICT

Neighborhood Associations: Irvington, Lloyd District, Sabin, Sullivan's Gulch
Stately **Irvington** (www.irvingtonpdx.com), a fashionable residential neighborhood in inner Northeast Portland, started its development in the late 19th century, when Portland's streetcar system expanded to the Eastside; the neighborhood was essentially completely built-up by the end of the 1930s. The neighborhood's first residents were generally middle-class tradespeople. (The city's upper classes mainly lived on the more established Westside.) For many of these early residents, the house they built or bought in Irvington was the first home they had ever

owned. Urban decay and rising crime in the 1960s and 1970s threatened the neighborhood's livability, but a renaissance that began in the 1980s and gathered steam in the 1990s is now essentially complete. Irvington is no longer a starter-home neighborhood by any stretch of the imagination. The average home costs more than twice the average in the city as a whole. Despite the high prices of even a fixer (if you can find one), Irvington is so desirable that some developers are demolishing existing houses to put one (or usually two) brand-new houses on the lot.

Along with the standard Eastside assortment of bungalows, "Old Portlands" (foursquares), barn-like Dutch colonials, and English cottages and Tudor-style homes, Irvington has fine examples of other early late-19th- and early-20th-century styles: Spanish colonial pseudo-villas, Victorians, large arts-and-crafts mansions, prairie-style homes, and plantation-style colonial revival homes. The annual Irvington Home Tour (www.irvingtonhometour.com) held each May shows off a selection of the neighborhood's historic houses. Not surprisingly, given the area's high property values, most homes here have been renovated, and nearly all have been well-tended. The area between Northeast 7th and 15th Avenues, which tends to have slightly more modest homes, was once considered a bit dicey, and revitalization has occurred more slowly there; it is perhaps the only part of Irvington with a more than negligible stock of fixers. (The area is rumored to have been "redlined" by real estate agents for years.) Many of Irvington's larger homes were turned into boarding houses for shipyard workers during the Second World War; most houses reverted to owner-occupied status after the war, but west of 15th Avenue many homes remained divided into two or three apartments. In addition, several apartment buildings, including lovely prewar walkup buildings but also some unattractive concrete structures, occupy the blocks just north of Northeast Broadway along the neighborhood's southern fringe.

The reasons for Irvington's popularity are obvious. It is a neighborhood of sidewalks, well-kept yards, gracious street trees, and attractive homes, yet it is

Irvington

Sabin

remarkably close to downtown Portland—parts of Irvington are scarcely more than a mile away from the central business district. Much of the neighborhood is reasonable walking distance from the MAX stop at Lloyd Center or from the Moda Center arena. Few major streets run through the core of Irvington, and those that do, like Knott (which also boasts some of the neighborhood's grandest homes) mainly carry neighborhood traffic, not commuters. These characteristics appeal to a wide range of buyers, from affluent empty nesters to families with children, who like the old-fashioned neighborhood vibe and the good-to-excellent set of public schools that serve Irvington. There is, however, only one park, Irving Park, in the neighborhood. The Irvington area has also become a popular choice for gay and lesbian couples in recent years.

Although most of Irvington proper is residential—a few retailers on 15th Avenue and Fremont Street and a smattering of B&Bs notwithstanding—the neighborhood is within walking distance of several shopping districts. Northeast Broadway, which forms Irvington's southern boundary, offers a dazzling array of shops, restaurants, bars, and services, ranging from independent bookseller Broadway Books to old-timey Helen Bernhard Bakery (since 1924, www.helen-bernhardbakery.com). Although the Northeast Broadway strip is not as trendy as certain other shopping districts—we're looking at you, Pearl District—it has a fair number of hip nightspots, such as the modernistic Pour Wine Bar & Bistro (www.pourwinebar.com) and the hip tiki bar (not a contradiction in terms, in this case) Hale Pele (www.halepele.com). The area just south of Broadway also includes the Lloyd Center mall and surrounding stores (see below). Moreover, the western half of Irvington is close to the burgeoning scenes on Martin Luther King Jr. Boulevard and Russell Street, the eastern half is within striking distance of Hollywood and Beaumont Village, and the northern tier is a short hop away from Alberta.

Northeast Fremont Street forms Irvington's northern boundary. This area was somewhat derelict little more than a decade ago, but today a small commercial district has sprung up at 15th and Fremont. Here you'll find a Whole Foods supermarket and a clutch of small shops and restaurants, such as County Cork Public House and, a few blocks to the east, the specialty nursery Garden Fever. These businesses are also represent the southern edge of the pleasant neighborhood north of Fremont, **Sabin**, which occupies the southern slope of Alameda Ridge. Both culturally and geographically, Sabin is a transition zone between Irvington and the funkier precincts of the Alberta Arts District. Homes in Sabin tend to be more modest and thus somewhat more affordable than those in Irvington, with a higher concentration of bungalows, foursquares, and English cottages, but average per-square-foot prices are only slightly lower. "Upper" Sabin, the area where the Alameda Ridge begins to rise, is dominated by the city's enormous Vernon water tank; nonetheless, some homes in the tank neighborhood have good views of downtown Portland, and the area surrounding the tank has been turned into a small "hydropark." The eastern part of the neighborhood blends fairly seamlessly into the lower part of the Alameda neighborhood. Sabin has a nice community feel and attracts many young families—Sabin School, the local elementary, is well-regarded—as well as straight and gay couples and some singles.

The **Lloyd District** is sort of an auxiliary downtown on the east bank, tucked between Northeast Broadway and Interstate 84. The center of the neighborhood is Lloyd Center, the city's oldest mall, which shelters the usual range of middle-brow stores. New mid-rise office buildings and hotels dominate the area to the west of the mall. Many of these hotels cater to attendees of events at the nearby Oregon Convention Center; the Moda Center arena (home court for the NBA's Trail Blazers) and Memorial Coliseum are in the western portion of the Lloyd District, known as the Rose Quarter. Some condos and apartments, including new multi-story buildings with views, along with the odd stranded house, provide residential options. There is plenty of construction going on in this area, and much more multifamily rental housing is on the way. While many Lloyd area residents love the convenience, some complain of high levels of perceived crime. (While you are unlikely to become a victim, for some reason the Lloyd District is a favorite

Lloyd District

Sullivan's Gulch

locale for gang members to shoot each other.) Indeed, the Lloyd District has one of the highest crime rates in the city, but its predominantly commercial character perhaps unfairly causes the per-capita crime numbers to skew higher.

To the east of Lloyd Center, the colorfully named **Sullivan's Gulch** neighborhood is squeezed between Northeast Broadway and the bluff overlooking Interstate 84 and the adjacent train tracks. (Interstate 84 was built in the actual gulch during the 1950s.) The neighborhood offers a melange of old and new condos and apartment buildings, mixed with bungalows, foursquares and other older single-family homes, many of which have been beautifully restored. Some of the apartments stand on the edge of the gulch with the freeway and train tracks essentially in the backyard. The buildings a bit farther north tend to be quieter, and offer quick access to the shops and services along Broadway. Most residents here are renters, and Sullivan's Gulch has some of the more affordable close-in rentals in town. As in other convenient Eastside neighborhoods, development has picked up here and new buildings are on the rise.

The southern half of this swath of Northeast Portland is extremely well connected to the rest of the city, both by road and by transit. The Eastside MAX line runs through the Lloyd District, and connects with the Interstate MAX line at the Rose Quarter Transit Center. The CL streetcar line runs from downtown over the Broadway Bridge, and loops through the Lloyd District before heading south to OMSI. Bus lines run along Northeast Broadway, Fremont, MLK, 15th Avenue, and 24th Avenue. Access to downtown Portland by road is 5 to 15 minutes, depending on traffic, via the Broadway Bridge or the Steel Bridge. These neighborhoods also have easy access to Interstate 5 and Interstate 84.

ALAMEDA, GRANT PARK, AND HOLLYWOOD

Neighborhood Associations: Alameda, Grant Park, Hollywood

Between 18,000 and 12,000 years ago, glacial Lake Missoula (in present-day Montana) formed behind a tongue of the ice sheet that covered much of the inland Northwest. Periodically, the lake broke through this ice dam, unleashing massive floods, each of which carried the volume of about 60 Amazon Rivers. These floods repeatedly scoured the Columbia Basin and flowed downstream to the sea past the future site of Portland, carrying and depositing massive amounts of debris. (Eddies of the Missoula Floods reached all the way up the Willamette Valley, burying much of the land in hundreds of feet of silt.) One of the many effects of these floods was to create the rock-filled escarpment that is now known as Alameda Ridge.

Alameda

The west end of the ridge rises in the Sabin neighborhood, and the crest runs east, just north of Fremont Street, eventually turning southeast to cross Fremont; it finally peters out in the Rose City Park neighborhood. The ridge's southern slope is fairly steep—most streets wind up the ridge rather than tackling the grade head-on—while the more gentle northern slope descends gradually toward the Columbia River. The highest section of ridge, west of Northeast 33rd Avenue, is the heart of the **Alameda** neighborhood. The neighborhood features a mix of older houses—bungalows, English Tudors, colonial revival, and stucco-sided, tile-roofed mission revival homes—on tree-lined streets with sidewalks. The houses on the ridge itself or high up on the southern slopes tend to be grand, genre-busting homes (what do you call an enormous arts-and-crafts home with half-timbered details and stucco siding?), often with rich architectural detailing, and most offer tremendous views over the city to the south and west (and in some cases of the Cascades to the southeast). These houses rarely go on the market, and when one does it usually sells for a princely sum.

Off the brow of the ridge, most Alameda houses are smaller (if not necessarily modest) and less expensive, although only compared to their ridgetop brethren; houses in Alameda in general are on average nearly twice the citywide figure, although prices are not rising as fast here as they are in some other neighborhoods. The houses north of the ridge tend toward the tidy bungalow model; some of these homes have views of Mount St. Helens from the upper floors. South of the ridge, housing styles are mixed, but English Tudors are more common, and homes on the southern slope are likely to have at least "territorial" views. More than 80% of Alameda residents own their homes, and houses are generally well-maintained and yards well-tended. Moreover, Alameda has a very low rate of violent crime; in some years, there are no reported violent crimes at all. The neighborhood is overwhelmingly residential, but most homes are within a reasonable walk of the shopping districts at Beaumont Village, further east on Fremont; Hollywood,

Grant Park

about a half-mile south, or the Alberta Arts District, about a half-mile north of the ridge. While the area has numerous long-time and in many cases elderly residents, Alameda Elementary School, on Fremont Street, is one of the most sought-after grade schools in the city, and the area attracts young families who can afford to live here.

Adjacent **Grant Park,** at the southern foot of Alameda Ridge, is a similarly family-friendly neighborhood, also filled with bungalows, English Tudors, cottages, Dutch colonials, and the like (albeit generally smaller than those in Alameda, and on smaller lots). The neighborhood takes its name from the large park at its center, which offers a playground, tennis courts, off-leash dog park, and picnic tables; thanks to the presence of Grant High School, there is also a quarter-mile running track, tennis courts, and a swimming pool. Children's author Beverly Cleary lived in the Grant Park neighborhood for much of her childhood, and several of her stories are set here. (Ramona "The Pest" Quimby lived on Klickitat Street.) Near the playground in Grant Park, a collection of bronze statues of several Cleary characters is set amid a children's play fountain (a popular gathering place for neighborhood families on hot summer days).

Grant Park has tended to attract white-collar professionals in recent years, especially professionals with families: it has one of the highest concentrations of families on the Eastside, due not only to its quiet, walkable streets and the amenities of Grant Park, but also to the traditionally desirable cluster of schools that serve the neighborhood, culminating at convenient Grant High. (A bit of history: the former Hollyrood Elementary, at the north end of the park, barely survived threats of outright closure in 2006, despite having the highest standardized test scores in the entire metropolitan area during the 2005–06 school year; it emerged controversially in rump form as the K–1 campus of the former Fernwood K–8 school, which was renamed the Beverly Cleary School in 2008.) The school cluster has become so popular that the Hollyrood and Fernwood buildings are coping with student numbers substantially in excess of their design capacities.

West of 33rd Avenue, the **Dolph Park** area, while nominally part of the Grant Park neighborhood, is essentially a transition zone between Irvington to the west and Grant Park proper to the east. Spiffy new street signs identify the neighborhood, although the term is not widely used or recognized outside (or necessarily inside) the Dolph Park area. Homes here are generally larger than those in Grant Park, but date from the same era and come in a similar range of styles. This sub-neighborhood is on the whole somewhat quieter than Grant Park proper, mainly because of its greater distance from the high school.

With the exception of a few small professional offices and the QFC super-market on Northeast 33rd Avenue, Grant Park is primarily residential. The library, shops, and restaurants of nearby **Hollywood**, however, are a short walk away. Cinematic-sounding Hollywood was named after the Hollywood Theatre (www. hollywoodtheatre.com), a 1926 movie palace that still stands (and still screens films and hosts special events) on Northeast Sandy Boulevard, Hollywood's main drag. Sandy slices through Hollywood diagonally from southwest to northeast, creating

Hollywood

oddly angled intersections where cross-navigation is difficult and building foot-prints go beyond squares and rectangles. As one of the city's few grid-busting arteries, Sandy carries fairly heavy traffic. Perhaps partially for this reason, Sandy was once a notorious haunt of streetwalkers; that element has mostly vanished from Hollywood, and the street is rapidly improving. Sandy now features several cafés, shops, restaurants, and other (legitimate) service providers, as well as a hulking new mixed-use Whole Foods supermarket/condo combo. The streets south of Sandy have an increasing number of retail stores and other businesses, too, including a relocated Trader Joe's; the Hollywood Farmers' Market (www.hollywoodfarmersmarket.org) is held in the Grocery Outlet parking lot every Saturday morning from May through November, and twice a month through winter.

Several restaurants and other businesses cluster within a block or two to the north of Sandy; Fleur de Lis Bakery, in the old library building at 40th and Hancock, is a favorite neighborhood gathering place. The new, mixed-use Hollywood Library on Northeast Tillamook, which includes a Beverly Cleary themed wall, stands in this area, as do a few smallish-scale condo and apartment buildings, including some nondescript 1960s-era apartments. Otherwise, the blocks between Sandy Boulevard and the foot of Alameda Ridge are filled mainly with 1920s-vintage bungalows, many of which have been restored beautifully. The homes tucked under the brow of Alameda Ridge north of Sandy Boulevard are shady in summer but can be a bit dark during winter. Hollywood has more rentals than in adjacent neighborhoods; it is also busier and has a somewhat higher crime rate, although the neighborhood becomes progressively more quiet as one moves north from Sandy.

The neighborhoods of central Northeast Portland have generally good bus service along North Broadway, Fremont Street, 33rd and 42nd Avenues, and Sandy Boulevard; eastbound and westbound MAX service is available from the Hollywood/Northeast 42nd Avenue Transit Center. By car, these neighborhoods are a 10-minute drive from downtown Portland at off-peak hours, and the airport is only 15 to 20 minutes away.

BEAUMONT VILLAGE, WILSHIRE PARK, AND ROSE CITY PARK

Neighborhood Associations: Beaumont-Wilshire, Rose City Park

Although the name is often used for the surrounding neighborhood as well, **Beaumont Village** refers to the three-quarter-mile stretch of Northeast Fremont Street between 33rd and 50th Avenues, on the plateau just north of Alameda Ridge. The street is lined with upscale (and a few downscale) boutiques, several restaurants, a brew pub, a hardware store, and Beaumont Market, a high-end but well-loved neighborhood grocery. While Beaumont Village lacks the high hipness quotient of some other eastside neighborhoods, it has variety enough to suit most non-hipster needs. (The area surrounding Beaumont Village has more families with young

Beaumont Village

children than, say, the Alberta area, and neighborhood businesses in general tend to be less edgy and more family-friendly.) Traditional one-story storefronts mix with oddities like the so-called Swiss House—a Tudor-style half-timbered building from the 1920s—and dramatic architectural statements like the hulking rust-colored block that is home to a Grand Central Bakery.

The walkable, tree-lined residential streets that branch off Fremont boast a bumper crop of bungalows and English-style homes, along with some Cape Cods and a few lost-looking ranches. Most homes are relatively modest, if not necessarily small. The grand homes concentrated along the section of Alameda Ridge that runs south of Fremont represent a significant exception to this generalization; many of these homes stand on curving streets on the brink of the ridge offering expansive southward views and are akin to the houses in Alameda proper. Some new and not entirely welcomed apartment buildings are rising along Fremont, but in general Beaumont Village has a palpable, cohesive community feel somewhat

Wilshire Park

reminiscent of a small town. In keeping with this vibe, an old-fashioned parade heads down the main drag during Fremont Fest in August.

A few blocks to the north of Fremont, the **Wilshire Park** neighborhood surrounds the 14-acre park of the same name. Homes around Wilshire Park are similar in style to those in Beaumont Village, but with more emphasis on English Tudors and a higher concentration of ranches. The area has been a desirable one for many years, so although home prices in the Beaumont-Wilshire neighborhood are not as jaw-dropping as in neighboring Alameda, the per-square foot price is similar.

To the east, the **Rose City Park** neighborhood is bungalow heaven, particularly south of Sandy Boulevard (although other older house styles certainly exist). Until a few years ago, Rose City Park was full of long-term residents, and was the sort of deep-rooted neighborhood where most of the front steps are covered in Astroturf. Few people moved in, and few people moved out—except perhaps into the neighborhood's Rose City Cemetery. (Rose City Park is where Alameda Ridge goes to die, too; it peters out at its eastern end at about 57th and Sandy.) The neighborhood's traditional insularity may explain why it long remained off the radar screen for most Portlanders. The area has undergone a turnover in the last few years, however. A minor influx of Southeast Asian immigrants, together with couples and young families that were priced out of neighborhoods with a similar feel, has helped diversify and energize the neighborhood, and Astroturfed steps are becoming a rare and kitschy sight. Prices have certainly risen here, but not as sharply as in some other neighborhoods, and Rose City Park, while not cheap, remains relatively affordable compared to the more sought-after neighborhoods a mile or two west. The Fremont Street commercial strip extends into Rose City Park; moreover, the once notoriously skanky section of Sandy Boulevard that bisects the neighborhood is being revitalized, and now features some decent restaurants and shops. Woodsy Normandale Park in the south part of the neighborhood has sports fields and a dog park. Rose City Park (the park, not the neighborhood) adjoins the Rose City Golf Course at the east end of the neighborhood; the park

Rose City Park

hosts live musical performances in summer. Homes in the southern part of the neighborhood endure noise from Interstate 84 and the adjacent railroad tracks.

While Beaumont-Wilshire and Rose City Park are farther (as the crow flies) from downtown Portland than some other Northeast neighborhoods, they're a relatively quick trip downtown by car—about 15 to 20 minutes on Broadway or Sandy, or (during non–rush hours) 10 minutes on Interstate 84—or by bus. Beaumont Village is reasonably close to the Hollywood Transit Center light rail stop, and the 60th Avenue stop is on the southern border of Rose City Park. These neighborhoods are also a short journey from the airport, yet are out of the normal airport flight path and are not typically subject to noise from low-flying planes.

THE ALBERTA ARTS DISTRICT AND CONCORDIA

Neighborhood Associations: Concordia, King (partial), Vernon, Woodlawn

Before a real estate agent with a flair for marketing coined the term "Alberta Arts District," there was simply Northeast Alberta Street, a minor east-west thoroughfare with some basic neighborhood shops and services and an abundance of boarded-up storefronts. In the 1990s, the sound of gunshots and the pulsing flash of police lights were just part of the neighborhood fabric, while the name of another neighborhood street, Killingsworth, became a sort of grim joke. And then something remarkable happened. Through a mysterious and apparently uncoordinated process involving artists priced out of the Pearl District, couples (gay and straight) who saw potential in the neighborhood's inexpensive and often dilapidated old houses, entrepreneurs dealing in exotic niche goods, and other so-called urban pioneers, the neighborhoods north and south of Alberta became the Next Big Thing. In the last few years, the transformation—or gentrification, depending on your point of view—of the neighborhood has become largely complete, and Next-Big-Thing status has migrated westward to North Portland. Some edginess remains, and crime isn't exactly nonexistent, but to see how far the neighborhood has come you need only recall that this part of town couldn't even support a supermarket in the late 1990s. There is now an upscale New Seasons on Northeast 33rd, while the Alberta Cooperative Grocery, www.albertagrocery.coop, is on Alberta proper.

This part of the city slopes gently northward from Alameda Ridge toward the Columbia River, and some residents opine that the area gets more light and has an airier feeling than neighborhoods like Hollywood that lie at the foot of the ridge's southern (steeper) slope. The modern heart of the neighborhood is the stretch of Northeast Alberta Street from MLK Jr. Boulevard east to 33rd Avenue. This newly christened "Alberta Arts District" is lined with a blend of upscale and aggressively countercultural establishments—hair salons (and a dog salon), clothing and knick-knack boutiques, and dozens of coffeehouses, bars, and restaurants—mixed in with long-standing businesses like Acme Glass.

Most businesses are locally owned, although rising rents threaten the viability of some smaller merchants. There are also several art galleries, although fewer than the "arts district" label would suggest. During the Last Thursday (lastthursdayonalberta.com) art walk, created in response to (or in mockery of) the Pearl's First Thursday and held on the last Thursday evening of each month, galleries and other businesses stay open late and the street becomes a freaky carnival of sorts. Close to a mile of Alberta Street is closed to traffic on Last Thursdays from May to September. Last Thursday has become somewhat controversial, in part because it draws so many non-locals, who cause parking and traffic problems and who are not necessarily respectful of the neighborhood. The Alberta Street Fair (www.albertastreetfair.com), held each August, is a bit like Last Thursday on steroids, and the neighborhood comes together at that time to celebrate its distinctiveness.

The blocks north and south of Alberta are primarily filled with bungalows, Old Portlands (foursquares), and homes in other early-20th-century styles. Many of these houses have been lovingly restored, while others were quickly remodeled

Alberta Arts District

and "flipped" for a quick profit as real estate prices in the neighborhood skyrocketed in the early and middle 'aughts. Still others are decidedly fixers. In addition to the older homes, some newer infill buildings, including new homes (built following teardowns or on vacant lots) and even some modern lofts, have been built in recent years. Alberta-area exteriors are notable for displaying a wider and brighter range of paint colors than those in more established neighborhoods. The neighborhood's transition started earlier in the zone south of Alberta Street (i.e., closer to the expensive homes on Alameda Ridge) than in the area to the north; the percentage of renovated homes is generally lower the farther north you go, but don't expect a bargain even on a rundown house within walking distance of Alberta. Keep in mind, too, that gentrification has not brought an end to crime or to urban annoyances like graffiti, and spending a small fortune for a beautifully restored bungalow with original woodwork and exquisite built-ins does not guarantee that your neighbor won't be selling drugs out of his house.

The heart of Alberta falls within the boundaries of the compact **Vernon** neighborhood. The northern and western part of the Alberta district technically falls within the **Woodlawn** area. This area tends to have smaller and less expensive homes than more southerly neighborhoods, but has many of the same characteristics. The neighborhood has the distinction (dubious or enviable, depending on your point of view) of being home to Oregon's first cannabis café, on Northeast Dekum. Stoners shouldn't get too excited (if that's even possible): the café is open only to members of NORML (a marijuana pro-legalization group) who have medical marijuana cards. More conventional businesses line Martin Luther King, Jr., Boulevard at the west end of the Woodlawn neighborhood, including a whole crop of new, trendy cafés, restaurants, and boutiques. Controversy surrounded plans for a new Trader Joe's grocery store to be built in a vacant lot at the intersection of MLK and Alberta Street; the company withdrew from the project in 2014 in the face of vocal (if not necessarily widespread) opposition by local community members opposed to gentrification. Natural Grocers is now expected to build and anchor a facility including commercial and retail space in the vacant lot. The gentrification process is less advanced in Woodlawn than in adjacent districts, and the neighborhood is still a bit rough around the edges. Freight trains run along tracks at the foot of the bluff near Lombard Street at the northern edge of the neighborhood, and train whistles and other noise bother some residents.

The **Concordia** neighborhood, named for Concordia University, includes the eastern half of the Alberta district (which is not an official neighborhood), but also extends further north and east. The blocks beyond the Alberta area consist of quiet, generally well-kept single family houses, with a couple of exceptions: Killingsworth Street, which runs parallel to Alberta several blocks to the north, is undergoing a revitalization of its own, with new businesses opening on a regular basis. The intersection with 33rd Avenue is particularly hopping, thanks to

Concordia

the presence of the New Seasons market, and the corner of Killingsworth and 31st has become one of the city's premier foodie destinations, boasting several top restaurants such as Beast, Cocotte, and DOC. Just to the north, McMenamins Kennedy School is an old elementary school that has been converted to a bar–hotel–movie theater complex; the clever remodel includes kid-height drinking fountains, blackboards in the guest rooms, and "Honors" and "Detention" bars. The tiled soaking pool, which is otherwise only open to overnight guests and paying members of the public, is available for neighborhood residents with picture ID to use for free. The mix of homes in "outer" Concordia is similar to the mix near Alberta, but the average home size is slightly smaller, and a few Cape Cods and ranches are thrown into the mix. Many of the old one-and-a-half-story bungalows have attic space that has been converted into office space, bedrooms, or luxurious (albeit low-headroom) master suites. Fernhill Park, at the eastern end of the neighborhood, with sports fields, a playground, and a wading pool, is the venue for free summer concerts.

The Alberta Area lacks significant woodsy greenspaces, but it has several attractive neighborhood parks, including Alberta Park and Woodlawn Park. While the area around Alberta Street is definitely urban and relatively close-in, the city's grid layout means there is no direct route to downtown Portland, which lies due southwest of the neighborhood. Cars and buses alike either have to travel west to Interstate 5 or Martin Luther King Jr. Boulevard and head south, or travel down 33rd Avenue to Broadway or Interstate 84 and head west. (To put it in geometrical terms, to get to downtown Portland you have to travel along two sides of an isosceles triangle rather than down the hypotenuse.) As a result, travel times are longer than the relatively short distance would suggest: about 15 minutes by car, and at least 20 minutes by bus. Several bus routes serve the area, but many transit trips involve a transfer to light rail.

OTHER NORTHEAST NEIGHBORHOODS

Neighborhood Associations: Cully, East Columbia, Madison South, Roseway, Sunderland

The neighborhoods that lie in the triangle from the Portland Airport vicinity to Interstate 205 and south to Interstate 84 are often overlooked in home searches, although some homes here offer excellent value. **Sunderland** and **East Columbia**, near the airport, are mainly industrial, although East Columbia includes an enclave of single-family contemporary homes near the Columbia Edgewater Country Club. Sunderland is home to the city's recycling yard as well as to Dignity Village, a semi-permanent, self-governing tent camp for the city's homeless. The northern tip of Sunderland touches the Columbia River, where some houseboats are moored. In contrast to these sparsely populated neighborhoods, **Cully** has a substantial population—about 13,000 people—and is one of the most diverse areas

Cully

of the city. The areas adjacent to the Rose City Park and Beaumont Village/Wilshire Park areas, north of Fremont and the Rose City Cemetery, offer some attractive small bungalows along with newer (but still small) ranch homes and some infill development. Many properties have large lots, and in some parts of the neighborhood you can almost image being in a rural area (if you squint and plug your ears). Indeed, in 2014 an errant black bear was removed from a tree here, which is not something that has happened in closer-in Northeast neighborhoods in recent years. The northern part of the neighborhood is largely light industrial, and this part of Cully sometimes suffers from airplane noise. Parts of the neighborhood are neat as a pin, while in others neatness is an exception. Much of the neighborhood lacks sidewalks, and many of the streets are unpaved. Moreover, while there are parks in adjacent neighborhoods, Cully itself is somewhat park-deficient; the main "park" is the grounds of Rigler Elementary School (which has an adjacent community garden). Many Cully residents complain that the city pays insufficient attention to the needs of their neighborhood. That said, there is some housing stock with good bones here, and per-square-foot housing prices are among the lowest in the city.

The **Roseway** neighborhood straddles a not very attractive, but slowly improving, section of Northeast Sandy Boulevard. The neighborhood has more than its share of "adult" shops on Sandy, but it also has some lovely bungalows, English-style cottages, Cape Cods, and ranches on quiet, walkable streets. Home prices here are a bit higher than in other outlying parts of Northeast Portland, but are substantially lower than in the more fashionable, closer-in neighborhoods. Roseway has good bus service along Sandy, Fremont, Prescott, and 82nd, and the neighborhood is reasonably close to the airport and main Eastside MAX lines. The adjacent **Madison South** neighborhood has somewhat newer homes on average than other neighborhoods west of Interstate 205, although there are still plenty of prewar homes "with character" here. In general, housing here is even less expensive than in Roseway, except for homes on Rocky Butte, the hill abutting Interstate

205 east of 82nd Avenue, which tend to be custom-designed structures with great views of downtown Portland, the Cascades, or (less appealingly) the airport. Rocky Butte homes are much pricier than homes elsewhere in the neighborhood, and some are valued at more than a million dollars. Rocky Butte features a summit lookout and some popular hiking and rock climbing locations. Madison South is also home to the Grotto, a peaceful Catholic garden/retreat that is famed for its Christmas light display and musical performances. The small neighborhood of **Sumner** just to the north has a few small cottages, but is dominated by light industrial facilities and various hotels, restaurants, and other sites associated with the nearby airport. Madison South and Sumner have excellent bus and MAX access.

NORTHEAST PORTLAND NEIGHBORHOOD INFORMATION

ZIP Codes: 97211, 97212, 97213, 97218, 97220, 97232,

Post Offices. Airport Mail Facility, 7460 NE Airport Way; Holladay Park Post Office, 815 NE Schuyler St; Piedmont Post Office, 630 NE Killingsworth St; Rose City Park Post Office, 2425 NE 50th Ave

Police Stations: Portland Police Bureau, North Precinct, 449 NE Emerson St, 503-823-5700 (non-emergency); East Precinct (for Madison South only), 737 SE 106th Ave, 503-823-4800 (non-emergency)

Emergency Hospitals: Legacy Emanuel Medical Center, 2801 N Gantenbein Ave, 503-413-2200, www.legacyhealth.org; Providence Portland Medical Center, 4805 NE Glisan St, 503-215-1111, www.providence.org

Libraries: Albina Library, 3605 NE 15th Ave, 503-988-5362; Gregory Heights Library, 7921 NE Sandy Blvd, 503-988-5386; Hollywood Library, 4040 NE Tillamook St, 503-988-5391

Parks: Major parks include Irving Park, Grant Park, Wilshire Park, Normandale Park, Rose City Park, Alberta Park, and Rocky Butte; www.portlandparks.org

Community Publication: *Hollywood Star*, www.star-news.info

Public Transportation: TriMet, 503-238-RIDE, www.trimet.org; extensive bus network on main streets, especially in close-in neighborhoods; Eastside and Airport MAX lines serve southern and eastern neighborhoods.

SOUTHEAST PORTLAND

Boundaries: North: East Burnside Street (official); Interstate 84 (unofficial); **West:** Willamette River; **South:** Milwaukie; **East:** 82nd Avenue (approximate)

Southeast Portland is in many ways the epitome of the image some people conjure up when they think of Portland: funky cafés, second-hand boutiques, tree-lined streets lined with old houses, plenty of aging hippies and bearded hipsters, bike riders galore, and one of the most consistently liberal voting records of any neighborhood in the country. While the Legalize Pot and Free Mumia crowds

Inner Southeast

are certainly a part of the neighborhood fabric, Southeast Portland is also the haunt of families, immigrants, students, professionals working for The Man, artisans, drug addicts, retirees, construction workers, and community and political activists of every stripe. Since not all of these types of people are usually found in the same place, it's safe to say that most people will feel at home somewhere in Southeast Portland—unless you're, like, too uptight, man.

INNER SOUTHEAST PORTLAND

Neighborhood Associations: Brooklyn, Buckman, Hosford-Abernethy, Kerns

The neighborhoods of inner Southeast Portland—the zone extending east of the Willamette River to roughly 28th Avenue—are a pastiche of tight-knit, generally laid-back urban environments where the neighborhood coffee shop is just around the block and there's always a new up-and-coming band at the bar down the street. These neighborhoods have perhaps the highest hipster quotient in the city, and (or but, depending on your point of view) also boast the country's highest percentage of residents who commute by bicycle.

The blocks closest to the river make up the **Central Eastside Industrial District**, a district zoned for commercial, warehouse, and light industrial use. In many ways it is the city's workshop, with many "artisanal" industries—tile makers, lampwrights, microdistilleries, specialty food companies, etc.—headquartered here, along with some less sexy but equally necessary businesses, like store fixture and used office furniture stores. Some worthy bars and eateries appear among the warehouses; cheeky, popular Bistro Montage (www.montageportland.com) lurks, troll-like, under the Morrison Bridge approach ramps, while the Produce Row Café (www.producerowcafe.com) has a popular outdoor beer garden. Formerly grimy Water Avenue is home to trendy Boke Bowl, the Bunk Sandwich Bar, Hair of the Dog Brewery, and Clarklewis restaurant. The stretch of East Burnside east of the bridge has gone from being a sketchy auxiliary skid row to hosting a bevy of upscale, trendy establishments, like the neo-mid-century Doug Fir Lounge (www.dougfirlounge.com) and celebrated restaurant Le Pigeon (www.lepigeon.com). This area has been unofficially rechristened as Lower Burnside (or, if you must, LoBu).

The Industrial District is also home to the Oregon Museum of Science and Industry (OMSI), which sits along the river almost directly beneath the clunky double deck of Interstate 5's Marquam Bridge. Unfortunately, Interstate 5 cuts off the rest of the Inner Eastside from its riverfront; the only river access between OMSI and the Steel Bridge is the Vera Katz Eastbank Esplanade. Opened in 2001, the Esplanade is a partly-fixed, partly-floating bike and pedestrian walkway that runs between the Hawthorne and Burnside bridges. Signs indicate where the main east-west streets would run (if they weren't on the other side of six lanes of roaring traffic). The Industrial District is essentially an industrial reserve, intended to maintain space where high-wage businesses can start and grow close to the city center, and housing developments are not allowed. Still, a few old Victorian houses, many of them beautifully (and colorfully) restored, linger poignantly among the industrial facilities and warehouses.

A few blocks in from the river, apartment buildings and other residential buildings start to become more common. In the **Kerns** and **Buckman** neighborhoods, to the north and south, respectively, of East Burnside Street, prewar walkup apartment buildings and duplexes mix with many old single-family homes and a crop of two-story 1960s-era apartment complexes randomly scattered through the neighborhoods; the latter have provided affordable housing for two generations of young people. A flurry of loft and apartment building construction is beginning to radically transform the streetscape along the main thoroughfares; because these buildings often lack adequate off-street parking, and the new residents are not as car-free as the developers would have people believe, finding on-street parking is becoming a problem in some areas. Kerns and Buckman both feature abundant commercial zones, including popular bars and

Inner Southeast

Ladd's Addition

restaurants. In particular, the intersection of East Burnside and 28th Avenue draws visitors from around the city to its strip of businesses, including boutiques, wine bars, acclaimed restaurants like Ken's Artisan Pizza (www.kensartisan.com), and cafés; the strip has been dubbed "Restaurant Row." For some reason most of the restaurants cluster on the east side of 28th. The second-run, multi-screen, deco-style Laurelhurst Theater is also at this intersection. A smaller commercial zone at Glisan and 28th includes popular Cuban restaurant Pambiche (www.pambiche. com) and the funky Laurelthirst Public House. The Buckman Portland Farmers' Market (www.portlandfarmersmarket.org) is held at Southeast Salmon Street and 20th Avenue on summer Thursday afternoons and evenings. Historic Lone Fir Cemetery, between Stark and Belmont Streets, is the final resting place for many of Portland's early movers and shakers; it also serves as a *de facto* greenspace for the surrounding neighborhood. For an impromptu history game, walk among the graves and try to match the names on headstones to Portland street names. The range of amenities, diverse housing options, and proximity to downtown Portland by bike make these neighborhoods popular choices with young singles and couples. Buckman and Kerns tend to be less popular with families and older couples and singles, in part because of the relative lack of parks, the somewhat transient young population, and the many busy thoroughfares that traverse these neighborhoods. Prices and housing options vary widely, although bargains are few; the vacancy rate is the lowest in the city, but average rents are not as high as the low vacancy rate might suggest.

Just south of the Buckman neighborhood, and north of Brooklyn, lies the **Hosford-Abernethy** neighborhood, the most well known portion of which is Ladd's Addition. South of Hawthorne Boulevard, between 12th and 20th Avenues, **Ladd's Addition** smashes the street grid of Southeast Portland with a series of diagonal streets and circles that slice the neighborhood into a group of circles, triangles, quadrilaterals, diamonds, and other shapes that would make any high school geometry teacher drool. The neighborhood has five rose gardens: a large one in the central circle, with four smaller, diamond-shaped gardens. Unfortunately, virtually no one from outside the neighborhood gets to see these gardens, because to the uninitiated they are impossible to find. On the plus side for residents, the confusing street layout ensures that few drivers try to take short cuts through the neighborhood, and those that do rarely attempt a second incursion. (The lack of car traffic makes the streets of Ladd's Addition a popular route for bicyclists, and there are frequent pulses of bike traffic down Ladd Avenue during morning and evening rush hours.)

The story behind the neighborhood's unusual geometry is that the developer, William Ladd (who was posthumously responsible for Laurelhurst, Eastmoreland, and several other notable Portland neighborhoods) supposedly sought to emulate Pierre L'Enfant's design for Washington, D.C., on a small scale. Ladd's Addition was platted in 1891, but due to an economic downturn no homes were built until 1905.

The homes that were built in Ladd's range from petite bungalows and Spanish-style homes with red tile roofs to enormous Arts and Crafts homes, with some postwar ranches and Cape Cods thrown in for chuckles. A few older garden court–type apartments can also be found here. The neighborhood has become very expensive, although a few choice houses in the neighborhood still await restoration (which doesn't mean they're cheap). The elm-shaded streets and grand old homes, combined with its location just over a mile from downtown Portland, make Ladd's Addition one of the most sought-after places to live in Southeast Portland. Needless to say, houses do not linger on the market here.

Most residents are either retired or are high-income professionals, including professionals with children. (The neighborhood's Abernethy Elementary School has an innovative curriculum and is highly regarded.) While the heart of Ladd's Addition is residential (barring the Palio Dessert and Espresso house on Ladd Circle, at the very center of the neighborhood, if you can find it), the entire neighborhood is within easy walking distance of the shops, restaurants, and cafés on Hawthorne Boulevard and on Division and Clinton Streets. In 2009 the American Planning Association named Ladd's Addition one of America's top 10 "Great Neighborhoods," citing its historical character, unique design, and bike- and pedestrian-friendliness. Indeed, Ladd's Addition represents a sort of idealized Portland—a leafy neighborhood of single-family homes, but within walking and biking distance to everything—that has become increasingly had to find in reality.

The gently rising area to the east of Ladd's Addition is known as **Colonial Heights**. The neighborhood's name does not refer to the houses themselves; while there are a few Dutch colonial houses in the neighborhood, the bulk of the housing stock is bungalows, English-style cottages, and other styles from the 1920s and 1930s, with a fair number of infill 1950s ranches mixed in. The neighborhood has an unusual number of churches, but is otherwise generally residential; as in Ladd's Addition, however, the shopping zones along Hawthorne Boulevard and Division Street are within a short walk of any point in the neighborhood.

Colonial Heights

Colonial Heights does sit on a small hill, and some homes have peek-a-boo views of downtown Portland and the West Hills. In general, home prices here are lower than in Ladd's Addition, but higher than some of the nearby neighborhoods to the east and south.

The **Clinton Street** neighborhood centers on the cluster of restaurants, bars, cafés, and the Clinton Street Theater (www.cstpdx.com) at Southeast 26th and Clinton, but the area popularly identified as Clinton Street reaches as far west as 12th Avenue. (Although Division Street is a main thoroughfare and carries substantially more traffic than Clinton Street, the prewar streetcars ran along Clinton, and locals continue to use the old name for the neighborhood.) The neighborhood housing stock consists mostly of small to mid-size bungalows with small but often lovingly landscaped yards, along with some 1960s apartment buildings and a smattering of warehouses and other commercial buildings, especially in the western end of the neighborhood. Many of the older homes have been renovated, while some haven't

Clinton Street

Brooklyn

seen a paintbrush in decades, although the former now outnumber the latter. A few modern condos, townhomes, and commercial buildings have gone up in the neighborhood, not all of which are to residents' liking, and new businesses are opening up and down Clinton Street and on a few intersecting streets.

New businesses have cropped up on Division Street, too, most notably the New Seasons supermarket, which is credited with helping spark the neighborhood's renaissance. The Seven Corners intersection, where SE Division, SE 20th, and SE Ladd all meet, is sometimes called the Seven Corners Progressive Vortex because of its concentration of progressive businesses. Just south on 21st, the venerable People's Food Co-op (www.peoples.coop) supplies the neighborhood with organic produce and bulk foods; the store also hosts one of the city's few year-round farmers' markets. Further east, Division becomes a restaurant row, lined with some of the city's most-lauded restaurants. (See "The Hawthorne, Belmont, and Division Street Districts" below.)

South of Powell Boulevard, historic **Brooklyn** began its existence in the 19th century as a working-class, largely Italian enclave centered on the neighborhood's extensive rail yards. The Italians are mostly gone, but the rail yards remain, and, between freight trains to the east and truck and commuter traffic on McLoughlin Boulevard to the west, this triangle-shaped neighborhood remains a transit hub. Brooklyn contains some warehouses and light industrial buildings, along with a few bars and restaurants and the Aladdin Theater, one of the best places in the city to see live music, on Milwaukie Avenue, but the bulk of the neighborhood is residential. Homes here range from grand Victorians and cute bungalows to apartments and a few postwar ranches. Many of the larger homes have been converted to multi-family use, and more than half of Brooklyn residents are renters. The neighborhood is a demographic mixed bag, with a mingling of families, singles, childless couples, and long-time elderly residents of widely varying income levels, which reflects its wide appeal to everyone from Aunt Petunia to international guitar gods. (Ex-Smiths guitarist Johnny Marr bought a house here when he moved from England to Portland to join indie band Modest Mouse.) Despite the neighborhood's working-class roots, the single-family houses for sale here don't boast working-class price tags: the average home price is somewhat higher than the city average. Prices are increasing in Brooklyn much faster than in most Portland neighborhoods, perhaps driven by the new MAX light-rail line through the eastern part of the neighborhood that is slated to open in late 2015.

All the Inner Southeast neighborhoods are within a 5-minute drive or 10-minute bus trip or bike ride of downtown Portland. The CL streetcar line from the Lloyd District to OMSI runs along MLK Jr. Boulevard (southbound) and Grand Avenue (northbound); an extension across the Tilikum Bridge to the South Waterfront District is scheduled to open in late 2015. The new MAX light-rail line to Milwaukie, also slated to begin service in late 2015, will include a Brooklyn station at SE 17th Avenue and Rhine Street.

LAURELHURST

Neighborhood Association: Laurelhurst

The imposing sandstone arches that mark the main entrances to Laurelhurst suggest that the neighborhood is special—or "high-class," as the Laurelhurst Company promised in its circa 1910 promotional materials. From the beginning, Laurelhurst was intended to be a relatively exclusive district. The company, a spinoff of the Ladd Estate Company (which was responsible for creating the Eastmoreland, Westmoreland, and eponymous Ladd's Addition neighborhoods in Southeast Portland), hired the Olmsted brothers to design the neighborhood's sinuous streets, and enforced a minimum home cost to keep the riff-raff out.

Nearly a century later, Laurelhurst is still one of the most sought-after (and thus expensive) neighborhoods on Portland's Eastside. Home prices are comparable to

Laurelhurst

prices in Alameda and Eastmoreland, and Laurelhurst's demographics and general feel are comparable to those neighborhoods in many respects. Laurelhurst is entirely residential, and the overwhelming majority of homes are single-family detached houses built between 1910 and the Second World War. Architecture runs the gamut of prewar styles, from foursquares to tile-roofed Spanish colonials, although bungalows of various sizes and configurations are the most common house types. Although many of these houses are quite grand, and some are bona fide mansions, lot sizes tend to be relatively small. Laurelhurst has an active neighborhood association that maintains constant vigilance, watching for developments that might affect the neighborhood's livability.

Demographically, Laurelhurst has a high concentration of affluent professionals, and the neighborhood is a mix of long-time residents and young families; many of the latter are attracted by the quality of the neighborhood's Laurelhurst Elementary School. Another attraction is Laurelhurst Park, which is sometimes referred to as the Portland equivalent of New York's Central Park. That comparison overstates things, but the park is undoubtedly lovely, and features a spring-fed lake, mature trees, a playground, and tennis and basketball courts. (Like Central Park, however, Laurelhurst Park is not entirely safe at night, although the neighborhood itself has a relatively low crime rate.) Laurelhurst's other notable landmark, Coe Circle, at the intersection of Northeast Glisan Street and César E. Chávez Boulevard, contains a gilded statue of Joan of Arc. Just west on Glisan, Holy Trinity Greek Orthodox Church hosts a popular Greek Festival each October.

Laurelhurst's curving streets are generally quiet, but busy Burnside, Glisan, and Stark Streets, and César E. Chávez Boulevard (renamed from 39th Avenue in 2009, not without controversy) all cut through or border the neighborhood, and Interstate 84 runs along the northern boundary. While these major thoroughfares bring traffic and noise concerns, they also ensure that the neighborhood is well-connected, with plenty of transit options. Several bus lines serve Laurelhurst, and the Hollywood/42nd Avenue MAX stop is a short walk away; downtown Portland is about a 10-minute drive down Burnside or on the freeway. There are no restaurants or other businesses within Laurelhurst proper, but most homes are within walking distance of at least one of the nearby business districts in Hollywood, the Belmont district, Burnside Street west of 32nd Avenue, or the restaurant row on Northeast 28th Avenue.

THE HAWTHORNE, BELMONT, AND DIVISION STREET DISTRICTS

Neighborhood Associations: Richmond, Sunnyside

Hawthorne Boulevard was known as Asylum Avenue until the late 1880s. Although a few people still call it that, presumably tongue-in-cheek, it is known today as the heart of the **Hawthorne District**, a strip of restaurants, bars, cafés,

Hawthorne District

and many kinds of shops that stretches for nearly 30 blocks from the vicinity of Ladd's Addition toward the base of Mount Tabor. Sometimes described as Portland's "Bohemian" neighborhood, or the Portland equivalent of Haight-Ashbury, Hawthorne has nonetheless lost much of its countercultural vibe in recent years (and, for that matter, the neighborhood has few immigrants from the Czech region of Bohemia). Yes, there are head shops and Grateful Dead–themed pubs along Hawthorne—and if there's a less attractive store logo than the prone-ancient-bearded-dwarf-hippie-with-bong picture that announces Smoking Glass, we've never seen it—but they are overwhelmingly outnumbered by a diverse host of other businesses.

There are far too many interesting establishments along Hawthorne to flag just one or two examples, but the heart of the business district is at 37th and Hawthorne, a spot that used to be called karma corner because you would inevitably run into old acquaintances (or boy- or girlfriends) there. This is still a danger, thanks to attractions like the Bagdad Theater and Pub on the southeast corner, or the Powell's Books branch on the north side of the street, which pull visitors from all over the city. The business district continues east of 39th Avenue/César Chávez Boulevard as far as 50th Avenue, although development is less dense here. The trendy bars at the upper end of Hawthorne are popular destinations for pub crawls; this stretch of the street is sometimes referred to as the Stumble Zone, for obvious reasons.

Paralleling Hawthorne six blocks to the north, **Belmont Street** has a similar, but smaller, selection of businesses. The Belmont Dairy mixed-use complex houses apartments, townhomes, and an upscale Zupan's supermarket; to either side and across the street are restaurants, coffeehouses, an old movie theater-*cum*-video arcade (the Avalon), antique stores, and boutiques. A Walgreen's on the corner of Belmont and 39th/César Chávez does a brisk late-night trade. The Belmont business district continues east of César Chávez in an intermittent, desultory way; highlights include Movie Madness (possibly the best video rental store in the Northwest, www.moviemadnessvideo.com) and the British-style Horse Brass Pub (www.horsebrass.com), which has a legendary beer selection and screens English Premier League soccer games.

Paralleling Hawthorne a few blocks to the south, **Division Street** is one of

Belmont Street

the city's most rapidly changing thoroughfares. The half-mile or so west of César Chávez has seen a boom in residential loft and apartment building construction, but at the same time it has evolved into perhaps the city's pre-eminent "restaurant row." This part of Division is home to restaurants as diverse as nationally renowned Pok Pok (www.pokpokpdx.com, Thai street food), Ava Gene's (www.avagenes.com, high-end rustic Italian), Xico (www.xicopdx.com, inventive Mexican-inspired cuisine), and Lauretta Jean's (www.laurettajean.com, handmade pies), to name just a few. Division does not yet have the shopping options that Hawthorne enjoys, but it has now surpassed Hawthorne in the eateries department.

The residential neighborhoods that flank Hawthorne, Belmont, and Division house a mix of twenty-something singles, original hippies and their latter-day wanna-bes, skate punks, professionals, blue-collar workers, and both bona fide and aspiring indie pop stars. A substantial number of families with children also live in the area, particularly east of 39th Avenue/César Chávez. The neighborhood south of Hawthorne, officially known as **Richmond**, has a higher proportion of homeowners than the blocks north of Hawthorne (officially known as **Sunnyside**), but single-family and multi-family dwellings are found throughout the area.

Most homes in this area are bungalows, foursquares, or other prewar types, although some new townhomes, custom homes, and tall, skinny detached homes on narrow lots are being built as infill or as replacements for dilapidated older homes, and apartment bunkers are being slapped up with seeming abandon on the main streets. The old streetcar line down Belmont, opened in the 1880s, was the first line on the Eastside, and the adjacent blocks have a higher concentration of Victorians than most other parts of the city. (The Pied Cow coffeehouse on Belmont occupies one of these.) There are also plenty of 1920s garden apartments and brick walkups, along with hulking 1960s-era low-rise apartment complexes and some spanking new condos like the strikingly modern (and controversial) Belmont Street Lofts. Particularly east of César Chávez, these streets also offer other varieties of old houses, including English Tudor–style cottages, Cape Cods, and even a few ranches. Peacock Lane, which parallels César Chávez one block to the east between Belmont and Stark, is a street of 1920s-vintage English cottages known for its annual holiday light display.

Thanks to the close-in location and the abundant local shopping and dining opportunities, the median price for a single-family home in this area is well above the city average, but less than in more exclusive, predominantly residential neighborhoods to the north. Homes are generally more expensive east of César Chávez and less expensive south of Division Street, in an area that has not been as popular for as long as the zone closer to Hawthorne Boulevard. The Waverly Heights neighborhood, west of César Chávez Boulevard between Division and Powell, was for many years a good bet for more affordable older homes, but the redevelopment on Division has pushed up prices in this area. For many people, these neighborhoods represent a good compromise between price, location, and urban amenities.

Throughout the area, home conditions and neighborhood "feel" can vary tremendously from one block to another: some blocks are lined with restored Craftsman bungalows with mature shade trees and laughing children on tricycles, while others have ramshackle houses with overgrown yards next to grim, windowless mystery buildings. Unless you are a fan of loud, late-night drunken conversations, you may want to avoid living within a block or so of the main commercial zones. Also be aware that on-street parking can be in short supply near Hawthorne, Belmont, and Division Streets. Many of the old houses in these neighborhoods maximize their small lot sizes by sharing a single driveway between two neighboring homes; often each house will have its own small garage at the rear of the lot.

These districts enjoy frequent bus service down Hawthorne, Belmont, Division, and Powell to downtown Portland, and north along 39th/César Chávez to the Hollywood MAX stop. It is a quick bike ride down designated low-traffic "bike boulevards" to downtown Portland, and these neighborhoods have one of the city's highest percentages of bike commuters. By car, it's a 10-minute shot west over the Hawthorne or Morrison bridges into downtown Portland.

Mount Tabor

MOUNT TABOR

Neighborhood Association: Mount Tabor

Mount Tabor, the tree-clad butte that dominates the landscape about four miles due east of downtown Portland, is home to one of the city's most diverse and popular parks. The park includes playgrounds, picnic areas, hiking trails, tennis courts, an off-leash dog park, and an extinct volcano. The park also has three open-air (but fenced-off) reservoirs, built in the late 19th and early 20th centuries. (The city's effort to cap the reservoirs for security reasons after the September 11 attacks met with a firestorm of opposition, and the reservoirs apparently will remain uncovered for now.) Mount Tabor offers fantastic, tree-framed views of Mount Hood, Mount St. Helens, and downtown Portland, too; the lawn on the west slope, just below the summit, is a favorite spot to watch the sun set over downtown and the West Hills, as the lights of Hawthorne Boulevard twinkle on 500 feet below.

Forest (and later, fruit orchards) covered Mount Tabor and the surrounding area until the late 19th century, when the Belmont streetcar line reached the neighborhood and significant residential development began. The western part of the neighborhood, especially the area between Hawthorne Boulevard and Stark Street just downhill from the park, contains some truly grand houses in a mix of styles ranging from Italianate and Queen Anne Victorian to Arts and Crafts and colonial revival. Many of these homes have views of the downtown skyline, and some have large yards with massive specimen trees—giant sequoias, monkey-puzzle trees, or European beeches, for example—that are now well over a century old. Interspersed with these elegant near-mansions are a host of more modest bungalows, foursquares, Dutch colonials, and English cottages; the first two styles are especially prevalent on the blocks south of Hawthorne, which are similar to the residential areas of the Hawthorne District proper and generally feature a younger mix of residents. High up on the north side of the hill, just below the northern

Sellwood

entrance to the park, Belmont passes through a separate enclave of bungalows and other prewar homes; in addition to easy access to the park, many of these homes have wonderful Mount Hood views. The slopes downhill and further north were developed much later, and include a large number of mid-century ranches, many with views north to Mount St. Helens. The slightly less fashionable blocks to the east and northeast of the park have a mix of prewar and mid-century homes, many of which have been restored in recent years; again, thanks to the salutary effects of elevation, many of these homes have views of Mount Hood and Interstate 205 (which, from a distance of about a mile, is actually not a bad prospect). In general, Mount Tabor home prices are higher than in the adjacent flatlands, but lower than in fashionable closer-in neighborhoods such as Irvington. About a third of the neighborhood residents rent; rentals are most common on the western and northern fringes of Mount Tabor.

Warner Pacific College, a Christian liberal arts college, has a campus on Southeast Division Street, adjacent to the south end of the park. (A proposed college expansion onto city-owned land generated heated neighborhood opposition, and appears to be dead.) Apart from a few small, isolated businesses, there are essentially no commercial areas within the Mount Tabor neighborhood, but most homes are within walking distance of a shopping district: the Hawthorne and Belmont districts on the west side, the burgeoning commercial district along Southeast Stark Street in Montavilla on the east side, and, on the north side, the QFC supermarket on Burnside Street and the Fred Meyer on Northeast Glisan Street, along with some smaller associated businesses.

It's a 10- to 15-minute drive or 20- to 25-minute bike ride from Mount Tabor west to downtown Portland. Buses run east-west along Burnside, Belmont, and Division Streets, and north-south along Southeast 60th Avenue; the northernmost part of the neighborhood is within walking distance of the MAX stop at Northeast 60th.

SELLWOOD & THE MORELANDS

Neighborhood Associations: Eastmoreland, Sellwood-Moreland

Eastmoreland lies south of (but technically includes) the classic campus of Reed College, with its old brick buildings and lawns filled with frisbee-throwing undergraduates. The neighborhood is worthy of its setting, with many truly grand homes on wide, tree-lined, curving streets that desultorily defy the city's grid. (Eastmoreland, like several other classic Eastside neighborhoods, was developed by the Ladd Estate Company, whose planners seemed to disregard the grid almost as a point of pride.) Most of the homes predate the Second World War, although unlike many other Southeast Portland neighborhoods, Eastmoreland has a relative dearth of Craftsman bungalows: the area mostly developed after the bungalow style had become passé. Instead, one finds an abundance of generally large, well-maintained Tudor, colonial revival, stone manor, and other traditional styles, and also some nicely designed mid century homes, mostly on corner lots that had remained vacant during the war. There are also a few bona fide mansions, as well as some more modest homes, particularly in the southern end of the neighborhood. Eastmoreland has a gracious, beautifully landscaped feel, with a strong sense of community spirit; the latter manifests itself in strident opposition to attempts to tear down existing homes to build infill dwellings that are deemed not in accord with the neighborhood character.

Eastmoreland is one of the most established and expensive neighborhoods on Portland's eastside, and residents are generally affluent—but demographically they include a mix of tenured professors, a few students and recent graduates, mid-career professionals, retirees, and young families. In addition to the lush grounds of many homes in the neighborhood, Eastmoreland greenspaces include the centrally located Berkeley Park, Crystal Springs Rhododendron Garden, the grounds of Reed College (including a small but surprisingly wild canyon), and Eastmoreland Golf Course. The grassy, shady median strip of Reed College Place

Eastmoreland

Westmoreland

is a popular walking route. There are virtually no businesses within Eastmoreland, but the neighborhood is a relatively short walk or drive from either Woodstock or Westmoreland (see below).

An unusual feature of the neighborhood is the Reed College nuclear reactor. The reactor produces very little heat, so despite the terrifying prospect of liberal arts students operating a nuclear reactor, a China Syndrome–style (or Modern Chinese Studies Syndrome–style) meltdown is not really a concern. A single bus line to downtown Portland serves the heart of Eastmoreland, although additional bus service is available on nearby streets.

To the west, across the railroad tracks and over busy McLoughlin Boulevard, is the aptly named **Westmoreland** neighborhood. Westmoreland was another Ladd development, but amazingly it is laid out according to the city grid. Milwaukie Avenue (which, although a named thoroughfare, runs north-south) is the neighborhood's main drag, with restaurants, shops, banks, a hardware store, the 1920s-vintage Moreland Theatre, and other establishments that give the neighborhood a small-town feel. The densest concentration of businesses is at the intersection of Milwaukie and Bybee Boulevard. The Moreland Farmers' Market (www.morelandfarmersmarket.org) takes place one block to the west of this intersection on Wednesday afternoons from mid-May through late October. On either side of Milwaukie, quiet, shady side streets are lined with bungalows, Old Portlands, and other older homes, with the odd 1950s ranch for the sake of variety. The western end of the neighborhood lies atop a bluff that overlooks Oaks Bottom Wildlife Refuge, with views of downtown Portland, the Willamette River, and the West Hills.

While it is connected both physically and in most Portlanders' minds to Westmoreland, **Sellwood** predates its neighbor to the north. The area was an independent city and early rival of Portland before it was annexed in 1893, and it has tried for more than a century to maintain its identity. Bustling commercial districts line Southeast Tacoma Street and 13th and 17th Avenues, and most establishments are locally owned. Sellwood is less consciously hip than close-in neighborhoods further north—Sellwood's best-known shopping experience is Antique Row, the parade of antique stores and malls along 13th Avenue—but the area offers everything from ethnic restaurants, bakeries, and children's clothing stores to paint stores, factory outlet stores, and drive-through fast-food joints. New Seasons on Tacoma is a favorite local supermarket.

Sellwood, like Westmoreland, is filled with attractive older homes, including Victorians, along with some newer commercial and apartment buildings. In general, the housing mix is more diverse in Sellwood than Westmoreland. Homes at the top of the bluff along the Willamette offer views north to downtown Portland. A few condo complexes, and even a new office park, overlook the Willamette River near the Sellwood Bridge; a community of houseboats provides a fully water-oriented living option. Just south of Sellwood, the small enclave of **Garthwick** lies within Clackamas County but is technically part of the city of Portland. This neighborhood is adjacent to Waverly Country Club and is full of formal, traditional-style homes. Apart from the wealthy anomaly of Garthwick, homes in Westmoreland and Sellwood are more affordable than those in Eastmoreland, but are not inexpensive and are appreciating more rapidly.

Sellwood and Westmoreland are home to all sorts of people—young professional couples, singles, retirees, blue-collar workers, and 1960s dropouts—but both are becoming known as great family neighborhoods, with plenty of events like the Moreland Monster March around Halloween. This area has some excellent parks: besides Oaks Bottom, which is a prime birdwatching spot along the Willamette River, there are woodsy Sellwood Park; Sellwood Riverfront Park just below it, with river access; and Westmoreland Park, which includes an artificial casting pond (and a spring-fed lake that frequently overflows its banks). The Springwater Corridor, a long-distance bike and pedestrian path, runs from OMSI south to Sellwood, loops around the neighborhood, then follows an old rail line to Boring in Clackamas County. Other family-friendly neighborhood features include the

Sellwood

Sellwood-Moreland Library in a new mixed-use building on 13th, which is walking distance from both Sellwood and Westmoreland, and century-old Oaks Amusement Park (www.oakspark.com), north of the Sellwood Bridge.

Speaking of the Sellwood Bridge, the rickety, two-lane span was long the weak link in the local transportation infrastructure. A properly sturdy replacement bridge is finally under construction and is scheduled to open in late 2015. In the meantime, a temporary bridge is in place. Other road connections north to downtown Portland or south to Clackamas County are reasonably efficient, but because railroad tracks and the high-speed thoroughfare of McLoughlin Boulevard cut off Westmoreland and Sellwood from the rest of the city, alternate routes are not plentiful. The new Orange Line MAX train to Milwaukie will run along McLoughlin Boulevard, with a stop serving Westmoreland/Eastmoreland and another at the east end of Sellwood. Bus service north to downtown Portland or south to the Milwaukie Transit Center is decent, if a bit pokey; bus service will likely be curtailed significantly once the MAX line starts running.

REED, CRESTON-KENILWORTH, AND WOODSTOCK

Neighborhood Associations: Creston-Kenilworth, Reed, Woodstock

Occupying a narrow swath of Southeast Portland south of Powell and east of the railroad tracks, the **Creston-Kenilworth** neighborhood is relatively close to the Division Street and Hawthorne Boulevard shopping districts, but is far enough south of them to be overlooked in home searches. The neighborhood is named for two city parks in the area; wooded Creston Park has a popular outdoor pool. The neighborhood is a mix of older homes, similar to that in the Hawthorne District, but with more apartment houses (and somewhat more homes in obvious need of maintenance). Some streets are lined with beautifully restored classic houses, while others could use many gallons of paint (and a lead remediation crew). While Powell Boulevard still has a ways to go, as the presence of several "exotic dancing"

Woodstock

establishments suggests, it has shed some of the seediness that has traditionally plagued it as new establishments like Hopworks Urban Brewery have moved in. The neighborhood shares many of the advantages and much of the vibe offered by the Hawthorne and Division Street districts, but at a lower price point that is much closer to the citywide median.

South of Holgate and west of 39th/César Chávez, the small **Reed** neighborhood is a mix of apartment complexes, some built in the 1960s, and small single-family homes (many rented by groups of students, wanna-be students, and others attracted by the proximity of Reed). Part of the neighborhood offers the standard Southeast Portland range of prewar houses, but a large section in the middle, known as Reedwood, is comprised of late 1960s-era ranch and two-story homes that were built on the site of a former botanical garden. Reed in general has well-maintained, nicely landscaped homes, but as in other neighborhoods, unwanted infill and teardowns are changing the neighborhood character. While most of the neighborhood is residential, César Chávez Boulevard hosts a popular Trader Joe's. The Brooklyn rail yards border both Reed and Creston-Kenilworth to the west, and can cause sleepless nights for noise-sensitive people.

Across 39th/César Chávez, to the southeast of Reed and just east of Eastmoreland—you could call it the land more east of Eastmoreland, in semi-palindromic fashion, but you would probably be the only one who called it that—lies increasingly popular **Woodstock**. The neighborhood's "downtown" is an unpretentious commercial strip along Southeast Woodstock Boulevard that contains about every kind of business you're liable to need on a daily basis: a gourmet coffeehouse, a hardware store, a supermarket, a pub, a wine store, and several restaurants, such as the popular Otto's Sausage Kitchen (www.ottossausage.com). A new Grand Central bakery and a New Seasons grocery, both indicia of a neighborhood's growing popularity among the relatively affluent, have recently opened here. Woodstock Park is a few blocks to the north. The streets nearby are lined with the kinds of homes that make Southeast Portland a popular place to live, such as bungalows and cute cottages, but they are generally smaller and much less expensive here than in trendier neighborhoods; the average home in Woodstock is in line with the Portland median price. Woodstock has an abundance of unpaved alleys, a feature that some residents like but that some people find surprising. The outer edges of the neighborhood include some ranch-style homes, and infill development is occurring on larger lots. Woodstock has a strong community spirit, and the Woodstock Festival and Parade brings the whole neighborhood out each July.

Bus service on the major streets is adequate in all three neighborhoods; it's a 15- to 30-minute ride to downtown Portland. By car, it takes about 10 to 20 minutes.

North Tabor

NORTH TABOR, SOUTH TABOR, AND MONTAVILLA

Neighborhood Associations: Montavilla, North Tabor, South Tabor

The **North Tabor** neighborhood, not coincidentally located just north of Mount Tabor, renamed itself a few years ago to make its position clear. (The previous name, Center, was far less descriptive, as the neighborhood is not really in the center of anything.) Northeast 60th Avenue bisects the North Tabor neighborhood, and serves as a useful demarcation line. West of here, the neighborhood fancies itself an eastern extension of Laurelhurst. While that perception is not strictly true (and certainly Laurelhurst residents don't see it that way)—for one thing, average home sizes are smaller here than in Laurelhurst, and the streets are straight—the neighborhood does contain many attractive older homes that would not be out-of-place in its western neighbor. There are some apartment buildings here, too, particularly near Interstate 84 and along Glisan near Providence Portland Hospital. This stretch of Glisan also features American Dream Pizza, home of the hand-twisted crust (when they're not too busy to bother).

East of 60th, the neighborhood becomes much more mixed, particularly north of Glisan. While there are still many older homes here, there are also apartments, duplexes, Cape Cods, ranches, and assorted new infill buildings, not all of which have been calculated to blend in well with their neighbors. There are also few sidewalks. Prices are lower in this part of the neighborhood, however, and some homes have views of downtown and the West Hills from atop Rosemont Bluff, at about 68th Avenue. The southern part of the neighborhood is reasonable walking distance to Mount Tabor Park.

Both Burnside and Glisan Streets have supermarkets and other businesses, and a small business node at 60th and Glisan has a few popular bars. The neighborhood has easy access to major highways and transit; bus lines run along Glisan, Burnside, and 60th, and the 60th Avenue MAX stop offers a quick trip downtown or to the airport. Because of the proximity of Interstate 84, traffic noise can be annoying in the northern fringe of the neighborhood.

On the opposite side of Mount Tabor, **South Tabor** is a fairly quiet, unassuming small neighborhood. Most homes here are relatively modest older houses, and the neighborhood is substantially less expensive than the Hawthorne-area neighborhoods just to the west but has a lower crime rate than neighborhoods to the southeast. Clinton Park, in the western part of the neighborhood, contains various sports fields and is a popular gathering place on summer evenings. Some new commercial and residential development is occurring here, driven in part by the creeping influence of the Division Street renaissance, and many residents are optimistic about the future of the neighborhood. In general, the western part of the neighborhood is considered more desirable and is certainly changing more rapidly than the eastern part.

To the east and southeast of North Tabor, the large **Montavilla** neighborhood (a contraction of "Mount Tabor Villa") contains both quiet neighborhoods of modest, well-kept single-family houses and the somewhat unpleasant strip mall that is 82nd Avenue, along with some associated apartment buildings. On average, Montavilla is one of Portland's least expensive neighborhoods—the median home price is well below the city median—but it also has a thriving and rapidly evolving commercial district along Stark Street east of Mount Tabor. New businesses like the Bipartisan Café, spruced-up old businesses like the restored Academy Theater (www.academytheaterpdx.com), and a farmers' market held on Sundays from June through October (www.montavillamarket.org) have helped attract new investment and new residents to the area.

Montavilla is a block-by-block kind of neighborhood, and while there are no longer any truly awful zones, some streets are much more attractive and have a palpably better vibe than others. In general, the neighborhoods just downslope of Mount Tabor within a few blocks of Stark Street are considered the most desirable and have seen the greatest influx of new residents, including families interested

Montavilla

in living close-in and but priced out of neighborhoods farther west. The neighborhood is fairly well-served by transit, with bus lines on Burnside, Glisan, Belmont, and 82nd, and MAX lines along Interstate 84 to the north and Interstate 205 to the east. By car, downtown Portland is about a 15-minute drive (without traffic) or a 30-minute bike ride.

OTHER SOUTHEAST PORTLAND NEIGHBORHOODS

Neighborhood Associations: Brentwood-Darlington, Foster-Powell, Mount Scott

Roughly south of Powell Boulevard and east of 52nd Avenue, the neighborhoods of Southeast Portland become less fashionable. This fact also means they become less expensive. Some people who make it their business to claim to know such things predict that these Southeast neighborhoods are destined to become the city's next hotspot. The process has already started in some neighborhoods, so you might want to get in while the getting's good. At the same time, parts of Southeast Portland are not for everyone. Many areas have a high crime rate, and 82nd Avenue has a long way to go before it overcomes its totally justified reputation as an enormous seedy strip mall; prostitution activity has historically been a major complaint of residents here. Even 82nd is beginning to improve, however, as an influx of Asian businesses, including the enormous Fubonn Mall (www.fubonn. com), start to replace the "lingerie modeling" shacks and windowless taverns.

Foster-Powell is a triangular and perhaps up-and-coming neighborhood between the major thoroughfares of Powell Boulevard and Foster Road. The neighborhood is home to both long-time residents and to recent immigrants with very different origins, as the business signs in Russian, Vietnamese, and Spanish attest, but it is also drawing in self-conscious urban pioneers who are on the lookout for bargains. Even Foster Road, which was for many years the red-headed stepchild of Southeast Portland thoroughfares, has begun to see some new cafés and other harbingers of demographic shift, particularly at its western end.

The **Mount Scott** neighborhood to the south centers on the tree island of Mount Scott Park, a shady park with a popular community center (which contains both a mini–roller rink and an awesome indoor pool complex, complete with an artificial "river"). The homes around the park are generally modest, but many have been fixed up nicely. (Note that not only is the Mount Scott neighborhood essentially flat, it is nowhere near Mount Scott itself. That prominent butte is in Clackamas County, near Clackamas Town Center.)

Hard against the Clackamas County line, the **Brentwood-Darlington** neighborhood has a relatively high rate of both property and violent crime. On the plus side, it vies for the title of the city's most affordable neighborhood, at least west of Interstate 205. Both the extreme western portion and extreme eastern portion of the neighborhood have access to the Springwater Trail Corridor, a multi-use bike path that runs from the Willamette River east to Gresham and Boring.

Bus service along the main east-west streets is good throughout these neighborhoods; the only north-south bus lines run along 82nd Avenue and 60th Avenue. MAX light-rail service runs along Interstate 205, not far to the east of 82nd.

SOUTHEAST PORTLAND NEIGHBORHOOD INFORMATION

ZIP Codes: 97202, 97206, 97213, 97214, 97215, 97232

Post Offices: Brooklyn Post Office, 1410 SE Powell Blvd; Creston Post Office, 5010 SE Foster Rd; East Portland Post Office, 1020 SE 7th Ave; Sellwood Post Office, 6723 SE 16th Ave

Police Station: Portland Police Bureau, Central Precinct (areas west of 39th/César Chávez), 1111 SW 2nd Ave, 503-823-3333 (non-emergency); East Precinct (areas east of 39th/César Chávez), 737 SE 106th Ave, 503-823-4800 (non-emergency)

Emergency Hospitals: Adventist Medical Center, 10123 SE Market St, 503-257-2500, www.adventisthealthnw.com; OHSU Hospital, 3181 SW Sam Jackson Park Rd, 503-494-8311, www.ohsu.edu/xd/health/; Providence Milwaukie Hospital, 10150 SE 32nd Ave, Milwaukie, 503-513-8300, www.providence.org; Providence Portland Medical Center, 4805 NE Glisan St, 503-215-1111, www. providence.org

Libraries: Belmont Library, 1038 SE César E Chávez Blvd, 503-988-5382; Holgate Library, 7905 SE Holgate Blvd, 503-988-5389; Sellwood-Moreland Library, 7860 SE 13th Ave, 503-988-5398; Woodstock Library, 6008 SE 49th Ave, 503-988-5399

Parks: Major parks include Mount Tabor Park, Laurelhurst Park, Westmoreland Park, Creston Park, Oaks Bottom Wildlife Refuge, Woodstock Park, and Crystal Springs Rhododendron Garden; www.portlandparks.org

Community Publications: *Southeast Examiner*, www.southeastexaminer.com; *The Bee*, www.thebeenews.com

Public Transportation: TriMet, 503-238-RIDE, www.trimet.org; comprehensive bus service, including frequent service routes, west of about 50th Avenue, with service on main routes east of 50th Avenue. Streetcar service along MLK Jr Blvd and Grand Avenue. Light rail runs along Interstate 84 and Interstate 205, and (beginning late 2015) along McLoughlin Blvd to Milwaukie.

NORTH PORTLAND

Boundaries: North: Columbia River; **West:** Willamette River; **South:** Willamette River; **East:** North Williams Avenue

Until relatively recently, Portland's "fifth quadrant"—the peninsula between the Willamette and Columbia rivers, where a wide deviation in the Willamette's course makes mincemeat of the city's Burnside-and-river-oriented directional system—was typically overlooked or avoided by newcomers and many long-time Portlanders alike. Crime rates in much of the area were sky-high, schools were perceived as appalling, and the urban fabric was in a general state of decay. While it's not exactly yuppie central—and most North Portlanders are fine with that—the district has undergone dramatic changes in the last five years. Buoyed in part by a new light rail line along Interstate Avenue, in part by soaring home prices in more traditionally fashionable parts of the city, and in part by urban renewal districts and investment incentives, North Portland experienced some of the city's fastest real estate appreciation over the last decade. New residents moved in with paint pails and big plans, and flippers did quick cosmetic makeovers, giving new life to formerly neglected homes. At the same time, many individual homes—and entire swaths of some neighborhoods—still await revitalization.

Of course, one person's revitalization is another person's gentrification, and not everyone in North Portland (or NoPo, as some boosters somewhat gratingly call it) welcomes the change. Rising housing prices have forced or enticed many long-time residents to move away, and some businesses are perceived as catering more to affluent new residents and visitors from other parts of the city than to actual local needs. Moreover, because many of the area's new residents are childless, some of the area's public schools suffer from declining enrollments and a continuing need for improvement. Still, the influx of newcomers has also brought (or coincided with) some positive changes, like a declining crime rate. In fact, North Portland no longer has any true no-go neighborhoods, although some streets are nicer than others and old perceptions die hard, especially in the suburbs. In sum, North Portland might be a great choice for people who are looking for relatively inexpensive housing in a newly "hot" or transitioning neighborhood, and who are willing to live with a bit of residual grittiness in exchange.

Boise-Eliot

BOISE-ELIOT, THE NORTH MISSISSIPPI DISTRICT, KING, AND OVERLOOK

Neighborhood Associations: Boise, Eliot, King (partial), Overlook

The **Boise** and **Eliot** neighborhoods, just east of Interstate 5 and the Willamette River in close-in North Portland, have undergone perhaps the swiftest and most dramatic renaissance of any neighborhood in the city. Once part of the independent city of Albina, these neighborhoods were originally built as middle-class housing for northern European immigrants. After the Vanport flood of 1948, which wiped out a World War II–era public housing project near the Columbia River, many former Vanport residents, mostly African-Americans, were relocated to Albina. (At that time, housing covenants and discriminatory real estate practices effectively barred African-Americans from most other parts of the city.) The neighborhood was almost entirely African-American by the 1960s.

Interstate 5 was plowed through the heart of Albina, and the community began a long decline.

Beginning in the 1990s, a few people from other parts of the city recognized what they considered the untapped potential of the then blighted, high-crime Boise and Eliot neighborhoods—a close-in location, a stock of classic old homes, and a commercial district (albeit one that was largely boarded up). Some started to buy and renovate homes and businesses. This influx has continued and accelerated, and today these neighborhoods are very much desegregated. Indeed, Boise Eliot (as the two neighborhoods are collectively called) is probably the most racially diverse neighborhood in the state. (The neighborhoods extend into Northeast Portland, but the character of the neighborhood does not change meaningfully from one quadrant to the other.)

North Mississippi Avenue, in the **Boise** neighborhood, is ground zero in the revitalization/gentrification of North Portland. The bustling part of the street is just a few blocks long, running roughly from Fremont Street to Skidmore Street.

North Mississippi Avenue

North Mississippi Avenue

In less than a decade, and really only in the last five years, the street has gathered an assortment of some of the city's most popular eateries (and beverageries) and a collection of shops that is, to put it mildly, eclectic: retail establishments include a lightbulb store (Sunlan, www.sunlanlighting.com), a small nursery and urban chicken farmer supply store (Pistils, www.pistilsnursery.com), and The Meadow (www.atthemeadow.com), which purveys chocolate, wine, flowers, and gourmet finishing salt varieties from around the world. The Rebuilding Center (www.rebuildingcenter.org), a popular source of recycled building materials and fixtures, dominates the south end of the strip.

North Mississippi's trendiness has spilled over onto other nearby Boise streets—North Williams Avenue now boasts hip restaurants like Lincoln (www.lincolnpdx.com) and the popular Fifth Quadrant pub, and a Grand Central Bakery location opened on Fremont—but not every commercial building is hipster fodder. The area is still full of mysterious old buildings with cracked, weedy parking lots.

Eliot neighborhood, to the south of Boise, is not yet as trendy as Boise, but it is getting there. Toro Bravo (www.torobravopdx.com) on Northeast Russell draws tapas hunters from across the city, and the nearby Wonder Ballroom features frequent live performances by local and nationally known acts. The southern portion of Eliot, along Interstate Avenue between Interstate 5 and the river, is primarily commercial and light industrial, but some trendy spots have opened here, too, such as Swedish restaurant Broder Nord (www.broderpdx.com).

The adjacent **King** neighborhood is technically in Northeast Portland, and much of it is generally considered part of the Alberta Arts area, but in terms of demographics, housing stock, and stage of development, the western part of King is much more akin to Boise-Eliot. King straddles, and is named for, Martin Luther King Jr. Boulevard, which, like North Missisipi, has undergone a significant transformation over the last few years. While MLK is a busier street, and could never become compact and quaint, it has attracted significant redevelopment capital, and hip new restaurants and cafés and creative businesses now stand alongside the tatty convenience stores and gas stations.

The Boise-Eliot and King neighborhood housing stock is as diverse as its commercial establishments, and includes everything from foursquares, Craftsman bungalows, tiny cottages, and a few old Victorians to converted churches, mixed-use buildings, apartments, and brand-new blocks of modernist condos on Mississippi Avenue itself. These neighborhoods are notable for relying less on taupe as part of an exterior color scheme than any other part of the city; homeowners are not afraid of bold colors or exuberant (but not necessarily weedy) gardens. Not every house has been redone, and there are still plenty of longtime residents living in dated but well-kept homes (along with some dated and dilapidated homes), but the gentrification juggernaut has resulted in a wave of renovation and new construction in the area. Many residents, both old and new, have already cashed out and moved on. The new denizens of the North Mississippi Avenue district fall predominantly into the "youthful hipster" or "creative class" demographics. The area has so far failed to attract a critical mass of new families, in part because some people consider the schools to be less desirable than those in some other parts of the city. This situation is slowly changing, however, and the neighborhoods are hardly devoid of children.

In terms of home prices, Boise has become shockingly expensive, at least in light of its relatively recent history, and is comparable to or even more expensive than some long-established desirable neighborhoods such as Sellwood. Rents are

King

slightly more manageable. Prices in Eliot and King, which have not been so thoroughly gentrified, are lower but still exceed the city average.

On the west side of Interstate 5, the **Overlook** neighborhood owes its name to its position atop Swan Island Bluff "overlooking" the port and the Willamette River. This area of stately street trees and gracious Craftsman bungalows, Old Portlands, and English Tudors became a hot real estate market when Adidas America opened its headquarters, Adidas Village, here in 2002. The opening of the Interstate MAX line, which runs through Overlook's eastern end, further primed the pump, and home prices in the neighborhood nearly doubled in the succeeding five years. Prices fell significantly here during the housing bust, and took much longer to recover here than in many other neighborhoods, so the median home price is not significantly higher than the citywide median. Overlook Park, at the edge of the bluff, is a 12-acre greenspace with a great view of the river and port, the Fremont Bridge, downtown Portland, and the West Hills. The homes along the lip of the bluff to the northwest share this view. The nearby Tudor-style Overlook House, built in 1927, today serves as a community center. The huge Swan Island industrial and port complex lies within Overlook's boundaries; most of the remainder of the neighborhood is residential, with commercial zones along Killingsworth Street and North Interstate Avenue. Some trendy new businesses have opened their doors, but older establishments, like The Palms Motor Hotel and the tiki-from-before-tiki-became-cool-again Alibi Restaurant, are still going strong. A century ago, this area was once the center of Portland's Polish community, and St. Stanislaus Polish Catholic Church on Interstate holds a Polish festival each September.

The true bargains in Overlook are gone, but the neighborhood still has some affordable fixers. Less than half of residents own their homes, so a fair number of rental properties are available if you're interested in metaphorically dipping your toes in the neighborhood water. The neighborhood attracts a mix of young singles, straight, gay, and lesbian couples, families, and professionals who work at Adidas.

Both Overlook and the Boise-Eliot neighborhood are extremely well-connected to the area's highway and transit system. Downtown Portland is only a short light-rail ride away on the Interstate MAX line; although the line does not run through Boise-Eliot, it is accessible from that neighborhood by a short walk over Interstate 5 on the Failing Pedestrian Bridge (which, despite the ominous name, is actually quite sturdy). These neighborhoods are generally bike friendly,

Overlook

and bike commuting downtown is eminently doable. The neighborhoods are very close to the Fremont Bridge on- and off-ramps and to Interstate 5, as well as to alternate north-south routes like Vancouver Avenue and North Interstate Avenue. The downside to this easy highway access is high levels of pollutants from auto exhaust; some studies have shown that residents of neighborhoods within a quarter-mile or so of Interstate 5, especially east (generally downwind) of the freeway, have higher rates of respiratory disease than people who live farther away from major highways.

ARBOR LODGE AND KENTON

Neighborhood Associations: Arbor Lodge, Kenton

The hits of the North Portland renaissance just keep on coming, and Arbor Lodge and Kenton are the latest neighborhoods to make it into the charts. These neighborhoods together occupy a large chunk of North Portland west of Interstate 5. Each straddles North Interstate Avenue and the MAX Yellow Line, which has helped increase the desirability of nearby homes (particularly to the west, farther from the freeway) and has spurred redevelopment up and down Interstate.

Arbor Lodge, which sounds quainter than it is, lies just north of Overlook, and shares a number of affinities with that neighborhood. Like Overlook, the western edge of Arbor Lodge lies along the Swan Island bluff, and homes along Willamette Boulevard have great downtown and Port of Portland views. Many of the streets in this part of the neighborhood have mature street trees and a few somewhat grand homes. The northern and eastern parts of Arbor Lodge have a mix of typically modestly sized Cape Cods and bungalows, many of which have been fixed up nicely. The ongoing redevelopment of Interstate Avenue has brought in new apartments, coffeehouses, restaurants, and other accouterments of the urban lifestyle, and is a relatively short bike ride or MAX ride from downtown Portland.

Arbor Lodge

Kenton

Also, rents and home prices tend to be slightly lower than in comparable neigh-borhoods of Southeast Portland, and this combination of factors has rendered this part of Arbor Lodge attractive to younger newcomers. Interstate Avenue also features a New Seasons supermarket, which along with the opening of the MAX line, is credited with sparking the renaissance of Arbor Lodge, and a giant new two-story Fred Meyer supermarket, which was a result of that renaissance. Arbor Lodge has started to attract married couples and young families, despite the less-than-ideal schools that serve the neighborhood; because prices here are more or less in line with the citywide median, given the amenities available in the area it can be an appealing place to buy a home when compared with other more expen-sive close-in neighborhoods. Some two-thirds of residents are homeowners.

Across rapidly evolving Lombard Street to the north, the **Kenton** neighbor-hood is best known for its kitschy giant statue of Paul Bunyan, which power-logged its way onto the National Register of Historic Places in early 2009, and as the home turf of embattled former mayor Sam Adams. The neighborhood began as a company town for a meatpacking plant—cattle were once driven along North Denver Avenue—but, as they say, times have changed. Instead of cattle, North Denver now hosts lowing herds of pubgoers and patrons of new restaurants like Cup & Saucer Café and Posies Café. Although the neighborhood is clearly on the upswing, and some boosters predict Kenton will be "the next Mississippi" (a ref-erence to the avenue, not the state), those boosters have been saying that for years; suffice to say Kenton has not yet been gentrified to the same extent. North Denver still has vacant storefronts, and Paul Bunyan appears to be ogling the strip club just across the MAX tracks. This residual grittiness/authenticity (along with the resulting more affordable home prices, well below the city median) is part of Kenyon's attraction to some people.

The main residential area centers on popular Kenton Park, which has a play-ground, sports fields, a wading pool, and vast expanses of grass. A few of the houses facing the park are quite imposing, but the bulk of the houses in the neighborhood, given its origin, are not especially grand. As in Arbor Lodge, there are plenty of bungalows, Cape Cods, and similar older-style houses; many homes have been spruced up in the last few years, while others nearby slowly molder. A few new townhomes have been built near the MAX station, and other new development is occurring along North Interstate. The trip to downtown Portland can take as little as 10 minutes by car or 20 minutes by MAX; bus lines run along the major streets, but typically connect with MAX rather than running all the way downtown.

ST. JOHNS AND UNIVERSITY PARK

Neighborhood Associations: Cathedral Park, St. Johns, University Park

St. Johns, the old neighborhood out near the end of the North Portland peninsula, has been the next big thing for years. In the meantime, other next big things— the Northeast Alberta and North Mississippi neighborhoods, for example—have taken off, while St. Johns has languished. But while St. Johns—named after James John, a settler whose morals were reputedly above reproach (or who was a crazy hermit, depending on what story you believe)—may not be red-hot, it's at least lukewarm. The area was a separately incorporated city from 1903 until 1915, when Portland annexed it, and the bones of its historic center remain, including the old City Hall. Given its relative proximity to downtown Portland (about 15 to 20 minutes away, traffic permitting), its old-fashioned, low-key "downtown," its com-

St. Johns Bridge

paratively affordable housing stock, and a distinctive icon in the form of the St. Johns Bridge (which, suspended between two Gothic-style towers, soars gracefully across the Willamette River here), it's hard to imagine that St. Johns could have remained off the radar indefinitely.

In fact, people here will tell you that St. Johns was never undiscovered; the current residents "discovered" it a long time ago. They will likely extol the community spirit of this tradition-ally working-class neighborhood and its locally owned businesses, and you may come away with the feeling that, if becoming the next "in" neighbor-hood means undergoing an influx of wisecracking hipsters, locals want none of it. That's not to say that St. Johns is static: portents of change are

St. Johns

already clearly visible in the main business district, which centers on North Lombard Street at Philadelphia Avenue. Established hangouts like Tulip Pastry Shop, with its six-decade-old doughnut recipe—the actual doughnuts are considerably fresher—rub facades with such new businesses as vegan-focused Proper Eats Market and Café. Or consider the juxtaposition on the north side of Lombard of Wayne's Barber Shop, which appears not to have changed in decades, with the The Olive & Vine, a purveyor of olive oils, gourmet sea salts, and other specialty foods, right next door. Across Lombard, the St. Johns Historic Twin Cinema and Pub (www.stjohnscinema.com) shows first-run movies at discount prices; the McMenamins St. Johns Theater and Pub a couple of short blocks away shows second-run movies at even cheaper prices. Mixed in with the seedy bars and old-time diners is Starbucks, the ultimate harbinger of shifts in neighborhood demographics.

However, these changes in demographics—from straight-up blue collar to a somewhat more diverse set of residents, including some young singles, older professionals, and families from out-of-state—that have driven the changes in the business mix have not resulted in whole-scale gentrification. Most newcomers to St. Johns seem to select the neighborhood for its actual characteristics, not its theoretical ones. Perhaps because of St. Johns' prior independent existence, innovations in the neighborhood seem to come from bottom-up effort rather than outside intervention. For example, two unique services have cropped up in the basement of the Red Sea Church on Lombard: the North Portland Preserve and Serve Library (www.preserveandserve.org) lends out kitchen equipment and utensils for home canning purposes, while Swap-n-Play Community Sharing (swapnplay.org) is an indoor/outdoor community playspace and used clothing/toys/household goods exchange depot (on the honor system).

Despite the ubiquitous signs of change and a can-do community spirit, St. Johns is not for everyone. The neighborhood is still a bit rough around the edges, and the crime rate remains relatively (although not dauntingly) high. Away from the St. Johns downtown area, Lombard Street has long been a grim, unwelcoming thoroughfare lined with check cashing establishments, smoky bars, fast food restaurants, convenience stores, and a few coffee shops, although this landscape, too, is changing. The neighborhood is virtually surrounded by industrial facilities and warehouses: this part of the lower Willamette has been a manufacturing and maritime center for close to a century, and St. Johns really boomed during the shipbuilding frenzy of the Second World War. At the same time, a fair number of natural areas are within or close to the neighborhood: woodsy Pier Park is on the northern fringes, Smith and Bybee Lakes (and the Columbia Slough, which connects them) form an important wetland, and Forest Park lies just across the St. Johns Bridge. From Kelley Point Park, at the very tip of the peninsula, you can ponder the confluence of the Willamette and Columbia Rivers.

In keeping with the neighborhood's working class roots, most houses are fairly modest structures; ranches, Cape Cods, and small cottages predominate, with a few old bungalows, foursquares, or Victorians thrown into the mix. There are also some apartment buildings, both old and new, including a few 1960s-era towers near the river, and quite a bit of infill has occurred, including some modern townhome developments. In short, the housing mix is varied—much more so than in most Portland neighborhoods—but the look and feel vary substantially from street to street. The median home price here is well below the citywide median, and St. Johns is perhaps the last "distinctive" old neighborhood in Portland that remains somewhat affordable. The apartment-heavy **Cathedral Park** neighborhood, named for the city park on the river under the cathedral-like eastern pier of the St. Johns Bridge, has higher home prices than St. Johns proper. Cathedral Park is technically a separate neighborhood but is functionally part of St. Johns.

The same cannot be said for **University Park**, a more traditionally genteel neighborhood that sits atop the bluff near the University of Portland. The neighborhood's name actually predates the current university—a Methodist institution called Portland University was established here in 1891, and the sale of neighborhood lots was intended to provide funds for the university's operation and

University Park

endowment. Streets were platted and named after colleges and universities, famous educators, and various Methodist worthies. The promoters of the subdivision were overzealous in some respects, dubiously promising that the "proximity of a large student body has a tendency to elevate the tone of all things." In other respects, their claims were underwhelming: the formal prospectus contained the helpful factoid that "University Park is entirely free from malaria."

While University Park is still free of malaria, an economic panic caused the subdivision scheme to founder, and the university closed. In 1901, the abandoned university reopened as a Catholic institution, which it remains to this day, and with better economic times the area around the campus gradually developed. As in St. Johns, housing styles here are a mix of many styles: Cape Cods, bungalows, ranch houses, small cottages, and a few Victorians. Homes along Willamette Boulevard have sweeping views over the Willamette toward downtown Portland and the West Hills. (The south side of Willamette Boulevard is parkland; only the north side is developed, so houses along Willamette do not perch on the edge of the bluff.) Average prices here are at least 50 percent higher than in St. Johns.

The streets in University Park run northeast-southwest and northwest-southeast, rather than north-south and east-west as in most of the city; this arrangement (which is also found in St. Johns) was supposed to ensure that houses catch the maximum amount of sunlight. Despite the proximity of the University of Portland, there are few apartments, and essentially no commercial district except for the relatively unappealing stretch of Lombard Street that forms the neighborhood's northern border. Columbia Park, on the neighborhood's eastern edge, is walking distance from most homes. Astor Elementary School, which serves University Park, is considered the best elementary school in North Portland, and one of the best in the city. The crime rate in University Park is lower than in other parts of North Portland.

Several TriMet bus lines serve St. Johns and University Park, but many trips involve long detours or transfers to the Yellow Line MAX, which does not serve the immediate area. The neighborhoods are a relatively short drive to downtown Portland, and some residents commute to Washington County via the St. Johns Bridge and Germantown Road or Cornelius Pass Road.

OUTER NORTH PORTLAND NEIGHBORHOODS
Neighborhood Associations: Bridgeton, Hayden Island, Humboldt, Piedmont, Portsmouth

The outer neighborhoods of North Portland are not as well known as close-in hotspots like North Mississippi, but many of them are changing just as rapidly. East of Interstate 5, the century-old foursquares and bungalows in the multicultural **Piedmont** and **Humboldt** neighborhoods are rapidly becoming popular. Humboldt basks in the reflected radiance of North Mississippi hipness (only a short walk or bike ride away to the south), but it has started to develop some neighborhood cachet of its own. Portland Community College's Cascade Campus is within Humboldt. Home prices here are nearly as high as in the Boise neighborhood, although rents tend to be lower. The next neighborhood to the north, **Piedmont**, is not as hip, and is accordingly somewhat less expensive. The neighborhood jewel of Piedmont is Peninsula Park, with a century-old rose garden, a swimming pool, and a community center. A few years ago, Piedmont would have attracted only urban pioneers, but the current of change keeps flowing northward, and the area is no longer a housing frontier.

Across Interstate 5 to the west, beyond Arbor Lodge and north of University Park, the working-class **Portsmouth** neighborhood includes New Columbia (www.newcolumbia.org), an 82-acre subsidized mixed-income housing development that is a showcase of environmentally sustainable design (and which replaced a notoriously crime- and gang-ridden old-style housing project).

North of the Columbia Slough, in the Delta Park area, most land is either used for commercial purposes or is parkland of some kind (if you define parkland broadly to include uses like golf courses, the Portland Meadows horse racing track, and Portland International Raceway). This area was the site of the community of Vanport, the largest public housing project in the United States, which was washed away in a devastating 1948 flood. Understandably, many people have since been reluctant to build here, but the **Bridgeton** neighborhood has housing right along the shore of the Columbia River, including some pricey new condominiums overlooking the water. Bridgeton also includes a large community of houseboats and live-aboard boats, a feature that **Hayden Island**—an actual island, in the Oregon portion of the Columbia River—shares. Hayden Island is best known as the site of a mall that attracts Washingtonians for tax-free shopping sprees and a nearby mobile home park, but east of Interstate 5 the island has a strong nautical character, with an abundance of docks and moorages, as well as some new, expensive condominiums, along Tomahawk Island Drive.

NORTH PORTLAND NEIGHBORHOOD INFORMATION

ZIP Codes: 97203, 97217, 97227

Post Offices: Kenton Post Office, 2130 N Kilpatrick St; Piedmont Post Office, 630 NE Killingsworth St; St. Johns Post Office, 8420 N Ivanhoe St

Police Stations: Portland Police Bureau, North Precinct, 449 NE Emerson St, 503-823-5700 (non-emergency)

Emergency Hospital: Legacy Emanuel Medical Center, 2801 N Gantenbein Ave, 503-413-2200, www.legacyhealth.org

Libraries: North Portland Library, 512 N Killingsworth St, 503-988-5394; St. Johns Library, 7510 N Charleston Ave, 503-988-5397

Parks: Major parks include Pier Park, Cathedral Park, Columbia Park, Peninsula Park, and Overlook Park; www.portlandparks.org

Community Publications: *St. Johns Review* (www.stjohnsreview.com)

Public Transportation: TriMet, 503-238-RIDE, www.trimet.org; bus service along major thoroughfares, and MAX service along Interstate Avenue line to downtown Portland

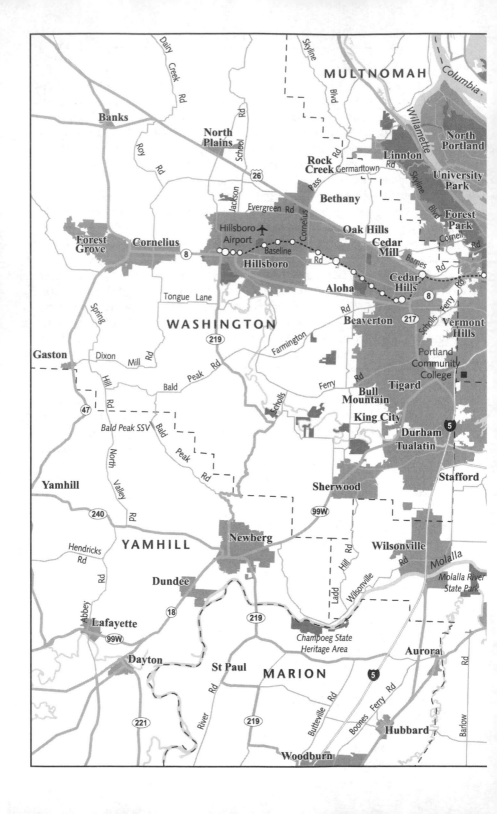

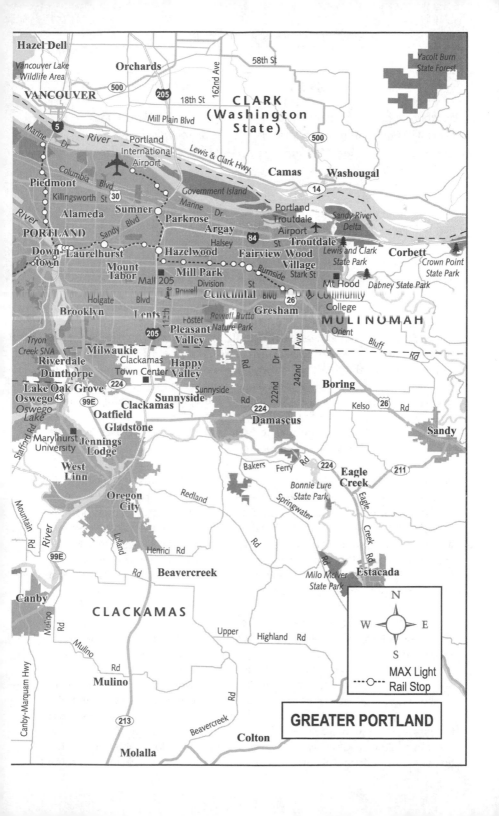

OUTER EAST PORTLAND

Neighborhood Associations: Argay, Centennial, Glenfair, Hazelwood, Lents, Mill Park, Parkrose, Parkrose Heights, Pleasant Valley, Powellhurst-Gilbert, Russell, Wilkes, Woodland Park, plus Maywood Park (independently incorporated)

Outer East Portland, or even just East Portland, is not an official designation. Still, the vast swath of the Portland grid that lies east of 82nd Avenue and especially east of Interstate 205 is palpably different from the rest of the city. It has its own school districts, its own neighborhood centers, its own concerns, and very different demographics. It is generally more socially and politically conservative, and also more ethnically and racially diverse, than other parts of Portland. It offers some of the lowest housing prices in the city; at the same time, a few neighborhoods have some of Portland's highest crime rates, while others are fairly peaceful, essentially suburban enclaves.

These neighborhoods were mostly rural until well into the 20th century; after the Second World War, they slowly filled up with middle-class homes, usually on large lots. Even after the area was mostly built-up, it remained unincorporated. Bit by bit, Portland has gradually annexed much of what used to be known as Mid-County (and Gresham annexed the rest from the opposite direction), but many residents feel neglected by the city. They point to the city's investment in places like the Pearl District and South Waterfront, and contrast those areas with the unpaved streets of their own neighborhoods.

Despite the area's underdeveloped infrastructure, much of the area is experiencing heavy infill development, in some cases on "flag lots"—lots behind an existing residence that are linked to the street by a skinny "panhandle" (or flag-pole) of property, which usually has a driveway. In some areas, especially near the Eastside MAX line, large apartment buildings and some mixed-use developments have been built. This tide of development is dramatically changing the character and the face of East Portland. The human faces of East Portland are changing, too. Many neighborhoods have experienced an influx of recent immigrants from East Asia, Russia and Ukraine, and Latin America.

The neighborhoods north of Halsey Street tend to feature ranch homes, split levels, contemporaries, and other standard postwar styles. Some neighborhoods, like **Argay**, **Wilkes**, and **Russell**, have postwar homes on the sort of curving streets and culs-de-sac that are common in suburban communities but are rare on the Eastside. The northern parts of the first two of these neighborhoods are largely devoted to commercial and light industrial uses. **Parkrose** has a larger number of older homes, mixed with a host of businesses that are more or less associated with the proximity of the airport. South of Interstate 84, slightly more affluent **Parkrose Heights** and **Woodland Park** have more older homes in a variety of styles—Cape Cods, bungalows, English-style cottages, and the like—along with ranches. The homes on the bluff (the "heights" that give the neighborhood its name) just south of the freeway have northward views of the Columbia River and the Washington Cascades. Some of the areas closest to the airport are plagued by aircraft noise. If the sound of jet engines bothers you, be sure to consult a map of flight paths (or just stand around outdoors and listen for airplanes) before committing to a house here. (On the plus side, Parkrose has a station on the Airport MAX line.)

Tucked in between Parkrose and Interstate 205, tiny **Maywood Park** (www.cityofmaywoodpark.com), with only 750 residents, is an independent city. Completely surrounded by (and functionally a part of) Northeast Portland, Maywood Park was incorporated in 1967 in an ultimately futile attempt to prevent Interstate 205 from being routed through the community. Most of the homes date to the late 1930s, and two-story cottages predominate. The neighborhood has an unusual abundance of mature trees, and although there are few sidewalks the streets are wide and traffic is light. Potential annexation to Portland is a perennial political issue here.

The neighborhoods south of Halsey are generally, if perhaps unfairly, considered less desirable. The central neighborhoods—**Hazelwood**, **Glenfair**, **Centennial**, and **Mill Park**—have some of the city's highest rates of violent crime. They are by no means no-go areas, however, and random violence is uncommon. Many blocks are quiet, respectable streets lined with ordinary-looking houses; apartment complexes border the main streets. These neighborhoods also offer access to the Eastside MAX line between Portland and Gresham, and several transit-oriented developments have sprung up along Burnside Street (along which the light rail trains run). Further south, **Powellhurst-Gilbert** also has above-average crime rates, but is nonetheless experiencing plenty of development, both infill and subdivisions of undeveloped land. This neighborhood, along with Hazelwood, Glenfair, Centennial, and Lents (see below), has the lowest median home prices in the city; they are among the few parts of Portland where it is still possible to buy a single-family home for under $150,000.

The **Lents** neighborhood was once notorious for poverty and high crime rates. While the neighborhood is not exactly thriving—it has no supermarket, and many neighborhood streets are unpaved—it has been designated an urban renewal zone and city funds have been allocated for redevelopment. In a hopeful sign, Lents has a new farmers' market that operates on Sundays from June through mid-October. The MAX Green Line from Gateway Transit Center south to Clackamas Town Center passes through Lents.

In Portland's southeasternmost corner, the **Pleasant Valley** neighborhood wraps around the base of Powell Butte, a prominent volcanic butte now protected as a nature park. Much of the neighborhood feels surprisingly rural, with horses grazing in pastures in some areas. This area also offers new homes in several developments. In addition to Powell Butte, the neighborhood is home to several other parks and natural areas, including Leach Botanical Garden (www.leachgarden.org). The Springwater Corridor, a bike and pedestrian trail that runs between downtown Portland and east Multnomah County, passes through both Lents and Pleasant Valley.

MAX lines along Burnside and Interstate 205 are a boon to transit users in outer East Portland. Bus transit is only available on the main east-west streets, with the exception of a north-south line along busy 122nd Avenue. Several different school districts serve the area: rapidly growing David Douglas School District (www.ddouglas.k12.or.us) serves the largest portion of outer Southeast, while Parkrose School District (www.parkrose.k12.or.us) covers Parkrose and the adjacent neighborhoods, Reynolds School District (www.reynolds.k12.or.us) serves part of outer Northeast Portland, and Centennial and the surrounding neighborhoods are part of Centennial School District (www.centennial.k12.or.us).

OUTER EAST PORTLAND NEIGHBORHOOD INFORMATION

ZIP Codes: 97216, 97220, 97230, 97233, 97236, 97266

Post Offices: Airport Mail Facility, 7460 NE Airport Way; Lents Post Office, 3850 SE 82nd Ave; Midway Post Office, 400 SE 103rd Ave; Parkrose Post Office, 4048 NE 122nd Ave

Police Station: Portland Police Bureau, East Precinct, 737 SE 106th Ave, 503-823-4800 (non-emergency); North Precinct (Parkrose, Argay, Wilkes), 449 NE Emerson St, 503-823-5700 (non-emergency)

Emergency Hospitals: Adventist Medical Center, 10123 SE Market St, 503-257-2500, www.adventisthealthnw.com; Kaiser Permanente Sunnyside Medical Center, 10180 SE Sunnyside Rd, Clackamas, 503-652-2880, www.kp.org

Libraries: Midland Library, 805 SE 122nd Ave, 503-988-5392; Rockwood Library, 17917 SE Stark St, 503-988-5396

Parks: Major parks include Powell Butte Nature Park, Beggars-tick Wildlife Park, Leach Botanical Garden, and Springwater Corridor Trail; www.portlandparks.org

Community Publications: *Mid-County Memo*, www.midcountymemo.com

Public Transportation: TriMet, 503-238-RIDE, www.trimet.org; bus lines on major east-west routes, and north-south on 122nd Ave. Eastside MAX on Burnside, Airport MAX service to Parkrose along Interstate 205; Green Line MAX service from Gateway to Clackamas Town Center along Interstate 205

SURROUNDING COMMUNITIES

WASHINGTON COUNTY

Washington County is simultaneously the epicenter of the Portland area's high-tech boom, a region of working farms and timberland, and a major residential area with a population in excess of half a million. The county is not without its problems; it has struggled to manage its rapid growth, and certain areas are notorious for traffic congestion, strip-mall sprawl, and other ills and inconveniences. Still, the region's dynamic economy, natural beauty, and high level of amenities continue to attract newcomers who wish to settle in a suburban location with a

Downtown Beaverton

relatively high quality of life, and for several years Washington County has been the fastest-growing county in the state.

BEAVERTON AND SURROUNDING AREAS

Portlanders have traditionally regarded Beaverton and the surrounding areas as the epitome of suburbia. While that stereotype has some truth—the area is decidedly suburban, with the good and bad aspects the term implies—it is becoming less accurate over time, and already by some measures is plain wrong. For example, Beaverton has a higher population density than Portland, and the West side light rail line brings commuters from Beaverton to downtown Portland in less time than it takes some people to drive in from outlying Portland neighborhoods.

Beaverton is the center of gravity for eastern Washington County, but tens of thousands of people live in areas that are immediately adjacent to, but not formally a part of, the city. Washington County is encouraging an eventual consolidation of services, and Beaverton, which has been on an annexation binge in recent years, is likely to swallow up many of the remaining unincorporated areas around it over the next 10 to 20 years. Beaverton's annexation plans are not without controversy—Nike, in particular, has fought the city's attempted annexation of its headquarters, in large part because the city's property taxes are higher than the county's—but there is an air of inevitability about them.

BEAVERTON

Boundaries: North: West Haven, Cedar Mill, Bethany, Oak Hills (unincorporated Washington County); **West**: Aloha (unincorporated Washington County); **South**: Tigard; unincorporated Washington County; **East**: Portland; West Slope, Raleigh

Hills, Garden Home (unincorporated Washington County); **Area**: 19.6 square miles; **Population**: 91,935

Well into the 20th century, Beaverton was a small town that functioned primarily as a service center for the surrounding farms, which succeeded the rich beaver dam meadows that gave the city its name. The region's produce traveled to market in Portland, seven miles away, at first over a plank road through the West

Beaverton

Hills where Canyon Road and the Sunset Highway now run, and later by train or truck. During the suburban boom following the Second World War, Beaverton became primarily a residential community, then further evolved into a center for new kinds of commerce, becoming the headquarters for multinational companies like Tektronix and Nike. (The latter company is actually located in unincorporated Washington County, literally across the street from, and essentially surrounded by, Beaverton.) New residents and new companies continued to pour in during the 1980s and 1990s, and the city is essentially fully built-out. Nonetheless, the city has continued to increase in population, both through organic growth and an aggressive annexation policy. Beaverton is already Oregon's sixth largest city (after Portland, Salem, Eugene, Gresham, and Hillsboro), and it is on track to become the second-largest city in the state within a decade or so.

Beaverton does not have a central business district per se; rather, outside the core residential areas, the whole city is a business district, with strip malls and office parks lining most of the main roads. That said, the traditional commercial center of gravity is the area around the tiny, hard-to-spot historic downtown, sometimes referred to as Old Town Beaverton, near the intersection of Southwest Hall Boulevard and Highway 10 (Beaverton-Hillsdale Highway/Farmington Road). This area includes a beautiful new public library, a swim center, a small park, and a number of small businesses like Beaverton Bakery (www.beavertonbakery. com); on Wednesdays and Saturdays during the summer the neighborhood hosts a wildly popular farmers' market (www.beavertonfarmersmarket.com) that bills itself as the largest agricultural-only farmers' market in Oregon. Beyond this small node, central Beaverton is a zone of supermarkets, not-so-super markets, big box stores, and chain restaurants. To the north along Cedar Hills Boulevard, the once nearly moribund Beaverton Mall has become the upscale Cedar Hills Crossing. The city has tried, only semi-successfully, to promote high-density, mixed-use developments near light rail stations; along with some old prewar homes and low-rise postwar apartment buildings that hang on in the area of the original town center, these transit-oriented developments are essentially the only residential options in the center of Beaverton.

Away from the sprawling center and the congested main roads, however, Beaverton wears a different face. The city is more ethnically and racially diverse than Portland, and has a higher population density but a lower crime rate; with 13 different neighborhood associations, there is almost literally something here for everyone. Home prices (and rents) within the city vary widely by neighborhood, but the citywide median price is not far off of the metro area average. Homes here tend to be pricier than in neighboring Tigard and Hillsboro, but less expensive than in Tualatin or Lake Oswego.

Beaverton

Much of the city's housing is new, but the ages of individual developments vary widely. Notably, roughly half the city's housing units are detached single-family homes; the other half are townhomes, apartments, and condominiums, most of which are relatively new. In keeping with this housing mix, the population is evenly split between renters and homeowners. Many Beaverton apartment complexes are massive mini-villages, with recreation centers, swimming pools, walking trails, and other amenities; these complexes almost always have vacancies, and are common places for newcomers to settle initially.

While every neighborhood in Beaverton has potential advantages, new-comers tend to land in one of a few areas. Hyland Hills, Ridgeview Heights, and other established subdivisions south and southwest of central Beaverton offer ranch, contemporary, split-level, and other postwar-era single-family homes with yards; most of these developments have homeowner associations, and some homes have distant views of Mount Hood. There are also a few mid-century modern "Rummer" homes in this area, as well as some newer homes on previously unbuilt parcels on the neighborhood fringes. Hyland Forest Park, in the middle of Hyland Hills, is a surprisingly wild, wooded park. Just to the west, Sexton Mountain in western Beaverton is a vortex of culs-de-sac, with mostly newer (1980s–1990s) homes on large lots. Many of these houses offer expansive views to the north and east, but despite the name not every house in this neighborhood is actually on the slopes of Sexton Mountain. Cooper Mountain, in the unincorporated area west of Sexton Mountain, has some very large, very expensive custom homes with views over the whole of the Tualatin Valley. Cooper Mountain is also home to a new, 231-acre nature park.

Back inside city limits, Southwest Beaverton has a sea of cookie-cutter newer homes, mostly multi-story structures on small lots along with some townhomes; the Murray Hill neighborhood in this area, which flanks Scholls Ferry Road, is a mix of newish single-family home developments, large apartment complexes, and commercial areas. These neighborhoods abut the urban growth boundary to the southwest, and the landscape changes from dense subdivisions to farmland quite abruptly.

Beaverton

The Greenway neighborhood west of Highway 217 is an established area of single-family homes and apartment complexes along the Fanno Creek Greenway; the neighborhood has a recreation center and offers quick access to the Washington Square area. Across town, the Five Oaks and Triple Creek neighborhoods of north-western Beaverton are mostly comprised of contemporary-style and newer homes on winding streets; this part of Beaverton is close to both the Sunset Highway and the Tanasbourne area of Hillsboro, and is popular with people who work at the region's high-tech employers. These neighborhoods are also close to the Nike and Tektronix campuses. Sandwiched between Five Oaks and central Beaverton, although not yet technically part of the city, the unincorporated area of **Cedar Hills** (not to be confused with Cedar Mill, north of the Sunset Highway) is a neighborhood of single-family homes dating anywhere from about 1950 to 1980 on mostly quiet, curving streets. Cedar Hills is close to the Sunset Highway and is a short drive or bus ride from the Sunset Transit Center MAX station; the area is home to the newly upscale Cedar Hills Crossing mall and a swarm of satellite shopping centers.

Beaverton has a wealth of parks, community centers, aquatic centers, and recreation complexes, including natural areas like Tualatin Hills Nature Park. The city does not have a parks and recreation department; park facilities are managed by the Tualatin Hills Park and Recreation District, www.thprd.org. The Beaverton School District (www.beaverton.k12.or.us) is the third largest district in the state, and covers a large swath of unincorporated Washington County. School quality varies dramatically, and includes both underperformers and some of the best public schools in the area.

Beaverton traffic is legendarily congested. Both the Sunset Highway and Highway 217 can be horrible during rush hour, and 217 is often bumper-to-bumper even on Saturdays. Main through streets aren't always much faster. Fortunately, Beaverton has excellent transit connections for a suburban community; buses run along the major streets, and the MAX line whisks commuters to downtown Portland in a little over 20 minutes. A new rush-hour commuter rail line to Tigard, Tualatin, and Wilsonville has two stations in Beaverton. Many jobs in the area are in suburban office parks and industrial campuses that can be inconvenient to reach by transit, and the majority of Beaverton commuters drive to work. Still, the city has a decent network of bike lanes and trails, and the percentage of residents who commute by bike is not much lower than the (legendarily high) percentage in Portland proper.

The city's website, and in particular its Map Center, is a useful resource for prospective residents.

Website: www.beavertonoregon.gov
ZIP Codes: 97003, 97005, 97006, 97007, 97008, 97225
Post Office: Beaverton Post Office, 4550 SW Betts Ave
Police Station: Beaverton Police Department, 4755 SW Griffith Dr, 503-526-2260 (general), 503-629-0111 (non-emergency dispatch), www.beavertonpolice.org
Emergency Hospitals: Providence St. Vincent Medical Center, 9205 SW Barnes Rd, 503-216-1234, www.providence.org; ; Kaiser Permanente Westside Medical Center, 2875 NW Stucki Ave, Hillsboro, 971-310-1000, www.kp.org

Library: Beaverton City Library: Main Library, 12375 SW 5th Ave, 503-644-2197; Murray Schools Branch, 11200 SW Murray Scholls Pl, 503-644-2197 (option 2); www.beavertonlibrary.org

Parks: More than 30 parks, open spaces, and recreational facilities, including Tualatin Hills Nature Park, Hyland Forest Park, Fanno Creek Park, and Greenway Park; Tualatin Hills Park and Recreation District, 503-645-6433, www.thprd.org

Community Publication: *Beaverton Valley Times*, www.beavertonvalleytimes.com

Public Transportation: TriMet, 503-238-RIDE, www.trimet.org; bus service on main routes to Hillsboro, downtown Portland, Tigard, and Southwest Portland. MAX light rail service to Hillsboro and downtown Portland; rush-hour commuter train service (WES) to Tigard, Tualatin, and Wilsonville

WEST SLOPE, RALEIGH HILLS, AND GARDEN HOME

Boundaries: **North**: Unincorporated Washington County; **West**: Beaverton; **South**: Tigard; Metzger (unincorporated Washington County); **East**: Portland; unincorporated Multnomah County; **Area**: 5.1 square miles; **Population**: Approximately 21,000

The three communities of West Slope, Raleigh Hills, and Garden Home lie in a narrow band between Beaverton and Portland, just west of the Multnomah County line. Residents of this mostly unincorporated area have Portland mailing addresses but generally enjoy lower Washington County property taxes. This odd (but advantageous) arrangement will change eventually, as the city of Beaverton is poised to annex the entire area in the next decade or so. All three neighborhoods are popular with families who appreciate living in a less dense suburban environment with abundant trees and recreational activities, but with easy access to Portland and Beaverton; the apartment complexes in Raleigh Hills are a common place for newcomers (including childless singles and couples) to land.

West Slope

West Slope is aptly named, as it sprawls across the west slope of the West Hills south of the Sunset Highway. The main drag here is Canyon Road, a rather unattractive strip mall that gathers car dealerships as it descends toward the flatlands of Beaverton proper. Some apartment complexes stand on or close to Canyon Road, but the neighborhoods on either side are largely comprised of single-family houses in styles ranging from tidy ranches, split-levels, and Cape Cods to large contemporary and custom-designed homes. The newest homes tend to cluster near the ridgetops north of Canyon Road. Many homes in this part of West Slope have excellent sunset views west over Beaverton to the Coast Range. South of Canyon Road, in flatter terrain, lie a public library and a neighborhood swim center.

Beaverton has already annexed much of West Slope, which is connected to the rest of the city by a narrow tendril of land that in some places is less than a block wide. To complicate matters, part of the neighborhood is in the Portland Public Schools district, and West Sylvan Middle School, which serves much of Portland's Westside, is technically in Beaverton.

Moving southeast, **Raleigh Hills** centers on the busy commercial area where Scholls Ferry Road and Oleson Road intersect Beaverton-Hillsdale Highway. The neighborhood was originally named Raleigh; the authors of *Oregon Geographic Names* observe that Raleigh Hills "sounds like a name coined by real estate operators." (The neighborhood is rolling, but not remarkably hilly except in its northern reaches.) Traffic on the main roads can be painfully congested during rush hour, and the concentration of shops and services draws traffic from surrounding neighborhoods. (For example, there are four supermarkets—a Safeway, New Seasons, a Fred Meyer, and a Walmart Neighborhood Market—along a short stretch of Beaverton-Hillsdale Highway.) On the plus side, the busy commercial strip along this road means that restaurants, shopping, and services are in easy reach. Many low-rise apartment complexes, quite a few with pools or other fairly upscale amenities, cluster along Beaverton-Hillsdale Highway and nearby

Raleigh Hills

Garden Home

sections of Scholls Ferry and Oleson roads. Off these main roads, Raleigh Hills is mostly comprised of a series of quiet and attractive subdivisions, with many well-kept ranch homes and some newer contemporary houses. North of Beaverton-Hillsdale Highway, there are some large, architect-designed homes on large wooded lots tucked into the hills. In the Vista Brook area, near the Portland Golf Club, east of Scholls Ferry Road, there is a high concentration of modernist post-and-beam "Rummer" homes, built by the Rummer Company in the 1960s essentially as design knockoffs of California Eichler homes. West of the golf club are some large new custom homes with Mount Hood views. As in West Slope, Beaverton has selectively annexed small portions of Raleigh Hills, although here only the width of a single street connects these areas to the rest of the city.

Still farther south, almost to the Tigard border, **Garden Home** features homes that are similar to, although in many cases more modest than, those in Raleigh Hills. Most houses here date from the 1950s through the 1980s; one-level or daylight ranches are the predominant, but certainly not the only, style. The southern parts of the neighborhood tend to have the newest homes, including some recent infill development. Portland has pulled a Beaverton in Garden Home, and extended a couple of annexation tentacles into Washington County. Garden Home has a large and popular recreation center and several small neighborhood parks and wooded areas; the attractive campus of the private Oregon Episcopal School has its own wetland, and the paved Fanno Creek Greenway Trail winds through part of the neighborhood Although it is very close to the office complexes and mall at Washington Square, Garden Home itself remains primarily an area of single-family homes; unlike West Slope and Raleigh Hills, the neighborhood has few businesses, with the exception of a shopping area clustered around the Lamb's supermarket at Oleson Road and Garden Home Road.

With the exception of parts of West Slope, most of this area is part of the Beaverton School District (www.beaverton.k12.or.us). The neighborhood is well connected by road to downtown Portland, Beaverton, and the Washington Square area, all of which are accessible if necessary without traveling on major highways. Be aware that it can be difficult to get around these neighborhoods without a car, although it is relatively easy to travel *out* of the neighborhoods by transit: bus service along the main east-west routes to Portland, Beaverton, or Tigard is adequate to good.

Websites: www.co.washington.or.us; www.beavertonoregon.gov
ZIP Codes: 97223, 97225
Post Office: West Slope Post Office, 3225 SW 87th Ave
Police Station: Washington County Sheriff's Office, East Precinct, 3700 SW Murray Blvd, Beaverton, 503-846-5900 (non-emergency), www.co.washington.or.us/sheriff/; Beaverton Police Department, 4755 SW Griffith Dr, 503-629-0111 (non-emergency dispatch), www.beavertonpolice.org
Emergency Hospital: Providence St. Vincent Medical Center, 9205 SW Barnes Rd, 503-216-1234, www.providence.org
Libraries: Garden Home Community Library, 7475 SW Oleson Rd, 503-245-9932, www.gardenhomelibrary.org; West Slope Community Library, 3678 SW 78th Ave, 503-292-6416, www.westslopelibrary.org
Parks: Community parks include Raleigh Park, Garden Home Park; part of Tualatin Hills Park and Recreation District, 503-645-6433, www.thprd.com
Community Publication: *Beaverton Valley Times*, www.beavertonvalleytimes.com
Public Transportation: TriMet, 503-238-RIDE, www.trimet.org; bus service to Portland, Beaverton, and Tigard

NORTH OF THE SUNSET HIGHWAY: WEST HAVEN, CEDAR MILL, OAK HILLS, BETHANY, AND ROCK CREEK

Boundaries: North: Unincorporated Washington County; **West**: Hillsboro; **South**: Sunset Highway (US 26); **East**: Portland; unincorporated Multnomah County; **Area**: approximately 10 square miles; **Population**: Approximately 43,000

The unincorporated neighborhoods west of the Multnomah County line and north of the Sunset Highway are generally residential and fairly affluent, with a highly educated population. These neighborhoods have become popular places for newcomers to settle, in large part because they offer relatively straightforward access to the major employment centers of Washington County and to downtown Portland (via the Sunset Highway or over the hills on Cornell Road or Barnes Road), because parks, shopping, and services are easily accessible, and because many new homes and apartments have been built here in recent years. Although it is densely developed, this area abuts the urban growth boundary, and rural landscapes are just a few minutes away. Home prices and rents are higher here than the metro area average, but the overall housing stock is in better condition than in some other suburban areas.

Just west of Portland and the
Multnomah County line, **West Haven**
is basically an extension of the Sylvan
area in Portland's West Hills. The main
thoroughfare, Barnes Road, is a busy
alternate route between Beaverton
and Portland; besides shopping
plazas, office parks, and a plethora
of apartment complexes, the Barnes
Road area is home to Providence St.
Vincent Hospital, the exclusive Catlin
Gabel School, and the Oregon College
of Art and Craft. Away from Barnes
Road, subdivisions of single-family
houses are tucked back into the woods
or draped across hillsides; some older
houses are fairly ramshackle, and other
houses are grand, architect-designed
structures, but most homes here are
relatively new, relatively middle-of-
the-road, relatively large structures.

West Haven

The far western part of the neighborhood is a sea of new townhomes and single-
family homes on relatively small lots. The Sunset Transit Center, an important
stop on the Westside MAX light rail line, is adjacent to the Sunset Highway on
the neighborhood's southern boundary; the northern terminus of Highway 217,
which runs south toward Tigard, is also here. Two bus lines serve the neighborhood, both of which connect to the Sunset Transit Center. The neighborhood in
general is not well suited to walking, other than within subdivisions, and parts of
it are very hilly.

To the northwest, abutting both West Haven and Portland's Forest Heights
neighborhood, **Cedar Mill** (www.cedarmill.org, not to be confused with Cedar
Hills, a neighborhood south of the Sunset Highway) was named for a sawmill that
operated here in the 19th century. Today, instead of forest, the neighborhood is
mix of quiet, established culs-de-sac with older, nicely landscaped ranch-style
or contemporary homes and large subdivisions of much newer townhomes and
single-family homes, typically in a "Craftsman-inspired" style. There are also a few
enormous custom homes on large lots. A commercial district along Cornell Road
also includes some apartment complexes and a parade of merchants eager to
meet all your everyday shopping needs; office complexes and other commercial facilities occupy the southern fringe of the neighborhood along the Sunset
Highway. The northern part of the neighborhood is known as **Bonny Slope**,
an area of new housing at the foot of the West Hills, close to the urban growth
boundary. Many of the homes in Bonny Slope have lovely views to the Coast

Cedar Mill

Range. Cedar Mill also has a Saturday morning farmers' market (www.cmfmarket. org) from June through September, which takes place near Sunset High on Cornell Road. There is bus service along Cornell Road and Saltzman Road, but much of the neighborhood has no regular transit service; recreational walkability varies, but unless you are on a main transit corridor you'll likely need a car to get around here. The Sunset Transit Center and MAX station is a short drive away just off Highway 26.

A bit farther to the northwest, **Bethany** is a sea of new housing developments. There are some high-density townhome and apartment developments, but the majority of the housing here consists of large, two-story homes in styles ranging from plain and boxy to "Craftsman-inspired" and somewhat adorned. Most lots are quite small, but open space is abundant and most streets have sidewalks; main routes have bike lanes. There is a small fishing pond (Bethany Pond) just off Northwest 185th Avenue. The neighborhood around Claremont Country Club is made up of custom, mainly single-story homes; nearby Bethany Village (www.

Bonny Slope

bethanyvillage.com) on Bethany Boulevard is a huge mixed-use development featuring housing, retail, and office space. The commercial center of the "Village" is a shopping complex with a supermarket, bank, and other essentials. The neighborhood is also close to the Rock Creek campus of Portland Community College. The agricultural fields of North Bethany were recently brought into the urban growth boundary, and a wave of development that will bring thousands of new homes to the area is just beginning. For now, the north (largely rural) and south (built-up) sides of Northwest Springville Road exist in stark contrast. Bethany might be a good place to start if you're looking for a brand-new home in Washington County.

The area of Bethany west of Northwest 143rd Avenue and south of West Union Road is known as **Oak Hills**. The homes here are generally older than those in the rest of Bethany, and consist mainly of contemporaries, ranches, and split-levels dating from the 1950s to the 1980s. The core of the neighborhood was built in the 1960s, in an early example of a planned unit development, and this part of Oak

Bethany

Hills was added to the National Register of Historic Places in 2013. The general vibe here is mid-century, including more than a score of Eichler-style homes built by the Rummer Company. Most streets have sidewalks, and some have bike lanes. Most homes in the neighborhood are situated on loops or dead-end streets off of Oak Hills Drive, which lazily circles a large community open space. The neighborhood association maintains a pool and gymnasium.

Portland Community College's Rock Creek campus is in the northwest fringes of Bethany, on the edge of the eponymous **Rock Creek** neighborhood (sometimes spelled Rockcreek). The community to the west is mainly residential, with winding streets and culs-de-sac centered on the Rock Creek Country Club. Most homes are two-story contemporary-style homes or one-level ranches, in many cases with cedar shake roofs; there are a few small-scale apartment buildings and duplexes in a similar style. In the southeast part of the neighborhood, where it blends into Oak Hills, there are a few streets lined with older ranch homes and split levels; an

Rock Creek

occasional forlorn old farmhouse reminds residents that these neighborhoods were once agricultural landscapes. Thanks to the presence of the community college, parts of both Bethany (including Oak Hills) and Rock Creek have decent bus service.

All these neighborhoods have excellent access to parks and open spaces, although these undeveloped parcels are not particularly large. Linear parks along stream or powerline corridors are especially common, and many homes back directly onto these greenspaces. Bethany in particular has a network of community trails. Homeowner associations maintain some parks; the remainder are part of the Tualatin Hills Park and Recreation District (www.thprd.com). These neighborhoods belong to the Beaverton School District (www.beaverton.k12.or.us); the district's Sunset High School is located in Cedar Mill, and Westview High School is in the Rock Creek area. The elementary schools in this part of the district are generally highly regarded, and include some of the best-rated schools in the Portland area.

Website: www.co.washington.or.us

ZIP Codes: 97006, 97225, 97229

Post Office: Cedar Mill Branch (contract post office), 12675 NW Cornell Rd, Suite B

Police Stations: Washington County Sheriff's Office, 215 SW Adams Ave, Hillsboro, 503-846-2700; East Precinct, 3700 SW Murray Blvd, Beaverton; 503-846-5900 (non-emergency), www.co.washington.or.us/sheriff/

Emergency Hospitals: Providence St. Vincent Medical Center, 9205 SW Barnes Rd, 503-216-1234, www.providence.org; Kaiser Permanente Westside Medical Center, 2875 NW Stucki Ave, Hillsboro, 971-310-1000, www.kp.org

Libraries: Cedar Mill Community Library, 12505 NW Cornell Rd, Suite 13, 503-644-0043, library.cedarmill.org; Oregon College of Art and Craft Library, 8245 SW Barnes Rd, 503-297-5544

Parks: Dozens of small parks and open spaces; part of Tualatin Hills Park and Recreation District, www.thprd.com

Community Publication: *Beaverton Valley Times*, www.beavertonvalleytimes.com
Public Transportation: TriMet, 503-238-RIDE, www.trimet.org; MAX service from Sunset Transit Center; several bus lines along main roads and to Portland Community College

ALOHA

Boundaries: North: Hillsboro; unincorporated Washington County; **West**: Hillsboro; unincorporated Washington County; **South**: Unincorporated Washington County; **East**: Beaverton; **Area**: 7.4 square miles; **Population**: 50,700

The most important thing to know about Aloha, the unincorporated area west of Beaverton, is that it has no connection to Hawaii. The name is pronounced "uh-LOW-uh," not "uh-low-HAH." According to *Oregon Geographic Names*, in 1912, the first postmaster "named the office Aloah after a small resort on Lake Winnebago in Wisconsin. During the application process the last two letters were transposed by the Post Office Department resulting in the shift from a midwest Indian name to a Hawaiian word." Ironically, Aloha has no particular resemblance to Wisconsin, either, and does not have any lakes, let alone lake resorts.

What Aloha does have is a sea—a sea of suburban housing. The area is not entirely residential—Metro has designated the center of Aloha as a regional "Town Center," and businesses and light industrial facilities of many kinds line busy Tualatin Valley Highway, including an Intel campus that was the first of many in Washington County, and some supermarkets and other retail businesses border Farmington Road—but the neighborhoods on either side of the highway are filled with postwar housing developments with plenty of culs-de-sac. The predominant housing style is the ranch in its various forms—standard ranch, daylight ranch, ranch with ill-advised second-story addition—along with some split-levels and contemporary-style homes. Lots are generally reasonably large without being gigantic. Some streets have sidewalks, although most do not. In short, Aloha should feel familiar to anyone who has spent much time in America's postwar suburbs.

Aloha has not yet experienced the surge of infill development that has transformed closer-in neighborhoods. Some new homes with views of the Tualatin Valley stand on the north slopes of Cooper Mountain, south of Farmington Road, and several newer developments have sprung up on the western fringe of the community, along SE 209th Street, but most Aloha homes are not especially new. Single-family homes make up the majority of housing options here, although there are some apartment complexes, especially in the eastern part of Aloha near the Beaverton border. In general, home prices and rents are slightly lower here than in other parts of Washington County, and (until Beaverton accomplishes its annexation ambitions) property taxes are lower, too.

Aloha is rich in neighborhood parks and open spaces, including a swim center and the bucolic Jenkins Estate in the district's extreme southwestern corner. Aloha is convenient to both Beaverton and Hillsboro, although automobile travel to other parts of the metro area can be time-consuming and inconvenient. (The MAX line runs along Aloha's northern border.) It is reasonably likely that Beaverton (and

Aloha

possibly Hillsboro) will annex much of Aloha in the next decade or two, but the area should remain unincorporated for the near future. Most of Aloha is within the Beaverton School District (www.beaverton.k12.or.us); the Hillsboro School District (www.hsd.k12.or.us) serves the western portion of Aloha.

Website: www.co.washington.or.us
ZIP Codes: 97006, 97007, 97078
Post Office: Aloha Post Office, 3800 SW 185th Ave
Police Stations: Washington County Sheriff's Office, 215 SW Adams Ave, Hillsboro, 503-846-2700; East Precinct, 3700 SW Murray Blvd, Beaverton; 503-846-5900 (non-emergency), www.co.washington.or.us/sheriff/
Emergency Hospitals: Tuality Community Hospital, 225 SE 8th Ave, Hillsboro, 503-681-1111, www.tuality.org; Providence St. Vincent Medical Center, 9205 SW Barnes Rd, 503-216-1234, www.providence.org/Oregon; Kaiser Permanente Westside Medical Center, 2875 NW Stucki Ave, Hillsboro, 971-310-1000, www.kp.org
Library: Aloha Community Library, 17455 SW Farmington Rd, Suite 25B, 503-259-0185, www.alohalibrary.org
Parks: More than 20 parks and open spaces; part of Tualatin Hills Park and Recreation District, 503-645-6433, www.thprd.com
Community Publications: *Beaverton Valley Times*, www.beavertonvalleytimes.com; *Hillsboro Argus*, www.hillsboroargus.com
Public Transportation: TriMet, 503-238-RIDE, www.trimet.org; bus service along Tualatin Valley Highway, Farmington Road, and 185th and 198th Avenues, with MAX light rail service along the community's northern edge

SOUTHEASTERN WASHINGTON COUNTY

The generally affluent southeastern chunk of Washington County has been one of the fastest-growing areas in the state over the last decade. Good schools, high-end shopping malls, access to parks and open space, and a concentration of nearby employers attract many new residents, as does housing that, while not cheap, is generally less expensive than housing in Lake Oswego, West Linn, or some other desirable suburban communities. On the downside, traffic congestion has increased markedly in recent years, both on the freeways (Interstate 5 and Highway 217) and on major city streets. If the suburban lifestyle appeals to you, and if you can handle the commute (or if you'll be working nearby), you may want to check out the cities and communities of this part of the metro area.

TIGARD

Boundaries: North: Beaverton; unincorporated Washington County; **West**: Beaverton; unincorporated Washington County; King City; **South**: Tualatin; Durham; **East**: Lake Oswego; Portland; **Area**: 12.2 square miles; **Population**: 50,500

Tigard

Tigard (pronounced TY-gird, and not like the Winnie the Pooh character Tigger) was called Butte until the end of the 19th century, when the town became known as Tigardville, and eventually just Tigard, after early Pioneers Wilson and Polly Tigard. For many years, Tigard was little more than a farm community and minor trade center. After the Second World War, however, Tigard began to develop into a bedroom community for Portland, only nine miles to the northeast. The completion of Interstate 5 (which forms Tigard's eastern border) in the 1960s fueled a boom in commerce and population that continues to this day.

Tigard's small, original downtown borders newly redeveloped Main Street, just off of Pacific Highway (Highway 99W), the congested, strip mall–lined road that leads from Portland to Sherwood and Yamhill County. The city hall, library, post office and a growing number of shops and restaurants are located in this area, but Tigard's commercial center of gravity has moved to the areas bordering the freeways that serve the city, Interstate 5 and Highway 217. At Tigard's northern tip stands Washington Square, the metropolitan area's largest and most upscale traditional mall, flanked by an honor guard of minor strip malls and commercial office buildings; at the city's southeastern corner is the region's premier "lifestyle" mall, Bridgeport Village. The zone between these two temples of commerce— essentially the eastern third of Tigard, within a few blocks of the freeways—is a mix of office parks, light industry, and big-box retailers, together with the occasional stray house or apartment building. The city has plans to increase the meager housing stock in the so-called "Tigard Triangle," the densely commercial and pedestrian-unfriendly zone between I-5, 217, and 99W.

Behind this bulwark of economic vitality lie the city's residential neighborhoods. With the exception of the Pacific Highway strip and parts of Scholls Ferry Road, most of the western two-thirds of the city is residential. Homes in central Tigard, south of "downtown," run the gamut of post-century styles, but the different subdivisions have very different flavors, depending on when and by whom they were built. Some areas are lined with ranch homes shaded by mature trees, others are comprised of clusters of tastefully painted newer townhomes, and still others feature basic two-story homes on stark culs-de-sac. One constant is that there are very few through streets, so traffic on residential streets tends to be light. Most blocks have at least a few families with children, with the exception of the neighborhood around Summerfield Golf Course, which is a 55+ residential community with some 1,700 residents. The southern end of the city is a landscape of culs-de-sac with newer, generally two-story homes, mixed with older ranches on older streets. This area is within walking distance of Cook Park, on the north bank of the Tualatin River.

West of Pacific Highway, most housing developments are less than 20 years old, and some are brand-new. In the northern reaches of the city, near Washington Square and along Scholls Ferry Road, there is a large stock of townhouses and apartment complexes, together with office parks, medical clinics, and other commercial buildings. Apartment buildings also abut stretches of Pacific Highway. Away from these areas, western Tigard is primarily an area of large, newer single-family homes. There are several high hills in this part of the city, and some houses have impressive views of Mount Hood. The median home price in Tigard is roughly in line with the metro-area average, and is higher than in Beaverton but lower than Tualatin, its immediate neighbors. You can expect to pay substantially above the city average price for a home that is larger than average, is relatively new, or offers a view.

Tigard's fast growth, combined with a similar level of growth in nearby suburbs, has resulted in significant traffic congestion. The nine-mile commute to downtown Portland takes 15 minutes on a good day or during off-peak hours, but it can last 45 minutes or more if there is an accident or other mishap. Highway 217 is no better, and Pacific Highway (99W) is notoriously slow. Buses serve Pacific Highway and some other main streets, but are often inconvenient except for commuters going to Portland, Tualatin, Washington Square, or Beaverton. There is no light-rail service—and given vocal opposition to the idea by some local groups, there isn't likely to be light rail service anytime soon—although the WES commuter train line between Beaverton and Wilsonville stops in downtown Tigard.

Tigard

Despite its congestion, Tigard is considered a desirable place for families, and roughly one-third of the city's households are families with school-age children. Most of the city is part of the well-regarded Tigard-Tualatin School District (www.ttsdschools.org); a small area in the northern portion of the city is part of the Beaverton School District (www.beaverton.k12.or.us). Tigard High School offers an International Baccalaureate program. Tigard has more than a dozen pleasant city parks, including Cook Park on the north bank of the Tualatin River, Summerlake Park in the northwest, and the greenways along Fanno Creek. The Tigard Farmers' Market (www.tigardfarmersmarket.com) is held in a parking lot near downtown Tigard on Sundays from mid-May through October. The highlight of the municipal calendar is the Tigard Festival of Balloons—these are major hot-air affairs, not birthday party–grade helium balloons—held each June.

Website: www.tigard-or.gov
ZIP Codes: 97223, 97224
Post Office: Tigard Post Office, 12210 SW Main St

Police Station: Tigard Police Department, 13125 SW Hall Blvd, 503-629-0111 (non-emergency)

Emergency Hospitals: Legacy Meridian Park Medical Center, 19300 SW 65th Ave, Tualatin, 503-692-1212, www.legacyhealth.org; Providence St. Vincent Medical Center, 9205 SW Barnes Rd, 503-216-1234, www.providence.org

Library: Tigard Public Library, 13500 SW Hall Blvd, 503-684-6537, www.tigard-or. gov/library

Parks: 24 city parks and open spaces, including Cook Park, Fanno Creek Park, and Summerlake Park; www.tigard-or.gov/community/parks/

Community Publications: The Times, www.tigardtimes.com; The Regal Courier, www.theregalcourier.com

Public Transportation: TriMet, 503-238-RIDE, www.trimet.org; eight bus lines along major routes to and from neighboring communities and downtown Portland; rush-hour commuter rail service (WES) to Beaverton, Tualatin, and Wilsonville

DURHAM

Durham is a tiny (265-acre) incorporated city of about 1,400 people wedged between Tigard and Tualatin along Upper Boones Ferry Road. The city is primarily residential, and although there are several office parks along Upper Boones Ferry, Durham has no retail establishments. (The city is, however, a short walk or drive to the Bridgeport Village shopping center just to the east.) Apart from a few small apartment complexes on Upper Boones Ferry, the city's housing is comprised of contemporary-style homes dating primarily from the 1960s to the 1980s. Most of these homes are on good-sized but not enormous lots on curving back streets and culs-de-sac, the names of which—Rivendell Drive, Woody End, Wilderland Court—suggest a developer with a Lord of the Rings fetish. Residents are justly proud of the city's canopy of mature conifers (a fact which is a bit ironic, as the city was named after a pioneer sawmill owner).

Durham is within the Tigard-Tualatin School District (www.ttsdschools.org). Durham Elementary School is actually just across the city limit in Tigard.

Website: www.durham-oregon.us

BULL MOUNTAIN

The unincorporated area of Bull Mountain occupies the ridgeline and slopes of the mountain of the same name west of Tigard. Bull Mountain has more than 10,000 residents, but its voters narrowly rejected incorporation in 2006 and the area has resisted wholesale annexation attempts by Tigard. Tigard has, however, selectively annexed small parcels in the eastern part of Bull Mountain, and is slowly annexing other areas where property owners request or agree to annexation.

Durham

The main road in Bull Mountain is, appropriately enough, Bull Mountain Road, which connects with 99W and runs east-west through the neighborhood. Access to most Bull Mountain homes is via the winding roads that branch north and south off of Bull Mountain Road. Several minor roads lead out of the neighborhood and down to Tigard and Beaverton, relieving traffic pressure on narrow Bull Mountain Road itself. Much of Bull Mountain consists of large, often custom-designed, homes with Mount Hood views, which may or may not be inside walled-in (although not necessarily gated) subdivisions. Newer homes here range from spacious to ostentatiously massive in size; many, if not most, are high up enough to have views of *something*, whether it be Mount Hood or the Tualatin Valley. There are also some neighborhoods of older ranches and split-levels, which are very nicely kept and landscaped with larger yards than many of the newer homes. The subdivisions in the western part of the neighborhood directly abut farmland.

Bull Mountain in general has higher home prices than neighboring Tigard or Beaverton, in large part because homes here tend to be relatively large and relatively new, with views. The neighborhood is extremely quiet; there are no townhouses or apartments and no major through highways, and public transportation is not available. Bull Mountain school children attend Tigard-Tualatin schools (www.ttsdschools.org). The unincorporated area has no public parks, although some subdivisions have their own greenspace areas.

KING CITY

Turn off busy Pacific Highway at Southwest Royalty Parkway, behind Grocery Outlet, and you will find yourself in King City, a 1960s-era retirement community of some 3,250 people. The streets, which generally have "royal" names—Imperial Avenue, King Richard Drive, Queen Victoria Place, etc.—wind around a semi-private golf course; watch for the "Golf Carts on Street" signs. Most homes are modest ranches and split-levels, and there are also some older condo complexes. Many

King City residences (and the golf course) have Mount Hood views. If King City sounds like your kind of place, you may have to wait a while: most properties have deed restrictions that require at least one owner to be over 55, and that bar anyone under 18 from living there. In recent years, however, King City has begun annexing nearby unincorporated areas to the south and west, and the deed restrictions don't apply in these new parts of the city. Look for the median age of King City residents (currently in the low 60s, down from 76 in 2000) to continue to decline in the future.

Website: www.ci.king-city.or.us

King City

TUALATIN

Boundaries: North: Tigard, Durham; **West**: Unincorporated Washington County; **South**: Unincorporated Washington County; **East**: Lake Oswego, unincorporated Clackamas County and Washington County; **Area**: 8.3 square miles; **Population**: 27,000

Tualatin (pronounced too-WALL-uh-tin), 12 miles south of downtown Portland, was once a sleepy small town on the south bank of the river for which it was named. Although it was incorporated in 1913, by 1970 the city still had fewer than 1,000 residents. Tualatin's population has since increased more than 25-fold, and the area continues to boom, with new residents drawn by the city's pleasant neighborhoods and greenspaces, strong public schools, family-friendly environment, and the growth of nearby high-tech businesses.

While Tualatin has no real downtown, the city is centered on the area just south of the Tualatin River, between Southwest Boones Ferry Road and Martinazzi Avenue. This area contains Tualatin Commons; built on the former site of a pet food factory, the development now includes an artificial lake, offices, restaurants, apartments, and a hotel. The city hall and library are also located here. (The library proudly displays the skeleton of a mastodon that was excavated nearby in the 1960s.) A self-guided Artwalk wends through the city center area, past public art (including the mastodon) and a few historic structures, and even such oddball attractions as a garden of poisonous plants. Nearby, a few older shopping plazas and apartment complexes blend into the new retail developments along Tualatin-Sherwood Road. The small part of the city that lies north of the Tualatin River contains most of Bridgeport Village, a popular upscale outdoor mall. (The rest of Bridgeport Village is in Tigard.)

Outside this concentration of commercial and medium-density residential developments, single-family homes comprise the bulk of the city's built-up area. Tualatin's residential districts generally feature medium-to-large homes on quiet, curving residential streets and culs-de-sac. The predominant housing style is one- or two-story Northwest contemporary or "shed" design; some homes have rather interesting architecture, and most have pleasantly landscaped yards with trees. There are a few older neighborhoods of ranch homes and split-levels; the newest neighborhoods cluster in southwest Tualatin. Some of these homes veer towards the McMansion end of the housing spectrum, with three-car garages and "great rooms." The real estate crash resulted in a number of completed, but largely unoccupied, developments in this part of the city; now that the market has recovered, and the available inventory has sold, some new developments are edging into the fields. There are also some townhomes and apartment complexes along Boones

Tualatin

Ferry Road near Interstate 5; and in East Tualatin near Legacy Meridian Park Hospital. The large planned development of Fox Hill perches above the Tualatin River in the easternmost part of the city. (East Tualatin is in Clackamas County.)

Tualatin

Because of Tualatin's popularity, housing prices are somewhat higher than in many other Washington County suburbs, although monthly rents are comparable. (Despite the preponderance of single-family homes, nearly half the population lives in rentals.) The city's main annual celebration is the Tualatin Crawfish Festival, which has survived for more than half a century despite the curse placed upon it by the Voodoo Queen of Acadiana in Louisiana, who felt perhaps overly protective of her region's claim to lifetime achievement in the field of crawfish. The city has a decent selection of community parks; Browns Ferry Park along the Tualatin River provides a launching point for canoes and kayaks.

The city's major streets and Interstate 5 are growing increasingly congested, and Tualatin Sherwood Road is ridiculously slow at certain times of day. Projected continued strong population growth in Sherwood and Wilsonville over the medium-term will continue to affect the traffic situation in Tualatin adversely. It's a 15-minute drive to downtown Portland at off-hours, but that figure doubles (or triples) at rush hour. Although the city is generally very car-dependent, Tri-Met offers express bus service to Portland, and there is a park-and-ride near Interstate 5. SMART runs buses between Tualatin and Wilsonville, and the WES commuter rail line between Wilsonville and Beaverton serves central Tualatin.

Almost all of Tualatin is part of the Tigard-Tualatin School District (www. ttsdschools.org), and Tualatin High School offers an International Baccalaureate program.

Website: www.tualatinoregon.gov
ZIP Code: 97062
Post Office: Tualatin Post Office, 19190 SW 90th Ave
Police Station: Tualatin Police Department, 8650 SW Tualatin Rd, 503-629-0111 (non-emergency)
Emergency Hospital: Legacy Meridian Park Medical Center, 19300 SW 65th Ave, Tualatin, 503-692-1212, www.legacyhealth.org

Library: Tualatin Public Library, 18878 SW Martinazzi Ave, 503-691-3074

Parks: 9 parks, including Browns Ferry Park, Atfalati Park, and Ibach Park; www.tualatinoregon.gov/recreation

Community Publication: *The Tualatin Times*, www.tualatintimes.com

Public Transportation: TriMet, 503-238-RIDE, www.trimet.org (bus service between Tualatin and Portland or Lake Oswego); SMART, 503-682-7790, www.ridesmart.com (bus service between Tualatin and Wilsonville); peak-hour commuter rail service (WES) to Wilsonville, Tigard, and Beaverton

SHERWOOD

Boundaries: North: Unincorporated Washington County; **West**: Unincorporated Washington County; **South**: Unincorporated Washington County; **East**: Tualatin; unincorporated Washington County; **Area**: 4.3 square miles; **Population**: 18,500

The outlying community of Sherwood, about 16 miles southwest of downtown Portland, is on the fringe of the metropolitan area, surrounded on three sides by the farms and wooded hills of rural Washington and Yamhill Counties. (The city is far enough out to have its own urban growth boundary.) It is also one of the fastest growing cities in the state. This growth has brought traffic congestion and

Tualatin

not-always-sensitive development; many outsiders experience Sherwood only along the two main through roads, Pacific Highway (Highway 99W), which is lined by strip malls, punctuated by the occasional large apartment complex, and Sherwood-Tualatin Road, which is flanked by industrial facilities and office parks and plagued by incessant truck traffic. The perception of the city these streets create is both unfortunate and inaccurate, as most of Sherwood is a quiet, pleasant suburban community with a small-town feel and strong community spirit.

The heart of this hidden city is Old Town Sherwood, a compact old-fashioned downtown where a beautiful new public library and a few new upscale businesses have started a minor revitalization. Old Town also hosts the Sherwood Saturday Market (www.sherwoodmarket.blogspot.com), held Saturday mornings from May through September. The adjacent Smockville neighborhood—Smockville was the original name of the town before its incorporation in 1892—is filled with bunga-lows and other older homes. Stella Olsen Park, at this neighborhood's western end, hosts concerts and outdoor movie screenings during the summer. Across the

Sherwood

railroad tracks to the southeast stands a mix of generally modest single-family homes ranging in age from early-20th-century cottages to ranches and contem-porary-style homes. The hills around Murdock Park, in Southeast Sherwood, are high enough to offer good views of the surrounding countryside; two-story con-temporary homes line the short, sometimes steep, streets. Newer tract homes dominate the southern and southwestern parts of the city. The newest devel-opments tend to be large, self-contained and walled-off (although not actually gated) blocks of large single-family homes, some of which have very small yards. The vast majority of Sherwood's housing stock consists of single-family homes, but some new apartment complexes have sprung up along Pacific Highway in the northern part of the city.

Despite Sherwood's substantial distance from the metropolitan center, real estate is not exactly cheap: the median home price is comparable to Tigard's, and quite a bit higher than prices in Beaverton or Hillsboro. The median household income, meanwhile, is higher than in most other metro-area communities. Traffic congestion can be (and usually is) a problem heading out of town toward Tigard or Tualatin; there is frequent (but not necessarily lightning-fast) bus service to Tigard and Portland. A new connector road between Interstate 5 and Highway 99W, which would bypass Tualatin-Sherwood Road, has been proposed to

Smockville Neighborhood

alleviate existing bottlenecks. Sherwood's biggest municipal festival is the annual Robin Hood Festival, complete with archery contest (but so far no "rob from the rich, give to the poor" event) (robinhoodfestival.org). (The city was named, either directly or indirectly depending on which story you believe, for England's Sherwood Forest.) The city is a popular choice for households with children, a fact reinforced in 2009 by *Family Circle* magazine naming Sherwood one of the top ten cities in the country for families. (Caveat: *Family Circle*'s screening criteria may not match yours.) Most of Sherwood is within the city's own school district (www.sherwood.k12.or.us); a small part of the northern portion of the city is within the Hillsboro School District (www.hsd.k12.or.us).

Website: www.sherwoodoregon.gov

ZIP Code: 97140

Post Office: Sherwood Post Office, 16300 SW Langer Dr

Police Station: Sherwood Police Department, 20495 SW Borchers Rd, 503-625-5523 (non-emergency)

Emergency Hospital: Legacy Meridian Park Medical Center, 19300 SW 65th Ave, Tualatin, 503-692-1212, www.legacyhealth.org

Library: Sherwood Public Library, 22560 SW Pine St, 503-625-6688, www.sherwoodoregon.gov/library

Parks: 12 public parks and open spaces, including Stella Olsen Park, plus Tualatin River National Wildlife Refuge

Community Publication: *Sherwood Gazette*, www.sherwoodgazette.com

Public Transportation: TriMet, 503-238-RIDE, www.trimet.org; one bus line with frequent service and one express bus line to Tigard and downtown Portland

WESTERN WASHINGTON COUNTY

Western Washington County blends the wonders of the modern world with the splendors of the natural environment. The tech employers of booming Hillsboro attract skilled workers from around the world, while just a few miles away you'll find fog-shrouded forested hills and world-class wineries. It's not perfect—traffic can be a nightmare, and increasing immigration and other demographic changes have caused growing pains and general strife about tax and land use issues—but western Washington County remains one of the fastest-growing parts of the state and is a major economic engine for the Portland area.

HILLSBORO

Boundaries: North: Unincorporated Washington County; **West**: Unincorporated Washington County; Cornelius; **South**: Unincorporated Washington County; **East**: Aloha (unincorporated Washington County), Beaverton; **Area**: 23.9 square miles; **Population**: 93,500

Hillsboro is not named for the city's terrain—the landscape could be described as "rolling" at best—but rather for early pioneer David Hill, who arrived in Oregon in 1842 and settled in this region by 1845. It's safe to say that Hill would be astonished if he could see what has happened to his old homestead. Over the last three decades or so, Hillsboro has grown from a sleepy agricultural service center and county seat to become the pulsing heart of the so-called Silicon Forest and the sixth largest city in Oregon. Computer-chip giant Intel, the largest private employer in the state, has several facilities in the city; the newest of these, the company's multi-billion dollar DX1 fab project, is scheduled to come online in 2015. Other technology companies with operations here include Epson, FEI, and Lattice Semiconductor. Most technology facilities are set in large industrial

Hillsboro

"campuses," which are heavily concentrated in the northeastern quarter of the city, close to the Sunset Highway. (In addition to "Silicon Forest," this part of Washington County is sometimes referred to as the Sunset Corridor.) Hillsboro's economic transition has caused a demographic transition as well: the city's population is becoming increasingly diverse, with many new Hispanic, East Asian, and South Asian residents (some of whom have come on H-1B visas to work at the region's tech companies).

The northeastern part of Hillsboro, besides harboring many industrial campuses and office parks, also has abundant shopping and residential options. The **Tanasbourne** district, which straddles Cornell Road west of 185th Avenue, includes the Streets of Tanasbourne (www.streetsoftanasbourne.com)—an upscale "lifestyle" mall—and a coterie of nearby retail hangers-on. The surrounding area is bursting with large residential developments, primarily apartment and townhome complexes with names that often follow this formula: Name = [(cutesy or made-up noun) + (general location or geographical feature) + e], e.g., "The Brookfordington at the Pointe." Most of the development in this area has occurred over the last 20 years, so housing units tend to be fairly new and complexes often have better-than-average amenities. The superabundance of apartments means that it's usually easy to find a vacancy in the area, and Tanasbourne attracts many newcomers, especially those who plan to work for Hillsboro employers.

Southwest of Tanasbourne is the much-lauded Orenco Station development, named for the Oregon Nursery Company that used to operate farms on the site. Orenco Station was one of the country's first suburban New Urbanist developments—mixed-use, transit-oriented, and pedestrian-friendly planned communities—with a residential mix including apartments, neo-traditional single-family homes with big front porches, and brick townhomes with Brooklyn-style stoops (but sanitized to avoid Brooklyn-style interactions—you talkin' to me?). Housing surrounds a "town center" with shops and restaurants. The Orenco "station" is the adjacent stop on the Westside light rail; downtown Portland is 40 minutes away by train. Orenco Station also hosts one of Hillsboro's three weekly farmers' markets, held on Sunday mornings during the summer months. Orenco Station has become so successful, in fact, that several other developments in the area have adopted the Orenco name to bask in the reflected glory of the original development; these other Orencos do not necessarily incorporate any elements of New Urbanist design.

West along Cornell Road, across from the Washington County Fairgrounds, Hillsboro Airport is home base for the local fleet of corporate jets, as well as less glamorous aircraft. As a result, airplane noise can be a concern for some residents. The neighborhoods west of the airport, around Hillsboro High School, have a mix of ranch and contemporary homes. The Jones Farm area, near an Intel campus of the same name, features newer two-story houses on culs-de-sac and dead-end streets; the small park at the center of the neighborhood is reserved for the use of residents only. Other parts of Northwest Hillsboro offer mostly two-story contemporary homes from the 1980s and 1990s, as well as some new housing developments on the fringe of the built-up area. This part of Hillsboro is growing in popularity, although it is a bit of slog from other parts of the metro area. Northwest Evergreen Road offers a stark example of the urban growth boundary in action: housing subdivisions spread out to the south, while working agricultural fields occupy the land to the north.

Downtown Hillsboro is a mix of businesses, apartment complexes, and city and county government buildings, including a modern civic center and the historic county courthouse. This is the western terminus of the Westside MAX line; the trip from here to downtown Portland takes about 50 to 55 minutes. Main Street is lined with small shops and eateries, which stay open late for the Tuesday Market, held on Tuesday evenings from June through August. Downtown also hosts a farmers' market on Saturday mornings from May through October; see www.hillsboromarkets.org for details. The residential neighborhoods surrounding downtown include some lovely restored bungalows and other older homes, leftovers from Hillsboro as it was when it was simply a county seat and not a major suburb and center of industry. The neighborhoods east of downtown feature ranches in varying states of repair and disrepair, mixed with some new apartment buildings; this area also contains small-scale cul-de-sac developments of newer

Hillsboro

homes, shoehorned into gaps in existing built-up areas. The areas further east, around Century High School, are mostly traditional suburban neighborhoods, with plenty of two-story, contemporary-style houses on short loops and dead-end streets.

Hillsboro is a demographic grab-bag of singles, families, students, elderly long-time residents, new immigrants from other countries, affluent high-tech workers, and low-paid agricultural laborers. (Farms, plant nurseries, and wineries still operate just beyond the urban growth boundary.) Like Beaverton, Hillsboro contains just about every kind of housing you could imagine, although Hillsboro is less expensive and not as densely populated as Beaverton, and homeowners make up a slightly higher percentage of the population. The Hillsboro School District (www.hsd.k12.or.us) is a mixed bag, with both excellent and mediocre schools. The city operates an extensive network of parks, recreation centers, "linear parks," and open spaces, including aptly named Noble Woods Park; Shute Park, which includes an aquatic center and library; and Rood Bridge Park, which has a put-in for canoes and kayaks along the Tualatin River. Jackson Bottom Wetlands (www.jacksonbottom.org) is an extensive area of marshland and bird habitat just south of downtown. Hillsboro is also home to the Hops, a minor-league baseball team that plays at Ron Tonkin Field, just south of the Sunset Highway.

Hillsboro has MAX light rail service to Beaverton and Portland, and a decent network of bus lines, but most residents get around by car, and the sprawling nature of development has resulted in significant congestion. The Sunset Highway commute to Portland can be a nightmare, while the slog along Tualatin Valley Highway to Beaverton is usually slow but manageable. People with jobs in or near Hillsboro are more likely to enjoy living here than people who work far away and intend to commute by car.

Website: www.ci.hillsboro.or.us
ZIP Codes: 97006, 97123, 97124
Post Office: Hillsboro Post Office, 125 S 1st Ave
Police Station: Hillsboro Police Department, 250 SE 10th Ave, 503-681-6190 (non-emergency); Tanasbourne Precinct, 20795 NW Cornell Rd, Ste 100, 503-615-6641
Emergency Hospitals: Tuality Community Hospital, 335 SE 8th Ave, Hillsboro, 503-681-1111, www.tuality.org; Kaiser Permanente Westside Medical Center, 2875 NW Stucki Ave, Hillsboro, 971-310-1000, www.kp.org
Libraries: Hillsboro Main Library, 2850 NE Brookwood Pkwy; Shute Park Branch Library, 775 SE 10th Ave; 503-615-6500, hillsboro.plinkit.org
Parks: More than 25 developed parks and facilities, including Noble Woods Park, Shute Park (and Shute Park Aquatic and Recreation Center), and Rood Bridge Park; 503-681-6120
Community Publication: *Hillsboro Argus*, www.oregonlive.com/argus
Public Transportation: TriMet, 503-238-RIDE, www.trimet.org; bus service on many major thoroughfares and light rail service east to Beaverton and downtown Portland

CORNELIUS

Boundaries: North: Unincorporated Washington County; **West**: Forest Grove; **South**: Unincorporated Washington County; **East**: Unincorporated Washington County; **Area**: 2.0 square miles; **Population**: 12,200

Cornelius

Cornelius is perhaps the least-known of Portland's sizable suburbs; ask the average Portlander what they think about Cornelius, and the response is likely to be, "Who?" (The "who," by the way, is the colorfully named Colonel T. R. Cornelius, who sounds like a character in an animated 1960s Christmas special but was actually a settler in the area in the 1840s.) It's not too surprising that Cornelius is not better known; it lacks any major landmarks, shopping centers, significant employers, or indeed regional destinations of any kind, and the city officially proclaims itself "Oregon's family town," a motto that is unlikely to garner tons of press. Cornelius serves as both a farm and forest service center and as a dormitory community of commuters to other parts of the region; in sum, it's a pretty quiet place.

The average household income in Cornelius is lower than in many other Washington County communities, in part because many residents are recent immigrants, but the flip side of the income coin is that housing is less expensive here than elsewhere in the county. Indeed, the median home price is among the lowest in the metro area, in part because of a lack of large, expensive homes to skew the data upward. Moreover, the crime rate is lower than in many other affordable parts of the metropolitan area.

State Highway 8 bisects the city in a couplet of one-way streets. The city has no real downtown, but the city hall and other public buildings are near the eastern end of the couplet, in the historic and recently spiffed-up center of the community. Most of the city's older, prewar homes are in this area, particularly south of Highway 8. The bulk of the city's housing stock consists of fairly modest single-family homes, ranging from small cottages (or mobile homes) to ranches and fairly large two-story homes. A fair number of houses painted unusual colors—magenta, chartreuse, purple, and pink, among others—enliven the rather conventional neighborhoods in the southwestern part of the city. Some new developments of large single-family homes have sprung up in the northeastern part of the city, off North 19th and 29th Avenues.

Part of Cornelius lies within the Forest Grove School District (www.fgsd.k12. or.us), while the eastern portion is part of the Hillsboro School District (www.hsd. k12.or.us); the city is considering starting its own school district so that all children from the city can go to the same high school.

Website: www.ci.cornelius.or.us

ZIP Code: 97113

Post Office: Cornelius Post Office, 1639 Baseline St

Police Station: Cornelius Police Department, 1311 N Barlow St, 503-359-1881 (non-emergency)

Emergency Hospital: Tuality Forest Grove Hospital, 1809 Maple St, Forest Grove, 503-357-2173, www.tuality.org; Kaiser Permanente Westside Medical Center, 2875 NW Stucki Ave, Hillsboro, 971-310-1000, www.kp.org

Library: Cornelius Public Library, 1355 N Barlow St, 503-357-4093

Parks: 10 city parks and open spaces; www.ci.cornelius.or.us

Community Publication: *Forest Grove News-Times*, www.forestgrovenewstimes. com

Public Transportation: TriMet, 503-238-RIDE, www.trimet.org; one bus line, with frequent service to Forest Grove, Hillsboro, and Beaverton

FOREST GROVE

Boundaries: North: Unincorporated Washington County; **West**: Unincorporated Washington County; **South**: Unincorporated Washington County; **East**: Cornelius; **Area**: 5.9 square miles; **Population**: 22,000

Forest Grove lies near the eastern foot of the Coast Range at the westernmost edge of the metropolitan area, 25 miles from Portland. While the city is not entirely unplugged from Washington County's high-tech economy—Viasystems, a circuit board manufacturer, is the city's largest employer, with 800 workers—Forest Grove

Forest Grove

remains an important agricultural service center. In addition to traditional farms and forestland—the city is named Forest Grove for a reason—the surrounding rural area includes several wineries, and even a sakery (SakeOne, www.sakeone. com). In many neighborhoods, farmland is literally just down the street, and the city feels much more like a small town than a suburb in an urban agglomeration of nearly two million people.

Forest Grove

The city's cultural center is Pacific University, chartered in 1849 as Tualatin Academy, which occupies a bucolic (and rapidly expanding) campus in the center of town. The adjacent historic downtown includes several antique stores and restaurants as well as the Forest Theater (www.actvtheaters.com), which shows second-run movies. A farmers' market is held on Main Street downtown on Wednesday evenings from May through October; during market season, downtown merchants stay open late on the first Wednesday of each month.

South of downtown, the extensive Clark Historic District is filled with old farmhouses, Queen Anne Victorians, Craftsman bungalows, and old cottages; some have been grandly restored, and while others have been neglected, the neighborhood feels a bit like it was lifted from a Norman Rockwell painting. North of downtown, small apartment complexes cluster around Pacific University. Further north, off the road to Banks, a few new multi-story duplexes and triplexes stand among modest ranches and smallish contemporary homes. The western end of town features winding streets and culs-de-sac with some new housing developments; the Coast Range looms scenically just to the west.

Strip malls and commercial uses dominate the area along Pacific Avenue east of downtown. The most impressive establishment in this part of town is McMenamins Grand Lodge (www.thegrandlodge.com); this former Masonic & Eastern Star Lodge has been restored and converted to the standard McMenamins combo of guest-rooms, multiple bars, a movie theater, and a soaking pool.

Forest Grove has several city parks and recreational facilities, including a popular aquatic facility, but the biggest recreational draws are Fernhill Wetlands, a prime bird-watching area in the city's southeast corner, and Henry Hagg Lake, a favorite swimming and boating destination in the foothills a few miles south of town. Many Forest Grove residents work in Hillsboro, a relatively manageable 20-minute drive away, but others face a long commute to workplaces elsewhere in the metro area. A single bus line runs from Forest Grove east to Hillsboro and Beaverton. There has been some discussion of extending light rail from Hillsboro to Forest Grove, but no firm plans (or, more importantly, funding commitments) have been made. The city is part of the Forest Grove School District (www.fgsd. k12.or.us).

Website: www.ci.forest-grove.or.us
ZIP Code: 97116
Post Office: Forest Grove Post Office, 1822 21st Ave
Police Station: Forest Grove Police Department, 2102 Pacific Ave, 503-629-0111 (non-emergency)
Emergency Hospitals: Tuality Forest Grove Hospital, 1809 Maple St, Forest Grove, 503-357-2173, www.tuality.org; Kaiser Permanente Westside Medical Center, 2875 NW Stucki Ave, Hillsboro, 971-310-1000, www.kp.org
Library: Forest Grove City Library, 2114 Pacific Ave, 503-992-3247, www. ci.forest-grove.or.us/city-hall/library.html
Parks: 9 city parks, including Lincoln Park (with skate park), plus an aquatic center
Community Publication: *Forest Grove News-Times*, www.forestgrovenewstimes.com
Public Transportation: TriMet, 503-238-RIDE, www.trimet.org; one bus line, with frequent service to Cornelius, Hillsboro, and Beaverton

OUTLYING WASHINGTON COUNTY COMMUNITIES

Beyond the urban growth boundary, past the last office parks and townhouse developments, Washington County remains largely rural, with an economy based on agriculture and forestry rather than high-tech industry. Several small towns and cities dot the hinterlands; these communities are generally growing in population, in large part because of a minor influx of commuters, but they have so far been spared the indignity of turning into purely dormitory suburbs.

Hazelnut groves and rich farmland surround the city of **North Plains** (www. cityofnp.org), located just north of the Sunset Highway. This city of about 2,000 people has a diminutive downtown with civic buildings—a city hall, a police station, a fire station, and a new wood-and-stone public library with ceilings made from clear hemlock—along with a couple of taverns, a market, and a hardware store. Other commercial establishments are in strip malls on Glencoe Road, just off the highway. Homes within city limits run the gamut from moss-covered, moldering shacks to developments of large new houses; a few multimillion-dollar estates lurk in the vicinity of world-class Pumpkin Ridge Golf Course just north of town. Many homes in the countryside outside of town have spectacular settings. The city expects to double in population by 2020.

North Plains holds an elephant garlic festival every year. Speaking of stinky things, North Plains is also the site of a large composting facility, which generated terrible odors until it stopped processing commercial food waste in 2013. Now, while parts of town get an occasional unpleasant whiff, the smell situation is much better. North Plains is part of the Hillsboro School District (www.hsd.k12.or.us).

A few miles further west, **Banks** (www.cityofbanks.org) lies near the eastern foot of the Coast Range, north of Forest Grove. Most businesses, schools, and government buildings, and many houses, are located on or just off the city's main street (conveniently named Main Street). At the north end of town, huge piles of logs along the railroad track await milling. Most homes within city limits are bungalows or early-20th-century styles, with the significant exception of some large new housing developments in the southern half of the city. Several wineries are nearby, and Banks is also the terminus of the 21-mile Banks-Vernonia State Trail (www.oregonstateparks.org), a multi-use linear trail built on an old railway line, which leads into the foothills of the Coast Range. Despite its small size and tiny population (about 1,900 people), Banks has its own school district (www.banks. k12.or.us).

Other rural Washington County communities include **Gaston**, near Henry Hagg Lake in the foothills of the Coast Range; **Laurel**, at the foot of the Chehalem Mountains south of Hillsboro; **Scholls**, an unincorporated, primarily agricultural community on the Tualatin River south of Hillsboro and north of Newberg; the logging town of **Gales Creek**, in a scenic valley northwest of Forest Grove; and **Roy**, known for its lavish holiday displays in December, when the entire town is tricked out with light bulbs and ostentatious holiday displays—look for clouds reflecting the glow on the western horizon. Bucolic **Helvetia** is representative of the rural

Scholls

Laurel

unincorporated areas in the rolling farmlands north of the Sunset Highway. Public transportation is essentially nonexistent in the rural areas of Washington County.

CLACKAMAS COUNTY

Portland's self-appointed tastemakers used to consider most of Clackamas County (with the affluent exceptions of Lake Oswego and West Linn, and especially the portion of Dunthorpe that spills over into the county) a bit beyond the pale, a sort of semi-rural backwater, populated by slack-jawed yokels, that lacked both the urban amenities of Portland and the dynamic economic growth that justified Washington County's existence. Such derisive nicknames as "Clackistan" were bandied about. (The widely publicized shenanigans of Clackamas County's Tonya Harding and Jeff Gillooly did not help to dispel this view.)

Anyone who still clings to this stereotype is behind the times. While many of the outlying areas remain fairly rural and admittedly (and proudly) not especially sophisticated, inner Clackamas County has experienced blistering population growth in recent years, and areas like Damascus are slated to accommodate much of the Portland area's projected population increase over the next 20 years. Parts of Clackamas County boast some of the highest average home prices in the region, and as for trendiness—well, for what it's worth, there are now dozens of Starbucks locations in the county, and nary a yokel in sight. Newcomers who once would never have given Clackamas County serious consideration are now settling there in droves. More are coming. You might be one of them.

SOUTHWEST CLACKAMAS COUNTY

The suburbs of southwest Clackamas County—the area south of Portland and west of the Willamette—have some of Oregon's highest per capita incomes and most coveted real estate. A few areas, such as much of Wilsonville and the Kruse

Way area of Lake Oswego, are regional commercial centers, but most of the land in this part of Clackamas County is devoted to residential (or outside the urban growth boundary, quasi-agricultural) uses.

DUNTHORPE AND RIVERDALE

These exclusive unincorporated neighborhoods occupy wooded hillsides, laced by sinuous roads, on the west bank of the Willamette River south of Portland. Although Dunthorpe and Riverdale lie mostly in Multnomah rather than Clackamas County, demographically they are more akin to Lake Oswego, their affluent neighbor to the south, than to Portland. Genteel **Dunthorpe** (together with the neighboring enclave of **Riverdale**) is known for large homes on large lots with correspondingly large price tags: A Dunthorpe fixer on acreage might go for a million dollars, if you're lucky. Home styles range from staid traditional to bold (but usually not too bold) contemporary. Because residents value privacy, properties are often fenced, walled, or hedged off, and many houses are not actually visible from the street. (This is not necessarily a bad thing—not everyone finds five-car garages attractive.) Many of the homes located along the Willamette River have boathouses or floating docks. That said, not every house in Dunthorpe is a splendidly isolated mansion, and there are some ranch-style and contemporary houses that would not seem out-of-place in surrounding communities.

The area has its own excellent school district, Riverdale School District (www. riverdaleschool.com), which consistently produces some of the highest test scores and college matriculation rates in the state. Riverdale Elementary School lies squarely in the middle of the neighborhood, off Riverside Drive, but Riverdale High School was built nearby in Southwest Portland (presumably to avoid the significant expense of condemning Dunthorpe real estate). Celebrities who have purchased homes here include various Portland Trail Blazers, actor Danny Glover, and Linus Torvalds, creator of the Linux open-source computer operating system.

LAKE OSWEGO

Boundaries: North: Portland; Dunthorpe; **West**: Tigard; **South**: West Linn; unincorporated Clackamas County; **East**: Willamette River; **Area**: 11.2 square miles; **Population**: 36,900

For many newcomers who can afford to live here, Lake Oswego represents the path of least resistance. It is the Portland version of an East Coast old-money suburb: affluent, tidy, woodsy, and generally quiet, with good schools and neighbors who keep the lawn mowed and the hedges trimmed. These features make it one of the most sought-after and prestigious places to live in the Portland area, with prices to match: the average home price here is higher than in any other city in the Portland metropolitan area. This concentration of wealth and (apparent) respectability also make Lake Oswego a subject of mockery in some quarters:

"Lake Big Ego" is one of the more printable derisive nicknames you might hear. "Lake O" certainly has its share of multimillion-dollar waterside homes and well-coifed Ferrari drivers, but it is actually more economically diverse than it appears to outsiders. While it's not a bargain-hunter's paradise by any definition, Lake Oswego contains a fair number of reasonably affordable apartments and unassuming single-family houses, especially in the city's western neighborhoods. The city has 21 neighborhood associations, and every last one of them is dedicated to preserving the quality of life in its own little slice of the city.

Lake Oswego centers on a three-and-a-half-mile lake, fed by a canal from the Tualatin River; the lake, officially named Oswego Lake, is managed by the Lake Oswego Corporation (www.lakecorp.com), an association of lakeshore residents, and is closed to public use. Unauthorized boaters can expect the aquatic equivalent of, "Hey you kids, get off my lawn!" The original settlement was a center for the iron industry—the ruins of the old iron foundry, the oldest on the West Coast, still stand in George Rogers Park on the Willamette River—but the area ultimately evolved into a community of summer cottages (a few of which still stand) on the shores of what was known until 1913 as Sucker Lake (not a great name from a real estate investment standpoint). Development for permanent housing began after the First World War, and accelerated during the suburban boom that followed the Second World War. Today the city is basically built out, with most development occurring as infill or in nearby unincorporated areas.

Lake Oswego's pleasant, small-scale downtown, at the northeast end of the lake, features a selection of upscale shops abutting Millennium Plaza Park, where a farmers' market (www.ci.oswego.or.us/farmersmarket/) takes place on Saturdays from mid-May through mid-October. Nearby Lakewood Center for the Arts is home to a theater (and a theater company) and hosts the annual Lake Oswego Festival of the Arts, held in June. The nearby **First Addition** neighborhood, one of the city's first residential neighborhoods, features Craftsman bungalows, English Tudor–style cottages, and other quaint prewar-style homes on walkable (but

Dunthorpe

largely sidewalk-less) streets. With its old homes and grid layout, First Addition would be a good choice for people who love the feel of Portland's Eastside neighborhoods but want to live in the suburbs. The neighborhood abuts the southern end of Tryon Creek State Natural Area.

Some apartments (and apartments that have been converted to condominiums) border Highway 43 and sprawl across the bluffs above the Willamette River or hover above the lake at its eastern end, but most waterfront (and water view) properties are single-family homes. Houses on or near the lakeshore sell at a substantial premium, as do homes along the Willamette River. A few charming old cottages and bungalows, and even some fairly nondescript ranches, remain here from a quieter era; however, many of these have been torn down to make way for enormous fenced-off quasi-mansions (or gated clusters of them). Some of these homes are true architectural gems, while others are notable mainly for their size and obtrusiveness. Homes with views on the wooded bluffs above the lake are somewhat less expensive, but hardly cheap. The quiet neighborhoods in the rolling hills north and south of the lake tend to feature winding streets lined with 1960s- and 1970s-era homes. In very broad terms, neighborhoods south of (and away from) the lake are slightly less expensive than neighborhoods north of the lake.

Lake Oswego

The western end of Lake Oswego, **Lake Grove**, has evolved into a major regional commercial center; the Kruse Way area, full of new Class A office space, acts as a satellite of downtown Portland, and Boones Ferry Road is lined with smaller-scale commercial developments, including restaurants and markets. This part of the city has many newer townhouse and apartment communities, together with single-family homes on the quieter side streets. These neighborhoods in general are the most affordable parts of the city for renters and buyers. The hillside **Mountain Park** neighborhood near Portland Community College's Sylvania campus features well-kept homes set on culs-de-sac and curving streets. Some homes are ranches or traditional-style homes, but others are custom-designed showpieces, ranging from modern houses clinging to the hillside to remarkable mid-century designs. The streets here seem to be in competition to see which has the most erudite name: Harvard Court and Princeton Court have nothing on Erasmus, Pericles, and Cervantes (which do not even deign to have designations as streets, or roads, or courts), while freedom-fighters gravitate to the heights of Nansen Summit, where Bolivar, Juarez, and Garibaldi frolic. Because the summit is the highest point for miles, homes on the upper slopes have expansive views (the subject of which depends on which direction the house faces). The lower part of the Mountain Park neighborhood has several unobtrusive apartment complexes where many newcomers seem to end up for a while.

In addition to (or despite) the prestige factor, many people move to Lake

Lake Oswego

Oswego for the excellent public amenities. The city runs a library, various community and senior centers, and many parks and natural areas. Lake Oswego skews old—the median age, like the median home price—is the highest in the region, but its excellent set of public schools is a major draw for families who can afford to live here. Lake Oswego School District (www.loswego.k12.or.us) operates nine elementary schools, two junior high schools, and two high schools (one recently rebuilt and the other remodeled). Although parts of Lake Oswego have decent bus service, and some neighborhoods have networks of paved walking trails, the city as a whole is quite car-dependent—outside the city center/First Addition area, many city streets are completely unwalkable, let alone bikeable—and the drive to Portland via often pokey Highway 43 or congested Interstate 5, while not the worst commute in the world, can be slow. The same is true for the commute to Washington County via Highway 217. (Although not a viable option for commuters, the Willamette Shore Trolley [oerhs.org/wst] a vintage trolley operated by the Oregon Electric Railway Historical Society, runs along the Willamette

River from downtown Lake Oswego to downtown Portland, with a shortened trip during Sellwood Bridge construction.) An actual streetcar from Portland to Lake Oswego was proposed, but plans were official suspended in 2012.

Lake Oswego

Website: www.ci.oswego.or.us

ZIP Codes: 97034, 97035

Post Offices: Lake Oswego Post Office, 501 4th St; Lake Grove Station, 15875 Boones Ferry Rd

Police Station: 380 A Ave, 503-635-0238 (non-emergency), www.ci.oswego.or.us/police

Emergency Hospital: Legacy Meridian Park Medical Center, 19300 SW 65th Ave, Tualatin, 503-692-1212, www.legacyhealth.org

Library: Lake Oswego Public Library, 706 4th St, 503-636-7628, www.lakeoswego-library.org

Parks: 24 developed and undeveloped parks and natural areas, including George Rogers Park, Foothill Park, Waluga Park, and Iron Mountain Park; www.ci.oswego.or.us/parksrec/

Community Publications: *Lake Oswego Review*, www.lakeoswegoreview.com

Public Transportation: TriMet, 503-238-RIDE, www.trimet.org; several bus lines with semi-frequent service within the city and to and from Portland, Oregon City, Tigard, and Beaverton

WEST LINN

Boundaries: North: Lake Oswego; **West**: Tualatin River, unincorporated rural area (Clackamas County); **South**: Willamette River, Tualatin River; **East**: Willamette River; **Area**: 8.1 square miles; **Population**: 25,800

West Linn is considered one of the most desirable, and is certainly among the most expensive, communities in the Portland area. Newcomers who are considering both cities often pick West Linn in preference to Lake Oswego as being both more down-to-earth and slightly less expensive. For many, the primary draw is the city's excellent schools—the West Linn–Wilsonville School District (www.wlwv. k12.or.us) has one of the best reputations (and some of the highest test scores) in the state. Add a relatively low crime rate and an abundance of parkland and natural areas, and the appeal is clear. The city has more than 25 parks and open spaces; most are small, neighborhood parks, with playgrounds and tennis courts, although a few larger parks, such as Wilderness Park and Willamette Park, draw visitors from the whole city. The city also encompasses the large Mary S. Young State Park along the Willamette River and the Nature Conservancy's Camassia Natural Area, a unique plateau region that was sculpted during ice age floods.

The Willamette River makes a great bend around West Linn, and forms the city's eastern and southern boundary. West Linn's neighborhoods occupy the mile and a half or so between the river and the crest of the range of hills that parallels the river to the west. Because of the river's bend, the city is shaped something like a chubby "V," with the point aimed at Willamette Falls and downtown Oregon City across the river. The northern arm of this V extends northward towards Lake

West Linn

Oswego and the attractive campus of Marylhurst University. Willamette Drive (State Highway 43) is the primary north-south artery here, but it is not a major commercial strip, although it is lined in places by a few nicely landscaped retail businesses, upscale supermarkets like Market of Choice, and small shopping centers. Uphill (west) of Willamette Drive, a few steep streets wind into the hills and lead to compact, rolling neighborhoods of loops and culs-de-sac lined with contemporary and custom multi-story homes. The hills (a southern spur of the Tualatin Mountains) top out at more than five hundred feet above the elevation of the river, so many of these homes have decks with dramatic views of the Cascade

North Willamette Neighborhood

Mountains. While luxury homes abound on the heights, there are also a few town-home developments and small-scale condo complexes. Back on the lowlands between Willamette Drive and the river lie neighborhoods of split-levels and well-kept ranches, many with river views or even river access. South of Mary S. Young State Park, in the Bolton neighborhood, there are many older homes—cottages, bungalows, and even a few grand Victorians.

The south half of West Linn is also a mix of old and new. Interstate 205 bisects this part of town, then crosses the river into Oregon City (as does Willamette Drive, on a much less impressive bridge built in 1922). On the bluff above the river, a few old houses, many in disrepair, have views of Willamette Falls as well as paper mills and other industrial facilities. The **Sunset** neighborhood, between Willamette Drive and the Interstate, features a range of newer and older homes (including some surprisingly shabby structures, and a few apartment buildings). To the west extend large developments of new, generally high-end—and, in some cases, truly enormous—homes. A new shopping center has sprung up to service these new developments, and the city hall relocated here in 1999. The **North Willamette** neighborhood, on the hills just above Interstate 205, comprises winding streets of newer contemporary and traditional-style homes; some large condo complexes occupy the lower slopes near the freeway. In general, this part of West Linn is the best choice for people looking for brand-new homes.

South of the Interstate, where the Tualatin River flows into the Willamette, is the historic **Willamette** neighborhood; this formerly important river landing features many houses from the late 19th and early 20th centuries. Period-appropriate false front facades decorate the commercial buildings—even the new ones—along Willamette Falls Drive, which features a concentration of restaurants, shops, and service providers. This area is the closest thing West Linn has to a traditional downtown. The blocks between here and the riverfront have heavy concentrations of historic homes, but newer homes and apartments have cropped up opportunistically over the years north of Willamette Falls Drive, and these parts of the neighborhood feature a wide range of architectural styles.

Despite its popularity, West Linn is not for everyone. In addition to its fairly high home prices, well above the metro-area median, the city is very car-dependent, and it can be a long and tedious commute to some of the more distant employment centers, whether via Interstate 205 or up Highway 43 to downtown Portland. Some residents complain that there is no real downtown; although there are a few office parks and other businesses near I-205 and along some of the main streets, the city is overwhelmingly residential—some 80% of the city is zoned for that purpose. In case you're wondering, there is no Linn (or East Linn, for that matter); West Linn got its name in 1854 when its predecessor, Linn City, was renamed.

Website: www.westlinnoregon.gov
ZIP Code: 97068
Post Office: Marylhurst Post Office, 17600 Pacific Hwy; West Linn Post Office, 5665 Hood St
Police Station: West Linn Police Department, 22825 Willamette Dr, 503-655-6214 (non-emergency), www.westlinnpolice.com
Emergency Hospitals: Providence Willamette Falls Hospital, 1500 Division St, Oregon City, 503-656-1631, www.providence.org Legacy Meridian Park Medical Center, 19300 SW 65th Ave, Tualatin, 503-692-1212, www.legacyhealth.org
Library: West Linn Public Library, 1595 Burns St, 503-656-7853, www.westlinn.lib.or.us
Parks: More than 25 parks and natural areas within city limits, including Willamette Park, Wilderness Park, and Mary S. Young State Park; www.westlinnoregon.gov/parksrec/
Community Publications: *West Linn Tidings,* www.westlinntidings.com
Public Transportation: TriMet, 503-238-RIDE, www.trimet.org; two bus lines with semi-frequent service to Oregon City or Lake Oswego/downtown Portland

West Linn

STAFFORD

The unincorporated zone between Lake Oswego, West Linn, Tualatin, and Wilsonville is one of the most scenic parts of the metropolitan area. This region of hills, woods, and fields, generally called Stafford, lies outside the metropolitan urban growth boundary, and so is lightly populated and nominally agricultural. The area's proximity to Portland—Interstate 205 runs right through Stafford (and features a Stafford exit, just southwest of Wankers Corner)—means that, in practice, most of the properties here are hobby farms. In particular, Stafford is horse country. Most properties are large, multi-acre spreads, and much of that acreage is devoted to horse barns, pastures, and other equestrian facilities. Many homes are situated on ridges, like Petes Mountain, to take advantage of expansive views of the Cascades and the Willamette and Tualatin valleys. Some areas of Stafford feel so sylvan and remote that it is difficult to accept that they're only half an hour from downtown Portland (in light traffic).

Stafford is likely to remain predominately semi-rural—or more accurately, quasi-rural, since most residents actually make their living in white-collar professions—for the immediate future (barring major changes in land use laws). Nonetheless, some small-scale developments are starting to crop up, such as the

Stafford

30-odd luxury homes of The Quarry at Stafford (built on the former site of an actual quarry). The Borland area has been designated as urban reserve land, meaning it may eventually be brought inside the urban growth boundary. Stafford is part of the West Linn–Wilsonville School District (www.wlwv.k12.or.us). Apart from a tiny commercial area at Wankers Corner (hold the snickers—it's pronounced "Wonkers"), at the intersection of Stafford Road and Borland Road, shopping and services are located primarily in surrounding communities. No public transportation serves the area.

WILSONVILLE

Boundaries: North: Unincorporated Washington County; **West:** Unincorporated Clackamas County; **South:** Willamette River (partial), unincorporated Clackamas County; **East:** Unincorporated Clackamas County; **Area:** 7.4 square miles; **Population:** 21,500

Wilsonville

The fast-growing suburb of Wilsonville is 17 miles south of Portland via frequently congested Interstate 5, which neatly bisects the city into east and west sides. The northern portion of the city is in Washington County, while most of Wilsonville is part of Clackamas County. Wilsonville historically had more jobs than residents: the city is home to technology companies like Mentor Graphics, Xerox Office Group, and FLIR Systems, as well as to various corporate distribution centers that are located here to take advantage of good freeway access and proximity to Portland. These businesses cluster on either side of the Interstate, especially in the northern part of the city. Major retail developments such as the massive Fry's Electronics complex and the adjacent Family Fun Center also border I-5, and drivers who never venture off the freeway can be forgiven for thinking that no one actually lives in Wilsonville at all.

In fact, not only do people live in Wilsonville, but the city has been for many years one of the fastest-growing communities in the metro area, with a 47 percent increase in population between 2000 and 2012. Home prices here are generally higher than in Tigard or Tualatin but lower than West Linn (with which Wilsonville shares a school district). Apartments comprise a relatively high percentage of the city's housing stock, with a concentration of complexes near Wilsonville Town Center, an agglomeration of decentralized shopping plazas, a park-and-ride lot, and Town Center Park on the east side of Interstate 5. On the edge of this quasi-downtown, Memorial Park slopes down to the banks of the Willamette River and features short climbing walls, an innovative playground, a tennis court, and a boat dock. The new developments to the north and northeast include some "apartment homes" and townhouses along with neighborhoods of very large single-family homes. Almost all of this development is of fairly recent vintage.

West of Interstate 5, beyond the office parks, light industrial facilities, distribution facilities, and the like, extend several quiet neighborhoods of townhomes and two-story, single-family contemporary-style homes, some of which overlook the Willamette. A few of these developments border shady alleys of hazelnut groves, which are almost certainly not long for this world. The big news in Wilsonville housing is the ongoing construction of master-planned community Villebois (www.villebois.com). Billing itself as "drawing inspiration from a compact French urban village," this walkable, mixed-use development includes hundreds of "green-built" residences in various traditional styles, arranged around a central park and village center. Villebois, which includes five different homeowner associations, associated with separate developers, is still being built out, and it may be a good choice for people looking to buy a new home in a planned community. The Wilsonville Farmers' Market (http://www.wilsonvillemarket.com), which runs Thursdays from mid-June to mid-September, takes place in a park within Villebois. Residents tend to like the development, but it is a bit out of the way, and is isolated not just from surrounding communities but from the rest of Wilsonville itself.

Across the Willamette, the **Charbonneau District** centers on a golf course, surrounded by one- and two-story contemporary houses, condos, and apartment complexes set amid trees, fountains, lakes, and—of course—fairways. (Fore!) The district contains a small village center with basic services; a few pathways link the disparate parts of the neighborhood, but most people walk heedlessly in the middle of the streets, which lack sidewalks and fortunately have light traffic. Charbonneau's only link with the rest of Wilsonville is Interstate 5's Boone Bridge over the Willamette; the city has proposed building a new foot/bike bridge between Charbonneau and Memorial Park, but no firm plans are in place.

Wilsonville

Charbonneau District

Wilsonville likes to think of itself as a family-friendly city, and about one-quarter of the city's residents are under 18. The highly regarded West Linn–Wilsonville School District (www.wlwv.k12.or.us), which covers most of the city, is a major draw for many parents. Students from the Charbonneau area attend schools in the Canby School District (www.canby.k12.or.us). Despite the abundance of jobs within the city limits, most residents don't actually work in the city, so traffic can be heavy in either direction during rush hour. The Boone Bridge over the Willamette River at Wilsonville is the only road bridge that crosses the river between Newberg and West Linn, and so it is a frequent traffic chokepoint. For some reason, Wilsonville is also the site of many accidents and traffic backups on Interstate 5. The city has its own public transit agency, **South Metro Area Regional Transit** (SMART; 503-682-7790, www.ridesmart.com), which provides bus service within Wilsonville and between the city and Portland, Salem, Tualatin, and Canby. TriMet's WES commuter rail service carries commuters to Wilsonville from Beaverton, via Tualatin and Tigard (and vice versa) during peak hours only; SMART buses connect with trains to carry commuters to and from the city's major employers.

Website: www.ci.wilsonville.or.us
ZIP Code: 97070
Post Office: Wilsonville Post Office, 29333 SW Town Center Loop E
Police Station: Wilsonville Station, Clackamas County Sheriff's Office, 30000 SW Town Center Loop E, 503-682-1012 (non-emergency)
Emergency Hospital: Legacy Meridian Park Medical Center, 19300 SW 65th Ave, Tualatin, 503-692-1212, www.legacyhealth.org
Library: Wilsonville Public Library, 8200 SW Wilsonville Rd, 503-682-2744, www. wilsonvillelibrary.org
Parks: 12 parks, trails, and natural areas, including Memorial Park, Town Center Park, and Graham Oaks Natural Area

Community Publications: *Wilsonville Spokesman*, www.wilsonvillespokesman.com
Public Transportation: South Metro Area Regional Transit (SMART; 503-682-7790, www.ridesmart.com) runs several free bus lines within the city, and operates commuter buses to Portland, Tualatin, Canby, and Salem; rush-hour commuter rail service (WES) to Tualatin, Tigard, and Beaverton

CLACKAMAS COUNTY—SOUTHERN SUBURBS

North-central Clackamas County—the suburban expanse east of the Willamette River and south of the city of Portland—contains the county's oldest communities and much of its existing population. This is one of the more affordable parts of the Portland area, but has more amenities than some other lower-cost suburbs.

MILWAUKIE
Boundaries: North: Southeast Portland; **West:** Willamette River; **South:** Oak Grove, Oatfield (unincorporated Clackamas County); **East:** Clackamas (unincorporated Clackamas County); **Area:** 4.8 square miles; **Population:** 20,700

Founded in 1847, Milwaukie—home of the Bing cherry, but billing itself as the Dogwood City of the West—was named after Milwaukee, Wisconsin (which later changed the spelling of its name, leaving its Oregon namesake with the original "ie" ending). For many years, Milwaukie was a fairly nondescript, under-the-radar suburb. Despite its proximity to Portland, Milwaukie did not experience the growth in population (and housing prices) that occurred in other area communities during the last two decades. However, due to its close-in location (and spillover from the adjoining popular Sellwood and Westmoreland neighborhoods in Portland), the city's real estate market posted some of the largest gains in housing prices in the Portland area in the last years of the bubble, and housing prices fell hard in the

Milwaukie

Milwaukie

ensuing crash. As of press time, Milwaukie housing prices are still well below their peak at the height of the bubble, and the median home price is one of the lowest in the metro area. At the same time, Milwaukie has good bones and plenty of community spirit; it is often overlooked as a relocation option, but it may be a smart choice for some newcomers. The city has a stock of single-family homes with large lots, and it has good road and transit connections to downtown Portland and the city's entire East Side.

A swath of railroad tracks and associated industrial facilities splits the city into two halves. (Noise from train whistles bothers some residents.) On the west side of the tracks, Milwaukie's small downtown (www.celebratemilwaukie.com) is changing, as new shops and service businesses join the old-line establishments, and row houses and apartment buildings spring up near the cute red brick city hall and Scott Park, where outdoor concerts are held in the summer. Downtown Milwaukie is something of a mecca for comic book fans, thanks to the presence of Dark Horse Comics (www.darkhorse.com) in an unassuming building on Main Street. One of the most vibrant farmers' markets in the Portland area takes place on Sundays during the summer (www.milwaukiefarmersmarket.com). Riverfront Park provides access to the Willamette, and hosts the Riverfest festival in July. The neighborhoods near downtown have a high concentration of older homes, with some apartment buildings and townhomes in the mix. The new Orange Line MAX light rail line will include stations at the north end and south end of downtown Milwaukie, and extensive commercial and residential development is likely to occur within walking distance of those stations.

Busy McLoughlin Boulevard cuts off downtown Milwaukie from the Willamette, but two nearby neighborhoods do border the river. To the north, large traditional-style homes—in some cases, bona fide mansions—line the narrow, winding streets around the private Waverly Country Club. Just south of downtown, the compact Island Station neighborhood features smaller, generally older homes that overlook (or are a short walk from) the river. Undeveloped Elk Rock Island is usually accessible by foot except during high water in winter and spring.

Milwaukie's east side is largely given over to modest single-family homes, mostly ranches, Cape Cods, and older cottages, with a few newer two-story homes and 19th-century farmhouses to spice up the mix. There are a few small commercial areas, as well as some clusters of bungalows in neighborhoods where the old streetcar lines used to run. Some new infill development is occurring along the city's far eastern fringe, where average lot sizes are larger. In addition, the northeastern portion of the city features popular North Clackamas Aquatic Park, a large indoor facility run by the local Parks & Recreation District (http://ncprd.com/aquatic-park). If you are considering property near Johnson Creek, be aware that the creek is subject to flooding. Some parts of Milwaukie have a relatively high property crime rate.

The new light rail line from downtown Portland to Milwaukie is scheduled to open in late 2015. In the meantime, bus service is decent to excellent throughout much of the city. Milwaukie is part of the North Clackamas School District (www.nclack.k12.or.us), the sixth largest in the state: the city has several elementary schools and its own middle and high schools. Several private schools, including the Portland Waldorf School, are also located here.

Website: www. milwaukieoregon.gov
ZIP Codes: 97222, 97267
Post Office: Milwaukie Post Office, 11222 SE Main St
Police Station: Milwaukie Police Department, 3200 SE Harrison St, 503-786-7400 (non-emergency)
Emergency Hospital: Providence Milwaukie Hospital, 10150 SE 32nd Ave, Milwaukie, 503-513-8300, www.providence.org
Library: Ledding Library, 10660 SE 21st St, 503-786-7580, www.milwaukieoregon. gov/library
Parks: Riverfront Park, Scott Park, and several other small parks maintained by the city; North Clackamas Central Park, Spring Park, and a few others are part of the North Clackamas Parks & Recreation District, www.ncprd.com
Community Publications: *Clackamas Review*, www.clackamasreview.com
Public Transportation: TriMet, 503-238-RIDE, www.trimet.org; multiple bus lines, with frequent service from Milwaukie Transit Center to Portland and Oregon City; MAX line under construction

OAK GROVE, JENNINGS LODGE, AND OATFIELD

Boundaries: North: Milwaukie; **West:** Willamette River; **South:** Gladstone; **East:** Clackamas (unincorporated Clackamas County); **Area:** 10 square miles; **Population:** Approximately 38,000

McLoughlin Boulevard (Highway 99E) achieves full strip mall glory in the expanse of unincorporated Clackamas County between Milwaukie and Gladstone. As you tool down the highway, it's easy to miss the quiet middle-class neighborhoods that extend to either side. To the west, between the highway and the Willamette River, lies the community of **Oak Grove**. Oak Grove developed along the trolley line that ran along what is now Arista Drive from 1893 until the 1950s, and the area contains a variety of homes of various ages, most on relatively large lots. The old trolley right-of-way has been converted into a six-mile bike and pedestrian trail.) River Road parallels McLoughlin to the west; the former is a much quieter and more pleasant thoroughfare than the latter, and is lined by homes and a few apartment buildings.

The bulk of Oak Grove's housing stock consists of fairly modest postwar Cape Cods, ranches, and related architectural styles, but some prewar homes survive near the trolley line, and larger contemporary and custom homes crop up near the Willamette River. A few homes on the river itself are lavish affairs, with boathouses and private docks, but on the whole Oak Grove lacks the outright mansions that line parts of the Willamette's west bank. The neighborhood has lots of trees and several parks; there are few sidewalks, but there's not much traffic off the main roads. Away from McLoughlin, there are relatively few commercial establishments. (The old commercial center of the community, on Oak Grove Boulevard, is mostly defunct.) Oak Grove will be the southern terminus of a new light rail line from downtown Portland, scheduled to open in the fall of 2015. Denser development, at least along McLoughlin (which the light rail line follows), seems likely, and some residents are afraid that the coming of the train will bring crime and alter the pleasant, quiet character of their neighborhood.

To the south, **Jennings Lodge** has a housing mix similar to Oak Grove, but with a greater proportion of bungalows and old farmhouses. River Road and McLoughlin begin to converge in Jennings Lodge, and the neighborhoods between become increasingly less insulated as one proceeds south.

East of McLoughlin Boulevard, the **Oatfield** neighborhood is draped over a ridge that runs parallel to the highway. (Oatfield was not named for any former agricultural land use, but rather for the Oatfields, a prominent pioneer family.)

Oak Grove

Oatfield

This area generally has newer and often larger homes than the neighborhoods west of McLoughlin; many homes along the ridge have views of the Willamette or the Cascades. East of Oatfield Road, some subdivisions feature split-levels and contemporary-style homes on winding culs-de-sac, a street feature not found in Oak Grove. Oatfield in general is somewhat more affluent than Oak Grove and Jennings Lodge, and housing prices are consequently slightly higher on average. The tiny enclave of **Johnson City** is an incorporated city composed entirely of a single mobile home park.

These neighborhoods have so far resisted periodic annexation attempts (we're looking at you, Milwaukie and Gladstone) and homegrown incorporation efforts. For now, the county provides the services that do exist—the area is part of the North Clackamas Parks and Recreation District, for example—but these three communities have their own water utility, the Oak Lodge Water District (www.oaklodgewater.org). (Get it? Oak Lodge serves *Oak* Grove and Jennings *Lodge*.) Oak Grove and the northern part of Oatfield are part of the North Clackamas School District (www.nclack.k12.or.us), while Jennings Lodge and the southern part of Oatfield belong to the Oregon City School District (www.orecity.k12.or.us). Considering its low density and absence of much in the way of regional destinations, the area has relatively good transit service: buses between Oregon City and Milwaukie run along River Road and Oatfield Road, and there is frequent bus service along McLoughlin Boulevard to downtown Portland. Some of these bus lines will likely terminate at the MAX station once the light rail line to downtown Portland opens.

Website: www.clackamas.us
ZIP Codes: 97222, 97267
Post Office: Oak Grove Post Office, 3860 SE Naef St
Police Station: Oak Lodge Sub-Station, Clackamas County Sheriff's Office, 2930 SE
    Oak Grove Blvd, 503-655-8211 (non-emergency)

Emergency Hospitals: Providence Milwaukie Hospital, 10150 SE 32nd Ave, Milwaukie, 503-513-8300, www.providence.org; Providence Willamette Falls Hospital, 1500 Division St, Oregon City, 503-656-1631, www.providence.org

Library: Oak Lodge Library, 16201 SE McLoughlin Blvd, 503-655-8543, www.clackamas.us/lib/

Parks: North Clackamas Parks & Recreation District, www.ncprd.com

Community Publications: *Clackamas Review*, www.clackamasreview.com

Public Transportation: TriMet, 503-238-RIDE, www.trimet.org; light rail from Oak Grove to Milwaukie and Portland (beginning fall 2015); bus service to Portland, Milwaukie, and Oregon City

GLADSTONE

Boundaries: North: Jennings Lodge, Oatfield (unincorporated Clackamas County); **West**: Willamette River; **South**: Clackamas River; **East**: Clackamas River; **Area**: 2.5 square miles; **Population**: 12,200

Gladstone is well-known for the parade of car dealerships along McLoughlin Boulevard, but once you get away from the guys in bad ties asking what it would take to get you into a vehicle today, the city has a different vibe. Gladstone was founded at the strategic confluence of the Willamette and Clackamas rivers; surrounded by water on three sides, it has a languid, small-town ambiance. This area was a gathering place of the original native inhabitants; a large maple known as the Pow-Wow Tree, which still stands on West Clackamas Boulevard near the north bank of the Clackamas River, was ostensibly a meeting spot for local tribes. Today, the river banks are equally popular with local anglers; Meldrum Bar Park, on the Willamette just downstream from the mouth of the Clackamas, is an especially esteemed spot for fishing.

Gladstone's extremely modest downtown, which manages to support a few stores and eateries and the beautifully restored Flying A Gasoline Station (which

Gladstone

no longer sells gas), is laid out in a strict grid north of the Clackamas River. Gladstone developed early, thanks to its proximity to Oregon City and the existence of a streetcar line from Portland, and for many years the city was the site of a popular Chautauqua, a sort of educational entertainment one-two punch that was popular in the late 19th and early 20th centuries. (Gladstone's Chautauqua closed in 1927, but the city still holds a festival by that name each summer.) Older houses from the city's early days perch on a bluff above the Clackamas River and line the streets for several blocks inland, mixed with opportunistically placed postwar homes. The riverfront area also has a few parks, including High Rocks Park (a favorite spot for swimming and notorious for occasional drownings).

Away from the river and north of downtown, a high ridge looms, and the city streets abandon the grid pattern as they wind uphill. Culs-de-sac lined with ranches, spacious split-levels and contemporaries occupy the slopes; near the top of the ridge, 1970s-era contemporary homes border the winding streets of Ridgegate and other woody, established neighborhoods. Some of these homes have expansive views of the Willamette and West Hills or of Mount Hood and the Cascades. Prices here are below the metro-area average, and on a per-square-foot basis represent some of the best values in the region.

Gladstone has its own school district (www.gladstone.k12.or.us), with one elementary, one middle, and one high school. Gladstone is not particularly close to major centers of employment, but neither is it ridiculously far away; various transportation options are available for northbound commuters, but only two road bridges cross the Clackamas River to the south and none cross the Willamette between Oregon City and the Sellwood Bridge in Portland. (Westbound commuters headed for Washington County or Wilsonville generally take Interstate 205, which runs through the eastern end of the city.)

Website: www.ci.gladstone.or.us
ZIP Code: 97027
Post Office: Gladstone Post Office, 605 Portland Ave
Police Station: Gladstone Police Department, 535 Portland Ave, 503-655-8211 (non-emergency)
Emergency Hospital: Providence Willamette Falls Hospital, 1500 Division St, Oregon City, 503-656-1631, www.providence.org
Library: Gladstone Public Library, 135 E Dartmouth St, 503-656-2411, www.gladstonepubliclibrary.wordpress.com
Parks: Eight parks, including Meldrum Bar Park, High Rocks Park, and Max Patterson Memorial Park
Community Publications: *Oregon City News*, www.oregoncitynewsonline.com
Public Transportation: TriMet, 503-238-RIDE, www.trimet.org; multiple bus lines, with service to Portland, Milwaukie, Oregon City, and Clackamas

Oregon City

OREGON CITY

Boundaries: North: Clackamas River; **West**: Willamette River; **South**: Unincorporated Clackamas County; **East**: Unincorporated Clackamas County; **Area**: 9.3 square miles; **Population**: 34,800

Historic Oregon City—the end of the Oregon Trail, first capital of the old Oregon Territory, oldest incorporated city in the western United States, home of the first American newspaper printed west of the Rockies (*The Spectator*), and terminus of America's first long-distance electricity transmission line (1889)—fell on hard times in recent years and is trying mightily to rise again. Until recently, the city has had trouble funding basic services like police and fire protection, but the Oregon City's old downtown is undergoing a remarkable renaissance and many neighborhoods are being spruced up. For people who are looking for an historic or quiet suburban community and don't mind things being a bit rough around the edges,

Oregon City

Oregon City might be a good choice. Home prices are rising here, but are still below the metro area average.

Oregon City's downtown occupies a narrow strip of level land on the Willamette River just downstream from Willamette Falls. The area near the falls was an important fishing ground for Native Americans, and it became the site of Oregon's first European settlement in 1829. By the 1840s, Oregon City had become a bustling town, and it was incorporated in 1844. When the Oregon Territory was created four years later, Oregon City became the capital. (That honor was transferred to Salem in 1852.) Willamette Falls fueled the city's initial industrial growth—the falling water powered lumber mills and flour mills especially—and to this day Oregon City has a palpable industrial feel. The defunct Blue Heron paper mill still stands at the south end of town, just below the falls, and the overall scene is reminiscent of an old New England mill town.

Oregon City is the seat of Clackamas County, and a few county government offices (including the courthouse) are still located in Oregon City's historic downtown, along with a variety of small shops, bars, restaurants, and other businesses. Although a few vacant storefronts remain, the downtown area is evolving into a more vibrant place, as new businesses inject fresh life into the district. Downtown Oregon City huddles at the foot of a near-vertical bluff, and one of the city's stranger sights is the Municipal Elevator, which resembles a flying saucer on a thick pillar. The elevator carries pedestrians up and down the face of the 90-foot bluff between the business district and literally named High Street at the clifftop.

The McLoughlin Historic District spreads for blocks across the relatively flat plateau at the top of the bluff. This area contains many lovingly restored houses from the 19th and early 20th centuries, an era when this neighborhood was Oregon City's most fashionable residential area. Although somewhat less fashionable today, it is easily the city's most distinctive (and to many observers, most attractive) neighborhood. Some of these historic houses still await loving attention. A few of the houses here have expansive views, but unfortunately a handful of nondescript 1950s- and 1960s-era commercial buildings occupy most of the view property at the brink of the bluff. Shops and restaurants border parts of Seventh Street, which runs through the heart of the district and is the commercial center for the neighborhood; the city hall, a repurposed Depression-era medical building, is also located here. Several of the historic houses, some of which date back to the 1840s, are open to the public.

In the southeast section of the historic district, Seventh Street (and the landscape as a whole) rises steeply to another relatively flat terrace, which stretches away toward the Clackamas County hinterlands. Here Seventh Street becomes Molalla Avenue and heads southward, flanked by supermarkets and shopping plazas. A diverse mix of newer subdivisions, old farmhouses, mobile home parks, ranch houses on culs-de-sac, apartments, and retirement communities sprawls across the this plateau. The library and police station are also located here, just off Molalla Avenue on Warner Milne Road; county offices are nearby, and one of the city's three farmers' markets (www.orcityfarmersmarket.com) takes place here on Saturdays from May to October. The outlying neighborhoods to the south and east feature predominantly newer homes, and a few brand-new new residential and commercial developments have risen on the fringes of the city. Some of these developments offer fine views of the Cascades. Clackamas Community College is in the city's far southeastern corner.

Back along the river, the Canemah Historic District clings to the steep slopes overlooking the Willamette just upstream from the falls. The neighborhood was

Canemah Historic District

once a bustling town, separate from Oregon City, and prospered as a place of portage around the falls. Today, it is eerily quiet, and is comprised of some historic homes, some new townhomes and single-family homes (generally built in a neo-traditional style), and some small ranch houses. Many of these homes have river views, while others are tucked back into dark hollows. Some barely improved roads lead to the neighborhood, which includes a pioneer cemetery dating from the 1830s, and the area is easy to miss.

Interstate 205 crosses the Willamette north of downtown Oregon City; some industrial facilities border the freeway, and the low-density Park Place neighborhood lies to the east. A large, upscale mixed-use development planned for the Clackamette Cove area—which sounds like the noise a waterfowl would make, but denotes the confluence of the Clackamas and Willamette Rivers—has been on-again, off-again for years, but currently seems to be moving forward. A park at the confluence itself includes a popular boat ramp.

Despite Oregon City's woes, the overall crime rate is not shockingly high. Still, some neighborhoods are plagued by drug dealing and property crime, so try to avoid choosing a residence sight-unseen. The Oregon City School District (www.orecity.k12.or.us) serves Oregon City and much of the outlying unincorporated area. Oregon City has decent transportation connections to the rest of the metropolitan area, both by car and by public transit. Amtrak's Cascades trains also stop here on their runs between Portland and Salem.

Website: www.orcity.org

ZIP Code: 97045

Post Office: Oregon City Post Office, 19300 Molalla Ave

Police Station: Oregon City Police Department, 320 Warner Milne Rd, 503-657-4964 (non-emergency), www.orcity.org/police

Emergency Hospital: Providence Willamette Falls Hospital, 1500 Division St, Oregon City, 503-656-1631, www.providence.org

Library: Oregon City Public Library, 606 John Adams St, 503-657-8269, www.orcity.org/library

Parks: More than 20 parks and trails, including Clackamette Park, Singer Creek Park, and McLoughlin Promenade; www.orcity.orgparksandrecreation

Community Publications: Oregon City News, www.oregoncitynewsonline.com

Public Transportation: TriMet, 503-238-RIDE, www.trimet.org; multiple bus lines within city to Oregon City Transit Center, and service between Oregon City and West Linn, Portland, Milwaukie, Lake Oswego, and Clackamas; service to Canby via Canby Area Transit (503-266-4022), and service to Molalla via South Clackamas Transportation District (503-632-7000, www.south-clackamastransportation.com).

CANBY

This center of the nursery industry—for plants, not babies—feels smaller and more isolated than it actually is. With a population of more than 15,000, Canby is no longer a small town, but the surrounding farmland helps the city maintain a countrified veneer. Indeed, Canby also houses the extensive Clackamas County Fairgrounds, home to the annual Clackamas County Fair and Rodeo.

Canby

The lack of a direct road connection across the Willamette to the southern part of the metropolitan area increases the city's sense of isolation; the rustic Canby Ferry, just north of town, is one of the last public ferries across the Willamette. In truth, while it's not exactly centrally located, Canby is only about 15 minutes from the bona fide suburbia of Oregon City, West Linn, and Wilsonville, and busy Highway 99E cuts right through town.

The city attracts a diverse set of newcomers, including many professionals who work in the south metro but want to live in a small, quiet city in the sticks. The surprisingly extensive downtown, just north of the railroad tracks and the highway, has a few restaurants and shops, a public library, and a cute red brick city hall. The adjacent neighborhoods have some lovely older homes that date from an era when Canby really was a small town. The rest of the city has homes in a variety of postwar styles, including some new subdivisions; houses on acreage lurk just outside the city limits. If you're looking for a truly small town, the neighboring city of **Barlow**, incorporated in 1903, has fewer than 150 residents.

Canby has its own school district (www.canby.k12.or.us) and its own transit agency, Canby Area Transit (503-266-4022), which provides bus service between Canby and Oregon City, Wilsonville, and Woodburn, as well as free bus service within Canby city limits.

Website: www.ci.canby.or.us

CLACKAMAS COUNTY—SOUTHEASTERN SUBURBS

The stretch of northern Clackamas County from Milwaukie east to Damascus was once a mostly rural landscape. By the 1980s, urban development filled much of the region east to Interstate 205; development slowly began to spill into the areas beyond, and by the late 1990s areas like Sunnyside and Happy Valley were

Clackamas

experiencing tremendous growth. This area, along with the new city of Damascus, is expected to continue to grow rapidly over the next two decades. Unfortunately, improvements in infrastructure have lagged behind population growth, and these areas are struggling to cope with crowded roads and classrooms. In contrast, much of the eastern part of this region is still semi-rural. Numerous newcomers select this part of Clackamas County because there are many new homes, and the area offers reasonably easy access both to Portland and to the Mount Hood region.

CLACKAMAS AND SUNNYSIDE

The unincorporated area known as **Clackamas** sits between Happy Valley and Milwaukie south of the Portland city limits. This area has no fixed boundaries that are popularly accepted (as opposed to census-designated), but "Clackamas" is generally understood to refer to the neighborhoods that extend along either side of Southeast 82nd Avenue in northern Clackamas County. The area is a mix of residential, commercial, and light industrial uses; 82nd Avenue itself is a long strip mall of questionable aesthetics.

Clackamas

Clackamas Town Center and neighboring Clackamas Promenade, at the intersection of 82nd Avenue and Sunnyside Road, is the retail and geographical heart of the area.

Residences in the Clackamas area run the gamut from squalid to luxurious. Low-rise apartment buildings and townhome complexes are abundant, and these often lie in close proximity to shopping plazas and other commercial facilities. Most single-family homes are solidly middle-class, although there are also some truly dilapidated affairs here; the neighborhoods west of 82nd Avenue are among the most affordable in the metropolitan area, but some pockets are plagued by crime problems.

The most expensive and desirable homes in the Clackamas area are located on Mount Scott, just east of Clackamas Town Center across Interstate 205. A warren of culs-de-sac and winding streets covers the lower slopes of this prominent hill; contemporary, custom, and neo-traditional homes, with a few stranded ranches and prewar homes, can all be found here. The neighborhood has lots of tiny wooded greenspaces, and many homes have good views west and north across the city to downtown Portland and the West Hills. Homes that are higher up are generally newer and larger; some of the largest houses are actually visible from downtown Portland, especially in late afternoon when their picture windows reflect the westering sun. Near the summit, with its cluster of antennas, stand a few brand-new, high-end homes with panoramic views east to Mount Hood.

Sunnyside (not to be confused with the neighborhood of the same name in the Hawthorne District of Portland) is a nearby unincorporated area; it extends along and to the south of Sunnyside Road, east of Clackamas Town Center and south of Happy Valley. There are some tidy older subdivisions in this area, but most housing here is quite new, in a range of styles and sizes from townhomes and apartment complexes to hulking three-story luxury homes with Mount Hood views. A few shopping plazas line Sunnyside Road. Forested Mount Talbert Nature Park, on a volcanic butte on the west side of the community, provides a large area of open space.

Parts of both Clackamas and Sunnyside are being selectively annexed by the city of Happy Valley, and the result is a discontinuous patchwork of incorporated and unincorporated areas. Although it is not centrally located, the entire Clackamas area is well-connected to the rest of the metropolitan area. Interstate 205 provides access to the southern suburbs and to Northeast Portland, while the Milwaukie Expressway (Highway 224) runs toward downtown Portland. TriMet buses cover most of the Clackamas area (although not up Mount Scott) and connect Clackamas to downtown Portland and to most destinations on the east side, and a light rail line runs along I-205 to Clackamas Town Center.

Sunnyside

Clackamas County agencies provide most public services in this area. The North Clackamas Park District manages local parks and public recreational facilities, including the popular North Clackamas Aquatic Park, which includes an indoor wave pool and diving well. North Clackamas School District (www.nclack. k12.or.us) provides public education.

Website: www.clackamas.us

HAPPY VALLEY

Boundaries: North: Portland; Gresham; unincorporated Multnomah County; **West**: Clackamas (unincorporated Clackamas County); **South**: Sunnyside (unincorporated Clackamas County); **East**: Damascus, unincorporated rural Clackamas County; **Area**: 8.3 square miles; **Population**: 16,500

If a high income alone can buy contentment, then Happy Valley is aptly named: the average household income is the highest of any city in the metro area, including Lake Oswego. At the same time, Happy Valley is one of the fastest-growing cities in Oregon, with new construction visible almost everywhere. In addition to growth through an influx of new residents, the city is expanding by annexing surrounding areas, and the city limits are weirdly discontinuous. (Happy Valley and Damascus recently reached an agreement about which unincorporated areas each city is entitled to gobble up.)

To the extent it has a center at all, Happy Valley is indeed centered in a valley

Happy Valley

along Mount Scott Creek, between Mount Scott on the west and Scouters Mountain on the east. The valley was once forestland and farmland, with a few houses on the valley bottom. The scene is very different today. Massive developments of large new homes sprawl up every hillside; styles range from "Northwest Lodge" to McMansions with giant entry arches and soaring great rooms, along with some basic, fairly nondescript (but still quite spacious) houses. Hillside (and especially hilltop) homes tend to be the largest and to command the highest prices. An eastward view is particularly coveted; because of Happy Valley's position closer to the Cascades, Mount Hood looms much larger from here than from Portland's West Hills. A few dazed-looking bungalows and ranches, the survivors of the original rural community, remain standing near Mount Scott Creek and along 147th Avenue, but the city's population has tripled in the last decade and virtually every structure here is less than 20 years old.

If Lake Oswego is the East Coast–style affluent suburb, Happy Valley is instant community, sunbelt-style, and as in parts of the sunbelt the real estate boom resulted in unsustainable real estate price increases. Parts of the city saw a wave of foreclosures after the bubble burst, but those unhappy times are largely in the past.

The city has a fair number of parks and open spaces amid the sea of housing; there is not much commercial activity in the heart of the city itself, but the shopping plazas of Sunnyside Road and the Clackamas area are a short drive away. Several retail centers have opened on Sunnyside in the southeast part of Happy Valley. The city is part of the North Clackamas School District (www.nclack.k12. or.us). A TriMet bus line runs along Sunnyside, and another provides service within Happy Valley and between Happy Valley and Clackamas Town Center, but the city is generally quite car-dependent.

Website: www.ci.happy-valley.or.us
ZIP Code: 97086
Post Office: Clackamas Post Office, 9009 SE Adams St, Clackamas
Police Station: Clackamas County Sheriff, Happy Valley Community Policing Center, 12915 SE King Rd, 503-760-0123 (non-emergency)
Emergency Hospital: Kaiser Permanente Sunnyside Medical Center, 10180 SE Sunnyside Rd, Clackamas, 503-652-2880
Library: Sunnyside Library, 13793 SE Sieber Park Way, www.clackamas.us/lib
Parks: Happy Valley Park, Happy Valley Nature Park, and several open spaces; North Clackamas Parks & Recreation District, www.ncprd.com
Community Publications: *Clackamas Review*, www.clackamasreview.com
Public Transportation: TriMet, 503-238-RIDE, www.trimet.org; limited bus service to Clackamas Town Center

DAMASCUS

A conversion will take place on the road to Damascus. In this case, there is no religious aspect; rather, fields will be converted to subdivisions on Sunnyside, Foster Road, Highway 212, and other roads to Damascus. Though it still looks mostly rural, make no mistake: Damascus is primed for radical change. (That's bucolic Damascus, Oregon, by the way, not its somewhat less bucolic namesake in Syria.) Metro's 2002 expansion of the urban growth boundary included Damascus, and a minor land rush is occurring in this semi-rural landscape of fields, berry farms, and modest country houses. Much of the region's growth in the next two decades is anticipated to occur here, and the area incorporated in 2004 to help deal with the anticipated population explosion. Since then the city has struggled to complete a comprehensive plan, and the city has been embroiled in waves of controversy and political infighting, including a vote to disincorporate and a fight over dean-nexation. Residential growth along existing thoroughfares is expected to begin as soon as water and sewer service is in place, although it will take many years to develop and finance infrastructure for the entire city, especially given the dysfunction in municipal government. For now, development is basically limited to parcels of one acre or more (i.e., parcels large enough for septic systems), although some denser development has occurred in the Carver area along Highway 224 where water and sewer lines already exist.. At the moment, the city offers a beautiful landscape, but a rather unhappy combination of relatively high taxes but few services.

As the area grows, transportation is likely to become a major issue; existing roads cannot handle projected traffic volumes. The first phase of the Sunrise Corridor freeway project linking Damascus to Interstate 205, and bypassing Highway 212, is under construction. TriMet buses run to the neighboring communities of Happy Valley and Estacada. The city is part of the Gresham-Barlow School District (www.gresham.k12.or.us), and has its own elementary and middle schools.

Website: www.ci.damascus.or.us

OUTER CLACKAMAS COUNTY

The outlying communities of Clackamas County lie in lovely rolling countryside at the western foot of the Cascade Mountains. Some homes here stand atop rises with views of Mount Hood or the Willamette Valley, others are tucked down into mossy forested hollows, and still others are part of subdivisions that wouldn't look out of place in a close-in suburb, but which invariably are just a short distance from the farm fields and forest land that still dominate the landscape. Generally speaking, these communities are popular with people who are looking for a rural or small-town environment within striking range of a large city, and with easy access to the abundant recreational opportunities in the nearby mountains. Commuting can be a major chore or worse if you work in downtown Portland or Washington County, but is quite doable if your job is in the eastern fringes of the metro area (e.g., Gresham or Oregon City).

Boring, which was named for early settler W. H. Boring and not for its lack of diversions, is a small, rural community set amid plant nurseries southeast of Gresham. The small town center at the intersection of Southeast 282nd Avenue and Highway 212 includes the Boring-Damascus Grange, which dates from 1896. The Boring farmers' market, held on summer Saturdays, is possibly the only one in Oregon to bill itself as "equine-friendly." Boring children attend Oregon Trail School District schools (www.oregontrailschools.com). (The school district is unlikely to adopt that phrase as its slogan.) Boring has very limited commuter bus service to Gresham; it is, however, favorably situated for hardy long-distance bike commuters at the end of the Springwater Trail Corridor that runs all the way to the Willamette River in Southeast Portland. Residents have a sense of humor about the name: Boring became paired (a sort of sister city relationship) with Dull, Scotland.

A few miles to the southeast, **Sandy** (www.ci.sandy.or.us) is well known to Portlanders as a pit stop for cheap gas, ski rentals, and doughnuts on the way to Mount Hood. It is also a growing, bustling small city of nearly 10,000 people, with its own urban growth boundary, public transit system, and school district (Oregon Trail School District, www.oregontrailschools.com). Mount Hood Highway (US 26) is the main drag through town; the lower end is lined with supermarkets and shopping plazas, but the highway divides and traffic slows when the road reaches the city's linear downtown area. Sandy offers a mix of housing, from 1950s-era ranches, apartment complexes, and brand-new luxury homes in Sandy proper to rural homes on acreage in the countryside nearby. Homes outside of town are sited in diverse settings, ranging from shady forest dells to hilltop pastures with views north to Mount St. Helens and east to Mount Hood. The surrounding area is dominated by plant nurseries, berry farms, and even a winery; to the east, toward Mount Hood, the land quickly transitions to forest. Sandy is the closest city to Mount Hood, and many residents are avid snowsport devotees. Sandy Area Metro buses (503-668-3466) connect Sandy to Gresham and Estacada.

About 10 miles south of Boring and Sandy, **Estacada** (www.cityofestacada. org) stands on the bank of the Clackamas River. From Highway 224, which wends its way up the Clackamas River Valley into the Cascades, Estacada doesn't look terribly attractive—the strip of businesses along the highway is definitely not the city's best face—but the small, old-fashioned downtown behind it is pleasant enough. Most of the city's houses stand on the hill behind downtown or are scattered in the forested areas nearby. Estacada's economy has traditionally been timber-dependent, and the city has not grown as quickly as some closer-in communities have. Although a boom in large homes on big plots of land outside town has caused average home prices in the area to rise significantly, Estacada is among the most affordable communities in the region. Estacada has its own school district (www.esd108.org), which serves a huge area of rural Clackamas County, including much of the Mount Hood National Forest. The Clackamas River offers abundant opportunities for fishing and boating, and Highway 224 leads deep into the heart of the Cascades. Although Estacada is decidedly outside the metropolitan area proper, a TriMet bus line runs between the city and Portland on weekdays.

Over the river and through the woods, truly rural **Colton** is enveloped in the lush foothills along Highway 211 southwest of Estacada. This is working timber country, complete with clearcuts and log trucks, as well as an abundance of Christmas tree farms, and the area has so far avoided an inrush of yuppies.

Molalla

Amenities are pretty much limited to a store and a restaurant at the crossroads. Colton has its own tiny school district (www.colton.k12.or.us), with an elementary school, a middle school, and a high school.

Heading back toward the lowlands, the much larger community of **Molalla** (www.cityofmolalla.com) is also a lumber town, but its economy is slowly diversifying and the town is attracting more residents who commute to the Portland and Salem metro areas. Molalla has a very scenic setting on a rolling site where the Cascade foothills (and their supplies of timber) meet the Willamette Valley. The comparatively large, bustling downtown offers a bonanza of businesses: hardware stores, restaurants, banks, and more. The city's generally well-kept homes include dwellings in old, newer, and newest styles. The city is regionally known for the Molalla Buckeroo Rodeo (www.molallabuckeroo.com), held each July at the rodeo grounds at the east end of town. Molalla has its own transit system, the South Clackamas Transit District (503-632-7000, www.southclackamastransportation.com), which connects the city to Canby and Oregon City by bus. **Mulino**, a few miles north of Molalla along the Cascade Highway (Highway 213), is not much larger than Colton—the community applied to the county for "hamlet" status in 2007—but it is certainly less remote. The Molalla River School District (www.molallariv.k12.or.us) serves both Molalla and Mulino.

Further north, a mile or two off Cascade Highway, just a few miles south of Oregon City, the hamlet of **Beavercreek** lacks much of a town center—there is a gas station, a fire station, a post office, and a couple of businesses, plus the Beavercreek Grange and historic Bryn Seion Welsh Church, the oldest Welsh church on the West Coast. Beavercreek is claimed to be the birthplace of the sport of geocaching (see the "Sports and Recreation" chapter for details). Homes on large lots or small farms occupy the rolling hills, and roughly 6,500 people live in the area. Some new developments are going up north of the community, especially near Cascade Highway, but Beavercreek as a whole remains decidedly rural. At the same time, it is only 15 minutes from Oregon City, and lies within the Oregon City School District (www.orecity.k12.or.us).

Other small outlying communities in Clackamas County include **Redland**, **Liberal**, **Eagle Creek**, and **Marquam**. Some people commute to the metropolitan area from the mountain communities between Sandy and Mount Hood—**Welches**, **Rhododendron**, **Zigzag**, **Wemme**, and **Brightwood**—but distance, hazardous winter weather, and heavy through traffic on Highway 26 make this option less attractive than it might sound.

EAST MULTNOMAH COUNTY

Residents of eastern Multnomah County—the communities that extend east of Portland's city limits—often grumble about being neglected. The county's population (and hence representation on the board of commissioners) is Portland-centric, and many of the 150,000-plus people in the rest of the county feel, rightly or wrongly, that their corner of the world doesn't get its proper share of funding. There is periodic talk of secession, either to form a new county, or to join Clackamas County, but the law is unfavorable and it is unclear that being tacked on to another populous county would provide any advantages. For now, fast-growing East County simmers in political disgruntlement, cooled only by the bitter winds that issue from the Columbia River Gorge in winter.

GRESHAM

Boundaries: North: Fairview; Wood Village; Troutdale; **West**: Portland; unincorporated Multnomah County; **South**: Unincorporated Multnomah County; unincorporated Clackamas County; Damascus; **East**: Unincorporated Multnomah County; **Area**: 23.4 square miles; **Population**: 109,000

Gresham

Gresham Station

Gresham (pronounced GRESH-um or, by true old-timers, GRAY-shum) is the fourth largest city in Oregon, but most Oregonians (or at least most Oregonians who live outside Gresham) seem blissfully unaware of this factoid. Ask the average Portlander what the fourth largest city in the state is, and they might guess Medford (no), Bend (not yet), or Beaverton (close but no cigar). In fact, many people in the Portland area largely ignore Gresham, except when they have to drive through it to get to Mount Hood. It is the butt of tasteless jokes, and the scene of gory crimes on local television news reports, and that is all.

The region's collective diss of Gresham is a shame. While the city does have its share of problems, including a frighteningly high crime rate in some areas, it also has plenty of quiet, middle-class neighborhoods, some decent schools, a charming, historic city center, a diverse population, and a light rail line with a straight shot to Portland. It is close to recreational opportunities on Mount Hood and in the Columbia River Gorge, it has easy access to Portland International Airport, and parts of the city have awesome views of the mountains. Moreover, real estate prices tend to be lower here than in most of Portland or its more fashionable suburbs. In short, while Gresham is far from a newcomer magnet, it is certainly worth a second glance.

Gresham's small downtown district (www.exploregresham.com) is surprisingly pleasant; the streets are lined with restaurants, shops, a few historic buildings (including a 1913 Carnegie Library, now a museum), and even a couple of day spas, and some new townhomes and loft-style residential buildings have been built here. There is a farmers' market here on Saturdays from May to October (www.greshamfarmersmarket.com). Downtown Gresham is the eastern terminus of the MAX Blue Line, and many residents rely on light rail to commute to jobs in Portland. (The city has vague plans to further energize this area with new "transit-oriented" development.) The area around downtown is an odd mix of housing and commercial development. Apartments and townhome developments line many of the main roads (and some of the minor ones), while older subdivisions of single-family houses dot the landscape; even within walking distance of downtown, there are neighborhoods of 1960s-era homes on winding streets and culs-de-sac. The general impression is that opportunistic developers built haphazardly whenever old Mrs. Brown's farm (or its equivalent) went up for sale, without really giving any thought to how or whether their developments related to one another. (This is not to say that the neighborhoods are necessarily unpleasant; some of them just seem stranded.) The new **Gresham Station** commercial development west of downtown has brought a bevy of national retailers and even some (relatively) high-end lofts and condos to the area.

Much of west-central Gresham consists of single-family homes mixed with high-density housing developments and apartments. Rents here are in many cases much lower than in close-in Portland neighborhoods, and the region has seen an influx of low-income workers who have been priced out of Portland by gentrification and rising rents. This area in general, and in particular the **Rockwood** neighborhood (which is being positioned as the "Gateway to Gresham"), has a reputation for gang activity and violent crime, although it's not exactly the South Bronx. There are also some quiet, residential, and perfectly safe areas here, so don't be put off by the bad rep. Some urban renewal activity is taking place in this part of the city, especially along Burnside Street where the MAX line runs. Much of the city's northern area, especially the districts adjacent to Fairview and Wood Village and flanking Interstate 84, is devoted to light industry.

In southwest Gresham, developments of newer homes—in some cases, brand-new homes—abut hobby farms just over the city line in unincorporated Multnomah County. This area, set in a valley on the west side of Gresham Butte, features a hodgepodge of styles, with a mix of ranches, contemporary homes, split-levels, some low-rise apartment complexes and townhome developments, and a few brand-new subdivisions. The homes on Gresham Butte itself (much of which is now protected as open space) tend to be newer and correspondingly

Gresham

more expensive, with views of the Washington Cascades (or, for houses on the eastern side of the butte, of Mount Hood).

The neighborhoods of southeast Gresham, like those of southwest Gresham, feature a mix of styles, although the average home is relatively new. The **Kelly Creek** neighborhood, off Orient Road, has experienced substantial new development right out to the city limits, where on Southeast 282nd Avenue you'll see dense developments right across the street from plant nurseries. This part of the city is well-positioned for quick trips to Mount Hood, and some homes have great views of the mountain looming to the southwest. Shopping plazas and light industrial facilities line the Mount Hood Highway (US 26) in this part of the city.

The Gresham-Barlow School District (district.gresham.k12.or.us) serves most of the city; students from the western fringe attend schools in the Centennial School District (www.centennial.k12.or.us), and the northern part of the city is part of the Reynolds School District (www.Reynolds.k12.or.us). Mount Hood Community College occupies a campus in the northeast corner of the city, and at least indirectly adds some cultural spice to the landscape. Gresham is reasonably well served by public transit; in addition to frequent MAX service, Tri-Met bus lines serve most of the main streets, and Sandy Area Metro buses run to Sandy. Interstate 84, which skirts Gresham to the north, is the main freeway route to Portland, but it can be very congested during rush hour, particularly between Interstate 205 and downtown Portland. Driving to Portland via the main east-west streets (Powell Boulevard, Division Street, Stark Street, Glisan Street, and Foster Road) can be slow and time-consuming, but it is a reasonable alternative if you are headed to Southeast Portland.

Website: www.greshamoregon.gov

ZIP Codes: 97030, 97080, 97230, 97233

Post Office: Gresham Post Office, 103 W Powell Blvd

Police Station: Gresham Police Department, 1333 NW Eastman Pkwy, 503-618-2318 (non-emergency)

Emergency Hospital: Legacy Mount Hood Medical Center, 24800 SE Stark St, Gresham, 503-674-1122, www.legacyhealth.org

Libraries: Gresham Library, 385 NW Miller Ave, 503-988-5387; Rockwood Library, 17917 SE Stark St, 503-988-5396; www.multcolib.org

Parks: More than 25 parks and natural areas, including Main City Park and Red Sunset Park, plus 8 miles of recreational trail; www.greshamoregon.gov/play/

Community Publications: *Gresham Outlook*, www.theoutlookonline.com

Public Transportation: TriMet, 503-238-RIDE, www.trimet.org; MAX light rail service to Portland and Washington County and bus service within Gresham and between Gresham and various points in Portland; Sandy Area Metro (503-668-3466, www.ci.sandy.or.us) runs buses from Gresham to Sandy

Fairview

FAIRVIEW, WOOD VILLAGE, AND TROUTDALE

Boundaries: North: Columbia River; **West**: Gresham; **South**: Gresham; **East**: Sandy River; **Area**: 3.5 square miles (Fairview); 0.9 square miles (Wood Village); 6.0 square miles (Troutdale); **Population**: 9,200 (Fairview); 3,900 (Wood Village); 16,500 (Troutdale)

The cities of Fairview, Wood Village, and Troutdale straddle Interstate 84 near the west end of the Columbia River Gorge, about 17 miles east of downtown Portland. These three "freeway-close" communities are sometimes lumped together—in this entry, for example—but all are separately incorporated and have different characteristics. Children from all three cities attend public schools in the Reynolds School District (www.Reynolds.k12.or.us). The median price of homes in these three communities is below the metro-area average, and is significantly lower than median prices in Washington County or the city of Portland.

Wood Village

The interstate runs right down the middle of **Fairview**, the closest of these three cities to Portland. The original heart of the city, just south of Interstate 84, is a relatively affordable neighborhood of Cape Cods, ranches, and (east of Fairview Avenue) some newer traditional and contemporary homes; across Halsey Street to the south, Fairview Village (www.fairviewvillage.com) is a new mixed-use, pedestrian-friendly, master-planned development with townhomes, single-family homes, apartments, shops, and offices. The new Fairview City Hall is also located here, and Salish Ponds Park provides nearby open space. North of Interstate 84, the shores of shallow Fairview Lake are lined with large, expensive new homes, most with private docks, and a small park with a canoe dock. A short distance to the north is Blue Lake Regional Park, a Metro-run park with a popular swimming beach.

The city of **Wood Village** sprang into being as a company town for the Reynolds Aluminum plant during the Second World War. Today, the city is best known as home of the disused Multnomah Greyhound Park (a.k.a. the "Dog Park") in the city's southeast corner; the park closed in 2004, and the site has been eyed for redevelopment. A plan to build a massive entertainment complex and casino on the site was defeated by voters in 2012. The adjacent Wood Village Town Center features a mix of retailers and specialty stores together with a new housing development. Most Wood Village homes are modest—unsurprisingly, given the city's origin—but not tiny or squalid.

Troutdale is the largest and most populous member of this civic trio. Troutdale's minuscule historic downtown borders the Historic Columbia River Highway, just up the hill and across the tracks from a very different shopping experience at the Columbia Gorge Factory Stores. Downtown Troutdale has several antique stores, restaurants and bars, and galleries, along with a couple of historic museums; a First Friday Art Walk takes place here, as does a farmers' and artists' market on Saturdays from April to mid-November. About a mile to the west on Halsey Street, the McMenamin brothers have converted the former Multnomah County Poor Farm

Troutdale

into the 38-acre Edgefield complex, with a hotel, several restaurants and bars, a brewery, a winery, a golf course, a movie theater, and a glassblowing studio. Troutdale's residential districts sprawl across the hills and bluffs south of downtown. A few older houses still stand in the old grid above the historic downtown, and relict farmhouses dot the rolling highlands, but most homes date from the 1950s onward. As one proceeds south and southwest, the housing stock grows generally newer, and contemporary homes on culs-de-sac dominate much of the southern half of the city. Many of the houses on the ridges on either side of Beaver Creek offer views of Mount Hood and the Sandy River. The subdivisions off Cherry Park Road, in the city's southwest, have newer homes and provide vistas across the Columbia River to the Washington Cascades (nice) and the Camas paper mill (less nice). The unincorporated zone between Troutdale and Gresham, in pretty countryside above the Sandy River south of the city, still has a definite rural feel.

These cities are literally at the doorstep of the Columbia River Gorge, and world-class hiking, windsurfing, and waterfall-gazing are only minutes away. At the same time, when the Gorge winds blow, Troutdale and vicinity take the brunt of the blast, and ice storms and snow storms, when they occur, are more severe. (Trees with weak limbs do not fare well here.) Besides the Gorge winds, occasional nuisances include low-flying planes from Troutdale Airport and occasional whiffs of the paper and pulp mill across the Columbia River in Camas, Washington. These cities offer a reasonably quick commute to Portland International Airport and its adjacent industrial zones, but traveling on Interstate 84 beyond Interstate 205 is very congested at peak times. Decent bus service exists, but coverage is fairly limited.

Websites: www.fairvieworegon.gov; www.ci.wood-village.or.us; www.ci.troutdale. or.us

ZIP Codes: 97024 (Fairview), 97060 (Wood Village and Troutdale)

Post Offices: Fairview Post Office, 1700 NE Market Dr; Troutdale Post Office, 647 SW Cherry Park Rd

Police Stations: Fairview Police Department, 1300 NE Village St, 503-674-6200 (non-emergency); Multnomah County Sheriff's Office, Wood Village City Hall, 2055 NE 238th Dr, 503-823-3333 (non-emergency); Troutdale Police Department, 234 SW Kendall Ct, 503-665-6129 (non-emergency)

Emergency Hospital: Legacy Mount Hood Medical Center, 24800 SE Stark St, Gresham, 503-674-1122, www.legacyhealth.org

Library: Fairview-Columbia Library, 1520 NE Village St, Fairview, 503-988-5655; Troutdale Library, 2451 SW Cherry Park Rd, 503-988-5355; www.multcolib.org/

Parks: Fairview: four small city parks, plus Metro's Blue Lake Regional Park; Wood Village: Donald R. Robertson City Park; Troutdale: more than 20 parks and open spaces, including Glenn Otto Park on the Sandy River and Columbia Park (www. ci.troutdale.or.us/parks-facilities/); the Columbia River Gorge National Scenic Area and several state and regional parks on the Sandy River lie just east of Troutdale

Corbett

Community Publications: Gresham Outlook, www.theoutlookonline.com
Public Transportation: TriMet, 503-238-RIDE, www.trimet.org; bus service to Portland and Gresham

CORBETT AND SPRINGDALE

The unincorporated community of Corbett lies on a rolling plateau between the Columbia and Sandy rivers near the western end of the Columbia Gorge, about 20 miles east of Portland. The area is largely a landscape of working farms, orchards, and wineries, with spectacular views of Mount Hood and the Columbia River from some places. Housing stock runs the gamut from old farmhouses and American vernacular homes to daylight ranches and huge new custom homes. The community's small commercial center lies on the Historic Columbia River Highway; Crown Point, the unofficial gateway to the Gorge, is just east of town. Although Corbett lacks big city amenities—or even small city amenities—it's a short drive from the eastern edge of the metropolitan area, and is close to recreational opportunities in the Gorge, on Mount Hood, and on nearby Larch Mountain. Corbett has its own small, highly sought-after school district (www.corbett.k12.or.us) with nationally ranked charter and regular high schools. Indeed, Corbett's strong public schools are a primary draw for many new residents, including residents who would not normally consider semi-rural living. Corbett can be extremely windy when the Gorge winds blow, and in winter it is the metro-area community most subject to ice and snow storms.

The low-density community west of Corbett and east of Troutdale along the historic highway is known as **Springdale.** The historic Springdale School in the center (such as it is) of Springdale is home to the Corbett Arts Program with Spanish.

Website: www.corbettoregon.com (unofficial)

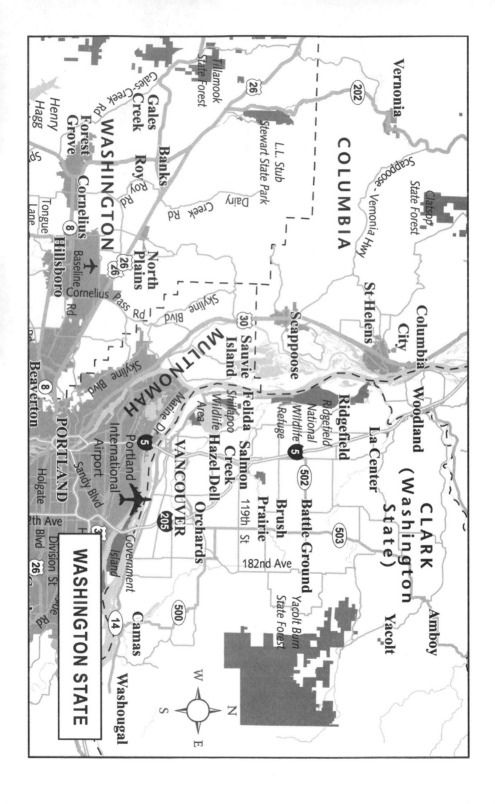

VANCOUVER AND CLARK COUNTY

Once upon a time, back in the 1840s, Clark County included all of what is now the state of Washington. Although the county has diminished dramatically in size since then, it has grown equally dramatically in population. A steady flow of settlers and homesteaders arrived throughout the second half of the 19th century, and the county's towns and cities started to expand in the early decades of the 20th, but the first big population boom occurred during the Second World War, when the Kaiser Shipyards in Vancouver employed nearly 40,000 people. During the war years, Vancouver's population exploded from 18,000 to 100,000; many of the new residents were housed in temporary facilities, and thousands of houses were thrown up in postwar years to accommodate the influx of wartime workers who decided to set down roots. More recently, nearby Portland's growth, along with Clark County's lower average home prices, the historic lack of an urban growth boundary to constrain sprawl, and the fact that Washington has no state income tax, combined to attract tens of thousands of new residents. Clark County's population now stands at about 440,000.

Unfortunately, job growth in Clark County has not kept pace with the area's explosive population growth. For more than a decade, Clark County's unemployment rate has been well above the Washington state average, and the jobs picture here has been worse than in other parts of the metro area. Many residents—about a third of the labor force—commute across the river to jobs in Portland. Rush-hour congestion along Interstate 5 between Vancouver and downtown Portland is, on average, the worst in the region, and the old Interstate Bridge is showing its age. A proposed new bridge, together with associated access ramp changes, was expected to have a price tag in the billions, and was finally killed by the Washington legislature, which refused to fund its share. The county's sprawling new developments have contributed to traffic congestion problems within the county as well, since road networks have not kept up with population growth.

Despite the congestion, Clark County remains an appealing destination for many newcomers. Although housing costs in places like Camas are well above the metropolitan average and new growth management laws in Washington are putting the brakes on willy-nilly rural development, Clark County as a whole has some of the most affordable homes in the metro area, and both rents and home prices are much lower than in Portland proper or its western and southern suburbs. Clark County's relative affordability has only increased following the post-bubble decline in real estate values, which hit Southwest Washington harder than the rest of the region. Washington is further fiscally attractive to some because it has no personal income tax, although it has high sales and property taxes. (If you live in Washington but work in Oregon, you will be subject to Oregon income tax.) Clark County is also perceived (at least in Clark County) as having better schools on the whole than Oregon does, with lower student-teacher ratios and more stable funding, although this generalization definitely is not true across the board. Clark County voters (especially North County voters) tend to be more politically conservative than their counterparts in Portland and its Oregon suburbs, although this generalization, too, does not paint a complete picture and is increasingly less true in Vancouver.

Vancouver and other large incorporated areas have their own neighborhood associations, which can be good resources for people planning a move. (A map of Vancouver associations is available at http://www.cityofvancouver.us/cmo/page/neighborhoods.) The unincorporated populated areas of Clark County also have neighborhood associations (see www.clark.wa.us/neighborhoods/associations.html).

County Website: www. clark.wa.us

VANCOUVER

Boundaries: North: Hazel Dell, Felida, Orchards (unincorporated Clark County); **West**: Vancouver Lake; Columbia River; **South**: Columbia River; **East**: Camas; unincorporated Clark County; **Area**: 49.9 square miles; **Population**: 167,500

Popularly relegated to the status of bland suburb to its much larger neighbor across the Columbia River, and dwarfed in public esteem by the more glamorous city of the same name in British Columbia, Vancouver USA (as the city has branded itself) has had trouble getting noticed. Civic boosters point out that if Vancouver were in Oregon it would be the second-largest city in the state, and emphasize that the city predates Portland by a couple of decades: the British Hudson's Bay Company established Fort Vancouver as its western headquarters in 1825. But until recently, the 'Couv has been treated like the quiet, homely sibling of its popular, wild sister south of the river. Then Washington legalized same-sex marriage and recreational marijuana, when both remained illegal in Oregon until 2014, and suddenly Portland looked decidedly old-fashioned in comparison.

Vancouver

Vancouver

Even without these decidedly liberal developments, Vancouver's stigma—if being thought of as completely unexciting is really a stigma—was already fading. Downtown redevelopment has given a breath of new life to the city's wheezing old commercial center, the city's restaurant and arts scene is growing, and annexations and a general influx of new residents have increased the city's population dramatically and have (at least theoretically) given it a bigger voice in the region.

Of course, many Vancouverites are happy with their city the way it is (or was). (In response to the common "Keep Portland Weird" bumper sticker, some vehicles have begun displaying stickers exhorting readers to "Keep Vancouver Normal.") Housing is more affordable here than in Portland, many neighborhoods have a great sense of community, the city is close to outdoor recreational opportunities, and there are plenty of amenities and mainstream shopping opportunities; at the same time, the cultural events and urban attractions of Portland lurk just across the river. A slim majority of Vancouverites oppose extending the light rail system to their city (or oppose paying for the extension, at any rate.) The potential downsides of living in Vancouver include high crime rates in some neighborhoods, a limited job base (and consequent high unemployment rate), sprawl and resulting car-dependency, airplane and/or train noise in some locations, and, for people who work in Oregon, Oregon income taxes and an increasingly congested commute. In short, Vancouver appeals to lots of people; whether you are one of those people depends on what exactly you're looking for.

Downtown Vancouver (www.vdusa.org), perched above the river just west of Interstate 5, manages the neat trick of being simultaneously down-at-heel and up-and-coming. Old pawn shops, check cashing joints, and windowless bars mix uneasily with new residential lofts, art galleries, and day spas, as well as a host of service businesses and office buildings. Once-seedy Esther Short Park has been transformed into a venue for outdoor music festivals, and also serves as the home of the city's farmers' market (www.vancouverfarmersmarket.com); an underutilized new convention center is nearby. A railroad track cuts off downtown

Vancouver from its waterfront, which the hulking Red Lion Hotel and its massive parking lot unfortunately dominate. It's too early to call downtown Vancouver trendy—or even to surmise that it will be trendy in the near future—but it has become a more attractive environment for residents and visitors than it was a few years ago.

Immediately to the north, the **Uptown Village** neighborhood (www. uptownvillage.com) offers a concentration of late-19th- and early-20th-century homes, including some cute bungalows, with several newer houses and apartment buildings mixed in. Dozens of small shops, restaurants, and service businesses line Main Street; the Clark County Historical Museum (www.cchmuseum.org), housed in an old Carnegie library, is also here. Community spirit is strong, and Uptown Village events include a St. Patrick's Day parade, a street festival, and outdoor summer movies.

North of Fourth Plain Boulevard, ranches, Cape Cods, and other postwar styles predominate, and the businesses along Main Street become more utilitarian. Houses east of Main Street tend to get some freeway noise; across Main, train noise becomes a potential problem as you move west. Just beyond the train tracks, the **Fruit Valley** neighborhood has a few residences, and even some stranded orchards, but the area is primarily industrial.

East of Interstate 5, the reconstructed palisades of Fort Vancouver (www.nps. gov/fova) stand anachronistically next to Pearson Airpark, a busy general aviation field. Nearby, the Vancouver Barracks, established in 1849 to guard the western end of the Oregon Trail, is still home to a Washington National Guard detachment; the grand Victorian houses of Officers Row, where General George Marshall and other military luminaries lived, have been converted to civic, nonprofit, and professional offices. While you cannot live in any of these places, you could live in the adjacent **Hudson's Bay** neighborhood, which includes historic structures and (mostly) small houses, along with some new row houses.

Vancouver

The other neighborhoods that lie between Interstates 5 and 205 contain a mix of single-family homes and small-scale apartments in a diverse range of styles and degrees of upkeep. Most homes here date from the 1940s to the 1970s, although some newer homes exist and infill development is occurring in certain areas. Homes along the Columbia have great views of the river, and in some cases of Mount Hood, as well as Portland International Airport just across the water. Unfortunately, these homes were built along a busy transportation corridor and suffer correspondingly from noise from trains, planes, and automobiles. Homes located on the upper slopes of the ridge that parallels the Columbia River north of Highway 14 also have views that extend to downtown Portland and the West Hills, but with somewhat less noise. In general, these homes tend to be large in size and high in price, and many have panoramic windows to take in the scene. On the plateau just behind the ridge lie several desirable neighborhoods, such as **South Cliff**. While much of the area north of the ridge features pleasant, middle-class housing, some neighborhoods have relatively high crime rates, particularly the neighborhoods near Fourth Plain Boulevard from Clark College to the Vancouver Mall.

Given their vintage, many of the neighborhoods in middle Vancouver lack sidewalks, but there is a liberal sprinkling of public parks. Although much of the Columbia River shore is awaiting redevelopment, the Waterfront Renaissance Trail runs along the river for five miles from downtown Vancouver.

The neighborhoods east of Interstate 205 were generally developed more recently than those west of the freeway, so homes and apartment complexes tend to be newer. This area features a mix of commercial, retail, and residential development. Many of these neighborhoods were annexed by the city of Vancouver in recent years. Residential options include large single-family homes along with townhouses and some apartment complexes. Mill Plain Boulevard as it runs through the **Cascade Park** neighborhood is this area's commercial heart. **Fishers Landing** and the surrounding area, at the city's far eastern end near Camas, are among the newest

Fishers Landing

and most popular neighborhoods in East Vancouver, but they are not to everyone's taste. Some brand-new residential and retail developments have cropped up around the Hewlett Packard facility in far northeastern Vancouver, on the outer fringes of Vancouver's urbanized area. Commuting into Oregon from East Vancouver can be a headache, although Portland International Airport and the surrounding industrial and commercial area is a short trip.

Two different school districts serve Vancouver. The Vancouver School District (www.vansd.org) covers the western half of the city; East Vancouver children attend Evergreen Public Schools (www.evergreenps.org). Both districts are quite large, with more than 20,000 students apiece. Evergreen schools have a slightly better reputation overall, but both districts contain excellent as well as not-so-great schools.

Website: www.cityofvancouver.us

ZIP Codes: 98660, 98661, 98662, 98663, 98664, 98682, 98683, 98684

Post Offices: Vancouver Post Office, 2700 Caples Ave, Vancouver; downtown Vancouver Post Office, 1211 Daniels St, Vancouver; Cascade Park Post Office, 304 SW Hearthwood Blvd, Vancouver

Police Stations: Vancouver Police Department, 605 E Evergreen Blvd, 360-487-7400 (non-emergency); West Precinct, 2800 NE Stapleton Rd, 360-487-7355 (non-emergency); East Precinct, 520 SE 155th Ave, 360-487-7500 (non-emergency)

Emergency Hospital: Southwest PeaceHealth Medical Center, 400 NE Mother Joseph Pl, Vancouver, 360-514-2000, www.peacehealth.org/southwest

Libraries: Vancouver Community Library, 901 C St, 360-906-5106; Cascade Park Community Library, 600 NE 136th Ave, 360-256-7782; Three Creeks Community Library, 800-C NE Tenney Rd, 503-906-4790; Vancouver Mall Community Library, 8700 NE Vancouver Mall Dr, Suite 285, 360-906-5106; www.fvrl.org

Parks: More than 60 city and county parks, trails, and recreational facilities, including Vancouver Lake Park, Marine Park, David Douglas Park, Haagen Park, the Burnt Bridge Creek Greenway, Columbia Springs Environmental Education Area, and Fort Vancouver National Historical Site; www.cityofvancouver.us/parksrec

Community Publications: *The Columbian*, www.columbian.com

Public Transportation: C-TRAN, 360-695-0123, www.c-tran.com; extensive service near downtown Vancouver and in the western half of the city, with service to and from major destinations in East Vancouver and surrounding suburbs, and commuter bus service to downtown Portland and the Delta Park and Parkrose MAX stations

CAMAS

Boundaries: North: Unincorporated rural area (Clark County); **West**: Vancouver; **South**: Columbia River; **East**: Washougal; **Area**: 12.6 square miles; **Population**: 21,000

Founded in the 1880s as a paper mill town on the north shore of the Columbia River, Camas has evolved into a booming suburb and minor center for high-tech enterprise, with new facilities for such companies as WaferTech and Sharp Micro-electronics. The city's population has more than doubled in the last 10 years, with new residents lured by relatively low taxes, access to open space (and buildable lots), and good public schools. In 2014, Camas collectively patted itself on the back when *Family Circle* named it one of the top ten towns in the country to raise a family. The Georgia-Pacific paper mill is still the city's primary landmark and one of its major employers; recently installed pollution control equipment has largely eliminated its once-legendary stench. Camas is a relatively easy 20-minute drive from Portland International Airport and its surrounding light-industrial area, but the commute to downtown Portland or Washington County can be grueling. Public transportation options from Camas are limited; some residents drive to transit centers in Vancouver or near the Portland Airport.

The city's old-school, vibrant downtown area (www.downtowncamas.com) includes a range of services, specialty shops, and restaurants; the 1920s-era Liberty Theater has reopened. Many downtown businesses stay open late for an evening "art walk" on the first Friday of each month.

The neighborhoods near downtown Camas feature small bungalows and other traditional home styles, which blend into ranches and other postwar designs as one travels outward from the old center. Many otherwise attractive homes near the riverfront suffer from railroad noise and proximity to industrial uses. A few lovely older homes stand on the banks of the Washougal River, which passes through the eastern end of the city. The majority of the city's housing stock

Camas

Camas

is fairly new, however, and choices run the gamut from small condos and apartments to massive custom homes with views of Mount Hood and the Columbia River. The new subdivisions on Prune Hill, an extinct volcanic cone in the western part of the city, offer particularly expansive views; in addition to a collection of assorted luxury homes, Prune Hill also has streets of somewhat more modest newer homes. The median home price in Camas is among the highest in the Portland area, and is significantly higher than in most of Clark County—some 60% more than in Vancouver, for example.

Camas has its own highly regarded school district (www.camas.wednet. edu). A full third of the city's population consists of children enrolled in public schools. Although the city has relatively few attractions of its own, it boasts a number of pleasant parks and offers easy access to the Columbia River Gorge and Gifford Pinchot National Forest. Lacamas Lake and its surrounding forested parklands and trails are especially popular.

The city's website has a useful page for newcomers (cityofcamas.us/index. php/ourcommunity/newresident) that includes information on setting up utilities, arranging a garbage hauler, and similar practical details.

Website: www.cityofcamas.us
ZIP Code: 98607
Post Office: Camas Post Office, 440 NE 5th Ave
Police Station: Camas Police Department, 2100 NE 3rd Ave, 360-834-4151 (non-emergency), www.cityofcamas.us/police
Emergency Hospital: Southwest PeaceHealth Medical Center, 400 NE Mother Joseph Pl, Vancouver, 360-514-200, www.peacehealth.org/southwest
Library: Camas Public Library, 625 NE 4th Ave, 360-834-4692, www.cityofcamas. us/library/

Parks: 12 parks, including Lacamas Park, Crown Park, Forest Home Park; www.cityofcamas.us/parks/

Community Publications: *Camas-Washougal Post-Record*, www.camaspostrecord.com

Public Transportation: C-TRAN, 360-695-0123, www.c-tran.com; limited bus service to Vancouver, Washougal, and downtown Portland

WASHOUGAL

Boundaries: North: Unincorporated rural area (Clark County); **West:** Camas; **South:** Columbia River; **East:** Unincorporated rural area (Clark County); **Area:** 5 square miles; **Population:** 14,200

Washougal

The easternmost significant community in the metropolitan area, Washougal, like Camas, is one of the fastest-growing communities in southwest Washington: the city's population has tripled since 1990. Although it is separately incorporated and has its own police department, library, and school district (www.washougal.k12.wa.us), Washougal can best be understood as an eastern extension of Camas. The city has a tiny old downtown on B Street, with a few other commercial establishments on E Street. The original center of Washougal lay between the Columbia and Washougal rivers, and the bulk of the city's older housing stock is here; many of the houses along the Washougal River have very pleasant settings. Newer houses with river views occupy the bluffs north of the Washougal River; quite a few of these houses are grand, custom-designed structures, and view lots on the hills are coveted. The area to the east of the city center—especially north of Evergreen Way and east of 32nd Street—has seen explosive residential growth in the last few years. Washougal is closer to Mount Hood than almost any other metro

Washougal

community, and on a clear late summer day residents can see crevasses on the mountain's glaciers.

Washougal suffers from some of the same commuting headaches as Camas, but weekend recreational opportunities are abundant: Steigerwald Lake National Wildlife Refuge and the Columbia River Gorge lie due east of the city. Much of the area along the Columbia is devoted to industrial uses, like the large port facility at the west end of town, but the three-mile Washougal Dike Trail leads east along the river from Steamboat Landing. Due to its proximity to the Gorge, Washougal is subject to occasional high winds and ice storms, and receives markedly more precipitation than Vancouver or Portland.

Website: www.cityofwashougal.us
ZIP Code: 98671
Post Office: Washougal Post Office, 129 Pendleton Way
Police Station: Washougal Police Department, 1320 A St, 360-835-8701 (non-emergency)
Emergency Hospital: Southwest PeaceHealth Medical Center, 400 NE Mother Joseph Place, Vancouver, 360-514-2000, www.peacehealth.org/southwest
Library: Washougal Community Library, 1661 C St, 360-835-5393, www.fvrl.org
Parks: More than a dozen parks and recreational facilities, including Steamboat Landing and Hathaway Park
Community Publications: *Camas-Washougal Post-Record*, www.camaspostrecord.com
Public Transportation: C-TRAN, 360-695-0123, www.c-tran.com; one bus line with limited service to Camas and Fishers Landing (East Vancouver)

UNINCORPORATED CLARK COUNTY: HAZEL DELL, LAKE SHORE, ORCHARDS, FELIDA, SALMON CREEK, AND BRUSH PRAIRIE

Along its northern fringe, the city of Vancouver transitions into several unincorporated communities, which in turn blend into one another in a band of urbanized area that extends seven or eight miles from east to west.

Immediately north of Vancouver, the community of **Hazel Dell** straddles Interstate 5; Hazel Dell Avenue, which runs parallel to the freeway a block or so to the west; and Highway 99, a frankly unattractive strip mall that parallels I-5 just to the east. The community was essentially rural into the 1940s, and a few large parcels, particularly east of Highway 99, still have a rustic feel. Most houses here, however, date from the 1950s to the present, and the housing mix here includes ranches, split-levels, and contemporary homes, many with lovingly landscaped yards. Most of the neighborhood is relatively flat, but a ridge offers some views of Portland and Mount St. Helens. A few developments of new homes and town-houses have cropped up in Hazel Dell, particularly in the northern half of the community. In general, the appearance of the neighborhood improves as one moves east or west from Interstate 5, so don't be put off by initial impressions. The southwestern part of the neighborhood offers easy access to the eight-mile, mixed-use Burnt Bridge Trail. The western edge of Hazel Dell borders Vancouver Lake, and the northwestern quadrant of Hazel Dell is also known as **Lake Shore**, and is considered one of the more desirable parts of the community. (Despite what the name suggests, there are no waterfront homes here.)

The string of communities to the east of Hazel Dell—**Walnut Grove, Minne-haha, Five Corners**, and **Orchards**—extend out past Interstate 205 into former farm- and timberlands. These areas have similar housing stock to Hazel Dell, but as you travel east and north the average home age declines precipitously. These communities have seen rapid development in recent years, and large subdivisions

Felida

Salmon Creek

and chain stores have replaced the fruit tree groves that gave Orchards its name. Home prices were never astronomical in these neighborhoods, even at the height of the last housing bubble, and this inner ring of unincorporated suburbia is one of the most affordable parts of the Portland metropolitan area. Note that despite the abundance of new construction and shiny new commercial establishments, a few neighborhoods have a lingering crime problem.

Northwest of Hazel Dell and west of Interstate 5, the tidy **Felida** neighborhood—named for the original 19th-century postmaster's cat (family Felidae)—has an abundance of newer homes on culs-de-sac. These communities have access to Vancouver Lake on the west and the Salmon Creek Greenway to the north; Lake Shore and Felida elementary schools have a good reputation, and many families are attracted to the area.

Just to the north and east, the **Salmon Creek** area groans under the weight of massive homes in expensive new subdivisions. Nearly all the construction in Salmon Creek is relatively new—in some cases brand-new—and generally upscale. The culs-de-sac along the north side of Salmon Creek's eponymous creek feature large contemporary homes and McMansions, some of which have grown up incongruously around mobile home parks. Some custom homes on large lots cluster along the bluff above Salmon Creek Greenway, especially at the western end. In addition to the abundant single-family homes, there are some townhomes and apartment complexes. New commercial developments have opened to serve the area's burgeoning affluent population.

Washington State University's Vancouver campus is in Salmon Creek, and its academic presence adds some cultural spice to a community that would otherwise be a fairly standard, if pleasant, suburban community. Salmon Creek's schools are widely considered among the best in the Vancouver School District. Interstate 205 splits off from Interstate 5 here, so Salmon Creek residents have their choice of southbound commuting options.

East of Salmon Creek, **Brush Prairie** still has a low population density and fairly rural ambiance, but new housing is going up along Highway 503. Given the growth of nearby Salmon Creek, Orchards, and Battle Ground, it seems likely that Brush Prairie is fated to experience increasing development in the future.

Vancouver School District (www.vansd.org) covers the western half of this area (i.e., Hazel Dell, Felida, and Salmon Creek); Orchards is part of Evergreen Public Schools (www.evergreenps.org), while Battle Ground Public Schools (www.battlegroundps.org) serve part of Brush Prairie; the remainder of Brush Prairie and some of the surrounding area is part of the Hockinson School District (www.hocksd.org). The city of Vancouver is widely suspected (or known) to covet this entire area, with the possible exception of Brush Prairie (which Battle Ground is slowly absorbing from the north). Most residents have been opposed to annexation in the past—the Clark County government already provides these communities with many of the services that incorporated areas enjoy—but circumstances could easily change.

BATTLE GROUND

Boundaries: North: Unincorporated Clark County; **West**: Unincorporated Clark County; **South**: Brush Prairie (unincorporated Clark County); **East**: Unincorporated Clark County; **Area**: 3.6 square miles; **Population**: 18,250

Battle Ground spreads across a scenic plain west of the Cascade foothills. A battle was never fought here—but today you will fight a battle just to get from the city to anywhere else. Battle Ground is the fastest growing city in Clark County, but it is not adjacent to any major highways, let alone mass transit options, so it takes at least 15 minutes, and often longer, just to get to Interstate 5 or 205. The city's population has quintupled since 1990, expanding by more than 20% in 1997 alone, and the road network simply has not kept up with the area's exploding

Battle Ground

growth. (Road widening projects now under way should improve the traffic situation somewhat in the near future.) To exacerbate the situation, the city statistically has only one job per two households, so most workers have to commute elsewhere. However, if you can live with the commute, Battle Ground is one of the most affordable metro-area communities.. It is very popular with families, and half the city's households include children under 18.

As one would expect, most homes in Battle Ground are relatively new; some are quite large, but there are also unostentatious developments of basic single-family homes and townhomes. A few old landmark homes remain from the town's early years, including the Henry Heisen House from the 1890s, Burdoin House from 1903, and the Rieck House, a 1920s bungalow. Supermarkets and other commercial services cluster along Main Street, especially near the intersection with Highway 503, but the majority of the city is residential. Battle Ground's main disadvantage—its relative isolation—is also one of its chief attractions. Fields and woodland surround the city, and recreational opportunities abound in the Cascade foothills, in places such as Battle Ground Lake State Park and Lucia Falls Park, Moulton Falls Park, and the Bells Mountain Trail on the East Fork of the Lewis River. The city's Battle Ground Public Schools district (www.battlegroundps.org) also serves several surrounding rural communities. Although growth has slowed from the heady days of the 1990s and 2000s, Battle Ground's population is expected to keep expanding steadily in the next decade.

Website: www.cityofbg.org
ZIP Code: 98604
Post Office: Battle Ground Post Office, 418 W Main St
Police Station: Battle Ground Police Department, 507 SW 1st St, 360-342-5200 (non-emergency)
Emergency Hospital: Legacy Salmon Creek Hospital, 2211 NE 139th St, Vancouver, 360-487-1000, www.legacyhealth.org
Library: Battle Ground Community Library, 1207 SE 8th Way, 360-687-2322, www.fvrl.org
Parks: 18 parks and trails, including Kiwanis Park and Fairgrounds Park; www.cityofbg.org
Community Publications: The Reflector, www.thereflector.com
Public Transportation: C-TRAN, 360-695-0123, www.c-tran.com; two bus lines with service to Vancouver, Delta Park (North Portland) and Yacolt

RIDGEFIELD, LA CENTER, AND WOODLAND

These three small cities are (for the time being) separated from one another, and from the sprawl emanating from Vancouver, by miles of woods and fields. **Ridgefield** (www.ci.ridgefield.wa.us) is one of the fastest-growing cities in Washington; fittingly, it was the birthplace of U-Haul, and quite a few of that company's trucks were used in the last few years to furnish the subdivisions that sprouted up in the fields along Pioneer Street. Ridgefield's tiny Old Town by the river has a few shops and cafés; radiating east and southeast from the town center and on the slopes behind, you can see everything from modest ranch houses and mobile home parks to brand new "Northwest Craftsman-style" homes. Houses on higher ground have good views west to the low Tualatin Mountains in Oregon. Working

La Center

farms, and even a winery, hem in the town on three sides, and it's possible to pick up rural acreage here; to the west, narrow Lake River and the Ridgefield National Wildlife Refuge separate Ridgefield from the mainstream of the Columbia River. Ridgefield still has a small-town feel, especially near the old center, but it's hard to ignore the new residential and commercial development. Ridgefield has its own school district (www.ridge.k12.wa.us).

La Center (www.ci.lacenter.wa.us) huddles on a hillside above the East Fork of the Lewis River; seen from a distance, the compact city center very faintly resembles a Northwest version of a Tuscan hill town. Unlike a Tuscan hill town, the town center has three card rooms offering poker and blackjack, but these establishments do not dominate the city. Houses are a variety of ages and styles, although there are few prewar homes left; some new construction is occurring around La Center, although noticeably less than in Ridgefield. The small La Center School District (www.lcsd.k12.wa.us) is well-funded and has an excellent reputation. The Cowlitz Tribe has proposed building a huge new casino complex near La Center, just off of Interstate 5, but plans have been tied up in court for years.

The small city of **Woodland** (www.ci.woodland.wa.us) lies along Interstate 5 about 20 miles north of Vancouver, and thus at the approximate northern limit of what most people would consider possible commuting distance from Portland. (Most of the city actually lies within Cowlitz County.) Houses here range from modest ranches to large custom homes on the banks of the Lewis River. While Woodland doesn't have many attractions, barring the lovely Hulda Klager Lilac

Yacolt

Gardens (www.lilacgardens.com), it is the gateway to the southern slopes of Mount St. Helens. Woodland has its own school district (www.woodlandschools.org).

Many newcomers choose these outlying areas because they are looking for small-town ambiance within striking distance of the amenities of a large city. Ironically, these attributes attract growth and sprawl, which in turn threaten to erode the small-town ambiance. (This dilemma is hardly unique to southwest Washington.) The continuing livability of these communities will likely depend on the way in which they manage (or attempt to manage) their growth.

As in other parts of Clark County, transportation is an issue of concern. If you don't have a job in these communities or nearby in Clark or Cowlitz Counties, be sure to test your anticipated commute before committing to buying a home here. C-TRAN's Connector service offers very limited service from La Center and Ridgefield to Vancouver, where transfers to the regular bus system are available.

AMBOY AND YACOLT

These northern Clark County communities offer acreage, quiet, and long, long commutes. With an economy traditionally based on logging and agriculture, this area remains in large part a working rural landscape; mud-splattered pickup trucks outnumber passenger cars, there is no Starbucks for miles, and the local grange is still active. Many residents, even those who are not farmers, keep horses, llamas, or other large animals. Most homes here are relatively modest ranch homes or old farmhouses on farms or large lots; a few new, ostentatious homes are going up in choice spots in the region's verdant valleys or on forested hillsides. Some homes have views of Mount St. Helens.

Each July, unincorporated **Amboy** hosts Territorial Days, which features such events as logging demonstrations and lawn mower drag races. **Yacolt**, best known for the devastating Yacolt Burn of 1902, the largest forest fire in Northwest history, was incorporated six years after the conflagration; it is the terminus of

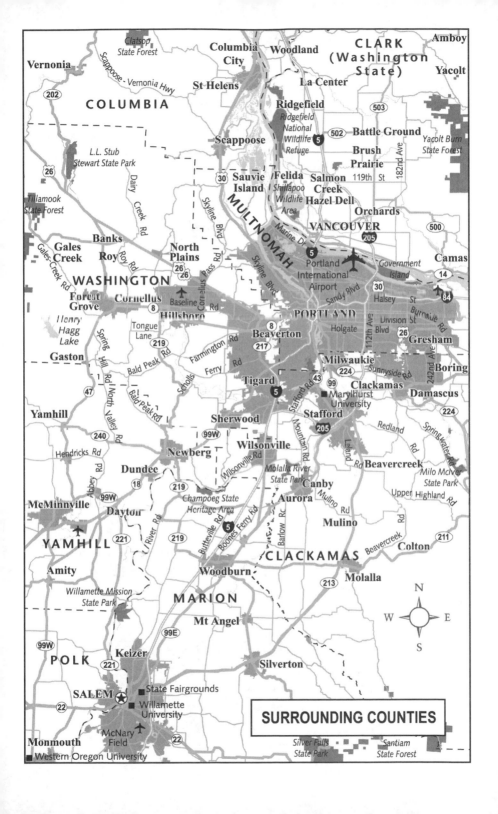

the Battle Ground, Yacolt, and Chelatchie Prairie Railroad, a scenic excursion train. Both communities offer a small range of essential services—groceries, auto repair, pizza, and the like—but most residents travel to Battle Ground or Vancouver for shopping. Yacolt has a primary school and Amboy has a middle school, both of which are part of the Battle Ground School District (www.battlegroundps.org). Public transportation is essentially nonexistent, barring a single bus line, running once per weekday in each direction, to Vancouver and North Portland.

OTHER OUTLYING COMMUNITIES

COLUMBIA COUNTY AND SAUVIE ISLAND

Sauvie Island (often referred to colloquially as "Sauvie's Island") lies at the mouth of the Willamette River, between Multnomah Channel and the Columbia River. Sauvie is a classic delta island—flat, rich farmland dotted with shallow lakes and sloughs—and despite its proximity to Portland, the island is wholly rural. The forested Tualatin Mountains rise to the west, and on clear days a procession of Cascade peaks appears in the east. The island is unincorporated, and has a single grade school—after sixth grade, island children go to school in Scappoose. A bridge over Multnomah Channel near the southern tip of the island provides the only road access to the mainland, and power outages are frequent during winter storms.

Sauvie Island is a popular choice for people who like isolation and crave a rural lifestyle, but island living doesn't come cheap: The median price of a home here is just about the highest in the metro area, and some spreads are in the multimillion-dollar range (although almost every dwelling comes with acreage). Moreover, isolation doesn't equal solitude; the island's beaches, wildlife refuges,

Sauvie Island

Scappoose

U-pick farms, and fall pumpkin patches and corn mazes attract hordes of visitors (and bicyclists, who enjoy the flat, scenic roads), and it can take a long time to get on or off the island on weekends in summer and autumn. A TriMet bus line with all-day service runs from the southern tip of the island to downtown Portland. (Note that more than half of Sauvie Island is actually within Multnomah County, but it has more affinities with predominantly rural Columbia County than with highly urbanized Multnomah County.)

The Columbia County line is a few miles north of the Sauvie Island Bridge. Columbia County has long been dependent on forest products and related industries for jobs; many long-time Portlanders don't think of it as part of the metropolitan area at all, even though Scappoose, the southernmost town in the county, is not much farther from downtown Portland than Wilsonville. The area is growing and evolving, however, with an influx of new residents who seek small-town living (and lower housing costs) within reach of jobs in the Portland area. Many of these new residents commute over the Tualatin Mountains to the tech centers of Washington County.

Scappoose (www.ci.scappoose.or.us) stands opposite the northern end of Sauvie Island, about 20 miles north of downtown Portland. This small city's older neighborhoods and commercial establishments cluster along Highway 30 and the train tracks that run beside it; a farmers' market takes place in the city center (such as it is) on Saturdays in season. There are some small developments of new homes in Scappoose proper, but most newer houses perch in the hills just west of town; some hillside homes have expansive views over Sauvie Island to the Cascades. Other houses are tucked away in shady canyons. Scappoose itself lacks river frontage, although Scappoose Bay to the north has a marina and some of the best flatwater kayaking in the state. About eight miles north, **St. Helens** (www.ci.st-helens.or.us), the county seat, *is* on the Columbia River, and takes advantage of its setting. The city's "Olde Towne" historic district spreads out along the riverfront, which also features a marina with a few houseboats; the city is located far enough

St. Helens

north that Mount St. Helens, not Mount Hood, dominates the eastern horizon. St. Helens's older homes are concentrated in this area. Newer homes spread out in subdivisions to the west, between the riverfront and Highway 30, and as in Scappoose many homes outside of town are set in hollows in the hills west of Highway 30. Just to the north of St. Helens, much smaller **Columbia City** (www.columbiacity.org) hugs the riverfront and the hillside just behind it.

The Scappoose School District (www.scappoose.k12.or.us) serves Scappoose and Sauvie Island; the St. Helens School District (www.sthelens.k12.or.us) covers St. Helens and Columbia City. Commuting to Portland is via Highway 30, which is not a freeway for most of the way and which carries a high volume of truck traffic. Commuters to Washington County face the choice of driving into Portland and out the frequently snarled Sunset Highway, or winding over the Tualatin Mountains on Cornelius Pass Road. Although St. Helens is essentially just across the river from Ridgefield, Washington, there are no highway bridges between Longview and Vancouver, so commuting to Clark County is not an easy or quick option (unless you own a boat and have access to docks on both sides of the Columbia). The only transit service in Columbia County is the Columbia County Rider (www.columbiacountyrider.com), which provides limited commuter service between St. Helens/Scappoose and downtown Portland, Longview, and Portland Community College's Rock Creek campus; the trip from St. Helens to any of these destinations takes about an hour.

County Website: www.co.columbia.or.us

YAMHILL COUNTY

Yamhill County, southwest of Portland, is the heart of Oregon's wine country. Yamhill County is a less-moneyed, more laid-back version of California's Napa

County, but don't let the dearth of Hollywood names fool you: winemakers here are serious about their product. The region is especially renowned for its Pinot Noir, which is among the very best in the world.

Of course, vineyards do not wholly, or even mostly, cover the county; the western half of the county encompasses a large, forested chunk of the Coast Range, while several small cities dot the landscape in the eastern half of the county. The closest of these cities to Portland is **Newberg** (www.newberg-oregon.gov), set picturesquely between the Willamette River and the Chehalem Mountains. This fast-growing city of about 23,000 people has an old-fashioned downtown (www.newbergdowntown.org), with a nearby neighborhood of historic homes (including Herbert Hoover's boyhood home, which is now a museum) featuring a number of impressive, century-plus-old landscape trees. The city has an abundance of more recently built homes, including hillside homes, as well as some brand-new developments and a large selection of apartment complexes. The presence of George Fox University ensures that Newberg has a more active cultural calendar than it otherwise would.

A few miles down the highway, the much smaller (and somewhat quainter) city of **Dundee** (www.dundeecity.org) features a couple of respected bistros and even some wineries right on the main drag. If you crave your own *terroir*—and if you don't know what that means, you probably aren't interested—expensive homes on grape-planted acreage are available just outside either city. Homes on the Chehalem Mountains or the Dundee Hills are especially coveted for viticulture, and offer incredible views across the Willamette Valley to the Cascades. Newberg Public Schools (www.newberg.k12.or.us) serve both communities.

Still farther down Highway 99W, **McMinnville** (www.ci.mcminnville.or.us) is the largest city in the county (about 33,000 residents). Like Newberg, McMinnville is undergoing substantial growth, and many new developments have sprung up around town. The city's pleasant downtown (www.downtownmcminnville.com) was largely built up during the period from 1880 to 1920, and is filled with

Newberg

restaurants, wine bars and cafés, interesting (and not-so-interesting) shops, the Mack Theater (opened in 1941), and the Hotel Oregon (another McMenamins restoration), with its popular rooftop bar. A farmers' market is held on Thursdays during the summer. The adjacent residential neighborhoods are filled with older homes, including some restored Victorians; more modern homes and low-rise apartment buildings dominate the rest of the city. Just south of downtown, Linfield College hosts an International Pinot Noir Celebration every summer. For now, the giant Spruce Goose airplane spreads its comically long wings at the Evergreen Aviation and

Dundee

Space Museum (www.evergreenmuseum.org), just outside town; the museum has an associated indoor waterpark that incorporates a rooftop Boeing 747. (The future of the museum/waterpark complex is in doubt at press time, due to the bankruptcy of Evergreen International Aviation.) McMinnville has its own school district (www.msd.k12.or.us). Although most areas of McMinnville are quite safe, a few neighborhoods are pretty dodgy, and the city has a surprisingly high rate of crime given its rural setting. That said, the city overall has a standard-issue small-town vibe; average housing prices are among the lowest in the Portland-Vancouver-Salem area.

Although they are by no means remote, the communities of Yamhill County aren't really close to any major cities. Newberg and Dundee are reasonable possibilities for commuters to jobs in Portland's southwestern suburbs, such as Tigard, Tualatin, or Wilsonville; McMinnville is within striking distance of Salem. If you're seriously considering a move to Yamhill County, be aware that Highway 99W, the main artery that connects Yamhill County to Portland, has a

McMinnville

chronic congestion problem. While it's not really a barrier to weekend sight-seeing, traffic congestion hampers commuters and dampens the area's economic growth. The state has begun construction on the first phase of an expressway that will bypass Newberg and Dundee, which is scheduled to open in 2017, but the remaining phases are unfunded; in other words, traffic will remain an issue, at least in the short-term. Yamhill County Transit Area (www.yctransitarea.org) provides limited bus service within Yamhill County and from county towns to Salem, Sherwood, and Hillsboro.

If you're looking for a small town in wine country, others worth checking out include **Amity**, **Yamhill**, **Carlton**, **Lafayette**, and **Dayton**.

County Website: www.co.yamhill.or.us

MARION COUNTY

The farmlands and rolling, wooded hills of Marion County lie smack-dab astride the mid-Willamette Valley, one of the nation's most productive agricultural regions. The region produces a range of crops, from iris bulbs to hazelnuts, and is perhaps best known as the home of the Marionberry, a tasty blackberry hybrid that was named after the county and has no relation to the former mayor of Washington, D.C. If you suffer from hay fever, beware: the central Willamette Valley has many grass farms, and in late spring high concentrations of grass pollen mean misery for allergy sufferers.

The town of **Aurora** (www.ci.aurora.or.us) began its existence in the 1850s as the Aurora Colony, a commune of German Christians—a Northwestern version of the Amana colonies. The commune eventually faded away, but left behind the nucleus of the city's historic district (www.auroracolony.com). Today, the historic district is packed with antique stores and small eateries; Aurora Mills Architectural

Aurora

Woodburn

Salvage (www.auroramills.com) and the Old Aurora Colony Museum are also located here. The neighborhood south of the historic center is a mix of century-old homes and postwar ranches. (A working train line runs nearby; beware if you're sensitive to rumbling and train whistles.) Some new housing developments are beginning to crop up on the outskirts of the city, but for now Aurora remains surrounded by agricultural land and the city maintains a laid-back, small-town atmosphere. The city is also home to a popular general aviation airport—the third busiest airport in the state—which makes Aurora (along with the nearby Charbonneau district of Wilsonville) a convenient place for avid private pilots to live. (Noise abatement procedures discourage pilots from overflying town.)

A public bus line links Aurora with Canby and the city of **Woodburn** (www.woodburn-or.gov), a major trade and service center for the northern Willamette Valley. Many Portlanders know Woodburn as the site of the Woodburn Premium Outlets mall just off Interstate 5, but there's much more to the city. Highway 99E, which parallels I-5 to the east, is a strip mall lined with supermarkets, chain restaurants, and *taquerias*, but the adjacent neighborhoods contain plenty of modest single-family homes and apartments. A busy set of train tracks abuts Woodburn's tiny downtown; to the west lies a pleasant district of historic homes on tree-lined streets. Some new housing developments are rising in the fields that surround the town. Woodburn's official nickname is "City of Unity," which reflects the city's unusually diverse population, including large contingents of Hispanics and Russian Orthodox Old Believers. If you happen to have a highly polluting car—and shame on you if you do—you should know that Woodburn is at the northern frontier of the zone where emissions tests are not required; residents of all Oregon towns and cities farther north have to take their vehicles to DEQ (Department of Environmental Quality) testing stations every two years. Northwest of Woodburn, the tiny, historic city of **St. Paul** (no website) is best known for its annual rodeo, held each year on July 4 (www.stpaulrodeo.com).

Charming **Silverton** (www.silverton.or.us), set amid fields and orchards at the edge of the Cascade foothills, is an increasingly popular destination for a day trip or weekend getaway, but it also attracts newcomers who like the scenic location and small-town vibe. Neighborhoods of old bungalows and cottages surround a traditional downtown, filled with murals illustrating the city's history; outlying areas feature ranches and newer contemporary homes, and true farm living is just outside the city. In terms of landscape, Silverton offers a mix of flat bottomland and rolling hills; hilltop homes feature gorgeous views of the nearby Cascades. Area attractions include the Oregon Garden and beautiful Silver Falls State Park. While too far from Portland for comfortable commuting for most people, Silverton may be a reasonable choice for people who work in Salem or at the southern end of the Portland metropolitan area (e.g., Wilsonville).

A few miles north of Silverton, charming, sleepy **Mt. Angel** (www.ci.mt-angel. or.us) celebrates its Swiss and German heritage with a glockenspiel in its small downtown area and a popular Oktoberfest (www.oktoberfest.org), held confusingly in September. Homes in Mt. Angel run the gamut from old farm cottages to large contemporary-style homes and everything in between, sometimes all on the same street. The landscape becomes rural within a mile or so in any direction. On a hill just east of town stands handsome Mt. Angel Abbey, home to a library designed by famed Finnish architect Alvar Aalto.

Salem (www.cityofsalem.net), Oregon's state capital and second-largest city, is not the urban dynamo one might expect. The city core, around the state capitol building, bustles with activity when Oregon's part-time legislature is in session, but has a quiet, small-town feel the rest of the year. Except for a few bars, downtown Salem mostly shuts down in the evening after the state workers go home, although that situation is gradually changing. A few good new restaurants draw evening diners year-round, and the (rather limited) selection of cultural offerings is slowly expanding; downtown Salem even hosts a talented improv troupe (Capitol City Theater, www.capitolcitytheater.com). The city has redeveloped part of the Willamette

Silverton

River waterfront into a park, there is a new convention center, and downtown has a handful of upscale condos. Can high-end restaurants and posh boutiques be far behind?

Maybe, maybe not. Virtually no one moves to Salem for its urban amenities, but more typically because they are attracted by the city's traditional-feeling, slow-paced vibe. In other words, in terms of attitude at least, Salem is an un-Portland, but it still enjoys both an attractive geographical location with access to abundant recreational opportunities, as well as reasonable proximity to Portland's urban attractions. As an added benefit, Salem remains the lowest-cost major housing market on the West Coast, and its relative affordability is definitely part of the city's appeal.

Salem Waterfront

Several historic districts with attractive old homes border the State Capitol and the Willamette University campus; the neighborhood near Bush's Pasture Park is particularly lovely. Hilly South Salem offers pleasant neighborhoods of postwar ranches and newer contemporary homes (some with mountain or valley views); prices here tend to be relatively high (for Salem). West Salem has an abundance of newer homes, with many of the McMansion variety, and prices here are also quite high by Salem standards. (Note that West Salem is in Polk County rather than Marion County.) South Salem and West Salem have traditionally been considered the most desirable parts of the city, but there are pleasant enclaves in other quadrants ars well. Home prices are generally lowest in North Salem and in the neighborhoods near Lancaster Drive, an extensive strip mall that parallels Interstate 5 on the city's east side.

Salem is a good bet for people who intend to work here or in a nearby community. The commute from Salem to Portland or Beaverton takes at least an hour—much longer if there's an accident—and traffic on Interstate 5 gets heavier every year. (The reverse commute from Portland to Salem is somewhat more manageable, but is still unpleasantly long.) Although many workers carpool or vanpool, there is little viable public transportation useful for commuters between the two cities; to get between the cities by bus, you would have to make multiple transfers and deal with two or three different transit agencies. Amtrak runs one northbound morning train and one southbound evening train; this option might work for commuters who work near Union Station in Portland.

If you are looking for a small town in this area, you might also consider **Hubbard, Gervais, Donald,** or **Scotts Mills**.

County Website: www.co.marion.or.us

THE COLUMBIA GORGE

The Columbia River Gorge, with its gobsmackingly dramatic scenery, is a popular destination for outdoor recreation, but for a select few it is also a place to call home. Although there are no sizeable communities between Troutdale/Washougal at the west end of the Gorge and Hood River/White Salmon, an hour east of Portland (in good weather), there are several small towns and numerous rural dwellings. Most Gorge dwellers live on the slightly less precipitous Washington side of the river, which also gets more winter sunshine. (This is not a feature of climate but a consequence of the steep cliffs on the Oregon side of the river blocking out light when the sun is at a low winter angle.) The largest town is **Stevenson** (ci. stevenson.wa.us), the county seat of Skamania County, which is transitioning from a logging town to a more tourism-based economy; other settlements include Carson and North Bonneville. The only hamlet of any size on the Oregon side is **Cascade Locks** (www.cascade-locks.or.us), at the southern end of the Bridge of the Gods near Bonneville Dam. In addition to houses in these small towns, homes of various sizes and ages are scattered among the hills and dells on the Washington side of the river; these range from newer houses on high benches of land with spectacular views to moldering old single-levels and mobile homes tucked into shady canyons. A few old cottages stand next to the Historic Columbia River Highway on the Oregon side.

All this sounds idyllic to some people, and it can be, but the fantasy of Gorge living may be more appealing than the reality, for several reasons. First, the Gorge is a designated National Scenic Area, with extremely strict land use laws; you can't simply buy a promising parcel of land and build a home, or necessarily even replace a dilapidated existing structure. Second, there is a limited economic base, which means that unless you have a home-based business you'll probably need to commute. And this fact leads to the third issue: because the Gorge funnels cold interior air westward in winter, ice and snow storms that don't affect Portland at all can cut off Gorge communities for days at a time. In addition, even during mild weather, the Gorge is subject to sustained strong winds that are great news for windsurfers but can be tedious or worrisome for residents. Wind speeds in excess of 100 miles per hour are not uncommon in exposed areas. If all that sounds enticing to you, then by all means consider living in one of the most spectacular settings in North America.

HERE WAS A TIME, YOU WILL BE ENDLESSLY REMINDED, WHEN Portland was considered one of the most affordable metropolitan areas in the country. No more. The steep and (at the time) seemingly inexorable rise in home prices that began in the late 1990s put the dream of home ownership beyond the reach of many Portlanders. Much of this spectacular rise in Portland real estate values was arguably due to newcomers bringing their equity from more expensive markets rather than to the robustness of the local economy. The median income had not (and has not) kept up with the price of housing, so many local workers were, and remain, completely priced out of the real estate market.

A noticeable slowdown in sales and in price appreciation and an increase in unsold inventory began in late 2006. Home prices peaked in mid-2007, and home prices began to decline noticeably in most parts of the metro area by 2008, although not evenly across the region and not to the extent experienced in such epicenters of the nationwide housing bust as Las Vegas, Phoenix, and Florida. By mid-2009, average home prices had declined by close to 20% from their peak, then began to rise, at first anemically, and then with more vigor. By 2014, housing prices in most parts of the metro area had recovered to, and in some places exceeded, their pre-crash levels. Even in the depths of the most recent housing bust, however, Portland real estate was hardly cheap, and in some popular close-in neighborhoods prices barely declined at all. The direction of real estate prices in the Portland area in the future is, of course, anyone's guess.

Regardless of whether home prices rise or fall, Portland's real estate is, and is likely to remain, the least expensive among the large metropolitan areas on the West Coast. If you plan to rent, Portland offers a wide range of rental housing types and prices (and landlord incentives in many large suburban complexes). Although the process of finding a place to live can be frustrating and time-consuming, remember that Portland is not, say, Manhattan or San Francisco. Eventually, you *will* be able to find a dwelling that works for you.

GETTING TO KNOW THE NEIGHBORHOOD

You should be able to narrow down your initial neighborhood options by considering factors such as the location of your new job, the availability of transit, your preferred housing type and style, the quality and location of schools, and the size of your housing budget. Once you come up with a short list of neighborhoods, how do you find out more detailed information about them? If you're looking for housing in the city of Portland, be sure to visit **www.PortlandMaps. com**, a free city-run website. Simply type in an address or intersection, and you'll be able to see detailed information about the size and assessed value of neighborhood housing stock, potential natural hazards in the area, reported crimes in the prior 12 months, airport noise, and a slew of other information; type in an actual address and you'll get details about the building (number of bedrooms, property taxes, permit history, roof type, and much more). Many of the larger suburban communities offer similar (but usually less comprehensive) online tools.

Another useful online tool is the **Street View** feature on Google Maps (www. maps.google.com; after you have entered an address and the location is highlighted with a red marker on the map, click on the marker and then choose Street View), which allows you to virtually explore the street-level landscape (via photos taken from Google's camera-equipped cars) for almost the entire metropolitan area; Street View is especially useful if you've narrowed your search down to a specific address or neighborhood. Note that Street View is not a real-time feature, so the view won't necessarily reflect current conditions—the screen will display the month and year the image was captured, if you're curious—but it should give you a decent sense of the look and feel of an area of interest.

Of course, you would be unwise to base your decision solely on maps, statistics, and photos taken by a goofy-looking vehicle. The best thing to do when house or apartment hunting is to visit prospective neighborhoods in person. Have breakfast or lunch at a local eatery and walk around—don't just circle around in your car. Talk to people in the neighborhood to get some subjective opinions. Find out if the services and conveniences you are accustomed to are available nearby, and pay attention to your comfort level: if you don't like the "feel" of the neighborhood, or if it just doesn't seem like a great fit for you, you might want to explore other options.

Also consider the commute. If you plan to drive to work, test drive the route during both morning and evening rush hours to be sure of what you're getting into. If you have a job in Wilsonville, at the south end of the metro area, it might be unwise to settle in Woodland, Washington, 53 miles to the north, unless you're a huge fan of podcasts or audiobooks. Many people are able to commute by bus or light rail, but the usefulness of transit depends on where you live, where you need to go, how long the trip takes, and what time of day you want to travel there. If you intend to commute by bike, plan some potential bike routes and do a trial ride from your prospective neighborhood. See the **Transportation** chapter for more details.

For tips on researching schools, see the **Childcare and Education** chapter.

CRIME AND SAFETY

In addition to proximity to work and/or amenities, "feel" of the neighborhood, and other subjective or individualized factors in choosing a place to live, you may also be concerned about crime. Every major city in the United States has its "good" and "bad" sections, and Portland is no exception. The good news here is that the violent crime rate in Portland is relatively tame by big city standards—the murder rate is substantially lower than the national average, for example. In 2013, the city recorded only 16 homicides, the lowest number since 1971. (The rape rate in Portland is much higher than the national average, but this statistic may reflect a higher reporting rate by victims rather than a greater incidence of rape.) In general, while random violence is not unknown, it is not especially common either—despite the impression the evening news, with its "if it bleeds, it leads" ethos, might convey.

For most Portlanders, property crime is a bigger concern. In the city, relatively high rates of burglary, auto theft, and larceny, fueled in part by the financial needs of methamphetamine addicts and other drug users, exceed the national average. Property crime rates overall have dropped slightly over the last few years, but certain neighborhoods remain plagued by frequent burglaries and car prowls. You can substantially reduce the likelihood that you will become a victim by taking some common-sense precautions, like locking your home and car—a shocking number of burglaries involve a burglar waltzing into a house through an unlocked door or open window.

The Portland Police Bureau's website (www.portlandonline.com/police) offers an online (nonemergency) crime reporting system that saves the citizen time and money. The site also provides a treasure trove of helpful information about crime and crime prevention. In particular, the online **CrimeMapper** tool (www.gis.ci.portland.or.us/maps/police/) is an excellent place to research crime rates in a given neighborhood; just type in an address, and you'll be shown the days, times, and locations of crimes reported in the previous 12 months in the immediate vicinity. (This feature is also available on the PortlandMaps.com site.) Several surrounding communities, including Beaverton (beavertonpolice.org/crime/maps_stats.aspx), have less robust versions of this tool. Police reports from a number of suburban cities, including Gresham, Canby, Troutdale, and Sherwood, appear on the somewhat clunky **CrimeReports.com** (www.crimereports.com) site. You can also call the local police or sheriff precinct or department that patrols your neighborhood of interest.

To find out if a registered sex offender lives in the neighborhood, visit the **Oregon Sex Offender Inquiry System** (sexoffenders.oregon.gov). In Washington, go to the website of the **Washington State Sex Offender Information Center** (ml.waspc.org).

RENTING VS. BUYING

In the long run, buying may be cheaper than renting, and you end up with an asset to show for it—but then again, as British economist John Maynard Keynes helpfully pointed out, in the long run we are all dead. Many newcomers buy a house or condo too soon after moving to town, only to discover that the neighborhood, the commute, or the home itself is more than they bargained for or is simply not to their liking. Especially in light of the recent fluctuations in home prices in Portland, it might be wise to rent to allow time to get to know the city before deciding where to put down permanent roots. If you have school-age kids, you might be in a hurry to get them settled into a school—but what do you do if you don't like the school? What if you come to hate the rain? What if your next-door neighbor's hobbies include storing rusted-out cars on blocks in the yard? For most homeowners, buying a home is the biggest transaction they'll ever undertake; it makes sense not to rush into a decision. And many people simply don't have the financial resources to buy a home or qualify for a mortgage. Of course, if you know where you'll be working and you know where you want to live, it can be a smart decision to buy a home—especially if you have enough money for a decent down payment.

For number-crunching assistance in deciding whether to rent or buy, try out one of the many online **rent vs. buy calculators**, such as the comprehensive calculator available at www.dinkytown.net/java/MortgageRentvsBuy.html.

RENTING

As in other cities, rents in Portland are subject to the law of supply and demand. During the depths of the last recession, the apartment vacancy rate exceeded 6%—not quite a renter's market, but a huge improvement over the 3% rate, which was essentially full occupancy—and rents had actually begun to decline after successive years of fairly steep increases. As a result, new construction ground to a halt. Then, as the economy recovered, demand for rental housing began to increase, vacancy rates plummeted, and rents began—you guessed it—to increase. New construction accordingly surged, but in the meantime, as of 2014 the Portland area has the second-tightest rental market in the country, with an overall vacancy rate of 3.5%, and vacancy rates of below 1% in certain popular areas such as close-in Southeast Portland. In short, bargains do not abound in the rental market. Some suburban areas have a higher vacancy rate (and lower rents), and in these areas it may still be possible to find incentives—a free month with a one-year lease, for example—to attract tenants.

FINDING A PLACE

Be prepared to pound some pavement. Start by scanning the online or print classifieds, but don't forget to go out and visit neighborhoods you're interested in and look for "For Rent" or "Vacancy" signs. In the current hot rental market, many landlords don't want or need to advertise; particularly in desirable, apartment-dense neighborhoods like Northwest Portland and Inner Southeast Portland, it is often easy enough to find tenants simply by hanging a sign outside a building for a day or two. Also check for vacancy notices tacked on bulletin boards at neighborhood coffeehouses or grocery stores. In suburban areas, look for signs on main roads, or call a complex's rental office and ask about upcoming vacancies.

ONLINE AND NEWSPAPER RESOURCES

The Internet has changed the way people find real estate, and that goes for rental properties, too. There are plenty of websites, such as **Move** (www.move.com), **Apartments.com** (www.apartments.com), and) **ForRent.com** (www.forrent.com), that list Portland properties for rent. One of the most popular sites, especially for small landlords, is **Craigslist** (www.portland.craigslist.org). Hundreds of ads are posted in the "apts/housing" section on a typical day; you can narrow your search based on number of bedrooms, rent amount, and whether cats or dogs are allowed, and you can search listings for specific terms (e.g., neighborhood names, fireplace, garage, etc.), but it still can be pretty overwhelming. Craigslist has a map feature, but it is pretty clunky. The useful **HousingMaps** mashup site (www.housingmaps.com) superimposes Craigslist ads that include an address or intersection on a Google map of Portland; this feature can be very useful if you are targeting specific neighborhoods or communities. HousingMaps allows you sort by the same criteria as Craigslist itself. Other potentially useful websites for fining rental housing include **Padmapper** (www.padmapper.com) and **Lovely** (livelovely.com). In addition to the commercial sites, **HousingConnections.org** (www.housingconnections.org) lists thousands of affordable, accessible, and special needs housing units in the Portland metropolitan area.

The old-fashioned way of finding out about rentals is to pore over newspaper classified ads. Be aware that many landlords and rental property managers use both online and newspaper advertising, and by the time a property appears in print it may already be "stale." The following publications have the best selection of classified ads, although the number of print ads has declined precipitously in recent years:

- *The Oregonian*; the Sunday edition of the biggest regional newspaper has the most comprehensive print rental and real estate listings for Portland and the surrounding communities. Rentals are listed by location, i.e., by city quadrant or suburban locale. Classifieds are available online at www.oregonlive.com. New listings appear daily in both the print and online versions of the classifieds.

- The **Portland Tribune** has skimpier listings than the *Oregonian*, but its online classifieds (www.community-classifieds.com) include listings from more than 20 community papers.
- **The Columbian** is the daily for Vancouver and Clark County, and is worth a gander if you're looking for rentals in southwest Washington; visit www.columbian.com for online classifieds.
- **Willamette Week**; this free news, arts and entertainment weekly is distributed each Wednesday. The paper often lists rental opportunities not included in the larger publications, but it is most valuable for those in search of short-term rentals, sublets, home share situations, or a roommate. To view ads online, visit www.wweek.com.

OTHER RENTAL PUBLICATIONS
Several companies publish free rental guides. Most list newer apartment complexes or apartments that are maintained by large property management companies. You can pick up rental guides at most grocery or convenience stores, or in some sidewalk vending boxes.
- **Apartment Guide**, www.apartmentguide.com
- **For Rent**, www.forrent.com

RENTAL PROPERTY MANAGEMENT COMPANIES

Rental property management companies manage multiple properties. These companies often list available properties on their websites, or you can call them to find out about upcoming vacancies. Here are a few of the larger rental property management companies in the Portland area:
- **Alliance Properties**, 503-350-1200, www.allianceproperties.net
- **American Property Management**, 503-284-2147, www.apmportland.com
- **Bluestone & Hockley**, 503-222-3800, www.bluestonehockley.com
- **Guardian Real Estate Services**, 503-802-3600, www.gres.com
- **Performance Properties**, 503-635-0099, www.ppirentals.com
- **Residential Property Management**, 503-245-8022, www.rpmpdx.com

PET-FRIENDLY RENTALS

Many landlords refuse to rent to tenants with pets, or at least with certain types of pets. (It's easier to find a landlord who will accept a cat or small dog than one who is willing to deal with your trio of Great Danes.) The **Oregon Humane Society** maintains an online list of pet-friendly rentals (www.oregonhumane.org/services/pet_friendly_rentals.asp); **Portland Pooch** has an online database of dog-friendly apartments (http://www.portlandpooch.com/directory/housing.htm). If your landlord allows pets, you will probably have to pay an additional deposit and/or a non-refundable pet fee based on the kind, number, and size of your animals.

SUBLETS AND SHARING

If you're having trouble finding a long-term place to live, or if there will be a significant gap between your arrival date and the date you can move into new digs, you may want to consider taking a short-term sublet. Sublets are most often available during the summer, but with luck you can find one at any time of year. Remember, however, that most leases say that a tenant can sublet only with the permission of the landlord. The original tenant generally remains responsible for unpaid rent and damage done to the apartment by the subtenant. If you're looking for a truly short-term situation, check out the **Temporary Lodgings** chapter.

If you're on your own, renting a room in an established group house can be a great way to get acquainted with the city without spending a whole lot on rent. Sometimes a group will get together and find a home, but more often one or two people will rent a house and then seek roommates through advertising or word-of-mouth referrals. The newspapers listed above (particularly *Willamette Week*) list ads for both sublet and sharing situations, as does **Craigslist** (www.portland. craigslist.org). (Craigslist also has a "housing wanted" category, if you're feeling proactive and lucky.)

While perusing ads for house sharing situations, keep in mind that "420 friendly" (a popular term in Portland listings) means that members of the household indulge in recreational marijuana use (or at least don't mind those who do). If that's not your scene, you should probably avoid responding to such ads.

MICRO APARTMENTS AND TINY HOUSES

If the high cost of rental housing has got you down, and you lead a reasonably ascetic existence and don't suffer from claustrophobia, you might consider a micro apartment (200 to 300 square feet or less, usually sharing a kitchen with other units) or tiny house or accessory dwelling unit (ADU). Several micro apartment buildings, which pack up to 50 or more individual units into a lot big enough for one or two houses, have risen in Portland since 2013. While the rent on a micro apartment is below the average rent for a studio, the per-square-foot cost can be much higher. So-called "tiny houses" or ADUs, which range from 800 square feet or so down to the size of a garden shed, are typically located in the back- or side-yard of an existing home. The attributes of tiny houses (other than size) vary tremendously; some ADUs are beautiful architect-designed structures, some are converted shipping containers, and others are ramshackle firetraps. Before agreeing to move into a tiny house, at a minimum make sure it meets health and safety standards. (Avoid dwellings powered by daisy-chained extension cords, for example.) Obviously, these living situations are not for everyone, but they can work well for the right person.

CHECKING IT OUT

You're on your way to the day's first rental appointment, you haven't had breakfast, the old college friends you're staying with keep quoting Ben Franklin ("Guests, like fish, begin to smell after three days"), your back is aching from a bad night's sleep on their decade-old futon, and 20 other people are waiting outside the prospective apartment when you drive up. You panic, take a quick glance around, like what you see, and grab an application. Three months later, you wonder how you landed in such a dump.

To avoid this scenario, tour each apartment with a clear idea of what you want. Consider making a checklist of specific things to look for; besides your personal musts and must-nots, here are a few specific questions you might want to keep in mind (or even write down ahead of time) to avoid aggravation later:

- If you're looking at an apartment, is it on the first floor? If so, does it have burglar bars? Can you open the bars from the inside in an emergency?
- Are the appliances clean and in working order? Do the stove's burners work? How about the oven? Does the kitchen sink have one or two basins? Is there sufficient counter and shelf space?
- Do the windows open, close, and lock? Do the windows, particularly the bedroom windows, face a busy street or noisy area?
- Are there enough closets or other storage areas? Are the closets big enough to accommodate your belongings? In an apartment building, is there secure storage elsewhere in the building, and is it free? If you have a bike, is there a secure place to store it overnight?
- Do the faucets and shower heads have adequate water pressure?
- Are there enough outlets for all your plug-in electronics and appliances? (In older buildings it is common to have only one or two outlets per room.) Is there a working phone and/or cable jack in the room where you plan to put a modem? If you plan to sign up for cable television, are there cable jacks in the rooms where you would watch TV?
- Does the building have a washer and dryer? If not, is there a laundromat nearby?
- If you have a car, is there off-street parking? Does it cost extra? Is there enough? Where do guests park? If parking is on-street, is parking easy to find? It's best to check out on-street parking in the evening, when people are home from work.
- Is there convenient access to public transportation and grocery shopping? How late do buses run, and do they run on weekends?
- Do you feel comfortable outside? Will you feel safe here at night?
- If you are looking at a basement apartment, check to see if there are any water stains along the walls.
- Does it smell funny? Someone may have sprayed the apartment for bugs, or there may be a mildew problem.
- If you are responsible for paying for utilities (see "Rental Agreements" below), what is the heat source? Electric space heating can be much more expensive

than gas heat. How well-insulated does the house or apartment seem to be? Are the windows single-pane or double-pane?

Finally, make sure you can afford the rent, along with the cost of any utilities you are responsible for. If everything passes muster, be prepared to stake your claim without delay!

STAKING A CLAIM

When you view a unit, come prepared. Bring your checkbook. If you are coming from out of state, or even if you aren't, you may be required to provide a cashier's check or money order instead of a check. Have cash on hand in case you cannot get to the bank and need to purchase a money order from a convenience store or check-cashing outlet. Often, the first qualified person to show up with a deposit is the person who gets the apartment. (Make sure you get a receipt for any money you pay.) Know your social security number, and have ready access to your references—both credit and personal—and your bank account information. Employment information is useful; if you have secured a job but haven't started work, ask your new employer to write a letter on company letterhead verifying your start date and salary.

If you find the unit or house you've been looking for, remember that it isn't just the early bird that gets the worm: it can also be the polite worm, the well-dressed worm, or the worm with the highest bid. It won't hurt to mention casually that you don't have a dog, cat, or monkey, and that you don't smoke or play the drums (assuming these things are true). Feel free to rave about the unit and how great it feels; after all, landlords have feelings too. If there is a garden, mention that you love gardening and have a very green thumb. If you do have a pet, get references from former landlords praising its good behavior. Keep in mind that landlords can request only non-smokers, they can prohibit pets other than service animals, and they can bar you from having overnight guests for more than a certain number of nights per year. (The number of nights should be reasonably high; the intent of the clause is to prevent unauthorized occupants from moving in. If you think you'll have lots of visitors, watch out for rental agreements containing such a clause, as it may not bode well for your landlord-tenant relationship.)

Almost all landlords or property managers will require a security deposit, usually equal to a month's rent, which will be refunded to you (less any damages) when you move out. Some landlords charge application or credit check fees ranging from $10 to $40 as a way to discourage frivolous rental applications; the fee is sometimes credited toward your deposit if your application is approved. Consider that most landlords will want your net monthly earnings to be at least three times the monthly rent; if you have no earnings, you'll probably need to show that you have sufficient liquid assets to be able to pay the rent. Landlords who charge a screening fee must provide written information about what they screen for. Look at the information and decide whether you think you'll qualify *before* you pay the fee. If you're not sure, be honest up front, explain the situation, and ask the landlord or property manager if they think you'll qualify. If they say no, it might not be worth your money.

Once your rental application is approved, then it's time to sign a rental agreement.

TENANT/LANDLORD RELATIONS

RENTAL AGREEMENTS

In Oregon, a rental agreement does not have to be in writing unless it is a lease for a fixed term, but you would be foolish not to get an agreement in writing. Review the rental agreement carefully before you sign it, and make sure that you understand key terms, such as:

- How much is the rent? To whom should it be paid? When is it due? If your rent is late, what are the penalties?
- When can the landlord increase the rent, and by how much? How much notice is required?
- Who pays for utilities such as electricity, gas, and water?
- Is the tenancy for a fixed period, such as six months or a year, or is the rental term indefinite? What is the move-in date?
- What repairs or cleaning has the landlord agreed to complete before you move in?
- What is the policy on subletting?
- Is a parking spot included? How many? Do they cost extra?
- What is the policy on repairs or maintenance?
- What is the policy on pets, smoking, or overnight guests?
- Is renter's insurance mandatory?
- If you are renting a house, who is responsible for mowing the lawn and maintaining the landscaping?
- What non-refundable fees are charged (cleaning fee, pet fee, etc.), and what is the policy for return of the security deposit?

Don't assume that the terms are completely nonnegotiable; many landlords are willing to make reasonable minor changes to their standard rental agreements. Make sure you get a copy of every document relating to your rental agreement, and keep them somewhere safe.

The type of tenancy you have is particularly important. If you have a **month-to-month tenancy**, either party can end the tenancy with 30 days' written notice, and a landlord can generally increase the rent at will (again, with 30 days' notice). If you have a tenancy for a fixed term, you have a **lease**. Most leases also provide that the rent is fixed for the lease term. If you have a lease, a landlord generally cannot evict you except for cause (such as your unexcused failure to pay rent); at the same time, you may not breach the lease without good cause (such as the landlord's breach of a material term of the rental agreement), even if you have what you think is a really good reason, like buying a house or moving to Tokyo.

If you must break a lease for reasons you can't blame on the landlord, you should expect to take a financial hit. You could try to sublet the unit for the remainder of the lease term, but keep in mind that the rental agreement may not allow sublets or your landlord may not approve the proposed subtenant. (Landlords must use the same criteria for sublessors as they do for other tenants.) Failing that, at a minimum you will lose your security deposit. Depending on the amount of rent at stake—the time remaining in the lease multiplied by the amount per month—and whether your lease specifies a fee for breaking the lease, your landlord might not bother to sue. Even if there is no specified fee for breaking a lease, you could, in theory, be sued for the full amount of rent you would pay through the remainder of the lease term (or until someone new moves in); in practice, as long as it's a reasonably lively rental market, landlords seldom bother chasing down a leasebreaker for only one or two months' rent. Keep in mind, though, that your next rental application will ask for contact information for your most recent landlord, so you'll be much better off if you negotiate an amicable deal. (One way to placate a jilted landlord is to recruit a new tenant yourself, to save the landlord the expense of advertising the vacancy.) If you need to leave before your lease expires, you should consult an attorney; the Oregon State Bar's Lawyer Referral Service (503-684-3763, 800-452-7636, www.osbar.org/public/ris/ris.html#referral) can provide referrals.

If possible, do a walk-through inspection of the property before you move in (or immediately after you take possession) to document the condition of the place. Get a copy of the inspection for your records.

LANDLORD-TENANT RIGHTS AND RESPONSIBILITIES

In the landlord-tenant relationship, both sides have rights and responsibilities. Some are obvious—the tenant is generally obliged to pay rent and not trash the place, and the landlord has to keep the building up to code. Some are less universally known: for example, contrary to what some renters (and landlords) believe, a landlord may not enter your apartment whenever he or she wishes, but usually has to give you 24 hours' notice (except in case of emergency). The following organizations provide a wealth of useful information about landlord-tenant issues:

- The **Community Alliance of Tenants**, 2710 NE 14th Ave, 503-460-9702, www. oregoncat.org, maintains a comprehensive database of information for tenants, and renter's rights information and handouts are available online. If you have a problem with your landlord, visit the website. If you can't find the information you're looking for, call the renter's rights hotline at 503-288-0130.
- **Legal Aid Services of Oregon provides a** legal information website (www. oregonlawhelp.org) with a useful section on housing law.

- The **Oregon State Bar** runs the Tel-Law service (503-620-3000, 800-452-4776), which offers basic recorded messages about legal subjects (including landlord-tenant law); this information is also available online at www.osbar.org/public/ legalinfo/tenant.html.

RENTER'S INSURANCE

Get it. The landlord's insurance generally covers damage to the building, not to your personal possessions. Renter's insurance provides relatively inexpensive protection against theft, water damage, fire, and in many cases, personal liability. Not only is renter's insurance a good idea (unless perhaps the total value of your possessions is less than the deductible), but some landlords require it. Most insurance companies that sell homeowner's insurance also sell renter's insurance. The **Oregon Insurance Division** provides useful consumer information about renter's insurance on its website (www.insurance.oregon.gov/DCBS/insurance/gethelp/ homeowner/Pages/home-rent.aspx), or you can call 503-947-7984 or 888-877-4894 and ask for a free copy of the Division's *Consumer Guide to Homeowner and Tenant Insurance* (also available online at www.oregon.gov/DCBS/insurance/ gethelp/Documents/).

BUYING

For most people, a home purchase is the biggest and most daunting transaction they will ever be involved in. Not only does it involve a pile of money and paperwork, but finding and buying a house, condo, or townhome is a complex and time-consuming process. Fortunately, the resources listed here—and a host of professionals in the area—can help you at every step: calculating your budget, choosing the right home in the right neighborhood, getting a mortgage, protecting your investment with adequate insurance, moving in, and making repairs and improvements. The **U.S. Department of Housing and Urban Development** has a useful online guide to buying a home at www.hud.gov/buying/index.cfm.

Many people move to Portland intending to buy a home, but find that the cost of real estate is just too high. Newcomers can avoid sticker shock by thoroughly researching home prices and neighborhoods before they arrive, and by keeping an open mind about the types of housing and the locations they are willing to consider. For instance, maybe you have your heart set on a big Craftsman-style house in the Irvington neighborhood, but you could live with a mid-century ranch in Milwaukie that's in your price range. Or perhaps that condo in the Pearl is way too expensive, but there's a townhome in Hillsboro that you can afford (and hey, you'll be working out in Washington County anyway). It's important to determine your priorities ahead of time, but be flexible (and realistic) when possible.

Homes in Portland come in many forms, from traditional single-family detached houses, usually with a yard of some kind, to various multiple ownership situations, primarily condos and townhomes. To a surprising extent, Portland has traditionally been a city of **single-family houses**, at least outside of downtown and its immediate environs. While infill development and duplex-ization over the years has made the generalization less true than it was, it is still easy to find houses in close-in neighborhoods (although they are no longer cheap by any measure). **Condominiums** are relatively new to Portland, and first became popular in Washington County and other outlying areas. More recently, a boom in high-end condo tower and "loft" construction in places like the Pearl District, the South Waterfront, and some of the main Eastside arterials, combined with the scramble to convert apartments to condos when real estate prices skyrocketed in the early and mid-2000s, means that condos are much more common than they used to be. When you buy a condominium, you are buying a unit within a larger complex; the complex is jointly owned and maintained, but the unit is yours to use, sell, or (usually) rent. (Keep in mind that monthly condo fees can be substantial.) In a **townhome**, another widespread form of multiple ownership, you own your unit and the land under it but you share one or more walls with adjacent attached units. Many townhomes have small back yards, while condos at most tend to offer decks or small patios.

Co-operative apartments are not common in Portland, but the area is home to an increasing number of **cohousing** projects. In these projects, which are sometimes called "intentional communities," each household owns its own unit but shares communal space such as a "common house." Cohousing residents often prepare and eat meals together and share gardening and other general maintenance responsibilities. Currently, there are five existing or developing cohousing projects in Portland. For more information about cohousing or for a list of locations, contact the Cohousing Association of the United States (www.cohousing. org) or the Northwest Intentional Communities Association (www.nica.ic.org).

POTENTIAL PITFALLS

When scouting for a home, be aware of the wide range of potential pitfalls. Not only will you have expenses for ongoing maintenance or necessary repairs (some of which a home inspection should uncover), but there may be issues specific to the property you're interested in. Many older homes feature disused underground storage tanks, which can be expensive to decommission. Some properties lie within conservation zones where regulations limit the owner's ability to build a deck or addition, for example. Other homes may have historic designations that affect remodeling options. Many homes in Southwest Portland and the outer Eastside neighborhoods are on unimproved streets, and the property owner is responsible for making (and paying for) repairs from the property line to the centerline of the public right-of-way. While a good real estate broker can help identify some of these issues, they should be on your personal radar screen before you get your heart set on a particular home.

Property taxes are another expense to consider. Oregon's unique property tax system makes it impossible to estimate property taxes based on market value alone; Washington's system is a bit more straightforward, but you should always check with your county assessor to find out the current property taxes on a specific property. (See **Money Matters** for information about property taxes.) Certain neighborhoods are **tax abatement areas** in which homebuyers, builders, or rehabbers pay reduced property taxes for a period of 10 years. Your real estate broker should be able to tell you which neighborhoods currently qualify. And speaking of taxes and other expenses…

GETTING YOUR FINANCIAL HOUSE IN ORDER

Assuming you aren't fortunate enough to be able to buy a house outright, you'll need to arrange a mortgage loan. It's a good idea to get pre-approved before looking for houses in earnest. Some sellers will not seriously consider an offer from a buyer who is not pre-approved, and the pre-approval process gives you a good idea of how much you can reasonably afford to spend on a house.

When you're ready to get pre-approved, go prepared with relevant financial documents and check your credit report in advance to make sure it is accurate. You can get one free copy of your credit report each year from each of the three major credit bureaus; visit www.annualcreditreport.com or call 877-322-8228. You are also entitled to a free credit report if you have been denied credit based on the contents of your credit report within the 30 days before your request. The national credit bureaus are:

- **Equifax**, 800-685-1111, www.equifax.com
- **Experian**, 888-397-3742, www.experian.com
- **TransUnion**, 800-888-4213, www.transunion.com

You might also want to check your FICO® score, the number that most lenders use to determine how creditworthy you are, and thus what interest rate you can get on your loan. The FICO score is available from Fair Isaac, the score's creators and overlords, at www.myfico.com. You may also be offered the chance to buy your score when you obtain a credit report. If the idea of having to pay to look at your own information—information that someone else is already profiting from—sticks in your craw, consider signing up for a credit monitoring service with a free 30-day trial period; you can usually get your credit score when you sign up. (Just remember to cancel before the free trial ends.)

It may be most convenient to get your pre-approval through a local bank, but shop around before you sign for your loan. While many banks offer competitive interest rates, mortgage brokers can often match or beat their best offers. Make sure you ask about closing costs, loan origination fees, and points when comparing interest rates. Of course, virtually no lender's loans are unique. Even in today's post-bubble environment of more stringent mortgage requirements, most lenders offer a variety of fixed-rate and adjustable-rate mortgage products and participate in government-insured VA and FHA loan programs, both of which allow for low down payments and have flexible qualifying guidelines.

If you need assistance with mortgage costs, several unique local resources are available. The **Portland Housing Center** (3233 NE Sandy Boulevard, 503-282-7744, www.portlandhousingcenter.org) provides homebuyer education and offers financial assistance to eligible buyers (generally, first-time buyers with below-median incomes). **Proud Ground** (5288 N Interstate Ave, 503-493-0293, www.proudground.org), formerly the Portland Community Land Trust, helps first-time homebuyers whose incomes are below the local median and who can't *quite* afford a house buy homes below the market rate.

ONLINE RESOURCES—MORTGAGES

The following sites might be useful in researching interest rates and loan programs:
- **Bankrate**, www.bankrate.com, allows you to compare mortgage and home equity loan interest rates, and offers several online mortgage and housing calculators.
- **Freddie Mac**, www.freddiemac.com, offers information on current mortgage averages.
- **Interest.com**, www.interest.com, includes advice for first-time home buyers, suggestions for finding the lowest interest rate, and current interest rate comparisons.

In addition, many real estate-focused sites such as **Zillow** (see "Househunting Resources" below) provide information on mortgages and lenders.

HOUSE HUNTING

WORKING WITH A REAL ESTATE AGENT

When an agent who has listed a home shows it to you, he or she is representing the seller, not you. If you want an agent who will act on your behalf, you will need to hire a buyer's agent. There is no substitute for the advice of a knowledgeable local real estate agent, and there usually is no downside to working with one when you're buying a home. (The buyer's broker's commission almost always comes out of the selling broker's commission; the exception is if you buy a property that is for sale by owner and the owner refuses to pay a commission to your agent.)

Probably the best way to find an agent is through a referral from a friend or co-worker. Failing that, you might consider agents who seem to have a lot of listings in your neighborhood of choice. Most agencies claim to serve the entire Portland area, but individual agents often specialize (or purport to specialize) in certain neighborhoods or in certain kinds of homes, and are not shy about advertising their specialties in community newspapers and on bus benches. While neighborhood knowledge is important, it's also important that your agent be someone you trust, who knows the market, and who listens to you. A good agent will interview you in detail about your needs and interests—not just your preferred price range, but every detail of your lifestyle. Are you planning to have any (or more) children? Do you need space in a basement to set up a media room, a model railroad, or an evil genius lair? Do you want to plant a garden, or would you prefer a small yard that requires little maintenance? Are you planning to commute by bike? The more information you can provide, the easier it will be for your agent to find a home that's a good match.

HOUSEHUNTING RESOURCES

In addition to the standard places for classified advertising listed in the "Renting" section above—newspapers, Craigslist, and the like—a wide range of online resources target prospective homebuyers. Most agents will send lists of properties to you by email as soon as they come on the market. In addition, or even before you decide to use an agent, you might find the following websites to be useful househunting resources:

- **Zillow**, www.zillow.com, purports to be able to give a market value for any house (based on recent sales in the neighborhood and the characteristics of the specific property) that is generally within 20% of the real market value. While the market values should be taken with a large grain of salt—a 20% margin of error on a $300,000 house represents $60,000, after all—the data on comparable sales in the target neighborhood are invaluable.
- **Trulia**, www.trulia.com, like Zillow, provides estimated market values for specific properties. It is useful to compare prices on both sites, as estimated values for the same property can differ significantly.
- **RMLS**, www.rmls.com, is the multiple listing service for the Portland area. The site includes a searchable database of most homes for sale; you can search by price, ZIP code, number of bedrooms, etc., but many search options—such as the list of "green" and energy efficient features—are only available to RMLS members (generally real estate brokers). Many real estate brokerages provide similar search functionality on their own websites.
- If you prefer to buy a home without an agent—or at least to buy from an unrepresented seller—check out sites that specialize in for sale by owner listings, including **HomesbyOwner.com** (www.homesbyowner.com/portland_or/), **FSBO.com** (www.fsbo.com), and **Owners.com** (www.owners.com).

PURCHASE AGREEMENTS AND CLOSING

A purchase agreement is a legally binding contract between the buyer and seller that states the price and all terms of the sale. Although most Oregon brokers start with a standard form, the purchase agreement is the most negotiable and variable document produced in the homebuying process. The purchase agreement is also the place where you, the buyer, can attach contingencies that protect you from being legally bound by the purchase agreement if, for example, the house you are buying does not pass its mechanical and structural inspection, the seller is unable to give you possession by a certain date, or you cannot obtain mortgage financing. Neither Oregon nor Washington regulates purchase agreements, but both states require sellers to provide certain property disclosures and a lead-paint disclosure.

Typically, once both parties have signed the purchase agreement, you will hire an independent home inspector or engineer to examine the foundation and overall structure, the HVAC and plumbing systems, and the roof. Also request that the inspector check for mold, particularly if the roof has been replaced recently or if there are signs of water damage in the basement. Your lender will appraise the house, but only to determine if it's worth enough to secure the loan.

If all goes well, eventually you'll close. Closings traditionally take place in the conference room of a title company, where you'll be asked to sign the tallest pile of papers you've ever seen. How do you avoid problems? First, schedule your closing at least six weeks from the date your purchase agreement was signed, then keep in contact with your lender to see if additional information is required. The week you close, your lender should send you a copy of the completed Settlement Statement, or HUD-1 form. (If the lender doesn't send it, ask for one. You have the legal right to see this form one business day before closing.) Compare the Settlement Statement to the good faith estimate of closing costs your loan officer gave you when you applied for the loan. The actual closing costs should not differ dramatically from the estimated costs. If they do, you may be getting scammed, although some costs, such as insurance premiums and the loan origination fee, can only be nailed down after your loan is approved because they are based on the amount of your loan and the final value of the property. It's a good idea to read the closing documents in advance; there won't be time at closing, and if any clauses cause you pause you'll have time to ask your lender about them or check with an attorney. Finally, make sure you bring the necessary papers—identification, proof of homeowner insurance, etc.—and a cashier's check to pay the balance of your down payment and unpaid closing costs.

INSURANCE

Your lender will require you to buy **homeowner insurance** to protect its investment (your home). Be sure the policy you choose adequately covers the house, its contents, and all outbuildings. A basic homeowner policy usually also includes liability insurance to protect you if someone is injured on your property, and living expense coverage that will pay for you to live elsewhere while the home is repaired or rebuilt. You may also want to purchase **earthquake coverage**, which most homeowner policies do not include. If your prospective home is in a floodplain, you'll need to purchase flood insurance from the **National Flood Insurance Program** (888-379-9531, www.floodsmart.gov).

You'll also need title insurance, which protects the lender in case your legal title to the property is faulty. (It doesn't protect you, though, so you may want to buy an owner's title policy. In Portland, it is usually customary for the seller to pay the premium on a buyer's title policy.) If you are putting down less than 20% as a down payment, you may also need mortgage insurance, which is required by many lenders as well as the FHA to cover them in case you default on the loan.

For advice on homeowner insurance from the **Oregon Insurance Division**, call 503-947-7984 or 888-877-4894 and ask for a free copy of the Division's *Consumer Guide to Homeowner and Tenant Insurance* (also available online at www.oregon.gov//DCBS/insurance/gethelp/Documents/).

WORKING WITH CONTRACTORS

If you intend to remodel or significantly alter the home you buy, you might want to enlist the services of an architect or structural engineer, who can give you a general sense of what options might be available for a particular house before you commit to a purchase. Once you buy a house, you'll face the problems of finding a reputable contractor, getting the work done in a timely and competent fashion, and paying for the remodel.

Accomplishing all these tasks can be a daunting proposition. It is not unheard-of for contractors to abscond with homeowners' money, and since Oregon currently requires most residential contractors to have only $15,000 in bond coverage, you could end up holding the bag—the empty bag that your money used to be in before you paid it to your contractor.

To help avoid this unpleasant scenario, the Oregon Attorney General and the **Oregon Construction Contractors Board** (CCB) suggest you take the following steps when dealing with any contractor:

• Check out the contractor in advance. It's always best to get recommendations from friends and family members who have had a good experience. Even a good recommendation, however, is no substitute for research. All contractors must be licensed, bonded, and insured. Check the contractor's license and history of complaints at the CCB's consumer website, www.hirealicensedcontractor.com, or call 503-378-4621. (In Washington, contact the state Department of Labor and Industries, 800-647-0982, https://secure.lni.wa.gov/verify/.) The Oregon Attorney General warns, "A devious contractor may tell you that he or she is licensed or may give you a false or outdated CCB number, so make sure to check on your own." Also check with the state Department of Justice or a nominally independent source such as the Better Business Bureau or Angie's List (888-888-LIST, www.angieslist.com). (See "Consumer Protection" in Helpful Services for more suggestions.) If the contractor provides references, check them.

• Get multiple written estimates. The Attorney General suggests getting at least three estimates. Make sure the bids are in writing. Don't automatically choose the lowest bid; make sure you compare the materials specified and the scope of the work, and be suspicious of unrealistically low bids.

- Get a written contract. Once you've selected a contractor, put your agreement in writing. Make sure the contract states what work is to be done, when it is to be done, and how much it will cost, and that sufficient details are included: "build addition, $80,000" won't cut it. Try to limit how much you have to pay upfront; you may be able to negotiate payments over the course of a long project once the contractor has completed certain phases. Don't sign the contract unless you understand it completely, and make sure all changes are in writing.

Even if you follow these steps scrupulously, you might still get scammed—there are no guarantees—but you'll substantially reduce your vulnerability.

BUILDING YOUR OWN HOME

If you dream of building your own home, you'll face a scarcity of large buildable lots within the urban growth boundary. In Oregon, you cannot simply buy a five-acre farm field in the exurbs and plunk down a house. The Portland area has a relative abundance of infill lots, although many of these lots are quite small or narrow and/or located on steep slopes. Keep in mind that building a huge house on a small city lot may not endear you to your new neighbors. You could also investigate doing a teardown of an existing, presumably dilapidated, house. If you must build a giant house on acreage, your best options are the rural exception zones outside the urban growth boundary in Oregon, or outer Clark County in Washington; in either case, be prepared for a *long* commute if you work in Portland.

EFORE YOU START YOUR NEW LIFE IN PORTLAND, YOU AND YOUR worldly possessions have to get here. Accomplishing that task can be expensive or cheap, complicated or simple, depending on how much stuff you've accumulated, where you're coming from, and how much of the heavy lifting you're willing to do yourself.

TRUCK RENTAL

If you plan to move your own belongings, you can simply rent a vehicle and hit the road. Look online or in the Yellow Pages under "Truck Rental" and then check the Web or call around for quotes. Even if you're dealing with a nationwide company, you might try calling the location nearest you to check pricing and availability. (Keep in mind that some of the national truck rental companies offer significant discounts for reserving a vehicle online.) If you just need a minivan or a small trailer, get quotes from a regular car rental company (listed in the **Transportation** chapter).

If you are comparing different moving options, factor in the cost of fuel— which, for a cross-country move, can equal or exceed the cost of the basic truck rental—insurance, accommodation, and food. If you need to move a car, also consider whether you prefer to tow the car (most truck rental companies offer trailers or other car-towing options), have it shipped by truck, or have someone else drive it. Many companies, not all of them reputable, will arrange shipment of your car for you. Directory sites such as **movecars.com** list companies that arrange for auto transport. The Federal Motor Safety Administration (FMCSA) has advised consumers of a dramatic increase in complaints against auto transporters and auto transport brokers, so (as always) research and caution are in order. To check on complaints against a specific auto transporter, or to file one, call the FMCSA at 888-368-7238 or visit www.protectyourmove.gov.

If you need a truck during peak moving season (between May and September) be sure to reserve one at least a month in advance, especially for one-way rentals. If you can, consider timing your move for the middle, rather than the end, of the month, because demand is lower then.

The following four national truck rental companies have multiple locations in the Portland area:

- **Budget**, 800-455-1332, www.budgettruck.com
- **Penske**, 888-996-5415, www.pensketruckrental.com
- **Ryder**, 800-297-9337, www.ryder.com
- **U-Haul**, 800-468-4285, www.uhaul.com

Once you're on the road, keep in mind that your rental truck may be a tempting target for thieves. If you must park the truck overnight or for more than a couple of hours, try to find a well-lit parking spot where you can keep an eye on it, and don't leave anything valuable in the cab.

COMMERCIAL FREIGHT CARRIERS AND CONTAINER-BASED MOVERS

If you don't want to drive a truck yourself, but you also don't want to hire a full-service mover, there's a third option: you can hire a commercial freight carrier to deliver a trailer or container to your home. You pack and load as much of it as you need, and the carrier delivers your trailer or container to your destination. In some cases, this option can be cheaper than renting and driving your own truck, especially when you consider the cost of fuel. **U-Pack Moving** (877-453-7274, www.upack.com) uses commercial 28-foot freight trailers. ABF charges by the linear foot, and you pay only for the linear feet you use (subject to a minimum charge). When you've finished loading, you install a plywood bulkhead; ABF fills the remaining space with freight, which is unloaded before the trailer is delivered to your new home.

U-Pack, **PODS** (877-770-7637, www.pods.com), **Door-to-Door Storage and Moving** (888-366-7222, www.doortodoor.com), **United Mayflower** (877-670-6061, www.unitedmayflower.com), **U-Haul**, and several other companies offer container-based moves. In this type of move, the carrier delivers plywood, metal, or fiberglass cubes or other containers to your home. You can generally take a few days to load the containers; when you're done loading, the company picks up the containers, transfers them to flatbed trucks, moves them to your destination city, and delivers them to your new home. You generally pay only to transport the containers you actually use, and, unlike a truck, the containers can be placed in storage at either end of the journey. However, a set of containers has a smaller storage capacity than a large truck, so this option may not work for people with many rooms full of belongings to move. In addition, some unusually long or tall pieces of furniture—grandfather clocks, for example—may not fit inside certain types of containers; if you have to move such items, ask the company for its containers' *interior* dimensions (as well as the dimensions of the "door") before you commit.

MOVERS

Probably the best way to find a mover is through a personal recommendation. Absent a reference from a trusted friend or relative, you can start with a search engine or the Yellow Pages. For long-distance moves, the **American Moving and Storage Association** (www.moving.org) keeps a list of certified movers that honor the organization's code of conduct.

Once you've identified potential movers, *do your homework*. The federal government eliminated the Interstate Commerce Commission in 1995. Currently, the Federal Motor Carrier Safety Administration (FMCSA), an agency of the Department of Transportation, is charged with regulating interstate moves, but it has only a handful of full-time investigators and has no authority to intervene on a consumer's behalf during a move. States do not have the authority to regulate interstate moving companies, and since the federal government basically won't, you're really pretty much on your own in your dealings with an interstate mover. Understandably, the interstate moving industry has degenerated into a largely unregulated free-for-all with thousands of unhappy, ripped-off customers. In fact, the Council of Better Business Bureaus reports that complaints against moving and storage companies rank near the top of all complaints received by their bureaus every year.

Watch out for shakedown schemes that begin with a lowball bid off the Internet and end with the mover holding your belongings hostage for a high cash ransom. Despite the fact that federal law says that movers cannot charge more than 10% over any written estimate, it is not unusual for unscrupulous movers to charge you several times their written estimates—and with your possessions in their possession, you may find yourself paying anyway, since companies that operate this way also won't tell you where they're holding your stuff.

For an informative—but potentially terror-inducing—read, check out the **MovingScam** website (www.movingscam.com). MovingScam.com provides sound, unbiased consumer education and is committed to bettering consumer protections in the moving industry. The site features a host of useful articles and recent moving news, and maintains a list of endorsed movers and reviews of moving experiences. Its message boards are tended by dedicated volunteers who respond promptly and knowledgeably to moving-related queries, free of charge. The FMCSA operates a similar website (www.protectyourmove.gov). This website provides one-click checking to make sure that an interstate mover is properly registered and insured. (You can get this information by phone at 800-832-5660.) The site also includes news of recent criminal investigations and convictions, offers links to local Better Business Bureaus, consumer protection agencies, state attorneys general, and state moving associations, and maintains a moving fraud prevention checklist. In general, consumer advocates and attorneys general around the country urge you to take precautions before hiring a mover by doing the following things:

- Make sure the mover is licensed and insured. If the companies you're interested in appear to be federally licensed, the next step is to contact the Better Business Bureau (www.bbb.org) and find out if the Bureau has a record of any complaints against them.
- Get several written estimates from companies that have actually sent a sales representative to your home to do a visual inspection of the goods to be moved. Don't worry about cost here; estimates should always be free. Don't do business with a company that charges for an estimate or wants to give you an estimate over the telephone. Do, however, make sure each company is giving you an estimate for approximately the same poundage of items to be moved, and for the same services. Finally, only accept estimates that are written on a document that contains the company's name, address, phone number, and signature of the salesperson. Note that estimates can be either binding or non-binding. A binding estimate guarantees the total cost of the move based upon the quantities and services shown on the estimate. A non-binding estimate is what your mover believes the cost will be, based upon the estimated weight of the shipment and the extra services requested. With a non-binding estimate the final charges will be based upon the services provided and the actual weight of your shipment. If you accept a mover's non-binding estimate, you must be prepared to pay up to 10% more than the estimated charges at delivery.
- Remember that price, while important, isn't everything, especially when you're entrusting all of your worldly possessions to strangers. Choose a mover you feel comfortable with.
- Ask for references—then check them.
- Be sure you understand the terms of the moving contract. Get everything in writing, including the mover's liability to you for breakage or loss. Consider whether to buy additional replacement insurance to cover loss or damage. Check your homeowner's or renter's insurance policy to see what, if any, coverage you may already have for your belongings while they are in transit. If the answer is "none," ask your insurer if you can add coverage for your move. You can purchase coverage through your mover. A mover's coverage, however, is normally based on the weight of the items being insured, not on their value. If you want to cover the actual value of your belongings, you will need to purchase "full value" or "full replacement" insurance. Though it's expensive, it's worth it—and you can lower the cost by increasing your deductible. Better yet, consider packing and moving irreplaceable, fragile or sentimental items, documents, and jewelry yourself. That way you can avoid the headache and heartache of possible loss or breakage of your most valuable possessions.
- Compile a detailed inventory of all items shipped and note their condition when they left your house. Take pictures of your important items, and be present for both the loading and unloading of your things. Since checking every item as it comes off the truck is probably impossible when you're moving the contents of an

entire house, write "subject to further inspection for concealed loss or damage" on the moving contract to allow for damage you may discover as you unpack.

- File a written claim with the mover immediately if any loss or damage occurs— and keep a copy of your claim, as well as all the other paperwork related to your move. If your claim is not resolved within a reasonable time, file complaints with the Better Business Bureau and appropriate authorities, as well. (See "Consumer Complaints—Movers," below.)

If you've followed the steps above and succeeded in hiring a reputable mover:

- Listen to what the movers say; they are professionals and can give you expert advice about packing and preparing. Also, be ready for the truck on both ends— don't make the movers wait. Understand, too, that there may be delays caused by factors—adverse weather, for example—that are beyond a carrier's control, and your belongings may not get to you at the time, or on the day, promised.
- Treat your movers well, especially the ones loading your stuff on and off the truck. Offer to buy them lunch, and tip them if they do a good job.
- Be prepared to pay the full moving bill upon delivery. The mover may require cash or a cashier's check. Some carriers will take VISA and MasterCard but it is a good idea to get written confirmation that you will be permitted to pay with a credit card; the delivering driver may not be aware of this arrangement and may demand cash.

INTRASTATE MOVES

If you are using a mover for a move that is wholly within Washington or Oregon, follow all the steps above for dealing with interstate movers: make sure they are licensed and insured, check with the Better Business Bureau, check estimates, check contracts, and check references. The regulatory entity for moves that start and end in Oregon is the **Oregon Department of Transportation, Motor Carrier Transportation Division** (MCTD) (503-378-5849, www.oregon.gov/ODOT/MCT/). The counterpart agency in Washington is the **Washington Utilities and Transportation Commission** (360-664-1160, 888-333-9882 for consumer complaints and information, www.wutc.wa.gov).

A complete list of state-authorized movers in Oregon is available from the MCTD at www.oregon.gov/ODOT/MCT/MOVERS.shtml. You can find out whether an Oregon moving company is licensed by calling 503-378-5985. The list of Washington-authorized moving companies is posted at www.wutc.wa.gov/consumers/movers/; follow the link to "Lookup Permitted Moving Companies" or call the commission at 360-664-1222 to ask if a specific company is registered.

PACKING AND ORGANIZING

Don't wait until the last minute to think about packing. You'll need plenty of boxes, tape, and packing material—probably more than you think. Moving and truck rental companies sell boxes, as do most office supply stores, but most grocery stores or liquor stores will let you scrounge some empty boxes. For foam "peanuts," bubble wrap, and other materials to protect fragile items, look in the Yellow Pages under "Packaging Materials"; if you have some especially fragile and valuable items, you might also want to look under "Packaging Service." Post-move listings on Craigslist (www.craigslist.org) often offer excess boxes and packing materials in the "free" category.

LOADING AND UNLOADING

If you are driving a rental truck or using a freight carrier, but you are disinclined to load and unload the truck yourself, many moving companies and independent businesses offer "pack and load" services. Companies that provide these services generally charge by the person/hour, with a minimum charge. (Call around, as hourly rates and minimums vary tremendously.) The same cautions that apply to hiring full-service movers apply equally to pack-and-loaders: try to get a recommendation from a trusted source, make sure the company is insured, and always check references. Beware of companies that use inexperienced temporary workers who may not be especially careful with either your belongings or your walls, and who may not pack your items securely in the truck—a fact which you may not discover until you unpack your crushed possessions at the end of your journey.

Because packing and loading do not involve the actual transport of goods, the businesses that provide these services are often unregulated. A 2003 Oregon law required pack-and-loaders in the state to have insurance and to register with the Oregon Department of Transportation, but 2009 legislation exempted pack-and-loaders who do not provide or operate a moving vehicle (or act as an agent for someone who does). Non-exempt pack-and-loaders are regulated as moving companies. Washington does not currently require pack-and-load companies to register with the state.

Whatever moving method you plan to use, make sure you'll have a spot at both ends of your move to park the truck or to place the trailer or containers. Some cities require a permit to park a truck or place containers on a public street; others don't require a permit, but will issue one so that you can reserve a parking place for your moving truck. You can get such a permit from the city of Portland's Office of Transportation, 503-823-7365, www.portlandonline.com/transportation (follow the link for "Get a Permit"), for a nominal fee.) If you are moving to or from a large apartment building, check with the manager to see if you need to reserve a time to load or unload.

STORAGE

Most communities have commercial storage facilities where you can rent a secure, climate-controlled self-storage locker—your own little warehouse—to keep items that don't fit in your home or that you only use occasionally. These can also be convenient places to store your belongings temporarily while you find a new home or while you prepare to sell your old one, and many have moving vans for rent. Find a storage facility online by using a search engine or searching online yellow pages (such as www.dexknows.com or www.yp.com) under "Household and Commercial Storage." Alternatively, check the tangible Yellow Pages under "Storage—Household & Commercial." Keep in mind that demand for storage surges in the prime moving months of May through September, so try not to wait until the last minute to look for a storage unit.

If you plan to open your storage locker only twice—the day you fill it and the day you empty it—then consider a suburban location that will be cheaper than facilities closer to the heart of a city. If you need more frequent access to your locker, location will matter, and so will access fees. Also note that some storage facilities only allow daytime access. Others have gates that only open when a car or truck triggers a weight-sensitive mechanism, which can be a problem if you don't own a car. Ask about billing and security deposits, too, and don't be late with payments: if you fall behind, the storage company will not dump your stuff on your doorstep—they'll auction it off.

Mobile or modular storage is more convenient, and more expensive, than self-storage. The company delivers a large container to your door, you load it, and the company hauls it away until you call for it. This can save you a lot of time and effort—it's one less round of unpacking, re-packing, and transport—but it's not good for easy access.

Portland and its suburbs are awash in storage possibilities. Your best bet for finding storage is to focus on a geographic location and then explore options within that general area. The biggest storage company in the Portland area is **Public Storage**, with more than 40 locations in the city and suburbs. Call 800-688-8057 or visit www.publicstorage.com for locations and quotes. Here are a few other storage companies that you can contact to start your search:

- **Downtown Self Storage,** 1305 NW Davis St, 503-388-4060, and 1304 NW Johnson St, 503-388-4061, www.downtownselfstorage.com, has two locations in the Pearl District.
- **Northwest Self Storage,** www.nwselfstorage.com, is a network of independent storage companies with more than two dozen locations in the greater Portland area; their website provides links and contact information for dozens of storage facilities in Oregon and Washington.
- **U-Haul Self-Storage,** 800-468-4285, www.uhaul.com, has several storage facilities in the area; U-Haul sometimes offers free storage for one month with a one-way truck rental.

CONSUMER COMPLAINTS—MOVERS

To file a complaint about an Oregon mover, contact the **Motor Carrier Transportation Division** (3930 Fairview Industrial Dr NE, Salem, 97302, 503-378-5849, www.oregon.gov/ODOT/MCT). For a bad move within Washington, contact the consumer affairs staff of the **Washington Utilities and Transportation Commission** at 888-333-9882, or visit www.wutc.wa.gov/fileacomplaint to use their online complaint form.

If yours was an interstate move, your options for government help are limited. The Federal Motor Carrier Safety Administration (FMCSA) recommends that you contact the Better Business Bureau in the state in which the moving company is licensed and that you register a complaint with that state's consumer protection office. You can also file a complaint directly with the FMCSA by telephone or online (888-DOT-SAFT [888-368-7238], nccdb.fmcsa.dot.gov). Don't expect much from the agency, however; the complaint hotline is essentially just a database and you will only hear from the FMCSA if it looks at your complaint and determines that enforcement action is warranted.

If satisfaction still eludes you, start a letter-writing campaign: to the state attorney general, to your congressperson, to the newspaper, to online review sites—the sky's the limit. (You won't necessarlly get results, but you might feel better.) If the dispute is worth it, and the moving company actually has assets or insurance and hasn't vanished into the ether, you can always hire a lawyer and seek redress through the courts.

TAX DEDUCTIONS

If your move is work-related, and your employer is not reimbursing your moving costs, some or all of your moving expenses may be tax-deductible. Though eligibility and specific requirements vary—depending, for example, on whether you have a job or are self-employed—you can generally deduct the cost of moving yourself, your family, and your belongings, even if you don't itemize deductions. To qualify for the deduction, your move must be employment-related; your new job must be at least 50 miles farther away from your former residence than your old job location; and you must work in the new location for at least 39 weeks of the first 12 months after your arrival.

In general, you can deduct:

- The cost of moving household goods from your old residence to your new one
- The cost of storing household goods in your new city for up to 30 consecutive days
- The cost of shipping your car
- The cost of moving your household pets
- The cost of your family's trip to your new residence (including transportation and lodging, but not meals)

Keep your receipts for these expenses.

If you take the deduction and then fail to meet the length-of-employment requirements, you will have to pay back the IRS (unless the failure is because your employer transferred you again or laid you off through no fault of your own). IRS publication 521 (available from the IRS website at www.irs.gov or by phone at 800-829-3676) provides full details of the moving expenses deduction. It's a good idea to consult a tax expert if you are unsure whether, or to what extent, your move qualifies for the deduction.

CHILDREN

Moving can be hard on children. Kids that move to a new city are suddenly isolated from their friends and have to start over in an unfamiliar school and community. According to an American Medical Association study, children who move often are more likely to suffer from such problems as depression, aggression, and low self-esteem. Often their academic performance suffers as well. Besides avoiding unnecessary moves, there are a few things you can do to help your children cope with these stressful upheavals:

- *Talk about the move with your kids.* Be honest but positive. Listen to their concerns. Involve them in the process as fully as possible.
- *Make sure the children have their favorite possessions* with them on the trip; don't pack "blankey" or "bear" in the moving truck.
- *Plan some fun activities* on the other end. Your children may feel lonely in their new surroundings, and some ready-made activities can help them feel more comfortable.
- *Keep in touch with family and loved ones* as much as possible. Photos, phone calls, and e-mail are important ways to maintain links to the important people you have left behind.
- *If your children are of school age, take the time to involve yourself* in their new school and in their academic life. Don't let them get lost in the shuffle.

For younger children, there are dozens of good books designed to help explain, or at least help ease the transition of, moving. These books include *Max's Moving Adventure: A Coloring Book for Kids on the Move* by Danelle Till, illustrated by Joe Spooner; *Alexander, Who's Not (Do You Hear Me? I Mean It!) Going to Move* by Judith Viorst; *Goodbye/Hello* by Barbara Hazen; *The Leaving Morning* by Angela Johnson; *Little Monster's Moving Day* by Mercer Mayer; *Who Will Be My Friends?* (Easy I Can Read Series) by Syd Hoff; *I'm Not Moving, Mama* by Nancy White Carlstrom, illustrated by Thor Wickstrom; and *The Berenstain Bears' Moving Day* by Jan and Stan Berenstain.

For older children, try *The Moving Book: A Kids' Survival Guide* by Gabriel Davis; *Amber Brown Is Not a Crayon* by Paula Danziger; *The Kid in the Red Jacket* by Barbara Park; *Hold Fast to Dreams* by Andrea Davis Pinkney; *Flip Flop Girl* by Katherine Paterson; and *My Fabulous New Life* by Sheila Greenwald.

PETS

Moving live animals across the country is stressful for everyone involved, whether animal or human. The *Pet-Moving Handbook* by Carrie Straub, available from First Books (www.firstbooks.com), provides practical answers for all your pet-moving questions and covers domestic and international moves via car, airplane, ferry, etc.

In general, driving your pets thousands of miles comes with its own set of challenges, including dealing with extreme weather (which could prevent you from leaving your pet in the car while you eat, for example) and finding pet-friendly overnight accommodation. If your pets go by air, you'll have to navigate the maze of regulations, services, and prices that each airline has devised for animal transport; some airlines will not transport pets at all, others allow them only in the cabin as carry-on luggage, and still others will only transport animals when outdoor temperatures are moderate. A few airlines have special climate-controlled pet care facilities at their hub airports, and will place pets in a climate-controlled cargo bay on the plane. At a minimum, you'll need to get a health certificate from your veterinarian.

Given the complications of moving animals over long distances, you might want to leave the task to professionals. The **International Pet and Animal Transportation Association** (903-769-2267, www.ipata.org) maintains a list of pet shipping companies. These companies, such as **WorldCare Pet Transport** (631-751-2297, www.worldcarepet.com), will make all the arrangements with airports, airlines, and the licensing authorities at your destination—and, of course, they will (or should) move your pet in accordance with the Animal Welfare Act and USDA specifications.

ONLINE RELOCATION RESOURCES

The following websites feature moving tips and links to movers, real estate leads, and other relocation resources:

- **American Moving & Storage Association**, www.moving.org, offers referrals to interstate movers, local movers, storage companies, and packing and moving consultants.
- **Sperling's Best Places**, www.bestplaces.net, compares quality-of-life and cost-of-living data for US cities.
- **First Books**, www.firstbooks.com, offers relocation resources and information on moving to Atlanta, Boston, Chicago, Dallas–Fort Worth, Houston, Los Angeles, Minneapolis–St. Paul, New York, Portland, San Francisco, Seattle, and Washington, D.C., as well as China and London, England. First Books also publishes the *Newcomer's Handbook for Moving to and Living in the USA*; *The Moving Book: A Kids' Survival Guide*; *Max's Moving Adventure: A Coloring Book for Kids on the Move*; and the *Pet-Moving Handbook*.
- **Move**, www.move.com, provides realty and rental listings, moving tips, and more.

- **The Riley Guide**, www.rileyguide.com/relocate.html, is an online moving and relocation clearinghouse with links to dozens of useful relocation-related sites.
- To learn more about your rights and responsibilities with respect to interstate moving, check out the **United States Department of Transportation** (USDOT) publication "Your Rights and Responsibilities When You Move," which is downloadable off the www.protectyourmove.gov website. The **State of Oregon** has created an online list of moving tips ("Consumer Guide to Moving"), available at oregon.gov/ODOT/MCT/movers.shtml. The **Washington Utilities and Transportation Commission** has compiled various fact sheets and consumer guides for moving at www.wutc.wa.gov/consumers/Pages/moverpublications.aspx.
- The **United States Postal Service** offers an online change of address form and general relocation information at moversguide.usps.com.
- **Worldwide ERC—The Workforce Mobility Association**, online at www.worldwideerc.org; if your employer is a member of this professional organization, you may have access to special services. Non-members can use the online database of real estate agents and related services.

O NCE YOU FIND A HOME FOR YOURSELF AND YOUR STUFF, YOU'LL want to find a home for your money (assuming you have any left at that point). Most financial institutions offer a variety of account options; fees (or their absence) often depend on the size of your balance. For major deposits, shop around for interest rates and perks, but for routine banking you'll be more interested in ATM fees and locations, online or mobile banking options, and direct deposit services (an increasingly common alternative to getting a paper paycheck). Small local banks or credit unions may have lower fees than their colossal national competitors, while offering you a more navigable bureaucracy if you need help. If you do most of your banking at lunchtime or on the way to work, make sure the bank you're interested in has convenient branches or ATMs. While virtually all banks and credit unions now offer some online banking services, some offerings are more robust than others; for example, some (but not all) banks now offer remote check depositing. If you currently have an account at a national bank with a Portland presence, check with a local branch; you may be able to keep your old account.

Once you decide on your new bank, it's usually a simple process to open a checking or savings account; generally you'll need photo identification, proof of address (if you haven't yet obtained an Oregon or Washington driver's license), your social security number, and money. Check with your prospective bank to find out what documents (and how much money) you'll need to bring with you.

Before you close your old bank accounts, keep in mind that many landlords and rental agencies will not accept a tenant who does not have a checking account, and some merchants will not accept the temporary checks most banks issue when you open an account, so it's probably wise to keep your old account current for at least a short time after you move.

BANK ACCOUNTS AND SERVICES

National, regional, and local banks all offer online and telephone banking, mortgages, and ATM, debit, and credit cards you can use practically anywhere in the world. Locally based banks, however, often specialize in (or at least advertise) personal service or special perks for customers; national banks generally offer the most comprehensive ATM networks and the widest array of services. In addition to the banks and credit unions listed below, many other banks (some with only one or two branches in the area) can be found online or in the Yellow Pages.

NATIONAL BANKS

These five large national banks have an extensive presence in the Portland area:
- **Bank of America,** 800-432-1000, www.bankofamerica.com, has dozens of branches and ATMs throughout the city and the surrounding suburbs.
- **Chase,** 877-68CHASE, www.chase.com, a newcomer to the region, became instantly pervasive following its 2008 acquisition of Washington Mutual; some banking centers are located inside Fred Meyer supermarkets.
- **Key Bank,** 800-539-2968, www.key.com, has more than two dozen branches in the Portland area.
- **US Bank,** 800-872-2657, www.usbank.com; once based in Portland, this bank's corporate headquarters have moved to Minneapolis, but it still has one of the most extensive ATM and branch networks in Oregon.
- **Wells Fargo,** 800-869-3557, www.wellsfargo.com; although it generated considerable ill will by closing branches across the region in the late 1990s, Wells Fargo has since re-established an extensive network of branches and ATMs in the Portland area.

LOCAL AND REGIONAL BANKS

- **Albina Community Bank,** 503-287-7537, 800-814-6088, www.albinabank.com, is a full-service community development bank with five branches; it invests its assets in lower- and middle-income communities in North and Northeast Portland.
- **Bank of Oswego,** 503-635-1699, www.bankofoswego.com, concentrates on offering personal service banking to the Lake Oswego area, with a branch in Sherwood.
- **Bank of the West,** 800-488-2265, www.bankofthewest.com, which operates in 20 Western and Midwestern states (plus Guam and Saipan), has branches throughout the metropolitan area; it is part of the French financial conglomerate BNP Paribas.
- **Banner Bank**, 800-272-9933, www.bannerbank.com, based in Walla Walla, Washington, has eight full-service branches in the Portland area.
- **Clackamas County Bank,** 503-668-5501, www.clackamascountybank.com, opened in 1911, serves Gresham, Boring, Sandy, and the communities of the Mount Hood foothills.

- **Columbia Bank,** 877-272-3678, www.columbiabank.com, based in Tacoma, has more than two dozen branches in the Portland area, and also has a strong presence on the Oregon Coast and in the inland Northwest.
- **Pacific Continental Bank,** 877-231-2265, www.therightbank.com, operates branches in western Oregon and Washington, including Portland, Beaverton, Tualatin, and Vancouver.
- **Umpqua Bank,** 866-486-7782, www.umpquabank.com, headquartered in southern Oregon, has dozens of branches in Portland and each of the major suburbs.
- **Washington Federal,** 800-324-9375, www.washingtonfederal.com, based in Seattle, has locations throughout Oregon and Washington, with eight branches in the Portland area.
- **West Coast Bank,** 800-895-3345, www.wcb.com, has more than two dozen branches in the area, primarily in the suburbs.

CREDIT UNIONS

Credit unions are an alternative to consumer banking. These nonprofit, cooperative institutions offer most of the same basic services banks do, but often with lower fees, higher interest rates, and more personalized service. Membership is generally limited to employees of certain companies or government agencies or to residents of a certain area. To find a credit union in Oregon or Washington that you are eligible to join, visit www.asmartercholce.org. Virtually any resident of the Portland metropolitan area is eligible to join at least one of the following four credit unions:

- **Columbia Credit Union,** 360-891-4000, 503-285-1521, 800 699 4009, www. columbiacu.org, has 12 branches in Clark County; anyone who lives or works in Washington State, or in Jantzen Beach/Hayden Island, Oregon (the northern fringe of North Portland), is eligible to join.
- **OnPoint Community Credit Union,** 503-228-7077, 800-527-3932, www. onpointcu.com, has 19 branches in the Portland area; membership is open to anyone who lives or works in Benton, Clackamas, Columbia, Crook, Deschutes, Jefferson, Lane, Linn, Marion, Multnomah, Polk, Washington, or Yamhill counties in Oregon or Clark or Skamania counties in Washington.
- **Rivermark Community Credit Union,** 503-626-6600, 800-452-8502, www. rivermarkcu.org, with four branches in the metro area, is open to residents (or family members of residents) of most counties in north-central Oregon, including Multnomah, Washington, Clackamas, and Yamhill.
- **Unitus Community Credit Union,** 503-227-5571, 800-452-0900, www.unituscu.com, has eight branches; you are eligible for membership if you live or work in any of 15 Oregon counties (including Multnomah, Washington, Clackamas, Marion, Polk, and Yamhill counties), or anywhere in Washington.

CREDIT CARDS

Despite its potential fiscal hazards, plastic is an increasingly common way to pay for goods and services—so much so that many Portland merchants will accept credit cards, but not personal checks. If you don't already have a credit card, you can compare credit card offerings—including interest rates, fees, special offers, and affinity features—at sites such as **CardHub.com** (www.cardhub.com) or **Bankrate.com** (www.bankrate.com/credit-cards.aspx).

VISA (www.usa.visa.com) and **MasterCard** (www.mastercard.us) cards are accepted by almost all merchants who take credit cards. **American Express** (www.americanexpress.com) and **Discover** (www.discovercard.com) cards are also widely accepted, though not universal.

Most department stores and other major retail chains issue charge cards, sometimes with lines of credit. Usually these accounts are issued automatically and instantly if you already have a VISA or MasterCard account, often in combination with a discount on purchases made on the day you apply. Store accounts may have lower fees (or no fees) and lower interest rates than major credit cards, and perks may include advance notice of sales, access to special services, and cardholder discounts. However, the instant discount may not be worth the hit to your credit rating that new accounts trigger, or the nuisance of keeping track of new cards.

You can also buy **prepaid charge cards**. These work like debit cards, so you can give them to a teenager or use them for Internet shopping and know that you can't lose any more money than the amount already encoded on the card.

If you prefer to use a credit card that allows you to earn frequent flier miles, be aware that many airlines have only limited service from Portland—usually to their hub cities—and that as a result it can be very hard to redeem miles for a seat. The airlines that have the most flights from Portland are Alaska Airlines, followed by Southwest Airlines, Delta Airlines, and United Airlines. For maximum flexibility, use a card that allows you to earn and redeem miles on one of those airlines or on a selection of carriers.

CONSUMER PROTECTION, IDENTITY THEFT, AND CREDIT REPORTS

Following a steady stream of disclosures of security breaches affecting major banks, retailers, websites, credit card companies, government agencies, and businesses that collect and sell personal data, it seems nearly impossible to do anything to protect yourself from either credit card fraud or identity theft—and yet, if you're a victim, a fraud such as identity theft can nearly ruin your life. Victims spend an average of 600 hours trying to repair their credit; it's a daunting task. For more information, contact the **Identity Theft Resource Center** at 888-400-5530 or www.idtheftcenter.org, or check out the Federal Trade Commission's identity theft website (www.consumer.ftc.gov/topics/privacy-identity).

That said, there is some good news: federal law generally limits your liability for unauthorized credit card charges to $50. Industry standards are even tougher and, in practice, consumers are often not held responsible for any unauthorized charges on their credit cards. The trick is to check your monthly statements carefully and notify your credit card company immediately when the charges are incorrect. So what else can you do to protect yourself? Security experts recommend several things. Don't print your full name and Social Security number on your checks, and don't carry your Social Security card in your wallet. Consider installing a locking mailbox if you don't have one already, and in any case don't let your mail sit in your mailbox any longer than absolutely necessary. Shred personal documents before recycling them. Finally, think twice before you make a financial transaction over the Internet. Convenient though it may be, security failures have been identified even on websites you might reasonably expect to be secure. Never send personal financial details through unencrypted email or submit them to an unsecured website. Finally, check your credit report periodically. You are entitled to one free credit report per year from each of the three major credit reporting companies, so if you request a report every four months from a different credit reporting company, you'll be able to keep tabs on your credit status for free. You can visit **www.annualcreditreport.com** for online access to all three.

The national credit bureaus are:

- **Equifax**, 800-685-1111, www.equifax.com
- **Experian**, 888-397-3742, www.experian.com
- **TransUnion Corporation**, 800-888-4213, www.transunion.com

TAXES

The Portland metropolitan area includes two states with very different tax systems. Oregon has no sales tax, but collects a relatively high income tax; Washington has no state income tax, but collects a relatively high sales tax and has a wide range of other taxes and fees; and homeowners in both states pay property taxes. If you live, work, and shop in the same state, the tax situation is fairly straightforward. However, Washington residents who work or shop in Oregon face special rules.

FEDERAL INCOME TAX

Federal tax forms and publications are available online at www.irs.gov; they can also be ordered from the IRS by telephone by calling 800-829-3676. Preprinted paper forms are available during filing season (January–April 15) at some public libraries. Although you'll have to go through a metal detector to get them, paper forms are also available at the downtown Portland IRS office, 1220 SW 3rd Avenue, 503-265-3501. You can get answers to your tax questions at this office, but some recent studies have found that the answer you get from an IRS representative often depends more upon the person giving it than on any clearly defined rule or regulation. (The same caution goes for advice provided on the IRS Tax Help Line, 800-829-1040.) The Service says it's working on standardizing responses.

Filing your tax return electronically can save you time and aggravation and can speed up your refund (if you're expecting one). Visit the IRS e-file site (www. irs.gov/Filing) for details, including a list of companies that offer tax software or online returns.

STATE INCOME TAX

Oregon's state income tax rate ranges from 5 to 9.9% of taxable income. Most tax-payers fall into the 9% marginal bracket, which kicks in at an extremely low level (taxable income of $8,150 for single filers and $16,300 for married filing jointly for the 2014 tax year). Taxable income above $125,000 for individuals and $250,000 for joint filers is taxed at 9.9%.

Tax forms and additional information are available from the **Oregon Department of Revenue**, 503-378-4988, 800-356-4222, www.oregon.gov/DOR.

Most (but not all) tax preparers and tax software publishers offer electronic filing for Oregon returns for a fee. Be aware that you will probably have to file an Oregon part-year resident tax return (Form 40P) for the year in which you move to Oregon; not all software publishers allow electronic filing for part-year returns, so check before committing to a program if electronic filing is important to you.

One unique aspect of the Oregon tax system is the "kicker." Whenever the state's two-year budget boasts a surplus of more than 2%, the entire surplus is refunded to taxpayers in odd-numbered years. The "kicker" kicks in more often than not, and many Oregonians look forward to receiving these tax refunds occasionally, typically every four to six years. (The checks are conveniently timed to arrive just before the December holidays.) While understandably popular, the kicker system is controversial, and has been criticized for preventing the state from maintaining a reserve fund for years in which revenues fall below estimates.

Oregon currently has no local personal income taxes for employees. A temporary Multnomah County income tax expired at the end of 2005.

Washington has no personal income tax for employees. However, cross-border commuters cannot evade Oregon income tax: Washington residents who work in Oregon must pay Oregon income tax on their earnings from Oregon employment, and Oregon residents who have jobs in Washington must pay Oregon income taxes.

SALES TAX

Oregon does not have a sales tax.

Washington charges both a state sales tax (currently 6.5%) and an array of local sales taxes (which the consumer sees as a single, combined number at the cash register). In Clark County, the total sales tax ranges from 7.7% in unincorporated areas to 8.2% in Vancouver and other incorporated municipalities.

Washington also collects—or attempts to collect—use taxes from its residents who purchase items from other states for use in Washington. For most Clark County residents, the use tax will affect them if they purchase goods via mail-order or over the Internet from retailers who do not collect Washington sales tax, or if they shop in Oregon. A complete description of Washington's use tax can be found on the **Washington Department of Revenue** website (http://dor. wa.gov/content/findtaxesandrates/usetax). Although Washington has stepped up enforcement of the use tax, the large number of big box retailers that lurk conveniently on the Oregon side of both Columbia River bridges in Portland suggests that not all Washingtonians are diligent about reporting their purchases.

If you are an Oregon resident, you may not have to pay sales tax on items you buy at a store in Washington. Washington law allows (but doesn't require) retailers to exempt taxes on certain sales to Oregonians. (The exemption does not apply to meals, services, or lodging, or to items that will be used within Washington.) If the merchant agrees not to charge you sales tax, you'll be asked to show photo identification, and you may have to fill out a tax exemption certificate. Most retailers in Clark County welcome customers from Oregon, and many are able to handle tax-free transactions. Merchants elsewhere in Washington, particularly small retailers, may not be set up to jump through the necessary tax exemption hoops, but it never hurts to ask.

PROPERTY TAXES

OREGON

In Oregon, county governments collect property taxes and distribute the funds to cities, school districts, and various special districts. The annual property tax is payable in thirds, with payments due on November 15, February 15, and May 15. A discount is available if you pay all or two-thirds of your annual tax by November 15. If you have a mortgage with an escrow account for taxes, your lender will pay the county directly.

Property taxes in Oregon generally increase at relatively low, predictable rates. Ballot Measure 5, passed in 1990, limited the overall property tax rate for education and general government purposes to $15 per $1,000 of assessed value. Voter-approved levies (for schools, libraries, or open space, for example) can (and do) raise property tax rates in some jurisdictions well above the Measure 5 limit, and the passage and expiration of various levies can cause your property tax bill to fluctuate significantly from year to year. Your property tax statement should have an itemized list of taxes, fees, and assessments from all the local taxing districts that provide services to your property. Some of these charges may not be based on assessed value.

In 1997, Ballot Measure 50 separated the taxable assessed value of a property from its real market value. Assessed value was initially set at 90% of a property's

1995 real market value, and subsequent increases in assessed value were limited to 3% per year. An exception to this rule is made for any improvements that raise the value of property by more than $10,000; if you buy a newly remodeled house, your property tax bill may be substantially higher than you expect. However, unlike in states such as California, a property's assessed value does not skyrocket to fair market value when the property is sold. If a taxpayer feels that the assessor incorrectly estimated the value of the property, he or she can file an appeal with their county's Board of Property Tax Assessment.

While these measures restrain increases in property taxes when real estate prices rise more than 3% per year, they can also result in assessed values so far below real market values that assessed values, and thus property taxes, can continue to increase even in a market downturn.

WASHINGTON

In Washington, counties collect property tax. Property tax bills go out in February, and half of the total tax is due April 30; perhaps to increase Halloween's scare factor, the other half is due October 31. As in Oregon, there is a statewide limit on the property tax rate—1% of market value, exclusive of voter-approved levies. Unlike in Oregon, however, a property's assessed value is the same as its current fair market value, and there is no limit on how quickly a property's assessed value can rise. (In Clark County, property values are reassessed annually.) Washington law generally limits the rate of increase in local levy amounts to 1% per year unless voters approve a higher increase, so in practice property taxes do not increase at the same rate as real estate values (and did not necessarily decrease during the last downturn in real estate values). As an added wrinkle, the 1% increase limit does not apply to individual homes, but only to the taxing district as a whole. Senior citizens and disabled persons may qualify for property tax exemptions or deferrals. Also note that homeowners generally qualify for a three-year exemption on the value of major remodels to single-family houses.

COUNTY OFFICES

For questions about assessments or property taxes for a specific property, check with your county's assessor:

- **Clackamas County Department of Assessment and Taxation**, 503-655-8671, www.clackamas.us/at/
- **Clark County (Washington) Department of Assessment**, 360-397-2391, www.co.clark.wa.us/assessor/index.html
- **Columbia County Assessor's Office,** 503-397-2240, www.co.columbia.or.us/ departments/assessors-office/assessors-home
- **Marion County Assessor's Office**, 503-588-5144, www.co.marion.or.us/ao/
- **Multnomah County Division of Assessment and Taxation**, 503-988-3326 (property tax information line), www.multcotax.org

- **Washington County Department of Assessment and Taxation**, 503-846-8741, www.co.washington.or.us/AssessmentTaxation/
- **Yamhill County Office of Assessment and Taxation,** 503-434-7521, www.co.yamhill.or.us/assessor/

OTHER TAXES AND FEES

If you are self-employed and you live within the TriMet transit district (which includes most of the Oregon portion of the metropolitan area), you will have to pay TriMet self-employment tax. This tax is collected by the Oregon Department of Revenue. Both Multnomah County and the City of Portland levy business taxes (described as a "license fee" in Portland) on net income. You may be subject to this tax if you're self-employed; businesses with less than $50,000 in gross revenue are exempt.

Although Washington has no income tax, the state levies a business and occupation (B & O) tax on gross (not net) business receipts. If you are self-employed, you will be subject to this tax. The B & O tax rate depends on the type of business activity you engage in. Full details are available at http://dor.wa.gov/content/find-taxesandrates/bandotax/. Washington also levies a hefty state and local excise tax on the sale of real estate. This tax is generally paid by the seller, so it won't initially affect you if you are moving to Washington from another state.

Several municipalities in the Portland area, including Oregon City, West Linn, and Lake Oswego, collect street maintenance fees from residents. At press time, Portland is also considering implementing a street fee.

STARTING A BUSINESS

Oregon's state government has created a streamlined multi-agency business startup toolkit, available at www.oregon.gov/business/Pages/toolkit.aspx, which is an excellent resource for prospective Oregon businesses. In addition, the Oregon Secretary of State's **Corporation Division** publishes "How to Start a Business in Oregon," a helpful guide to opening a business in the state. The booklet is available online at sos.oregon.gov/business/pages/staring-business.aspx, or by calling the Corporation Division at 503-986-2200. The **Portland Development Commission** (503-823-3200) operates a web portal (www.pdc.us/for-businesses.aspx) that is useful for existing or planned Portland businesses.

If you want to start a business in Washington, you must file an application for a Master Business License with the state. The Washington **Department of Revenue** website (bls.dor.wa.gov/startbusiness.aspx) contains useful information about the business startup and licensing process. You may also need a local business license. The **Clark County** website (www.co.clark.wa.us/aboutcc/new_clarkcounty/startingbusiness.html) lists several resources for people thinking of starting a business in the area.

NOW THAT YOU'VE FOUND THE HOME OF YOUR DREAMS — OR AT LEAST a place to hang your Gore-Tex jacket—you'll need to get the utilities turned on, get connected to the Internet and/or cable TV, and get rid of the pile of trash and recycling you've accumulated during your move. And you'll need to get a new driver's license and register your car (if you have one). And you'd better register to vote. You might want to subscribe to a newspaper. And you'll probably want a library card. And…well, moving in is just the first step to getting settled in Portland.

UTILITIES

A few large utilities (and several small ones) serve the two states and seven counties that make up the greater Portland metropolitan area. In most cases, you won't be able to choose which company provides your water, electric, cable, or gas service, so there's no point in comparing prices. You can usually sign up for service directly with the utility, either by telephone or online. If you are unsure about which specific utility serves your new address, check with your new city or county government, your realtor, or your property manager. Whichever utility company serves your new home, call the one-call utility locator service for your area before you start digging in your new yard. In Oregon, call the **Oregon Utility Notification Center** at 800-332-2344, or visit the center online at www.digsafelyoregon. com; in southwest Washington, contact the **Washington Utility Notification Center**, 800-424-5555, www.callbeforeyoudig.org.

ELECTRICITY

Two large investor-owned utilities and one public utility district (PUD) provide electricity to most of the Portland metropolitan area. The primary electric utility for most of the city of Portland and its suburbs in Oregon is **Portland General**

Electric (PGE) (503-228-6322, 800-542-8818 for customer service, 503-464-7777, 800-544-1795 to report outages and emergencies, www.portlandgeneral.com). Owned from 1997 to 2006 by Enron, and thus one of that company's few real assets, PGE is now a stand-alone company. To start service, call customer service or visit www.cs.portlandgeneral.com.

Pacific Power (888-221-7070 for customer service and new accounts, 877-508-5088 for outages, www.pacificpower.net), serves most of Northeast Portland and a portion of downtown Portland. Pacific Power is the local business name of PacifiCorp, a major power company that is part of Berkshire Hathaway Energy.

In Clark County, Washington, electricity is delivered by **Clark Public Utilities** (360-992-3000 or 800-562-1736 for customer service, 360-992-8000 for outages, www.clarkpublicutilities.com), a customer-owned PUD.

A few PUDs, member-owned electric cooperatives, and municipal power companies provide electricity to outlying communities in Oregon:

- **Canby Utility**, 503-266-1156, is Canby's independent, city-owned utility.
- **Columbia River PUD**, 503-397-0590, www.crpud.net, provides electric service to much of Columbia County, including Scappoose and St. Helens, and a small part of northern Multnomah County.
- **Forest Grove Light and Power**, 503-992-3250, www.forestgrove-or.gov/city-hall/light-a-power.html, is a department of the city of Forest Grove; it provides electricity to Forest Grove and part of the surrounding area.
- **McMinnville Water & Light**, 503-472-6158, www.mc-power.com, is the municipal utility company for the city of McMinnville.
- **Salem Electric**, 503-362-3601, www.salemelectric.com, serves portions of Keizer and Salem (primarily West Salem).
- **West Oregon Electric Cooperative**, 503-429-3021, 800-777-1276, www.westoregon.org, serves rural areas of Clatsop, Columbia, Tillamook, Washington, and Yamhill counties.

Most local utilities offer **green power** or renewable energy options to residential customers. PGE has two programs: **Green Source** and **Clean Wind. (See www.greenpoweroregon.com.)** Pacific Power's version is the **Blue Sky** program, which offers similar options. The Clark Public Utilities program is called **Green Lights**. Contact your utility or visit its website for additional information and costs.

NATURAL GAS

Many houses and apartments in the Portland area do not use gas at all; some homes have electric furnaces and water heaters—a holdover from the days when the region's hydropower was ridiculously cheap—and a few older homes still have oil furnaces. If your home has a natural gas furnace, stove, or water heater, **NW Natural** is almost certainly your provider. To activate new service, call 503-226-4211 or 800-422-4012 or visit www.nwnatural.com/service.

HEATING ASSISTANCE

In Oregon, the **Low Income Home Energy Assistance Program** (503-986-2000, www.oregon.gov/OHCS/Pages/SOS_Low_Income_Energy_Assistance_Oregon. aspx) helps low-income households pay heating bills during the winter months; for details about other heating assistance options, visit **Heat Oregon** (503-612-6300, www.heatoregon.org). Washington has a similar program with an identical name, the **Low Income Home Energy Assistance Program** (360-725-2857, www. commerce.wa.gov/Services/individualassistance/Low-Income-Home-Energy-Assistance-Program/). Additional heating assistance programs, funded by the federal government or utility companies, may be available; visit the federal site, www.liheap.ncat.org, or call 866-674-6327.

Washington has a disconnection moratorium rule that allows low-income households that have exhausted all other alternatives to keep their heat on from November 15 through March 15. To qualify, you must follow certain procedures, including contacting the utility and trying to work out a payment plan. Contact the **Washington Utilities and Transportation Commission** (800-333-9882, www.wutc.wa.gov/consumer) for details. Oregon does not have a similar moratorium rule; if you are unable to pay your utility bills during the winter, contact your utility directly to work out a payment plan to avoid disconnection.

TELEPHONE

AREA CODES

Portland and its Oregon suburbs have two area codes, **503** and **971**. The 971 area code was introduced in 2000 as an "overlay" area code for the Portland metropolitan area, and there is no geographic division between the two area codes. Telephone companies are required to exhaust their supply of 503 prefixes before assigning a 971 area code, and currently 971 numbers are mostly assigned to cell phones. As a result, the 503 area code is still by far the most common—so much so that many residents and businesses still only give out seven-digit numbers, with the "503" implied.

Because these two area codes overlap, you must dial the full ten-digit telephone number, including the area code (but not including an initial "1"), when you make a local call. To complicate matters, the 503 area code encompasses large parts of northwest Oregon outside the metro area, including Salem and the north coast; calls to these areas are toll calls, and you'll need to dial a "1" before the area code. There is unfortunately no way to tell from the area code alone whether a 503 number is a local or distance call.

The area codes for the rest of the state are **541** and **458**; in the Willamette Valley, the geographic area covered by these codes begins just south of Salem. The 458 area code is even less common than 971, which is to say you will encounter it rarely, if at all. Like callers in northwest Oregon, callers from the 541 area code region also need to dial the full ten-digit telephone number.

The area code for southwest Washington is **360**. Currently, it is not necessary to dial the area code first when making local calls to a 360 number. The implementation of a proposed new 564 overlay area code for western Washington has repeatedly been delayed.

LANDLINE PHONE SERVICE

Century Link has a virtual monopoly on local residential telephone service in Portland and much of the suburban area. You can order new residential service online at www.centurylink.com/home/phone/, or by calling 866-642-0444. **Frontier Communications** (www.frontier.com, 800-921-8101) is the incumbent carrier in Yamhill County, most of Washington County (except for North Plains, which is Century Link territory), Gresham, Sandy, Happy Valley, Wilsonville, and Silverton, and for much of Clark County, Washington.

A few competitors offer alternatives to the main carriers for local phone service, although these newcomers primarily serve business rather than residential customers. In addition, **Comcast** offers cable-based phone service (see **Cable Television**, below), and if you have a broadband connection you can choose to use Internet-based phone service (see **VoIP**, below).

A few Clackamas County communities are served by independent telecom companies:

- **Beaver Creek Cooperative Telephone Company**, 503-632-3113, www.bctelco.com, provides telephone, wireless, cable television, and Internet service in Oregon City and Beavercreek.
- **Canby Telecom**, 503-266-8111, www.canbytel.com, provides telephone, Internet, and digital television (via DSL) service in Canby.
- **Colton Telephone & Cable TV**, 503-824-3211, www.colton.com, offers the services its name suggests, along with Internet service, in Colton.
- **Molalla Communications Company**, 503-829-1100, molalla.net, offers a similar range of services in Molalla.

In Washington, local telephone service is open to competition. Although **Century Link** and **Frontier** are the dominant local carriers in Clark County, consumers can use one of several other companies for residential phone service; check the listings in the front of the phone book or go to the **Washington Utilities and Transportation Commission** website, www.wutc.wa.gov/telecom, to find authorized telecommunications companies.

LONG-DISTANCE AND INTERNATIONAL SERVICE
AND PREPAID CALLING CARDS

You are under no obligation to use your local phone company for long-distance service. Many companies now offer unlimited long-distance calls for a flat fee, which can be a good deal if you make lots of long-distance calls. (Local phone companies often offer their customers "bundle" discounts on unlimited long-distance plans.) Otherwise, analyze your typical calling patterns and select a plan that offers the best deal based on the time of day and average duration of your calls. You can research and compare long-distance plans at websites such as **www. saveonphone.com** and **www.tollchaser.com**.

While the ubiquity of mobile phones (and the decline in public pay phones) has made **prepaid calling cards** largely obsolete, some convenience stores and corner markets still sell these cards in denominations of $5 and up. Some of these card companies advertise rates as low as 1.2 cents a minute. Those rates apply to actual talking time, though—with per-call charges and surcharges for using a pay phone, you'll deplete the card balance rapidly if you make lots of short calls. Still, prepaid cards can be cheaper than many long-distance plans if you tend to make only a few long calls.

Making international calls from your home phone can be shockingly expensive. Most long-distance companies offer general or country-specific international calling plans; there is often a monthly charge, so these plans work best for people who make frequent international calls, especially to a single country. For occasional international calling, consider an international prepaid calling card. Alternatively, sign up for a web-based calling program such as **Skype** (www.skype.com), which offers very low international rates.

VOIP

Voice over Internet Protocol, or VoIP, allows people with broadband connections to make voice telephone calls over the Internet, including international calls, for a flat monthly fee. The biggest players in this market have traditionally been **Skype** (www.skype.com) and **Vonage** (www.vonage.com), but most major and some minor telephone, cable, and Internet providers now offer VoIP service, and a host of standalone VoIP providers has arisen. VoIP may be a good value if you make many long-distance calls. However, VoIP has some downsides: it won't work during a power failure or if your broadband connection goes down, it can suffer from poor sound quality, and your location cannot always be identified if you call 911 (although this last issue is slowly being resolved). Given these pitfalls, it may be advisable to keep a conventional landline or a cell phone for emergencies or power outages.

WIRELESS PHONE SERVICE

Portlanders, like urbanites around the world, increasingly view cell phones as a necessity. A growing number of residents have dropped their traditional long-distance service, or have even abandoned landlines entirely, preferring to rely instead on their cell phones (and their carriers' national rate plans) for all voice communication. This approach has potential pitfalls—for example, wireless reception in hilly neighborhoods can be spotty or nonexistent, and service can be inconsistent even in areas with otherwise adequate coverage—but it may be a good solution if you plan to get a mobile phone anyway. Keep in mind that vast swaths of the rural Northwest lack any coverage at all, and Oregon is one of the only states in the country where analog-compatible phones are still necessary in some remote areas. To be sure that you're not stuck with a cell phone that won't work where and when you need it, confirm that your provider will allow you to test the phone for a trial period after you start service and to return the phone if reception is unacceptable. (Not all carriers accept returns, and some who do charge a restocking fee.)

Check the Yellow Pages for a complete list of cellular providers, and research the latest deals on service plans between companies. Be prepared to swallow a one- to three-year contract for the best monthly rates; if you don't need a free or subsidized phone, and you don't make lots of calls, a pay-as-you-go plan may be a better deal. The largest cellular carriers in the Portland area are:

- **AT&T Wireless**, 888-333-6651, www.wireless.att.com
- **Cricket Wireless**, 800-274-2538, www.mycricket.com
- **Sprint**, 866-866-7509, www.sprint.com
- **T-Mobile**, 800-866-2453, www.t-mobile.com.
- **Verizon Wireless**, 800-256-4646, www.verizonwireless.com

Most of these carriers have stand-alone stores as well as mall-based kiosks throughout the Portland area. Some electronics and office supply stores, large retailers like Fred Meyer, Target, Costco, and Walmart, and online merchants like **Amazon.com** sell phones and service plans on behalf of one or more carriers. In addition, Century Link and Frontier offer discounts for bundling cell and landline services; check with your prospective carrier for details.

INTERNET SERVICE

Your telephone or cable provider should be annoyingly eager to also provide you with Internet service. The bundled services they offer can often be good deals; however, it's worth shopping around for an Internet Service Provider (ISP) that will best support your particular needs (for web hosting, for example, or national dial-in access if you travel frequently). Be sure to check out local ISPs as well as the big national providers; local companies sometimes offer less expensive (and more responsive) service than big players like MSN, AOL, or Earthlink.

If you're deciding between DSL and cable broadband service, be sure to compare the speeds of the services available in your specific neighborhood. Ask your neighbors about their experiences, and consider whether the room in which you plan to place your modem already has a phone or cable jack in place. (It can be expensive to add new jacks.)

WI-FI (F)
Portland's experiment in free municipal Wi-Fi ended badly in 2008 when MetroFi, the private company that had a contract to provide Wi-Fi access across 95 percent

of the city, pulled the plug, citing high costs and lower-than-expected ad revenue. In a rare display of fiscal restraint, the city refused to pay MetroFi $9 million to keep what was a pretty mediocre service going. Wi-Fi service is now fairly ad hoc: coffee shops, bars, libraries, and other establishments throughout the metropolitan area are Wi-Fi hotspots that provide free or paid wireless access to their patrons. A few sites like **www.wifipdx.com** provide lists of Portland Wi-Fi hotspots. The **Personal Telco Project** (www.personaltelco.net) is an all-volunteer effort to create a public (as opposed to municipal) Wi-Fi network in Portland; check their website for hotspot listings.

CABLE AND SATELLITE TELEVISION

CABLE TELEVISION
Comcast (800-934-6489, www.comcast.com) has a monopoly on traditional cable television service in Portland and most suburban areas. **Frontier** has the cable franchise in east Multnomah County, and also offers FiOS television service over fiber-optic lines to many of its telephone subscribers in Washington County. (See **Landline Phone Service**, above, for contact and service area information.) There are several small franchises in outlying areas, and Beavercreek, Colton, and Molalla, have municipal cable systems; Canby offers digital television over its municipal DSL lines.

SATELLITE TV
Satellite television is available throughout the region from **Direct TV** (855-852-4388, www.directv.com) and **Dish** (855-852-4388, www.dish.com).

WATER AND SEWER

Portland takes great pride in its drinking water system, although the system's reputation took a hit in 2014 when a system-wide boil-water alert was issued due to potential bacterial contamination. Generally speaking, though, the city boasts some of the highest-quality tap water in the country because its primary source is the protected Bull Run watershed near Mount Hood. (The city's backup source is drinkable but somewhat less pristine groundwater from a well field near the Columbia River.) Most Portlanders drink water directly from the tap; some people filter their water, which is a wise practice, especially if you live in an older home that may have lead in the water lines.

To set up water service in the city of Portland, contact the **Portland Water Bureau** (503-823-7770, www.portlandonline.com/water). Residential bills come every three months, with a monthly billing option for customers who sign up for electronic billing. Water bills include sewer and stormwater utility charges. The stormwater charge is based on the estimated volume of runoff from roofs and paved areas on your property. Through the Clean River Rewards program, homeowners and businesses can qualify for a discount on the stormwater charge if they take certain steps to prevent rainwater from flowing into streets or sewers. Visit www.cleanriverrewards.com for details.

Outside Portland, most incorporated cities provide municipal water and sewer service to their residents (in some cases, using Portland water). To sign up or for more information, contact your city hall or visit your city's website (see the **Useful Phone Numbers and Websites** chapter). Many unincorporated areas obtain water service from nearby municipal systems or from special water districts. The largest of the latter, **Tualatin Valley Water District** (503-642-1511, www.tvwd.org), serves nearly 200,000 residents in eastern Washington County, including parts of Beaverton, Hillsboro, and Tigard.

If you're concerned about the quality of your local tap water, or if you just want more information about it, you can contact your water utility and ask for a copy of their annual report (which is usually posted online); alternatively, contact the Environmental Protection Agency (call the safe drinking water hotline, 800-426-4791, or go to www.epa.gov/safewater).

CONSUMER PROTECTION–UTILITY COMPLAINTS

Try to resolve billing or other disputes with your phone, gas, or electric company on your own. If a problem persists, contact the Consumer Services Section of the **Oregon Public Utility Commission** (PO Box 1088, Salem, OR 97308-1088, 503-378-6600 [Salem], 800-522-2404 [Oregon outside Salem], www.puc.state.or.us/Pages/consumer/index2.aspx). OPUC's website includes an explanation of the complaint procedure and a complaint form that you can submit online.

In Washington, contact the consumer affairs staff of the **Washington Utilities and Transportation Commission** (P.O. Box 47250, 1300 South Evergreen Park Drive SW, Olympia, WA 98504, 800-333-9882), or visit www.wutc.wa.gov/fileacomplaint to use their online complaint form. Note that these agencies only regulate investor-owned utilities, so if you have a dispute with a public utility district or municipal utility, you'll have to work out the problem with the utility.

TRASH AND RECYCLING

If you're renting, you can skip much of this section—Oregon law requires landlords to provide garbage and recycling collection—but if you're buying a home you'll need to arrange for trash pickup.

OREGON

TRASH

Metro, the Portland area's regional government, coordinates solid waste disposal and supports programs to increase recycling and reduce waste across the region. Local cities and counties franchise actual garbage pickup to a host of private companies. To find your garbage hauler, visit Metro's "Find your garbage hauler" page at www.oregonmetro.gov/hauler or call 503-234-3000. Contact your hauler directly to set up garbage hauling service and to find out about available container sizes and monthly charges.

If you need to dispose of a large item—like that moldy, squirrel-infested sofa that the old owner of your new house "forgot" to take off the front porch—you can load it in your car, truck, or trailer, cover it with a tarp, and haul the thing to one of Metro's transfer stations:

- **Metro Central Station, 6161 NW 61st Ave, Portland**
- **Metro South Station, 2001 Washington St, Oregon City**

For directions and hours, call Metro Recycling Information at 503-234-3000 or visit www.oregonmetro.gov/tools-living/garbage-and-recycling. Alternatively, you can have a private company deliver (and take away) a large drop box; do a web search or look in the Yellow Pages under "Garbage & Rubbish Collection." Rates are generally uniform between companies for the same services, and depend on the size of the box and the type of waste you plan to put inside. If you're looking to expend less effort but more money, call a service like 1-800-GOT-JUNK, which will send a crew to clean up your mess for you and whisk it away.

If you live in Washington County, two other privately operated locations might be more convenient. The **Forest Grove Transfer Station** (1525 B Street, Forest Grove, 503-992-1212) accepts the same kinds of materials for disposal or recycling as Metro's transfer stations. Visit www.wmnorthwest.com/transferstation/forestgrove.htm for hours and fee information. The **Hillsboro Landfill** (3205 SE Minter Bridge Road, Hillsboro) accepts only "dry waste" (i.e., no kitchen waste or other materials that could decompose rapidly and cause odor or vector problems) and some recyclables. Call 503-640-9427 or visit www.wmnorthwest.com/landfill/Hillsboro.htm for hours, fees, and details about what kinds of waste the landfill will accept.

CAN IT BE REUSED OR RECYCLED?

If you don't want materials that are still potentially usable, you can call Metro Recycling Information at 503-234-3000 to talk with a recycling specialist who will help you find a convenient option for recycling, reusing, or disposing of the unwanted item. Alternatively, visit Metro's interactive "Find a Recycler" web page (www.oregonmetro.gov/findrecycler), which features information about hundreds of reuse and recycling options across the region. (The call center maintains the database used for both the hotline and the Find a Recycler web tool, so you'll get the same information by phone or online.) The database is updated on almost a daily basis, so information is as current as possible.

RECYCLING

Franchised garbage haulers pick up **curbside recycling** and **yard debris/compost.** Each local government regulates curbside recycling and determines what materials are accepted, although glass, paper, metal, and plastic bottles and tubs can be recycled at the curb throughout the region. Some jurisdictions offer more comprehensive recycling options than others.

In Portland, the **Bureau of Planning and Sustainability** (503-823-7202, www.PortlandOnline.com/bps/recycle) administers the city's curbside recycling and compost/yard debris pickup programs. In Portland, recycling and yard debris/kitchen waste are picked up weekly, but garbage is picked up every other week. For information about curbside recycling in other parts of the metro area, visit www.oregonmetro.gov/tools-living/garbage-and-recycling/recycling-home-0, call Metro at 503-234-3000, or contact your local government.

More ambitious recyclers can go beyond the limited range of materials recycled at the curb; to learn where to recycle packing peanuts, block styrofoam, old batteries, antifreeze, and other hard-to-find-a-home-for items, contact—you guessed it!—Metro at www.oregonmetro.gov/findrecycler or 503-234-3000. Metro also accepts recyclables at its transfer stations.

If your new home will be In an outlying area beyond Metro's jurisdiction, contact your city or county government directly to find out how to set up garbage and recycling service. If you're going to live someplace *really* remote, you may have to haul your own garbage to the dump!

WASHINGTON

Waste Connections Inc. (360-892-5370, www.wcnorthwest.com) provides trash, recycling, and yard debris pickup in most of Clark County. Call them or visit their website to set up service. The city of Camas hauls garbage for city residents; visit ci.camas.wa.us/index.php/pwgarbage or call 360-834-2462 for details. For general information on garbage collection, recycling, and yard debris collection in Clark County, visit www.co.clark.wa.us/recycle.

Clark County has three transfer stations:

- **Central Transfer Station**, 11034 NE 117th Ave, Vancouver, 360-256-8482
- **Washougal Transfer Station**, 4020 S Grant St, Washougal, 360-835-2500
- **West Van Materials Recovery Center**, 6601 NW Old Lower River Rd, Vancouver, 360-737-1727

ELECTRONICS RECYCLING AND HAZARDOUS WASTE DISPOSAL

Electronic waste, such as television sets, computers, computer monitors, and the like, contains such heavy metals as lead, mercury, and cadmium and should not be thrown out. If the item still works, consider donating it to a nonprofit such as **Free Geek** (1731 SE 10th Ave, 503-232-9350, www.freegeek.org), an organization that rebuilds used electronics and provides them to people and organizations in need.

To learn how to recycle electronic waste in the Portland area, visit Metro's electronics recycling web page at www.oregonmetro.gov/findrecycler and select "electronics" from the list of recyclable items, or call 503-234-3000. If you live in

Oregon outside Multnomah, Clackamas, and Washington counties, the Oregon Department of Environmental Quality's website (www.oregonecycles.org) has useful information about e-cycling (computer and electronics recycling); you can also call 888-532-9253 to find a collection site near you. The Washington Department of Ecology posts similar information at www.ecy.wa.gov/programs/swfa/ eproductrecycle/.

Household hazardous waste such as paint, solvents, or chemicals is not safe to toss in the trash and should be disposed of properly. If you generate or inherit such materials in the Portland area, you can take your household hazardous waste to Metro for free, safe disposal or recycling. Metro has two hazardous waste acceptance facilities, which are adjacent to the two transfer stations listed above and are open Monday through Saturday. For information and directions, call 503-234-3000 or visit www.oregonmetro.gov/hhw. In Clark County, household hazardous waste can be taken to the **Central Transfer and Recycling Center** on weekends from 8 a.m. to 4 p.m., or the **West Van Materials Recovery Center** on Friday or Saturday from 8 a.m. to 4 p.m.; the Washougal Transfer Station accepts hazardous waste from 8 a.m. to 4 p.m. on the third Saturday of every month. (See the listings above for contact info.) Both Metro and Clark County organize frequent community hazardous waste collection events from March through November.

Of course, you should properly dispose of your electronic and hazardous waste *before* you move to Portland; it's illegal and unsafe to transport hazardous waste, and getting rid of bulky electronics you no longer use will reduce the amount of stuff you have to move. Call 1-800-RECYCLE to find out where you can recycle electronics or dispose of hazardous waste in your area.

AUTOMOBILES

DRIVER'S LICENSES AND STATE ID CARDs

OREGON
You must obtain an Oregon driver's license when you become an Oregon resident. (The law does not specify a time limit or grace period.) You must be at least 16 to obtain a driver's license. If you have a valid license from another U.S. state or territory, Canadian province, South Korea, or Germany, and you're over 18, you will only need to pass a written test and an eye exam; a driving test is generally not necessary, although the DMV has the authority to require one. (Be aware, however, that the Oregon written exam has the reputation of being comparatively challenging.) Bring proof of identity with your full legal name (including your current out-of-state license); proof of current residence (such as lease or mortgage documents, a credit card or utility bill, or a bank statement); proof of legal presence in the United States (such as a passport or birth certificate or appropriate visa); and cash or check for the license fee (currently $60) to a regular or full-service **Oregon Driver and Motor Vehicles Services Division** (DMV) office.

Motorcycle endorsements cost $144; you'll need a valid motorcycle endorsement from another U.S. state or territory or Canadian province.

To get a state identification card, bring proof of identity and residence and the $44.50 fee to a DMV office. You can obtain additional information about driver's licenses and state ID cards from the **DMV** (503-299-9999 [Portland area], www.oregon.gov/ODOT/DMV/). The helpful brochure "Quick Tips for Doing Business with DMV" is available in PDF format at www.odot.state.or.us/forms/dmv/6841.pdf.

You can get a new Oregon driver's license at any of the following Portland-area DMV offices:

*   10280 SW Park Way, Beaverton
*   10 82nd Dr, Gladstone
*   2222 E Powell Blvd, Gresham
*   1300 SW Oak, Suite H, Hillsboro
*   3 SW Monroe Pkwy, Suite D, Lake Oswego
*   1502 SW Sixth Ave, Portland (Downtown)
*   8260 N Interstate Ave, Portland (North)
*   1836 NE 82nd Ave, Portland (Northeast)
*   8710 SE Powell Blvd, Portland (Southeast)
*   37395 Hwy 26, Sandy
*   14240 SW Galbreath Dr, Sherwood
*   500 N Columbia River Hwy, Ste 400, St. Helens

A complete list of regular and express DMV offices in Oregon is available online at www.oregon.gov/ODOT/DMV/pages/offices/index.aspx. Not every office offers all DMV services.

WASHINGTON

You must get a Washington driver's license within 30 days of the date you establish residency in the state. If you meet certain qualifications you can pre-apply online, but ultimately you'll need to go to a driver's licensing office with proof of identity (including your unexpired out-of-state license), your social security number (if you don't have it memorized), and the license and application fees (currently $35 plus a $54 issuance fee). Most, but not all, offices now accept credit cards. If you already have a license from another state, British Columbia, Germany, or South Korea, you'll need to complete an application and pass a vision test, but you won't need to take a written or driving test unless your out-of-state license is expired.

To get a state identification card, you'll need to go to a licensing office with proof of identity and $54. More information about driver's licenses and state ID cards is available from the **Washington Department of Licensing**, 360-902-3900, www.dol.wa.gov/driverslicense/. Two full-service licensing offices serve Clark County:

*   9609 NE 117th Ave, Vancouver, 360-576-6060
*   1301 NE 136th Ave, Vancouver, 360-260-6288

OWNING A CAR

It is true that it is possible to live and move about happily in Portland without a car. It is also true that most Portland households own at least one car, and that trying to make your way around the suburbs without one can be a lonely, stressful, and time-consuming endeavor. Assuming you're in the car-owning majority, there are several steps you'll need to take to become a happy (or at least legal) Portland motorist.

AUTOMOBILE REGISTRATION

OREGON

You are required to register and title your car(s) in Oregon when you become an Oregon resident. You can register your vehicle at any of the state DMV offices listed above; to save time, try to combine errands and get a driver's license during the same visit. You'll need to bring the title and (for most vehicles) proof that your car has passed an emissions test (see below). If there is a lien on your car (if the car is financed, for example), you'll need permission from the security interest holder. You'll also need to have a VIN inspection; this brief procedure can be performed at any full-service DMV office or can be done during your emissions test. Oregon does not require a safety inspection, and registration is a fixed amount (currently $86 per year for passenger cars, plus an extra $19 for residents of Multnomah County); fees are not based on a vehicle's weight or value. Registration is good for two years.

Be sure to bring a checkbook or enough cash to cover the registration, title, license plate, and VIN inspection fees; the DMV does not accept credit cards. If you have a passenger vehicle and you're not getting specialty or personalized plates, expect to pay a total of about $194 for a two-year registration on a used car; the cost for new vehicles will be higher. Full information on titling and registering a vehicle in Oregon is available on the **Oregon DMV** website (www.oregon.gov/ODOT/DMV/pages/vehicle/titlereg.aspx) or by calling 503-299-9999.

WASHINGTON

You must title and register your vehicle within 30 days of moving to Washington. (You'll need to show your Washington driver's license, so take care of that first.) To register a vehicle, you will need to submit your current title, a notarized Vehicle Certificate of Ownership Application, and possibly proof that the vehicle has passed a Washington emissions test (see below). You will also need to pay a host of fees and charges, including title fees, subagent fees, a one-time VIN inspection fee, and a registration fee. Registration fees alone, which are based on vehicle, range between $43.75 and $63.75 for most vehicles. More details about vehicle registration, including specific fees, are available from the **Department of Licensing** (360-902-3770, www.dol.wa.gov/vehicleregistration/). Additional fees can easily equal or exceed the registration cost.

To register, visit or mail your paperwork and fees to any vehicle licensing office. There are ten vehicle licensing offices in Clark County; a complete list is available online at https://fortress.wa.gov/dol/dolprod/vehoffices/. (Note that Washington driver's licensing offices cannot process vehicle registrations.)

AUTOMOBILE INSURANCE

In **Oregon**, the legally required (and woefully inadequate) minimum liability insurance coverage is $25,000 per person/$50,000 per crash for bodily injury to others; $20,000 per crash for damage to the property of others; personal injury protection coverage of $15,000 per person; and uninsured motorist coverage of $25,000 per person/$50,000 per crash for bodily injury. You do not need to bring proof of insurance with you when you register your car (unless you are taking a driving test or have previously been convicted of driving without insurance), but you will need to certify that the vehicle has at least the legally required minimum insurance coverage. You must carry proof of insurance in your vehicle at all times; electronic proof is acceptable.

Washington's mandatory insurance requirements for bodily injury or property damage to others are the same as Oregon's, except that the property damage minimum is only $10,000; personal injury protection and uninsured motorist coverage are not required. You must carry proof of insurance in your vehicle at all times.

EMISSIONS TESTING

In general, any vehicle brought into the Portland metropolitan area must pass an **emissions test** before it can be registered. Once your car is registered, you'll need to have it re-tested every two years.

OREGON

In Oregon, pre-1975 vehicles, motorcycles, and all vehicles registered outside the Portland metropolitan area and the Rogue Valley in Southern Oregon are exempt from testing. The testing fee is $21, payable by cash, credit card, money order, or debit card only; checks are not accepted. Testing hours vary; generally, vehicle inspection stations are closed on Sundays and Mondays, and stay open late on Wednesday nights. There are six inspection stations, known as "clean air stations," in the Portland area:

- **Clackamas,** 9350 SE Clackamas Rd (near intersection with SE 82nd Dr, off I-205 just north of the 212/224 exit))
- **Gresham**, 1200 SW Highland Dr (near 182nd Ave and Powell Blvd)
- **Northeast Portland**, 7701 NE 33rd Dr (between Columbia Blvd and Marine Dr)
- **Scappoose**, 52751 NE 1st (just off Hwy 30)
- **Sherwood,** 14962 SW Tualatin-Sherwood Rd (east of Sherwood off Pacific Hwy)
- **Sunset/Hillsboro**, 5130 NW Five Oaks Dr (off Cornelius Pass Rd, just north of the Sunset Hwy/US 26)

You can check out the crowd on online "lane cams" on the DEQ website, or call 971-673-1630, before you go. Clean Air Stations are normally busiest on Tuesdays, so a visit on Wednesday evening, Thursday, or Friday will result in a shorter wait time. For complete details of Oregon's emissions testing program, including station hours and program requirements, visit the **Department of Environmental Quality Vehicle Inspection Program** website (www.deq.state.or.us/aq/vip/) or call 503-229-5066 or 877-476-0583.

WASHINGTON

If you live in a non-rural part of Clark County, your car will probably have to pass an emissions test. Vehicles less than 5 or more than 25 years old are exempt from testing, as are certain hybrid vehicles with a city fuel economy rating of at least 50 miles per gallon and diesel passenger vehicles weighing three tons or less. Note that Washington requires emissions tests every two years; the model year of your car determines whether your car gets tested in even or odd years. If you move to Washington with a car that would not otherwise have to be tested during the year you move, you can wait a year to get it tested (but you'll have to register the vehicle right away regardless).

The inspection fee is $15, payable by cash, local check, or credit or debit card. Complete information is available from the **Washington Vehicle Emissions Program** (253-395-1177, emissiontestwa.com). Two emissions inspection stations, operated by a private contractor, serve Clark County:

- **West Vancouver,** 14110 NW 3rd Ct., Vancouver, 360-574-3731
- **East Vancouver**, 1121 NE 136th Ave, Vancouver, 360-254-2173

Inspection stations are open weekdays from 8:30 a.m. to 5 p.m. (Thursdays until 6 p.m.), and Saturdays from 8:30 a.m. to 2 p.m.; they are closed Sundays, state holidays, the day before Christmas, and during inclement weather (such as snowstorms). Reservations are not available, but current wait times are posted at www.emissiontestwa.com/e/waittime.aspx. Waits are generally shortest on Mondays and in the middle of each month.

PARKING

Several close-in Portland neighborhoods, including portions of Nob Hill, Goose Hollow, the Central Eastside Industrial District, Lair Hill, and the Homestead neighborhood near OHSU, are part of the city's **Area Parking Permit Program**. The proximity of these areas to downtown, combined with their lack of parking meters, make them attractive places for commuters to park; at the same time, many people who live and work in these neighborhoods do not have off-street parking, so as a consequence on-street parking is in short supply to begin with. The city introduced a permit program to address this potential problem. You generally cannot park in these zones for more than a specified length of time (typically 90 minutes or two hours) during the day, but residents of each zone, and people who work there, can purchase zone parking permits that exempt their cars from the visitor parking time limit. (Street signs explain visitor parking restrictions, so don't worry too much about accidentally parking in a permit-only zone.) To find out whether your new address is in an Area Parking permit zone, or to learn how to apply for a permit, visit www.portlandoregon.gov/transportation/38744 or call the Portland **Office of Transportation** at 503-823-5185.

Some municipalities in the Portland area require you to obtain a permit to park overnight on a public street. Check with your county or city government to see if a permit is necessary in your neighborhood.

For information about parking garages, meters, towing, and park-and-ride lots, see the **Transportation** chapter.

OWNING A BICYCLE

Formalities for bicyclists are few. In Oregon, helmets are required for riders under 16. Washington has no statewide helmet requirement, but Vancouver requires riders of all ages to wear helmets. Bicyclists must use lights between dusk and dawn and follow all applicable rules of the road. Bicycle registration is not required.

See the **Transportation** and **Green Living** chapters of this book for more details on being a Portland bicyclist.

VOTER REGISTRATION

Oregon is a vote-by-mail state. There are no polling places; the state mails a ballot to the address where you are registered, you complete the ballot, and you mail it back to the county elections office or drop it off at a designated ballot drop box. Clark County, Washington, also conducts elections by mail.

You can register to vote in either state when you get your driver's license. Alternatively, mail-in voter registration forms are available at libraries, community centers, and other public buildings, and are also available online (oregonvotes.org in Oregon; vote.wa.gov in Washington).

In **Oregon**, mail or drop off your voter registration form at your county elections office (see below). If you are a first-time Oregon voter, your registration must be postmarked at least 21 days before an election for you to be eligible to vote in that election.

In **Washington**, mail completed forms to your county election department. If you already have a Washington driver's license or ID card, you can register online. The deadline to register by mail is 29 days before an election. If you are not registered to vote in another Washington county, you can register in person at your county elections department up to 8 days before an election.

The following are the county elections offices in the Portland area:
- **Clackamas County Clerk, Elections Division,** 1710 Red Soils Ct, Suite 100, Oregon City, 97045, 503-655-8510, www.clackamas.us/elections/

- **Clark County Elections Office**, PO Box 8815, 1408 Franklin St, Vancouver, WA 98666-8815, 360-397-2345, www.clark.wa.gov/elections/
- **Columbia County Elections Department**, Columbia County Courthouse, 230 Strand St,
- **St. Helens**, 97051, 503-397-7214, www.co.columbia.or.us/departments/elections-department/elections-home
- **Marion County Clerk, Elections Division**, 4263 Commercial St SE #300, Salem, 97302, 503-588-5041, 800-655-5388, www.co.marion.or.us/co/elections
- **Multnomah County Elections Division**, 1040 SE Morrison St, Portland, 97214, 503-988-3720, www.mcelections.org
- **Washington County Elections Division,** 3700 SW Murray Blvd, Ste 101, Beaverton, 97005, 503-846-5800, www.co.washington.or.us/elections/
- **Yamhill County Clerk and Elections**, 414 NE Evans St, McMinnville, 97128, 503-434-7518, www.co.yamhill.or.us/clerk/

Full information about voter registration, political parties, and election dates is available from the **Oregon Secretary of State, Elections Division** (866-ORE-VOTE, oregonvotes.org) or the **Washington Secretary of State** (360-902-4180, 800-448-4881, vote.wa.gov).

POLITICAL CONTRIBUTIONS TAX CREDIT

Oregon taxpayers who make certain political contributions are eligible to claim a state tax credit for the amount of the contribution, subject to an annual maximum of $100 for a joint return or $50 for a single or separate return. Complete details are available from the **Oregon Department of Revenue** (503-378-4988, 800-356-4222; www.oregon.gov/DOR/PERTAX/).

Since Washington has no personal income tax, it does not offer a similar state tax credit.

PUBLIC LIBRARIES

Each county in the Portland area operates its own library system. The library systems are online, so you can scan for titles, place requests, check your borrowing records, and renew titles from home. (Phone renewals are also available.) In addition to physical books, most area library systems now allow patrons to check out or use ebooks, streaming services, and other media. Policies vary from library to library, but generally to get a library card you'll need to fill out an application form and present photo identification; applicants younger than 13 must get a parent's signature (but don't have to show photo ID). If you don't yet have an Oregon or Washington driver's license, you'll need to show a utility bill, credit card bill, or other financial or quasi-official piece of mail that shows your local address. Check out the **Neighborhoods** chapter of this book or visit the appropriate system's website to find the library nearest you.

Most of the library systems in the region belong to the Metropolitan Inter-library Exchange, or **MIX**, which means that if you live anywhere in Multnomah, Washington, Clackamas, or Clark Counties (as well as several other counties outside the metropolitan area), you can get a free library card from any library in the region. Note that MIX does not include community libraries in Columbia, Marion, or Yamhill Counties (which do not have countywide systems), but does include much of southwest Washington. The separate **Oregon Library Passport Program** encompasses public libraries throughout Oregon, as well as some academic libraries. Information on these programs is available from your local branch.

The following are the main library systems in the Portland area:

- **Multnomah County Library,** 503-988-5402, www.multcolib.org, with 19 libraries, serves the city of Portland and its eastern suburbs. It is the oldest public library system west of the Mississippi, and it is also, per capita, among the nation's busiest: library patrons check out or renew some 25 million titles annually, an average of more than 30 items for each county resident.
- **Washington County Cooperative Library Services,** 503-846-3222, www.wccls.org, is a cooperative network of 17 city, community, and specialty libraries in Washington County.
- **The Library Information Network of Clackamas County,** 503-723-4888, www.lincc.org, is an organization of 13 county and city libraries in Clackamas County.
- **Fort Vancouver Regional Library District**, 360-906-5106, www.fvrl.org, covers a large swath of Southwest Washington, including nearly all of Clark County (with the exception of the city of Camas, which operates its own public library).

Some academic libraries at Portland-area colleges and universities are open to the public and may allow borrowing privileges. For a list of colleges in the region, see the **Higher Education** chapter.

PASSPORTS

Getting a passport can take upward of six weeks, so be sure to give yourself plenty of time. If you're leaving the country imminently, you can pay an extra fee and receive two-week expedited service; if you need even faster service, search the Internet for passport expediting services.

If you don't currently have a valid passport, apply in person at any passport acceptance facility (a designation that includes many post offices and other government offices). To find the facility nearest you, check the government pages of the phone book or search by ZIP code at the State Department's Passport Acceptance Facility page (iafdb.travel.state.gov). You must submit two identical full-face passport photos of yourself, proof of U.S. citizenship (such as an original or certified birth certificate, an expired passport, or a naturalization certificate), a completed passport application and proper payment, and a driver's license or other valid form of photo identification. Complete information is available at travel.state.gov/content/passports/english.html.

Many Portlanders travel to **Canada**—Vancouver in British Columbia is only about 6 hours away by car (traffic permitting) and is a popular long weekend destination. Currently, U.S. citizens traveling by land or sea must show a full U.S. passport, a U.S. Passport Card (PASS), or other authorized document such as a state-issued "enhanced" driver's license. (A regular driver's license won't cut it anymore.) U.S. citizens traveling by air must present a U.S. passport.

A single parent traveling with children, or grandparents or other guardians traveling with children, should carry proof of custody or letters from the non-accompanying parent(s) authorizing travel out of the country. (These documents are in addition to proof of the child's citizenship.) Hunters may take ordinary rifles and shotguns into Canada (provided they are declared), but fully automatic and assault-type weapons are prohibited. A complete list of restricted and prohibited firearms can be found at the RCMP's **Canadian Firearms Program** website (www. rcmp-grc.gc.ca/cfp-pcaf/). In addition, anyone with a criminal record (including a drunk driving conviction) should contact the Canadian embassy or nearest consulate before going to Canada. For complete information about traveling to Canada, peruse the **Consular Services** web page of the U.S. mission to Canada (canada.usembassy.gov/consular-services.html).

PRINT AND BROADCAST MEDIA

TELEVISION

For broadcast (i.e., free) television, the Portland market features the major national networks plus a few independents. Of course, if you've ordered cable or satellite TV, the channels will differ from those given here. The main local television stations are:

- **Channel 2: KATU** (pronounced K-2) (ABC), www.katu.com
- **Channel 6: KOIN** (CBS), www.koin.com
- **Channel 8: KGW** (NBC), www.kgw.com
- **Channel 10: KOPB** (Oregon Public Broadcasting, PBS affiliate), www.opb.org
- **Channel 12: KPTV** (Fox), www.kptv.com
- **Channel 24: KNMT** (Trinity Broadcasting), www.tbn.org
- **Channel 32: KRCW** (CW), portlandscw32.com
- **Channel 49: KPDX** (MyNetworkTV), www.kpdx.com

Most of these stations now have multiple digital channels with different simultaneous programming.

RADIO

From jazz to punk, country to classical (and classic rock), NPR's "All Things Considered" to Rush Limbaugh, Portland's radio menu offers something for almost every taste (or absence thereof). In addition to the usual fungible selection of

Clear Channel stations and other nationally programmed radio fodder, Portland boasts several excellent independent, locally owned stations. Here's a brief guide to what's available on the Rose City's radio airwaves; remember that most radio stations now stream programming over the Internet, so you can try out local stations even before you move to Portland.

NEWS, TALK, AND SPORTS
- **KBNP**, 1410 AM, www.kbnp.com (business and finance)
- **KEX**, 1190 AM, www.1190kex.com (news and syndicated talk)
- **KMTT**, 1080 AM, www.1080thefan.com (sports and sports talk)
- **KPAM**, 860 AM, www.kpam.com (local and syndicated talk)
- **KPOJ**, 620 AM, www.foxsportsradion620.com (sports and sports talk)
- **KUFO**, 970 AM, www.freedom970.com (conservative talk)
- **KUIK**, 1360 AM, www.kuik.com (local and syndicated talk)
- **KXL**, 101.1 FM and 750 AM, www.kxl.com (talk, sports)
- **KXTG**, 750 AM, www.750thegame.com (sports)

MUSIC (COMMERCIAL)
- **KBFF,** 95.5 FM, www.live955.com (top 40)
- **KFBW**, 105.9 FM, www.1059thebrew.com (classic rock)
- **KGON**, 92.3 FM, www.kgon.com (classic rock)
- **KINK**, 101.9 FM, www.kink.fm (album-oriented rock)
- **KKCW**, 103.3 FM, www.k103.com (soft rock)
- **KKOV**, 1550 AM, www.sunny1550.com (adult standards)
- **KKRZ**, 100.3 FM, www.z100portland.com (top 40)
- **KLTH**, 106.7 FM, www.portlandoldies.com ('60s and '70s)
- **KNRK**, 94.7 FM, 947.fm (alternative)
- **KRSK**, 105.1 FM, www.1051thebuzz.com (adult contemporary, top 40)
- **KUPL**, 98.7 FM, www.kupl.com (country)
- **KWJJ,** 99.5 FM, ww.thewolfonline.com (country)
- **KXJM**, 107.5 FM, www.jammin1075.com (hip-hop, rhythmic top 40)
- **KYCH**, 97.1 FM, www.charliefm.com (miscellaneous pop)

PUBLIC AND MEMBER-SUPPORTED RADIO
- **KBOO**, 90.7 FM, www.kboo.fm (progressive/alternative community radio)
- **KMHD**, 89.1 FM, www.opb.or/kmhd/ (jazz)
- **KOPB**, 91.5 FM, www.opb.org (Oregon Public Broadcasting: NPR, PRI, news, talk, and public affairs)
- **KPSU**, 1450 AM, www.kpsu.org (college radio from Portland State University)
- **KQAC**, 89.9 FM, www.allclassical.org (classical)
- **KXRY**, 91.1 FM, www.xray.fm (eclectic mix of local DJs and progressive talk)

CHRISTIAN
- **KBVM**, 88.3 FM, www.kbvm.com (Catholic broadcasting)
- **KFIS**, 104.1 FM, www.1041thefish.com (contemporary Christian music)
- **KKPZ**, 1330 AM, www.kkpz.com

- **KLVP**, 97.9 FM, www.klove.com (adult contemporary Christian)
- **KPDQ**, 93.9 FM, www.kpdq.com

SPANISH LANGUAGE
- **KGDD**, 93.5 FM, 1520 AM, www.lagrande.mx
- **KRYP**, 93.1 FM, www.931elrey.com
- **KSZN**, 1230 AM
- **KWIP**, 880 AM, www.kwip.com

CHILDREN'S PROGRAMMING
- **KDZR**, 1640 AM (Radio Disney)

NEWSPAPERS AND MAGAZINES

Whether your interest is restaurants, parenting, bicycling, anarchism, or New Age living, there is a local (and probably free) newspaper or magazine for you. In addition to the publications listed below, the freebie racks at local libraries and natural foods stores groan under the weight of dozens of niche magazines and newspapers. (There are fewer than there used to be; an unfavorable advertising climate and the growth of the Web have driven many long-established print publications out of business.)

The *Oregonian* (www.oregonlive.com/oregonian) is Portland's long-established "serious" news daily. Like many metropolitan dailies nowadays, its quality is wildly inconsistent, but the *Oregonian* occasionally wins Pulitzer prizes. It is the only Oregon newspaper with a statewide circulation. In 2014 it converted from a traditional full-size broadsheet format to a more compact, 11" x 15" format. It also discontinued daily home deliveries; it currently prints papers daily, but delivers papers only on Wednesday, Friday, Saturday, and Sunday. Subscribers have online access to the digital edition daily. Upstart competitor the *Portland Tribune* (www.portlandtribune.com), part of the local Pamplin Media Group empire, is published in hard copy form on Tuesdays and Thursdays; founded in 2001, the *Tribune* focuses primarily on local and regional news, and is available for free at many locations around the metropolitan area. Pamplin Media also publishes community weeklies that serve most of the major suburbs; the combined efforts of the conglomerate's news staff are posted online on a rolling basis. Across the Columbia River, the Vancouver *Columbian* (www.columbian.com) covers communities in Clark County seven days a week. If the local papers are insufficiently urbane for your taste, the *New York Times* (www.nytimes.com) offers home delivery of its Northwest regional edition.

Business news junkies may enjoy perusing the *Portland Business Journal* (bizjournals.com/portland/) and the *Daily Journal of Commerce* (www.djcoregon.com). The *Wall Street Journal* (online.wsj.com) is available for delivery in some parts of the metro area.

Willamette Week (www.wweek.com) is a free weekly that covers the local arts and entertainment scene and dabbles (often successfully) in serious journalism; its coverage of local politics is in some cases superior to that of mainstream newspapers. Copies are available at supermarkets, record stores, stand-alone kiosks, and restaurants and cafés throughout Portland and in some of the suburbs. The *Willy Week*'s edgier-than-thou weekly competitor, the *Mercury* (www.portlandmercury.com), is likely to annoy most readers over the age of 30, but its coverage of the local music scene is excellent. *Just Out* (www.justout.com), an arts and entertainment paper that covers events of interest to Portland's gay and lesbian community, comes out (so to speak) monthly.

Several local glossy monthlies beckon from newsstands and supermarket checkout aisles. *Portland Monthly* (www.portlandmonthlymag.com) covers shopping, dining, personalities, getaways, and current events in the metro area for a readership with apparently substantial disposable income; despite the preponderance of ads, the writing can be entertaining and informative. *1859* (www.1859oregonmagazine.com), named for the year of Oregon's statehood, is a bimonthly statewide lifestyle magazine with a self-described mandate to showcase "the breadth of the Oregon experience." The editorially slighter bimonthly *Oregon Home* (www.oregonhomemagazine.com) caters to the nesting and home-remodeling crowd. If you're interested in the movers and shakers of the local economy, *Oregon Business* (www.oregonbusiness.com) will keep you in the loop. Monthly community papers like the *Southwest Portland Post* (www.swportlandpost.com), the *Southeast Examiner* (www.southeastexaminer.com), and *The Bee* (inner Southeast Portland, www.readthebee.com) cover items of local interest to the various quadrants of the city; these publications are typically delivered to area residents for free, and are also available at libraries and local shops.

Several papers and magazines report on events of interest to specific ethnic communities, including the *Asian Reporter* (www.asianreporter.com), *El Hispanic News* (www.elhispanicnews.com), and *Oregon Jewish Life* (www.ojlife.com); the *Portland Observer* (www.portlandobserver.com) and the *Skanner* (www.theskanner.com) emphasize coverage of events of interest to the city's African-American community.

Portland is awash in a sea of regional special-interest publications, including various activity-centric 'zines, New Age and alternative health magazines like *New Connexion* (www.newconnexion.net), and such parenting publications as *Portland Family Magazine* (www.portlandfamily.com) and *Metro Parent* (www.metro-parent.com). If your only dependent is a dog, then *Spot* (www.spotmagazine.net) is your newspaper. The *Portland Alliance* (www.theportlandalliance.org) and the *Peaceworker* (www.peaceworker.org) preach leftist politics to the converted. Scores of other niche publications await your discovery and/or avoidance at public places around the city.

KNOWING WHERE TO GO FOR A PARTICULAR SERVICE IS PARTICULARLY important when you move to a new city or state. The following information, which includes details about various services, including renting furniture, hiring a housekeeper, pest control, shipping services, and consumer protection, might make your life a bit easier. This chapter also includes sections about services for the disabled, seniors, new residents from abroad, and gay and lesbian life.

RENTAL SERVICES

If you need to furnish a home right away and you don't have time to shop for the perfect furniture and appliances, or if you won't be in town for more than a couple months, you can rent practically anything you need. Be careful, though: if you rent household items for more than a few months, you will almost always end up paying more than if you had bought new furniture. In addition to the furniture rental establishments listed below, you might consider home staging services, or even rent-to-own businesses like **Aaron's** (www.aarons.com) or **Rent-A-Center** (800-665-5510, www.rentacenter.com). Be aware, though, that even credit purchases are usually cheaper in the long run than "rent-to-own" plans. Use these services sparingly.

The following are two long-established rental outfits in the area:

- **Cort Furniture Rental**, 9495 SW Cascade Ave, Beaverton, 503-520-8800, 888-360-2678, www.cort.com
- **People's Furniture Rental**, 11035 SW 11th St, Suite 290, Beaverton, 800-922-1231, www.peoples1.com

DOMESTIC SERVICES

As with any service, satisfied friends and trusted colleagues are the best sources of recommendations for domestic service providers. Failing that, **Angie's List**

(888-888-LIST, www.angieslist.com) advertises itself as a list of plumbers, auto mechanics, painters, and the like recommended by members, but you should still check references as you would (or should) with any contractor or service provider. There is a fee to join. Free online review sites like **Yelp** (www.yelp.com) are another good resource, but don't take every review, positive or negative, at face value.

For other goods and services, take a look at the **Shopping for the Home** chapter.

HOUSE CLEANING

You might decide to use a house-cleaning service on a one-off basis (before you move into a new house, for example) or on an ongoing basis. Before you employ any cleaner or cleaning service, be sure to check references and only use cleaners who are insured. (Agencies that employ bonded and insured cleaners usually say so in their advertisements.) Personal recommendations are your best source for finding cleaners, but of course cleaning services are also listed online and in the Yellow Pages (under "House Cleaning").

If you're trying to minimize the use of chemicals in your home, several companies such as **Domestica** (503-222-2334, www.domesticaclean.com) use only nontoxic, environmentally safe products to clean your home.

PEST CONTROL

While typical Oregon pests lack the horrifying cachet of, say, hissing cockroaches, they can nonetheless be troublesome to have around the house. In the insect department, dampwood termites and carpenter ants, if left unchecked, can cause structural damage, and other insects can be nuisances. Mammals that sometimes pose problems include possums, raccoons, skunks, bats, squirrels, mice, moles, or even nutria, huge, non-native rodents from Argentina that resemble giant beavers with enormous orange teeth. (This is true.) Rats often infest areas where invasive English ivy has established itself, and the inaccessible (to humans) spaces between parallel neighboring fences.

If these critters have invaded your home or yard and setting traps yourself has not worked or is not an option, consider calling an exterminator, or visit www. pestweb.com for comprehensive information about dealing with your unwelcome houseguests. If your problem requires a professional solution, consult one of the many services listed online or under "Pest Control Services" in the Yellow Pages. If your problem is with furry creatures, many services offer live trapping. You're unlikely to want that solution for insects, but the following services claim to use less toxic (although not necessarily nontoxic) chemicals:

- **All Natural Pest Elimination**, 877-662-8449, www.nobuggy.com
- **Alpha Ecological**, 503-972-8733, 800-768-9424, www.alphaecological.com
- **Bugaboo Pest Control**, 503-289-0576, www.bugaboopest.com
- **EcoCare**, 503-222-5566, www.pestcontrol.com

POSTAL AND SHIPPING SERVICES

Portland's main post office is located just north of downtown, near Union Station, at 715 Northwest Hoyt Street (the main entrance is on Glisan). Hours of operation are Monday through Friday, 8 a.m. to 6:30 p.m., and Saturdays from 8:30 a.m. to 5 p.m. Neighborhood post offices are more convenient for most people, but tend to have shorter hours. To find your local post office (including contract post offices housed in local businesses), or to look up ZIP codes or postal rates, call 800-ASK-USPS (800-275-8777) or visit www.usps.com. The Airport Mail Facility at 7640 Northeast Airport Way (503-335-7920) is open weekdays from 8:30 a.m. to 10 p.m., 9:30 a.m. to 9 p.m. on Saturdays, and 11 a.m. to 9 p.m. on Sundays.

If you're between addresses and need a place to receive mail, you can rent a box at a local post office or choose a private mail receiving service. Many of the private services allow call-in mail checks and mail forwarding, but they often charge more than the post office.

MAIL RECEIVING SERVICES

Look in the Yellow Pages under "Mail Boxes-Rental" to find the most conveniently located private mail receiving services. The following services have multiple locations in the Portland area:

- **Postal Annex+**, 800-767-8252, www.postalannex.com
- **The UPS Store**, 800-789-4623, www.theupsstore.com

SHIPPING SERVICES

In addition to parcel shipment and next-day or second-day delivery, most of the familiar national shipping services offer freight service for large items.

- **DHL**, 800-225-5345, www.dhl-usa.com
- **FedEx**, 800-463-3339, www.fedex.com
- **United Parcel Service (UPS)**, 800-742-5877, www.ups.com
- **United States Postal Service**, 800-275-8777, www.usps.com

JUNK MAIL AND TELEMARKETING

A deluge of junk mail will almost certainly follow you after you move, and everyone from the phone company to your mortgage lender will be anxious to sell your name to marketers. To curtail the onslaught, write to the junk mail overlords at **Direct Marketing Association** (DMAChoice, Direct Marketing Association, P.O. Box 643, Carmel, New York 10512) to request a form, or obtain or submit an online form at www.dmachoice.org. (Either way, they'll charge you $1 for the privilege of removing your name from mailing lists; online, you'll have to navigate through the propaganda explaining why direct mail advertising is the best thing since indoor plumbing.) Most—but not all—businesses and charities that send junk mail will exclude addresses registered with this service, but it may take 30 to 90 days for junk mail to slow. Registration with the DMA will not deter marketers that do not buy the organization's preference lists.

The major credit bureaus share an opt-out line that allows you to reduce the volume of prescreened offers for credit and insurance that you receive. Call 1-888-5-OPTOUT (888-567-8688) or visit www.optoutpresecreen.com to have your name removed from mailing lists that the credit bureaus sell to direct-mail marketers.

You can stop those annoying dinnertime calls from legitimate commercial telemarketers (but not charities, political organizations, or rogue boiler room operations that scorn the law) by adding your number to the Federal Trade Commission's **National Do Not Call Registry**. Call 800-382-1222 or visit www.donotcall.gov.

AUTOMOBILE REPAIR AND MAINTENANCE

Finding a trustworthy mechanic is often difficult, to say the least. The best way to find a good shop is to ask coworkers, neighbors, and friends, particularly those with the same make of car, for recommendations. Shop around for a mechanic before you need one; if you wait until your car is virtually immobile, you're likely to be tempted to take it to the nearest chop shop. Auto dealerships are generally reliable, if pricier than independent mechanics; at least they have the parts, equipment, and (one hopes) expertise to service the cars they sell.

If you're considering an independent shop, you may want to check with the Better Business Bureau to see if any complaints have been filed against it. (See "Consumer Protection" below.) If it's just advice you need, consider tuning in to Tom and Ray Magliozzi (better known as Click & Clack), the guys on National Public Radio's Car Talk program. Although the Magliozzis have retired, and Tom passed away in November 2014, old programs are rebroadcast on KOPB (91.5 FM) on Saturdays at 10 a.m. and Sundays at 11 a.m. The "Mechanics Files" page of the Car Talk website (www.cartalk.com/mechanics-files/) is a database of recommended (and reviled) mechanics, as reviewed by Car Talk listeners.

If the question isn't who will repair your car, but rather who to call to have it towed, you'll find lots of options listed online and in the Yellow Pages under "Towing-Auto." To avoid a frantic search for towing companies after you've broken down, consider joining an automobile club. The **American Automobile Association (AAA)** (contact AAA of Oregon/Idaho, 888-422-2503, www.oregon.aaa.com) is the best-known club; it offers towing services, travel guides and maps, and lists of approved mechanics, among other services. The local club now offers roadside assistance for bicycles as well as motor vehicles. The lesser-known (and locally based) **Better World Club** (866-238-1137, www.betterworldclub.com) offers similar services, and bills itself as "America's only eco-friendly auto club." Many national service station chains and insurance companies also offer road service plans.

HEALTH CARE

HEALTH INSURANCE

At press time, the contours of the health insurance landscape in the Northwest and nationwide are changing. The Affordable Care Act, a.k.a. Obamacare, now requires most Americans to have health insurance coverage or pay an annual penalty. Because the law also, among other things, requires plans to offer certain minimum features and prohibits denial of coverage based on pre-existing conditions, both the range and cost of available plans is very much in flux. For now, employer-sponsored plans cover most Oregonians (and Washingtonians) who have private health insurance. If your employer doesn't provide coverage, or if you're self-employed (or unemployed), you'll need to shop around for health insurance. The new online health insurance exchanges somewhat simplify this process. **Cover Oregon** (www.coveroregon.com, 855-268-3767) is the Oregon gateway to the insurance exchange. (Cover Oregon became infamous nationally after it spent hundreds of millions of dollars building a website through which no one was ever able to complete an insurance enrollment; hundreds of thousands of Oregonians had to mail in enrollment forms. The state eventually gave up on developing its own exchange, and the Cover Oregon website now connects to the federal exchange.) **Washington's** health exchange is accessible at 855-923-4623, www.wahealthplanfinder.org. Be sure to compare deductibles and co-pays, the percentages covered for various procedures, restrictions on which doctors and hospitals you can use, the extent of prescription drug coverage, and exemptions for pre-existing conditions. Insurance premiums can vary dramatically from one company to another. Subsidies are available for lower-income workers.

The **Insurance Division** of the Oregon Department of Consumer and Business Services (350 Winter St NE, Salem, 97301, 503-947-7984, 888-877-4894, www.insurance.oregon.gov) regulates health insurance in Oregon. A range of consumer publications, including health insurance buyer's guides and complaint statistics for various insurers, is available for download at the Division's website; visit www.insurance.oregon.gov/consumer/health-insurance/health.html or call 503-947-7984 or 888-877-4894 to request publications by mail. In Washington, the **Office of the Insurance Commissioner** (PO Box 40255, Olympia, Washington, 98504, 800-562-6900, www.insurance.wa.gov) provides similar services; health insurance information for consumers is available at www.insurance.wa.gov/consumers/health/index.shtml.

HEALTH CARE PLANS

The following seven companies have traditionally provided the vast majority of private health insurance coverage in Oregon. Most of these companies also operate in southwest Washington.

- **Health Net**, 888-802-7001, www.healthnet.com.

- **Kaiser Permanente**, 877-488-3590, www.buykp.org
- **LifeWise Health Plan of Oregon**, 800-290-1278, www.lifewiseor.com
- **Moda**, 888-392-2940, www.choosemoda.com
- **PacificSource Health Plans**, 855-330-2792, www.pacificsource.com
- **Providence Health Plans**, 503-574-7500, 800-988-0088, www.providence.org/healthplans/
- **Regence BlueCross Blue Shield of Oregon**, 888-734-3623, www.regence.com

HEALTH CARE ASSISTANCE PROGRAMS

Medicare is the federal government's health insurance program for people age 65 and older and qualified disabled individuals of any age. For information about Medicare eligibility or to apply for Medicare benefits, call the **Social Security Administration** at 800-633-4227 or visit ssa.gov/medicare. You cannot yet apply for Medicare online. In Oregon, volunteers at the **Senior Health Insurance Benefits Assistance Program** (SHIBA; 800-722-4134, www.oregon.gov/DCBS/SHIBA/) provide free, individualized counseling about Medicare and related programs, including Medicare-supplement insurance and long-term care insurance. Their website lists contact information for SHIBA sites around the state, or you can call them for more information. **Washington's** similar SHIBA program (see below) is not limited to Medicare advice.

The **Oregon Health Plan** is the state's version of the federal government's Medicaid program. Administered by the Oregon Health Authority, the Oregon Health Plan provides health coverage for working people with very low incomes, as well as people with disabilities. Call 800-699-9075 or visit www.oregon.gov/OHA/healthplan for information about coverage and eligibility requirements.

Washington's **Statewide Health Insurance Benefits Advisors** (SHIBA) network dispenses advice and distributes information on a range of health insurance matters, including private insurance as well as government programs such as Medicare and Medicaid. Information is available from the SHIBA website (www.insurance.wa.gov/shiba/) or by calling the HelpLine at 800-562-6900.

COMPLAINTS

For insurance-related complaints, contact the Oregon Insurance Division's **Consumer Advocacy Unit** (503-947-7984, 888-877-4894, www.insurance.oregon.gov), which can help with resolving complaints. Their website includes an online complaint form. In Washington, contact the Insurance Commissioner (800-562-6900, www.insurance.wa.gov/complaints-and-fraud/).

FINDING A DOCTOR

If your job includes health benefits, your insurance plan or HMO may require you to use a participating doctor or facility (or may pay a reduced benefit if you use a medical care provider who is "out-of-plan"). If you have a choice of physicians, there's no substitute for word-of-mouth; if you can, ask for a referral from a friend or trusted coworker. If that option is unavailable, such websites as www. drscore.com and www.healthgrades.com purport to rate physicians, but the ratings should probably be taken with a grain of salt (and an aspirin, then call them in the morning). The **Oregon Medical Board** (971-673-2700, 877-254-6263, www.oregon.gov/OMB/) regulates physicians in Oregon; contact them or visit the website to check on a doctor's credentials and history of lawsuits or professional sanctions, or to make a formal complaint about a doctor or other medical professional. In Washington, the state's **Health Systems Quality Assurance Commission** (360-236-4700, www.doh.wa.gov/hsqa/professions/medical/default. htm) provides a somewhat equivalent service.

Portland is a national center for alternative and naturopathic medicine. As always, a personal recommendation is the best way to find a health care provider. Failing that, try the "Find a Physician (ND)" tool on the **Oregon Board of Naturopathic Medicine** site (www.oregon.gov/OBNE/), or call them at 971-673-0193. You could also visit one of the clinics at the **National College of Natural Medicine** (503-552-1551, www.ncnm-clinic.com).

HOSPITALS

- **Adventist Medical Center**, 10123 SE Market St, 503-257-2500, www.adventisthealthnw.com
- **Doernbecher Children's Hospital at OHSU**, 3181 SW Sam Jackson Park Rd, 503-494-8311, http://www.ohsu.edu/xd/health/services/doernbecher/
- **Kaiser Permanente Westside Medical Center**, 2875 NW Stucki Ave, Hillsboro, 971-310-1000, www.kp.org
- **Kaiser Permanente Sunnyside Medical Center**, 10180 SE Sunnyside Rd, Clackamas, 503-652-2880, www.kp.org
- **Legacy Emanuel Medical Center**, 2801 N Gantenbein Ave, 503-413-2200, www.legacyhealth.org
- **Legacy Good Samaritan Medical Center**, 1015 NW 22nd Ave, 503-413-7711, www.legacyhealth.org
- **Legacy Meridian Park Medical Center**, 19300 SW 65th Ave, Tualatin, 503-692-1212, www.legacyhealth.org
- **Legacy Mount Hood Medical Center**, 24800 SE Stark St, Gresham, 503-674-1122, www.legacyhealth.org
- **Legacy Salmon Creek Medical Center**, 2211 NE 139th St, Vancouver, 360-487-1000, www.legacyhealth.org
- **Oregon Health & Science University (OHSU) Hospital and Clinics**, 3181 SW Sam Jackson Park Rd, 503-494-8311, www.ohsu.edu/xd/health/
- **Providence Milwaukie Hospital**, 10150 SE 32nd Ave, Milwaukie, 503-513-8300, www.providence.org/Oregon/

- **Providence Portland Medical Center**, 4805 NE Glisan St, 503-215-1111, www.oregon.providence.org
- **Providence St. Vincent Medical Center**, 9205 SW Barnes Rd, 503-216-1234, www.oregon.providence.org
- **Providence Willamette Falls Hospital**, 1500 Division St, Oregon City, 503-656-1631, www.oregon.providence.org
- **Southwest PeaceHealth Medical Center**, 400 NE Mother Joseph Pl, Vancouver, 360-514-2000, 503-972-3000, www.peacehealth.org/southwest/
- **Tuality Community Hospital**, 335 SE 8th Ave, Hillsboro, 503-681-1111, www.tuality.org
- **Tuality Forest Grove Hospital**, 1809 Maple St, Forest Grove, 503-357-2173, www.tuality.org

AFFORDABLE HEALTH CARE

COMMUNITY AND PUBLIC CLINICS

Community clinics and some public health clinics offer free or low-cost treatment to low-income individuals and families; some clinics use sliding fee scales based on income.

- The **Coalition of Community Health Clinics** (503-546-4991, www.coalition-clinics.org) is a coalition of community clinics located throughout the city of Portland. Their comprehensive website includes links to non-member clinics, including clinics that provide low-cost dental and chiropractic services.
- **Free Clinic of SW Washington**, 4100 Plomondon St, Vancouver, 360-313-1390, www.freeclinics.org
- The **Multnomah County Health Department** (www.multco.us/health) operates several safety-net clinics in Portland and Gresham; for clinic appointments call 503-988-5558.
- The **Wallace Medical Concern** (503-489-1760, www.wallacemedical.org), is based in the Rockwood area of East Portland/Gresham, and also operates a mobile medical clinic five days a week as well as an Old Town clinic on Thursday evenings.

PHARMACIES

Most hospitals and large clinics have their own pharmacies. So do most major supermarkets, discount stores, and warehouse stores, including **Fred Meyer** (800-576-4377, www.fredmeyer.com/pharmacy/), **Safeway** (877-723-3929, www.safeway.com), **Albertsons** (877-932-7948, www.albertsons.com), **Walmart** (http://www.walmart.com/cp/pharmacy/5431), **Bi-Mart** (541-344-0681, www.bimart.com), **Costco** (800-607-6861, www.costco.com), and **Target** (877-798-2743, www.target.com). In addition to such national drugstore chains as **Rite Aid** (800-748-3243, www.riteaid.com) and **Walgreens** (800-925-4733, www.walgreens.com),

Portland still has a fair number of friendly, independently owned pharmacies; just walk or drive around your neighborhood, or look in the Yellow Pages under "Pharmacies" for locations.

The following pharmacies are open **24 hours**. Many emergency hospitals also have 24-hour pharmacies on-site.

* **Rite Aid**: 2021 NW 185th Ave, Hillsboro, 503-645-7704; 10860 SE Oak St, Milwaukie, 503-652-8058
* **Walgreens**: 14600 SW Murray Scholls Dr, Beaverton, 503-579-1878; 13939 SW Pacific Hwy, Tigard, 503-670-9812; 1950 NE Burnside Rd, Gresham, 503-674-8482; 1905 SE 164th Ave, Vancouver, 360-885-2938

ADVANCE DIRECTIVES

An advance directive allows you to state your wishes for medical care in the event that you are unable to make decisions for yourself; it also allows you to designate a person who will make health care decisions on your behalf. If you already have an advance directive in another state, it is a good idea to complete the form in your new state to ensure your wishes are honored. **Oregon** advance directives are available online at www.oregon.gov/DCBS/insurance/SHIBA/topics/pages/advancedirectives.aspx; hard copies are available from Oregon Health Decisions (503-692-0894, 800-422-4805, www.oregonhealthdecisions.org), or from most hospitals. You can download a **Washington** health care directive at a number of websites, including that of the Washington State Medical Association (www.wsma.org/advance-directives); hard copies are available from hospitals or physicians.

HEALTH LAW—PROTECTING PRIVATE INFORMATION

A variety of federal and state laws, most notably the federal Health Insurance Portability and Accountability Act of 1996 (HIPAA), restrict health care providers' ability to use and disseminate personal health information. The general rule is that a provider cannot share your health information with a third party unless you have given your written consent or there is a law that authorizes the provider to share your information. If you believe your right to privacy of medical records has been violated, you can file a complaint with the United States Department of Health and Human Services at their **Region X Office for Civil Rights** in Seattle. For details on how to file a complaint, visit www.hhs.gov/ocr/privacy/hipaa/complaints/ or call 800-368-1019.

CONSUMER PROTECTION

The best way to avoid becoming a victim of fraud is to work to prevent it in the first place. Read all contracts down to the smallest print, save all receipts and cancelled checks, get the names of telephone sales and service people with whom you deal, date every paper you sign, make sure contractors are properly licensed and bonded, and check with the Attorney General's office or the Better Business Bureau for complaints before you do business with a company.

Sometimes, despite your best efforts and suspicious nature, you'll get ripped off. You negotiate, calmly but firmly and with documents in hand, but to no avail. What can you do? First, contact the local **Better Business Bureau** at 503-212-3022 (Oregon) or 206-431-2222 (Washington) or online at www.bbb. org/alaskaoregonwesternwashington/. This organization will keep a permanent record of unresolved complaints, but its first priority is to encourage its affiliated businesses to address all reasonable complaints promptly and thoroughly. The BBB will not get involved until you have exhausted the usual channels of complaint—contacting the supervisor, manager, or owner, for example. You can also file a complaint—or threaten to file a complaint—with the **Federal Trade Commission** (877-382-4357, www.ftc.gov) or with the agency responsible for consumer protection in the state where the offending business is located:

- **Oregon Department of Justice, Office of the Attorney General**, 503-378-4320, 877-877-9392 (toll-free in Oregon), www.doj.state.or.us/consumer/
- **Washington State Office of the Attorney General,** 800-551-4636 (to request that a complaint form be mailed to you), www.atg.wa.gov/FileAComplaint.aspx

If all else fails, you can go to court—unless your contract provides for mandatory arbitration. (You did notice that arbitration clause in paragraph 37 when you read the contract in full, right?) You can file a small claims action without an attorney in cases where the amount at issue is $7,500 or less ($5,000 or less in Washington). Contact the clerk of court in your county for details. The **Oregon State Bar** has useful information about consumer protection and small claims court on its website (www.osbar.org), and also operates a lawyer referral service; call 503-684-3763 or 800-452-7636, or visit the website for details. In Clark County, Washington, contact the Clark County Bar Association's **Southwest Washington Lawyer Referral Service** at 360-695-0599.

SERVICES FOR PEOPLE WITH DISABILITIES

GETTING AROUND

CARS
To obtain a disabled person parking permit, contact the Oregon **DMV** (503-299-9999, www.oregon.gov/ODOT/DMV/pages/driverid/disparking.aspx). (In Washington, apply to the state **Department of Licensing**, 360-902-3770, TTY 360-664-8885, www.dol.wa.gov/vehicleregistration/parking.html.)

The car rental companies listed in the **Transportation** chapter can usually accommodate special needs with 48 to 72 hours' notice.

PUBLIC TRANSPORTATION

Given at least 24 hours' notice, most local and national passenger carriers will make any needed accommodations for passengers with special needs.

TriMet is fully accessible; buses have ramps or power lifts, light rail (MAX) cars and the Portland Streetcar have extending ramps, and WES commuter train car floors are flush with the platform. Stations have Braille signage, and bus operators announce stops in advance; computerized recordings announce stops on MAX and the Portland Streetcar. Service animals are allowed on all public transit. People with disabilities travel at reduced fares. For more information, visit TriMet's accessibility page (www.trimet.org/access/) or call 503-962-2455 (TTY 711).

TriMet's **LIFT** paratransit program offers shared-ride transportation for people whose disabilities prevent them from using fixed-route public transportation. Call 503-962-8000, option 2 (TTY 711) for details or visit www.trimet.org/lift/. Portland's aerial tram is also fully accessible.

Ride Connection (503-226-0700, www.rideconnection.org) helps older adults and people with disabilities with transportation to jobs, medical appointments, shopping, or local transport hubs. Their **RideWise** program helps people with disabilities to travel independently on public transportation.

In Clark County, **C-TRAN** (360-695-0123, www.c-tran.com) operates lift-equipped buses. C-TRAN also operates the C-VAN paratransit service; visit www.c-tran.com/c-tran-services/c-van-and-accessible-service or call 360-695-8918 (TTY 360-695-9715) for details.

AIR TRAVEL

The **U.S. Department of Transportation** publishes a free booklet entitled *New Horizons: Information for the Air Traveler with a Disability*, also available online at www.airconsumer.ost.dot.gov/publications/horizons.htm. For more information, call the DOT **Disability Hotline** at 800-778-4838 (TTY 800-455-9880).

TRAVEL RESOURCES

- **Adventures Without Limits**, 1341 Pacific Ave, Forest Grove, 503-359-2568, www.awloutdoors.com, designs outdoor adventure activities for people of all abilities.
- **The Boulevard** (www.blvd.com) is a web portal for disability resources that includes a section on accessible travel and recreation.
- Eugene-based **Mobility International USA** (541-343-1284, www.miusa.org) publishes several guides to international travel, exchange, and development for people with disabilities.
- **Society for Accessible Travel & Hospitality**, 212-447-7284, www.sath.org

COMMUNICATION

Telecommunications Relay Service allows deaf and hard-of-hearing individuals to communicate with hearing people through a trained operator using a text telephone (TTY). The relay operator translates both parties' words verbatim and is required by law to keep all conversations strictly confidential. The service is free. To use the service, dial **711** from any phone or call 800-735-1232 (from Oregon) or 800-833-6388 (from Washington).

Access Services Northwest, 503-457-5000, www.asnwonline.com, and **Northwest American Sign Language Associates**, 503-267-4861, www.nwasla. com, provide sign language interpreters and other communication facilitation services for deaf, hard-of-hearing, and hearing individuals in Oregon and southwest Washington.

INDEPENDENT LIVING

Independent Living Resources (2410 SE 11th Ave, 503-232-7411, TTY 503-232-8408, www.ilr.org) offers up-to-date information about, and advocates for, accessible housing, transportation, employment, and other community resources. The **Washington State Independent Living Council** (800-624-4105, wasilco.org) coordinates independent living centers in Washington. (There are none in Southwest Washington at press time, however.)

ADDITIONAL RESOURCES

The most comprehensive sources of information for people with special needs are **www.disAbility.gov**, a portal to hundreds of federal government sites and related links, and the **International Center for Disability Resources on the Internet**, www.icdri.org. A few local resources include:

- **The Arc of Multnomah-Clackamas** (503-223-7279, www.thearcmult.org) provides information and referrals for people with developmental or mental disabilities. **The Arc of Southwest Washington** (360-254-1562, www.arcswwa. org) performs the same role in southwest Washington.
- The website of **Multnomah County Aging and Disability Services** (multco.us/ ads) includes a comprehensive database of services and resources for people with disabilities. It also operates a 24-hour helpline (503-988-3646).
- **Disability Rights Oregon** (503-243-2081, 800-452-1694, www.droregon.org) provides legal advocacy and protection for Oregon residents with disabilities. This organization provides information and advice about issues including civil rights, special education, rights to services, health care, and guardianship. The **Alliance of People with Disabilities** (206-545-7055, 866-545-7055, www.dis-abilitypride.org) offers similar services to Washington residents.
- **The Oregon Department of Human Services' division for Aging and People with Disabilities** (503-945-5811, 800-282-8096, www.oregon.gov/DHS/sp-

wpd/) has assembled a wealth of useful information and helpful links on their website. In Washington, the state's **Aging and Long-Term Support Administration**, 360-725-2300, www.altsa.dshs.wa.gov, provides a similar function.

SERVICES FOR SENIORS

The federal government's **Senior Citizens' Resources** web page (www.usa.gov/Topics/Seniors.shtml) is a useful starting place for general information for seniors, including tips on consumer protection, health, housing, and finances. In Oregon, contact the state Department of Human Services' **Aging and People with Disabilities** division (503-945-5811, 800-282-8096, www.oregon.gov/DHS/spwpd) for information about services for Oregon seniors. In southwest Washington, the **Southwest Washington Agency on Aging and Disabilities** (888-637-6060, www.helpingelders.org) is a helpful resource.

- Seniors with mobility difficulties or disabilities should peruse the "Getting Around" section of Services for People with Disabilities, above. Note that TriMet and other public transit agencies charge a reduced fare for "honored citizens." The following are a few more local resources for older adults.
- **Adult Placement Network**, 503-659-2029, www.adultplacementnetwork.com, is a referral agency for retirement homes, assisted living facilities, and other housing options for older adults who cannot or choose not to live alone.
- **Aging and Disability Resource Connection of Oregon**, 855-673-2372, www.adrcoforegon.org, helps connect seniors to local services.
- **Meals-on-Wheels**, 503-736-6325, www.mealsonwheelspeople.org, provides nutritious hot lunches to people over the age of 60 at dozens of meal sites in Multnomah, Washington, and Clark counties, and delivers hot lunches to seniors who are unable to come to a meal site.
- **Metropolitan Family Service**, 1808 SE Belmont St, 503-232-0007, www.metfamily.org, reaches out to older adults through programs that encourage and assist with independent living and provide volunteer opportunities for seniors.
- Multnomah County's **Aging and Disability Services** (503-988-3646, multco.us/ads) provides information about services for seniors, and in some cases operates those services (such as cooling centers for seniors in extremely hot weather).
- Portland State University's **Senior Adult Learning Center**, 503-725-4739, www.sites.google.com/a/pdx.edu/salc/home, provides continuing education for seniors and allows people over 65 to audit regular PSU classes for free.
- The website of **Seniors Housing Together** (seniorshousingtogether.com) offers tips on selecting housing options for seniors. If you are looking for a shared housing situation for older adults, **Let's Share Housing** (503-719-5444, www.letssharehousing.com) is a good place to start.

SERVICES FOR INTERNATIONAL NEWCOMERS

According to the U.S. Census Bureau, more than 300,000 Oregonians were born in other countries. The Portland area is home to tens of thousands of immigrants, including substantial communities from Mexico, Southeast Asia, Russia, Ukraine, West and East Africa, and the Indian subcontinent.

If you are one of these international newcomers, or if you want to be, a variety of helpful information is available online at the **U.S. Citizen and Immigration Services** website (uscis.gov). If you have specific questions, you can also contact the USCIS national customer service center (800-375-5283, TTY 800-767-1833). (Once you know what you need to do, you'll inevitably have to fill out paperwork.)

If you need legal aid in immigration matters, you can contact one of the following organizations:

- **Catholic Charities Immigration Legal Services**, 2740 SE Powell Blvd # 2, 503-542-2855, www.catholiccharitiesoregon.org/services_legal_services.asp
- **Immigration Counseling Service**, 519 SW Park, Suite 610, 503-221-1689, www.immigrationcounseling.org
- **Sponsors Organized to Assist Refugees (SOAR)**, 7931 NE Halsey St, Suite 314, 503-284-3002, www.emoregon.org/soar.php

International newcomers who are experiencing culture shock can get a quick overview of American culture, etiquette, expectations, and quirks in the *Newcomer's Handbook for Moving to and Living in the USA* by Mike Livingston, published by **First Books**. Call 503-968-6777 or visit www.firstbooks.com to order a copy.

CONSULATES

Most foreign consulates on the West Coast are located in San Francisco, Los Angeles, and/or Seattle. The following countries have honorary consuls in Portland, who may or may not be able to assist citizens of the nations they nominally represent: Austria, Barbados, Belgium, Canada, Cyprus, Czech Republic, Denmark, France, Germany, Guatemala, Iceland, Italy, Latvia, Liechtenstein, Lithuania, Luxembourg, Malaysia, the Netherlands, New Zealand, Norway, the Philippines, Romania, South Korea, Thailand, and the United Kingdom. Addresses and telephone numbers for most of these honorary consulates are listed in the Yellow Pages under "Consulates & Foreign Governments"; unlisted consuls are unlikely to be of much use to foreign nationals.

There are two full consulates in Portland:

- **Consulate General of Japan**, 2700 Wells Fargo Center, 1300 SW 5th Ave, 503-221-1811, www.portland.us.emb-japan.go.jp
- **Consulate of Mexico**, 1305 SW 12th Ave, 503-274-1442, consulmex.sre.gob.mx/portland/

GAY AND LESBIAN LIFE

Portland regularly appears in top-ten lists of the best cities in the U.S. for gays and lesbians. While the "studies" that generate these lists are generally based less on rigorous analysis than on a desire for page views and magazine sales, Portland's inclusion comes as no surprise. For many years, the city has had a large, thriving gay, lesbian, bisexual, and transgender (GLBT) community. By some estimates, nearly 10% of inhabitants of Portland proper self-identify as gay, lesbian, or bisexual. Rainbow flags and "Queer Nation" bumper stickers are common in neighborhoods in much of the city (and to a lesser extent, in some of the suburbs), and Sam Adams, mayor from 2009 to 2013, was the first openly gay mayor of a large U.S. city.

While Portland is on the whole a tolerant and friendly home for gay singles, couples, and families, homophobia and discrimination certainly exist. In 2007 Oregon passed legislation outlawing discrimination based on sexual orientation or gender identity in housing, employment, public education, and public accommodations, with some exemptions for religious organizations. (Washington passed a similar law in 2006.) A 2004 Oregon ballot measure amending the state constitution to ban gay marriage passed with nearly 57% of voters in favor (although majorities in two counties, including Multnomah County, voted against the measure). This ban was overturned in federal court in 2014, but by then attitudes toward same-sex marriage in Oregon (as elsewhere in the country) had changed dramatically, and a planned 2014 ballot measure to repeal the ban—a measure the court decision made unnecessary—was widely expected to pass. Across the Columbia, Washington voters had already legalized same-sex marriage by referendum in 2012.

GLBT RESOURCES

The biweekly arts, entertainment, and news magazine *Just Out* (www.justout. com) is an indispensable source of information about Portland's GLBT community. **Portland's Gay and Lesbian Yellow Pages** (www.PDXGayYellowPages.com), available for free at many area libraries, bookstores, and business, lists gay-owned or gay-friendly businesses, and includes listings for local GLBT clubs and organizations. (Otherwise, beyond being smaller than the phone company's Yellow Pages and having generally more interesting ads, it's really just a phone directory.) There are too many organizations that address the concerns and interests of GLBT community in Portland to list them all here, but the following organizations are a good starting point:

- **Basic Rights Oregon**, 503-222-6151, www.basicrights.org, works for equal rights for gays and lesbians.
- **PFLAG (Parents and Friends of Lesbians and Gays)**, 503-232-7676, www. pflagpdx.org, sponsors monthly meetings and discussions; visit www.pflagpdx. org for information.

- **Portland Area Business Association (PABA)** (www.paba.com) works to build business and career opportunities in the GLBT community.
- **Pride Northwest** (503-295-9788, www.pridenw.org) organizes and promotes Portland's annual Pride festival, held in downtown Portland each June.
- The **Q Center** (4115 N Mississippi Ave, 503-234-7837, www.pdxqcenter.org) is a community center for GBLT and Questioning individuals.
- **Sexual Minority Youth Resource Center** (2450 NE Sandy Blvd, Suite 100, 503-872-9664, www.smyrc.org) provides counseling and a free drop-in center for GLBT and questioning youth under age 24.

A MOVE TO A NEW CITY ALMOST ALWAYS INCLUDES RUNNING LOTS OF errands—from buying new curtains to replacing mops and brooms that didn't make it into the moving truck. Portland offers plenty of shopping choices, from major national department stores and big-box behemoths to hole-in-the-wall thrift shops and unique local boutiques. If you've moved from somewhere other than Alaska, Montana, New Hampshire, or Delaware, you'll be delighted to find that Oregon does not (yet) have a state sales tax. (If you've moved to Washington, you're out of luck; see **Money Matters** for more details.)

SHOPPING DISTRICTS AND MALLS

NEIGHBORHOOD SHOPPING DISTRICTS

Portlanders are rightly proud of the variety and distinctiveness of their city's neighborhood shopping districts. While almost every city neighborhood has its own commercial node, some of these districts are larger and more diverse than others. The following are the main shopping districts that draw visitors from beyond the surrounding neighborhoods. Most of these districts have formal business organizations with websites.

- **Alberta Arts District**, NE Alberta St between Martin Luther King Jr Blvd and 33rd Ave, www.albertamainst.org; since about 2000, this area has blossomed from a somewhat sketchy neighborhood into a thriving zone of cafés, boutiques, wellness centers, and art galleries. This mile-long strip offers a funky mix of businesses—including such unusual attractions as a grilled cheese–vending school bus (the Grilled Cheese Grill, NE 11th and Alberta, 503-206-8959, www.grilledcheesegrill.com) and a high-end vegan gourmet *prix fixe* restaurant (Natural Selection, 3033 NE Albert Ave, 503-288-5883, www.naturalselectionpdx.com). The neighborhood hosts an evening art fair on the last Thursday of each month.

- **Downtown Portland**, www.downtownportland.org; downtown Portland has about every kind of good and service you might need, in almost every price range. Unfortunately, the stores are scattered all over the place, not in a nice little row, although the traditional center of gravity for downtown shopping is the area surrounding Pioneer Courthouse Square. Downtown shopping options include independently owned establishments; national chains, including some upscale chains such as Tiffany & Co.; and such department stores as Nordstrom, Macy's, and H&M. Most downtown stores are an easy stroll from transit; if you're driving, many downtown merchants will validate parking at certain garages.
- **Hawthorne District**, SE Hawthorne Blvd between 12th and 58th Avenues (greatest concentration of businesses between 32nd and 39th/César Chávez), www.thinkhawthorne.com; the Hawthorne District has long had a reputation as Portland's hippie shopping district, but the area actually offers a quite diverse shopping experience (the occasional bong store and tie-dye establishment notwithstanding). For several blocks, restaurants, bars, cafés, theaters, and many gift and specialty shops line the street. The district is on the whole quite laid-back and unpretentious (especially compared to, say, the Pearl), although chains are moving in and a few new, somewhat incongruous lofts have been built. A similar but slightly more compact shopping district extends along **Belmont Street** (www.belmontdistrict.org), which runs parallel to Hawthorne Boulevard a few blocks to the north. Paralleling Hawthorne a few blocks to the south is the burgeoning **Division Street/Clinton Avenue** district (www. divisionclinton.com), which has a few boutiques but is best known for its restaurants, several of which are among the very best in the city.
- **Multnomah Village**, centered on the intersection of SW Capitol Hwy and 35th Ave, www.multnomahvillage.org; the "Village in the heart of Portland" harbors an eclectic range of specialty shops, antique stores, and restaurants, cafés, and pubs. Its Southwest Portland location means it tends to be less hipster-focused and more family-oriented than some Eastside shopping districts.
- **North Mississippi,** North Mississippi Ave between Mason St and Fremont St, www.missisippiave.com; like the Alberta Arts District, North Mississippi Avenue was a down-and-out neighborhood not many years ago. Its subsequent transformation into a vibrant commercial district is, depending on your point of view, either an urban success story or an example of relentless gentrification. Either way, the result from the visitor's perspective is an eclectic and booming collection of restaurants and interesting shops, including a comic book store, a gourmet salt shop, a small nursery, a pizza joint/pub that hosts a weekly spelling bee, and a light bulb superstore.
- **Northeast Broadway**, NE Broadway between Grand Ave and 28th Ave (www. nebroadway.com); Northeast Broadway businesses cater both to residents of the adjacent (and generally affluent) Irvington neighborhood and to people from other parts of the city who come to shop and dine here. This district runs eastward from the Lloyd Center shopping mall area towards Hollywood, and

includes a mix of unassuming old-line businesses such as Helen Bernhard Bakery (since 1924; 1717 NE Broadway, 503-287-1251, www.helenbernhardbakery.com), trendy bars, a variety of dining establishments, and some hot boutiques.

- **Northwest Portland (Nob Hill)**, NW 21st and 23rd Avenues, from Burnside St north to Vaughn St, www.nwpdxnobhill.com; Northwest Twenty-Third (sometimes derisively called Trendy-Third) Avenue (and, to a lesser extent, Northwest Twenty-First Avenue, which runs parallel two blocks east) is one of the brightest stars in Portland's shopping firmament. The street is lined with a dazzling range of stores, with an emphasis on clothing, household goods, antiques, and knick-knacks of all kinds, as well as restaurants and cafés that cater to all tastes and budgets. Chains such as Pottery Barn, Urban Outfitters, and Restoration Hardware have made inroads here in recent years, but many stores remain locally owned (or at least small-scale). Street parking can be hard to find on weekends and evenings, but the area is eminently walkable and easily accessible by bus and streetcar.
- **Pearl District**, north of West Burnside St, between 8th Ave and Interstate 405, 503-227-8519, www.explorethepearl.com. Call it frou-frou, call it trendy, call it spendy—and you'd be right. The Pearl is not a neighborhood in which to seek bargains. Barring a few businesses such as Powell's Books that predated the neighborhood's transformation into a playground for the affluent, options generally range from upscale independent stores to upscale chain stores, although a few shops, bars, and restaurants do actually cater to patrons with an average income. That said, the Pearl offers lots of unique merchandise that cannot be found anywhere else in Portland. Shops and restaurants are sprinkled liberally throughout this expansive but densely built-up neighborhood, which makes the Pearl a great destination for a walking/shopping/gourmet food sampling expedition.
- **Sellwood/Westmoreland**, centered on SE 13th Ave and Tacoma (Sellwood) and SE Milwaukie Ave at Bybee (Westmoreland) (www.sellwoodwestmoreland.com); Sellwood and Westmoreland are two separate districts only half a mile apart, and both offer a mix of interesting boutiques, popular restaurants, art galleries, and plenty of antique stores. Although it is not particularly far away from the city center, the area remains off the radar screen for many Portlanders, and so is (on the whole) less self-consciously trendy than some close-in shopping zones.
- **St. Johns (www.stjohnsmainstreet.org)**; the "downtown" area of St. Johns along North Lombard St at the east end of the St. Johns Bridge is a funky blend of businesses: places that seemingly have not changed since the Eisenhower presidency stand next to quirky, hip boutiques, vegan and ethnic restaurants, laid-back coffeehouses, and two different independent movie theaters. Still, everyone seems to get along just fine. This area still draws relatively few shoppers from the rest of Portland, but its splendid isolation is definitely coming to an end.

Shopping districts in most communities outside Portland tend to be of the strip mall variety, but some of the older, more established suburbs such as Milwaukie,

Beaverton, Forest Grove, Troutdale, Hillsboro, Oregon City, and Gresham (www. gresham.org) have walkable downtown shopping districts; Vancouver's Uptown Village district (www.uptownvillage.com) is also worth a visit.

While not a shopping district per se, the **Portland Saturday Market** (503-241-4188, www.portlandsaturdaymarket.com) functions as an outdoor weekend bazaar from March through Christmas. It is located under the west end of the Burnside Bridge and in a specially built plaza stretching southward, along the river.

MALLS

Although Portland's neighborhood shopping districts are fantastic, that doesn't mean the vast seas of pavement surrounding the area's malls are empty. Indeed, at the more popular malls it can be hard to find a parking space at all on weekends or during the holiday shopping season. If nothing else, malls are a great place to stretch your legs (and your credit limit) if you fear going out in the winter drizzle.

In addition to its ongoing love affair with traditional indoor malls, Portland is getting plugged into the one of the country's newest shopping trends, the "lifestyle mall," which features upscale retailers in faux–Main Street settings:

- The **Streets of Tanasbourne** mall in Hillsboro (NW Cornell Rd at Stucki Ave, 503-533-0561, www.streetsoftanasbourne.com), which opened in 2004, was the local avatar of this trend.
- Perhaps the area's prime example is **Bridgeport Village** (503-968-1704, www. bridgeport-village.com), which opened in 2005 at Lower Boones Ferry/Bridgeport Rd and Interstate 5 (exit 290), straddling the Tigard-Tualatin border and across the freeway from Lake Oswego. In addition to national retailers such as Anthropologie and Crate and Barrel, Bridgeport Village has attracted several local retailers, including Mario's (clothing). The complex also includes spas, salons, several restaurants, and cafés, with a Whole Foods supermarket across the street. Bridgeport Village is popular enough to cause traffic backups on I-5.

The success of these initial developments is likely to spawn imitators, and indeed, older indoor malls such as Washington Square, Clackamas Town Center, and Cedar Hills Crossing have revamped their exteriors to make them more open and accessible from the outside and less forbiddingly featureless.

Here's a list of the major traditional shopping malls in the Portland area:

- **Cedar Hills Crossing**, 3205 SW Cedar Hills Blvd, Beaverton, 503-643-6563, www.cedarhillscrossing.com; once upon a time this was the nearly moribund Beaverton Mall. Following a major redesign several years ago, it is now Cedar Hills Crossing, and boasts a crowded multiplex and such indicia of relevance as a Powell's bookstore and a New Seasons supermarket.
- **Clackamas Town Center**, 12000 SE 82nd Ave, Clackamas, 503-653-6913, www. clackamastowncenter.com; Clackamas Town Center is one of the area's primary suburban shopping centers. Anchored by a Macy's, Sears, Nordstrom, and JC

Penney, Clackamas Town Center offers few surprises. The mall proper expanded by some 250,000 square feet in 2007, adding a "lifestyle center" zone, and several satellite shopping centers have sprung up around it, including Clackamas Promenade just across the street.

- **Lloyd Center Mall**, NE Multnomah St at 11th Ave, 503-282-2511, www.lloydcentermall.com; one of the first enclosed malls in the country, Lloyd Center, in close-in Northeast Portland, is Portland's primary "urban" mall. In addition to the usual mall shops, department stores (Nordstrom, Macy's, Sears), discount stores (Marshall's, Ross Dress for Less), a food court, and a multi-screen cinema, Lloyd Center houses an ice skating rink smack-dab in the middle of the mall.

- **Pioneer Place**, 700 SW 5th Ave, 503-228-5800, www.pioneerplace.com; this downtown Portland mall is fairly unobtrusive (partly because it lacks an adjacent surface parking lot, and partly because much of it is underground). As a result, Pioneer Place manages to function reasonably well as part of the downtown shopping scene. Most of the stores are relatively upscale, and the only department store anchor is H&M. A new Apple Store, on the site of the former Saks Fifth Avenue, is a striking addition to the downtown streetscape. The underground food court gets ridiculously crowded during weekday lunch hours.

- **Washington Square**, 9585 SW Washington Square Rd, Tigard, 503-639-8860, www.shopwashingtonsquare.com; along with Clackamas Town Center, Washington Square is one of the two dominant traditional suburban malls in the Portland area. Both malls have the same four anchor department stores (although Washington Square's Nordstrom is the largest in the state). Washington Square's overall retail mix is somewhat more upscale than most other area malls, reflecting the relative affluence of its Washington County surroundings.

- **Westfield Vancouver**, 8700 NE Vancouver Mall Dr, Vancouver, 360-892-6255, westfield.com/Vancouver/; better known as the Vancouver Mall, this mall near the intersection of Interstate 205 and State Route 500 is a pretty standard issue suburban shopping complex.

OUTLET MALLS AND FACTORY STORES

Factory discount stores often stock overruns and imperfect goods. While they can offer great bargains, shoppers should pay special attention to merchandise quality. There are two major outlet malls within a 45-minute drive of Portland. **Columbia Gorge Premium Outlets** (450 NW 257th Ave, Troutdale, 503-669-8060, www.premiumoutlets.com/columbiagorge/), with 45 stores, is just south of Interstate 84 at exit 17. **Woodburn Premium Outlets** (1001 Arney Rd, Woodburn, 503-981-1900, www.premiumoutlets.com/woodburn/), a 100-plus store complex of "craftsman-inspired" storefronts at exit 271 on Interstate 5, sometimes backs up traffic on the freeway for miles.

In addition to the outlet malls, several local companies operate stand-alone factory outlet stores:

- **Columbia Sportswear Outlet Stores,** 1323 SE Tacoma St, 503-238-0118; 3 Monroe Pkwy #H, Lake Oswego, 503-636-6593
- **Danner Factory Store,** 12021 NE Airport Way, 503-251-1111
- **Hanna Andersson Outlet Store,** 7 Monroe Pkwy, Lake Oswego, 503-697-1953
- **Nike Factory Store,** 2650 NE Martin Luther King Jr Blvd, 503-281-5901
- **Pendleton Woolen Mills Outlet Store,** 2 Pendleton Way, Washougal, 360-835-1118

DEPARTMENT STORES

Most Portland-area department stores are attached to malls, although there are a few stand-alone establishments.

- **JC Penney,** Clackamas Town Center, 503-653-8830; Washington Square, 503-620-0750; Vancouver Mall, 360-254-3800; Columbia Tech Center, 19005 SE Mill Plain Blvd, Vancouver, 360-253-9550; www.jcpenney.com; JC Penney sells everything from vacuum cleaners and mattresses to clothing and cosmetics.
- **Kohl's,** seven Portland-area stores, 866-887-8884, www.kohls.com; Kohl's competes with Sears and JC Penney, and runs sales almost continuously on everything from clothing to coffee makers.
- **Macy's,** six Portland-area locations (including downtown Portland), 800-289-6229, www.macys.com. In 2006, Macy's, which had never had a Portland presence, bought long-time Portland department store chain Meier & Frank. To some local consternation, it changed the names of all Meier & Frank stores to Macy's (as it had done with other acquisitions, such as Marshall Field's in Chicago) and "Macified" the stores and their product lines. Many Portlanders still refer to Macy's stores as Meier & Frank.
- **Nordstrom,** 701 SW Broadway, 503-224-6666; Lloyd Center, 503-287-2444; Washington Square, 503-620-0555; Clackamas Town Center, 503-652-1810; Vancouver Mall, 360-256-8666, www.nordstrom.com; thanks to its reputation for superb customer service, Nordstrom dominates the local market for high-end clothing and shoes.
- **Sears,** Lloyd Center, 503-528-3200; Clackamas Town Center, 503-786-5200; Washington Square, 503-620-1510; Vancouver Mall, 360-260-4200; www.sears.com; known for Craftsman power tools, Sears no longer sells the Craftsman bungalows and other kit homes that are scattered around many of Portland's early–20th century eastside neighborhoods. The store is a mainstay for family clothing, appliances, and home electronics.

DISCOUNT DEPARTMENT STORES

Some upscale departments stores (such as Nordstrom—see Nordstrom Rack, below) have their own outlets where they sell discontinued, overstocked, or slightly irregular merchandise at reduced prices. Such goods are also sold through discount outlets such as Marshall's, Ross Dress for Less, and T.J. Maxx. Other discount chains—Target, Kmart, and Walmart—carry name-brand goods, but generally not the designer labels available at upscale department stores.

- **Fred Meyer**; most Fred Meyer supermarkets have an attached department store for non-grocery items. See "Supermarkets" below for details.
- **H&M**, five Portland-area stores, 855-466-7467, www.hm.com/us
- **Kmart**, four Portland-area stores, 866-562-7848. www.kmart.com
- **Marshall's**, Lloyd Center, 503-287-6441; 16200 SW Pacific Hwy, Tigard, 503-620-7230; 881 NE 25th Ave, Hillsboro, 503-547-2841; 10257 NE Cascade Pkwy, 503-249-8132; 2077 NE Burnside St, Gresham, 503-492-7121; www.marshallsonline.com
- **Nordstrom Rack**, 245 SW Morrison St, 503-299-1815; 18100 NW Evergreen Pkwy, Beaverton, 503-439-0900; 8930 SE Sunnyside Rd, Clackamas, 503-654-5415; 9175 SW Cascade Ave, Beaverton, 971-327-6161; www.nordstrom.com
- **Ross Dress for Less**, 17 Portland-area stores, 800-945-7677, www.rossstores.com
- **Saks Fifth Avenue Off Fifth**, 7455 SW Bridgeport Rd, Tualatin, 503-620-6536, www.saksoff5th.com
- **Target**, 14 Portland-area locations, 800-440-0680, www.target.com
- **T.J. Maxx**, 604 SW Washington St, 503-224-1417; 2135 N Parker Ave, 503-240-9412; 11370 SE 82nd Ave, 503-653-7913; 3805 SW 117th Ave, Beaverton, 503-641-1828; 8635 SW Tualatin-Sherwood Rd, Tualatin, 503-612-0000; 8101 NE Parkway Dr, Vancouver, 360-256-9606; www.tjmaxx.com
- **Walmart**, nine Portland-area stores, www.walmart.com

And don't forget membership warehouse stores such as **Costco** and **Bi-Mart**. They offer low prices on food, electronics, cameras, small appliances, housewares, and automotive supplies. Membership fees apply, and you don't get—or pay for—the level of service you expect from a regular department store. See the "Food" section below for more details.

HOUSEHOLD SHOPPING

In addition to the businesses listed below, most department stores (and many discount department stores) carry a wide range of household goods, from mattresses and sheets to home electronics and appliances. A category-defying option for furniture, accessories, and Swedish ginger cookies is **IKEA**, which is located just off I-205 at the Portland International Airport exit (10280 Cascades Pkwy, 888-888-4532, www.ikea.com). The store's ridiculously large sign is hard to miss from the freeway, especially at night.

APPLIANCES, COMPUTERS, AND ELECTRONICS

Although many of the national big-box electronics chains with Portland stores have gone "el foldo" in the last couple of years, Portland nonetheless boasts an impressive array of electronics and household appliance stores. In addition to the stores listed below, for appliances, you might consider home improvement retailers such as **Home Depot** and **Lowe's** (see "Hardware and Paint" below) or department stores like **Sears**. For computers, also check prices and offerings at office supply chains such as **Office Depot** (13 Portland-area stores, 800-463-3768, www.officedepot.com), **Staples** (five Portland-area stores, 800-333-3330, www. staples.com), and **OfficeMax** (seven Portland-area stores, 800-283-7674, www. officemax.com); all three of these companies frequently place advertising inserts in the Sunday *Oregonian*.

For specialist or smaller-scale computer dealers, look online or check the Yellow Pages under "computers"; look for other home electronics and appliance retailers under "Appliances," "Stereo & Hi Fi-Dealers," and "Television-Dealers," or try one of these stores:

- **Apple Store**, Pioneer Place, 450 SW Yamhill St, 503-265-2010; Bridgeport Village, Tigard, 503-670-8400; Washington Square, Tigard, 503-495-2080; www.apple.com
- **Basco Builders Appliance Supply Company**, 1411 NW Davis St, 503-226-9235, www.bascoappliances.com
- **Best Buy,** eight Portland-area stores, 888-237-8289, www.bestbuy.com
- **Bose Showcase Store**, Pioneer Place, 503-224-5772, www.bose.com
- **DeWhitt Appliance**, 12518 NE Airport Way, 503-546-4212, www. dewhittappliance.com
- **Echo Audio**, 1015 SW Washington St, 503-223-2292, 888-248-3246, www. echohifi.com
- **Fred's Sound of Music Audio/Video**, 3760 SE Hawthorne Blvd, 503-234-5341, www.fredsoundofmusic.com
- **Fry's Electronics**, 29400 SW Town Center Loop, Wilsonville, 503-570-6000, www.frys.com
- **The Mac Store**, 700 NE Multnomah St, 800-689-8191; Cedar Hills Crossing, Beaverton, and Clackamas Town Center, Clackamas; www.themacstore.com; as the name suggests, this Pacific Northwest chain is another Apple retail specialist.
- **NW Natural Appliance Center**, 2610 SE 8th Ave, 503-220-2362, www. nwnaturalappliances.com; this is the gas company's appliance showroom, so don't come looking for electric cooktops here.
- **Pearl Audio Video**, 1038 NW Johnson St, 503-222-2599, www.pearlaudiovideo.com
- **Radio Shack**, 800-843-7422, www.radioshack.com, has 18 stores in the area.
- **Spencer's Appliances**, 7115 NE Glisan St, 503-254-7977, www. spencersappliancesonline.com, sells new and used appliances.
- **Standard TV & Appliance**, 1205 NE 33rd Ave, 503-542-5120; 5240 SW 82nd Ave, 503-777-3377; 3600 SW Hall Blvd, Beaverton, 503-619-0500; www. standardtvandappliance.com; Standard has one of the area's widest selections

of major appliances. Standard also sells used appliances at 5240 SE 82nd Ave, 503-777-3377, www.stvausedappliance.com.

- **Stark's Vacuums**, eight Portland-area locations, 800-230-4101, www.starks.com
- **Stereotypes Audio**, 1401 SE Morrison St, 503-280-0910, www.stereotypesaudio.com
- **Vern L. Wenger Company Video/Audio**, 5904 SW Beaverton-Hillsdale Hwy, 503-292-9211, www.wengersvideoaudio.com
- **Video Only**, 1900 N Hayden Island Dr, 503-283-3400; 8200 SE Sunnyside Rd, Clackamas, 503-653-8200; 12000 SW Canyon Rd, Beaverton, 503-520-0520; www.videoonly.com

CARPETS, RUGS & TILE

Portland has scores, if not hundreds, of carpet and tile retailers, ranging from discount warehouses to small stores that specialize in antique Persian rugs. For a complete list, look online or in the Yellow Pages under "Carpet & Rug Dealers" or "Tile-Ceramic-Contractors & Dealers." If you're in the market for gorgeous, high-end designer tile, be sure to check out the showroom of Portland-based **Pratt & Larson Tile and Stone** (1201 SE 3rd Ave, 503-231-9464, www.prattandlarson-or.com).

FURNITURE

A home furnishings showroom may be one of the first places you visit as you try to fill the empty spaces of your new home or apartment. There are plenty of furniture stores waiting for you, both in the city and in the strip malls and shopping centers of almost every suburban community. Simply do an online search or check the Yellow Pages under "Furniture-Retail" for a complete listing. Many department stores also offer good selections of traditional home furnishings. If you're looking for something beyond standard pieces in traditional styles, Portland has a plethora of options, with a heavy concentration in the Pearl District and on the Inner East Side. Here's a partial list of stores to try:

- **Altura Furniture**, 3500 N. Mississippi Ave, 503-288-2228, www.alturafurniture.com, sells locally crafted, contemporary solid wood furniture.
- **Beam & Anchor**, 2710 N Interstate Ave, 503-367-3230, www.beamandanchor.com, sells "warm industrial" housewares.
- **Design Within Reach**, 1200 NW Everett St, 503-220-0200, www.dwr.com; offers a wide selection of modern furniture, including authorized reproductions of classic designs such as the Eames lounge and ottoman.
- **Eclectic Home**, 2259 NW Raleigh St, 503-224-0551, www.eclectichome.com, sells "sustainable" furniture and organic mattresses.
- **Eco PDX**, 2289 N Interstate Ave, 503-287-8181, www.ecopdx.com, offers handcrafted furniture from salvaged tropical lumber.

- **Hip,** 1829 NW 25th Ave, 503-225-5017, www.ubhip.com, specializes in the kind of clean-lined Euro-style furniture that's perfect for your new condo in the Pearl.
- **Hive,** 820 NW Glisan St, 503-242-1967, www.hivemodern.com, carries a wide selection of modern furniture, lighting, and accessories.
- **The Joinery,** 4804 SE Woodstock Blvd, 503-788-8547, www.thejoinery.com, builds beautiful dressers, tables, and other pieces from certified sustainably harvested wood.
- **Mitchell Gold + Bob Williams,** 1106 W Burnside St, 503-972-5000, www. mgbwhome.com, sells furniture best described as "modern traditional" from a highly visible showroom on West Burnside.
- **Natural Furniture,** 800 NE Broadway, 503-284-0655, www.naturalunfinished-furniture.com; Natural Furniture sells ready-to-finish tables, chairs, bookcases, and other wood furniture.
- **Portland Furniture,** 908 NW 23rd Ave, 503-546-5468, www.portlandfurnitureonline.com, has a wide selection of living room, dining room, and bedroom furniture in styles ranging from respectably traditional to uber-modern.

HARDWARE AND PAINT

As they do nearly everywhere in America, **Home Depot** (www.homedepot.com) and **Lowe's** (www.lowes.com) dominate Portland's home improvement market. These stores offer everything from paint and wallpaper to lumber, lighting, flooring, countertops, appliances, and plumbing fixtures under one very expansive roof. But the big boys haven't yet put neighborhood hardware stores and specialty retailers out of business; Portland and the surrounding communities still have quite a few traditional hardware stores, many of them affiliated with **Ace** (www.acehardware.com) or **True Value** (www.truevalue.com). Do a web search look in the Yellow Pages under "Hardware-Retail" or "Building Materials-Retail" or go for a walk in your neighborhood to find more options. Most hardware stores (as well as Home Depot and Lowe's) now carry paint and can match colors, but for the best quality and a wider (or at least different) selection you may want to try a specialty paint store (listed in the Yellow Pages under "Paint-Retail"). Here are a few paint and hardware options:

- **A-Boy Plumbing & Electrical,** 503-287-0776, www.aboysupply.com, is a locally owned chain with three locations in the Portland area.
- **Chown Hardware,** 333 NW 16th Ave, 503-243-6500, www.chown.com, has knowledgeable staff members and a vast selection of hardware and fixtures.
- **Green Depot,** 819 SE Taylor St, 503-222-3881, www.greendepot.com, sells no-VOC paints and stains.
- **George Morlan Plumbing Supply,** 2222 NW Raleigh St, 503-224-7000, 5529 SE Foster Rd, 503-771-1145, 12585 SW Pacific Hwy, Tigard, 503-624-7381, www.

georgemorlan.com; this is a veritable supermarket of plumbing fixtures, supplies, and related items.

- **Miller Paint Co.**, 503-255-0190, www.millerpaint.com, is a local company with more than 20 stores in the Portland area.
- **Mr. Plywood**, 7609 SE Stark St, 503-254-7387, www.mrplywoodinc.com, is a basic, close-in lumber yard and building supply store.
- **Parr Lumber**, www.parr.com, is a local hardware company with nine Portland-area retail yards.
- **Rodda Paint**, www.roddapaint.com, is another local paint manufacturer with multiple stores in the Portland area; among the featured paint lines is Devine Color, a unique "color from the Northwest" high-end specialty interior paint designed by Gretchen Schauffler, a nationally recognized Portland-area artist, color consultant, and entrepreneur.
- **WC Winks Hardware**, 200 SE Stark St, 503-227-5536, www.winkshardware. com; chased out of the Pearl District several years ago by gentrification, Winks stocks obscure hinge types, door pulls, and other hard-to-find hardware. It is also closed on weekends.
- **Woodcrafters**, 212 NE 6th Ave, 503-231-0226, www.woodcrafters.us; a woodworker's Disneyland, Woodcrafters sells tools, blades, and cabinet hardware, and has probably the city's best selection of millwork and moldings.

HOUSEWARES, KITCHENWARE, AND LINENS

If the department stores don't have just what you're looking for, one of these specialty stores might:

- **Bed, Bath & Beyond**, eight Portland-area stores, 800-462-3966, www. bedbathandbeyond.com
- **Crate & Barrel**, Bridgeport Village, Tigard, 503-598-9005, www.crateandbarrel.com
- **French Quarter Linens**, 530 NW 11th Ave, 503-282-8200, www.frenchquarterlinens. com; luxuriate in high thread counts and the silkiness of fine Egyptian cotton at this purveyor of European bedding and towels.
- **Indigo Traders**, 7878 SW Capitol Hwy, 503-780-2422; 6532 SW Capitol Hwy, 503-972-6020; www.indigotraders.com; this store specializes in Mediterranean and Middle Eastern textiles and glassware.
- **Kitchen Kaboodle**, 800-366-0161, www.kitchenkaboodle.com; this local kitchenware chain has four stores in the area, and also sells furniture.
- **Mirador Kitchen & Home**, 2106 SE Division St, 503-231-5175, www. miradorkitchenandhome.com, sells an eclectic collection of natural (e.g., made from organic fibers) linens, kitchenware, canning supplies, and other items for the home.
- **Natural Spaces**, 5331 SW Macadam Ave, 503-695-6177, www.naturalspaces. com, offers natural linens and products made from recycled glass.

- **Please Be Seated**, 8309 SE 13th Ave, 503-595-1736, www.pleasebeseatedpdx. com, has a little bit of everything for the table: linens, china, glassware, and more.
- **Sur la Table**, 1102 NW Couch St, 503-295-9679; 390 N State St, Lake Oswego, 503-636-2181; Bridgeport Village, Tigard, 503-968-8015; www.surlatable.com
- **Williams-Sonoma**, 338 NW 23rd Ave, 503-946-2300; Washington Square, Tigard, 503-684-2784; www.williams-sonoma.com

LAMPS AND LIGHTING

Many building supply stores, hardware stores, and furniture stores sell light fixtures. In addition, lighting "superstores" such as **Lamps Plus** (9369 SE 82nd Avenue, 503-788-7772; 8748 SW Hall Boulevard, Beaverton, 503-641-7546; www. lampsplus.com) and **Globe Lighting** (five Portland-area stores, 800-689-1000, www.globelighting.com) carry thousands of different light fixtures. For something a bit out-of-the-mainstream, or for historical reproduction lighting, try one of the following stores:

- **Ferguson**, 824 NW 18th Ave, 503-222-1144, www.ferguson.com, stocks not only lighting, but bath and kitchen fixtures and appliances.
- **Porteco Lighting**, 1401 SE Morrison St, 503-719-5011, portecolighting.com, carries an assortment of low-voltage and energy-efficient lighting.
- **Rejuvenation**, 1100 SE Grand Ave, 503-238-1900, www.rejuvenation.com; this Portland-based company manufactures reproduction light fixtures from periods ranging from the early electric era to the "atomic age" of the mid-20th century.
- **Schoolhouse Electric**, 2181 NW Nicolai St, 503-230-7113, www. schoolhouseelectric.com; another period lighting maker, Schoolhouse Electric casts many of its shades from the original early–20th century molds.
- **Sunlan Lighting**, 3901 N Mississippi Ave, 503-281-0453, www.sunlanlighting. com, stocks almost every conceivable type of light bulb, including a range of full-spectrum bulbs to brighten up those pesky Portland winters.

MATTRESSES AND FUTONS

For a standard, mass-produced mattress, your cheapest options are generally department stores or such chains as **BedMart Mattress Superstores** (888-840-4282, www.bedmartmattresssuperstores.com), **Mattress World Northwest** (503-594-0550, www.mattressworldnorthwest.com), and **SleepCountry USA** (888-887-5337, www.sleepcountry.com), all of which have multiple Portland-area locations. At any of these establishments, you'd be very unlucky to drop in on a day without a mattress sale in progress. For a futon or custom-made mattress, try one of the following stores:

- **Cotton Cloud Futons and Mattresses**, 701 NE Broadway, 503-335-0758, www. cottoncloudfutons.com
- **Eclectic Home**, 2259 NW Raleigh St, 503-224-0551, www.eclectichome.com

- **Mulligan Mattress Co.**, 1200 SE 7th Ave, 503-222-3723, ww.mulliganmattress. com, offers custom-built mattresses made with natural latex and organic cotton.
- **Rock Soft Futon**, 3200 SE Hawthorne Blvd, 503-236-0921, www.rocksoftfuton.com

GARDEN CENTERS AND NURSERIES

Thanks to Portland's mild, maritime climate, many kinds of plants thrive here. A single small urban yard might contain a rose bush, a windmill palm tree, an alpine rock garden, a eucalyptus tree, a dwarf Japanese maple, a yucca, and an ancient rhododendron. As you might imagine, gardening is a popular pastime here, and there are plenty of in-town garden centers, both large and small, that cater to the horticulturally inclined. Beyond the urban fringe, horticulture is a major part of Oregon's agriculture industry, and Portland's hinterlands are dotted with tree and plant nurseries. Some of these nurseries are highly specialized, and many sell directly to the public.

Here are a few of the more popular local garden centers and nurseries:
- **Cistus Nursery**, 22711 NW Gillihan Rd, Sauvie Island, 503-621-2233, www. cistus.com; billing itself as "the home of zonal denial," Cistus sells hardy sub-tropicals and southern hemisphere plants that can (and do) grow in Portland.
- **Cornell Farm**, 8212 SW Barnes Rd, 503-292-9895, www.cornellfarms.com, has a wide selection of shrubs and annual and perennial garden plants.
- **Dennis' Seven Dees** and **Drake's Seven Dees**, four Portland-area garden centers, www.dennis7dees.com, 503-777-7777; www.drakes7dees.com, 503-292-9121. (The "seven dees" stand for the first initials of the founders' children, not the era of disco and bell bottoms.)
- **Garden Fever**, 3433 NE 24th Ave., 503-287-3200, www.gardenfever.com, sells specialty plants, seeds, and garden accouterments.
- **Joy Creek Nursery**, 20300 NW Watson Rd, Scappoose, 503-543-7474, www. joycreek.com; this nursery 18 miles north of Portland is worth the trip to buy unusual cultivars and hard-to-find plant species.
- **Livingscape Nursery**, 3926 N Vancouver Ave, 503-248-0104, www.livingscape. com; this small urban nursery stocks ornamentals, edible plants, and a wide range of Northwest natives.
- **Pistils**, 3811 N Mississippi Ave, 503-288-4889, www.pistilsnursery.com; this small neighborhood nursery focuses on locally and sustainably grown plants, and carries chicks in spring for urban poultry farmers.
- **Pomarious Nursery,** 1920 NW 18th Ave, 503-490-6866, www.pomariousnursery. com, focuses on boxwood and textural plants.
- **Portland Nursery**, 5050 SE Stark St, 503-231-5050, 9000 SE Division St, 503-788-9000, www.portlandnursery.com; Portland Nursery has huge selections of both garden-variety and unusual plants, and is one of the best close-in sources for trees and large shrubs.

SECOND-HAND SHOPPING

Shopping for second-hand stuff is a thrifty, sometimes quirky, and generally environmentally sound activity, and consequently is a favorite pastime of many Portland residents. What better way to spend a drizzly afternoon than searching for treasures that (usually) cost so little?

ANTIQUE DEALERS

Portland is chock-full of stores that sell original and reproduction antiques (and that generally identify which is which, so you don't need to fear embarrassment when you show up with your treasure on *Antiques Roadshow*). The city's largest concentration of such stores is on Antique Row, an extended parade of stores and antique malls that stretches along Southeast 13th Avenue in Sellwood, but dozens of antique dealers are scattered throughout the city, with additional notable clusters in the Hawthorne District, the inner East Side, the Pearl District, and Northwest/Nob Hill. Many suburban communities, especially historic communities such as Aurora and Forest Grove or affluent suburbs such as Lake Oswego, also have antique stores.

ARCHITECTURAL SALVAGE

You never know what you might find at Portland's architectural salvage stores; a single establishment could have everything from Victorian oak mantels to rows of 1950s movie theater seats. Inventories change often, so you may need to check in frequently if there's something in particular you're looking for.

- **Aurora Mills Architectural Salvage**, 14971 1st St NE, Aurora, 503-678-6083, www.auroramills.com
- **Habitat ReStore,** pdxrestore.org, operated by Habitat for Humanity, has three Portland-area stores.
- **Hippo Hardware**, 1040 E Burnside St, 503-231-1444, www.hippohardware.com
- **Northwest Salvage and Second Hand House**, 7402 NE St Johns Rd, Vancouver, 360-694-0662
- **Old Portland Hardware and Architectural**, 700 NE 22nd Ave, 503-234-7380, www.oldportlandhardware.com
- **Rejuvenation**, 1100 SE Grand Ave, 503-238-1900, www.rejuvenation.com; best known for its reproduction light fixtures (see **Lamps and Lighting**, above), Rejuvenation also sells original salvaged hardware and house parts.
- **The ReBuilding Center**, 3625 N Mississippi Ave, 503-331-1877, www.rebuildingcenter.org, markets high-quality salvaged, surplus, and green building materials and provides jobs for residents of North Portland. Because they are often called in to dismantle and salvage reusable building materials from homes, you have a good shot at finding a match for your own old doors here.

GARAGE SALES AND FLEA MARKETS

If your idea of the perfect Saturday afternoon is spending a few hours poking through tubs of other people's flotsam, you're in luck. Most Portland garage and yard sales take place from May through September, but there are always at least a few sales on any given weekend. In addition to the widely used sign-on-the-utility-pole method, garage sales are advertised in the *Oregonian* classifieds (available online at www.classifieds.oregonlive.com under "Garage-Yard and Estate Sales") and on Craigslist (portland.craigslist.org/gms/).

Portland's **flea markets** come and go, and some of the more fleeting flea markets seem suspiciously like clearinghouses for stolen goods, but the legitimate versions can offer good deals. Keep an eye on the classifieds for large semi-regular events at such places as the Memorial Coliseum. Two established weekend indoor markets to try are **M & M Swap Meet**, 346 SW Walnut St, Hillsboro, 503-040-0091, which is largely geared to Hispanic shoppers, and the diverse **Fantastic Flea Market**, 19340 SE Stark St, 503-618-9119, www.fantasticfleamkt.com.

VINTAGE AND SECOND-HAND STORES

There is a fine line between "antique" and "vintage." There is an equally fine line between "vintage" and "junk." Portland has an abundant selection of places to try your hand at distinguishing between the two qualities, as well as plenty of ordinary second-hand stores. If you poke around any Portland neighborhood, you're bound to find at least one or two vintage or second-hand stores where you can try your shopping luck. Online maps listing some (but by no means all) Portland vintage stores are available from www.shopvintageportland.com/maps. Be aware that the stock at most vintage and thrift stores turns over frequently, so be ready to buy if you find something you want. (Conversely, if you like the store but didn't find what you were looking for, try again in a few days.) Here are a few suggestions to get you started, although these really just scratch the surface of Portland's vintage scene:

- **Bombshell Vintage**, 811 E Burnside St, 503-239-1073, www.bombshellvintage-clothing.com, is a great place to look for vintage dresses and World War II–era fashions as well as absurd '70s duds.
- **City Liquidators**, 823 SE 3rd Ave, 503-230-7716, www.cityliquidators.com, carries everything from a rotating stock of used and new commercial furniture (very useful if you need to furnish an office) to boxes of artificial flowers. Several other unrelated businesses in the immediate area also sell used office furniture.
- **Decades Vintage Company**, 328 SW Stark St, 503-223-1177, www.decadesvintage.com, sells everything from original 1950s eyeglass frames to vintage men's Hawaiian shirts.
- **Goodwill**, 1943 SE 6th Ave, 503-238-6165, plus more than two dozen other Portland-area locations, www.meetgoodwill.com; you're unlikely to find a cheap

Matisse now that Goodwill has started selling its most valuable donated goods on eBay, but you can still find some good used stuff here. Goodwill's three area outlet stores, a.k.a. "The Bins," which overflow with jumbled masses of cheap, unsorted goods, are infamous for their treasure hunting possibilities.

- **Red Light Clothing Exchange**, 3590 SE Hawthorne Blvd, 503-963-888, redlightclothingexchange.com, has many racks of used (although not necessarily vintage) clothes.
- **Xtabay**, 2515 SE Clinton St, 503-230-2899, xtabayvintage.blogspot.com, primarily sells mid-century clothing and accessories.

FOOD

MAJOR SUPERMARKET CHAINS AND WAREHOUSE STORES

Almost every neighborhood in the Portland metropolitan area is only a short distance from one or more major chain supermarkets. **Fred Meyer** (800-576-4377, www.fredmeyer.com) probably has the most pervasive presence; known to three generations of Portlanders as "Freddy's," the chain was indeed founded by a man named Fred G. Meyer in downtown Portland in 1922. Most Fred Meyer stores offer one-stop shopping for food, hardware, toys, sporting goods, small appliances, low-end household furniture, and the like. The chain is now owned by Ohio-based Kroger, as is the more upscale and less ubiquitous **QFC** (Quality Food Centers) supermarket chain (800-576-4377, www.qfc.com). **Safeway** (877-723-3929, www.safeway.com) runs neck-and-neck with Fred Meyer for local market dominance. Both **Albertsons** (877-932-7948, www.albertsons.com) and **Thriftway** (www.thriftwaystores.com) also have numerous stores in the area. (Thriftway stores are individually owned, and their names often bear identifiers, as in Bales Thriftway or Lamb's Thriftway.) Walmart has opened eight **Walmart Neighborhood Markets**, www.walmart.com, in the area, primarily in suburban locations, with more on the way; these stores have much smaller footprints than the company's better-known superstores, and focus on food rather than non-edible plastics. Bellingham, Washington–based **Haggen** (www.haggen.com) has expanded into the Portland area in recent years, with stores in Beaverton, Hillsboro (Tanasbourne), Oregon City, and Tualatin.

A few discount supermarkets such as **WinCo Foods** (12 area stores, www.wincofoods.com, no credit cards, bag your own groceries, open 24 hours) and **Grocery Outlet** (14 area stores, www.groceryoutlet.com) can be found in outlying neighborhoods and in surrounding communities.

Two warehouse store chains in the Portland area, **Costco** (seven Portland-area locations, 800-774-2678, www.costco.com) and **Bi-Mart** (nearly 20 Portland-area stores, 541-344-0681, 800-456-0681, www.bimart.com) offer good deals on bulk foods and other household items. (Sam's Club does not have any local stores.)

Both stores have membership requirements. Call ahead or check out their websites for details.

SMALL AND SPECIALTY SUPERMARKET CHAINS

Low prices and convenience are consumers' most-cited reasons for shopping at large chains. However, don't miss out on the unique offerings of Portland's smaller supermarket chains, most of which boast larger selections of natural and locally produced foods, organic and specialty produce, and esoteric wines and cheeses than the big chain stores do—for a modest price premium, of course.

Zupan's Markets (3301 SE Belmont St, 503-239-3720; 2340 W Burnside St, 503-497-1088; 7221 SW Macadam Ave, 503-244-5666; 16380 Boones Ferry Rd, Lake Oswego, 503-210-4190; www.zupans.com) and Eugene-based **Market of Choice** (8502 SW Terwilliger Blvd, 503-892-7331; 5639 Hood St, West Linn, 503-594-2901; www.marketofchoice.com) both focus on relatively affluent shoppers, and the food selection reflects this fact. Market of Choice has one of the best supermarket cheese selections in town.

Portland is an ideal breeding ground for natural foods supermarkets. Locally owned **New Seasons Market** (www.newseasonsmarket.com) has 13 supermarkets in the Portland area, with more on the way. New Seasons focuses on natural foods, but still stocks staples such as Hershey's chocolate syrup. New Seasons has higher prices than the major chain stores, but its customer service is outstanding and the wheels on the shopping carts actually revolve freely. National natural foods supermarket chain **Whole Foods** (eight area stores, www.wholefoodsmarket. com) boosted its meager local presence when it purchased erstwhile competitor Wild Oats, then promptly rebranded or closed that chain's seven Portland-area stores. (A bit of history: Wild Oats had itself purchased local chain Nature's Fresh Northwest in 1999; after the acquisition, disaffected refugees from Nature's started New Seasons.) **Natural Grocers** (http://www.naturalgrocers.com/), a Colorado-based newcomer to the region, currently has stores in Beaverton, Clackamas, and Gresham, and plans to open a market in Northeast Portland as well.

While it's not really a full-service supermarket, California-based **Trader Joe's** (eight Portland-area stores, www.traderjoes.com) is an indispensable stop for many foodies, pleasing both gourmets and gourmands. Famous for its inexpensive wine (so-called two-buck chuck, now up to $3), Trader Joe's offers a giant selection of packaged and frozen foods and specialty items, many branded under its own private label. It offers a wide selection of bread and dairy products, but its fresh produce selection is relatively limited.

FOOD CO-OPS

Besides offering unsprayed produce and the gamut of "free" foods—gluten-free, pesticide-free, cruelty-free, free-range, etc.—co-ops sell many foods in bulk, allowing you to buy the exact one tablespoon of celery seed that you need to make your favorite tempeh marinade. Co-ops sell shares to members, and some allow you to volunteer at the store for a discount on groceries, but non-members are welcome as well. There are three co-ops with four locations in Portland:

- **Alberta Cooperative Grocery**, 1500 NE Alberta St, 503-287-4333, www. albertagrocery.coop, offers a diverse selection of foods.
- **Food Front Cooperative,** 2375 NW Thurman St, 503-222-5658; 6344 SW Capitol Hwy, 503-546-6559; www.foodfront.coop, has some of the city's best and freshest produce, and stocks many specialty foods from local vendors.
- **People's Food Co-Op**, 3029 SE 21st Ave, 503-232-9051, www.peoples.coop, is probably the kind of place you think of when you think of a co-op. Besides its vast bulk foods section and selection of organic foods, this venerable co-op (which has expanded into a "green" remodeled space) hosts a year-round farmers' market on Wednesdays.

SPECIALTY FOODS

Portland and its suburbs harbor many specialty food stores. Here are some of the best-known examples to get you started:

- **Beaumont Market**, 4130 NE Fremont St, 503-284-3032; a classic neighborhood market, Beaumont Market provides a fine selection of groceries, produce, meat, beer and wine.
- **Benessere**, 907 SW 9th Ave, 503-206-5317; 1428 NE Broadway St, 503-281-6389; www.benessereoil.com; these two locations sell a mind-boggling selection of olive oils, and also offer a great place to start a balsamic jihad.
- **Bob's Red Mill Whole Grain Store,** 5000 SE International Way, Milwaukie, 503-607-6455, www.bobsredmill.com; this is basically the factory store for this nationally known miller of whole and stone-ground grain and seed products. And yes, Bob is a real person.
- **Cacao**, 712 SW Salmon St, 503-274-9510; 414 SW 13th Ave, 503-241-0656; www.cacaodrinkchocolate.com; Portland has a fine selection of chocolate makers, many with their own storefronts. Cacao sells chocolates from several of these local chocolatiers, plus various gourmet and single-origin chocolates from around the world.
- **Cheese Bar**, 6031 SE Belmont St, 503-222-6014, www.cheese-bar.com, has the widest cheese selection in town, with a focus on artisanal cheeses; don't come here looking for Velveeta and cans of Cheez Whiz.
- **City Market,** 735 NW 21st Ave, 503-221-3007, offers an outstanding (but expensive) selection of imported cheeses, fresh fish, fresh pasta, and sausages and pâtés from multiple vendors.
- **Food Fight**, 1217 SE Stark St, 503-233-3910, www.foodfightgrocery.com, is an only-in-Portland (OK, maybe it would work in a few other places, but not many) phenomenon: a vegan convenience store.

- **Foster & Dobbs**, 2518 NE 15th Ave, 503-284-1157, www.fosteranddobbs.com, sells artisanal food products, with an emphasis on cheese, wine, and cured meats.
- **Gartner's Country Meat Market**, 7450 NE Killingsworth St, 503-252-7801, www.gartnersmeats.com, is one of the city's most popular non-nightclub meat markets. Gartner's not only sells meat but will also butcher your dead moose, elk, or deer.
- **Lamb's at Stroheckers**, 2855 SW Patton Rd, 503-223-7391, www.lambsmarkets. net; while it sounds like a vendor of young sheep, Stroheckers is actually an up-scale grocery store perched high up in Portland's West Hills, with a specialty and imported foods selection that reflects its affluent surroundings. The store base-ment features a well-regarded wine cellar.
- **Pastaworks**, 3735 SE Hawthorne Blvd., 503-232-1010, www.pastaworks.com; best known for its fresh pasta, Pastaworks also sells meats, cheeses, produce, wine, and various local and imported grocery items.
- **Penzey's**, 120 NW 10th Ave, 503-227-6777; 11787 SW Beaverton-Hillsdale Hwy, Beaverton, 503-643-7430; 11322 SE 82nd Ave, 503-653-7779, Clackamas; www. penzeys.com; this Wisconsin-based spice chain has three Portland-area outposts.
- **Proper Eats Market and Café**, 8638 N Lombard St, 503-445-2007, propereats. wordpress.com, sells local organic produce and vegan groceries; its kitchen serves prepared vegan and vegetarian food.
- **Sheridan Fruit Co.**, 409 SE Martin Luther King, Jr Blvd, 503-236-2114, www. sheridanfruit.com; this Portland institution dates back more than 90 years. Besides fruit (and vegetables), Sheridan's stocks wine, meat, and bulk and spe-cialty food items.
- **Stone Cottage Herbs**, 8609 SE 17th Ave, 503-719-6658, www.herbsspicesteas. com, sells nearly 1000 types of spices, herbs, and teas.

MAKE-AND-TAKE MEAL ASSEMBLY

An option that might be more of a bargain than you'd expect is **make-and-take meal assembly**, where the store does the prep and all you do is the assembly. The now popular national concept actually originated in the Pacific Northwest in 2002. A couple of the more popular companies follow. You can also go to the website for Easy Meal Prep Company (www.easymealprep.com), an industry asso-ciation, for updated lists and locations.

- **Dream Dinners**, 360-804-2020, www.dreamdinners.com
- **Thyme Management**, 503-380-5775, www.thymemanagement.com, operates out of a commercial kitchen in Old Town.

FARMERS' MARKETS, COMMUNITY-SUPPORTED AGRICULTURE, AND COMMUNITY GARDENS

If you're searching for the freshest fruits and vegetables, your best bet is to buy directly from the growers. Portlanders enthusiastically support local farmers' markets, which are generally open one day a week in season (usually Wednesday, Thursday, Saturday, or Sunday). Most local farmers' markets are generally open from May through September or October, although some remain open through November or December and a handful, such as the Hillsdale and People's markets, operate year-round. In addition to fresh produce from local farmers, offerings typically include locally produced cheese and cured meat, fresh bread, and fresh meat or seafood. Arts and crafts vendors are common at some markets, banned at others. For a more or less complete statewide list of farmers' markets, visit www. oregonfarmersmarkets.org.

The following farmers' markets are located in the city of Portland:

- **Cully Farmers' Market**, 5027 NE 42nd Ave, 503-284-6823, www. cullyfarmersmarket.com; open June–September, Thursdays, 4 p.m.–7 p.m.
- **Hawthorne Evening Market**, SW César E Chávez Blvd at Lincoln St, 541-602-9730, www.hawthorneeveningmarket.com; open May-October, Saturdays, 4:00 p.m.-7:30 p.m.
- **Hillsdale Farmers' Market**, Wilson High School–Rieke Elementary School parking lot, SW Capitol Highway at Sunset Blvd, 503-475-6555, www. hillsdalefarmersmarket.com; open May–November, Sundays, 10 a.m.–2 p.m., and December–April, two Sundays per month, 10 a.m.–2 p.m.
- **Hollywood Farmers' Market**, NE Hancock St between 44th and 45th, 503-709-7403, www.hollywoodfarmersmarket.org; open May–September Saturdays, 8 a.m.–1 p.m.; October-November, Saturdays, 9 a.m.–1 p.m.; and December-April, first and third Saturdays of the month, 9 a.m.–1 p.m.
- **Lents International Farmers' Market**, SE 92nd Ave and Foster Rd, 503-282-4245, www.lentsfarmersmarket.org; open mid-June–October, Sundays, 10 a.m.–3 p.m.
- **Lloyd Farmers' Market**, NE Holladay St between 7th and 9th Avenues, 503-730-8637, www.lloydfarmersmarket.net; open year-round (except between December 25 and January 1), Tuesdays, 10 a.m.–2 p.m.
- **Montavilla Farmers' Market**, 7600 SE Stark St, 503-810-7413, www. montavillamarket.org; weekly late June–October and the Sunday before Thanksgiving, Sundays, 10 a.m.–2 p.m.
- **Moreland Farmers' Market**, SE Bybee Blvd at 14th Ave, 503-341-9350, www. morelandfarmersmarket.org; open mid-May–late October, Wednesdays, 3 p.m.–7 p.m.
- **OHSU Farmers' Market**, MacKenzie Hall Courtyard, OHSU, 503-494-8792, www. ohsu.edu/farmersmarket/; open June–September, Tuesdays, 10 a.m.–2 p.m.
- **Parkrose Farmers' Market**, 12505 NE Halsey St, 503-341-1402, www. parkrosefarmersmarket.org; May–October, Saturdays, 8 a.m.–2 p.m; also open Wednesdays, 2 p.m.–7 p.m., July-early September.
- **People's Farmers' Market**, People's Food Co-Op, 3029 SE 21st Ave, 503-232-9051, www.peoples.coop/farmers-market; open year-round, Wednesdays, 2 p.m.–7 p.m.

- **Portland Farmers' Market—Buckman**, SE Salmon St at 20th Ave, 503-241-0032, www.portlandfarmersmarket.com; open May–September, Thursdays, 3 p.m.–7 p.m.
- **Portland Farmers' Market—Downtown**, Winter Shemanski Park, South Park Blocks at SW Salmon St, 503-241-0032, www.portlandfarmersmarket.org; open, May–November, Wednesdays, 10 a.m.–2 p.m.; and January–February, Saturdays, 10 a.m.–2 p.m.
- **Portland Farmers' Market—Kenton**, N Denver Ave at McClellan St, 503-241-0032, www.portlandfarmersmarket.org; open June–September, Fridays, 3 p.m.–7 p.m.
- **Portland Farmers' Market—King**, NE 7th Ave at Wygant, 503-241-0032, www.portlandfarmersmarket.org; open May–November, Sundays, 10 a.m.–2 p.m.
- **Portland Farmers' Market—Northwest**, NW 19th Ave at Everett St, 503-241-0032, www.portlandfarmersmarket.org; open June–September, Thursdays, 2 p.m.–6 p.m.
- **Portland Farmers' Market—Pioneer Courthouse Square**, Pioneer Courthouse Square, SW 6th Ave at Morrison St, 503-241-0032, www.portlandfarmersmarket.org; open mid-June–August, Mondays, 10 a.m.–2 p.m.
- **Portland Farmers' Market—PSU**, South Park Blocks between SW Montgomery St and SW Harrison St, 503-241-0032, www.portlandfarmersmarket.org; open April–October, Saturdays, 8:30 a.m.–2 p.m., and November–mid-December, Saturdays, 9 a.m.–2 p.m.
- **St. Johns Farmers' Market**, St. Johns Plaza, N Lombard St at Philadelphia Ave, 503-877-5368, www.sjfarmersmarket.com; May–October, Saturdays, 9 a.m.–2 p.m.
- **South Waterfront Farmers' Market**, Eliza Caruthers Park, 3508 SW Moody Ave, 503 972 3289, www.southwaterfront.com/farmers-market.html; open June–October, Thursdays, 2 p.m.–7 p.m.
- **Woodstock Farmers' Market**, Key Bank, 4600 SE Woodstock Blvd, 971-208-5522, woodstockmarketpdx.com; open June–October, Sundays, 10 a.m.–2 p.m.

In addition to the markets in Portland proper, there are farmers' markets in the following surrounding communities:

- **Battle Ground** (www.bgvillage.com)
- **Beaverton** (503-643-5345, www.beavertonfarmersmarket.com)
- **Boring** (503-293-5016)
- **Bull Mountain** (503-314-2955, tbmfm.org)
- **Camas** (360-838-1032, www.camasfarmersmarket.org)
- **Canby** (503-263-5151)
- **Cedar Mill** (503-913-7733, www.cmfmarket.org)
- **Clackamas-Sunnyside** (503-704-4212, www.windancefarmsandart.com)
- **Damascus** (503-929-9482, www.damascusfreshandlocalmarket.com)
- **Estacada** (503-309-0846, www.estacadafarmersmarket.com)

- **Fairview** (503-704-4212, www.windancefarmsandart.com)
- **Forest Grove** (503-992-0078, www.adelantemujeres.org/fg-farmers-market/),
- **Gresham** (503-341-4153, www.greshamfarmersmarket.com)
- **Happy Valley** (503-504-8615, www.sunnysidefarmersmarket.com)
- **Hillsboro** (503-844-6685, www.hillsboromarkets.org)
- **Lake Oswego** (503-675-3985, www.ci.oswego.or.us/parksrec/lake-oswego-farmers-market)
- **Milwaukie** (503-407-0956, www.milwaukiefarmersmarket.com)
- **Oregon City** (503-734-0192, www.orcityfarmersmarket.com)
- **Sandy** (503-489-2173)
- **Scappoose** (503-543-3469, www.scappoosefarmermarket.com)
- **Sherwood** (503-971-998-6431, sherwoodmarket.blogspot.com)
- **Tigard** (503-619-6048, www.tigardfarmersmarket.com)
- **Troutdale** (503-704-4212, www.windancefarmsandart.com)
- **Tualatin** (503-333-9192, www.tualatinfarmersmarket.com)
- **Vancouver** (360-737-8298, www.vancouverfarmersmarket.com)
- **West Linn** (503-349-0015www.westlinnfarmersmarket.org)
- **Wilsonville** (503-778-0261, www.wilsonvillemarket.com)

As a supplement or alternative to your nearest farmers' market, you might consider community-supported agriculture (CSA). In CSA, you buy "harvest shares" from a local farm, and in return you receive a proportionate amount of the farm's production, usually on a weekly basis during the growing season. For information about CSA and a list of local farms that participate in CSA programs, visit the website for the **Portland Area CSA Coalition** (www.portlandcsa.org).

Interested in growing your own, but don't have a yard? Check out the **Community Gardens** page on the Portland Parks and Recreation website, www.portlandoregon.gov/parks/39846.

HOME DELIVERY

If you're after supermarket goods but don't want to fight supermarket crowds, **Safeway** (www.shop.safeway.com) offers home delivery to some areas. For bins of fresh organic produce and natural groceries delivered to your door, try **Organics to You**, 503-236-6496, www.organicstoyou.org, or **Grocery Getter Organic**, 971-285-3270, www.ggetter.com.

ETHNIC MARKETS

The small grocery stores full of delicacies from other parts of the world that are scattered around Portland and its surrounding communities reflect the region's growing ethnic diversity. Interestingly, the majority of ethnic food stores of all kinds are located in suburban communities, a fact that mirrors the current pattern of immigrant settlement in Oregon (as well as the generally high housing prices and rents in close-in neighborhoods). Although many local supermarkets offer a selection of foods for ethnic cooking, try some of the stores below for a more authentic experience (and remember, this is a very incomplete list):

- **Portland World Foods**, 9845 SW Barbur Blvd, 503-244-0670; 830 NW Everett St, 503-802-0755, www.portlandworldfoods.com; it initially seems like an ordinary supermarket, stocked with a standard range of groceries and produce, but a few minutes spent perusing shelves filled with such Middle Eastern products as carob molasses and candied mulberries, not to mention the tasty baklava at the deli, will cure you of your delusion.
- **Caribbean Spice,** 4516 NE 42nd Ave, 503-493-2737, sells groceries produced throughout the tropical world, from West African fufu flour to Caribbean hot sauces.
- **Dashen International Groceries**, 3022 NE Glisan St, 503-234-7785; former-ly Becerra's, this store sells hard-to-find Mexican and other Latin American groceries.
- **Fiji Emporium**, 7814 N Interstate Ave, 503-240-2768, www.fijiemporium.com, sells East Indian and Australian (!) foods.
- **Fubonn**, 2850 SE 82nd Ave, 503-517-8899, www.fubonn.com; this complex of shops, restaurants, and a supermarket bills itself as the largest Asian shopping center in Oregon.
- **India Supermarket**, 17235 NW Corridor Ct, Beaverton, 503-617-9999, cheenibori.com, is one of several Indian markets in the Beaverton/Hillsboro area.
- **International Food Supply**, 8005 SE Stark St, 503-256-9576, www.internation-alfoodsupply.com, concentrates on Mediterranean and Middle Eastern foods. It shares owners with the Portland World Foods markets.
- **Martinotti's**, 404 SW 10th Ave, 503-224-9028, martinottis.ypguides.net, has an eclectic selection of European (especially Italian) imports; put your Christmas marzipan order in early.
- **Merkato Ethiopian Music and Food**, 2605 NE MLK Jr Blvd, 503-331-9283, is one of several East African markets in this part of Northeast Portland.
- **Roman Russian Food Store**, 10918 SE Division St, 503-408-7525, is one of numerous stores on the east side that sell imported food from Russia, Eastern Europe, and the Caucasus.
- **Uwajimaya**, 10500 SW Beaverton-Hillsdale Hwy, Beaverton, 503-643-4512, www.uwajimaya.com; the sole Oregon outlet of a Seattle-based chain, Uwaji-maya offers a vast selection of Asian groceries and goods, as well as some of the area's best fresh seafood. A potential second Portland-area store in Old Town-Chinatown has been rumored for years.

BAKERIES

Fifteen years ago, really high-quality artisan bread was as scarce in Portland as two weeks of sunny days in January (which is to say, quite scarce). While the climate hasn't changed much since then, the city now boasts an enviable collection of places to buy truly outstanding bread and other baked goods. Here are a few of the most highly regarded bakeries in town:

- **Baker & Spice**, 6630 SW Capitol Hwy, 503-244-7573, www.bakerandspicebakery.com; the bakery's **Cakery** is a few doors down in the same complex, 6306 SW Capitol Hwy, 503-546-3737, www.bakerandspicecakery.com
- **Grand Central Baking Company**, seven Portland locations, www.grandcentralbakery.com
- **Ken's Artisan Bakery**, 338 NW 21st Ave, 503-248-2202, www.kensartisan.com
- **Pearl Bakery**, 102 NW 9th Ave, 503-827-0910, www.pearlbakery.com
- **Roman Candle Baking Company**, 3377 SE Division St, 971-302-6605, www.romancandlebaking.com
- **St. Honoré Boulangerie**, 2335 NW Thurman St, 503-445-4342, 3333 SE Division St, 971-279-4433; 315 1st St, Lake Oswego, 503-496-5596, www.sainthonorebakery.com
- **Little T American Baker**, 2600 SE Division St, 503-238-3458; 1022 W Burnside St, 503-894-8258; www.littletbaker.com

A growing number of dedicated gluten-free retail bakeries have opened in and around Portland the past several years, including **Kyra's Bake Shop**, 460 5th St, Lake Oswego, 503-212-2979; **New Cascadia Traditional**, 1700 SE 6th Ave, 503-546-4901, www.newcascadiatraditional.com; **Petunia's Pies and Pastries**, 610 SW 12th Ave, 503-841-5961, www.petuniaspiesandpastries.com; and **Tula**, 4943 NE MLK Jr Blvd, 503-764-9727, www.tulabaking.com.

WINE, BEER, AND LIQUOR

In both Oregon and Washington, wine and beer are sold at convenience stores and supermarkets, but in Oregon hard liquor is only available at bars and state-licensed liquor stores. Washington voters approved privatized liquor sales in 2012, and many grocery stores now sell hard liquor. (Washington has one of the highest tax rates on distilled spirits, so privatization has not led to lower prices, and many liquor-loving Washingtonians travel to Oregon liquor stores to buy in quantity.) Most markets of any size carry a good range of domestic beer (including micro-brews) and the most popular import brands; for one of the city's best selections of bottled beers, try **Belmont Station**, 4500 SW Stark St, 503-232-8538, www.belmont-station.com. While some supermarkets also have surprisingly good wine selections, the area's wine shops are great for more esoteric offerings, and usually offer personalized recommendations and in-store wine tastings. Here's a partial list of Portland wine shops:

- **Blackbird Wine Shop**, 4323 NE Fremont St, 503-282-1887, www.blackbirdwine.com
- **Cork**, 2901 NE Alberta St, 503-281-2675, www.corkwineshop.com

- **E & R Wine Shop**, 6141 SW Macadam Ave, 503-246-6101, www.erwineshop.com
- **Great Wine Buys,** 1515 NE Broadway, 503-287-2897, www.greatwinebuys.com
- **Liner & Elsen**, 2222 NW Quimby St, 503-241-9463, 800-903-9463, www.linerandelsen.com
- **Mt. Tabor Fine Wines**, 4316 SE Hawthorne Blvd, 503-235-4444, www.mttaborfinewines.com
- **Oregon Wines on Broadway**, 515 SW Broadway, 503-228-4655, 800-943-8858, www.oregonwinesonbroadway.com
- **Portland Wine Merchants,** 1430 SE 35th St, 503-234-4399, www.portlandwinemerchants.com
- **Sip D'Vine**, 7829 SW Capitol Hwy, 503-977-9463, www.sipdvine.com
- **Vino**, 137 SE 28th Ave, 503-235-8545, 888-922-8545, www.vinobuys.com
- **Vinopolis Wine Shop**, 1610 NW Glisan St, 503-223-6002, www.vinopoliswineshop.com
- **Wizer's Fine Wines**, 330 1st St, Lake Oswego, 503-636-1414, wizers.com
- **Woodstock Wine & Deli**, 4030 SE Woodstock Blvd, 503-777-2208, www.woodstockwineanddeli.com

Perhaps you prefer to cut out the middleman and go directly to the source—i.e., wineries and brewpubs. For a list of wineries in the region check out the online directories of **Willamette Valley Wineries** (www.willamettewines.com) or the **Oregon Wine Board** (www.oregonwine.org); for Portland-area craft breweries, go to the **Oregon Brewers Guild's** Portland brewery list (oregoncraftbeer. org/breweries/portland-area/). If your taste runs more to hard cider, there are several cideries in the region; **Wandering Aengus Ciderworks** (503-361-2400, www. wanderingaengus.com), near Salem, has occasional open houses. There is even a sakery in the western suburb of Forest Grove: **Saké One**, 820 Elm St, Forest Grove, 503-357-7056, www.sakeone.com. Portland is also a center of the burgeoning craft distillery movement. The granddaddy of local distillers, **Clear Creek Distillery** (2389 NW Wilson St, 503-248-9470, www.clearcreekdistillery.com, tastings available), produces some of the world's best fruit eaux-de-vie and brandies. Most of the dozen-plus new kids on the block occupy warehouses in inner Southeast Portland, in an area known (to some) as distillery row, and focus on gin, vodka, and other spirits. Several companies, including **House Spirits Distillery** (2025 SE 7th Ave, www.housespirits.com) and **New Deal Distillery** (900 SE Salmon St, 503-234-2513, www.newdealdistillery.com), have tasting rooms. Check out www. distilleryrowpdx.com for a complete list of distillers.

EATING OUT

A comprehensive listing of Portland restaurants would double the size of this book. Since you're interested in a guide, not a paperweight, suffice it to say that Portland has restaurants for every type of palate and pocketbook, with more opening all the time. For current restaurant reviews and recommendations, try **Willamette Week's Restaurant Guide**, published each fall in print form and available online at wweek. com. The **Oregonian** online restaurant guide is available at www.oregonlive.com/dining/; the paper's Friday A&E section includes full and capsule restaurant reviews. **Citysearch** (portland.citysearch.com) is another popular, if not always reliable, site for restaurant listings; **Yelp** (www.yelp.com) and **Urban Spoon** (www.urbanspoon. com) also feature user-generated reviews and ratings.

Don't forget Portland's ridiculously eclectic food cart scene; the highest concentrations of food carts are located downtown to serve the lunch hour crowd, but they can also be found in scattered "pods" around the eastside. Local blog **foodcartsportland.com** maintains an up-to-date list of food carts.

OTHER SHOPPING

ART SUPPLIES

- **Blick Art Materials, 1115 NW Glisan St, 503-223-3724;** 2710 Cedar Hills Blvd, Beaverton, 503-646-9347; www.dickblick.com
- **Collage**, 1639 NE Alberta St, 503-249-2190; 7907 SE 13th Ave, 503-777-2189, www.collagepdx.blogspot.com
- **Columbia Art & Drafting Supply**, 1515 E Burnside St, 503-232-2216, www.columbia-art.com
- **Muse Art + Design**, 4220 SE Hawthorne Blvd, 503-231-8704, museartanddesign.com
- **Oblation Papers and Press**, 516 NW 12th Ave, 503-223-1093, www.oblationpapers.com

BOOKS

For a list of local bookstores, see the **Cultural Life** chapter.

CIGARS

If you must indulge, **Rich's Cigar Store** (820 SW Alder, 503-228-1700, 800-669-1527, www.richscigarstore.com) is the long-time source for fine tobaccos. Established in 1894, Rich's has a walk-in humidor and, for nonsmokers, stocks more than 2,500 periodicals from around the world. **Broadway Cigar Company** (locations in Northeast Portland, Lake Oswego, and Camas, www.broadwaycigar. com, 503-473-8000) sells cigars and accessories, includes a walk-in humidor, and provides a well-appointed smoking lounge.

FOR CHILDREN

Children's clothing, furniture, and toys are available at most department stores and discount stores. Such spelling-challenged national retailers as **Babies "R" Us,**

Toys "R" Us (both at www.toysrus.com), and **Gymboree** (www.gymboree.com) all have multiple stores in and around Portland. Portland also has many independent stores that specialize in children's stuff. Here are a few:

- **Black Wagon,** 3964 N Mississippi Ave, Portland, 866-916-0004, www.blackwagon.com, serves up large helpings of hip designer clothes, toys, and bedding for the 0–6 crowd.
- **Child's Play**, 2305 NW Kearney St, 503-224-5586, www.childsplayportland.com, has a wide selection of toys and books.
- **Finnegan's**, 820 SW Washington St, 503-221-0306, www.finneganstoys.com, is the largest non-chain toy store in town, with a truly tremendous selection of toys and games.
- **Grasshopper**, 1816 NE Alberta St, 503-335-3131, www.grasshopperstore.com, sells an eclectic assortment of children's books, clothes, and toys.
- **Kids at Heart**, 3445 SE Hawthorne Blvd, 503-231-2954, www.kidshearttoys.com, sells high-quality children's toys and books.
- **OMSI Science Store**, Oregon Museum of Science and Industry, 1945 SE Water Ave, 503-797-4626, www.omsi.edu/science-store; not exactly a children's store, the gift shop at OMSI nonetheless carries a huge selection of science-related toys, kits, and assorted gadgets for kids of all ages.
- **Polliwog**, 234 NE 28th Ave 503-236-3903, www.polliwogportland.com, offers clothing and accessories for newborns to first-graders.
- **Posh Baby**, 916 NW 10th Ave, 503-478-7674, www.poshbaby.com; not for bargain hunters, this Pearl District store sells strollers, toys, furniture, and accessories.
- **Spielwerk Toys**, 7556 SE 13th Ave, 503-736-3000, 3808 N Williams Ave, 503-282-2233, www.spielwerktoys.com, specializes in classic, old-school wooden toys and creative aids.
- **Thinker Toys**, 7784 SW Capitol Hwy, 503-245-3936, www.thinkertoysoregon.com, in Multnomah Village, sells a large selection of toys, games, and kits for preschoolers to high schoolers.

MUSIC

The quality and range of music sellers in Portland is truly astounding. In addition to the standard assortment of mall chain stores, big-box retailers, and book/record/DVD purveyors, there are nearly two dozen independent record and CD shops in the city of Portland alone. Southeast Hawthorne Boulevard boasts the largest concentration of these shops, but every Eastside neighborhood seems to have at least one claustrophobic but much-loved used record store. Many of Portland's indie record shops specialize in specific genres—punk is a particular favorite—while others practically define the word eclectic; virtually any music store in the city is worth a browse. The biggest, best-known independent store is **Music Millennium**, 3158 E Burnside St, 503-231-8926, www.musicmillennium.com, which hosts frequent in-store shows.

PARTY SUPPLIES

Got balloons for that housewarming party? If not, you could visit your local supermarket's customer service desk. Better yet, pay a visit to **Lippman Company**, 50 SE Yamhill St, 503-239-7007, www.lippmancompany.com. This festive establishment offers 12,000 square feet of party favors, pirate gear, balloons, costumes, and other party supplies in the Eastside Industrial District. Come for the helium tanks, stay for the practical joke selection.

PHOTO SUPPLIES AND PROCESSING

When your photo processing needs go beyond 35mm prints, **Blue Moon Camera and Machine**, 8417 N Lombard St, 503-978-0333, www.bluemooncamera.com, in the heart of St. Johns, processes all kinds of arcane and rare film types. As a further gesture to iconoclasm, Blue Moon also sells refurbished manual typewriters. The more mainstream **Pro Photo Supply**, 1112 NW 19th Ave, 503-241-1112, 800-835-3314, www.prophotosupply.com, also has a photo lab and sells cameras, lenses and other accessories, photo paper, and ink.

RAINWEAR

At some point, you'll need good rainwear. You should be able to find something appropriate at any discount or full-service department store, at sporting goods stores (see **Sports and Recreation** for a list), or from mail order suppliers such as Land's End (www.landsend.com) or L.L. Bean (www.llbean.com). Or you might try one of the following sportswear retailers:

- **Columbia Sportswear**, 911 SW Broadway, 503-226-6800, www.columbia.com, is the company's downtown flagship store; also consider checking out Columbia Sportswear's outlet stores in Sellwood, Lake Oswego, and Woodburn Premium Outlets. (See "Outlet Malls" above.) If you've just arrived from a desert clime, Columbia has a store at the airport.
- **The North Face**, 1202 NW Davis St, 503-727-0200, www.thenorthface.com, has lots of high-end mountaineering gear, as well as a selection of jackets made from expensive waterproof/breathable fabrics.
- **Patagonia**, 907 NW Irving St, 503-525-2552, www.patagonia.com, has pricey, nicely made activewear, including rainwear.

ODD AND HARD-TO-FIND GOODS AND SERVICES

DIAPER SERVICE

Unless you plan to wash 'em yourself, **Tidee Didee** (503-777-3856, www.tideedidee.com) is the only game in town for handling non-disposable diapers.

FURNITURE RESTORATION AND REPAIR

Did you unpack the moving truck only to find that it was a bad idea to pack your unpadded "claw" sculpture next to that Stickley dresser? Portland has many furniture hospitals, most of which are listed online in the Yellow Pages under "Furniture-Repair and Refinish."

E VEN IN FAMILIAR SURROUNDINGS, FINDING QUALITY CHILDCARE AND good schools is one of the most challenging and overwhelming tasks parents face, and a move to a new area compounds the difficulty. With time and effort, however, it is usually possible to find a good situation for your child, whether it is in-home or on-site daycare, a nanny, an after-school program, or a good public or private school. The keys, of course, are research and persistence, and perhaps a bit of luck. Keep in mind that even institutions with the best reputations may not be suited to your child's individual needs. Get comfy with the phone book and the web, and, perhaps most important, prepare to talk with other parents.

CHILDCARE

Probably the best way to find a good childcare provider is by referral from someone you know and trust. As a newcomer, however, you may not have such resources at your disposal. A good place to start your research is one of several local childcare resource and referral agencies that can help you find and select childcare providers. Call 866-227-5529 or visit www.ccrr-mc.org in Multnomah County; 800-624-9516, ww.caowash.org in Washington and Columbia counties 866-371-4373, clackesd.k12.or.us/ece/ccrr.html in Clackamas County; 360-750-9735, 800-282-0874, www.esd112.org/ccrr in Southwest Washington.

In Oregon, the **Oregon Employment Department** (www.oregon.gov/ EMPLOY/CCD/) regulates childcare providers. There are several options for care, and each is subject to different regulations. A **childcare center** is a facility other than a private home that provides care for more than 13 children; such centers must be state-certified, are subject to mandated adult-child ratios, and must offer a program of age-appropriate activities. A **certified family childcare home**, which is subject to similar requirements, is a facility in the provider's family residence that provides care for a maximum of 16 children, including the provider's children.

Family childcare homes that care for no more than 10 children (including the provider's children) need only be licensed with the state; certification is not required. A wide range of small-scale childcare providers are exempt from licensing requirements, including providers who care for no more than three children (in addition to the provider's own children), nannies and others who provide care in a child's home, and caregivers who provide care on an occasional basis only or who are related to the child. Programs run by government agencies are also exempt, as are preschools (i.e., facilities that offer an educational curriculum for children from three years old through kindergarten-age) that provide care for less than four hours per day. To check on the licensing status of a childcare provider or find out about complaints, call the Child Care Division's hotline at 800-556-6616.

Washington requires virtually anyone who is paid to care for children on a regular basis to be licensed (unless the children are related to the caregiver). The **Washington Department of Early Learning** (www.del.wa.gov) regulates childcare providers in that state. To check the license status and complaint history of a childcare provider, visit the department's website or call 866-482-4325.

In addition to the required state certifications, you may want to look for childcare centers that are accredited by third-party organizations like the **National Association for the Education of Young Children** (NAEYC), www.naeyc.org.

WHAT TO LOOK FOR IN CHILDCARE

When searching for the best place for your child, be sure to visit prospective providers—and make an appointment. A security-conscious caregiver should not let a random stranger on the premises unannounced; a staff member should accompany you at all times. In general, look for a safe and clean environment and a caring attitude. Are areas that children use child-proofed? Are the kitchen, toys, and furniture clean and safe? Are outdoor play areas fenced and free of hazards? Observe other kids at the facility. Do they seem happy? Are they well behaved? Is the adult-child ratio acceptable? Ask for the telephone numbers of parents who use the service and talk to them. It's a good idea to request a daily schedule—look for both active and quiet time, and age-appropriate activities. Keep in mind that wet Portland winters don't allow for daily outdoor play. Is there an adequate covered space for active play in winter? Does the facility have adequate insurance? Finally, understand that a license does not necessarily guarantee quality childcare. It is your responsibility as a parent to make sure that the caregiver delivers the standard of care you expect.

NANNIES AND AU PAIRS

NANNIES
Hiring a nanny is generally the most expensive childcare option, but under the right circumstances it can be a very rewarding arrangement for everyone involved. In the Portland area you can expect to pay at least $400 a week for a full-time

nanny—more (and sometimes much more) for a nanny with more experience or who will be expected to care for multiple children or do housework.

Several agencies help match nannies with families. While these services tend to charge significant placement fees, many agencies perform background checks or psychological testing (for the nanny, not you) during the applicant screening process. Nannies are not state-licensed, and screening processes vary, so you may want to ask each agency about its specific screening criteria. Most agencies can also help with temporary childcare needs. Local nanny placement agencies include:

- **A Brilliant Nanny**, 4110 SE Hawthorne Blvd #157, 503-459-4055, www.abnanny.com
- **Care Givers Placement Agency**, 10211 SW Barbur Blvd, Suite 203A, 503-244-6370, www.cgpa.com
- **Karoline's Nannies**, Vancouver, 360-721-0902, www.karolinesnannies.com
- **Northwest Nannies**, 11830 SW Kerr Pkwy, Suite 330, Lake Oswego, 503-389-5568, www.nwnanny.com

If you are contracting directly with your nanny for his or her services, rather than going through an agency, you'll have to get an employer identification number from the IRS and pay certain taxes, including social security, Medicare, and possibly unemployment insurance tax, and you'll have to withhold income tax—unless of course you're planning on being nominated for a high-profile federal job and would like a good scandal to torpedo your nomination, in which case by all means neglect to pay taxes for your nanny. You'll also need to carry workers' compensation, which you may be able to purchase through your homeowner's or automobile insurance provider. Several companies offer assistance with childcare employment taxes, including **HomeWork Solutions** (800-626-4829, www.nanitax.com) or **GTM Payroll Services** (800-929-9213, www.gtm.com/household/).

Be sure to check references before hiring a nanny. Although most agencies run background checks, if you're not using an agency or if you simply want a second opinion, several companies can perform pre-employment screening. Look in the Yellow Pages under "Employment Screening" or "Background Screening," or type "employment screening" into your search engine for links.

AU PAIRS

Au pairs are young adults, usually college-age women, visiting the United States with a special visa status that allows them to provide childcare and light housekeeping in exchange for room and board, international airfare, and a weekly stipend. The host family benefits from cultural exchange as well as relatively inexpensive childcare, but the placement usually only lasts one year and an au pair might not offer the same level of maturity and experience as a career nanny. Keep in mind that the au pair will be in a foreign country and will be interested in traveling and meeting people her age, but may not have fully considered how restricted her free time will be. At the same time, many parents have unrealistic expectations of their au pair, and assume that she will be a combination nanny, babysitter, and full-time housekeeper, with few outside interests or social engagements. That said, the au pair arrangement can be a great experience for those families and au pairs who understand the trade-offs of the system and have the same expectations for their year together.

The US State Department's **Bureau of Educational and Cultural Affairs** (202-203-5096, j1visa.state.gov/programs/au-pair) regulates au pair placement agencies and maintains a current list of designated sponsor agencies. The following are some of the approved national au pair agencies that can connect you with a local placement coordinator:

- **Au Pair in America**, 800-928-7247, www.aupairinamerica.com
- **AuPairCare**, 800-428-7247, www.aupaircare.com
- **Cultural Care Au Pair**, 800-333-6056, www.culturalcare.com
- **EurAuPair**, 800-333-3804, www.euraupair.com
- **Go Au Pair, 888-287-2471, www.goaupair.com**
- **InterExchange Au Pair USA**, 800-287-2477, www.interexchange.org/au-pair-usa

SCHOOL-AGE PROGRAMS

Many organizations offer care to school-aged children before and/or after school hours and during school vacations. In many cases, care is provided on-site at an elementary school, or at a nearby location to which children are transported by bus after school. Check with your child's school for convenient options. Note that school-age programs that are operated by a public school or other government agency are exempt from state certification requirements (but the programs may choose to be certified anyway).

SCHOOLS

There are hundreds of public and private schools in the Portland area, and choosing the right one for your child can be a complicated and time-consuming task. While the public school systems in Portland and in many of the surrounding communities rely primarily on neighborhood-based schools (i.e., schools that draw from a set attendance area), they also offer a growing number of magnet programs and specialty schools; add transfer options, private schools, and charter schools into the mix and the range of options is dizzying. Fortunately, there are some sources that can help with your initial search.

The **Oregon Department of Education** is responsible for statewide curriculum, instructional, and assessment testing programs. The department issues an annual statewide report card that covers every public school in the state. The annual report cards are available from the Department's website (www.ode.state.or.us), which also offers a tremendous amount of additional information about public education in Oregon. In Washington, the office of the **Washington Superintendent of Public Instruction** (www.k12.wa.us) plays a similar role and issues report cards for schools in that state.

The **Chalkboard Project** (www.chalkboardproject.org) is another good source of information about Oregon public schools. This organization is involved in a side project, the **Open Books Project** (www.openbooksproject.org), which allows parents—and others—to track how educational funding dollars are spent in Oregon; the website includes report cards for each school and district, provides information about statewide educational spending and spending by district, and allows for district-by-district comparisons.

Other sources for gathering specific information about schools include **Great Schools** (www.greatschools.org), a nonprofit organization dedicated to providing clear and objective information about local schools; and the **National Center for Educational Statistics** (www.nces.ed.gov), a federal center that collects and analyzes information from states. Information on private schools is notoriously hard to come by; they are not subject to state curriculum requirements, and do not have to release certain information (such as standardized test scores or teacher credentials) that public schools are required to disclose.

When researching schools, bear in mind that statistics and summary progress assessments paint a picture that is at best incomplete. While objective measures may help support or guide your decision, there is really only one way to choose a school, public or private, that is right for your child: visit.

When visiting a school, pay attention to your gut reaction. Ask yourself these questions:

- Am I comfortable here? Will my child be comfortable here?
- Does the school feel safe? Are the bathrooms clean and free of graffiti?
- Do the students seem to be engaged? Is student work on display?
- Are classrooms crowded? (Class sizes can vary enormously from school to school.) Do teachers appear to be overworked?
- Are adults present throughout the building and grounds?
- Are desks, instructional materials, and computers plentiful and up-to-date?
- Does the school offer academic and extracurricular opportunities for students to explore their own special interests, such as art, music, sports, or science?
- In an elementary school, pay attention to the way the children are moving around—are they interacting naturally, but staying on task? In a middle school or high school, notice how students interact with each other and with teachers at the beginning and end of class, and in the halls.
- Ask elementary teachers about reading and math groups and find out if children move up as they build skills.
- Are parents encouraged to volunteer? To paraphrase JFK, ask not only what your school can do for your child, but what you can do for your child's school. The level of parent and community involvement in a school is one key to that school's success.

PUBLIC SCHOOLS

Public schools in the Northwest face many challenges, including rapid growth in districts on the urban fringe, declining enrollments in inner cities, and an increasingly diverse student population. In Oregon, a roller-coaster ride of inconsistent (and often inadequate) funding over the last decade or so has exacerbated these problems. As the *Oregon Blue Book*, the state's official government directory, succinctly puts it, "Oregon public school finance is unique and very complicated for several reasons." In a nutshell, mandatory property tax limits reduced local governments' ability to fund schools, and today about two-thirds of the money for public schools comes directly from the state. While state funding has helped reduce the disparity in resources between districts, it leaves school funding vulnerable to economic cycles and competing demands for limited revenue (despite a state constitutional amendment, passed in 2000, which requires the legislature to appropriate sufficient funds to allow schools to meet legally established quality goals). State funding also means that communities which place a high value on their schools have only a limited ability to increase support for those schools using local tax revenues.

A funding crunch in Oregon during the recession of the early 2000s led some districts to cut electives, increase class sizes, and (most infamously) lop several days off the school year to reduce costs. In response to this deterioration in school services, some parents placed their children in private schools or simply moved to more affluent school districts. An improved economy—and in many districts, voter-approved property tax levies—helped stabilize school funding until the most recent recession, beginning in 2008, led once again to declining tax revenues and mounting pressure on school budgets in both Oregon and Washington. The financial picture has improved somewhat with the economy in recent years, but fundamental school funding issues, which are hardly unique to the Northwest, have not been resolved. That said, some districts are in a much better financial position than others.

Unlike in many states, school district boundaries in Oregon and Washington do not necessarily correspond to city or county boundaries. For example, five different school districts serve the city of Portland, and the Portland Public Schools district draws from both Multnomah County and a small portion of Washington County.

Both Oregon and Washington have educational service districts (ESDs), which generally encompass multiple districts and which provide certain programs and services that are too costly or specialized for districts to provide on their own. Most parents don't deal directly with ESDs.

PORTLAND PUBLIC SCHOOLS

The Portland Public Schools district—the largest of five districts that encompass parts of the city of Portland, and the most populous school district in the state—serves some 47,000 students. Although enrollment had declined for many years, it has recently stabilized and has even begun to increase slightly for several years. Close to 85% of Portland children attend public school, and Portland remains one of the few large cities in America in which the middle class has not largely abandoned the public schools. To be sure, Portland Public Schools is emerging from a time of great uncertainty and turmoil that included state funding cuts, a round of school closures, controversy over standardization and core curriculum issues, and a narrowly averted teachers' strike in 2014. Immediate challenges include a high dropout rate, several consistently low-performing schools, and equity issues between schools and neighborhoods; state report card ratings run the gamut from "needs improvement" to "outstanding." That said, some Portland schools are among the best in the state.

The school district website (www.pps.k12.or.us) includes a great deal of information about individual schools (click on "schools" in the horizontal menu) and about school choices, with a handy look-up function to find the neighborhood school for a specific address (www.pps.k12.or.us/departments/enrollment transfer/6478.htm). Your child is guaranteed a spot at your neighborhood school. The Enrollment and Transfer Center is a great resource; send an email to enrollment-office@pps.k12.or.us or call 503-916-3205.

REGISTRATION

To register your child, go to your assigned neighborhood school or approved transfer school. (Keep in mind that the school that is closest or most convenient to your residence may not necessarily be your neighborhood school.) Call first to make sure the staff member you need to see will be available, and bring the following documents:

- A completed Student Registration form, available in hard copy from the school or online at www.pps.k12.or.us/departments/enrollment-transfer/6808.htm.
- Proof of the student's age (e.g., a birth certificate or passport). Children who are five years or older by September 1 may enroll in kindergarten.
- Records of immunization for diphtheria, tetanus, hepatitis B, chicken pox, polio, hemophilus influenza type B (HiB), mumps, measles, and rubella, unless you are seeking an exemption for religious or medical reasons. There are specific requirements for each grade level.
- Proof of residence: You must provide two or more recent documents showing your name and current home address, such as utility bills, credit card bills, a rental agreement, or the deed to your home. A driver's license is not acceptable to show proof of residence.
- The name and contact information for any previous school your child attended outside the Portland Public Schools district.

You can register at any time, but it is better for everyone (including your child) if you register as early as possible. Most schools hold informational meetings and provide tours for prospective parents during the winter months.

TRANSFERS

If you would prefer that your child attend a school other than your neighborhood school, you can apply for a transfer. Transfer applications are due in late winter. Popular schools generally have more transfer applications than open slots, and applicants are selected by lottery in the spring; in an average year, more than three-quarters of applicants get into one of their top choices, if not necessarily their first choice. A few schools, particularly those with new and expanding programs, including language immersion programs, may have spaces available in select grades until late August. (Be aware that, as a newcomer and given the timetable for transfer requests, your child will likely have to attend your neighborhood school initially unless he or she is not yet school age.) For details about the transfer process, visit www.pps.k12.or.us/departments/enrollment-transfer/schoolchoice.htm or call the Enrollment and Transfer Center at 503-916-3205.

MAGNET SCHOOLS AND LANGUAGE IMMERSION PROGRAMS

Portland has several magnet and charter schools that concentrate on arts, math and science, or other disciplines; contact the school district for specifics. In addition, language immersion programs are available in Spanish, Russian, Japanese, and Mandarin Chinese. (The Mandarin kindergarten-to-college immersion program, which begins at Woodstock Elementary School and continues at Hosford Middle School, Cleveland High School, and the University of Oregon, was the first of its kind in the United States.) For more information, contact the Portland Public Schools Immersion Coordinator at 503-916-6255.

SUBURBAN DISTRICT SCHOOLS

The suburban districts in the Portland area defy generalization. Some are huge, with thousands of students, and others are tiny; some have sparkling new facilities and adequate budgets, others have frankly decrepit buildings and are struggling financially; some have some of the highest test scores and graduation rates in the state or country, and others—well, not so much. In fact, school conditions and academic performance can vary dramatically not only between but within districts, so research is in order.

Registration procedures are fairly uniform throughout the Portland area—go to the appropriate school and present an enrollment form, proof of residence, immunization records, proof of the child's age, and prior school contact information. Contact your school district for specific enrollment requirements and information.

The following are the main school districts in the four-county metropolitan area:

OREGON

Beaverton School District

16650 SW Merlo Rd
Beaverton, OR 97006
503-591-8000
www.beaverton.k12.or.us

The Beaverton School District, the third-largest in the state, educates more than 39,000 students from the city of Beaverton, part of Tigard, and many of the surrounding unincorporated areas of Washington County (and a tiny portion of Multnomah County). The district as a whole has a very good reputation—its overall academic performance is among the best of the state's large school districts—although some schools are much better than others. In addition to the standard offerings at its 33 elementary, 8 middle, and 5 high schools, the district has a wide range of "option" schools, including the International School, which is part of the International Baccalaureate program, the Arts & Communication Magnet Academy for grades 6–12; a Science and Technology High School; and a Health & Science School for grades 6–12, which follows the "Expeditionary Learning" model.

Canby School District

1130 S Ivy St
Canby, OR 97013
503-266-7861
www.canby.k12.or.us

The Canby School District has more than 5,000 students from Canby and much of the surrounding (primarily rural) area, including the Charbonneau District of Wilsonville.

Centennial School District

18135 SE Brooklyn St
Portland, OR 97236
503-760-7990
www.centennial.k12.or.us

This jurisdiction-busting district containing 10 schools plus an alternative school for grades 7–12 serves outer Southeast Portland, western Gresham, and portions of unincorporated Multnomah and Clackamas counties.

Corbett School District
35800 E Historic Columbia River Hwy
Corbett, OR 97019
503-261-4200
www.corbett.k12.or.us

This tiny, highly regarded 1,100-student district in eastern Multnomah County has one elementary, one middle, one high school, and one charter school, all at the same location, plus an offsite K–8 arts with Spanish program. The high school has an impressive Advanced Placement program and is generally considered to be one of the best schools in the state.

David Douglas School District
1500 SE 130th Ave
Portland, OR 97233
503-252-2900
www.ddouglas.k12.or.us

The David Douglas School District serves more than 10,000 students in a large swath of East Portland (east of Interstate 205 and west of the Centennial School District). This part of the city is experiencing significant immigration from Mexico, Eastern Europe, and Southeast Asia, and district enrollment is growing at a rapid rate. Roughly one-quarter of students are English language learners. David Douglas High, with some 2,700 students, has the largest enrollment in the state.

Forest Grove School District
1728 Main St
Forest Grove, OR 97116
503-357-6171
www.fgsd.k12.or.us

The Forest Grove School District covers 200 square miles in the city of Forest Grove, part of the adjacent city of Cornelius, and nearby unincorporated areas. It educates 5,800 students.

Gladstone School District
17789 Webster Rd
Gladstone, OR 97027
503-655-2777
www.gladstone.k12.or.us

The Gladstone School District largely (but not entirely) corresponds with the boundaries of the city of Gladstone. With one elementary, one middle, and one high school (which has only about 730 students), this is one of the smallest suburban districts.

Gresham-Barlow School District
1331 NW Eastman Pkwy
Gresham, OR 97030
503-261-4550
district.gresham.k12.or.us

The Gresham-Barlow school district serves a socioeconomically and ethnically diverse student population in much (but not all) of Gresham and the new city of Damascus. The district has nearly 12,000 students in 22 schools (including three charter schools); performance varies from school to school.

Hillsboro School District
3083 NE 49th Pl
Hillsboro, OR 97124
503-844-1500
www.hsd.k12.or.us

The fourth-largest district in Oregon, Hillsboro School District educates more than 20,000 students in much of western Washington County; in addition to the city of Hillsboro, the district includes all or part of North Plains, Cornelius, and unincorporated areas from Aloha south to the edge of Sherwood. There are 25 elementary schools, 4 middle schools, and 4 high schools (as well as an alternative school and a charter school). As one might expect, school performance and offerings vary substantially within the district. Hillsboro High (aka Hilhi) has an International Baccalaureate program.

Lake Oswego School District
2455 Country Club Rd, PO Box 70
Lake Oswego, OR 97034
503-534-2000
www.loswego.k12.or.us

This well-funded, sought-after district includes six elementary schools, two junior high schools, and two high schools. The district boasts some of the highest test scores and high school graduation rates in the state.

North Clackamas School District
4444 SE Lake Rd
Milwaukie, OR 97222
503-353-6000
www.nclack.k12.or.us

North Clackamas School District extends from Milwaukie and Oak Grove in the west to Happy Valley and Sunnyside in the east. Schools within the district vary widely in quality, from excellent to mediocre at best.

Oregon City School District

1417 12th St
Oregon City, OR 97045
503-785-8000
www.orecity.k12.or.us

This sprawling district encompasses Oregon City and large sections of unincorporated Clackamas County, including Jennings Lodge, Beavercreek, and Redland.

Parkrose School District

10636 NE Prescott St
Portland, OR 97220
503-408-2100
www.parkrose.k12.or.us

The Parkrose School District can trace its origins to the 1880s. Today, it serves a smallish area of Northeast Portland, primarily east of Interstate 205, with four elementary schools, a middle school, and a high school.

Reynolds School District

1204 NE 201st Ave
Fairview, OR 97024
503-661-7200
www.reynolds.k12.or.us

Reynolds School District serves the east Multnomah County cities of Fairview, Troutdale, and Wood Village, as well as portions of outer Northeast Portland and northern Gresham. Reynolds High, the district's only high school, has the second-highest enrollment in the state.

Riverdale School District

11733 SW Breyman Ave
Portland, OR 97219
503-262-4840
www.riverdaleschool.com

Riverdale School District serves perhaps the most affluent area in Oregon, and test scores, graduation rates, and college attendance prospects are correspondingly high. Riverdale Grade School serves students in kindergarten through eighth grade; older students attend Riverdale High School, located near Lewis and Clark College in Portland.

Sherwood School District
23295 SW Main St
Sherwood, OR 97140
503-825-5000
www.sherwood.k12.or.us

This generally well-regarded school district in southwestern Washington County has three elementary schools (plus a charter school), two middle schools, and one high school.

Tigard-Tualatin School District
6960 SW Sandburg St
Tigard, OR 97223
503-431-4000
ttsdschools.org

Tigard-Tualatin School District, which covers most of the cities of Tigard and Tualatin, as well as the surrounding communities of Durham, Bull Mountain, and Metzger, is one of the most sought-after districts in the state. Average student performance, school ratings, and test scores are generally high throughout the district. Both of the district's high schools—Tigard High School and Tualatin High School—offer International Baccalaureate programs.

West Linn–Wilsonville School District
22210 SW Stafford Rd
Tualatin, OR 97062
503-673-7000
www.wlwv.k12.or.us

The West Linn–Wilsonville School District covers the two non-adjacent cities of West Linn and (most of) Wilsonville, as well as the unincorporated areas that lie between them. This well-regarded district has nine elementary schools, three middle schools (two in West Linn and one in Wilsonville), and a high school in each city, along with a grades 4–8 charter school and the Arts & Technology High School.

WASHINGTON

Battle Ground Public Schools
11104 NE 49th St
Brush Prairie, WA 98606
360-885-5300
www.battlegroundps.org

Battle Ground Public Schools has some 11,000 students in Battle Ground and the surrounding unincorporated areas of Clark County, including parts of Brush Prairie, Amboy, and Yacolt.

Camas School District
841 NE 22nd Ave
Camas, WA 98607
360-335-3000
www.camas.wednet.edu

The growing Camas School District, one of the most sought-after districts in Southwest Washington, serves the city of Camas and part of unincorporated Clark County. The district has six elementary schools, two middle schools, and a new high-tech high school.

Evergreen Public Schools
13501 NE 28th St
Vancouver, WA 98668
360-604-4000
www.evergreenps.org
The generally well-regarded Evergreen Public Schools system serves the eastern half of Vancouver and much of nearby unincorporated Clark County. The district has more than 26,000 students, and is the fourth-largest school district in Washington. Mountain View High, one of six high schools in the district, offers 24 Advanced Placement classes (one of the highest totals in the Northwest).

Hockinson School District
17912 NE 159th Ave
Brush Prairie, WA 98606
360-448-6400
www.hocksd.org

This largely rural district includes most of Brush Prairie and parts of the surrounding areas of unincorporated Clark County, and offers one elementary, one middle, and one high school.

Vancouver School District
2901 Falk Rd
Vancouver, WA 98661
360-313-1000
www.vansd.org

The Vancouver School District educates more than 22,000 children in the western half of the city of Vancouver and a large chunk of unincorporated Clark County. The district has several magnet schools, including the Vancouver School of Arts & Academics, which boasts a 99% graduation rate.

Washougal School District
4855 Evergreen Way
Washougal, WA 98671
360-954-3000
www.washougal.k12.wa.us

Washougal's school district boundaries encompass not just the area within city limits, but also a sizeable portion of the rural Columbia Gorge eastward into Skamania County. The district has three elementary schools, two middle schools, and two high schools (including an alternative high school).

PRIVATE AND PAROCHIAL SCHOOLS

The Portland area is home to many excellent private and parochial schools. The following are some of the better known (but by no means the only) private schools in the region.

- **Catlin Gabel School** (P–12), 8825 SW Barnes Rd, 503-297-1894, www.catlin.edu
- **Central Catholic High School** (9–12), 2401 SE Stark St, 503-235-3138, www.centralcatholichigh.org
- **French American International School** (P–8), 8500 NW Johnson St, 503-292-7776, www.faispdx.org
- **German American School of Portland** (P–5), 3900 SW Murray Blvd, Beaverton, 503-626-9089, www.gspdx.org
- **The International School** (P–5), 025 SW Sherman St, 503-226-2496, www.intlschool.org
- **Jesuit High School** (9–12), 9000 SW Beaverton-Hillsdale Hwy, 503-292-2663, www.jesuitportland.org
- **La Salle Catholic College Preparatory** (9–12), 11999 SE Fuller Rd, Milwaukie, 503-659-4155, www.lsprep.org
- **L'Etoile French School** (P–5), 68 SW Miles St, 503-715-1258, www.letoilefrenchschool.com
- **Northwest Academy** (6–12), 1130 SW Main St, 503-223-3367, www.nwacademy.org

- **Oregon Episcopal School** (P–12), 6300 SW Nicol Rd, 503-246-7771, www.oes.edu
- **Portland Jewish Academy** (P–8), 6651 SW Capitol Hwy, 503-244-0126, www.portlandjewishacademy.org
- **Portland Waldorf School** (P–12), 2300 Harrison St, Milwaukie, 503-654-2200, www.portlandwaldorf.org
- **St. Mary's Academy** (9–12), 1615 SW 5th Ave, 503-228-8306, www.stmaryspdx.org
- **Summa Academy** (K-8), 2510 SW 1st Ave, 503-287-1785, summainstitute.org

A complete list of nonpublic schools in Oregon is available in the Oregon Department of Education's **Oregon School Directory** (www.ode.state.or.us/pubs/directory/), and in Washington from the Washington Superintendent of Public Instruction's **Office of Private Education** (www.k12.wa.us/PrivateEd/).

HOMESCHOOLING

Parents who have misgivings about public schools have the right to take their children's education into their own hands. Many parents believe that they are best qualified to design an educational program that will engage and challenge their children, responding to each child's unique psychological and intellectual traits. Homeschooling is especially popular among strongly religious parents who object to the secular nature of public schools, and among liberal parents who object to, among other things, public schools' increasing reliance on corporate sponsorship.

Teaching is not easy—you will need a lot of time and energy to plan and execute a study program that will enable your children to earn a high school diploma at home—but there are plenty of organizations and resources to help you. The **Oregon Home Education Network** (503-321-5166, www.ohen.org) and the **Washington Homeschool Organization** (425-251-0439, www.wash-homeschool.org) are good places to start.

CHARTER SCHOOLS

Many school districts in Oregon, including Portland, offer public charter schools—schools run autonomously, but with the (sometimes grudging) approval or sponsorship of the local school board. At press time, there were over 120 charter schools statewide. Unlike most public schools, charter schools, which are bound by their own charter agreements, are free from some traditional school regulations. For more information about charter schools in Oregon, including a current list of charter schools, visit the **Oregon Department of Education** charter school page at www.ode.state.or.us/go/charterschools/, or contact the **League of Oregon Charter Schools** (503-838-3636, www.oregonleaguecharters.org), the state's charter schools association.

Washington voters approved a charter school initiative in 2012. The state is currently in the early years of implementing the law, and at press time only a handful of charter schools had opened, none of which are located in Southwest Washington. Up-to-date information is available from the **Washington Charter Schools Association** (www.wacharters.org).

THE PORTLAND METROPOLITAN AREA IS HOME TO MORE THAN A dozen colleges and universities, five community college systems, and a dazzling number of specialized degree-granting (and non–degree-granting) institutions.

Nineteen of Oregon's accredited, not-for-profit private colleges and universities belong to or are affiliated with the **Alliance of Oregon Independent Colleges and Universities**; the association's website (www.oaicu.org) includes school profiles and general information about attending a private college. Of the seven institutions that constitute the public **Oregon University System** (www.ous.edu), only one—Portland State University—is based in Portland. (Oregon Health & Science University [OHSU], also in Portland, is an OUS affiliate.) The system's flagship campuses, University of Oregon (in Eugene) and Oregon State University (in Corvallis), while not within reasonable commuting distance of Portland, have tens of thousands of alumni in the area and offer lectures, professional courses, and extension courses through local satellite centers (503-412-3696, pdx.uoregon.edu, and 503-553-3400, oregonstate.edu/portlandmetro/, respectively). The **Oregon Institute of Technology** (OIT) has a Wilsonville campus, and **Washington State University** has a campus in Vancouver. Addresses below are in Oregon unless otherwise noted.

REDUCED OUT-OF-STATE TUITION OPTIONS

Unlike some states, Oregon and Washington do not have a full reciprocity agreement that allows residents of one state to attend public colleges or universities in the other state at a reduced tuition rate. However, residents of certain "border" counties in Oregon (including Multnomah, Washington, Clackamas, and Columbia Counties) are eligible to pay resident tuition rates at Washington State University–Vancouver for course loads of eight credits or less. Similarly, residents of "border" counties in Washington (including Clark County) are eligible to pay resident tuition at Portland State University (for course loads of eight credits or less) at certain OHSU programs, and the OIT Wilsonville campus. Residents of either state qualify for resident tuition status at some of the other state's community colleges.

The **Western Interstate Commission for Higher Education** (WICHE) manages student exchange programs for 15 western states, including Washington and Oregon. Washington and Oregon residents may qualify for resident or reduced nonresident tuition at certain programs in certain institutions in other WICHE states. A complete description of the various exchange programs and their (fairly complex) rules is available on the WICHE website (www.wiche.edu/StudentExchange).

SAVING FOR COLLEGE

Oregon taxpayers who have pre–college-age children may be interested in Oregon's 529 college savings plans. These plans allow individuals to open special accounts to invest for college; earnings are exempt from state and federal tax, as are withdrawals for qualified educational purposes (tuition, room and board, supplies, etc.). Money in a 529 plan can be used at practically any college or university in the country, not just at Oregon institutions. In addition, contributions to an Oregon 529 plan are deductible on Oregon state tax returns; for tax year 2014, joint filers may deduct up to $4,530, and others may deduct up to $2,265 per year. These amounts are indexed for inflation and should rise each year. (Note that the tax deduction is also available to Washington residents who work in Oregon and pay Oregon income taxes.) Further information is available from the **Oregon 529 College Savings Network** (www.oregon529network.com).

Oregon's 529 plan received some bad press a few years ago when its supposedly ultra-conservative bond portfolios suffered huge losses. Funny story—it turns out the outside fund manager invested the funds not in bonds, but in toxic derivatives, credit default swaps, and other investments of questionable wisdom. The state sued the manager, and a different money manager is now in charge.

Washington does not have a college savings plan, but it does have a **Guaranteed Education Tuition** program (www.get.wa.gov), which is essentially a tax-advantaged prepaid tuition plan. Washington residents (and Oregon residents) are generally eligible to contribute to 529 plans run by other states. For more information on other states' 529 plans, visit www.savingforcollege.com or www.collegesavings.org.

PORTLAND-AREA UNIVERSITIES AND COLLEGES

- **Concordia University**, 2811 NE Holman St, Portland, 97211, 503-288-9371, 800-321-9371, www.cu-portland.edu; a private Lutheran college, Concordia University, part of the national Concordia University System, offers degrees in arts and sciences, education, management, and theology. Enrollment: about 3,100.

- **Corban University**, 5000 Deer Park Drive SE, Salem, 97317, 503-581-8600, www.corban.edu; this private Christian college in Salem offers more than 50 undergraduate majors, as well as graduate programs in education, business administration, and counseling. Enrollment: about 1,100.
- **George Fox University**, 414 N Meridian St, Newberg, 97132, 503-538-8383, 800-765-4369, www.georgefox.edu; founded by Quakers in 1891, this private Christian university offers more than 50 undergraduate, graduate, and seminary degree programs at its residential campus in Newberg (southwest of Portland) and at satellite campuses in Portland, Salem, and Redmond (Central Oregon). Enrollment: about 3,500.
- **Lewis and Clark College**, 0615 SW Palatine Hill Rd, Portland, 97219, 503-768-7040, 800-444-4111, www.lclark.edu; this private liberal arts college with an excellent national reputation occupies a rolling, wooded campus in the hills of Southwest Portland. In addition to its College of Arts and Sciences, Lewis and Clark is home to a Graduate School of Education and Counseling and to one of Oregon's three law schools, which has a renowned environmental law program. Enrollment: about 3,700.
- **Linfield College,** 900 SE Baker St, McMinnville, 97128, 800-640-2287, www.linfield.edu; a Baptist liberal arts college, Linfield is located in the small city of McMinnville, about 45 minutes southwest of Portland. Enrollment: about 2,600.
- **Marylhurst University,** 17600 Pacific Hwy (Hwy 43), Marylhurst, 97036, 503-636-8141, 800-634-9982, www.marylhurst.edu; this coeducational Catholic university in Portland's southern suburbs (between Lake Oswego and West Linn) serves working adults who want to earn an undergraduate or graduate degree or professional certification but require a flexible timetable. Marylhurst is known for its small class sizes, generous credits for life experience, and distance learning options. Enrollment: about 1,600.
- **Multnomah University**, 8435 NE Glisan St, 97220, 877-251-6560, www.multnomah.edu; formerly Multnomah Bible College, Multnomah University focuses on bible studies, and also offers master's degrees in divinity. Enrollment: about 900.
- **Oregon College of Art and Craft**, 8425 SW Barnes Rd, Portland, 97225, 503-297-5544, 800-390-0632, www.ocac.edu; this small art college offers bachelor's and master's degrees in craft-related disciplines. Enrollment: about 180.
- **Oregon Health & Science University,** 3181 SW Sam Jackson Park Rd, Portland, 97239, 503-494-8311, www.ohsu.edu; this gleaming complex of hospitals, research laboratories, clinics, and classrooms perches atop Marquam Hill just south of downtown Portland, and is one of the city's most recognizable landmarks (especially at night, when it blazes with light). OHSU comprises medical, dental, and nursing schools, as well as a science and engineering graduate school located on a separate campus in Beaverton. Enrollment: about 2,800.
- **Oregon Institute of Technology, Wilsonville**, 27500 SW Parkway Ave, Wilsonville, 97070, 503-821-1250, www.oit.edu/wilsonville; OIT, also known as

Oregon Tech, has its main campus in Klamath Falls, in southern Oregon. The small Wilsonville campus offers degree programs in certain engineering and information technology fields. Enrollment: about 4,100 (all campuses)

- **Pacific Northwest College of Art,** 1241 NW Johnson St., Portland, 97209, 503-226-4391, www.pnca.edu; located in the heart of the trendy Pearl District, PNCA offers B.F.A. and M.F.A. degrees in several art-related majors, including painting, photography, and communication design, and also runs continuing education and certificate programs. Enrollment: about 600.
- **Pacific University,** 2043 College Way, Forest Grove, 97116, 503-352-6151, 877-722-8648, www.pacificu.edu; Pacific University, one of the state's oldest post-secondary institutions, has an extensive and beautiful campus in the western suburb of Forest Grove. The school offers degrees in dozens of undergraduate majors, as well as graduate degrees in education, optometry, pharmacy, and several other disciplines. Enrollment: about 3,500.
- **Portland State University,** P.O. Box 751, Portland, 97207, 503-725-3000, 800-547-8887, www.pdx.edu; PSU, which anchors the southern end of downtown Portland's Park Blocks, boasts the largest overall college or university enrollment in Oregon. Largely a commuter school, PSU offers over 200 undergraduate and graduate programs at several different schools and colleges, ranging from the College of Liberal Arts and Sciences to the nationally known College of Urban and Public Affairs. PSU also offers extension and continuing education classes to the community at large. Enrollment: about 30,000.
- **Reed College,** 3203 SE Woodstock Blvd, Portland, 97202, 503-771-1112, www.reed.edu; Reed, regarded as one of the top liberal arts colleges in the country, has a reputation for both academic rigor and social permissiveness. (Some locals refer to Reed, perhaps enviously, as a 4.0 party school.) The school occupies a lovely residential campus, complete with canyon and ivy-clad brick buildings, in Southeast Portland. Enrollment: about 1,400.
- **University of Portland,** 5000 N Willamette Blvd, Portland, 97203, 503-943-7147, www.up.edu; this large Catholic institution, which sits atop a bluff overlooking the Willamette River in North Portland, is consistently ranked among the top regional universities in the West. In addition to its College of Arts & Sciences, which offers dozens of possible undergraduate and graduate degrees, the university has schools of nursing, education, engineering, and business administration. Enrollment: about 3,900.
- **Warner Pacific College,** 2219 SE 68th Ave, Portland, 97215, 503-517-1000, www.warnerpacific.edu; this small Christian liberal arts college is located on the south slope of Mount Tabor in Southeast Portland; Warner Pacific also offers master's programs in management and organizational leadership, education, and religion. Enrollment: about 1,600.
- **Washington State University–Vancouver,** 14204 NE Salmon Creek Ave, Vancouver, WA 98686, 360-546-9788, www.vancouver.wsu.edu; this young, relatively small branch of the state's land grant university offers 20 different

undergraduate degrees and 11 graduate degrees; it occupies a sprawling new campus in outer northeast Vancouver. Enrollment: about 3,000.

- **Willamette University,** 900 State St, Salem, 97301, 503-370-6300, www. willamette.edu; founded in 1842 (and thus the oldest college in the western United States), Willamette is located in Salem, about an hour south of Portland; although primarily a liberal arts college, it has graduate schools of management and education and is home to one of Oregon's three law schools. Enrollment: about 2,700.

AREA COMMUNITY COLLEGES

These community colleges offer two-year degrees and collectively serve tens of thousands of students in the Portland region. They also offer a wide range of adult education and special-interest courses to local residents.

- **Chemeketa Community College,** Salem, 503-399-5000, www.chemeketa.edu, is the community college for Salem and the mid–Willamette Valley (including Marion County and much of Yamhill County).
- **Clackamas Community College,** Oregon City, 503-594-6000, www. clackamas.edu, serves most of the populated portions of Clackamas County (except Lake Oswego, Boring, Damascus, and Sandy); there are satellite campuses in Harmony (Clackamas Town Center) and Wilsonville, and extension classes are offered in Canby, Estacada, and Molalla.
- **Clark College,** Vancouver, 360-699-6398, www.clark.edu, serves Vancouver and Clark County, Washington; the main campus is near downtown Vancouver, with a satellite campus at the Columbia Tech Center in eastern Vancouver. Some classes are held at WSU–Vancouver and at Town Plaza on East Mill Plain Blvd.
- **Mt. Hood Community College,** Gresham, 503-491-6422, www.mhcc.edu, has a vast district that covers eastern Multnomah County (including outer Northeast Portland) and parts of Clackamas County from Damascus and Boring to the summit of Mount Hood; the main campus in Gresham has a satellite in Northeast Portland.
- **Portland Community College,** Portland, 971-722-6111, 866-922-1010, www. pcc.edu, serves Lake Oswego, most of the city of Portland, all of Washington County, and parts of Columbia and Yamhill counties; the four main campuses are Cascade (in North Portland), Rock Creek (off the Sunset Highway in the western suburbs near Hillsboro), Sylvania (in outer Southwest Portland), and Southeast Portland at Division St and 82nd Ave, with several additional centers located in Portland, Newberg, and Washington County. Community education classes take place at dozens of sites around the area.

OTHER DEGREE-GRANTING INSTITUTIONS

The Portland area supports dozens of other institutions of higher or continuing education. Some of these institutions, like Le Cordon Bleu College of Culinary Arts (www.chefs.edu), National College of Natural Medicine (www.ncnm.edu), Oregon College of Oriental Medicine (www.ocom.edu), and Mount Angel Seminary (www. mountangelabbey.org/seminary/) offer specialized instruction in specific disciplines; others are run by national for-profit corporations and focus on career or business education. You can find a complete list of approved degree-granting programs in Oregon on the website of the state Student Assistance Commission's **Office of Degree Authorization** (www.oregonstudentaid.gov/oda.aspx). A similar list for Washington is available from the **Washington Student Achievement Council** (www.wsac.wa.gov).

P ORTLAND REGULARLY SHOWS UP IN THE TOP TWO PLACES IN LISTS OF the country's most canine-friendly burgs, as compiled by sources such as *Dog Fancy* (authoritative!) and *Forbes* (less authoritative). While such rankings are largely meaningless, Portland is a great place for pet lovers. The city's human-to-dog ratio is reportedly approaching four to one, and the city has undergone a multi-year boom in dog-friendly events and businesses. A **Doggie Dash** run (www.oregonhumane.org/doggiedash/) is held each May, canine day care centers seem to be springing up on every other block, and the four **Lucky Labrador Brewing Company** pubs (www.luckylab.com) welcome dogs at their outdoor tables. (Cats are at least as popular as dogs in Portland, but being more self-sufficient and less gregarious, they require fewer public amenities.) Note that you'll have to find another home for your gorilla, lion, bear, crocodile, etc.—dangerous or exotic pets became illegal in Oregon in 2010.

PET LICENSES

In Multnomah County (which includes the city of Portland), both dogs and cats must be licensed within 30 days of becoming "resident" in the county. To license your pet, you'll need to pay a fee, which varies depending on the duration of the license, the type of animal, and whether it has been spayed or neutered; one-year licenses range from $12 to $30, with discounts available for (human) seniors. You'll also need to provide proof that your pet has a current rabies vaccination. Licenses are available from veterinary clinics or directly from **Multnomah County Animal Services** (503-988-7387, www.multcopets.org/licensing-information). Newcomers to the county can get a free 60-day "starter" license online at the MCAS website.

Pet licensing requirements across the Columbia River are similar. Licenses are required for dogs, cats, and wild animals that are kept in Vancouver, unincorporated Clark County, or the town of Yacolt. License information and applications are available online or by phone from **Clark County Animal Protection and Control** (360-397-2489, www.clark.wa.gov/development/animals/licenses.html), or from various licensing agents. Most other incorporated areas in Clark County, including Camas, require municipal licenses for dogs; check with your city hall for specific requirements.

In Clackamas, Columbia, Marion, Yamhill, and Washington counties, in Oregon, licenses are required for dogs only. Generally, as in Multnomah and Clark counties, fees vary depending on whether the pet is sterile or fertile, and you must provide evidence of rabies vaccination.

- **Clackamas County Dog Services**, 13141 SE Hwy 212, Clackamas, 503-655-8628, clackamas.us/dogs/
- **Columbia County Clerk**, 230 Strand St, St. Helens, 503-397-3935, www.co.columbia.or.us/clerk
- **Marion County Dog Services**, 3550 Aumsville Hwy SE, Salem, 503-588-5233, www.mcdogs.net
- **Washington County Animal Services**, 1901 SE 24th Ave, Hillsboro, 503-846-7041, www.co.washington.or.us/hhs/AnimalServices/
- **Yamhill County Dog Control**, Yamhill County Fairgrounds, 2070 Lafayette Ave, McMinnville, 503-434-7538, www.co.yamhill.or.us/dog-control

VETERINARY CARE

Satisfied friends and neighbors are the best sources of veterinarian referrals. If you can't get a personal recommendation, look in the Yellow Pages, do an Internet search, or contact the **Oregon Veterinary Medical Association** (503-399-0311, 800-235-3502, www.oregonvma.org), which offers a "find a vet" service. (In Washington, contact the **Washington State Veterinary Medical Association**, 425-396-3191, 800-399-7862, www.wsvma.org.)

PET HOSPITALS

- **Banfield, The Pet Hospital** (866-894-7927, www.banfield.com) is a national chain that started in Portland and is still headquartered here; they have 20 locations in the metro area.
- **VCA Animal Hospitals** (800-VCA-PETS, vcahospitals.com) has ten area hospitals.

VETERINARY EMERGENCY CARE

Dove Lewis (www.dovelewis.org) operates a 24-hour emergency animal hospital at 1945 NW Pettygrove St (emergency line 503-228-7281).

Other area emergency veterinary clinics that are open nights and weekends include:

- **Columbia River VetERinary Specialists**, 6607 NE 84th St, Ste 109, Vancouver, 360-694-3007, www.columbiarivervetspecialists.com
- **Emergency Veterinary Clinic of Tualatin**, 19314 SW Mohave Ct, Tualatin, 503-691-7922, www.evcot.com
- **Salem Veterinary Emergency Clinic**, 3215 Market St NE, Salem, 503-588-8082, www.salemervet.net
- **St. Francis 24 Hour Pet Hospital**, 12010 NE 65th St, Vancouver, 360-253-5446, www.stfrancis24hr.com
- **Tanasbourne Veterinary Emergency**, 2338 NW Amberbrook Dr, Beaverton, 503-629-5800, www.tanasbourneveter.com
- **VCA Northwest Veterinary Specialists**, 16756 SE 82nd Dr, Clackamas, 503-656-3999, www.northwestvetspecialists.com
- **VCA Southeast Portland Animal Hospital**, 13830 SE Stark St, 503-255-8139, www.vcahospitals.com/southeast-portland

PET ADOPTION

If you want to adopt a pet, a local animal shelter is a good place to begin. Cats and dogs will come with their first vaccinations and a discount coupon to have them spayed or neutered. Area shelters include:

- **Animal Aid,** 5335 SW 42nd Ave, 503-292-6628, www.animalaidpdx.org
- **Bonnie L. Hays Small Animal Shelter,** 1901 SE 24th Ave, Hillsboro, 503-846-7041, www.co.washington.or.us/hhs/AnimalServices/AnimalShelter/
- **Cat Adoption Team**, 14175 SW Galbreath Dr, Sherwood, 503-925-9903, www.catadoptionteam.org
- **Clackamas County Dog Services**, 13141 SE Hwy 212, Clackamas, 503-655-8628, www.clackamas.us/dogs
- **Columbia Humane Society,** 2084 Oregon St., St. Helens, 503-397-4353, www.columbiahumane.org
- **Family Dogs New Life Shelter**, 9101 SE Stanley Ave, 503-771-5596, www.familydogsnewlife.org
- **Homeward Bound Pets**, 10605 SE Loop Rd, McMinnville, 971-237-1604, www.hbpets.org
- **Humane Society for Southwest Washington**, 1100 NE 192nd Ave, Vancouver, 360-693-4746, southwesthumane.org
- **Marion County Animal Shelter**, 3550 Aumsville Hwy SE, Salem, 503-566-6966, www.mcdogs.net
- **Multnomah County Animal Shelter**, 1700 W Historic Columbia River Hwy, Troutdale, 503-988-7387, www.multcopets.org
- **Oregon Humane Society**, 1067 NE Columbia Blvd, 503-285-7722, www.oregonhumane.com
- **PAWS Animal Shelter**, 1741 Willamette Falls Dr, West Linn, 503-650-0855, www.facebook.com/PAWSOregon

- **Pixie Project**, 510 NE MLK Jr Blvd, 503-542-3433, www.pixieproject.org
- **Willamette Humane Society**, 4246 Turner Rd SE, Salem, 503-585-5900, www.whs4pets.org

You can also try such online resources as **Petfinder** (www.petfinder.com) and **Adoptapet.com.**

OTHER RESOURCES FOR PET OWNERS

Several publications and websites focus on pet-related service providers, upcoming events, and news of interest to Portland-area pet owners. Check out **Portland Pooch** (www.portlandpooch.com), the **Oregon Humane Society**'s Services directory (www.oregonhumane.org/services/overview.asp), and the Oregonian's **Oregon Pets** section (www.oregonlive.com/pets/) or pick up a copy of *Spot* (www.spotmagazine.net) at your local library or pet supply store. You might just learn about some new, indispensable service. (Pet psychics? Who knew?)

PET SITTERS, DOGGIE DAY CARE, AND KENNELS

Not counting in-home doggie day care centers, the city of Portland harbors dozens of doggie day care and canine "social clubs," most of which seem to have pun-based names. (Example: **Virginia Woof Dog Daycare Center**, 1520 E Burnside Street, 503-224-5455, www.virginiawoof.com.) The suburbs have several dozen more, and new facilities open seemingly every month. As with most services, it's best to get a personal recommendation for a pet sitter, doggie day care provider, or kennel. The Oregon Humane Society publishes a useful list of "Questions to Ask When Considering a Dog Day Care," available at www.oregonhumane. org/services/documents/Daycare_s_000.pdf.

For up-to-date listings of doggie day care centers and pet sitters, check out **Portland Pooch**'s online list at http://www.portlandpooch.com/directory/ daycare/listings.htm. **Pet Sitters International** (www.petsit.com) and **Portland Petsitters** (www.portlandpetsitters.com) also offer online listings of pet sitters. Ads for in-home or private doggie day care are sometimes posted in the community/pets forum of craigslist.com, although as with any Craigslist ad, *caveat emptor*. For kennels (including cat-only boarding facilities), search www.findpet-care.com (which also has daycare listings), or check the Yellow Pages under "Pet Boarding" or "Dog and Cat Kennels." Portland Pooch's online list of dog kennels is at www.portlandpooch.com/directory/boarding.htm. If you need to board your pet because you're leaving the city by air, the unique **Airpet Hotel** (6212 NE 78th Ct, Suite B, 503-255-1388, www.airpethotel.com) allows you to "park, board your pet, and board your plane."

DOG PARKS

Portland has more public off-leash areas per capita than any other city in the country—33 as of 2014, up from only 4 in 2000. (Sadly, the explosive growth of off-leash areas in Portland was partly the result of increasing conflict between dog-owning and non–dog-owning park users; this conflict culminated most visibly and tragically with the fatal poisonings of more than a dozen dogs in Laurelhurst Park in 2003.) Nine of these areas are fully fenced, dedicated off-leash areas, eight are unfenced areas that are open during most park hours, and the remaining 16 are open for off-leash use during specific hours only. The **Portland Parks and Recreation** off-leash program website (www.portlandoregon.gov/parks/38287) lists off-leash areas, hours, and regulations, and provides links to maps of each specific park and the off-leash area within each park.

Outside Portland, off-leash areas have been established in Beaverton, Happy Valley, Hillsboro, Milwaukie, Tigard, Lake Oswego, Wilsonville, Vancouver, and several other suburbs, as well as in some area state parks. **PortlandPooch.com** has created an up-to-date, comprehensive online map of dog parks in the Portland region; visit www.portlandpooch.com/dogparks/map.htm, and click on any location marker to find the name and location of the dog park, with a description of the off-leash area. A companion comparison chart, which includes user ratings for each park, is located at www.portlandpooch.com/dogparks/comparison.htm.

THE AVERAGE TRANSPLANT TO PORTLAND IS UNLIKELY TO NAME "CUL-
tural life" as his or her primary motivation for moving here. But Portland
has an incredibly vibrant arts and entertainment scene—in some respects,
arguably the best in the country for a city of its size—and it's filled with big and
small arts venues that offer high-caliber and occasionally world-class performances in practically any artistic genre you could name. It also tends to attract
enough young artists of all kinds to give the local arts scene a surprisingly avant-
garde flavor.

This chapter also covers **Museums**, **Literary Life**, and **Culture for Kids.**

WHAT'S GOING ON?

The **Willamette Week** and the **A&E** insert in the Friday **Oregonian**, available
weekly in paper form or online at www.wweek.com and oregonlive.com/enter-
tainment respectively, offer the most complete listings of upcoming performing
arts events, exhibit openings and closings, film screenings, dance clubs, and the
like. The weekly **Portland Mercury** (www.portlandmercury.com) is a runner-up.

TICKETS

As in most US cities, tickets to the majority of cultural events in Portland can (or
must) be bought through ticket leviathan **Ticketmaster** (866-448-7849, online
at www.ticketmaster.com, or at retail outlets, including many area Fred Meyer
stores). For especially popular events, such as major rock concerts, you may
have no choice but to buy from Ticketmaster. However, for many events and
performances you can avoid paying the hefty extra Ticketmaster service fees by
purchasing tickets directly at the box office of the event venue.

Several local venues use the ticket service **TicketsWest** (800-992-8499, www. ticketswest.com), which has retail outlets at most Safeway supermarkets, as well as Music Millennium.

Events at the Moda Center, the Arlene Schnitzer Concert Hall, and several other performing arts venues are sold through **ComcastTix** (www.ComcastTIX. com). You may occasionally encounter one of several other online ticket services, including **TicketWeb** (www.ticketweb.com) and the "fair trade" ticket service **Brown Paper Tickets** (800-838-3006, www.brownpapertickets.com).

If you have your heart set on going to a sold-out performance, a ticket broker can usually accommodate you, but expect to pay a significant premium for the privilege. Look in the Yellow Pages under "Ticket Sales—Entertainment & Sports," or check out online sites like craigslist.org, eBay (www.ebay.com), www.ticketsnow.com, or www.stubhub.com.

CONCERT HALLS AND THEATERS

Most of Portland's "high" cultural events—major theatrical productions, dance and classical music performances, and the like—take place at the five venues listed below, collectively the "Portland'5 Centers for the Arts." Portland also has an impressive range of high-quality alternative performance spaces, and many events are held in the city's churches and synagogues, in high school and college campus theaters and auditoriums, at neighborhood community or cultural centers, or in cafés and rock clubs. Some smaller theater companies have their own dedicated performance spaces.

- **Arlene Schnitzer Concert Hall**, 1037 SW Broadway, 503-248-4335, www. portland5.com/arlene-schnitzer-concert-hall; the "Schnitz" is part of the downtown Portland Center for the Performing Arts complex on Broadway. This ornate, formal concert hall, decorated in rococo finery, hosts Oregon Symphony performances; lectures; various classical, dance, and theatrical productions; and the occasional rock concert.
- **Brunish Theatre**, 1111 SW Broadway, 503-248-4335, www.portland5.com/ brunish-theater; this small, flexible space in the downtown Portland Center for the Performing Arts complex sees a diverse set of small-scale performances, primarily plays.
- **Dolores Winningstad Theatre**, 1111 SW Broadway, 503-248-4335, www. portland5.com/winningstad-theatre; another star in the Portland Center for the Performing Arts constellation, this small Elizabethan-style theatre hosts a variety of theatrical productions, and is an especially popular venue for Shakespeare plays.
- **Keller Auditorium**, 222 SW Clay St, 503-248-4335, www.portland5.com/keller-auditorium; formerly the Civic Auditorium, the Keller Auditorium provides a home for the Portland Opera, the Oregon Ballet Theatre, and most touring Broadway shows that come through Portland.

- **Newmark Theatre**, 1111 SW Broadway, 503-248-4335, www.portland5.com/ newmark-theatre, is an intimate, Edwardian-style theater.

PERFORMING ARTS

While the lists below include almost all the city's professional performing arts companies, and many of its major nonprofessional organizations, they are by no means exhaustive.

DANCE

- **Bobery (www.bobery.com), formerly Hot Little Hands,** is a small dance company that gives infrequent but highly regarded performances, including presentations of original works.
- **BodyVox**, 1201 NW 17th Ave, 503-229-0627, www.bodyvox.com, is a dynamic, innovative modern dance company that is based in Portland but frequently tours around the country.
- **Oregon Ballet Theatre**, 818 SE 6th Ave, 503-222-5538, www.obt.org; this nationally recognized professional ballet company performs a series of shows every two to three months. The OBT's Christmastime *Nutcracker* performances are wildly popular. The OBT also operates a ballet school.
- **Polaris Dance Theatre**, 1501 SW Taylor St, 503-380-5472, www.polarisdance. org, is a contemporary dance company that also offers classes at its dance center in downtown Portland.
- **White Bird**, 503-245-1600, www.whitebird.org, brings regional, national, and international contemporary dance companies to Portland.

MUSIC

SYMPHONIC, OPERA, CHAMBER MUSIC

Portland's classical music resources are surprisingly good, and some of its professional performers are of national or international caliber. Besides offering many options for traditional classical fare, Portland is a center of the burgeoning alt-classical scene. Moreover, Portland attracts more musicians and singers than it can support professionally, so even nonprofessional groups put on performances of surprisingly high quality.

- **Beaverton Symphony Orchestra**, 503-819-4664, www.beavertonsymphony. org; this amateur orchestra focuses on the "great works" of classical music.
- **Chamber Music Northwest**, 503-294-6400, www.cmnw.org; CMNW is not a performance group, but rather an organization devoted to bringing high-caliber chamber music artists to Portland to perform. It arranges events throughout the year, but the culmination of its efforts is a summer chamber music festival held at Reed College and the Catlin Gabel School.

- **Classical Revolution**, www.classicalrevolutionpdx.org; with a rallying cry of "chamber music for everyone," Classical Revolution is one of the best known of several alt-classical or underground classical ensembles in Portland. They give frequent non-stuffy performances.
- **Friends of Chamber Music**, 503-224-9842, www.focm.org, brings several world-class chamber ensembles to Portland each year.
- **Opera Theater Oregon**, www.operatheateror.wordpress.com, is a local alternative opera company that gives frequently rollicking and always unconventional performances, such as *Das Rheingold* rescripted as a Baywatch episode.
- **Oregon Symphony**, 503-228-1353, www.orsymphony.org; the Oregon Symphony, now more than a century old, is one of the largest and most highly regarded orchestras in the country. In addition to its performances of classical standards and the occasional contemporary piece, the Symphony presents a yearly pops series with guest non-classical performers. Most performances take place at the Arlene Schnitzer Concert Hall.
- **Portland Baroque Orchestra**, 503-222-6000, www.pbo.org; one of the best orchestras of its kind in the world, the Portland Baroque Orchestra indeed plays Baroque music, including some obscure pieces. PBO uses only original period instruments or reproductions.
- **Portland Cello Project**, www.portlandcelloproject.com, is another alt-classical group. PCP performs around the country and collaborates frequently with non-classical artists. Plenty of cellos? Yes. Talented musicians? Yes. Traditional performances? No.
- **Portland Chamber Orchestra**, 503-771-3250, www.portlandchamberorchestra.org, is the oldest professional-amateur chamber orchestra in the United States.
- **Portland Columbia Symphony Orchestra**, 503-234-4077, www.columbiasymphony.org, composed of both professional and semiprofessional musicians, performs several concerts from autumn through spring of each year.
- **Portland Opera**, 503-241-1802, www.portlandopera.org; based in the Keller Auditorium, the Portland Opera is regarded as one of the top opera companies in the United States. While most of its productions are time-tested works, it also stages some innovative and contemporary productions, such as *Nixon in China* and Philip Glass's *Galileo Galilei*.
- **Portland Piano International**, 503-228-1388, www.portlandpiano.org, brings world-class pianists to Portland for recitals.
- **Portland Taiko**, 503-288-2456, www.portlandtaiko.org; neither purely music nor wholly dance, this group's performances incorporate elements from multiple disciplines based around the taiko, a traditional Japanese drum.
- **Third Angle New Music Ensemble**, 503-331-0301, www.thirdangle.org, presents new chamber music.
- **Vancouver Symphony Orchestra**, 360-735-7278, www.vancouversymphony.org; billing itself as "America's Vancouver Symphony" (to avoid confusion with

the organization of the same in Vancouver, British Columbia), the Vancouver Symphony is the leading orchestral group in Southwest Washington.

CHORAL

Portland is rich in vocal music groups of all ages and abilities. The following list provides a glimpse of some of the city's choral groups that offer public performances.

- **Cappella Romana**, 503-236-8202, www.cappellaromana.org, performs works of Byzantine complexity—literally. The group's focus is music of the Byzantine and Eastern Orthodox traditions, and most of their singing is in Greek or Russian.
- **Choral Arts Ensemble of Portland**, 503-488-3834, www.caeportland.com, performs a diverse range of choral music.
- **In Mulieribus**, www.inmulieribus.org, is a female vocal ensemble that primarily performs pre-1750 works.
- **Oregon Repertory Singers**, 503 230 0652, www.orsingers.org; both the quality and the sheer volume of this 60-voice choir will knock your socks off.
- **Portland Gay Men's Chorus**, 503-226-2588, www.pdxgmc.org, gives an eclectic series of performances each year.
- **Portland's Singing Christmas Tree**, 503-244-1344, www.singingchristmastree. org; a seasonal phenomenon, Portland's Singing Christmas Tree is actually a group of human singers arranged in the shape of a conifer and not a caroling evergreen.
- **Portland Symphonic Choir**, 503-223-1217, www.pschoir.org; this accomplished and well-respected choir offers a full program of choral performances each year. (The group's annual Wintersong! celebration is a particular highlight.)

CONTEMPORARY

For all the diversity of the city's arts community as a whole, Portland's contemporary music scene gets the most national press. Portland is currently an alternative music hotbed; the city groans under the collective weight of scores of talented indie bands virtually no one has heard of. Some locally based bands like the Shins, the Decemberists, and the now-disbanded Sleater-Kinney have achieved international success, and plenty of up-and-coming acts like Blitzen Trapper, Blind Pilot, and Portugal. The Man are getting there, and the city's alternative music pedigree stretches from proto-garage band The Kingsmen (immortalized by their one hit, "Louie Louie") through Elliott Smith and Everclear. However, Portland is also one of the jazz, blues, and acoustic music hotspots of western North America, and the area boasts accomplished contemporary musicians working in almost every genre (or blending them—Pink Martini, which has legions of fans as far away as France, mixes classical, pop, and Latin influences, among others).

Given the range of the local music scene, it's not surprising that the majority of Portland's live music venues are at least moderately cross-genre, and some venues, such as the Crystal Ballroom and Mississippi Studios, take pride in presenting a diverse slate of acts. The venues listed below generally offer live music at least four or five nights a week. Many bars, restaurants, pubs, and nightclubs offer live music on a less-frequent basis, especially on weekends. A statewide smoking ban for bars and restaurants means that you won't come home after a gig with your hair and clothes smelling like a Vegas ashtray.

ARENAS

Rock and pop superstars tend to play in the city's sports arenas, both located in the Rose Quarter/Lloyd District area of Northeast Portland:

- **Memorial Coliseum**, 300 Winning Way, 503-797-9619, www.rosequarter.com
- **Moda Center**, One Center Court, 503-797-9619, www.rosequarter.com. (The Moda Center was long known as the Rose Garden, and you'll still hear most people call it that. Do not confuse the Rose Garden arena with the International Rose Test Garden in Washington Park. More than one newcomer has made the mistake, and the potential for confusion is exacerbated on the occasions where the Washington Park rose garden hosts outdoor summer concerts.)

CABARET

While many of Portland's bars, restaurants, nightclubs, and performance spaces offer an occasional cabaret performance, the city's only dedicated cabaret (as distinct from strip clubs that call themselves cabarets) is **Darcelle XV** (208 NW 3rd Avenue, 503-222-5338, www.darcellexv.com), which has staged female impersonator cabaret shows since the late 1960s.

FOLK, ACOUSTIC, BLUEGRASS, CELTIC

- **Aladdin Theater**, 3017 SE Milwaukie Ave, 503-234-9694, www.aladdin-theater.com; the Aladdin is one of the city's most comfortable concert venues—it actually is a theater, with full seating, plus tasty food and good beer—and gets its fair share of big-name touring folk, rock, and country acts. The seating arrangement is ideal for enjoying folk acts and singer-songwriters, but renders crowd surfing and mosh pit formation impractical.
- **Alberta Street Pub**, 1036 NE Alberta St, 503-284-7665, www.albertastreetpub.com, hosts acoustic, Celtic, and bluegrass performances most nights.
- **Biddy McGraws**, 6000 NE Glisan St, 503-233-1178, www.biddymcgraws.com; despite the name, Biddy's features more than just Irish music (although there is plenty of that).
- **Kells**, 112 SW 2nd Ave, 503-227-4057, www.kellsirishportland.com, has live Irish music every night of the week.
- **White Eagle Saloon**, 836 N Russell St, 503-282-6810, www.mcmenamins.com/whiteeagle; this purportedly haunted McMenamins tavern has live acts almost every night, along with some all-ages weekend afternoon shows.

JAZZ & BLUES

For complete information on local events and gigs, check out the websites of the **Jazz Society of Oregon** (www.jsojazzscene.org) and the **Cascade Blues Association** (cascadeblues.org).

- **Andina**, 1314 NW Glisan St, 503-228-9535, www.andinarestaurant.com; this upscale and deservedly popular Peruvian restaurant in the Pearl District has live jazz and Latin music almost every night.
- **Jimmy Mak's,** 221 NW 10th Ave, 503-295-6542, www.jimmymaks.com, is widely regarded as Portland's foremost live jazz venue, and is graced by occasional performances by living legends of jazz.
- **Tillicum Club**, 8585 SW Beaverton-Hillsdale Hwy, 503-327-8147, www.thetillicum.com; this unpretentious restaurant/bar on the fringe of the suburbs hosts regular live performances, with an emphasis on blues.
- **Tony Starlight's**, 1125 SE Madison St, 503-517-8584, www.tonystarlight.com; if you can ignore the cheesy name, Tony Starlight's offers a good selection of jazz performances, including traditional jazz and swing.
- **Wilf's**, Union Station, 800 NW 6th Ave, 503-223-0070, www.wilfsrestaurant.com; who would have guessed that a restaurant in an Amtrak station would have such great live music with an atmosphere to match?

ROCK, POP, ALTERNATIVE

This category is a catch-all for all the diverse styles spawned from rock-and-roll or R&B—punk, pop, surf, rockabilly, hip hop, alternative, indie, metal, speed metal, death metal, and so on. As noted above, most "rock" clubs also host shows by other types of performers.

- **Alberta Rose Theatre**, 3000 NE Alberta St, 503-764-4131, www.albertarosetheatre.com; this 1920s-vintage theatre, a former movie house, features a diverse slate of acts, including the occasional living legend blowing through town.
- **Ash Street Saloon**, 225 SW Ash St, 503-226-0430, www.ashstreetsaloon.com; live music seven nights a week in a non-trendy, saloon atmosphere.
- **Crystal Ballroom**, 1332 SW Burnside St, 503-225-0047, www.crystalballroompdx.com; the Crystal Ballroom (a bona fide, actual ballroom) is locally famous for its sprung floor and psychedelic wall murals. Many local, national, and international acts headline here. The cool kids hang out in Lola's Room, one floor down.
- **Dante's**, 350 W Burnside St, 503-226-6630, www.danteslive.com; one of Portland's most eclectic clubs, Dante's hosts everything from cabaret to punk in a dark space with lots of red décor and a few open flames. (Get it?)
- **Doug Fir Lounge**, 830 E Burnside St, 503-231-9663, www.dougfirlounge.com; worth visiting for the underlit floor alone, this hip Eastside bar hosts an impressive roster of shows, including performances by artists of national renown.
- **Duff's Garage**, 1635 SE 7th Ave, 503-234-2337, www.duffsgarage.com; this Southeast Portland venue presents bands running the stylistic gamut from roots rock and rockabilly to country, jazz, and blues.

- **The Goodfoot**, 2845 SE Stark St, 503-239-9292, www.thegoodfoot.com; this Southeast pub hosts frequent live performances, including more funk and soul acts than most Portland venues.
- **Hawthorne Theatre**, 1507 SE 39th Ave, 503-233-7100, www.hawthornetheatre. com, an all-ages venue in the Hawthorne District, has (almost) nightly live shows.
- The **Laurelthirst Public House**, 2958 NE Glisan St, 503-232-1504, www. laurelthirst.com; this comfy pub/restaurant on the edge of the Laurelhurst neighborhood is more than just a clever name: local and some touring bands play here almost every night.
- **Mississippi Studios,** 3939 N Mississippi Ave, 503-288-3895, www. mississippistudios.com; this intimate club on North Mississippi Avenue hosts everything from vintage jazz to alternative bands like Franz Ferdinand.
- **Roseland Theater**, 8 NW 6th Ave, 503-230-0033, www.roselandpdx.com; the Roseland pulls in some big-name national and international acts. Depending on the evening bill, you could mix with punks, hipsters, teeny-boppers, Rastafarians, aging hippies, or all of the above.
- **Star Theater**, 13 NW 6th Ave, 503-345-7892, www.starrtheaterportland.com, is a former movie house–turned strip club–turned music venue is a relative newcomer to the Portland gig scene, but some relatively well-known national acts have played here already.
- **Wonder Ballroom**, 128 NE Russell St, 503-284-8686, www.wonderballroom. com; the historic Wonder Ballroom is yet another venue with a remarkably diverse slate of performers, including some national acts.

THEATER

Portland has many, many theater companies and ensembles; some go a year or more between productions. For a (relatively) complete list of area theater groups, as well as notices of upcoming events, visit the website of the **Portland Area Theater Alliance** (www.patagreenroom.org).

Here are some companies that produce plays on a more or less regular basis:
- **Action Adventure Theater**, www.actionadventure.org; this nonprofit collective offers unique productions that are often semi-improvised.
- **Artists Repertory Theatre**, 1515 SW Morrison, 503-241-1278, www.artistsrep. org; this accomplished professional nonprofit company stages a regular program of serious and comedic plays in its intimate downtown theater.
- **The Broadway Rose Theatre Company**, 12850 SW Grant Ave, Tigard, 503-620-5262, www.broadwayrose.com; the Broadway Rose, a professional theatre company based in Tigard, focuses on Broadway musicals.
- **CoHo Productions**, 2257 NW Raleigh St, 503-220-2646, www.cohoproductions. org; this award-winning company puts on an always-intriguing slate of plays at its intimate performance space in Northwest Portland (which it shares on occasion with other local and touring theatrical organizations).

- **defunkt theatre**, Back Door Theater, 4319 SE Hawthorne Blvd, 503-481-2960, www.defunktheatre.com, produces innovative, intriguing, and sometimes edgy plays.
- **Do Jump! Extremely Physical Theater**, The Echo Theatre, 1515 SE 37th Ave, 503-231-1232, www.dojump.org; when this genre- and gravity-defying troupe of "actorbats" performs, the result is part theater, part dance, and part circus. (DoJump! also offers lessons in theater and what can best be described as creative movement.)
- **Hand2Mouth Theatre**, 210 SE Madison St, Ste 11, 503-235-5284, www. hand2mouththeatre.org; this lively company produces somewhat barebones but well-executed original productions.
- **Hillsboro Artists Regional Theatre**, 185 SE Washington St, Hillsboro, 503-693-7815, www.hart-theatre.org; this community theater puts on several productions each year in western Washington County.
- **Imago Theatre**, 17 SE 8th Ave, 503-231-9501, www.imagotheatre.com, known best for its imaginative, long-running production *Frogz*, Imago focuses on physical theatre and oddball costumes and sets. Most of their original productions delight both children and adults.
- **Lakewood Theatre Company**, 368 S State St, Lake Oswego, 503-635-3901, www.lakewood-center.org; Lakewood Theatre Company has an active calendar of generally noncontroversial productions.
- **Miracle Theatre Group**, 425 SE 6th Ave, 503-236-7253, www.milagro.org, is a group of three Latino arts and culture organizations—Miracle Mainstage, Teatro Milagro, and Community Artes—that present English-language, Spanish-language, and bilingual productions.
- **Northwest Classical Theatre Company**, The ShoeBox Theater, 2110 SE 10th Ave, 971-244-3740, www.nwctc.org; the Northwest Classical Theatre Company focuses on the plays of Shakespeare and other established playwrights.
- **Playback Theater**, 503-719-6328, www.playbacktheaterpdx.com; you tell your story, the actors and musicians play it back for you.
- **Portland Actors Ensemble**, 503-467-6573, www.portlandactors.com; this troupe is best known for its free summer Shakespeare-in-the-Park performances in Portland public parks.
- **Portland Center Stage**, Gerding Theater at the Armory, 128 NE 11th Ave, 503-445-3700, www.pcs.org, is one of the Northwest's largest and most respected theater companies; its productions range from classic dramas to contemporary comedies (and vice versa).
- **Portland Playhouse**, 602 NE Prescott St, 503-488-5822, puts on some pretty edgy shows in a small former church in Northeast Portland.
- **Profile Theatre**, 1515 SW Morrison St, 503-242-0080, www.profiletheatre.org; each season, Profile Theatre produces a series of plays from a single playwright. (The 2015 season honored American playwright Sarah Ruhl.)

- **Theatre Vertigo**, Shoebox Theatre, 2110 SE 10th Ave, 503-306-0870, www. theatrevertigo.org, takes on a diverse mix of old and new works.
- **Third Rail Repertory**, 503-235-1101, www.thirdrailrep.org, is a permanent ensemble that stages serious (and tragicomic) plays with a high level of professionalism.
- **Triangle Productions**, 1785 NE Sandy Blvd, 503-239-5919, www.trianglepro. org, now celebrating its 25th season, continues its mission "to entertain and educate through the celebration and presentation of contemporary live theatre, and to promote diversity and tolerance through the presentation of accessible, high-quality productions addressing a broad range of social and political issues."

COMEDY AND IMPROV

GQ magazine has rated Portland the least funny city in America. Given that *GQ*, while unintentionally hilarious, is not a humor magazine, this rating should not trouble you and in fact is quite heartening. There is plenty of funny business going down in town. In addition to the listings below, the **Bridgetown Comedy Festival** (www. bridgetowncomedy.com) brings a raft of comics to town each spring.

COMEDY CLUBS
Many bars and clubs hold occasional stand-up and open-mike nights, but **Harvey's Comedy Club**, 436 NW 6th Ave, 503-241-0338, www.harveyscomedyclub. com, and **Helium Comedy Club**, 1510 SE 9th Ave, 888-643-8669, www.helium-comedy.com, are the best places to see actual and would-be stand-up comics, including some touring headliners.

IMPROV AND SKETCH COMEDY
A combination of stand-up comedy and acting, improvisational theater uses audience suggestions to create a scene, which is then played for laughs. Sketch comedy is generally scripted, but often has a similar freewheeling feel. Most improv and sketch comedy groups perform on weekends only; call ahead or check websites as times and locations change frequently.

- **The 3rd Floor**, www.the3rdfloor.com
- **Brainwaves**, 503-520-8928, www.brainwavesimprov.com
- **The Brody Theater**, 16 NW Broadway, 503-224-2227, www.brodytheater.com
- **ComedySportz**, 1963 NW Kearney St, 503-236-8888, www.portlandcomedy.com
- **Curious Comedy Theater**, 5225 NE Martin Luther King, Jr Blvd, 503-477-9477, www.curiouscomedy.org
- **Funny Business,** 503-703-3026, www.funnybusinesspdx.com
- **The Liberators**, www.liberatorsimprov.tumblr.com
- **The Unscriptables**, 2432 SE 11th Ave, 503-841-6734, www.theunscriptables.com

FILM

Portland offers a variety of cinematic experiences, from first-run Hollywood block-busters to art house and foreign films. Look in the daily or weekly newspapers (or on their websites) for movie listings and show times, or peruse www.portland-movietimes.com.

Portland and its suburbs have an abundance of multiplexes that show main-stream releases: the main chain is **Regal Cinemas** (www.regmovies.com), which has more than a dozen multiplexes in the metropolitan area, but several other multi-screen cinemas are owned by other chains such as **Cinemark** (www.cinemark.com). A few independent or neighborhood theaters also screen first-run movies, including the **Moreland** (6712 SE Milwaukie Ave, 503-236-5257, www.morelandtheater.com), the **St. Johns Cinema and Pub** (8704 N Lombard St, 503-286-1768, www.stjohnscinema.com), and **Cinetopia** (three locations, one in Beaverton and two in Vancouver, www.cinetopia.com), which offer several comfy auditoriums (some with leather seats or pillow pits); each location has an on-site restaurant. In addition to movies in traditional formats, there is a four-story-tall screen at the **Empirical Theater** at the Oregon Museum of Science and Industry (OMSI, 1945 SE Water Ave, 503-797-4640, www.omsi.edu/empirical-theater).

Portland is also blessed with a wealth of second-run movie houses. While these are especially common on Portland's East Side, they also exist in such suburbs as Milwaukie, Gresham, and Vancouver. A true Portland experience is watching a movie in one of the **McMenamins** "theater pubs" (movie line 503-249-7474, www.mcmenamins.com), which serve pizza and beer in the restored buildings—for example, the theater at the Kennedy School on Northeast 33rd Avenue, once an elementary school auditorium, is filled with sofas and armchairs. The ornate Bagdad Theater on Southeast Hawthorne was once a true 1920s movie palace (and is rumored to be haunted); its audio and video systems were recently upgraded, and it is currently the only movie outpost in the McMenamins empire to show first-run movies.

The cinemas listed below screen independent, foreign, classic, documentary, and other non-mainstream films. If nothing at the theaters catches your fancy, Portland is also home to one of the country's best video rental stores, **Movie Madness** (4320 SW Belmont St, 503-234-4363, www.moviemadnessvideo.com).

- **Cinema 21 Theatre**, 616 NW 21st Ave, 503-223-4515, www.cinema21.com
- **Clinton Street Theater and Brewpub**, 2522 SE Clinton St, 503-897-0744, www.cstpdx.com
- **Fifth Avenue Cinema**, 510 SW Hall St, 503-725-3551, www.5thavenuecinema.org
- **Hollywood Theatre**, 4122 NE Sandy Blvd, 503-281-4215, www.hollywoodtheatre.org
- **Living Room Theaters**, 341 SW 10th Ave, 971-222-2010, pdx.livingroomtheaters.com

- **Northwest Film Center**, Whitsell Auditorium, 1219 SW Park Ave, 503-221-1156, www.nwfilm.org
- **Regal Fox Tower Stadium 10**, 846 SW Park Ave, 503-221-3280, www.regmovies. com

FILM FESTIVALS

In addition to the following established festivals, Portland frequently hosts one-off film and video festivals and international film festivals with rotating venues.
- **Cascade Festival of African Films**, 971-722-5711, www.africanfilmfestival.org
- **Fresh Film Northwest**, 503-221-1156, www.nwfilm.org/festivals/freshfilm
- **HP Lovecraft Film Festival**, www.hplfilmfestival.com
- **Northwest Filmmakers' Festival**, 503-221-1156, www.nwfilm.org/festivals/ nwfest
- **Oregon Independent Film Festival**, www.oregonindependentfilmfest.com
- **Portland Film Festival**, www.portlandfilmfestival.com
- **Portland International Film Festival**, 503-221-1156, www.nwfilm.org/ festivals/piff/
- **Portland Jewish Film Festival**, www.pdxjff.org
- **Portland Lesbian and Gay Film Festival**, 503-223-4515, www.plgff.org
- **Portland Oregon Women's Film Festival**, www.powfest.com
- **Reel Music Festival**, 503-221-1156, www.nwfilm.org/festivals/reelmusic/

NIGHTCLUBS & DISCOS

Many of Portland's bars and nightclubs have live music on some nights. Some are hipster dives, others are simply bars with a DJ, and still others are full-fledged dance clubs. The Portland club scene changes almost weekly: once-hot spots fall out of favor, new clubs draw the city's bright young things and/or suburbanites in baseball caps, owners get indicted or skip town. Here's a current sampling of Portland nightclubs:
- **Aalto Lounge**, 3356 SE Belmont St, 503-235-6041, www.aaltoloungepdx.com
- **Andrea's Cha-Cha Club**, 832 SE Grand Ave, 503-230-1166, www.grandcafepdx. com
- **Couture, 28 NW 4th Ave**, 503-484-5959, www.coutureultralounge.com
- **Crush**, 1400 SE Morrison St, 503-235-8150, www.crushbar.com
- **East End**, 203 SE Grand Ave, 503-232-0056, www.eastendportland.com
- **Fez Ballroom**, 316 SW 11th Ave, 503-221-7262, www.fezballroom.com
- **Harlem PDX, 220 SW Ankeny St**, 971-333-1220, www.harlempdx.com
- **Holocene**, 1001 SE Morrison St, 503-239-7639, www.holocene.org
- **Jones, 107 NW Couch St**, 971-271-7178, wwwjonesbarportland.com
- **The Knife Shop at Kelly's Olympian**, 426 SW Washington St, 503-228-3669, www.kellysolympian

- **Rotture**, 315 SE 3rd Ave, 503-234-5684, www.rotture.com
- **Splash, 904 NW Couch St**, 503-893-5551, www.splashbarpdx.com
- **Tube**, 18 NW 3rd Ave, 503-241-8823
- **Valentine's**, 232 SW Ankeny St, 503-248-1600, valentinespdx.com
- **Whiskey Bar**, 31 NW 1st Ave, 503-227-0405, www.whiskeybarpdx.com

VISUAL ARTS

ART GALLERIES AND MUSEUMS

Given the vibrancy of Portland's arts scene, it's a bit surprising that the city has only a handful of art museums with permanent exhibits:

- The **Blue Sky Gallery**, 122 NW 8th Ave, 503-225-0210, www.blueskygallery.org, formerly the Oregon Center for the Photographic Arts, exhibits photographic images from local, national, and international photographers.
- The **Museum of Contemporary Craft**, 724 NW Davis St, 503-223-2654, www. museumofcontemporarycraft.org, founded in 1937, occupies a new space on the North Park Blocks, after moving from its longtime home on Lair Hill.
- **Portland Art Museum**, 1219 SW Park Ave, 503-226-2811, www.portlandartmu-seum.org; when Portlanders speak of "*the* art museum," this is what they mean. The Portland Art Museum is the oldest art museum in the Northwest, and holds significant collections of European, American, and East Asian painting and sculpture, Native American art, and silver; the museum is also home to the Jubitz Center for Modern and Contemporary Art. In addition to its permanent exhibits, the museum holds frequent temporary exhibits and hosts traveling international exhibitions.

Most area colleges have gallery spaces that host rotating exhibits; the best known of these are **Cooley Art Gallery** at Reed College (3203 SE Woodstock Blvd, 503-777-7251, www.reed.edu/gallery/) and the **Art Gym** at Marylhurst University (17600 Pacific Hwy [Hwy 43], Marylhurst [between Lake Oswego and West Linn], 503-699-6243, www.marylhurst.edu/theartgym/). In addition, the **Portland Institute for Contemporary Art (PICA)** (415 SW 10th Ave, Suite 300, 503-242-1419, www.pica.org) sponsors frequent exhibits of contemporary art—broadly defined to include film, dance, drama, and other art forms.

Portland's art scene really thrives in its galleries, some of which have received national acclaim. The city has scores of art galleries showcasing everything from traditional to cutting edge art; they reach critical mass in the Pearl District and Northwest Portland. A fairly complete list of galleries is available at the **Portland Art Dealers Association** website (www.padaoregon.org), and the local arts & entertainment papers include listings of galleries and their current exhibits.

ART WALKS

Several neighborhoods with a high concentration of galleries host evening art walks, when galleries stay open late and various forms of live entertainment usually take place. On **First Thursday** (the first Thursday of each month), Pearl District galleries welcome the art-loving throngs, although the focus of this neighborhood tradition has shifted somewhat from art to bar-and-restaurant hopping. See www.firstthursdayportland.com for details. The Alberta Arts District hosts a similar **Last Thursday** (www.lastthursdayonalberta.com), which is just as much a "scene" as First Thursday, but of a very different and more bohemian kind.

Other neighborhood art walks include **First Fridays** in the Central Eastside (www.facebook.com/1FPDX) and Multnomah Village; Mississippi Avenue's **Second Thursday**; and **Hump Day** (www.humpdaypdx.com) in Inner Southeast on the second Wednesday of each month. Far less frequent is the annual two-day **Southeast Area ARTWalk** (www.seportlandartwalk.com), which includes the Hawthorne and Division/Clinton Street districts. Several suburban communities also sponsor semi-regular art walks.

For a different kind of art walk, the Regional Arts and Culture Council and the Portland Visitors Association produce a self-guided **walking tour** of Portland's outdoor public art; visit racc.org/public-art/ to download a copy or call 503-823-5111 to have a copy mailed to you.

MUSEUMS

For art museums and galleries, see the preceding pages.

CULTURE AND HISTORY

In addition to the museums listed below, many of the older communities in the Portland area maintain small museums of pioneer life or have historic houses that are open to the public.

- **Clark County Historical Museum**, 1511 Main St, Vancouver, 360-993-5679, www.cchmuseum.org; nearly a century old, this museum houses exhibits of Clark County's rich history, ranging from Native American societies to the coming of European traders and pioneers through the development of modern Vancouver.
- **Fort Vancouver**, 1501 E Evergreen Blvd, Vancouver, 360-816-6200, www.nps.gov/fova/; years before Portland was a gleam in its coin-tossing founders' eyes, Fort Vancouver served as the administrative center of the British Hudson Bay Company's fur-trading empire, which stretched from Alaska to California.
- **Museum of the Oregon Territory**, 211 Tumwater Dr, Oregon City, 503-655-5574, www.clackamascountyhistory.org; Oregon City was the original capital of the Oregon Territory, and this museum's high points are the exhibits that reveal everyday life during Oregon's territorial and early statehood periods.

- **Oregon Historical Society**, 1200 SW Park Ave, 503-222-1741, www.ohs.org; this vast repository of artifacts and documents also presents permanent and temporary exhibits about Oregon history, including the large and elaborate "Oregon My Oregon" exhibit. Entrance is free for Multnomah County residents.
- The **Oregon Jewish Museum**, 1953 NW Kearney St, 503-226-3600, www.ojm.org, focuses on the history and experience of the Jewish community in the Pacific Northwest from pioneer days to the present; the museum also houses the Oregon Holocaust Resource Center.
- **Oregon Maritime Museum**, Waterfront Park at Pine St, 503-224-7724, www.oregonmaritimemuseum.org; housed on a retired sternwheeler floating on the Willamette River downtown, the Oregon Maritime Museum highlights Portland's rich past (and present) as a major port and maritime center.
- **Oregon Nikkei Legacy Center**, 121 NW 2nd Ave, 503-224-1458, www.oregonnikkei.org, highlights the history and contributions of Japanese-Americans in the Pacific Northwest.
- **Oregon Rail Heritage Foundation**, 2250 SE Water Ave, 503-233-1156, www.orhf.org, preserves historic locomotives and rolling stock at the Brooklyn Rail Yard; the foundation runs Oregon Pacific Railroad cars to and from Oaks Park on summer Saturdays.
- **Pittock Mansion**, 3229 NW Pittock Dr, 503-823-3623, www.pittockmansion.org; this chateauesque mansion near the summit of the West Hills was built in the early twentieth century for an Oregon pioneer-cum-newspaper baron.
- **Portland Police Museum**, 1111 SW 2nd Ave, 16th Floor, 503-823-0019, www.portlandpolicemuseum.com; housed on the 16th floor of the city's justice center (i.e., jail building and police headquarters), this museum showcases the history of the Portland Police Bureau and the experiences of individual officers. Exhibits include the original jail cell from the St. Johns Police Station.
- **Washington County Museum**, 120 E Main St, Hillsboro, 503-645-5353, www.washingtoncountymuseum.org; this museum of Washington County history is located in the Hillsboro civic center complex.

SCIENCE AND TECHNOLOGY

- **Evergreen Aviation & Space Museum**, 500 NE Captain Michael King Smith Way, McMinnville, 503-434-4185, www.evergreenmuseum.org; the museum's extensive collections are in turmoil because of the bankruptcy of Evergreen International Airlines, but for now this museum's big attraction—and it is truly a *big* attraction—is Howard Hughes's Spruce Goose, by some measures the largest airplane ever built.
- **Oregon Museum of Science and Industry (OMSI)**, 1945 SE Water Ave, 503-797-4000, 800-955-6674, www.omsi.edu; housed in a large facility on the east bank of the Willamette River, OMSI has several galleries devoted to science and technology. Most of the exhibits are interactive, and many are tailored to

children. OMSI also gives tours of the USS *Blueback* submarine, which is permanently docked outside the museum, and hosts frequent visiting exhibits.

- **Rice Northwest Museum of Rocks & Minerals**, 26385 NW Groveland Dr, Hillsboro, 503-647-2418, www.ricenorthwestmuseum.org; modestly housed in the founders' former home in an out-of-the-way corner of Hillsboro north of Highway 26, this is nonetheless one of the nation's finest museums of rocks and minerals.
- **World Forestry Center Discovery Museum**, Washington Park, 4033 SW Canyon Rd, 503-228-1367, www.worldforestry.org; this mostly hands-on museum focuses on forestry and the ecology of forests around the world generally and in the Pacific Northwest in particular. The smokejumper harness exhibit and the "raft ride" are particularly popular with children.

OFFBEAT MUSEUMS

With the demise of the 24-Hour Church of Elvis, Portland lost its most beloved, or at least most famous, oddball attraction. Fortunately, the city continues to host a few offbeat museums.

- **The Hat Museum**, 1928 SE Ladd Ave, 503-232-0433, www.thehatmuseum.com (by reservation only); the name of this museum speaks for itself.
- **Ping Pong's Pint-Sized Puppet Museum**, 906 SE Umatilla St, 503-233-7723, www.puppetmuseum.org; not just a museum of puppets, this unique establishment also hosts puppet live puppet shows.
- **Stark's Vacuum Museum**, 107 NE Grand Ave, 503-232-4101, www.starks.com/vacuum-museum; tucked away inside the headquarters store of Stark's Vacuums is a museum of vacuums. The staff are used to visitors who joke that the museum's exhibits suck.

ARCHITECTURE AND WALKING TOURS

Portland has traditionally been pretty conservative when it comes to architecture (the much-despised Michael Graves–designed Portland Building, an early exemplar of Postmodernism, notwithstanding). That conservatism is rapidly evaporating, and some remarkable new structures have risen over the last decade or so. (The federal courthouse downtown, capped by a soaring "wing," is one example of this.) Moreover, much of the city's historic architecture is both well-preserved and noteworthy. The **Architecture Foundation of Oregon** has produced a *Look Around Guide* to 41 different notable architectural sites in Portland; the guide is available for download at www.af-oregon.org. The **Architectural Heritage Center** (701 SE Grand Ave, 503-231-7264, www.visitahc.org) focuses on historical preservation; in addition to providing information about Portland's historic structures and hosting architectural history exhibits in its gallery space, the Center is a great resource if you've bought a vintage home.

Portland is a great city for strolling, but if you're looking for something a bit more organized and informative, contact **Portland Walking Tours** (503-774-4522, www.portlandwalkingtours.com); their tours focus on downtown and the surrounding neighborhoods, but they also offer tours of outlying neighborhoods on request. For a journey through the infamous **Shanghai tunnels** of Old Town, where (so the story goes) drunken bar patrons were unknowingly "crimped" to crew for free on trans-Pacific sea voyages, contact the Cascade Geographic Society at 503-622-4798 or visit www.shanghaitunnels.info.

LITERARY LIFE

With its gunmetal gray winter skies and frequent drizzle, Portland is a great bookstore town. Area residents flock to book groups, book signings, and fiction, non-fiction, and poetry readings (often given by well-known local authors). In addition to bookstore- and library-hosted events, **Literary Arts** (925 SW Washington St, 503-227-2583, www.literary arts.org) sponsors lectures and readings by local, national, and international authors and poets; its Portland Arts & Lectures series usually brings several Pulitzer Prize winners to the city. The highlight of the local literary calendar is **Wordstock** (www.wordstockfestival.com), an annual festival that features lectures, writers' workshops, and a book fair.

BOOKSTORES

While the city has chain bookstores like Barnes & Noble, many residents are fiercely loyal to Portland's independent booksellers. The largest of these is **Powell's Books** (1005 W Burnside St, 503-228-4651, 800-878-7323, www.powells.com), the largest bookstore in North America, which sells both new and used books and occupies an entire city block in the Pearl District. (Powell's also has two large satellite stores, at 3723 SE Hawthorne Blvd, and at Beaverton's Cedar Hills Crossing mall, 3415 SW Cedar Hills Blvd, as well as a small store at the airport.) Most best-selling authors who come to Portland on book tours make an appearance at Powell's, although smaller independent bookstores sometimes snag big-name writers for in-store readings and book signings.

The following is a selection of general-interest and specialty booksellers in Portland proper. Many of these stores, like Powell's, sell used as well as new books.

GENERAL-INTEREST BOOKSTORES
- **Annie Bloom's Books**, 7834 SW Capitol Hwy, 503-246-0053, www.annieblooms.com
- **Barnes & Noble Booksellers**, five area stores, www.barnesandnoble.com
- **Broadway Books**, 1714 NE Broadway, 503-284-1726, www.broadwaybooks.net
- **Powell's** (see above)
- **St. Johns Booksellers**, 8622 N Lombard St, 503-283-0032, www.stjohnsbooks.com
- **Wallace Books**, 7241 SE Milwaukie Ave, 503-235-7350

SPECIAL-INTEREST BOOKSTORES
- **A Children's Place**, 4807 NE Fremont St, 503-284-8294, www.achildrensplacebookstore.com
- **Green Bean Books**, 1600 NE Alberta St, 503-954-2354, www.greenbeanbookspdx.com (children's)
- **In Other Words**, 14 NE Killingsworth St, 503-232-6003, www.inotherwords.org (women's and feminist)
- **Laughing Horse Book and Film Collective**, 12 NE 10th Ave, 503-236-2893 (progressive politics)
- **Monograph Bookwerks**, 5005 NE 27th Ave, 503-284-5005, www.monographbookwerks.com (fine arts)
- **Mother Foucault's**, 523 SE Morrison St, 503-236-2665 (literature, philosophy, theory, politics)
- **New Renaissance Bookshop**, 1338 NW 23rd Ave, 503-224-4929, www.newrenbooks.com (New Age)
- **Reading Frenzy**, 3628 N Mississippi Ave, 503-274-1449, www.readingfrenzy.com (independent presses)

USED BOOKSTORES
For fairly complete listings of used bookstores and used book–related events in the area, visit the website of the Portland Area Used Booksellers Association (www.pauba.org).
- **Another Read Through**, 3922 N Mississippi Ave, 503-208-2729, www.anotherreadthrough.com
- **Bingo Used Books**, 3366 SE Powell Blvd, 503-231-4091, www.bingousedbooks.com
- **Booktique**, 3975 Mercantile Blvd, Lake Oswego, 503-699-9109, www.ci.oswego.or.us/library/shop-booktique
- **Cameron's Books & Magazines**, 336 SW 3rd Ave, 503-228-2391, www.cameronsbooks.com
- **Daedalus Books**, 2074 NW Flanders St, 503-274-7742
- **Hawthorne Boulevard Books**, 3129 SE Hawthorne Blvd, 503-236-3211
- **Longfellow's Books**, 1401 SE Division St, 503-239-5222, www.longfellowspdx.com
- **Paper Moon Bookstore**, 4707 SE Belmont St, 503-239-8848, www.papermoonbookstore.com
- **Title Wave**, 216 NE Knott St, 503-988-5021, www.multcolib.org/titlewave/ (Multnomah County Library surplus)

LIBRARIES

Portland-area public libraries host frequent literary events and exhibitions. See the **Getting Settled** chapter for a list of library systems in the region.

CULTURE FOR CHILDREN

Portland has so many cultural opportunities for kids they may become surly, disinterested teenagers long before they can take advantage of them all. The *Oregonian's* weekly A&E supplement lists events and activities of interest to families.

The following listing of child-oriented organizations and places represents only a small part of what Portland has to offer its young residents. In addition to organizations that are geared specifically to children, many of the "grownup" groups in town offer special performances for children. The Oregon Symphony, for example, puts on a Kids Concert series every year. Several museums that are not specifically "children's" museums offer a wide range of child-friendly exhibits; OMSI and the World Forestry Center Discovery Museum have particularly extensive kid-oriented displays. And don't forget about the children's bookstores, listed above under "Special Interest Bookstores." For more ideas on ways to entertain the young'uns, including family and holiday festivals, see **A Portland Year**.

MUSIC

- **Metropolitan Youth Symphony**, 503-239-4566, www.playmys.org; the Metropolitan Youth Symphony comprises several hundred young musicians (in several different groups) from throughout the metropolitan area, with an age range of six years through college.
- The **Oregon Children's Choir & Youth Chorale**, 503-534-0226, www.occyc.org, consists of three choirs divided by grade level; membership is by audition only, and the two older groups embark on summer tours to national or international destinations.
- **Portland Boychoir and Ovation!**, 503-697-3872, www.portlandchoirs.org; a choir for boys ages 6 to14 and a training choir for girls ages 11 through 14 feed into Ovation!, a mixed vocal ensemble for high schoolers.
- **Portland Symphonic Girlchoir**, 503-226-6162, www.girlchoir.com, comprises multiple ensembles for girls 5 to 18 years old.
- **Portland Youth Philharmonic**, 503-223-5939, www.portlandyouthphil.org; the country's oldest youth orchestra has come a long way from its roots as the "Sagebrush Symphony." The organization now encompasses two full orchestras as well as a string orchestra and a wind ensemble. Membership is by open audition, and the musicians occasionally embark on national and international tours.

MUSEUMS AND OUTDOOR ATTRACTIONS

- **Bonneville Fish Hatchery** off I-84, exit 40, west of Cascade Locks, 541-374-8820; the fish hatchery adjacent to Bonneville Dam (which can be an interesting destination for older kids in its own right) includes a sturgeon viewing pond with underwater viewing windows that allow visitors to peer at a variety of impressive fish, including Herman the Sturgeon, a 12-footer.

- **Kidd's Toy Museum**, 1300 SE Grand Ave, 503-233-7807, www.kiddstoymuseum. com; no, it's not misspelled—this museum houses more than 10,000 toys from the collection of Frank Kidd, including many toys that would be too unsafe, well-made, and/or outright racist to be marketed today.
- **Oaks Park**, 7805 SE Oaks Park Way, 503-233-5777, www.oakspark.com; this old-school amusement park (open summer only) and roller rink (open year-round) along the Willamette in Sellwood has entertained generations of Portland children.
- **Oregon Zoo**, Washington Park, 4001 SW Canyon Rd, 503-226-1561, www.oregonzoo.org; the Oregon Zoo continues to expand its offerings. Besides the usual collection of animals from around the world—including a renowned herd of Asian elephants and an associated elephant museum—the zoo has several exhibits devoted to the fauna of the Pacific Northwest. The zoo also hosts frequent festivals and concerts.
- **Portland Children's Museum**, Washington Park, 4015 SW Canyon Rd, 503-223-6500, www.portlandcm.org; this is the city's largest kid-centric museum, and it has a correspondingly large array of theme play areas/exhibits, including a dig pit, "market," water play area, clay studio, etc.
- **Safety Learning Center and Fire Museum and the Historic Belmont Firehouse**, 900 SE 35th Ave, 503-823-3741, www.jeffmorrisfoundation.org (open Wednesdays, the second Saturday of each month, and by advance arrangement); the city's oldest working firehouse focuses on life safety education, but also includes the requisite fire pole, fire engine, and other hands-on firehouse accouterments.

THEATER AND DANCE

- **Krayon Kids Musical Theatre Company**, 503-656-6099, www.krayonkids.org, based in Oregon City, organizes musical productions cast entirely with kids.
- **Northwest Children's Theater and School**, 1819 NW Everett St, 503-222-4480, www.nwcts.org; based in the Northwest Neighborhood Cultural Center, Northwest Children's Theater stages several youth-oriented productions each year and offers acting, theater, and film and video classes for children.
- **Oregon Children's Theater**, 1939 NE Sandy Blvd, 503-228-9571, www.octc.org; the Oregon Children's Theater is Oregon's largest nonprofit professional children's theater company, and puts on several productions each year, generally in one of the large downtown theaters. The OCT offers acting and production classes and workshops for children ages four and older.
- **Tears of Joy Puppet Theatre**, 503-248-0557, www.tojt.org; most Tears of Joy productions are designed (or at least suitable) for children, but a few of its performances are definitely adults-only.

P ORTLAND IS A GREAT SPORTS AND RECREATION TOWN, PARTICULARLY for weekend warriors who like playing games as much as (or more than) they like watching them. Portland doesn't have many major professional teams—the city government has called Portland the most under-served professional sports market in the country—but the area's abundant recreational opportunities more than make up for the lack of big-league luster. Besides taking advantage of a great environment for year-round outdoor recreation, Portlanders also engage in some quirky quasi-sports, like geocaching (which was invented here). Unless you're into something really esoteric like ice kiting, you're bound to find congenial surroundings for whatever pastime literally or figuratively floats your boat.

Health clubs and sporting goods stores are listed at the end of this chapter.

PROFESSIONAL AND SEMIPROFESSIONAL SPORTS

As of 2014, Portland has only two "big five" professional sports teams—the Trail Blazers National Basketball Association franchise and the highly popular Portland Timbers Major League Soccer franchise, which together get most of the sports media and fan attention in town. The city nonetheless offers a decent range of opportunities to watch talented athletes play various games. If you need a (relatively) close-by major league baseball or NFL fix, you'll have to make the trek north to Seattle to see the Mariners or the Seahawks in action.

BASEBALL

Portland is the largest metropolitan area in the United States without a major league baseball team. Various civic boosters periodically launch efforts to lure an existing or expansion team to Portland, and came reasonably close to wooing the relocating Montreal Expos (a team that Washington, D.C., ultimately bagged;

they're now the Nationals). Portland lost its AAA team, the Portland Beavers, in 2010, when their stadium was remodeled for Major League Soccer and no area city would step up to the plate to fund a new stadium. For now, Portland has to be content with Class-A short-season baseball, which has the advantage of being less expensive and arguably more fun to watch than major league baseball. The **Hillsboro Hops** (www.hillsborohops.com), a farm team for the Arizona Diamond-backs, relocated to Hillsboro from Yakima, Washington, in 2013. The Hops play at Ron Tonkin Stadium (4460 NW 229th Ave, Hillsboro), just off the Sunset Highway; a free shuttle runs from the Orenco Station MAX stop on game days. Their Class-A short-season rivals, the **Salem-Keizer Volcanoes** (www.volcanoesbaseball.com), affiliated with the San Francisco Giants, play adjacent to I-5 just north of Salem.

BASKETBALL

The **Portland Trail Blazers** (www.blazers.com) won their only NBA champion-ship in 1977. Since then, the Trail Blazers have fielded some strong teams that have vied for and won the NBA Western Conference title, as well as mediocre ros-ters that included players who had run-ins with the law. (The latter circumstance begat the "Jail Blazers" nickname.) Still, the Blazers enjoy strong (if not neces-sarily broad-based) community support even when their record is abysmal; the bandwagon grows more substantial when the Blazers do well, as when, against all expectations, they made the Western Conference finals in 2014. The Blazers play in the Moda Center, formerly (and still widely) known as the Rose Garden. Tickets are available through the team website or by calling the Blazer Ticket Line (844-RIP-CITY).

The Portland area is also home to two International Basketball League teams, the **Portland Chinooks** (www.ibl.com/Portland_chinooks) and their presumably hated cross-town rivals, the **Vancouver Volcanoes** (www.ibl.com/Vancouver_vol-canoes). While IBL basketball is purportedly fast-paced and high-scoring, and certainly more affordable to attend than NBA games, you'll be hard-pressed to find many people other than diehard sports fans who have heard of either team.

FOOTBALL

In 2014, the **Portland Thunder** (www.portlandthunder.com) began life as an expansion team in the Arena Football League. The Thunder play home games in the Moda Center. Single-game tickets are available by calling 503-789-7673.

HOCKEY

The "major-junior" **Portland Winter Hawks** (www.winterhawks.com) compete in the Calgary-based Western Hockey League, which mainly comprises teams based in western Canadian cities. The team has reliably won the Western Conference Championship in most recent years. The Winter Hawks enjoy a fiercely loyal fan base, and games can be rowdy (although actual fights are generally confined to the players). Half-time activities, which sometimes involve hapless fans slipping around on the ice in a quest for some prize, can be surprisingly entertaining in a low-key way. During their fall and winter season, the Winter Hawks play home games in the Memorial Coliseum or the adjacent Moda Center in the Rose Quarter of Northeast Portland. Tickets are available online, by calling 503-236-4295, or at the Memorial Coliseum and Rose Quarter box offices on game nights.

Portland is frequently named as a contender for an NHL franchise when and if the league expands, but don't hold your breath.

SOCCER

The **Portland Timbers** (www.portlandtimbers.com) are an MLS (Major League Soccer) team. The season runs from April to September. The Timbers play home games at Providence Park (1844 SW Morrison St, 503-553-5400, www.providenceparkpdx.com). The Timbers enjoy the most consistently enthusiastic fan base in town, and at home games the Timbers Army section of the stadium (the north end) is both a visual and aural phenomenon. Chainsaw-wielding lumberjack Timber Joey slices through a log when the Timbers score. Tickets are available through the team website, by calling 503-553-5555, or from the Providence Park box office.

The **Portland Thorns** (www.timbers.com/thornsfc) play in the National Women's Soccer League. They won the league championship in 2013. Like the Timbers, the Thorns play home games at Providence Park.

COLLEGIATE AND HIGH SCHOOL SPORTS

Portland lacks the sort of college sports powerhouses that vie for national championships in football and basketball. The nearest Pac-12 schools are Oregon State University in Corvallis (about 90 minutes away), and the University of Oregon in Eugene (two hours south), and those schools' athletic programs suck up most of the state's college sports money and attention. That said, most nearby colleges and universities field intercollegiate teams in at least one sport. Probably the most watchable teams, at least for non-alumni, are the **University of Portland Pilots** women's and men's soccer teams. (The women's squad won the 2005 Division I NCAA championship, and has won several conference championships since then.) For more information, visit www.portlandpilots.com.

High school sports can be exciting, and not just for players and their friends and parents. In addition to football, baseball, basketball, and soccer, some schools offer lacrosse, water polo, and other less mainstream sports. Most high school athletic activities in Oregon are coordinated through the Oregon School Activities Association (www.osaa.org). (In Washington, the equivalent organization is the Washington Interscholastic Activities Association, www.wiaa.com.) For news coverage of Portland high school athletics, check out the sports section of the *Oregonian* or visit highschoolsports.oregonlive.com.

PARTICIPANT SPORTS AND OUTDOOR RECREATION

If you ask Portlanders what they love about city, you're liable to hear them rhapsodize about the great selection of outdoor recreational opportunities. From watching the sunset over the city from Mount Tabor Park to climbing Mount Hood, and from walking around the block to running the Portland Marathon, hundreds of activities are available for every level of athletic ability.

For general information about local parks, pools, community centers, tennis courts, or community athletic programs, start with your local parks department. In the city of Portland, contact **Portland Parks and Recreation** (503-823-PLAY, www.portlandparks.org). Contact information for other communities' parks departments is listed in the **Useful Phone Numbers and Websites** chapter.

BICYCLING

In Portland, bicycling is wildly popular, both as a recreational activity and as a means of transportation. (For information about bike routes, bike commuting, and getting around by bicycle generally, see the **Transportation** chapter.) Portland has an abundance of bike lanes and "bike boulevards"—streets with low traffic volume and, often, obstacles to through car traffic—and a developing system of paved off-street trails allows bicyclists to ride fairly long distances without having to dodge motorized vehicles. The longest of these urban trails is the 17-mile Springwater Corridor, which runs from the east bank of the Willamette River to Boring as part of the still incomplete 40-Mile Loop (see www.40mileloop.org for details); other off-street trails include the Eastbank Esplanade and the Willamette Greenway; a long trail paralleling Marine Drive on the south shore of the Columbia River; and some not especially peaceful trails that parallel Interstate 205 and part of the Sunset Highway. Just west of the metro area, the **Banks-Vernonia State Trail** is a 21-mile rails-to-trails project that has been converted into a linear state park; see www.oregonstateparks.org/park_145.php for more information. Serious riders can practice, or race, on the scarily banked **velodrome** at Alpenrose Dairy in southwest Portland (6149 SW Shattuck Rd, www.obra.org/track/).

Bike touring possibilities outside Portland are legion. Thanks to the region's urban growth boundary, densely populated areas rather quickly give way to farmland and forest, laced with paved roads that, in many cases, have relatively low traffic volume. Your route could lead through flat farmland, shady valleys in the Cascade foothills, and rolling vineyard country—all in one day. Pancake-flat Sauvie Island is an especially popular nearby destination; the fact that the island is reachable by public transportation (bikes allowed) adds to the appeal.

Road biking gets much of the press in Portland, but the region has outstanding mountain biking opportunities, too. **Forest Park** is a justly popular destination, with options for riders of various abilities. (Bikes are restricted to designated trails, and concerns about erosion and conflicts with hikers on steep, narrow trails mean singletrack is currently limited to a sole 0.3-mile stretch.) **Fat**

Tire Farm (2714 NW Thurman St, 503-222-3276, www.fattirefarm.com) is conveniently located virtually next door to the park; the store rents mountain bikes and can point out appropriate routes. Besides the miles of trails in Forest Park, there are plenty of lesser-known routes, including singletrack and doubletrack trails, outside the city; take a look at a mountain biking guidebook for suggestions, or contact the Northwest Trail Alliance (see contact information below).

RESOURCES

The city of Portland's **Office of Transportation** posts extensive information on its website (www.gettingaroundportland.org) about bicycling in Portland, including bike maps and routes, a list of bicycle-related organizations and shops, and suggested bike touring itineraries; click on the "Active Transportation" link. Several bike-related nonprofits, including the **Bicycle Transportation Alliance** (503-226-0676, www.btaoregon.org), the **Community Cycling Center** (1805 NE 2nd Ave, 503-288-8864, www.communitycyclingcenter.org), and **Shift** (www.shift2bikes.org), are very helpful sources of information for Portland bicyclists.

EVENTS

If you like to bike in a group, or at least to follow an organized (and supported) itinerary, consider signing up for one of the many organized recreational rides that take place around the area. The biggest of these are **Cycle Oregon** (503-287-0405, www.cycleoregon.com), a week-long tour through a scenic part of the state—the itinerary changes each year—and the **Seattle to Portland Bicycle Classic** (cascade.org/ride-major-rides/group-health-stp), a one- or two-day pedal between the two cities. Some of the many shorter bike tours that attract more casual riders include the **Worst Day of the Year Ride** (www.worstdayride.com), held in typically rainy and chilly February (the 2014 ride was cancelled due to a rare snowstorm); and **Providence Bridge Pedal** (503-281-9198, www.bridge-pedal.com), which wends its way across all ten of Portland's Willamette River road bridges. Each year, the city sponsors several **Sunday Parkways** events, in which streets in a particular neighborhood are closed off to cars and thrown open to bikes. **ORbike** (www.orbike.com) maintains the most complete and up-to-date online list of bicycling events in the area.

BICYCLE CLUBS

The following organizations organize rides and events around the area.
- **Northwest Trail Alliance**, www.nw-trail.org
- **Oregon Bicycle Racing Association**, www.obra.org
- **Portland Velo**, www.portlandvelo.net
- **Portland Wheelmen Touring Club**, 503-666-5796, www.pwtc.com
- **Vancouver Bicycle Club**, www.vbc-usa.com

BIRDING

Whether you're an experienced birder who's new to Portland or someone investigating the activity for the first time, the **Audubon Society of Portland** (5151 NW Cornell Rd, 503-292-6855, www.audubonportland.org) is a great place to start. The Society has its own 180-acre sanctuary adjacent to Forest Park in the West Hills, which includes an interpretive center, a care center for injured birds, and a store that sells field guides and other birding essentials. The Society's website has an extensive library of information about local birding, including updated rare bird alerts.

BOATING

The **Oregon State Marine Board** (503-378-8587, www.boatoregon.com) provides a wealth of information about boating in the state, including current boating regulations, navigational hazards, and water access points. Its website is useful for both motorized and non-motorized boaters. The **Washington Recreation and Conservation Office** (360-902-3000) maintains its state's boating portal at boat. wa.gov.

CANOEING AND KAYAKING

Sea kayaking, whitewater kayaking, and canoeing are very popular throughout the Northwest. Non-motorized watercraft are generally permitted on any navigable body of water, but accessible public launch points may be hard to find. Popular nearby places for paddling include the Columbia Slough in North and Northeast Portland; coastal rivers and bays, such as Tillamook Bay; lakes and reservoirs, such as Blue Lake in Fairview (a good spot for fledgling canoeists); and the Clackamas, Tualatin, Molalla, Sandy, Columbia, and Willamette rivers.

It is possible to make some epic river trips to or from Portland; if you have the time, you can float downstream on the mostly flat water of the Willamette for well over a hundred miles from Eugene to Portland, with a single portage at Willamette Falls in Oregon City. On the Columbia, the 146-mile Lower Columbia Water Trail (www.columbiawatertrail.org) leads from Bonneville Dam to Astoria. (Be aware that paddling the Columbia can force you to contend with strong winds, surprisingly large waves, treacherous currents, and oceangoing ship traffic.) Some skilled ocean kayakers seeking saltwater brave the open Pacific, but others regularly head north to the protected waters of Puget Sound or southern British Columbia. If you're looking for an outfitter or guided trip, visit the website of the **Oregon Guides and Packers Association** (www.ogpa.org). For more specific information and suggested routes, check out one of the guidebooks listed in **A Portland Reading List** or contact one of the following local clubs:

- **DragonSports USA**, www.dragonsports.org (dragon boat paddling)
- **Lower Columbia Canoe Club**, www.l-ccc.org
- **Oregon Kayak and Canoe Club**, www.okcc.org

- **Oregon Ocean Paddling Society (OOPS)**, www.oopskayak.org
- **Pacific Northwest LGBT Kayaking Club**, www.outkayaking.org
- **Willamette Rowing Club**, www.willametterowing.com

RENTALS

If you'd like to dabble in paddling and don't want the hassle of transporting a boat, you can rent a watercraft from one of the following locations, all of which are located within easy carrying distance of a launch point:

- **Alder Creek Kayak & Canoe** (www.aldercreek.com) has three Portland-area locations: near OMSI on the east bank of the Willamette River (1515 SE Water St, 503-285-1819), at Jantzen Beach on the Columbia (200 NE Tomahawk Island Dr, 503-285-0464), and at Brown's Ferry Park in Tualatin, on the Tualatin River (6855 SW Nyberg Ln, 503-691-2405, open Memorial Day–Labor Day only).
- **Portland River Company** (www.portlandrivercompany.com) has a rental facility on the west bank of the Willamette at Willamette Park in South Portland (6600 SW Macadam Ave, 503-459-4050).

MOTORBOATS

Many Northwesterners own motorboats; small boats with outboard motors that can be transported by trailer and used for fishing are particular popular and versatile, although you'll also see folks with ski boats, jet skis, and motor yachts. Major rivers and larger lakes and reservoirs generally have convenient boat ramps or other access points; the **Oregon State Marine Board** provides a list of access points on its website (www.oregon.gov/osmb/pages/access/acess.aspx), or contact them at 503-378-8587 to have a hard copy of the *Oregon Boating Facilities Guide* mailed to you. For Washington water access points, check the website of the **Recreation and Conservation** office (www.rco.wa.gov/maps/), which also offers a free *Washington Water Cruiser* app.

Several marinas for larger boats are located along the Columbia River or on Multnomah Channel; the **RiverPlace Marina** (503-241-8283) is on the Willamette, right downtown. Most marinas offer motorboat rentals to qualified boaters.

If you're bringing in a boat from out-of-state, you'll need to register it. In Oregon, the **Oregon State Marine Board** coordinates boat registration; in Washington, you'll need to go through the **Washington Department of Licensing** (360-902-3770, www.dol.wa.gov/vehicleregistration/registerboat.html).

SAILING

Sailing on Portland-area rivers and lakes is enjoyable and can be challenging, but it is also constricting. The open North Pacific is often stormy, and the only access from Portland to the ocean is over the treacherous Columbia Bar. (Serious sailors who can afford it keep boats moored in Puget Sound, two to three hours north of Portland, which gives them access to hundreds of miles of protected sailing grounds.) For local sailing opportunities, including classes and races, contact the

Island Sailing Club (515 NE Tomahawk Island Dr, 800-303-2470, www.islandsailingclub.com) or the Willamette Sailing Club (6336 SW Beaver Ave, 503-246-5345, www.willamettesailingclub.com).

WHITEWATER RAFTING

Oregon is full of classic whitewater trips: the Deschutes River in central Oregon; the Snake River in Hells Canyon, on the Oregon-Idaho border; the McKenzie River, east of Eugene; the Owyhee River in remote southeastern Oregon; and the Rogue and Umpqua rivers in southern Oregon. Exciting whitewater is available closer to Portland on the Clackamas River, only an hour away; the North Santiam River, east of Salem; and the Wind, White Salmon, and Klickitat Rivers on the Washington side of the Columbia River Gorge. Commercial rafting companies operate on all of these streams; check online or in the Yellow Pages under "Rafts & Raft Trips" for company listings or visit the **Oregon Guides and Packers Association** website (www.ogpa.org). For more specific information on whitewater rafting in Oregon, contact the **Northwest Rafters Association** (www.nwrafters.org).

FENCING

If fencing means more to you than simply yard enclosure or the sale of stolen goods, you're in luck. Portland has several clubs and facilities for fencers of all abilities. *En garde!*
- **Northpointe Gymnastics & Fencing**, 6707 NE 117th Ave, Vancouver, 360-254-7958, www.northpointegym.com
- **Northwest Fencing Center**, 4950 SW Western Ave, Beaverton, 503-277-2237, www.nwfencing.org
- **Oregon Fencing Alliance**, 503-467-9891, www.oregonfencing.org
- **PDX Fencing**, 5645 SW Arctic Dr, Beaverton, 503-644-7739, www.pdxfencing.com
- **Salle Trois Armes**, 8517 NE Lombard St, 503-285-2962, www.fencingcenter.org
- **Studio of American Fencing**, 4048 NE 42nd Ave, 503-249-2884, www.saf.pair.com

FISHING AND HUNTING

In addition to the range of outdoor and sporting goods stores in the Portland area (see "Sporting Goods Stores" towards the end of this chapter), September 2014 saw the opening of the first Portland area Cabela's, a Nebraska-based, nationally known hunting and fishing superstore, in Tualatin just off I-5.

FISHING

The fishing and shellfishing opportunities available in Oregon are nothing short of amazing. In the Portland area, you can find salmon, trout, and other game fish in nearly every river and reservoir, including the Willamette River as it flows through downtown Portland. (You wouldn't be wise to eat bottom feeders from the lower Willamette unless your idea of a delicious meal includes not-so-delectable PCBs.)

The **Oregon Department of Fish and Wildlife** (ODFW) (4034 Fairview Industrial Dr SE, Salem, 503-947-6000, www.dfw.state.or.us) regulates fishing and hunting activity in Oregon, and is the best place to go for general information about license requirements and current regulations and restrictions. (In Washington, the equivalent agency is the **Washington State Department of Fish and Wildlife**, 360-902-2200, wdfw.wa.gov.) In Oregon, everyone 14 or older needs a license to fish; angling license fees range from $9 (for residents aged 14 to 17) to $116 (for an annual nonresident license with Columbia River Basin endorsement). One-day to seven-day licenses are available at reduced prices. Shellfish collection requires a separate license; fees range from $7 to $20.50. (Washington requirements and prices are similar.) Licenses are available at most sporting goods stores and many grocery stores.

ODFW also publishes useful pamphlets (most of which are available online) on a variety of fish and wildlife topics; they're not going to reveal anyone's secret fishing hole, but they can point you in the right direction. Their pamphlet *50 Places to Go Fishing Within 60 Minutes of Portland* (also available on the ODFW website) is a useful starting point.

HUNTING

Inner-city Portland isn't really a pickup-and-gun-rack kind of place (although there are certainly residents who enjoy hunting), but hunting, including bowhunting, is a popular activity in some surrounding areas, particularly in the Cascade foothills, the Coast Range, and the mountains of eastern Oregon. Targets range from such big game as deer, elk, or bear to waterfowl, rabbits, and quail. Check with **ODFW** for current regulations and license or tag requirements.

GEOCACHING AND ORIENTEERING

A relatively new activity that has only been around since 2000, geocaching actually originated just outside Portland in the town of Beavercreek. It is essentially a high-tech game of hide-and-seek, in which a collection of objects is "cached" at specific coordinates and the seeker uses a global positioning system to find the cache. (Geocaching etiquette requires that if you take something from the cache, you leave something else in its place.) For information about geocaching in the area, check out **Oregon Geocaching**, www.oregongeocaching.org.

Orienteering is decidedly less high-tech, and involves point-to-point route-finding, sometimes over difficult or brushy terrain, using only a map and (usually) a compass. The **Columbia River Orienteering Club** (www.croc.org) organizes orienteering events in the Portland area.

GOLF

It's admittedly no Florida or Phoenix, but Portland harbors some surprisingly good golf courses. Even the weather helps the reasonably hardy golfer here: mild temperatures and incessant precipitation for most of the year keep the fairways green, and if you don't mind the rain, you can pretty much golf all winter. Also, you usually don't need to schedule summer tee times to avoid the midday heat, and given the infrequency of thunderstorms in western Oregon you are unlikely to be struck by lightning while hoisting your putter into the air in triumph after your impressive birdie on the eighth hole. If you're serious about your golf game, consider joining the **Oregon Golf Association** (www.oga.org), which also covers southwest Washington.

Below is a list of the public or semi-private golf courses within Portland, as well as some of the most popular courses in surrounding communities. Because one person's putt-putt is another's Pebble Beach, we've made no attempt to rank the courses, and there is a challenge here for every skill level. For a complete list of area courses check the Yellow Pages or use the Oregon Golf Association's **Course Finder** tool (www.exploreoregongolf.com). For detailed course descriptions, including photos, visit **Oregon Golf** (www.oregongolf.com).

- **Broadmoor Golf Course**, 3509 NE Columbia Blvd, 503-281-1337, www.broadmoor-1931.com
- **Camas Meadows Golf Club**, 4105 NW Camas Meadows Dr, Camas, 360-833-2000, www.camasmeadows.com
- **Charbonneau Golf Club**, 32020 SW Charbonneau Dr, Wilsonville, 503-694-1246, www.charbonneaugolf.com
- **Claremont Golf Club**, 15800 NW Country Club Dr, 503-690-4589, www.claremontgolfclub.com
- **Colwood National Golf Club**, 7313 NE Columbia Blvd, 503-254-5515, www.colwoodgolfclub.com
- **Eagle Landing Golf Course,** 10220 SE Causey Ave, Happy Valley, 503-698-8020, www.theaerieateaglelanding.com (short course)
- **Eastmoreland Golf Course**, 2425 SE Bybee Blvd, 503-775-2900, www.eastmorelandgolfcourse.com
- **Forest Hills Golf Course**, 36260 SW Tongue Ln, Cornelius, 503-357-3347, www.golfforesthills.com
- **Glendoveer Golf Course**, 14015 NE Glisan St, 503-253-7507, www.playglendoveer.com
- **Heron Lakes Golf Course**, 3500 N Victory Blvd, 503-289-1818, www.heronlakesgolf.com
- **Langdon Farms Golf Club**, 24377 NE Airport Rd, Aurora, 503-678-4653, www.langdonfarms.com
- **Lake Oswego Golf Course**, 17525 Stafford Rd, Lake Oswego, 503-636-8228, www.lakeoswegogolf.org
- **Meriwether National Golf Club**, 5200 SW Rood Bridge Rd, Hillsboro, 503-648-4143, www.meriwethergolfclub.com
- **Mountain View Golf Course**, 27195 SE Kelso Rd, Boring, 503-663-4869, www.mtviewgolfclub.com

- **Pumpkin Ridge Golf Club**, 12930 Old Pumpkin Ridge Rd, North Plains, 503-647-4747, www.pumpkinridge.com
- **Quail Valley Golf Course**, 12565 NE Aerts Rd, Banks, 503-324-4444, www.quailvalleygolf.com
- **RedTail Golf Course**, 8200 SW Scholls Ferry Rd, 503-646-5166, www.golfredtail.com
- **The Reserve Vineyards & Golf Club**, 4805 SW 229th Ave, Aloha, 503-649-8191, www.reservegolf.com
- **Rose City Golf Course**, 2200 NE 71st Ave, 503-253-4744, www.rosecitygc.com
- **Stone Creek Golf Club**, 14603 S Stoneridge Dr, Oregon City, 503-518-4653, www.stonecreekgolfclub.net
- **Tri Mountain Golf Course**, 1701 NW 299th St, Ridgefield, 360-887-3004, www.trimountaingolf.com
- **Wildwood Golf Course**, 21881 NW St Helens Rd, 503-621-3402, www.golfingwildwood.com

Farther afield, the region around Bend in **Central Oregon** is a major golf destination, as is, to a lesser extent, the **Oregon Coast**.

HIKING AND WALKING

The amount of green you see on an Oregon state map speaks for itself. The majority of the state is public land, much of it national forest, and thousands of miles of hiking trails lace the region. It's not necessary to venture very far to get a hiking fix, however; almost every neighborhood in Portland is within hailing distance of a walking path or hiking trail. The longest and "wildest" trails are in the West Hills, especially in Washington Park and Forest Park. (The Wildwood Trail runs for 28 miles along the spine of the West Hills, from near the Oregon Zoo to the northern reaches of Forest Park, crossing paved roads only a few times along the way.) Many of the trails in the region are interconnected, and given world enough and time you could walk all the way across the state.

Portland is also a great city for urban rambles, especially near downtown and on the East Side, where sidewalks are abundant. If you like some direction to your walks, buy, beg, or borrow one of the walking or hiking guides described in **A Portland Reading List**, or visit peripatetic guidebook writer William L. Sullivan's website (www.oregonhiking.com). For something more structured and informative, try one of the tours offered by **Portland Walking Tours** (503-774-4522, www.portlandwalkingtours.com). (Note that their "Epicurean Excursion" to various foodie destinations is unlikely to promote weight loss.)

Walk About (www.walkaboutmag.com), a free publication available at many natural food supermarkets and sporting goods stores, lists events of interest to Northwest walkers. If you prefer to walk with a partner or group, look into the following organizations:

- **Columbia River Volkssport Club** (www.walking4fun.org) organizes recreational walks, usually about six miles in length, in scenic locations around the Portland area.
- Although best known as a mountaineering club, the **Mazamas** (527 SE 43rd Ave, 503-227-2345, www.mazamas.org) sponsor frequent hikes, including some for beginning hikers.
- Portland-based **Racewalkers Northwest**, www.rwnw.org, organizes local training walks and racewalk competitions.
- **Wonders of Walking**, 503-282-1677, www.wondersofwalking.com, sponsors various recreational and competitive walking events in the Northwest.

Portland Parks and Recreation (www.portlandparks.org) also organizes walks and hikes, as do many environmental organizations, including the **Sierra Club's** local Columbia Group (www.oregon.sierraclub.org/groups/columbia/).

HORSEBACK RIDING AND EQUESTRIAN SPORTS

Most equestrian activities necessarily take place outside of Portland, although there are some trails in the larger parks, such as Forest Park, that allow horses. If you're interested in trail rides, try **Flying "M" Ranch** (23029 NW Flying M Rd, Yamhill, 503-662-3222, www.flying-m-ranch.com). For more serious trail riding, the nonprofit **Oregon Equestrian Trails** (www.oregonequestriantrails.org) is an excellent resource. If you're looking for riding lessons, or if you actually own or want to own a horse, check out the listings at **Oregon Horse** (www.oregonhorse.net) or the **Oregon Horse Directory**, produced annually by Oregon Horse Country (www.oregonhorsecountry.com).

HOT AIR BALLOONING

Several area companies will carry you into the sky in a hot air balloon (and bring you back down again). Try **Portland Rose Hot Air Balloon Adventures** (Lake Oswego, 503-638-1301, 877-934-6359, www.portlandroseballoons.com), **Vista Balloon Adventures** (Newberg, 503-625-7385, 800-622-2309, www.vistaballoon.com), or **Pacific Peaks Balloon Company** (Tigard, 503-590-5250, www.pachigh.com). Regardless of a company's headquarters location, flights generally launch from outlying areas.

ICE SKATING

Portland lacks the convenient frozen ponds of, say, Minneapolis, so ice skating necessarily takes place in indoor rinks. All of the rinks below offer public skating, skate rentals, and lessons; most sponsor hockey, speedskating, and other ice-related activities. Please be tactful and bear in mind that Tonya Harding jokes wore out their welcome long ago.

- **Lloyd Center Ice Rink**, Lloyd Center Mall (lower level), 503-288-6073, www.lloydcenterice.com
- **Mountain View Ice Arena**, 14313 SE Mill Plain Blvd, Vancouver, 360-896-8700, 503-235-8176, www.mtviewice.com
- **Sherwood Ice Arena**, 20407 SW Borchers Dr, Sherwood, 503-625-5757, www.sherwoodicearena.com
- **Winterhawks Skating Center**, 9250 SW Beaverton-Hillsdale Hwy, 503-297-2521, www.winterhawksskatingcenter.com

Amateur figure skaters may be interested in the **Portland Ice Skating Club** (www.pisc.org). If ice skating is too strenuous for your taste, try **curling**. The Evergreen Curling Club (503-430-0910, www.evergreencurling.org) has its own curling facility in Beaverton, and stands ready and willing to help you out.

MUSHROOM HUNTING

If you know the difference between a morel and a false morel—or if you'd like to—consider joining the **Oregon Mycological Society** (www.wildmushrooms.org). OMS organizes frequent mushroom hunts and educates its members about mushroom identification and other mycological issues. OMS puts the "fun" in fungi!

PAINTBALL & LASER TAG

If shooting at people is your hobby, and you want to keep it legal, paintball and laser tag are among your few available non-military options. Here are a few establishments that will facilitate your murderous predilections:
- **Action Acres**, 10381 S Mulino Rd, Canby, 503-266-5733, www.actionacrespb.com
- **Impact Action Spots**, 19265 SW Schaber Ln, Tualatin, 503-213-3230, www.impactactionsports.com
- **LaserPort**, 6540 SW Fallbrook Pl, Beaverton, 503-526-9501, www.laserportofbeaverton.com
- **Splat Action Paintball**, 32155 S Grimm Rd, Molalla, 503-467-1855, www.splataction.com
- **Ultrazone Laser Tag**, 16074 SE McLoughlin Blvd, Milwaukie, 503-652-1122, www.ultrazoneportland.com

RACQUET SPORTS

Many city and suburban public parks have outdoor tennis courts, the majority of which are lighted. Given the inevitable heartbreak and soggy tennis balls that result from playing on a court full of puddles, Portland thankfully also has its share of indoor courts. The following indoor courts are public facilities:

- **Lake Oswego Indoor Tennis Center**, 2900 Diane Dr, Lake Oswego, 503-635-5550, www.ci.oswego.or.us/parksrec/indoor-tennis-center
- **Portland Tennis Center**, 324 NE 12th Ave, 503-823-3189
- **St. Johns Racquet Center**, 7519 N Burlington Ave, 503-823-3629, www.stjohnsracquetcenter.org

There are several private racquet clubs in the area, too; check online the Yellow Pages under "Tennis Courts-Private" for listings. In addition, some of the larger health clubs feature racquetball and squash courts.

ROCK CLIMBING AND MOUNTAINEERING

ROCK CLIMBING

The area around Portland is blessed with many good rock climbing and bouldering options, ranging from climbs in abandoned quarries to ascents of towering natural cliffs; a few decent outdoor sites are within city limits, notably Rocky Butte quarry in Northeast Portland. The **Portland Rock Climbs** website (www.portlandrockclimbs.com) describes other nearby climbing sites and offers links to local climbing groups. Smith Rock State Park in Central Oregon (www.oregonstate-parks.org or www.smithrock.com) is one of the premier climb destinations in the country.

If you want to learn to climb, or just need to keep your skills up, try one of the following rock gyms. (Rock gyms are also good sources of information on local climbing options and routes.)

- **The Circuit Bouldering Gym**, 6050 SW Macadam Ave, 503-246-5111, www.thecircuitgym.com
- **Planet Granite**, 1405 NW 14th Ave, www.planetgranite.com
- **Portland Rock Gym**, 21 NE 12th Ave, 503-232-8310, www.portlandrockgym.com
- **Stoneworks Climbing Gym**, 6775 SW 111th Ave, Beaverton, 503-644-3517, www.belay.com

In addition, some area health clubs and even outdoor stores (REI) have climbing walls.

MOUNTAINEERING

The Northwest offers abundant possibilities for serious mountaineers. The most obvious local destination is glacier-covered Mount Hood, reputedly one of the world's most-climbed peaks. At 11,240 feet, Mount Hood is not especially high, but it is a challenging and potentially treacherous climb that should not be attempted lightly: people die on the mountain every year. Other tempting (and potentially deadly) glaciated Cascade volcanoes include Mount Jefferson, Mount Adams, Mount Baker, and Mount Rainier.

The **Mazamas** (527 SE 43rd Ave, 503-227-2345, www.mazamas.org) is the area's largest mountaineering club; the group has a large clubhouse in Southeast Portland and offers excellent classes on mountaineering basics.

RUNNING AND JOGGING

The surprising numbers of lycra-clad bodies sloshing down the street in the damp winter pre-dawn attest to the local popularity of recreational running. (Unlike in some higher-crime cities, the people you see dashing down the street usually aren't running away from anything, except perhaps their inner demons.)

RESOURCES

Although it's in the business of selling running shoes and apparel, the **Portland Running Company** (two area stores, www.portlandrunningcompany.com) also offers training tips, lists suggested routes, sponsors group runs, and provides links to area running organizations and events.

EVENTS

Recreational and competitive running (and walking) events take place all year. They run the gamut from seasonal activities like **First Run** (held at midnight on New Year's) or the **Turkey Trot** (on Thanksgiving Day) to such themed events as the **Hippie Chick Half-Marathon** (for women only) or the dreaded **Lake of Death Relay**. The two biggest running events on the local calendar are the **Hood to Coast Relay** (503-292-4626, www.hoodtocoast.com in August, which wends its weary way from Timberline Lodge on Mount Hood to the Oregon Coast, and the **Portland Marathon** (503-226-1111, www.portlandmarathon.org), held in October. Most Northwest races and running events are listed on **www.racecenter. com**, which also offers online registration.

RUNNING CLUBS

- **Complete Running Club**, 503-593-1396, www.crpusa.com
- **Oregon Road Runners Club**, www.orrc.net
- **Portland Frontrunners**, www.portlandfrontrunners.org (gay/bi/lesbian running club)
- **Runner Chick Training Club**, 971-409-8461, www.runnerchicktrainingclub. com (women only)
- **Team Red Lizard Running Club**, www.redlizardrunning.com

SKATING AND SKATEBOARDING

In Portland, skates and skateboards are a recognized form of transportation, and the city has actually designated a few "preferred skating routes" downtown. The website for the city's **Office of Transportation** lists rules and safety suggestions for skaters who use public streets. Visit www.portlandoregon.gov/transportation/ article/405782 for more information.

ROLLER SKATING/IN-LINE SKATING

In-line skating remains a popular activity on Portland's paved paths, particularly along the downtown waterfront and on the Eastbank Esplanade, and it looks like old-school roller skates may be making a comeback, too. If you prefer to skate indoors, the **Oaks Skating Rink** at Oaks Amusement Park in Sellwood (7805 Oaks Park Way, 503-233-5777, www.oakspark.com/roller-skating.html) boasts a 20,000-square-foot wooden floor. **Indoor Goals** (16340 NW Bethany Ct, Beaverton, 503-629-9500, www.indoorgoals.com) hosts inline hockey leagues.

SKATEBOARDING

Portland's a totally sick place to get your ollie on, bro. (Note: to a skateboarder, this is a good thing.) Not only is skateboarding legal on public streets (see above), but skateparks are increasingly common, even in suburban communities. The city of Portland has approved a master plan for the development of a network of 19 skateparks; visit the website of **Skaters for Portland Skateparks** (www.skateportland.org) for details. The granddaddy of all Portland skateparks is the legendary and semi-official **Burnside Skatepark** (burnsideskatepark.blogspot.com), which lurks under the east side of the Burnside Bridge like a gnarly concrete troll.

Skateoregon (www.skateoregon.com) offers comprehensive information about skate parks throughout the state and beyond.

SKYDIVING

If you're the sort of person who gets a rush out of jumping out of planes, or if you think you might be, try **Skydive Oregon**, 12150 S Hwy 211, Molalla, 503-829-3483, 800-934-5867, www.skydiveoregon.com.

TEAM SPORTS

BASKETBALL

Many gyms, community centers, and even city parks have indoor (or at least covered) basketball courts, and pick-up games are easy to find. If you're after a more structured experience, **PortlandBasketball.com** (www.portlandbasketball.com) the area's largest adult basketball league, averages more than 250 teams (including co-ed teams) that encompass every age and skill level. Local park and recreation districts and health clubs also organize adult basketball leagues.

HOCKEY

Most area ice rinks can point you in the right direction for ice hockey leagues. (See "Ice Skating" above.) For information about organized roller hockey, contact **Indoor Goals** (16340 NW Bethany Ct, Beaverton, 503-629-9500, www.indoor-goals.com).

SOCCER

Soccer is undoubtedly the most popular team sport in Portland. Most youth soccer leagues in Portland proper are under the auspices of the **Portland Youth Soccer Association** (503-646-6683, www.portlandyouthsoccer.com). In the suburbs and the rest of the state, the **Oregon Youth Soccer Association** (503-626-4625, 800-275-7533, www.oregonyouthsoccer.org) oversees the majority of youth soccer leagues and games; the OYSA's counterpart across the Columbia is **Washington Youth Soccer** (877-424-4318, www.washingtonyouthsoccer.org). Adult footballers bow to the mighty **Oregon Adult Soccer Association** (503-292-1814, www.oregonadultsoccer.com), which coordinates various soccer leagues, including those in the **Greater Portland Soccer District** (www.gpsdsoccer.com). In Washington, the **Washington State Adult Soccer Association** (425-485-7855, www.wssa.org) deals with adult soccer play. **Northwest United Women's Soccer** (www.oregonwomenssoccer.com) organizes women-only leagues in metro Portland.

Several indoor soccer facilities organize league play on astro-turfed, hockey rink–like fields. Portland-area indoor soccer arenas include **Portland Indoor Soccer** (418 SE Main St, 503-231-6368, www.pdxindoorsoccer.com); the **Mittleman Jewish Community Center** (6651 SW Capitol Hwy, 503-244-0111, www.oregonjcc.org); **Salmon Creek Indoor Sports** (110 NW 139th St, Vancouver, 360-571-7628, www.scsoccerarena.com); **Soccerplex** (8785 SW Beaverton-Hillsdale Hwy, 503-297-4145, www.soccerplex.com); **Indoor Goals** (16340 NW Bethany Ct, Beaverton, 503-629-9500, www.indoorgoals.com); and **Tualatin Indoor Soccer** (11883 SW Itel St, Tualatin, 503-885-9300, www.tualatinindoor.com).

Futsal, a Brazilian variant of indoor soccer that dispenses with walls, is growing in popularity. Dedicated venues for the sport include:
- **Portland Futsal,** 3401 SE 17th Ave, 503-238-8725, www.portlandfutsal.com
- **Rose City Futsal**, 5010 NE Oregon St, 503-734-2382, www.rosecityfutsal.com

SOFTBALL AND BASEBALL

The **Portland Metro Softball Association** (PMSA) (www.portlandsoftball.com) offers one-stop shopping for all your organized softball needs. PMSA coordinates play for thousands of players and hundreds of teams, including men's, women's, and co-ed teams. The **Northwest Independent Baseball League** (www.nwibl.org) has a roster of adult baseball teams, including semi-pro teams.

OTHER TEAM SPORTS

CRICKET
- **Oregon Cricket League**, www.oregoncricketleague.org, for those who prefer their British sport with more tea breaks and fewer cracked ribs

FOOTBALL
- **Portlandfootball.com,** www.portlandfootball.com, is a dedicated flag football league.
- **Portland Steelheads**, www.portlandfooty.com, Australian rules football

LACROSSE
- **Lacrosse Northwest,** 503-295-7774, www.laxnw.com, youth and adult lacrosse
- **US Lacrosse** (Oregon chapter), www.oregonlax.com, youth and adult lacrosse

MULTI-SPORT
Portlandia satirized these adult sports leagues in a sketch involving an adult hide-and-seek league:
- **Recesstime Sports Leagues,** 503-381-5056, www.recesstimesports.com, organizes leagues in dodgeball, kickball, ping pong, and bowling.
- **Underdog Sports Leagues,** 503-282-1155, www.underdogportland.com, sponsors coed kickball, flag football, dodgeball, volleyball, bowling, and mini golf leagues.

RUGBY
- **Oregon Rugby Sports Union Club,** www.orsu.org, men's and women's rugby
- **Portland Rugby Club,** www.portlandrugby.org, men's and women's rugby

ULTIMATE FRISBEE AND DISC GOLF

Many Portland parks have adequate space for a casual game of Frisbee. If Ultimate Frisbee is your game of choice, the **Portland Ultimate Flying-Disc Federation** (www.portlandultimate.org) coordinates league play and designates times and places for pick-up games.

Disc golf is played at a growing number of Portland-area parks. **Oregon Disc Golf** (www.oregondiscgolfcom) maintains an up-to-date list of Pacific Northwest disc golf courses on its website, and provides detailed descriptions of each course as well as links to regional disc golf events, leagues, and clubs.

WATER SPORTS

SCUBA DIVING

While there are no real recreational dive sites in Portland proper—you wouldn't really want to encounter the sorts of things you might find in the murky lower Willamette—the area nonetheless nurtures an active dive community. Hood Canal in Washington State (an arm of Puget Sound) is a popular dive destination that's not too far away, and there are plenty of challenging dives off the Oregon Coast. High-altitude lakes in the Oregon Cascades, such as Crater Lake and Waldo Lake, offer visibility approaching 100 feet and are popular destinations for divers with proper equipment and training. If you'd like to get certified in advance of a trip to someplace like Belize or Palau, check with one of the clubs listed below for recommendations, or look online or in the Yellow Pages under "Scuba Diving Instruction" for a list of scuba schools.

The following are a few local scuba resources and dive clubs. (If you're looking for a different kind of dive club, perhaps one with dim lights and plenty of Pabst Blue Ribbon, try looking under "Nightclubs and Discos" in the **Cultural Life** chapter.)

- **Northwest Dive Club**, www.nwdiveclub.com
- **Oregon Scuba Club**, www.oregonscuba.com
- **Pacific NW Scuba**, www.pnwscuba.com

SURFING/WINDSURFING/KITEBOARDING/STAND-UP PADDLEBOARDING

Surfing at the Oregon Coast is at best a full wetsuit proposition. Much of the coastline is viable surfing territory for the suitably skilled and equipped, but many Oregon surfers are reluctant to divulge the locations of their favorite breaks. (Be aware that surfers in certain towns are notorious for a "locals only" attitude, especially when they encounter vehicles with out-of-state plates.) For basic information about surfing in Oregon, visit **www.oregonsurf.com**. One professional surfing event, the Nelscott Reef Tow (www.nelscottreef.com), in which jet skis tow surfers into position, takes place off Lincoln City.

Some of the world's best **windsurfing** is found in the nearby Columbia River Gorge; the sheer-sided gorge serves as a wind tunnel for air moving between the Columbia Basin and the Willamette Valley, which means that afternoon winds are generally strong and reliable. The Oregon windsurfing capital is Hood River, about an hour east of Portland. The town is filled with windsurf-related businesses—even the local Full Sail brewery is named in honor of the sport. Hood River and the Oregon Coast are both major destinatiosn for **kiteboarding**, a sport in which a rider on a small kiteboard or surfboard is pulled along by a large kite or sail; sustained gusts or large waves can give the rider serious air-time.

Any boardsport store can help with rental equipment or lessons. If you're a first timer, it's probably most efficient to start in Hood River. In Portland, try **Gorge Performance** (7400 SW Macadam Ave, 503-246-6646, www.gorgeperformance.com).

Stand-up paddleboarding (SUP) has become very popular in the last few years, thanks in part to its gentle learning curve and its suitability to a wide range of locations and water conditions. Warm summer days even see SUPers maneuvering around the Willamette River downtown like confused gondoliers. Boardsport stores and even canoe and kayak stores typically offer SUP sales, rentals, and lessons.

SWIMMING

SWIMMING BEACHES

When the first wave of hot weather strikes Portland, many people head for nearby streams like the Sandy River and Clackamas River. Because the rivers are usually still frigid and full of snowmelt, however, drownings and deaths by hypothermia (often exacerbated by excessive alcohol consumption) make the news every year. That said, water temperatures usually warm up nicely by July in most area lakes and rivers. The Pacific is a different story; only the very hardy (or foolhardy) can stand to remain in the ocean in Oregon for very long without a wetsuit.

Public **swimming beaches** in the Portland region include:

- **Blue Lake Regional Park**, 20500 NE Marine Dr, Fairview, 503-665-4995, www. oregonmetro.gov/parks/blue-lake-regional-park, has a very popular swimming beach.
- **Henry Hagg Lake**, 503-846-8715, www.co.washington.or.us/hagglake/, at Scoggins Valley Park in Gaston, south of Forest Grove, nestles in the foothills of the Coast Range; the water here warms up into the mid-70s in high summer, but watch out for sudden drop-offs.
- **Rooster Rock State Park**, 503-695-2261, www.oregonstateparks.org, hugs the shore of the Columbia River east of Troutdale (at Exit 25 off Interstate 84). The park offers two swimming beaches, one of which is a designated clothing-optional beach.
- **Sauvie Island** has a couple of beaches on the Columbia River (basically at the end of the island's road). The beaches, which can be steep when water levels are low, offer interesting views of passing barges and oceangoing cargo ships; nearby Collins Beach (an officially designated clothing-optional beach) offers views of a different kind.
- **Vancouver Lake**, 6801 NW Lower River Rd, Vancouver, 360-619-1111, www. clark.wa.gov/parks-trails/vancouverlake.html; the lake has a designated swimming area, and water quality is regularly monitored for excessive amounts of *E. coli* bacteria and blooms of toxic blue-green algae. (That is supposed to make you feel safe, by the way.) The lake is closed to swimming when bacteria counts exceed acceptable levels.

SWIMMING POOLS

Portland Parks and Recreation operates six indoor pools (open year-round) and seven outdoor pools (open mid-June through early September). Pools have scheduled times for lap swimming, open play, family play, and water exercise classes; the indoor pools at Mt. Scott Community Center and Southwest Community Center have separate children's water play areas with spraying water toys and 115-foot waterslides. For information call 503-823-SWIM or visit www.portland-oregon.gov/parks/38284.

If you live outside Portland, check with your local parks and recreation department (listed in the **Useful Phone Numbers and Websites** chapter) for aquatic centers and outdoor pools in your area. Note that many area health clubs also have swimming facilities.

WINTER SPORTS

Sometime in November, as raindrops keep falling on their heads and white flakes start to pile up in the Cascades, the thoughts of many Portlanders turn to winter sports. Transplants from outside the Northwest will notice four distinctive features of snow in this region. First, it tends to be heavy and wet: particularly at lower elevations on the west side of the Cascades, Oregon's climate is not cold and dry enough to reliably produce the kind of powder that falls in the Rockies, and the result is sometimes referred to derisively as "Cascade concrete." Second, there's usually lots of the stuff: even in an average year snowfall totals exceed 40 feet in places like Crater Lake, while in exceptional years truly monumental levels can accumulate. (In February 1999, the Mount Baker ski area in Washington state had to close for several days because 70 feet of snow had buried the chair lifts.) Third, it sticks around: several ski areas regularly stay open into June, and Timberline's Palmer Snowfield, high on Mount Hood, is open almost year-round. (Timberline is a popular summer training center for Olympic skiers and snowboarders.) And last, it doesn't fall much at low elevations: to get your snow fix, you'll have to head east and uphill.

SNO-PARK PERMITS

If you plan to ski, snowboard, snowshoe, or just play in the snow, you'll need to get a **Sno-Park permit**. If you park in a designated Winter Recreation Area—and most places you'll park for winter sports and snow play will be so designated—between November 15 (December 1 in Washington) and April 30, you must display a permit inside your windshield. (The fees from the permit program pay for snow removal in the parking areas.) You can buy a permit at some government offices and most ski areas and sporting goods stores. One-day permits for Oregon cost $4, three-day permits cost $9, and season permits cost $25; in Washington, one-day permits cost $20 and seasonal and special groomed trail permits cost $40. Vendors generally charge an additional convenience fee. Oregon honors Sno-Park permits issued by California and Idaho (and vice-versa). Neither Washington nor Oregon honors the other state's Sno-Park permits.

For more information, or for a map of winter parking areas where permits are required, visit www.oregon.gov/ODOT/DMV/pages/vehicle/sno_park_permits. aspx (for Oregon) or www.parks.wa.gov/winter/permits/ (for Washington).

For information about chain and traction tire requirements for winter driving, see the **Transportation** chapter.

DOWNHILL SKIING AND SNOWBOARDING

The most popular and developed ski areas in the state are on Mount Hood and elsewhere in the northern Oregon Cascades, one to four hours from Portland. The closest ski areas to Portland are:

- **Cooper Spur Mountain Resort**, 541-352-6692, www.cooperspur.com; this old-school, family-friendly ski area on the east side of Mount Hood has one chair lift, a rope tow, and an inner tube tow.
- **Hoodoo**, 541-822-3799, www.hoodoo.com; closer to Salem and Eugene than to Portland, Hoodoo offers five lifts and two rope tows serving 800 skiable acres, with a good mix of beginner, intermediate, and advanced runs.
- **Mt. Bachelor**, 541-382-2442, 800-829-2442, www.mtbachelor.com; not really a day trip, Mt. Bachelor is 20 miles west of Bend, in Central Oregon. Despite the distance from Portland, Mt. Bachelor's weather (sunnier than Mount Hood) and generally good snow conditions, combined with nearly 3,700 acres of skiable terrain, make it a popular destination. Mt. Bachelor is usually open into late spring.
- **Mt. Hood Meadows**, 503-337-2222, 800-SKI-HOOD, www.skihood.com; with 11 lifts, including five high-speed quads, Meadows is the largest ski area on Mount Hood. Including a snowcat skiing option, Meadows has almost a 4,000-foot vertical, and its location on the mountain's east side gives it noticeably more sun. On the downside, it's a slightly longer drive from Portland than Timberline or Skibowl.
- **Mt. Hood Skibowl**, 503-272-3206, 800-SKI-BOWL, www.skibowl.com; this large ski area has a large number of black diamond runs and is the closest ski area to Portland; because of its relatively low base elevation, snow conditions can be iffy during winter warm spells. In summer, Skibowl turns into an adrenaline sports park.
- **Summit Ski Area**, 503-272-0256, www.summitskiarea.com; perched above the rest area at Government Camp, near Mount Hood, this small ski, snowboard, and tubing area opened in 1927 and is the oldest ski area in the Northwest. Summit is good for beginning skiers, but not very challenging for anyone beyond novice level.
- **Timberline**, 503-272-3158, 800-547-1406, www.timberlinelodge.com; with an annual average snowfall of more than 400 inches, Timberline usually has the deepest snow base of any Oregon ski area, and has a stunning setting high on the south slope of Mount Hood. Fans of *The Shining* will recognize Timberline's Depression-era lodge.

Most of Oregon's large ski areas, and some of the small ones, offer night skiing. Mt. Hood Skibowl claims to have the largest night ski area in the country. If you don't own your own equipment, rentals are available at outdoor stores in the Portland area; in Sandy, Welches, and other communities along Highway 26 on the way to Mount Hood; and at the ski areas themselves.

Farther afield, several ski areas in eastern and southern Oregon have small or nonexistent crowds. **Anthony Lakes** (www.anthonylakes.com), in the Blue Mountains near Baker City, usually has the best powder and some of the most challenging terrain in the state. Many diehard Portland skiers and riders make the seven-plus-hour trek north to British Columbia's **Whistler Blackcomb** resort (www.whistlerblackcomb.com), venue for most of the outdoor events of the 2010 Winter Olympics.

Several Portland-area ski and snowboard clubs sponsor outings, races, lessons, and social events. For a fairly complete list of local clubs, visit the **Northwest Ski Club Council** website, www.nwskiers.org.

NORDIC AND TELEMARK SKIING

The mid-to-high elevations of Oregon's national forests are laced with Nordic (cross-country) ski trails for all abilities. Extensive trail networks radiate out from Government Camp on Mount Hood, Santiam Pass east of Salem, and in the Mount Bachelor area near Bend. There are several good guidebooks to cross-country ski routes in Oregon and Washington (see **A Portland Reading List** for suggestions). Telemark skiers have abundant opportunities as well; for a memorable experience, do a spring ascent of Mount St. Helens on a clear day, and ski most of the way down (permit required).

Novice snowshoers (and occasionally large dogs) sometimes obliterate ski tracks on some cross-country routes. To guarantee a clear trail, try one of the following groomed trail networks:

- **Cooper Spur Nordic Center** (541-352-6692, www.cooperspur.com), near Cooper Spur Ski Area on the east side of Mount Hood, has 6.5 kilometers of groomed trails.
- **Mount Hood Meadows Nordic Center** (503-337-2222, 800-SKI-HOOD, www.skihood.com), off Highway 35 on the southeast side of Mount Hood, maintains 15 kilometers of groomed trails.
- **Mount Bachelor Nordic Center** (800-829-2442, www.mtbachelor.com), near Bend in central Oregon, offers 56 kilometers of groomed trails, and includes a Nordic freestyle terrain park.
- **Teacup Lake Nordic** (www.teacupnordic.org) offers a 20-kilometer network of groomed trails off Highway 35 on the east side of Mount Hood.

If you'd like to hobnob with likeminded skiers, contact the Portland chapter of the **Oregon Nordic Club** (www.onc.org/pdx-onc) or the **Bergfreunde Club** (503-245-8453, www.bergfreunde.org).

SNOWSHOEING

Snowshoeing has exploded in popularity in the last five years, The sport has several attractions: it's free (apart from the cost of renting or buying the snowshoes), it requires no special skills or training, and it can be done pretty much anywhere there is a snowed-over road or trail. If you're following a ski trail, please be courteous and keep to one side to avoid obliterating ski tracks.

If you'd like to try snowshoeing, but don't want to set out on your own, **Portland Parks and Recreation** (503-823-PLAY, www.portlandparks.org) offers several snowshoe excursions each winter.

SNOWMOBILING

Snowmobiling is allowed on many national forest roads and trails; access is generally from sno-parks or from private resorts. For more information, contact the **Oregon State Snowmobiling Association**, www.oregonsnow.org.

OTHER RECREATIONAL ACTIVITIES

AUTOMOBILE RACING

- **Portland International Raceway** (West Delta Park, 1940 N Victory Blvd, 503-823-7223, www.portlandraceway.com) hosts a variety of auto races and other motorsport events.
- The **Woodburn Dragstrip** (7730 Highway 219, Woodburn, 503-982-4461, www.woodburndragstrip.com), located in the Willamette Valley between Portland and Salem, generally limits its offerings to drag races.

BILLIARDS AND POOL

Many bars around Portland have pool tables, but for a dedicated pool hall ambiance try one of the following establishments:
- **Hot Shots Westside Family Billiards**, 4900 SW Western Ave, Beaverton, 503-644-8869, www.hotshotspool.com
- **Rialto Poolroom Bar & Café**, 529 SW 4th Ave, 503-228-7605, www.rialtopoolroom.com
- **Sam's Billiards**, 1845 NE 41st Ave, 503-282-8266, www.portlandpoolhall.com
- **Uptown Billiards Club**, 120 NW 23rd Ave, 503-226-6909, www.uptownbilliards.com

BOWLING

Some might argue that it's more a sport (or a way of life) than a pastime, but however you classify it, bowling is a popular activity. Most bowling alleys host at least one, and usually several, bowling leagues; check with the alley for signup information, or visit the website of the **U.S. Bowling Conference Greater Portland** (www.gpusbc.com). Alleys are sometimes completely reserved for tournaments, league play, or birthday parties, so check the alley's website or call first to find out when open bowling is available. If ordinary bowling is too tame for your taste, most area lanes offer glow-in-the-dark bowling and other jazzed-up versions of the game.

The Portland metropolitan area has about two dozen bowling alleys; the lanes listed below are the most centrally located. Some close-in alleys, such as the venerable Hollywood Bowl, have closed in recent years to make way for retail developments and apartment complexes. For more suburban options, look online or peruse the Yellow Pages listings for "Bowling."

- **AMF Pro 300 Lanes,** 3031 SE Powell Blvd, 503-234-0237, www.amf.com/pro300lanes/
- **Grand Central Restaurant and Bowling Lounge**, 808 SE Morrison St, 503-236-2695, www.thegrandcentralbowl.com

There is also a little-known bowling alley in the **Viking Gameroom** in the basement of the Smith Memorial Student Union at Portland State University (www.pdx.edu/gameroom/bowling). There are only six lanes, but the prices cannot be beat.

If you prefer your bowling outdoors, the **Portland Lawn Bowling Club** (www.portlandlawnbowling.org) has a clubhouse and green in Westmoreland Park, at Southeast 22nd Ave and Bybee Blvd. If your tastes lean to the even more esoteric, note that this green is also used by the **Portland Pétanque Club**, www.pdxpetanque.org. The **Portland Bocce League** (www.portlandbocce.com) plays on the bocce courts on the North Park Blocks.

CASINOS

The Oregon Lottery (www.oregonlottery.org) promotes scratchoffs, Powerball tickets, and the video poker machines that infest every darkly lit tavern in town (while halfheartedly reminding Oregonians that lottery games should not be played for investment purposes). For real casino games like blackjack and dollar slots you'll have to visit a tribal casino. Indian casinos are among the state's biggest attractions, and although there are no casinos in the metropolitan area, other than three cardrooms in La Center in northern Clark County, the following establishments are within a two-hour drive:

- **Chinook Winds Casino Resort**, 1777 NW 44th St, Lincoln City (Oregon Coast), 541-996-5825, 888-CHINOOK, www.chinookwindscasino.com

- **Indian Head Casino**, 3236 Hwy 26, Warm Springs (Warm Springs Reservation), 541-460-7777, www.indianheadgaming.com
- **Spirit Mountain Casino**, 27100 SW Salmon River Hwy, Grande Ronde (west of Salem), 503-879-2350, 800-760-7977, www.spiritmountain.com

CHESS

The **Portland Chess Club** (503-246-2978, www.pdxchess.com) organizes tournaments and casual play for all ages. Local organizations that focus on younger players include the **Oregon Scholastic Chess Federation** (www.oscf.org) and **Chess for Success** (www.chessforsuccess.org). **Northwest Chess** (www.nwchess.com) is an excellent source of information about chess in the region, including chess news, tournaments, activities, and club listings.

DANCING

If you're interested in pursuing dance moves that go beyond random nightclub gyrations, you'll have plenty of company. Portland harbors a wide range of dance-oriented clubs that offer lessons, organize competitions, and host dances. **Portland Dancing** (www.portlanddancing.com) is a clearinghouse of information on clubs and events, and covers styles ranging from Lindy Hop to country line dancing and from salsa and tango to Israeli folk dancing. You can also check *Willamette Week* or the A&E section of the Friday *Oregonian* for dance events and get-togethers. For formal dance instruction, check online or look in the Yellow Pages under "Dance Instruction."

HORSE RACING

The horses are on the track from October through May at **Portland Meadows** (1001 N Schmeer Rd, 503-285-9144, www.portlandmeadows.com) at Delta Park in North Portland.

MODEL RAILROADING

The **Columbia Gorge Model Railroad Club**, 2505 N Vancouver Ave, 503-288-7246, www.cgmrc.com, owns its own building, which contains a truly amazing 500+ square foot scale model of train lines in the Columbia River Gorge. Farther south, you might want to look into **Pacific Northwest Live Steamers**, 503-829-6866, www.pnls.org, which operates Shady Dell Train Park just east of Molalla, open to the general public May through October.

YOGA

In addition to the private studios listed below, **Portland Parks and Recreation** (503-823-PLAY, www.portlandparks.org) offers yoga classes at many of its facilities;

check its website or its seasonal printed catalogs for details. Some health clubs also offer yoga classes to members, as do many spas and wellness centers. While yoga is probably the most popular "alternative" fitness regimen in Portland, the city is replete with studios for Pilates, CrossFit, and other forms of non-traditional strength and fitness training. The following is a non-comprehensive list of establishments that are solely yoga studios:

- **Amrita**, 0110 SW Bancroft St, 503-552-YOGA, www.dayafoundation.org
- **Bikram Fremont Street**, 4831 NE Fremont St, 503-284-0555, www.bikramfremontstreet.com
- **Gudmestad Yoga Studio**, 3903 SW Kelly, Suite 210, 593-223-8157, www.gudmestadyoga.com
- **The Movement Center**, 1021 NE 33rd Ave, 503-231-0383. www.mcyoga.com
- **North Portland Yoga**, 55 NE Farragut St #1, 503-995-3570, www.northportlandyoga.com
- **OmBase**, 6357 SW Capitol Hwy, 503-922-3100, www.ombase.org
- **Portland Yoga Arts**, 4400 NE Glisan St, 503-287-1078, www.portlandyogaarts.com
- **Yoga Bhoga**, 1028 SE Water Ave #265, 503-241-5058, www.yogabhoga.com
- **Yoga Pearl**, 925 NW Davis St, 503-525-9642, www.yogapearl.com
- **The Yoga Project**, 1229 SE Nehalem St, 503-235-1155, www.theyogaproject.org
- **Yoga Shala**, 3808 N Williams St, 503-963-YOGA; www.yogashalapdx.com
- **Yo Yo Yogi**, 1306 NW Hoyt St, Ste 101, 503-688-5120, www.yoyoyogi.com

HEALTH CLUBS

Portland is full of health clubs and gyms. Most have workout equipment, conditioning classes, and personal training programs, and some offer swimming pools, yoga, specialized workouts, and childcare. Call or visit the club you're interested in to get details on their programs.

If you work for a reasonably large organization, ask human resources about membership discounts for fitness clubs. Note that the health club business is generally one without fixed prices; the dripping person on the adjacent treadmill may have paid twice as much or half as much as you did. Also, it pays to read the fine print on any agreement; the terms "annual membership" and "no fees" may not mean what you think they do. Even if everything looks good, the fitness business has some shady operators that have been known to skip town and padlock clubs; try to avoid paying for a year in advance, for example. Be aware that many clubs offer frequent promotions—membership fee discounts or waivers, the first month at half price, free seven-day passes, and the like—so if you're in no hurry to join a club it might be worth waiting to see if a better deal comes up.

The following partial list of Portland health clubs should help you start your search. For a complete list, do an online search for clubs in your desired neighborhood, or check the Yellow Pages under "Health Clubs." In addition to private clubs, many municipal community centers have exercise facilities; check with your local parks and recreation department for details.

- **Cascade Athletic Club**, 9260 SE Stark St, 503-257-4142; 2456 SE Powell Blvd, Gresham, 503-618-4142; 19201 SE Division St. Gresham, 503-665-4142; 16096 SE 15th St, Vancouver, 360-597-1100; www.cascadeac.com; a FitLife network member (see below)
- **ClubSport Oregon**, 18120 SW Lower Boones Ferry Rd, Tigard, 503-968-4500, www.clubsports.com/Oregon; a FitLife network club
- **Curves**, 800-848-1096, www.curves.com; this worldwide network of franchised women-only fitness clubs has more than 40 locations around the metropolitan area.
- **East & West Side Athletic Clubs**, 555 SW Oak St, 503-222-7800; 9100 SE Sunnyside Rd, Clackamas, 503-659-3846; 4606 SE Boardman, Milwaukie, 503-659-3845; www.eastsideathleticclub.com; these clubs are FitLife network members.
- The **FitLife Club Network** includes dozens of independent fitness clubs in Oregon, Washington, and Montana, including some 20 clubs in the Portland metro area. Members of each club get reciprocal use of other member clubs. Visit www.fitlifeclubs.com or call 503-445-6235 for a list of network clubs.
- **Hollywood Fitness**, 5223 NE Sandy Blvd, 503-281-4776, www.hollywoodfitness.net
- **The Green Microgym**, 1237 NE Alberta St; 7703 SE 13th Ave; 503-933-2230, www.thegreenmicrogym.com; where else can you ride a stationary bike that generates electricity for the building? A separately licensed green gym (The Green Microgym Belmont, 828 SE 34th Ave, Ste B, 503-313-6216, www.thegreenmicrogymbelmont.com) is located in the Belmont Street neighborhood.
- **LA Fitness**, www.lafitness.com, has 11 locations in the region.
- **Lloyd Athletic Club**, 815 NE Halsey St, 503-287-4594, www.lloydac.com; a FitLife network club
- **Loprinzi's Gym**, 2414 SE 41st Ave, 503-232-8311, www.loprinzisgym.com; this unpretentious, old-school-style neighborhood gym offers affordable, pay-as-you go memberships.
- **Mittleman Jewish Community Center**, 6551 SW Capitol Hwy, 503-244-0111, www.oregonjcc.org
- The venerable **Multnomah Athletic Club**, 1849 SW Salmon St, 503-223-6251, www.themac.com, has long been a place where Portland's movers and shakers could, well, move and shake, as well as hobnob. The eight-story clubhouse and 600-car parking garage remind you that you are not in Kansas anymore, as does the ban on "manual labor work clothes" in the lobby areas. (Seriously.) Sadly for would-be Gatsbys, with a few exceptions (e.g., legacy members and spouses of current members) MAC membership is by annual lottery.

- **Nautilus Plus OC**, 10466 SE Main St, Milwaukie, 503-659-4111; 1715 S Beavercreek Rd, Oregon City, 503-657-7717; www.nautilusoc.com
- **Northwest Women's Fitness Club**, 2714 NE Broadway, 503-287-0655, www.nwwomensfitness.com
- **Sunset Athletic Club**, 13939 NW Cornell Rd, 503-645-3535, www.sunsetac.com; a FitLife network club
- **24 Hour Fitness**, 800-224-0240, www.24hourfitness.com, has 14 locations in the Portland area.
- **West Coast Fitness**, 2640 NE Alberta St, 503-288-4500; 2310 N Lombard St, 503-688-5130; 7522 N Lombard St, 503-283-5404; www.pdxgym.com; a FitLife network club
- The **YMCA** (www.ymcacw.org) has three family fitness centers: 9685 SW Harvest Ct, Beaverton, 503-644-2191; 11324 NE 51st Circle, Vancouver, 360-885-9622; 23000 SW Pacific Hwy, Sherwood, 503-625-9622

SPORTING GOODS STORES

Whether you're heading out of town for a two-week backpack on the Pacific Crest Trail or spending an hour at the park with a Frisbee, you may need to go shopping first. Portlanders take their sports and recreational activities seriously, so there's no shortage of places to find just the right equipment. The following list should get you started. If you're not sure whether you want or need to buy an expensive item, inquire about testing or renting.

- **Andy and Bax**, 324 SE Grand Ave, 503-234-7538, www.andyandbax.com, sells military surplus goods as well as more mainstream camping and outdoor equipment.
- **Big 5 Sporting Goods**, 800-898-2994, www.big5sportinggoods.com, has 10 stores in the Portland-Vancouver area.
- **Cabela's**, 7555 SW Nyberg St, Tualatin, 503-822-2000, www.cabelas.com, specializes in hunting and fishing equipment and clothing.
- **ClimbMax Mountaineering**, 626 NE Broadway, 503-816-0207, 800-895-0048, www.climbmaxmountaineering.com, is one of the best mountaineering equipment stores in the United States.
- **Dick's Sporting Goods**, 877-846-9997, www.dickssportinggoods.com, has five Portland-area locations.
- **Montbell**, 902 SW Yamhill St, 971-271-8871, www.montbell.us; the U.S. flagship store for Japanese outdoor equipment company Montbell.
- **Mountain Hard Wear**, 722 SW Taylor St, 503-226-6868, www.mountainhardwear.com
- **Mountain Shop**, 1510 NE 37th Ave, 503-288-6768, www.mountainshop.net
- **Next Adventure**, 426 SE Grand Ave, 503-233-0706, nextadventure.net, sells both new and used equipment.

- **Oregon Mountain Community**, 2975 NE Sandy Blvd, 503-227-1038, www. omcgear.com
- **Play It Again Sports**, 9244 SW Beaverton-Hillsdale Hwy, 503-292-4552; 8101 NE Parkway Dr, Vancouver, 360-260-9440; www.playitagainsports.com; these stores focus on used (and thus generally affordable) sports equipment, but they also stock some new sporting goods.
- **REI**, 1405 NW Johnson St, 503-221-1938; 7410 SW Bridgeport Rd, Tualatin, 503-624-8600; 2235 NW Allie Ave, Hillsboro, 503-617-6072; 12160 SE 82nd Ave, Clackamas, 503-659-1156; www.rei.com; Seattle-based REI (short for Recreational Equipment Incorporated) is the country's largest consumer cooperative. Members receive an annual dividend based on their total purchases over the previous year.
- **Snow Peak,** 410 NW 14th Ave, 503-697-3330, www.snowpeak.com; this is the North American flagship store for a Japanese outdoor equipment company.
- **Sports Authority**, www.sportsauthority.com, is the country's largest sporting goods retailer; there are five stores in the metro area.
- **US Outdoor Store**, 219 SW Broadway, 503-223-5937, www.usoutdoor.com

GREENSPACES

P ORTLAND'S LANDSCAPE IS A VISIBLE MANIFESTATION OF VARIOUS GEO-
logical forces: volcanic eruptions, grand shifts and collisions of the earth's
crustal plates, tremendous ice age floods, enormous landslides, and the
ceaseless flow of two major rivers and dozens of tributary streams. Add to this mix
a permanently snow-capped peak on the skyline and a lush forest canopy, and it's
easy to get distracted by the grandeur of the city's surroundings and to think of
the region as one enormous park.

Hundreds of city, regional, state, and national parks and forests and other
greenspaces provide abundant opportunities for enjoying the area's natural
beauty. Some of these parks are little more than expanses of grass, maybe with
a swing set or a softball diamond thrown in; others, like Mount Hood National
Forest, include vast tracts of roadless wilderness. For suggested guidebooks to
parks and hiking trails in the region, see **A Portland Reading List.**

PARKS

CITY PARKS—PORTLAND

Portland is richly endowed with parks of all sizes and descriptions. The city maintains more than 250 park and recreation facilities that cover in total about 10,000
acres. The city's original park plan, drawn up by John Olmsted in 1904, called for a
series of parkways, city squares, and many types of parks. While the plan was never
fully realized—Southwest Terwilliger Boulevard is the only parkway in Olmsted's
plan that was actually built, for example—the city did take his advice and buy up
large chunks of land for use as parkland. Today, nearly every neighborhood has at
least one neighborhood park, and hardly any point in the city is more than a few
blocks from a park or open space of some kind (although some neighborhoods,
particularly those in outer East Portland and the inner Eastside, are considered

park-deficient). For a complete list of city parks, visit the **Portland Parks and Recreation** website at www.portlandparks.org, or call the bureau at 503-823-PLAY (503-823-7529).

Downtown Portland is laid out with greater attention to commerce than to outdoor recreation, but it has a few locally important parks. **Tom McCall Waterfront Park** occupies the west bank of the Willamette River from RiverPlace north to the Steel Bridge. Until the 1970s, a highway ran along the riverfront; today, lunch hour joggers do. On sunny days the park is crowded with runners, walkers, rollerbladers, idlers, and, in some areas, unabashed drug dealers. The park hosts frequent music and food festivals during the summer months. Although the park borders the river, the downtown seawall makes direct access to the water difficult. A few blocks inland, the shady **South Park Blocks**, chock-a-block with heroic statues and other public art pieces, extend through the southern half of downtown from Portland State University to Salmon Street; after a few blocks' interruption by buildings and a somewhat austere public square capping an underground parking garage, the arrangement continues in the **North Park Blocks**, which run from Ankeny Street to Glisan Street in the Pearl District. A few other small parks, such as **Keller Fountain Park** at 3rd and Clay and **Lownsdale** and **Chapman** squares near the county and federal courthouses—not to mention Pioneer Courthouse Square, the city's "living room"—make convenient lunch spots for downtown office workers. To the north, in the Pearl District, **Tanner Springs Park** and **Jamison Square** give the neighborhood's condo dwellers some breathing space.

In the forested hills just west of downtown, **Washington Park** encompasses a variety of attractions: hiking trails, the International Rose Test Garden, the Oregon Zoo (503-226-1561, www.oregonzoo.org), two museums, a Vietnam Veterans Memorial, the Oregon Holocaust Memorial, tennis courts, soccer fields, one of the city's best playgrounds, and the Japanese Garden (see "Gardens" below). To the north, a series of smaller parks—Hoyt Arboretum (see "Gardens"), the grounds of city-owned Pittock Mansion, and **Macleay Park**, which includes the popular Balch Creek Trail—connect Washington Park with **Forest Park**, the city's largest and wildest park. This 5,000-acre gem extends along the spine and eastern slopes of the low Tualatin Mountains, which run northwest from downtown Portland. The park is a favorite haunt of hikers, joggers, mountain bikers, and the occasional elk or cougar. The 30-mile Wildwood Trail runs from Washington Park into the northern reaches of Forest Park; it's part of the 40-mile loop (see "Regional Trails" below).

Besides the green gem of Tryon Creek State Natural Area (see below), Southwest Portland has several parks that contain wooded areas in the West Hills, including **Marquam Nature Park, Marshall Park, George Himes Park**, and **Keller Woodland**, adjacent to an especially scenic portion of Terwilliger Boulevard. **Council Crest Park** perches atop the highest hill in Portland, and offers expansive views in almost every direction; in the early 20th century, Council Crest was the site of a popular amusement park, complete with roller coasters, and was linked to downtown Portland by trolley. **Willamette Park**, in the Johns Landing neighborhood, is one of the few parks in Portland with direct access to the Willamette River; it's a popular location for launching boats. In the more suburban precincts of Vermont Hills, 90-acre **Gabriel Park** has a host of recreational facilities, including a large skate park and the popular Southwest Community Center.

The eastside grid features dozens of parks of various sizes. Almost every neighborhood has its own park; indeed, several neighborhoods are known by the name of the local park. Such is the case with one of the loveliest parks in Portland, **Laurelhurst Park**. Designed in 1912, the park is planted with now-mature specimen trees, such as giant sequoias, coast redwoods, and native Douglas firs, which border broad "meadows" and recreation areas; the grounds center on a shallow lake that is popular with ducks. Further east, nearly 200-acre **Mount Tabor Park** includes an extinct volcano—look for evidence of the old crater near the carved-out basketball courts—as well as acres of second-growth forest; miles of jogging paths, hiking trails, and winding roads cut into the side of the hill; a playground; tennis courts; an amphitheater; and three controversial open-air reservoirs. Mount Tabor offers excellent views, and the lawn just west of the summit is a popular place to watch the sunset over downtown and the West Hills, with the bright lights of Hawthorne Boulevard stretching away below. Other major parks in Southeast Portland include **Sellwood Park, Clinton Park, Westmoreland Park, Woodstock Park, Lents Park**, and the extensive **Powell Butte Natural Area**.

North and Northeast Portland lack the wooded hill parks of other parts of the city, but they have an abundance of popular neighborhood parks. **Grant Park, Irving Park, Wilshire Park, Alberta Park, Fernhill Park**, and **Normandale Park** are major parks in Northeast Portland; **Peninsula Park, Overlook Park, Columbia Park**, and **Pier Park** are some of the prime parks in North Portland. **Cathedral Park**, under the east end of the St. Johns Bridge, hosts a popular jazz festival each July; the park also has boat launching facilities. **Kelley Point Park** occupies the tip of the North Portland peninsula at the confluence of the Willamette and Columbia rivers. **Delta Park**, which is chock-full of sports fields, sits on the former site of Vanport, a large community that was washed away in a 1948 flood. Several miles to the east, just off Interstate 205 in Northeast Portland, **Rocky Butte** has some of the best rock climbing in Portland and offers a panoramic view from the summit.

REGIONAL TRAILS

The Portland area has a reasonably extensive trail network that links various parts of the metropolis. The primary component of the regional trail system is the **40-Mile Loop** (www.40mileloop.org) of walking and biking trails, which, although incomplete, is now substantially longer than 40 miles. The largest links in this chain are the Eastbank Esplanade and other trails along both sides of the Willamette from downtown Portland south to the Sellwood Bridge; the Springwater

Corridor from Southeast Portland east to Gresham and Boring; the Wildwood Trail through Washington Park and Forest Park (hikers only); and a path along the Columbia River, off Marine Drive in Northeast Portland. Other major regional trails include the bikeway that parallels Interstate 205, the Fanno Creek Trail in Washington County, and the trails along the north side of the Columbia River in Vancouver and Washougal. The **4T Trail** (www.4t-trail.org)—the four Ts are trail, tram, trolley, and train—combines hiking trails in the Council Crest area of the West Hills with rides on MAX, the Portland Streetcar, and the Portland Aerial Tram.

CITY, COUNTY, AND REGIONAL PARKS—SURROUNDING COMMUNITIES

Most incorporated communities in the Portland area have a parks department that deals with city parks and natural areas; these suburban parks are primarily of interest to the residents of nearby neighborhoods. In addition to the municipal departments, there are several multi-community park districts and county park departments in the region. The **Tualatin Hills Park and Recreation District** (503-645-6433, www.thprd.org) manages more than 200 parks and 35 miles of trails in Beaverton and the surrounding areas. The crown jewel of this network is **Tualatin Hills Nature Park** (503-629-6350), a natural area of more than 220 acres, with five miles of trails, that is located essentially in the middle of Beaverton. **Washington County Parks** (503-846-8881) operates three facilities, of which the only one of any size is the expansive **Scoggins Valley Park/Henry Hagg Lake** in the foothills of the Coast Range; the lake is a popular destination for swimming and boating in summer.

    North Clackamas Parks & Recreation District (503-742-4348, www.ncprd.com) covers a large swath of northern Clackamas County from Milwaukie to Happy Valley and south to Gladstone. The **Clackamas County Parks Department** (503-742-4414, www.clackamas.us/parks/) operates several county parks, including popular **Barton Park** on the Clackamas River.

    Across the Columbia, **Clark County Parks** (360-397-2285, www.clark.wa.gov/publicworks/parks/index.html) administers dozens of neighborhood, community, and regional parks and trails in Clark County. Major regional parks include **Lacamas Park** and the adjacent Lacamas Lake Greenway and Lacamas Heritage Trail, near Camas; **Moulton Falls Park** and **Lucia Falls Park**, together with the 7.5-mile Bells Mountain Trail, on the East Fork of the Lewis River outside Battle Ground; and **Vancouver Lake**, a large lake on the west side of Vancouver that is popular for swimming, windsurfing, rowing, and kayaking.

    Metro manages many greenspaces and natural areas, including undeveloped sites, in the Portland area; for a fairly complete list, visit www.oregonmetro.gov and click the link for "Parks and Venues." In North Portland, **Smith and Bybee Wetlands Natural Area** (503-797-1850) is a major surprise; this 2,000-acre expanse of lakes, sloughs, and surrounding wetlands is just a few minutes from downtown Portland,

and is essentially surrounded by commercial and industrial facilities, but is rich in wildlife, including bald eagles. You can explore the park on a paved trail or by non-motorized boat. One of the most popular developed sites is **Blue Lake Regional Park** (503-665-4995) in Fairview, which encompasses a large, swimmable lake near the Columbia River. **Oxbow Regional Park** (503-663-4708), on the lower Sandy River about 20 miles east of downtown Portland, includes a stand of old-growth forest; you can watch Chinook salmon spawn here in the fall. Metro also manages the historic **Lone Fir Cemetery** at the intersection of Stark and Morrison in close-in Southeast Portland; this pleasant enclosed burial ground contains not only the graves of notable early settlers but also abundant grass and some 500 trees, and serves as a de-facto park for many residents in the immediate area.

There are no Multnomah County–run parks; Metro took over management and ownership of the county's parks in the 1990s.

GARDENS

Portland's temperate, maritime climate is ideal for gardening. Both visitors and locals alike delight in the region's public gardens, botanical gardens, and arboreta.

- **Crystal Springs Rhododendron Garden**, SE 28th Ave at Woodstock Blvd, 503-771-8386, www.portlandonline.com; this picturesque, nearly 10-acre garden of rhododendrons, azaleas, and related woody plants surrounds a small lake in Southeast Portland. You'll have plenty of company here in May.
- **Elk Rock Garden of the Bishop's Close**, 11800 SW Military Ln, 503-636-5613, www.elkrockgarden.org; this beautiful 13-acre garden, originally a private estate and now the office grounds of the bishop of the Episcopal Diocese of Oregon, overlooks the Willamette River in Dunthorpe.
- **The Grotto**, NE 85th Ave at Sandy Blvd, 503-254-7371, www.thegrotto.org; a combination garden and religious shrine, the National Sanctuary of Our Sorrowful Mother is a peaceful 62-acre retreat in Northeast Portland.
- **Hoyt Arboretum**, Washington Park, 4000 SW Fairview Blvd, 503-865-8733, www.hoytarboretum.org; laced by 12 miles of trails, Hoyt Arboretum displays more than 1,200 different species of trees and shrubs from around the temperate world. Visit the grove of coast redwoods, admire the magnolia blossoms in spring, or hunt for unusual specimens, like the collection of southern beech (*Nothofagus*) trees from South America and Tasmania.
- **Hulda Klager Lilac Gardens**, 115 Pekin Rd, Woodland, WA, 360-225-8996, www.lilacgardens.com, is filled with lilac blooms, and those who admire lilac blooms, in late April and early May.
- **International Rose Test Garden**, Washington Park, 400 SW Kingston Ave, 503-227-7033, www.rosegardenstore.org; many photographers take their iconic picture-postcard image of Portland, showing Mount Hood looming behind downtown skyscrapers, from the International Rose Test Garden in Washington Park. But the garden offers more than just a pretty panorama; it displays nearly

10,000 rose plants, representing more than 550 varieties of roses, in several sub-gardens, including a Shakespeare Garden and a garden of miniature roses.

- **Lan Su Chinese Garden,** NW 3rd Ave at Everett St, 503-228-8131, www.lansugarden.org, occupies a city block in Chinatown. Based on traditional Chinese garden design, this garden features a series of courtyards and pavilions, linked by bridges and winding pathways, set around an artificial lake.
- **Leach Botanical Garden,** 6704 SE 122nd Ave, 503-823-9503, www.leachgarden.org; located a bit off the beaten path in outer Southeast Portland, Leach Botanical Garden is nonetheless one of the finest public gardens in the state with more than 2,000 species of North American, and particularly Northwestern, native plants on display in an informal, naturalized setting.
- **Portland Japanese Garden,** Washington Park, 611 SW Kingston Ave, 503-223-1321, www.japanesegarden.com; one of the finest and most authentic Japanese gardens in North America occupies the hillside just above the International Rose Test Garden. This is an especially appealing spot to wander in spring, when the cherries are in bloom, or in autumn, when the leaves of Japanese maples turn orange and crimson.

NATIONAL AND STATE FORESTS

NATIONAL FORESTS

The mountain ranges of the Pacific Northwest are blanketed in forests, and ten national forests contain much of the timberland (or clear-cut former timberland, as the case may be) in western Oregon and Washington. Four of these national forests are reasonably close to the Portland area.

- **Mount Hood National Forest** (503-668-1700, www.fs.usda.gov/mthood/) covers more than a million acres of the northern Oregon Cascades east of Portland, including Mount Hood and most of the surrounding mountain region. Hikers, bikers, climbers, campers, loggers, anglers, mushroom hunters, and participants in winter sports of all kinds are all heavy users of the Mount Hood National Forest, but nearly a fifth of the forest is designated wilderness area where crowds are greatly diminished.
- To the south, **Willamette National Forest** (541-225-6300, www.fs.usda.gov/willamette/) encompasses the central Oregon Cascades west of the Cascade Crest, including the Mount Jefferson Wilderness, Detroit Lake, and other popular recreational areas within a two-hour drive of Portland.
- **Siuslaw National Forest** (541-750-7000, www.fs.usda.gov/siuslaw/) occupies a discontinuous stretch of the northern and central Coast Range, including some sites along the coast itself.
- **Gifford Pinchot National Forest** (360-891-5000, www.fs.usda.gov/gpnf/), in the southern Washington Cascades, includes some remote, little-visited regions,

as well as the blockbuster attraction of **Mount St. Helens National Volcanic Monument** (360-449-7800, www.fs.usda.gov/mountsthelens). The monument includes the volcanic crater itself, the blast zone that was devastated by the 1980 eruption, and much of the relatively untouched south side of the mountain. Two visitor centers provide interpretive context for this still-active volcano.

Most recreational activities in the national forests now require users to purchase a daily or annual **Northwest Forest Pass**. You must display this pass in your car when you park at a trailhead or other area where the pass is required. Passes are available from Forest Service offices and some retail stores; you can also order the pass online or by telephone from Nature of the Northwest (971-673-2331, www.naturennw.org). Daily passes are $5 and annual passes cost $30. Alternatively, the interagency **America the Beautiful** pass, which covers national forest fee areas (including trailheads for which the Northwest Forest Pass would otherwise be required), national parks, and other federal lands nationwide, costs $80 for one year (store.usgs.gov/pass/).

STATE FORESTS

The **Oregon Department of Forestry** manages nearly 800,000 acres of forestland around the state. The closest state forest to Portland is **Tillamook State Forest** (503-357-2191, www.oregon.gov/ODF/tillamookstateforest/) in the Coast Range about an hour west of the city. Beginning in 1933, this area was the site of a series of massive forest fires that ultimately devastated 355,000 acres of timberland. The forest today is almost entirely hand-planted second-growth; recreational opportunities include hiking, mountain biking, fishing, camping, and horseback riding. The Tillamook Forest Center (866-930-4646, 503-815-6800, www.tillamookforest center.org) provides interpretation of the forest and its history, and has a popular replica of a fire lookout tower. To the north, less-developed **Clatsop State Forest** (503-325-5451, www.oregon.gov/odf/field/astoria/state_forest_management/recreation_main.aspx) has a few hiking trails and campgrounds.

In Washington, the **State Department of Natural Resources** manages several state forests. The only state forest in Southwest Washington is **Yacolt Burn State Forest** (360-577-2025, www.dnr.wa.gov/AboutDNR/ManagedLands/Pages/amp_rec_yacolt_burn_state_forest.aspx), which, like Oregon's Tillamook State Forest, was once consumed by a massive, devastating fire. Yacolt Burn State Forest has trails for hiking and mountain biking, but it is especially popular with off-road vehicle enthusiasts.

COLUMBIA RIVER GORGE NATIONAL SCENIC AREA

The **Columbia River Gorge National Scenic Area** (541-308-1700, www.fs.usda. gov/crgnsa) is one of Portland's favorite playgrounds, featuring outstanding scenery and unique geology. Recreational opportunities abound; as the National

Scenic Area's website declares in dry, bureaucratic prose: "Hiking, mountain biking, windsurfing, camping, fishing, boating, wildlife watching, birding, wild-flower viewing, photography, picnicking, rock climbing. You can do all this and more in the Columbia River Gorge National Scenic Area." While the description is accurate, please do not try to do all these activities simultaneously.

The National Scenic Area is a patchwork of federal, state, municipal, and private land; some 20 Oregon and Washington state parks within the NSA protect some of the Gorge's most scenic and popular destinations. (See "State Parks" below for contact information.) A Northwest Forest Pass is required at many trail-heads and parking areas in the Gorge.

STATE AND NATIONAL PARKS

STATE PARKS

OREGON

Oregon has 234 state parks and recreation areas, including several in the Portland area. A full list and map is available online from the **Oregon State Parks** website, www.oregonstateparks.org, or call the State Parks Information Center at 800-551-6949. The following are the most popular state parks near Portland:

- **Banks-Vernonia State Trail**, in the Coast Range west of Portland, is a 21-mile "linear park" based on a former railroad line that has since been turned into a multi-use trail.
- **Government Island State Recreation Area**, in the Columbia River near the Interstate 205 bridge, is accessible by boat only; the island's small sandy beaches make tempting destinations on a hot summer day.
- **L.L. Stub Stewart State Park** is Oregon's newest full-service state park. Opened in 2007, the 1,800-acre park in the Coast Range foothills includes hiking and equestrian trails and two disc golf courses.
- **Mary S. Young State Recreation Area**, on the west bank of the Willamette River in West Linn, is a pleasant park full of forests, fields, and riverside, linked by eight miles of trails.
- **Milo McIver State Park**, on the Clackamas River near Estacada, offers excellent boating, hiking, fishing, and camping opportunities.
- **Molalla River State Park** near Canby protects 566 acres of riparian wetlands where the Molalla River flows into the Willamette. The park is a popular site for boating, birdwatching, and other wildlife viewing, and hiking.
- **Tryon Creek State Natural Area** (503-636-9886, SW Terwilliger Blvd, www.try-onfriends.org); this 650-acre, hilly, wooded park in Southwest Portland protects the watershed of Tryon Creek. Several miles of shady trail lace the park, and a nature center provides interpretive materials and trail maps.

WASHINGTON

Washington maintains nearly 140 state parks and recreation areas; visit www. parks.wa.gov or call 360-902-8844 for details. Apart from the parks in the Columbia River Gorge (see above), only three state parks are close to the Portland area:

- **Battle Ground Lake State Park,** just east of Battle Ground, centers on a small lake of volcanic origin (a sort of miniature Crater Lake) that is a popular spot for swimming and camping.
- **Paradise Point State Park** is a water-centered park on the Lewis River; the proximity of Interstate 5 makes the park less inviting than it might otherwise be.
- **Reed Island State Park**, in the Columbia River east of Camas, is a 510-acre island that is accessible only by boat.

NATIONAL PARKS

Several national parks and monuments lie within a day's drive of Portland, including **Crater Lake National Park** in the southern Oregon Cascades, **Oregon Caves National Monument,** and **Cascade Siskiyou National Monument** in southwestern Oregon, **Mount Rainier National Park** southeast of Seattle, **Olympic National Park** on the Olympic Peninsula west of Seattle, and **North Cascades National Park** on the Canadian border. (See **Quick Getaways** for more information.)

WILDLIFE REFUGES

Oaks Bottom Wildlife Refuge, on the east shore of the Willamette River near Sellwood and Westmoreland, is a 141-acre urban wildlife refuge managed by the city of Portland. It is an excellent site for birdwatching—look for great blue herons, the official city bird. Less than a mile from downtown Hillsboro, **Jackson Bottom Wetlands Preserve** (503-681-6206, www.jacksonbottom.org) encompasses some 635 acres of wildlife-rich wetlands with more than four miles of hiking trails.

The U.S. Fish and Wildlife Service manages the **Tualatin River National Wildlife Refuge** in Sherwood (503-625-5944, fws.gov/tualatinriver), which hosts almost 200 bird species, although it protects less than 1% of the river's watershed. In Washington, the 5,300-acre **Ridgefield National Wildlife Refuge Complex** (360-887-4106, www.fws.gov/ridgefieldrefuges/) includes four refuges along the Columbia River in Southwest Washington. Significant portions of the refuge are closed to the public, and other areas are open only at certain times of year.

OTHER GREENSPACES

- The **Audubon Society of Portland** (503-292-6855, www.audubonportland.org) owns a 150-acre preserve along Balch Creek, below Cornell Road in Northwest

Portland. Trails are free to use and are open daily from dawn to dusk. Audubon also manages the Ten Mile Creek Sanctuary on the Oregon Coast.

- The federal **Bureau of Land Management** (Oregon state office: 503-808-6001, www.blm.gov/or/) manages about two million acres of land in Western Oregon. West of the Cascade crest, most BLM land is timberland, and in many areas it is interspersed with Forest Service parcels in a checkerboard pattern. The most popular BLM facility near Portland is Wildwood Recreation Site (503-622-3696) on the Salmon River near Welches on the western slopes of Mount Hood.
- **The Nature Conservancy** owns or manages 46 sites in Oregon, including three in the Portland area; visit www.nature.org/Oregon/ for a complete list of preserves open to the public, including directions and access restrictions. Several schools and colleges maintain public open space; scholastic natural areas include **Reed College's** small but surprisingly wild canyon and the wetlands on the **Oregon Episcopal School** campus.
- **Sauvie Island**, while it is not a park but rather a working agricultural/residential landscape, is nonetheless a popular destination for biking, beachgoing, and wildlife viewing and has several small parks and wildlife reserves.
- The region's navigable **rivers**—the Willamette, the Columbia, the Tualatin, the Sandy, the Molalla, and the Clackamas—provide exciting water-based recreational opportunities, including canoeing and kayaking, powerboating and jetskiing, whitewater rafting, and sailing.

YOU'VE FOUND A PLACE TO LIVE, UNPACKED, AND GOTTEN SETTLED into your new home. Now it's time to get involved in the community. This chapter lists a variety of options for community involvement, from volunteering, to social clubs, to places of worship.

COMMUNITY INVOLVEMENT

Volunteering for an organization that does work you care about is a satisfying way to make a difference in your new community while at the same time meeting people who share similar interests.

VOLUNTEER MATCHING AND PLACEMENT

The following organizations coordinate many volunteer activities in the Portland area. Contact them and they will help you find an organization in need of your time and talents.

- **Clackamas County Volunteer Connection**, 503-650-5779, www.co.clackamas. or.us/socialservices/volunteer.html, matches volunteers with volunteer opportunities from more than 200 community partners in Clackamas County.
- **Earth Share of Oregon**, a federation of environmental nonprofit organizations, lists current volunteer opportunities on its website; call 503-223-9015 or visit www.earthshare-oregon.org/get-involved/volunteer/ for more information.
- **Hands on Greater Portland**, 503-200-3355, www.handsonportland.org, matches volunteers with 200 nonprofits and other community organizations in Multnomah and Clackamas counties.
- **Volunteer Connections**, 360-694-6577, www.hsc-wa.org/volunteer-center, co-ordinates volunteer matching in Clark County.
- **Volunteer Match**, www.volunteermatch.org, allows you to search for volunteer opportunities by distance from any ZIP code.

In addition, the "Community" section of the *Oregonian's* online classified section (classifieds.oregonlive.com) lists organizations that need volunteers for specific projects.

AREA CAUSES

Portland has hundreds, if not thousands, of nonprofit organizations that provide a range of services, and many of them are in constant need of volunteer help. The following list is just a sample of the organizations that use volunteers; some have structured volunteer programs with training sessions and schedules, while others are grateful when you walk in off the street and help sort donated clothing for an hour. In addition to the organizations listed in this chapter, keep in mind that many of the community institutions listed elsewhere in this book rely on volunteers.

Note that you may be greeted with caution when you offer your services to an agency that deals directly with children. Don't take it personally; since you care enough about children to volunteer in an after-school program or summer camp, you understand the agency's duty to check your references and perhaps run a criminal background check.

If you have special skills (legal or medical training; experience with web design, desktop publishing, writing and editing, or accounting; a license to drive large trucks and buses; or a background in catering and the know-how to prepare meals for 400 people), be sure to mention them. Don't be shy. Any nonprofit organization will be happy to hear from you.

AIDS AND HIV
- **Cascade AIDS Project**, 208 SW 5th Ave, #800, 503-223-5907, www.cascadeaids.org
- **Ecumenical Ministries of Oregon HIV Services**, 2941 NE Ainsworth St, 503-460-3822, www.emoregon.org/HIV-day_center.php
- **Our House**, 2727 SE Alder St, 503-234-0175, www.ourhouseofportland.org

ALCOHOL AND DRUG DEPENDENCY
- **Lines for Life**, 5100 SW Macadam Ave, Suite 400, 503-244-5211, 800-282-7035, www.linesforlife.org

ANIMALS
- **Audubon Society of Portland**, 5151 NW Cornell Rd, 503-292-6855, www.audubonportland.org
- **Cat Adoption Team**, 14175 SW Galbreath Dr, Sherwood, 503-925-8903, www.catadoptionteam.org
- **Feral Cat Coalition of Oregon**, 503-797-2606, www.feralcats.com
- **Oregon Humane Society**, 1067 NE Columbia Blvd, 503-285-7722, www.oregonhumane.org

- **The Pixie Project**, 510 NE Martin Luther King, Jr Blvd, 503-542-3432, www.pixieproject.org
- **Project Pooch**, 503-697-0623, www.pooch.org

CHILDREN AND YOUTH
Besides the organizations listed below (and other nonprofits focused on children and youth), almost any public school will have volunteer opportunities.

- **Big Brothers Big Sisters Columbia Northwest**, 1827 NE 44th Ave, Suite 100, 503-249-4859, www.bbbsnorthwest.org
- **Boys and Girls Aid Society**, 018 SW Boundary Ct, 503-222-9661, boysandgirlsaid.org
- **Boys and Girls Clubs of Portland Metropolitan Area**, 7119 SE Milwaukie Ave, 503-232-0077, bgcportland.org
- **Children's Home Society of Washington**, 206-695-3200, 800-456-3339, www.chs wa.org
- **I Have a Dream Oregon**, 2916 NE Alberta St, Suite D, 503-287-7203, www.dreamoregon.org
- **Janus Youth Programs**, 707 NE Couch St, 503-233-6090, www.janusyouth.org
- **R.E.A.P. (Reaching and Empowering All People)**, 503-688-2784, www.reapusa.org
- **Schoolhouse Supplies**, 2735 NE 82nd Ave, 503-249-9933, www.schoolhousesupplies.org

CULTURE AND THE ARTS
Practically every institution listed in the "Cultural Life" chapter relies to some extent on volunteers. The **Regional Arts and Culture Council** (411 NW Park Ave, Suite 101, 503-823-5111, www.racc.org) lists volunteer opportunities on its website.

DISABILITY
- **Disability Rights Oregon**, 610 SW Broadway, Suite 200, 503-243-2081, www.droregon.org
- **Independent Living Resources**, 1839 NE Couch St, 503-232-7411, www.ilr.org
- **Special Olympics Oregon**, 5901 SW Macadam Ave, Suite 200, 503-248-0600, www.soor.org

ENVIRONMENT
- **The City Repair Project**, 2800 SE Harrison St, 503-235-8946, www.cityrepair.org
- **Community Energy Project**, 422 NE Alberta St, 503-284-6827, www.communityenergyproject.org
- **The Freshwater Trust**, 65 SW Yamhill St, Suite 200, 503-222-9091, www.thefreshwatertrust.org

- **Friends of Trees**, 3117 NE Martin Luther King Jr Blvd, 503-282-8846, www.friendsoftrees.org
- **Northwest Environmental Advocates**, 503-295-0490, www.northwestenvironmentaladvocates.org
- **Sierra Club (Oregon Chapter)**, 1821 SE Ankeny St, 503-238-0442, www.oregon.sierraclub.org
- **SOLVE,** 2000 SW 1st Ave, Suite 400, 503-844-9571, 800-333-SOLV, www.solv.org
- **Tualatin Riverkeepers**, 11675 SW Hazelbrook Rd, Tigard, 503-218-2580, www.tualatinriverkeepers.org

GAY AND LESBIAN
- **Basic Rights Oregon**, 310 SW 4th Ave, Suite 300, 503-222-6151, www.basicrights.org
- **Q Center**, 4115 N Mississippi Ave, 503-234-7837, www.pdxqcenter.org

HEALTH AND HOSPITALS
Most hospitals and community clinics welcome volunteers; just give the nearest institution a call, or contact one of the following organizations:
- **African American Health Coalition**, 2800 N Vancouver Ave, Suite 100, 503-413-1850, www.aahc-portland.org
- **American Red Cross, Oregon Chapters**, 3131 N Vancouver Ave, 503-284-1234, www.oregonredcross.org

HUNGER, HOMELESSNESS, AND POVERTY
- **Central City Concern**, 503-294-1681, www.centralcityconcern.org
- **Community Warehouse**, 3969 NE Martin Luther King Jr Blvd, 503-235-8786, www.communitywarehouse.org
- **Food Not Bombs**, www.foodnotbombs.net/oregon.html
- **Growing Gardens**, 2003 NE 42nd Ave #3, 503-284-8420, www.growing-gardens.org
- **Habitat for Humanity**, 1478 NE Killingsworth St, 503-287-9529, www.pdxhabitatportlandmetro.org
- **JOIN**, 1435 NE 81st Ave, Suite 100, 503-232-2031, www.joinpdx.com
- **Meals-on-Wheels**, 7710 SW 31st Ave, 503-736-6325, www.mealsonwheelspeople.org
- **Metropolitan Family Service**, 1808 SE Belmont St, 503-232-0007, www.metfamily.org
- **Neighborhood House**, 7780 SW Capitol Hwy, 503-246-1663, www.nhpdx.org
- **Northeast Emergency Food Program**, 4800 NE 72nd Ave, 503-284-5470, www.emoregon.org/NE_food_program.php
- **Operation Nightwatch**, 1432 SW 13th Ave, 503-220-0438, www.operationnightwatch.org
- **Oregon Food Bank**, 7900 NE 33rd Ave, 503-282-0555, www.oregonfoodbank.org

- **Outside In**, 1132 SW 13th Ave, 503-535-3800, www.outsidein.org
- **p:ear**, 338 NW 6th Ave, 503-228-6677, www.pearmentor.org
- **Portland Homeless Family Solutions**, 1838 SW Jefferson St, 503-915-8307, www.pdxhfs.org
- **Portland Rescue Mission**, 111 W Burnside St, 503-647-7466, www.portlandrescuemission.org
- **REACH Community Development**, 4150 SW Moody Ave, 503-231-0682, www.reachcdc.org
- **Sisters of the Road**, 133 NW 6th Ave, 503-222-5694, www.sistersoftheroadcafe.org
- **Transition Projects**, 665 NW Hoyt St, 503-280-4700, www.tprojects.org

INTERNATIONAL RELIEF AND DEVELOPMENT

- **Medical Teams International**, 14150 SW Milton Ct, Tigard, 503-624-1000, 800-959-4325, www.medicalteams.org
- **Mercy Corps**, 45 SW Ankeny St, 503-896 5000, 800-292-3355, www.mercycorps.org

LITERACY

- **Financial Beginnings**, 9600 SW Capitol Hwy, Ste 150, 800-406-1876, www.financialbeginnings.org
- **Start Making a Reader Today (SMART)**, 101 SW Market St, 971-634-1634, 877-598-4633, www.getsmartoregon.org

MENTORING AND CAREER DEVELOPMENT

- **Dress for Success Oregon**, 1532 NE 37th Ave, 503-249-7300, www.dressforsuccessoregon.org
- **Oregon Tradeswomen**, 3934 NE MLK Jr Blvd #101, 503-335-8200, www.tradeswomen.net
- **Service Corps of Retired Executives (SCORE)**; Portland: 601 SW 2nd Ave, Suite 950, 503-326-5211, www.scorepdx.org; Vancouver: 4001 Main St, Ste 120, Vancouver, 360-699-1079, www.scorevancouver.org

POLITICS

In addition to the various large and small political parties that are active in the area, Portland has many nominally nonpartisan political organizations, most of which are focused on one or more particular issues (the environment, gay rights, homelessness, etc.) and are thus listed in the appropriate section. The **City Club of Portland** (901 SW Washington St, 503-228-7231, www.pdxcityclub.org) is a non-partisan—but well-connected—group that focuses on public affairs.

REFUGEES AND IMMIGRANTS
- **Immigrant and Refugee Community Organization**, 10301 NE Glisan St, 503-234-1541, www.irco.org
- **Sponsors Organized to Assist Refugees** (SOAR), 2906 NE Glisan St, 503-284-3002, www.emoregon.org/soar.php

SENIORS
- **Elders In Action**, 1411 SW Morrison St, Ste 290, 503-595-7533, www.eldersinaction.org
- **Meals-on-Wheels**, 7710 SW 31st Ave, 503-736-6325, www.mealsonwheelspeople.org
- **Metropolitan Family Service**, 1808 SE Belmont St, 503-232-0007, www.metfamily.org
- **Northwest Pilot Project**, 1430 SW Broadway, Suite 200, 503-227-5605, www.nwpilotproject.org
- **Ride Connection**, 503-528-1720, www.rideconnection.org

WOMEN'S SERVICES
- **Bradley-Angle House**, 5432 N Albina Ave, 503-232-1528, www.bradleyangle.org
- **Portland Women's Crisis Line**, 503-232-9751, www.pwcl.org
- **Sexual Assault Resource Center**, 4900 SW Griffith Dr, Suite 100, Beaverton, 503-626-9100, www.sarcoregon.org

CHARITABLE GIVING

Not everyone can give time or talent to a good cause. Another way to help is to donate something that virtually every charity needs: money. Before donating, consider checking out the charity's fiscal responsibility and its ratio of overhead to program spending; if the charity spends 95% of its money on fundraising efforts and overhead and 5% on program delivery, you might want to pass. Third-party watchdog sites like **Charity Navigator** (www.charitynavigator.org), **Guidestar** (www.guidestar.org), or the Better Business Bureau's **Wise Giving Alliance** (www.give.org) can help you assess a charity's performance.

MEETING PEOPLE

As a rule, Portlanders are friendly and not particularly reticent; you can usually start a conversation with a stranger without being immediately suspected of having an ulterior motive, and people you meet in social settings are more likely than not to be chatty (sometimes unnervingly so). That said, as a newcomer, it's not always easy to meet people with similar interests. Volunteer organizations (see "Community Involvement" above), cultural events (see **Cultural Life**), recreational sports clubs (see **Sports and Recreation**), and, for the spiritually inclined, religious groups (see "Places of Worship" below) are all excellent places to meet new friends. The arts and entertainment papers (see "What's Going On?" in **Cultural Life**) are full of event listings. Dating and matchmaking services, let alone online social networking sites like Facebook and LinkedIn, are beyond the scope of this book, but the following are some suggestions for making friends and meeting people in your new home.

ALUMNI GROUPS

Most local, regional, and large national colleges and universities have alumni groups in Portland. If there's no organized alumni group, you should be able to find other graduates of your school living in the area. Check with your alma mater's alumni or development office, or just wait around: eventually, they'll find you.

BUSINESS GROUPS

If you have a particular professional focus, there is probably a business group for you. Most of these groups exist in whole or in part for networking purposes, so social events are usually frequent.

POLITICAL GROUPS

Whether you're a government-out-of-my-hemisphere Libertarian or a fist-pounding Trotskyite, or even if your political leanings fall somewhere in between those extremes, you're bound to find a *simpatico* political group in town. If you hate politics, consider founding a Portland Apathy Association—assuming you can be bothered.

OUTDOOR ADVENTURES

Several organizations, including Portland Parks and Recreation, organize outdoor adventures—hikes, snowshoe treks, rafting trips, and more. You can often find out about trips by checking out the bulletin boards of sporting goods stores. The **Mazamas** (527 SE 43rd Ave, 503-227-2345, www.mazamas.org and the **Trails Club of Oregon** (503-233-2740, www.trailsclub.org) maintain very active calendars of outdoor events.

SPECIAL INTERESTS

It seems like every niche interest has a club, from the **Portland Skyliners Tall Club** (503-222-7373, www.tall.org/clubs/or/portland/) for women over 5'10" and men over 6'2" to the **Society for Creative Anachronism's** Kingdom of An Tir (www.antir.sca.org) for medieval re-creationists (and recreationists). (Would-be knights or damsels of above-average height can go wild and join both clubs!) Just do a web search for your favorite interest or characteristic, or even your favorite celebrity, and you're bound to come up with something.

For a calendar of upcoming meetings from clubs and groups of all kinds, check out the listings at **www.meetup.com**; just type in your ZIP code, type in a subject, and you'll likely have dozens of options to choose from.

PLACES OF WORSHIP

The Pacific Northwest is, by some measures, the most unchurched region in the United States. A low rate of weekly church attendance, however, does not translate to a lack of spirituality or an absence of places of worship. The Portland area has hundreds of houses of worship representing every major faith and denomination (and a host of minor ones, too). If you are at all religiously inclined, you'll almost certainly be able to find a spiritual home.

If you belong to a congregation in your old hometown, your religious leader might be able to refer you to a kindred congregation in Portland. In addition to web resources, the Yellow Pages has extensive listings under "Churches," "Synagogues," and "Mosques"; the church listings are organized by denomination and include sections for nondenominational, interdenominational, and independent churches as well as metaphysical centers.

The following interfaith agencies, representing congregations working together to address hunger, homelessness, and other urban problems, also might be able to refer you to a congregation that fulfills your spiritual needs:

- **Ecumenical Ministries of Oregon**, 0245 SW Bancroft St, Suite B, 503-221-1054, www.emoregon.org
- **Interfaith Council of Greater Portland**, 3956 NE Couch St, 503-238-1155, www.ifcgp.org

The list of resources below is by no means complete, and it is not a substitute for the Yellow Pages or newspaper listings, but it includes local and regional societies or associations for a range of religious groups.

ALTERNATIVE WORSHIP—NEW AGE SPIRITUALITY, PAGANISM, AND MORE

For a comprehensive guide to New Age spiritual centers, Ayurveda, meditation, mysticism, and other spiritual resources, visit the website for *New ConneXion* magazine (www.newconnexion.net) or pick up a free copy at area libraries, bookstores, or natural food stores. Wiccans, pagans, and other adherents of *really* old-time religion currently lack a local umbrella organization, but a web search for whatever strain of spirituality/paganism you're interested in should reveal a group or two in the area.

BAHA'I

- **Portland Baha'i Center**, 8720 N Ivanhoe St, 503-289-6331, www.portlandbahai.org

BUDDHIST

Various sects of Buddhism are represented in the Portland area, but there is no overarching resource dedicated to Portland Buddhists collectively. The Seattle-based **Northwest Dharma Association** (206-441-6811, www.northwestdharma.org) also covers Portland-area groups and events.

CHRISTIAN

The following major denominations have an organized local or regional presence. Independent and nondenominational churches are, by definition, not part of a denomination, and so have no collective regional organization; the same is true for many small denominations with relatively few adherents in the area, as well as some larger groups, such as Christian Scientists and Jehovah's Witnesses, which are governed from a national headquarters.

APOSTOLIC

The worldwide **Apostolic Faith Church** (503-777-1741, www.apostolicfaith.org) is headquartered in the Woodstock neighborhood of Southeast Portland.

ASSEMBLIES OF GOD

- **Oregon Ministry Network of the Assemblies of God**, 503-393-4411, www.oregonag.org

BAPTIST

- **American Baptist Churches of the Central Pacific Coast**, 503-228-8394, www.vibrant-life.net
- **CB Northwest**, 503-669-1515, www.cbnw.org (Conservative Baptist)
- **Northwest Baptist Convention**, 360-882-2100, www.nwbaptist.org (Southern Baptist)

CATHOLIC

- **Archdiocese of Portland**, 503-234-5334, www.archdpdx.org

CHURCH OF GOD

- **Association of the Churches of God**, 503-393-3510, 800-873-7729, www.orwacog.org

CHURCH OF JESUS CHRIST OF LATTER-DAY SAINTS (MORMONS)

The Mormons are one of the largest denominations in Oregon. There are many local churches scattered around the area. The regional Temple (13600 SW Kruse Oaks Blvd, Lake Oswego, 503-639-7066, www.lds.org) is hard to miss: its giant marble spires loom just west of Interstate 5 near the Highway 217 interchange.

EMERGING CHURCHES

So-called "emerging churches" are nondenominational, often loosely organized, and definitely non-hierarchical. Services take place in schools, community centers, or even pubs. Here are a few local examples.

- **Bread and Wine**, Portland, www.breadandwine.org
- **Evergreen Community**, Portland, evergreenpdx.org
- **Imago Dei**, Portland, 503-231-5096, www.imagodeicommunity.com
- **The Pearl Church**, Portland, 503-709-2571, www.pearlchurch.org

EPISCOPAL

- **Episcopal Diocese of Oregon**, 503-636-5613, 888-346-2373, www.diocese-oregon.org

FRIENDS (QUAKERS)

Several Society of Friends groups meet in the local area. The **Multnomah Monthly Meeting** (503-232-2822, www.multnomahfriends.org) encompasses some (but not all) local Friends worship groups.

LUTHERAN

- **Evangelical Lutheran Church in America** (ELCA), Oregon Synod, 503-413-4191, www.oregonsynod.org
- **Northwest District of the Lutheran Church–Missouri Synod**, 503-288-8383, 888-693-5267, www.nowlcms.org

MENNONITE

- **Pacific Northwest Mennonite Conference**, 503-522-5324, 888-492-4216, www.pnmc.org

METHODIST

- **Oregon-Idaho Conference of the United Methodist Church**, 503-226-7931, 800-593-7539, www.umoi.org

NAZARENE

- **Oregon Pacific District of the Church of the Nazarene**, 503-581-3950, www.orpac.org

ORTHODOX

- **Pacific Northwest Deanery**, Diocese of the West, The Orthodox Church in America, 415-567-9378, www.dowoca.org

PRESBYTERIAN

- **Synod of the Pacific**, Presbyterian Church USA, 800-754-0669, www.synodpacific.org

SEVENTH-DAY ADVENTIST

- **Oregon Conference of Seventh-Day Adventists**, 503-850-3500, www.oregonconference.org

UNITARIAN UNIVERSALIST

- **Pacific Northwest District of the Unitarian Universalist Association**, 425-957-9116, www.pnwd.org

UNITED CHURCH OF CHRIST

- **Central Pacific Conference of the United Church of Christ**, 503-228-3178, www.cpcucc.org

WESLEYAN

- **Northwest District of the Wesleyan Church**, 307-756-9482, www.northwestdistrict.org

GAY AND LESBIAN SPIRITUAL GROUPS

The **Community of Welcoming Congregations** (503-665-8741, www.welcomingcongregations.org) is an association of more than 100 congregations in Oregon and southwest Washington that welcome worshipers of all sexual orientations and gender identities.

HINDU

There is no centralized source of information on Hinduism in Portland. Two good places to look into are the **Vedanta Society of Portland** (1157 SE 55th Ave, 503-235-3919, www.vedanta-portland.org), which is a branch of the Ramakrishna Order of India, and the **Portland Hindu Temple** (Brahma Premananda Ashram), 11515 SW Hall Blvd, Tigard, 503-598-3073, www.portlandhindutemple.org.

ISLAMIC

The **Islamic Society of Greater Portland** (www.isgponline.com) sponsors social and community events for members of the local Muslim community; its website includes links to local mosques and Islamic schools.

JAIN

• **Jain Society of Oregon**, 503-292-1965, www.jainworld.com/society/Oregon.htm

JEWISH

The **Jewish Federation of Greater Portland** (6680 SW Capitol Hwy, 503-245-6219, www.jewishportland.org) is a great resource for the Jewish community. The organization's comprehensive website lists local events and contains links to Jewish resources, agencies, camps, schools, and congregations, including Conservative, Reform, Orthodox, Reconstructionist, Sephardic, and unaffiliated congregations in the metropolitan area and elsewhere in the Northwest.

B Y NOW, YOU'VE PROBABLY HEARD A FEW NOT ESPECIALLY FUNNY jokes about Oregon rain. One old saw holds that Oregonians don't tan— they rust. Another states that Portland's rainy season only runs from September 1 to August 31. Yet another asks, "What do you call two consecutive days of rain in Portland?" (Answer: the weekend.) Then there's the story about the hapless fellow waiting to be admitted into hell. He watches anxiously as Satan throws almost every soul in line ahead of him into the fiery pit, but notices that every so often the devil chucks someone off to the side instead. Intrigued, he summons up the courage to peep, "Excuse me, Prince of Darkness, but I notice that you seem to be throwing some people off to the side instead of into the inferno." "Oh, them," the devil replies ruefully. "They're from Portland. They're too wet to burn." Har har har. Endless rain. How very droll.

It *does* rain a lot in Oregon. Rumors of a nine-month deluge, however, are greatly exaggerated. The sun comes out *sometimes*, even in winter, and summers are typically glorious. And even if the weather's often wet and gray, it's somewhat comforting that the region's best known climatic feature is its drizzle rather than, say, category 5 hurricanes, killer tornadoes, or paralyzing blizzards.

Which is not to say that Portland is not at risk from natural disasters. All that rain sometimes begets mudslides and floods, and the area is subject to earthquakes, volcanic eruptions, forest fires, and the occasional ironic drought. It's all part of the price you pay for living in a paradise—a soggy, geologically unstable paradise.

WEATHER AND CLIMATE

According to the Portland office of the **National Weather Service** (www.wrh. noaa.gov/pqr/), Portland enjoys or endures, depending on your point of view, on average, about 36 inches of precipitation per year (at the official reporting station at Portland International Airport—downtown Portland tends to be slightly wetter). Portland's total annual rainfall is less than that of most cities in the

Northeast and Southeast—Miami's average rainfall is more than 50% higher. The difference, of course, lies in the number of rainy days. Portland's precipitation rarely comes in the form of brief cloudbursts; rather, like the quality of mercy in *The Merchant of Venice*, it droppeth as the gentle rain from heaven upon the place beneath. Stated more bluntly and less elegantly, it falls over long, gray weeks of intermittent drizzle and light rain, resulting in an average of more than 150 days per year with measurable precipitation. Here's the bad news in statistical form, showing 30-year normals, courtesy of the National Weather Service:

Month	Normal Precipitation (in Inches)	Mean Number of Days with Precipitation (.01 inch or more)
January	4.88	18
February	3.66	15
March	3.68	18
April	2.73	16
May	2.47	14
June	1.7	9
July	0.65	4
August	0.67	4
September	1.47	7
October	3.00	13
November	5.63	19
December	5.49	19
Yearly Total	**36.03**	**155**

You'll notice that more than 90% of the city's total rainfall falls from September to May. While the uneven distribution of rainfall during the year does mean the winter months are that much soggier, it also means that summers tend to be dry—newcomers who arrive during July and August are often shocked to find the city a patchwork of brown lawns. So when the pitter-patter of rain on your windows for the umpteenth day in a row threatens to drive you to suicide (or to the sunny environs of Las Vegas, which for some people amounts to the same thing), think hopefully of the blue skies and warm days of July.

While you may struggle to believe it in November and December, Portland is actually one of the drier locations in northwest Oregon. (Even within the city limits, rainfall amounts vary dramatically, and the official observation station at the airport often receives less rain than downtown Portland, and substantially less rain than the highest elevations in the West Hills.) Frequent moisture-laden storms off the Pacific Ocean drop 60 to 80 inches of rain each year on most coastal communities, and when the storm clouds hit the Coast Range and begin to rise and condense, the rain really begins to pour down. Some locations high in the Coast Range average nearly 180 inches of rain each year—that's five times as much as Portland gets! By the time a storm reaches the Willamette Valley and the Portland area, much of the moisture has already been wrung out of the clouds. (This "rain-shadow" effect is why Portland tends to get gray skies and drizzle rather than constant downpours.) Then, when the storm hits the Cascade foothills and the clouds once again begin to rise, cool, and condense, precipitation amounts rise correspondingly. The high Cascades get more than 100 inches of "rain-equivalent" precipitation, but at that elevation it mostly falls as hundreds of inches of snow. By the time the storm passes to the east side of the mountains, there is usually very little moisture left, which is why much of central and eastern Oregon is high desert.

Despite its proximity to the Cascade Mountains and its northerly latitude—more than 45 degrees north latitude, about the same as Minneapolis and Montreal—Portland is not a snowy city. That is not to say that heavy snowfall never occurs. December 2008 was exceptionally snowy, with 19 inches of the white stuff recorded at the airport; some parts of the metro area got more than three feet of snow, and the city was essentially shut down for several days. The winter of 2013–14 was bookended by two significant snowstorms, one of which prompted the city of Portland to send out an emergency message asking residents to stay home. Such wintry events are quite rare, however. The Portland Airport averages only about 6 inches of snow per year, and in some winters there's no snow at all on the valley floor. Elevations over 500 feet, including much of the West Hills, often get more snow than downtown Portland or the East Side (or get snow when those places do not), but even at higher elevations a heavy snowfall is rare in the metropolitan area. Near the Gorge and in the Cascade foothills, snow is much more common, although even there it is not a regular occurrence.

You may notice that extended forecasts seem to call for snow far more often than snow actually falls. According to local weatherman Matt Zaffino, "It comes down to basic climatology and geography, and Portland snow storms have to buck both to really have a chance." Moisture usually comes from the west, out of the relatively warm North Pacific, while cold Arctic air from the North American interior has to get past the natural barriers of the Rockies and the Cascades. Often, during the winter, a computer model will predict that everything is coming together perfectly to produce several inches of snow, but ultimately either the moisture or the cold air fails to arrive. Explains Zaffino, "everything has to fall into place just right, and against the natural tendency of our weather patterns, to produce a big Willamette Valley snow storm." The relative scarcity of snow means that anything more than a dusting of snow results in school closures and massive traffic disruptions. If you're from a snowy part of the world, you'll probably find this behavior amusing, frustrating, or both.

Although snow is rare, ice storms do occur with some frequency, particularly in East Portland, Gresham, Troutdale, Camas, and other communities near the western end of the Columbia River Gorge. Cold air rushing through the Gorge from eastern Oregon sets the stage for ice storms by creating a layer of sub-freezing air at ground level, with warmer air at altitude. When a storm moves in from the west, precipitation begins to fall as rain, but the rain turns to ice while falling (or freezes on contact with the ground). While ice storms can be treacherous, the effects are usually short-lived (although every few years heavy ice accumulations bring down branches all around eastern Multnomah County).

The same maritime influence that brings frequent precipitation to Portland also gives the city relatively mild temperatures. Here are the average high and low temperatures for each month, again courtesy of your friends at the National Weather Service:

Month	Normal High	Normal Low
January	47	35.8
February	51.3	36.3
March	56.7	39.6
April	61.4	43.1
May	68	48.6
June	73.5	53.6
July	80.6	57.8
August	81.1	58
September	75.8	53.1
October	63.8	46
November	52.8	40.5
December	45.6	35.2

The hottest temperature ever recorded in Portland was 107; the lowest was −3. In an average year, however, the mercury may hit 100 on one or two days in summer, and fall to the mid-teens on the coldest winter nights. In general, summer days are not terribly muggy; a 95-degree day in Portland may be more comfortable than an 85-degree day in Atlanta. Still, the city is subject to occasional extremes (or what Portlanders consider extremes), particularly when continental airmasses infiltrate western Oregon, and the weather can deviate significantly, in either direction, from the region's normal climatic averages. For example, the summer of 2009 brought more 90-degree-plus days (24) than any other on record, including two consecutive days with a high of 106 degrees at Portland International Airport; just a few months later, December 2009 featured a period of record-breaking cold. Similarly, 2014 featured the coldest February on record, immediately followed by one of the warmest springs.

As a result of its complex topography, the Portland metropolitan area has many microclimates. The West Hills receive more rain than the surrounding lowlands (and create a miniature rain-shadow for downtown Portland), while Cascade foothill towns like Sandy and Estacada average more than 55 inches of rain each year. Downtown Portland and the densely populated East Side demonstrate a heat island effect; forested areas outside the heart of the city are noticeably cooler on hot days and cool down more rapidly on clear nights. Areas near the Columbia River tend to be breezy, and therefore cooler in the summer; the eastern part of the metropolitan area, near the mouth of the Columbia River Gorge, is subject to fierce winds whipping down the Gorge from the interior in the winter. The lesson here is to choose your location carefully if you have strong preferences about weather. For detailed information about Oregon weather and climate, including fun facts about record-shattering events, visit the website of the **Oregon Climate Service**, www.ocs.oregonstate.edu.

AIR POLLUTION

Portland is not an especially smoggy city, and most of the region's air quality problems are seasonal. On hot, still summer days, emissions from cars and industry, together with emissions from other sources (such as boat and lawnmower engines, and even paint fumes), react with oxygen to create ground level ozone or smog. To help combat the problem, vehicle emission tests are required in the Portland metropolitan region, including Clark County, Washington. (See the **Getting Settled** chapter for testing requirements and locations.) For the most part, however, Portland meets national standards for clean air.

Air toxics are a more insidious problem. For example, in winter, particles associated with smoke from wood stoves and fireplaces can build up in the air and cause health problems, and particulate pollution from burning diesel fuel can be a problem at any time of year. The new cleaner-burning diesel fuel and more-efficient diesel engines required by the EPA should help decrease particulate pollution over the next few years.

The Oregon Department of Environmental Quality's **Air Quality Division** (503-229-5696, www.oregon.gov/DEQ/AQ/) is charged with enforcing federal, state, and local air quality laws. The DEQ provides current air quality reports for various locations in and around Portland on its website (www.deq.state.or.us/aqi/index.aspx). The department offers the following tips for improving air quality:

- Drive less.
- If you use a woodstove, use an efficient, EPA-certified model, and dry firewood at least six to twelve months before burning it.

- During hot weather, refuel your vehicle during cooler evening hours, and make sure your gas cap seals properly.
- Wait until temperatures decrease and breezes pick up before you mow the lawn or use gasoline-powered garden equipment.
- Consider using non-gasoline powered equipment, like a manual push mower or electric mower instead of a gasoline-powered lawn mower.

NATURAL DISASTERS

Natural disasters happen. The City of Portland has put together cheerful online maps showing your relative danger of being swept away in a landslide, scorched by wildfire, or pulverized in an earthquake; just visit **Portland Maps** (www.portlandmaps.com), type in any address or intersection, click on "Maps," then click "Hazard." A similar mapping feature is available for most of the Oregon portion of the metropolitan area at hazardmap.oregonmetro.gov.

MUDSLIDES

Mudslides are one of the most common natural disasters in northwest Oregon. (According to the Oregon Department of Geology and Mineral Industries, 9,500 landslides occurred in the state during the exceptionally soggy period from February 1996 through January 1997.) The same steep hills that offer residents spectacular views also render their homes and roads vulnerable to mudslides during extended periods of heavy rain. While they are certainly not an everyday occurrence, mudslides happen often enough to warrant concern if you live (or are considering living) on or near a steep slope. The 2014 Oso landslide in Washington state, which killed dozens of people, is a reminder of how devastating a landslide can be.

Geologists warn that steep bluffs and hillsides where earth movement has occurred in the past or where geology favors such movement are most at risk. Such conditions exist in large swaths of the West Hills and other hilly parts of the metropolitan area. If you are considering buying a home in a potentially slide-prone area, you might want to consult with a geologist or geotechnical engineer to analyze the property in question. Be aware that most homeowner's policies will not cover damage or destruction to your home caused by a landslide. Separate (usually expensive) landslide policies are available, but even these policies might not cover damage in all circumstances (e.g., if human actions contributed to the slide). If you live in a potentially slide-prone area, check with your insurer, and read the fine print carefully.

WILDFIRES

Western Oregon occasionally experiences drought conditions, which in turn set the stage for dangerous wildfires. While large fires are more prevalent in the drier eastern half of the state, forested neighborhoods in the Portland area, including close-in neighborhoods in the West Hills, are theoretically at risk from wildfires. The National Fire Protection Association offers tips on protecting your home from wildfire on its web site, www.firewise.org.

EARTHQUAKES AND TSUNAMIS

Oregonians live in a geologically unstable region. Earthquakes measuring at least 5 on the Richter scale hit northwest Oregon in 1962, 1964, and 1993—the last of these, centered near Salem, damaged the state Capitol building—and the Nisqually Earthquake that struck the Puget Sound region in 2001, which had a magnitude of 6.8 and caused an estimated $2 billion in damage, reminded Portlanders that bigger quakes are by no means impossible in the Northwest. Several faults run right through the metropolitan area, including one that runs directly under downtown Portland, and a large temblor on any of those faults could potentially cause significant damage and loss of life. More troubling, geologists advise us that it is only a matter of when, not if, the "Big One"—a megathrust quake of a magnitude of 9 or more—occurs along the Cascadia subduction zone 90 miles or so off the Oregon coast. The last time that happened, on January 26, 1700, some coastal areas dropped several feet in elevation, and the resulting tsunami waves pummeled the Northwest coast and even caused serious damage as far away as Japan. A similar quake today would cripple the infrastructure of the Northwest west of the Cascades, and could cause tens of thousands of deaths from Northern California to British Columbia.

For more light bedtime reading about earthquake hazards in the region, visit the website of the **Pacific Northwest Seismic Network** (www.pnsn.org), which includes data about the location and magnitude of recent (generally very small) area quakes. Also remember that earthquake coverage is not usually part of a standard homeowner's insurance policy; be sure to look into purchasing earthquake insurance if you own, or plan to own, a home here, and consider doing a full or partial seismic retrofit.

While it isn't really an issue in Portland proper, the entire Northwest coast is a potential **tsunami** danger zone. Signs in Oregon coastal communities point the way to evacuation routes; if you're at the coast and you feel an earthquake, head inland to higher ground immediately. The threat is not merely theoretical, nor limited to Cascadia subduction zone events; the 1964 Good Friday Earthquake in Alaska generated a tsunami that struck the Oregon coast, causing significant property damage and drowning four campers on the beach at Newport.

VOLCANIC ERUPTIONS

Four major, non-extinct volcanoes—Mounts Hood, St. Helens, Adams, and Rainier— are visible from downtown Portland. While three of those volcanoes are inactive (although not extinct), Mt. St. Helens, only 50 miles away, erupted spectacularly on

May 18, 1980. The blast blew the top 1,300 feet off the mountain and sent a plume of ash as far east as Oklahoma. The United States Geological Survey's **Cascades Volcano Observatory** in Vancouver, Washington, provides abundant information about the region's volcanoes on its website (vulcan.wr.usgs.gov).

While Portland is far enough from all of these volcanoes that an eruption is unlikely to cause widespread destruction in the city itself, significant disruption is certainly possible. In particular, if Mount Hood were to erupt, Portland's source of municipal water (the Bull Run reservoirs on the west side of the mountain) could become unusable.

EMERGENCY PREPAREDNESS

The Oregon Trail Chapter of the **American Red Cross** offers a suite of disaster preparation tools on its website (www.redcross.org/or/Portland/preparedness). The Red Cross recommends taking the following steps to get ready for potential disasters:

MAKE A PLAN

- Research the kinds of disasters that could happen in the Northwest, and talk with your family about them.
- Learn how to use emergency equipment, such as fire extinguishers, and know how to shut off utility service to your home. Pick two places to meet in case of an emergency, one right outside your home and one outside your neighborhood.
- Put together a disaster kit and a stockpile of emergency supplies.
- Make a list of emergency contact numbers and tell everyone in your household where the list is kept.
- Practice your plan and maintain your supplies in a state of readiness.

BUILD A KIT

Put together a disaster supply kit with water (one gallon per person, per day) and a three-day supply of non-perishable food. The kit should include:

- A complete first-aid kit and first-aid reference guide
- Portable battery-operated radio and spare batteries
- Flashlights and spare batteries
- Blankets and extra clothing, including rain gear and sturdy shoes
- A three-day supply of critical medication and a spare pair of eyeglasses
- Comfort items for children, such as toys, games, stuffed animals
- Food, water, and carrying cages and other supplies for pets
- Plastic sheeting, duct tape, a pocket knife, matches, rope, a whistle, and other survival gear
- A Crescent wrench, screwdrivers, a hammer, an axe, and other essential tools

- Sanitation supplies, such as toilet paper, soap, detergent, bleach (for water purification), diapers, feminine sanitary supplies, trash bags, and pre-moistened towelettes
- Copies of important documents and a stash of emergency cash

It may seem like a hassle to prepare so thoroughly for a disaster, given the seemingly low risk of catastrophe. However, as the Red Cross's booklet *Together We Prepare Oregon* points out, "The greatest risk here in Oregon could be complacency, as many people are not aware of the potential for natural and manmade disasters in our communities. By taking these simple steps, you can help prepare your family, community, neighborhood school and workplace."

P ORTLAND ENJOYS A NATIONAL REPUTATION AS A LEADER IN PROGRES-
sive transportation policy, and rightly so, but that doesn't mean you'll find
a utopia of limitless transit options and constantly free-flowing freeways.
Some parts of the region are ill-served by buses (and not at all by light rail), and if
you need to drive on major highways at peak hours, you will certainly encounter
traffic congestion. If you have moved here from, say, Los Angeles, you may dismiss
Portlanders as lightweights, but the perception that traffic conditions are getting
worse has prompted cries of woe-is-me from commuters and truckers alike. In
fact, traffic congestion has gotten measurably worse over the last two decades.
While the *average* commute is not terrible, at least when measured against bigger
cities, Portland has among the most unreliable commute times in the country,
according to a 2013 study by Texas A&M. For example, a commute that takes 20
minutes under normal conditions can, on any given day and often for no apparent
reason, take 45 minutes. The good news, if you want to call it that, is that although
congestion in Portland is getting worse, it is not getting worse as fast as it is in
other cities. That fact may not console you as you sit motionless on Interstate 5 at
5 p.m., but you can take consolation in the thought that traffic should be speeding
along again in an hour or two.

Lots of hand wringing about transportation is going on in the area, particularly about transportation in growing suburban communities, with the transit
boosters facing off against the road builders (and with most people seemingly
in the middle). The perceived problem is in part a deliberate regional choice to
preserve existing neighborhoods and expand transit options rather than build
big new freeways. The proposed Mount Hood Freeway, which would have oblit-
erated many neighborhoods in Southeast Portland (along with 1% of the city's
housing stock), was killed off in the 1970s. The money that would have gone
toward freeway construction was diverted to other projects instead, most notably
the Eastside MAX project. The prevailing anti-freeway ethos means that roadway

construction has not kept pace with population growth; instead of drastically expanding freeway capacity, Portland's transportation planners have tinkered with the system, for example adding metered on-ramps to smooth the flow of merging traffic. At the same time, most highway engineers will tell you that freeway capacity fills up shortly after it is created, and the result is that Portland's rush hour features congested four- and six-lane freeways instead of congested ten- or twelve-lane freeways.

For several years, the regional government, Metro, has been working on a comprehensive transportation plan to figure out how to accommodate the 725,000 newcomers it predicts will arrive by 2035. This new plan should help determine what the future mix of transportation options should be, whether and where to expand highways, and how to deal with aging transportation infrastructure. While you may not be in a position to determine the region's transportation future, as a newcomer you at least have the chance to influence your personal transportation future: if you don't want to spend a lot of time in traffic, consider living close to your workplace or someplace where you're likely to have access to convenient public transportation. If you choose to commute across the metropolitan area, or to live in an outlying area and work in Portland, accept that traffic congestion is not likely to improve much in the future. Good luck with those gas prices, too.

BY CAR

The U.S. Census Bureau estimated in 2014 that 59.5% of workers living in the city of Portland commuted to work by car, alone. The figure for the metro area as a whole is closer to 70%. That percentage seems to have declined slightly, and it's lower than in some other metropolitan areas, but the fact remains that most people in the Portland area get around primarily by car.

MAJOR FREEWAYS

As you get to know Portland, you'll find alternatives to the freeways, highways, and major thoroughfares (unless you have to cross a bridge, in which case your options are limited). Until then, here are some of the major traffic arteries.

- **Interstate 5** is the main north-south highway artery, not just for the Portland area, but for the entire West Coast. It travels through the southern suburbs and Southwest Portland, crosses the Willamette at the south end of downtown, and runs along the east bank of the river, then due north through North Portland and across the Columbia River into Vancouver. The northbound stretch of I-5 north of downtown during the evening commute is typically the most congested section of highway in the metro area.
- **Interstate 84** (the Banfield Freeway), the main east-west artery on the east side, runs from Interstate 5 just across the river from downtown Portland to outer

Northeast Portland, through Fairview, Wood Village, and Troutdale, into the Columbia River Gorge, and ultimately on to Idaho. The I-5/I-84 interchange is often extremely congested.

- The **Sunset Highway** is the name for US Highway 26 west of downtown Portland. It runs over the West Hills at Sylvan and skirts the northern fringes of Beaverton and Hillsboro before losing its freeway characteristics and continuing on to the coast. According to the Oregon Department of Transportation, traffic on the Sunset is the most inconsistent in the area: one day, the commute is relatively free-flowing, and the next day it's an ever-living nightmare. During peak hours, the latter condition is more common than the former. Be aware that east of I-405, US 26 is not a freeway; it crosses the Ross Island Bridge to Southeast Portland and becomes Powell Boulevard. At the eastern edge of Gresham, it again becomes a limited-access highway—the Mount Hood Highway—and runs to Sandy and eventually continues (as a regular highway) over the shoulder of Mount Hood to Central Oregon.
- **Interstate 405** (technically the Stadium Freeway, although you'll rarely hear it called anything other than 405) loops around the west side of downtown Portland. In its short existence it branches off of Interstate 5 just south of downtown, connects with the Sunset Highway, skirts downtown, the Pearl District, and the Northwest Industrial District, crosses over the Willamette on the Fremont Bridge, and reconnects with I-5 north of the I-84 interchange.
- **Interstate 205** is the closest thing Portland has to a beltway (albeit only a half-beltway). This 37-mile eastern alternate to I-5 branches off that highway in Tualatin, loops through West Linn and Oregon City, and travels north through Clackamas and East Portland before passing near the airport and crossing over the Columbia into eastern Vancouver. It eventually rejoins I-5 in Salmon Creek, Washington. I-205 is a useful bypass if you're traveling north or south through the metro area and you want to avoid downtown, although the I-5 through route encompasses a shorter distance. I-205 is officially named the War Veterans Memorial Freeway, but almost no one ever calls it that.
- **Highway 217** connects the Sunset Highway north of Beaverton with Interstate 5 in Tigard. Traffic is often stop-and-go here, even on weekends, and the short distances between on- and off-ramps tend to exacerbate congestion.
- **Washington State Highway 14** runs from downtown Vancouver east along the Columbia River to Camas, and continues into the Gorge as a two-lane highway.
- Some non-freeway major arteries include the **Milwaukie Expressway** (Highway 224), which links Milwaukie and Clackamas; **McLoughlin Boulevard** (Highway 99E), which runs from Southeast Portland through Milwaukie to Oregon City; **Pacific Highway** (Highway 99W), which connects Tigard and Southwest Portland with Yamhill County; **Highway 30**, which runs from Northwest Portland north to Linnton, St. Helens, and ultimately Astoria; and **Washington State Highway 500**, a major east-west arterial in northern Vancouver.

MAJOR BRIDGES

If you need to cross either the Willamette River or the Columbia River, the bridges can be a major chokepoint. There are currently no tolls for any metro-area bridges, although tolling is being considered for whatever new bridge might one day be built across the Columbia.

COLUMBIA RIVER

Only two bridges cross the Columbia in the Portland area.

- The **Interstate Bridge** carries I-5 over the Columbia between Portland and Vancouver. It has no shoulders, and its drawbridge is occasionally raised to allow ship traffic to pass. Plans to replace the bridge with a new multi-modal span at an estimated cost of several billion dollars, known as the Columbia River Crossing project, or CRC, died (for the time being) in 2013 for lack of funding.
- Interstate 205 crosses the river at the **Glenn Jackson Bridge** east of the airport.

WILLAMETTE RIVER

Several bridges span the river in or near downtown Portland. From north to south, the **Broadway**, **Steel**, **Burnside**, **Morrison**, **Hawthorne**, and **Ross Island** bridges carry local traffic between the east side neighborhoods and downtown. With the exception of the Ross Island, all of these bridges are drawbridges of one kind or another, and passing barge or other boat traffic can cause auto traffic backups; the Hawthorne Bridge, with a lower road deck, tends to get raised more often than the others. Two double-decker freeway bridges also bracket the downtown waterfront. At the south end, Interstate 5 crosses the river on the hulking, unlovely **Marquam Bridge**, which has the redeeming quality of offering an excellent view of downtown. The much more elegant **Fremont Bridge** carries I-405 over the river at the north end of downtown.

Tilikum Crossing, a new bridge between the Ross Island and the Marquam bridges, is scheduled to open in fall 2015. The Tilikum will carry light rail trains, streetcars, buses, bikes, pedestrians, and emergency vehicles, but will be closed to private cars and trucks.

The only road bridge over the Willamette downstream (north) of the Fremont Bridge is the **St. Johns Bridge**, a beautiful suspension bridge opened in 1931 that connects the St. Johns neighborhood of North Portland with the Linnton neighborhood on the west bank. The new **Sauvie Island Bridge** spans Multnomah Channel north of Linnton.

South of downtown, the narrow, aging **Sellwood Bridge** links Sellwood on the east bank with Macadam Avenue (Highway 43) south of the Johns Landing area. After years of planning, the Sellwood Bridge is being replaced with a new structure in the same location; the new bridge is scheduled to open in fall 2015. Upstream (south) of the city of Portland, three other road bridges cross the river in the metro area—the **Boone Bridge** for I-5 at Wilsonville and the **I-205 (George Abernethy)** and **Highway 43** bridges between West Linn and Oregon City.

The **Canby Ferry** (toll required) shuttles passenger vehicles (and passengers) across the river north of Canby.

TRAFFIC REPORTS

Most Portland radio and television stations provide frequent traffic updates during morning and evening rush hours, but you'll need to know the nicknames of area highways to make heads or tails of the information. (See "Major Highways" and "Major Bridges" above.) Frequent bottlenecks with non-obvious meanings include "Delta Park," meaning the section of I-5 just south of the Interstate Bridge in North Portland; the "Tunnel," where Highway 26 (a.k.a. the Sunset Highway) passes through the Vista Ridge Tunnel just west of downtown; and the "Terwilliger curves" (or often just "the curves"), the stretch of Interstate 5 south of downtown where the highway goes around a series of relatively sharp curves near the Terwilliger Boulevard exit. (The latter location, where the speed limit drops from 55 to 50, is reputed to have the highest traffic accident rate of any spot on Interstate 5 between Canada and Mexico.)

The Oregon Department of Transportation's **tripcheck.org** website has a map showing current freeway speeds, construction, and expected delays; you can also check out the view from one of ODOT's many strategically placed highway cameras. Across the Columbia River, the Washington State Department of Transportation posts traffic information at www.wsdot.wa.gov/traffic. A new Google Maps service shows real-time traffic conditions. Go to maps.google.com, type in the location you're interested in (e.g., Beaverton), and click on the "Traffic" button in the upper right corner of the map. Various color codes indicate current speeds: green means more than 50 mph, orange 25–50 mph, red means pretty darn slow, and gray denotes a lack of data. In general, the evening commute is slightly worse than the morning commute, but freeways are typically free-flowing by 7 p.m.

PARKING

Street parking is free in most suburban communities, except in a few older commercial districts that still have street meters. In Portland, you'll have to pay to park downtown and in the Pearl District, Old Town/Chinatown, the South Waterfront neighborhood, and in parts of Northwest Portland and a few sections of the Inner East Side, such as the Lloyd District/Rose Quarter neighborhood. Some neighborhoods require parking permits; if you don't live or work in the neighborhood, you'll be limited to two hours or so of free parking. (See **Getting Settled** for details.)

Most street meters in downtown Portland and other close-in neighborhoods have been replaced by high-tech, solar-powered SmartMeters. Look for a Smart-Meter at the center of the block instead of next to your parking space; to pay, you select the amount of time you plan to park (up to the maximum time allowed) and insert cash, a credit or debit card, or a reusable smart card (available from various vendors). There is a $1 minimum charge for credit and debit cards. The machine spits out a receipt, which you then set gingerly in place between the glass and the weatherstripping on the inside of the door window on the sidewalk side of your car, making sure the print is facing the exterior. Try to avoid either jamming the receipt so deep that it disappears into the window well or placing it so precariously that it drops off into the vehicle interior when you shut the door. The receipt shows the expiration time; if you return to your car with time remaining, you can park in another spot until time is up. (Just be sure the receipt is still on the sidewalk side of the car.)

Parking garages are abundant downtown and in the Pearl District. Around the periphery of downtown and in Old Town/Chinatown, surface parking lots predominate. Many lots cater to commuters and charge relatively high rates for short-term parking on weekdays, but the city-owned **Smart Park** garages (www.portlandonline.com/smartpark/) charge low hourly rates for three hours or less, and many downtown merchants will validate parking for two hours with a minimum purchase. You can find Smart Park garages in the following locations:

- SW 1st Ave at Jefferson St
- SW 3rd Ave at Alder St
- SW 4th Ave at Yamhill St
- SW 10th Ave at Yamhill St
- O'Bryant Square, SW Stark St at 9th Ave
- NW Davis St at Naito Pkwy

Star Park (www.star-park.com) also has several lots of its own with reasonable hourly rates.

TOWED VEHICLES

Hope that your car is never towed from a parking lot against your will. The City of Portland imposes some minor regulations on towing companies—the so-called "temper fee," imposed on people who manifest anything more than mild bemusement when they see their car being towed away, is not allowed, for example—and 2007 state legislation imposed a few obligations on predatory towers (see http://www.doj.state.or.us/consumer/pages/towing.aspx), but beyond those limited protections you're stuck with the whims of what former Portland City Commissioner Randy Leonard, a man no stranger to temper tantrums, once called "a cowboy industry with few rules."

DRIVING RULES AND HABITS

Oregon and Washington don't have many unusual traffic rules. Northwesterners are generally pretty good about following rules of the road—crazy drivers are invariably dismissed as California transplants—and you may be pleasantly surprised at the ease with which you can merge onto highways. Surveys repeatedly find Portland motorists to be among the most courteous drivers in the country, based on assessments of the frequency of road-rage behaviors in major U.S. cities. (*Portlandia* satirized the painfully polite Portland driver in the "No, you go" sketch involving two drivers at a four-way intersection; each driver insists that the other go first, leading to an hours-long stalemate.) At the same time, polite driving doesn't necessarily equate to competent driving; for example, you may be infuriated by cars that travel in the fast (passing) lane going just below the speed limit, even when there is nothing in front of the car and nothing preventing the car from moving into the slow lane. The single car lane in each direction on the downtown transit mall also confuses many people — disproportionately people in cars with Washington plates. (Hint: if you're in a lane that says "Buses Only" or are driving on light rail tracks, you shouldn't be there.) Many drivers turning left at signals seem disinclined to move forward into the intersection before a gap in the traffic materializes, only to speed away when the light turns yellow, leaving the cars behind them to wait for a new cycle. There are just some regional habits you'll have to learn to live with. And, as elsewhere in the country, you'll see plenty of people flouting state laws prohibiting talking on a cell phone or texting while driving.

Be aware of one-way streets, especially in downtown Portland. Red-light and speed cameras are used in Portland and some surrounding jurisdictions, so keep your speed down and don't try to run yellow lights. Don't attempt to pump your own gas in Oregon, where self-help of that kind is illegal. (Oregon and New Jersey are the only states that ban self-service at retail gas stations.) In winter, you are required to carry chains or have traction tires—generally studded tires that tear up roads and make a distinctive clacking sound on dry pavement—when you travel through snow zones. (Snow zones include most of the state's mountainous regions, but even some urban roads, like West Burnside Street as it crosses the West Hills, or SW Sam Jackson Park Road as it winds upward to OHSU, meet the definition during rare snowy weather.) During ice or snow storms, chains or traction tires may be required (although four-wheel-drive and all-wheel-drive vehicles with all-weather tires are usually exempt from this requirement except when conditions are unusually severe).

CAR SHARING

If you want the freedom of driving a car without the trouble and expense of owning one, consider joining a car-sharing service.

- **Car2Go** (877-488-4224, www.car2go.com) offers two-seater Smart cars for $0.41 per minute or $15/hour; the company's cars are ubiquitous in the city center.
- **Zipcar** (866-494-7227, www.zipcar.com) places vehicles in strategic locations throughout Portland and in some suburban communities. Zipcar members determine their monthly driving needs, and choose an hourly or monthly rate

plan; costs for the "occasional driver" plan begin at $8 per hour. The company pays for gas, insurance, and maintenance.

CARPOOLING

Local governments offer significant incentives to employers to arrange carpools or vanpools. If you're interested in carpooling but your employer doesn't sponsor carpools, and you don't already know someone you can share a ride in with, visit **Drive Less Connect** (www.drivelessconnect.com) or, in Southwest Washington, the **Clark Country Trip reduction Office** (360-487-7733, www.clarkcommute. com) for online ride matching. If you can get 5 to 15 carpool buddies together, and your group meets some basic requirements (e.g., you commute at least 10 miles or through a congested corridor), Metro's **VanPool** program (http://www.oregon-metro.gov/tools-living/getting-around/share-ride/vanpool) will subsidize part of the cost to lease a van. **C-Tran** has a similar vanpool service for Clark County commuters; visit http://www.c-tran.com/vanpool.html or call 360-906-7510. (C-Tran's program currently has a waiting list.)

Carpools qualify for reduced parking rates in designated spots in downtown Portland, the Lloyd District, and the Pearl District. The only HOV (High-Occupancy Vehicle) or carpool lane in the Portland area is on I-5 northbound north of downtown, and occupancy restrictions apply from 3 p.m. to 6 p.m. only.

CAR RENTAL

The following car rental companies have multiple locations in the metropolitan area. For smaller companies and airport-only options, check online or look in the Yellow Pages under "Auto Renting."
- **Avis**, 800-633-3469, www.avis.com
- **Budget**, 218-7992, www.budget.com
- **Dollar**, 800-800-4000, www.dollar.com
- **Enterprise**, 800-261-7331, www.enterprise.com
- **Hertz**, 800-654-3131, www.hertz.com
- **Thrifty**, 800-334-1705, www.thrifty.com

BY BIKE

Despite its wet, chilly fall and winter weather and hilly terrain in some neighborhoods, Portland is perhaps the most bike-centric large city in America. *Bicycling* magazine and other granters of accolades have repeatedly named Portland the best overall cycling city in the country, and although it's no Amsterdam, Portland is a reasonably easy place to get around by bike. The U.S. Census Bureau estimated in 2014 that 6.1% of Portland commuters traveled by bike, and on a typical weekday some 7,000 to 8,000 bicycles cross into downtown on the Hawthorne Bridge. The city currently has 181 miles of striped bike lanes, 79 miles of bike paths, and 59 miles of "neighborhood greenways"—shared-use city streets with low auto traffic volume and (sometimes) obstacles to through car traffic on which bicycles are given priority. The city has (unfunded) plans to triple this mileage by 2030, and suburban areas already add many more miles of trails and bike lanes to the total.

If you're interested in commuting or otherwise getting around by bicycle, even on a part-time basis, a host of organizations stand ready to help. The Portland **Bureau of Transportation** (503-823-5490, www.gettingaroundportland. org) provides extensive bicycling information, both online and in hard copy, and holds frequent workshops designed to inform and encourage nascent cyclists. The following nonprofits are also excellent resources for actual and prospective bicyclists:

- **Bicycle Transportation Alliance**, 618 NW Glisan St #401, 503-226-0676, www.btaoregon.org
- **Community Cycling Center**, 1805 NE 2nd Ave, 503-288-8864, www.communitycyclingcenter.org
- **Shift**, www.shift2bikes.org

The Portland Office of Transportation publishes several neighborhood bike maps, as well as the fairly comprehensive (and free) citywide *Portland by Bicycle* map and guide, which includes an inset map of Beaverton and Vancouver bike routes. These maps are available in hard copy or as PDFs at www.portlandoregon. gov/transportation/39402. Multnomah (503-988-5050), Washington (800-537-3149), Clackamas (503-742-4500), and Clark (360-397-6118) Counties all publish county-level bike maps, but the best region-wide map is *Bike There*, available for $9 at most bike shops, bookstores, and some natural foods supermarkets and co-ops. A free map of Vancouver bike routes is available from the city's Transportation Services office; call 360-487-7700 to request one or search for "Vancouver bike map" on www.cityofvancouver.us. Many other suburban communities publish their own bike maps. For something higher-tech, try www.bycycle.org or Google Maps, both of which offers online bike directions. For the Google option, go to maps.google.com, input your desired start and end points for directions, and click on the cyclist icon. Be aware that these services will not always send you on the most bike-appropriate route, so use your judgment.

Many businesses have bicycle parking for patrons and/or employees, and some downtown parking garages have free covered bike parking. For information about bike locker rentals downtown and in the Lloyd District, call 503-823-5345. In addition, bike storage lockers are available at some transit centers and MAX stations; call 503-962-2104 for details or visit www.trimet.org/howtoride/bikes/lockersavailable.htm.

Two-wheeled, single-seat bicycles are allowed on all public buses and light rail trains in the Portland area, as well as WES Commuter Rail, the Portland Streetcar, and the Aerial Tram. (Tandems, trikes, rickshaws and the like are not permitted.) Buses have a fold-down front rack with space for two bikes, and trains have designated areas for bicycles. For details on how to take your bike on public transit, call 503-238-RIDE or visit www.trimet.org/howtoride/bikes/.

BICYCLE SAFETY

The Oregon Department of Transportation produces the *Oregon Bicyclist Manual*. While at times overly basic—the first of the "Four Basic Principles" presented in the manual is "Maintain Control of Your Bicycle," and the list of "Practices to Avoid" includes the helpful hint, "Don't dart out suddenly into the roadway"—the booklet does contain a useful rundown of rules of the road for bicyclists. The manual is available for download online from the DOT's Bicycle and Pedestrian Program (visit www.oregon.gov/ODOT/HWY/BIKEPED and click on the "Publications" link), or you can order a copy by calling 503-986-4175. The Portland Office of Transportation publishes the slightly less patronizing *A Guide to Your Ride*.

Vancouver is the only city in the metro area that requires bicyclists of all ages to wear helmets. Although helmets are not required for cyclists 16 years and older in Oregon, you would be very unwise not to wear one. (Some hipsters, as well as a contingent of people who have had bicycling thrust upon them following a DUII conviction, seem to think that helmets look uncool, but do you know what else is uncool? Permanent brain damage.) For more information about helmets, visit the **Bicycle Helmet Safety Institute** website (www.helmets.org).

ROADSIDE ASSISTANCE

Roadside assistance for bicyclists? You bet! **Better World Club** (866-238-1137, www.betterworldclub.com) has offered bike roadside assistance for several years; bicycle-only plans start at about $40 per year. **AAA of Oregon and Southern Idaho** (800-444-8091, www.oregon.aaa.com) joined the bandwagon in 2009 and now offers bicycle service to its Plus-level members; AAA does not have a bike-only plan.

WALKING AND SKATEBOARDING

Much of Portland is ideal walking territory, with plentiful sidewalks and short blocks. The **Office of Transportation** publishes nifty maps of walking routes in different parts of the city; visit www.gettingaroundportland.org for details. If your own two feet aren't good enough for you, it is legal to skate, skateboard, or ride a (non-motorized) scooter on any street or sidewalk in Portland, except downtown, where you'll have to stick to streets. (Certain downtown streets have been designated as skate routes.) Visit www.portlandoregon.gov/transportation/article/405782 for more information.

PUBLIC TRANSPORTATION

TriMet (503-238-RIDE, www.trimet.org) is by far the largest transit agency in Oregon. TriMet operates a bus network that serves most of the Portland metropolitan area, the MAX light rail system, and a single-line, suburban commuter rail service. The system averages more than 300,000 weekday boardings, with over 100 million boardings annually. While those numbers are impressive, whether and how well the system will serve *you* depends on where you live, where you need to go, when you need to depart or arrive, and how much time you have to get there. Recent service cuts, fare increases, and the elimination of a fareless zone downtown have caused ridership to decline slightly over the last few years.

TriMet has scrapped its traditionally zone-based fare scheme, and now a single fare is valid for the entire system. At press time, a single two-hour ticket costs $2.50 and an all-day ticket is $5. Youths under 18 (or in high school) pay $1.65 for a two hour ticket, honored citizens (i.e., the elderly and disabled) pay $1, and children under 7 ride free. Fares generally increase each September.

You can pay a single cash fare or buy an all-day ticket when you board a bus; bills are accepted, but exact change is required. Tickets are also available from the self-service vending machines at MAX stations; some of these machines accept credit cards. You can buy books of tickets and monthly passes at the **TriMet Ticket Office** at Pioneer Courthouse Square downtown (701 SW 6th Avenue) or at many area supermarkets and convenience stores. You can also order tickets and passes online at www.trimet.org. TriMet now offers mobile ticketing apps for both iPhone and Android devices, and these phone-based tickets are becoming increasingly popular (and less subject to glitches than during their initial rollout).

From 1975 until January 3, 2010, all public transportation was free within an area known as Fareless Square, which ultimately encompassed a 330-square-block area that included most of downtown Portland between the Interstate 405 loop and the Willamette River. Budgetary constraints and anecdotes of drug dealing and other criminal activity on buses in the fareless zone, combined with the opening of new light rail service on 5th and 6th Avenues, prompted TriMet to eliminate Fareless Square and replace it with a **Fareless Rail Zone**, which was itself discontinued in 2012. A fareless zone no longer exists for any form of TriMet transportation. This fact still confuses tourists using out-of-date guidebooks, but confusion doesn't count as a valid fare.

Ride Connection (503-226-0700, www.rideconnection.org) facilitates travel for older adults and people with disabilities, both by helping with independent travel on public transit and by providing public transit alternatives.

Other regional transit agencies serve southwest Washington and outlying areas in Clackamas County. These agencies currently operate buses only; see "Bus" below for specifics.

LIGHT RAIL

The **Metropolitan Area Express (MAX)** light rail system currently has four lines with a total of 52 miles of track, with those numbers set to increase to five lines and nearly 60 miles of track in late 2015. MAX is the backbone of the transit system in that, although light rail accounts for about a bit more than a third of all trips on TriMet, most bus lines connect with MAX. (Some riders have complained that what was formerly a single bus trip now requires a transfer to MAX.) See pages 538–539 for a system map.

The 33-mile **Blue Line** runs from Hillsboro in the west to Gresham in the east, via Beaverton, downtown Portland, and Northeast Portland. The eastern portion of this line, from Portland to Gresham, was the region's first light rail line when it opened in 1986. The Westside MAX opened in 1998. If, for some reason, you wanted to ride the line from end to end, it would take about an hour and a half.

The **Red Line** serves Portland International Airport. This line, opened in 2001, shares tracks with the Blue Line from Beaverton Transit Center to Gateway Transit Center in Northeast Portland, then runs the 5.5 miles to the airport on a spur line. It takes about 40 minutes to get to the airport terminal from downtown Portland.

The **Yellow Line** runs from Portland State University along the downtown transit mall (5th and 6th Avenues) to Union Station, crosses the Willamette on the Steel Bridge to the Rose Quarter, then heads north along Interstate Avenue to the Expo Center in North Portland, just south of the Columbia River. It takes about half an hour to travel the length of the line.

The **Green Line**, opened in September 2009, runs from Portland State University to Clackamas Town Center. The line shares track with Yellow Line trains in downtown Portland from PSU to Union Station, crosses the Steel Bridge (like all MAX trains currently) and uses the Blue Line/Red Line tracks between the Rose Quarter and Gateway Transit Center; the line then branches off and runs south from Gateway to Clackamas Town Center along Interstate 205. The journey from downtown to Clackamas takes about 40 minutes.

The 7.3-mile **Orange Line** from downtown, across the new Tilikum Crossing bridge, and through Southeast Portland to Milwaukie and Oak Grove, is scheduled to open in the fall of 2015.

A lack of funding, combined with opposition in some suburban communities, means that further expansion of the light rail system is in doubt, at least in the immediate future. An extension of the Yellow Line to Vancouver, Washington, was rejected by Clark County voters. Plans for other lines, including a line along Barbur Boulevard to Tigard and a Blue Line extension to Forest Grove, among others, are still ongoing, but construction is a decade or more away and the result (if any) might be a dedicated bus lane rather than a rail line.

COMMUTER RAIL

The **Westside Express Service (WES)**, a 14.7-mile commuter rail line from Wilsonville to central Beaverton, opened in 2009. This suburb-to-suburb line, one of the few such lines in the country, makes intermediate stops in Tualatin, Tigard, and southeast Beaverton. It operates during weekday rush hours only. The train connects with MAX in Beaverton, and offers free WiFi and reclining seats, but the line has been something of a fiscal disaster: the Colorado railcar manufacturer TriMet selected to build the trains went out of business mid-project, and ridership, although increasing, has been well below projections, with only about 2,000 riders per weekday using the service. For more information visit www.trimet.org/wes/.

BUS

TriMet runs 80 bus lines, including 13 "frequent service" lines, through the metro area. Almost all buses run to or from either downtown Portland or one of 16 regional transit centers. Bus service runs the gamut from frequent and excellent to nonexistent: lines with heavy ridership, or that serve major corridors, run at least every 15 minutes on weekdays (and more often during rush hour), while other lines provide commuter service only, sometimes in only one direction. Most bus lines fall somewhere in between these service extremes. Major service cuts in September 2009 eliminated some routes and reduced frequency or days of service on many others. These changes are likely to be permanent as the agency continues to focus on rail-based projects to the detriment of basic bus service.

Most bus stops on "frequent service" lines have printed time point information at the stop, and most major bus stops on other lines have schedules posted for the lines that stop there. Every official stop has a stop identification number. In theory, you can obtain up-to-the-minute arrival information by calling 503-238-RIDE (503-238-7433) and entering the stop ID number. If your bus is stalled or broken down somewhere, however, it can be "arriving in three minutes" for half an hour or more. TriMet makes its system information available on an open-source basis, and dozens of third-party programmers have created useful applications for transit tracking from smartphones. Visit www.trimet.org/apps for details.

In downtown Portland, most bus lines run down the recently redeveloped transit mall (southbound on 5th Avenue and northbound on 6th Avenue).

In addition to TriMet, the following transit agencies provide bus service in the Portland metropolitan area:

- **C-TRAN**, 360-695-0123, www.c-tran.com, provides bus service in Clark County, including commuter service between Vancouver and downtown Portland as well as to the Expo Center and Parkrose MAX stations.
- **Canby Area Transit**, 503-266-4022, www.ci.canby.or.us/transportation/CAThomepage.htm, provides service within Canby and between Canby and Oregon City and Woodburn (via Aurora).

- **Columbia County Rider**, 503-366-0159, www.columbiacountyrider.com, provides shuttle service between Scappoose, St. Helens, and Rainier, and limited commuter service between downtown Portland and St. Helens and Scappoose. Buses also connect St. Helens/Scappoose with Portland Community College's Rock Creek campus, Vernonia with Hillsboro and Beaverton, and Rainier with Longview/Kelso, Washington.
- **Salem-Keizer Transit**, 503-588-2877, www.cherriots.org, runs buses within Salem and adjacent Keizer, and to some outlying areas, and operates an express bus route to Wilsonville and another to Grande Ronde and the Spirit Mountain Casino.
- **Sandy Area Metro (SAM)**, 503-668-3466, www.ci.sandy.or.us/transit, runs buses within Sandy and links Sandy to Gresham (and therefore the MAX light rail system) and Estacada.
- The **South Clackamas Transportation District**, 503-632-7000, www.southclackamastransportation.com, serves Molalla and runs between Molalla and Canby, and to Clackamas Community College.
- **South Metro Area Regional Transit (SMART)**, 503-682-7790, www.ridesmart.com, serves Wilsonville. In addition to fareless routes within the city, SMART runs buses that connect Wilsonville with Portland, Tualatin, Salem, and Canby.
- **Yamhill County Transit Area**, 503-474-4910, www.yctransitarea.org, provides limited bus service within Yamhill County and between Yamhill County and Salem, Sherwood, Tigard, and Hillsboro.

PORTLAND STREETCAR

The Portland Streetcar (www.portlandstreetcar.org) runs desultorily on two close-in lines. The modern, primarily Czech-made trains are the pokey little puppies of the transit system: they get you there, but at a leisurely speed. The NS Line runs between Northwest Portland and the South Waterfront district, via the Pearl District, downtown Portland, and Portland State University. The newer CL line runs from downtown Portland over the Broadway Bridge to the Lloyd District, then down Martin Luther King Jr. Boulevard (southbound) and Grand Avenue (northbound) to the Oregon Museum of Science and Industry (OMSI). In late 2015, an extension of this line will run from OMSI over the Tilikum Bridge to connect with the NS Line in South Waterfront. It takes just over half an hour (more or less) to ride either line from one end to another. Although the lines are owned by the city of Portland, TriMet and some C-TRAN tickets and passes are valid on the streetcar. A streetcar-only fare is $1 for two hours. An annual streetcar-only pass costs $200.

Streetcar lines have also been proposed for various other routes, including Burnside and Couch streets, Hawthorne Boulevard, Powell Boulevard, and Northeast Broadway, but budgetary obstacles are likely to doom or delay any new routes for at least a few years.

PORTLAND AERIAL TRAM

Portland's sleek, expensive aerial tram opened in 2007 to fanfare and criticism. Two futuristic, Swiss-made silver pods travel the 3,000 linear (and 500 vertical) feet between the Oregon Health & Science University (OHSU) campus high on "Pill Hill" and the Center for Health and Healing in the rapidly developing South Waterfront district. Critics include many neighborhood residents, who do not appreciate tram cars passing back and forth high overhead (thus giving passengers birds'-eye views of back yards), and fiscal watchdogs, who note that the tram cost $57 million, more than triple the original estimated cost. (OHSU picked up the bulk of the cost, with the city of Portland kicking in several million dollars.) The tram is not really a convenient transit option unless you're headed to or from OHSU, but on a clear day it offers a heck of a view.

Tram tickets currently cost $4.35 round-trip; OHSU staff, patients with appointments, and children six and under ride free. Tickets are only sold at the lower station. (It's an open secret that this system results in a useful loophole: If you board at the top and ride down one-way, as a practical matter you won't need to pay, although technically you are required to have a valid ticket.) An annual pass costs $100. Although the tram is nominally part of Portland's public transit system, regular TriMet tickets and transfers are not valid (although monthly and annual TriMet and C-TRAN passes and annual Portland Streetcar passes are accepted). The tram runs weekdays from 5:30 a.m. to 9:30 p.m. and on Saturdays from 9 a.m. to 5 p.m.; the tram operates on Sunday afternoons from 1 p.m. to 5 p.m. during the summer only. Bikes are permitted and, as one would expect from a mode of transport that serves a hospital, the Aerial Tram is fully accessible. For more information, visit www.gobytram.org.

PARK & RIDES

There are more than 60 park & ride lots in TriMet service territory. You can park at these lots for free (usually for up to 24 hours) and take a bus or MAX train to your destination. Note that some of the more popular park & ride lots fill up early, and you have no guarantee of finding a parking space. Also, many of these lots are provided by churches or other private entities and are intended for weekday use only. For a list of park & ride locations, visit www.trimet.org/parkandride/, or call 503-238-RIDE. C-TRAN has six park & rides in Clark County; visit www.c-tran.com or call 360-695-0123 for locations.

TAXIS

Unless you're downtown or at the airport, you'll probably need to telephone for a cab rather than hail one on the street. The following are the major (but not the only) Portland taxi companies:
- **Broadway Cab**, 503-333-3333, www.broadwaycab.com

- **Green Cab and Green Shuttle**, 503-234-1414, www.portlandgreencabtaxishuttle.com
- **Radio Cab**, 503-227-1212, www.radiocab.net
- **Union Cab**, 503-222-2222, www.unioncabpdx.com

At press time, car-share services such as Uber and Lyft do not operate in Portland (and are in fact illegal), although these companies have begun to lobby city hall for legitimacy. In November 2014, Uber began serving the cities of Beaverton, Gresham, Hillsboro, and Tigard.

REGIONAL/NATIONAL TRAVEL

AIR TRAVEL

Portland International Airport (503-460-4234, 877-739-4636, www.pdx.com) is one of the country's more pleasant major airports; its airport code, PDX, is often used as shorthand for the entire Portland metropolitan area. The airport is located in northeast Portland, just south of the Columbia River. There are several concourses for passenger flights, but only one terminal.

The check-in and security screening process is usually not the nightmare it can be at some airports, but the official advice is to arrive at least two hours before your flight is scheduled to depart. In most cases, you won't need nearly that much time unless you're traveling at peak hours, but at least the airport shops and restaurants are above average, and in many cases are outposts of local businesses like Powell's Books, The Real Mother Goose, and Elephant's Deli. You'll often encounter live entertainment at PDX—pianists, guitarists, singers, perhaps even a harpist or roaming accordion player. You can also hook up to free wireless Internet service in most parts of the airport, or let the kids work off pre-flight energy at one of the two play areas in the terminal.

Members of certain airline mileage plans, travelers with special needs, and travelers going from Portland to Seattle can go through an "express lane" at the security checkpoint. Most airlines also participate in the TSAPre√expedited screening program. Security requirements are constantly in flux, so check with your airline for the latest information on check-in procedures, availability of curbside check-in, and identification requirements. For up-to-date regulations on the handling of liquids, electronics, shoes, and other potentially dangerous objects, visit the **Transportation Security Administration** website (www.tsa.gov).

Because Portland is not a national hub, no one airline dominates the market; however, PDX serves as a regional hub for Alaska Airlines, which together with Southwest and Delta, carries about two-thirds of all passengers who come through the airport. There are nonstop flights from Portland to most major metropolitan areas in the United States and to most mid-size cities (and some small cities) in the West; in addition, there are nonstop international flights to Tokyo, Amsterdam,

Guadalajara, Vancouver, and Calgary, and seasonal nonstops to Frankfurt, Reykjavik, Puerto Vallarta, and Los Cabos.

The following airlines serve Portland:

- **Air Canada**, 888-247-2262, www.aircanada.com
- **Alaska Airlines**, 800-252-7522, www.alaskaair.com
- **American Airlines**, 800-433-7300, www.aa.com
- **Condor**, 800-524-6975, www.condor.com
- **Delta Air Lines**, 800-221-1212, www.delta.com
- **Frontier Airlines**, 800-432-1359, www.flyfrontier.com
- **Hawaiian Airlines**, 800-367-5320, www.hawaiianair.com
- **Icelandair**, 800-223-5500, www.icelandair.com
- **JetBlue Airways**, 800-538-2583, www.jetblue.com
- **SeaPort Airlines**, 888-573-2767, www.seaportair.com
- **Southwest Airlines**, 800-435-9792, www.southwest.com
- **Spirit Airlines**, 001-401-2200, www.spirit.com
- **United Airlines**, 800-864-8331, www.united.com
- **US Airways**, 800-428-4322, www.usairways.com
- **Virgin America**, 877-359-8474, www.virginamerica.com
- **Volaris**, 866-988-3527, www.volaris.com

GETTING TO AND FROM THE AIRPORT

TriMet's Red Line **MAX** (light rail) trains run directly to the terminal; the airport station is just east of baggage claim. At press time, a one-way ticket to or from downtown Portland is $2.50 for adults, and the trip takes about 35 to 40 minutes.

If you're driving, make your way to Interstate 205 and take the exit for Airport Way West, then follow Airport Way to the terminal. Sandy Boulevard makes a good alternative route during the evening rush hour; take Sandy to Northeast 82nd Avenue, and go north to Airport Way. Travel time from downtown Portland is about 20 to 40 minutes, depending on traffic. When it reaches the terminal, the airport roadway splits into two levels: the upper roadway is for departures, and the lower roadway is for arrivals. Stopping is allowed only for active pick-up or drop-off of passengers and loading or unloading luggage. If you need to park, see "Airport Parking" below.

Taxis, door-to-door shuttles, charter buses, long-haul shuttles, and courtesy shuttles for airport hotels, off-airport parking and car rental facilities, and long-term parking lots depart from the lower roadway outside baggage claim. Many downtown hotels offer shuttle service to or from the airport; call ahead for times, costs, and companies. (Transport may be free or at a reduced rate if you are a hotel guest.) For a list of door-to-door shuttle services and other airport transportation options, visit www.portofportland.com/PDX_Grnd_Trnsprtn.aspx or call the airport's ground transportation office at 503-460-4686.

AIRPORT PARKING

The airport **parking garage** is connected to the terminal by tunnels and skyways, so it's convenient for parking when curbside drop-off or pick-up won't do. Parking is $3 per hour; people on expense accounts and other big spenders can park here for $27 per day. People with larger expense accounts and no time to lose can use **Gold Key valet parking** for $10 per hour or $30 per day, with optional car washing and detailing services. Motorcycle and bicycle parking is free. The **long-term parking** garage is next to the short-term garage; it's a longer walk from the terminal, but shuttles run frequently; parking is $21 a day. The red and blue **economy lots** are not walking distance from the terminal; you'll have to rely on the shuttle bus, but parking is only $10 per day. (If you park for a week, the seventh day is free.)

Various **off-airport lots** also serve PDX travelers. You can browse off-airport lots and make parking reservations at www.airportparkingreservations.com; they charge a booking fee on top of the parking cost. In many cases, unless you have a coupon or other discount, the off-airport lots are only marginally cheaper than the official economy lots. (Online searches typically uncover various coupons, with ever-changing promotions, for these lots.) If you have a very early departure or very late arrival, many airport hotels offer hotel and parking packages that often are no more expensive than the cost of a room; you can usually leave your car at the hotel for a week or more. Some (but not all) of these deals are available from www.parksleepfly.com; alternatively, just call an airport hotel directly or visit its website. (See **Temporary Lodgings** for some suggested airport hotels.)

TRAIN

Amtrak passenger trains stop at historic Union Station, just north of downtown at the northern end of Portland's Transit Mall. The popular **Cascades** service (www.amtrakcasacades.com) runs from Eugene to Vancouver, British Columbia, via Seattle. Currently there are four Cascades trains a day in each direction from Portland to Seattle, and two trains in each direction between Portland and Eugene. Scheduled travel time to Seattle is about three-and-a-half to four hours, which is slightly longer than the driving time between the cities if there's no traffic; since the Amtrak train shares tracks with freight trains, the train is subject to delays. Given the likelihood of traffic congestion, however, especially north of Olympia, and the certainty of aggravation, the train is a great alternative to driving (or for that matter, to flying) if you're headed from one downtown to the other. Locally, the Cascades service also stops in Oregon City and in Vancouver, Washington. Two more round-trips per day between Portland and Seattle are scheduled to start in 2017, and planned track improvements should cut travel time between the cities by up to an hour.

The **Coast Starlight** from Seattle to Los Angeles via Oakland passes through Portland once per day in each direction. Just a few years ago, it was not uncommon for the Coast Starlight to arrive 10 hours or more behind schedule, and the train's chronic tardiness gave it the nickname "Starlate." More recently the train's on-time performance has improved. The **Empire Builder** runs once daily to and from Chicago via Spokane, the Idaho panhandle, the southern border of Glacier National Park, various destinations in eastern Montana and North Dakota, Saint Paul, and Milwaukee. The trip takes a minimum of 46 hours, and sleeping compartments and a dining car are available.

For schedules, fare information, and reservations on Amtrak trains, visit www. amtrak.com or call 800-USA-RAIL (800-872-7245). Be sure to ask about promotions and discounts.

INTERCITY BUS

Portland's **Greyhound** terminal (503-243-2361) is located at 550 Northwest Sixth Avenue, just south of Union Station. Greyhound buses can take you from Portland to any major city along the Interstate 5 corridor between Canada and Mexico. Greyhound buses also run east to Spokane via Washington's Tri-Cities, and southeast to Boise, Idaho, and Salt Lake City, via Pendleton. For schedules and reservations visit www.greyhound.com or call the national reservation number, 800-231-2222.

Bolt Bus (877-265-8287, www.boltbus.com), a slightly more upscale brand than its parent company Greyhound (and frankly, what isn't?), runs up to eight trips a day from Portland to Seattle (with continuing service to Vancouver, British Columbia) and two trips a day south to Eugene. Tickets can be as low as $1 (at least one seat per bus trip), and the buses feature Wi-Fi, electric outlets for electronics, and reserved seats.

Additional options for regional intercity bus transport include:

- **Amtrak Thruway** buses (800-872-7245) run south to Salem and Eugene. Tickets for these services can be reserved on the Amtrak website (www.amtrak.com).
- The **Central Oregon Breeze** (800-847-0157, 541-389-7469, cobreeze.com) runs daily buses between Portland and Bend (twice daily in summer).
- **Northwest POINT** (541-484-4100, 800-442-4106) operates Amtrak Thruway buses between Portland and Cannon Beach, Seaside, and Astoria.
- **Valley Retriever** (541-265-2253) connects Portland to Newport via McMinnville, Salem, Albany, and Corvallis.
- **The Wave** (503-815-8283, www.tillamookbus.com) offers twice-a-day trips between Portland and Tillamook, connecting with local coastal bus routes.

MOST PORTLANDERS ARE PROUD OF THEIR CITY'S REPUTATION FOR environmental leadership, and with good reason. Portland regularly garners accolades for its green policies, and the state government is trying hard to establish Oregon as a leader in green business and renewable energy. Of course, not everyone in the area is on board with the whole sustainability thing—we're looking at you, guy in the Hummer with the "I Am the Scourge of Bicycles" bumper sticker—and the very word "sustainability" has been overused (and misused) to the point where it risks losing any specific meaning, or worse, is used as cover for products, projects, and services that upon analysis are not really "sustainable" at all. If you're reading this chapter, however, you're probably interested in reducing your environmental impact. There are plenty of local resources and lots of like-minded people to help you out.

GREENING YOUR HOME

The quickest and easiest way to have a green home is to buy one that is no bigger than you need—smaller homes consume fewer resources—and that is already well-insulated and energy-efficient, that incorporates nontoxic and sustainably produced materials, or that has features like solar-assisted water heating. Since 2007, the local real estate Multiple Listing Service, **RMLS** (www.rmls.com), has allowed prospective home buyers to include green home features in their searches. (This search option is currently only available to licensed real estate agents and other RMLS members.) Assuming you're not lucky enough to move into an existing eco-dwelling, there's plenty you can do to make your home more environmentally friendly.

GREEN REMODELING

Portland's **Bureau of Planning and Sustainability** (1900 SW 4th Avenue, Suite 7100, 503-823-7700, www.portlandoregon.gov/bps/) publishes a *Green Home*

Remodeling Guide, available for download at its website. Other green building materials are also available from the office.

In many cases, the greenest building materials are those that someone else has already used. The **ReBuilding Center** (3625 N. Mississippi Avenue, 503-331-1877, www.rebuildingcenter.org) stocks used building materials that have been donated or salvaged from "deconstructed" buildings. **Habitat ReStore** (10445 SE Cherry Blossom Drive, 503-283-6247; 13475 SW Millikan Way, Beaverton, 503-906-3823; 10811 SE Mill Plain Boulevard, Vancouver, 360-213-1313; www.pdxrestore.org) also sells donated used and new construction materials, and proceeds go to Habitat for Humanity. You might consider poking around the region's architectural salvage stores (see **Shopping for the Home** for listings).

If it's new materials you're after, **Green Depot** (819 SE Taylor Street, 503-222-3881, www.greendepot.com) carries everything from cork and marmoleum flooring to recycled glass tiles, recycled cotton batt insulation, and low-flow plumbing fixtures. If you're doing structural work, consider using green-certified wood products; the **Forest Stewardship Council** (www.fscus.org) is a widely known certification program. Use nontoxic or least-toxic glues and finishes whenever possible; local paint companies **YOLO Colorhouse** (877-493-8276, www.yolocolorhouse.com), **Devine Color** (888-693-3846, www.devinecolor.com), **Miller Paint** (multiple area stores, www.millerpaint.com), and **Rodda Paint** (multiple area stores, www.roddapaint.com) produce quality zero-VOC (volatile organic compounds) and low-VOC paint.

ENERGY EFFICIENCY

Reducing your home's energy consumption, particularly its consumption of energy produced by fossil fuels or other non-renewables, is probably the single most effective way to create a greener home. In most homes, furnaces and air conditioners, appliances, and lighting are the biggest energy hogs, and you'll get the most bang for your buck by weatherizing your home and making these systems work more efficiently. The following steps are typically recommended for boosting your home's energy efficiency:

- Insulate and weatherize your home. Poorly insulated walls, ceilings, and floors allow heated or cooled air to escape from your house, needlessly raising your energy use (and energy bill). Also seal ductwork, insulate hot water pipes in non-conditioned spaces, and seal or caulk leaks around doors, windows, pipes, vents, attics, and crawlspaces. Replace or repair leaky old windows. These steps will also reduce drafts and increase comfort levels in your home.
- Upgrade your heating and cooling systems. Old furnaces and air conditioning units are usually much less efficient than new models. Once you've insulated and weatherized your home, consider replacing old units with new, efficient units, and make sure that they are properly sized for your home. A program-

mable thermostat can also help reduce energy consumption by adjusting the inside temperature automatically when you're at work or asleep.

- Upgrade inefficient appliances. Replacing old, inefficient washing machines, dishwashers, water heaters, and especially refrigerators with more efficient models can have a major effect on your energy consumption (and, in the case of washing machines and dishwashers, on your water consumption, too).
- Install efficient lighting. Compact fluorescent light bulbs use 75% less energy and last up to ten times longer than standard incandescent bulbs. They also generate less heat. For an assurance of quality, choose ENERGY STAR® bulbs.

Fortunately, you don't have to figure out how to accomplish these things on your own. **Energy Trust of Oregon** (866-368-7878, www.energytrust.org) can help make your home more energy-efficient. They offer cash incentives to help you pay for energy-saving improvements, and their website includes a free online home energy use analyzer tool. You can also schedule a free on-site home energy review (complete with installation of complimentary compact fluorescent light bulbs and low-flow showerheads). For a comprehensive whole-house energy assessment and energy recommendations, consider hiring an Energy Trust–certified contractor to do a Home Performance with ENERGY STAR analysis.

Energy Trust provides energy efficiency services and cash incentives for Oregon customers of Portland General Electric, Pacific Power, NW Natural, and Cascade Natural Gas. Many other utilities offer similar services and incentives. When you're ready to start investing in energy efficiency, low-cost loans and utility or manufacturer rebates are available for some projects, and in many cases the **Oregon Department of Energy** (503-378-4040, 800-221-8035, www.oregon.gov/energy) offers state tax credits as well. Federal tax credits are also available; visit the federal government's **Energy Star** website (www.energystar.gov) or talk to your accountant for details.

Energy Trust offers energy efficiency services and cash incentives for certain types of improvements to customers of NW Natural in southwest Washington. If you live in Washington and are not a NW Natural customer, contact your local utility for help with energy audits and information about financial incentives for making your home more efficient. (Because Washington has no state income tax, it does not offer tax credits to homeowners.)

RENEWABLE ENERGY

Consider buying green power from your local utility; look in the "Utilities" section of the **Getting Settled** chapter for details. If you are interested in going further in your support of renewables, not only can you make your home more energy-efficient, but you can make energy in your home. Despite the cloudy climate, **solar energy**, including solar water heating and photovoltaic electricity, is actually quite viable in Portland; depending on your home's location, wind power or geothermal heating systems may also be potential options. **Solar Oregon** (www. solaroregon.org), a local nonprofit, offers a monthly workshop on how to go solar, and its website provides useful information about solar power. Significant federal and state tax credits and other incentives are available for purchasing renewable energy systems; contact **Energy Trust** for specific information.

WATER CONSERVATION

Although you've moved to a supposedly rainy city, water conservation is still important: July and August can be virtually rainless, and even in years with abundant precipitation a reduction in water use means that we can get by with fewer storage facilities, pipes, sewer treatment facilities, and new water sources. Plus, because water rates are high, and Portland's household sewer charge (which is even higher than the water charge) is tied to your water consumption, you'll save money, too. For water conservation tips, visit the website of the **Regional Water Providers Consortium** (www.conserveh2o.org) or click on the "conserve water" tab on the **Portland Water Bureau's** website (www.portlandoregon.gov/water). The Portland Water Bureau will also send its customers free water conservation devices; use their online order form or call 503-823-4527.

LANDSCAPING

Don't forget to make your home green on the outside, too (and we're not talking about paint color). Reduce or eliminate pesticides and chemical fertilizers, and use as little supplemental water as possible. (The resources listed in "Water Conservation" above also have handy tips for water-smart irrigation.) The regional government entity **Metro**, which is responsible for, among other things, managing waste in the metropolitan area, provides useful information about natural gardening techniques, including composting. Visit Metro's "Yard and Garden" page at www.oregonmetro.gov/tools-living/yard-and-garden, or call 503-234-3000 to request brochures.

Landscaping with native plants is a great way to reduce your yard's environmental impact. Because native plants are adapted to the local climate and soils, they often practically take care of themselves; at the very least, they don't require constant watering and fertilization. **PlantNative** (503-248-0104, www.plant-native.com) and the Portland chapter of the **Native Plant Society of Oregon** (www.npsoregon.org/chapters/po.html) are good resources for learning how to use native plants in your yard. For more ambitious gardeners, the Three Rivers Land Conservancy has a comprehensive **Backyard Habitat Certification Program** (503-699-9825, www.trlc.org/backyard-habitat-certification-program/); watch for the yard signs proclaiming certification. And for goodness' sake, don't plant English ivy or other highly invasive species in your yard; contact the **No Ivy League** (503-823-3681, www.noivyleague.com) for details on why doing so is very naughty.

ENVIRONMENTALLY FRIENDLY PRODUCTS AND SERVICES

Your pocketbook is one of your most powerful weapons in the environmental fight. Your decision to support environmentally friendly businesses not only helps those businesses, but indirectly creates additional consumer demand for environmentally benign choices (a demand that could ultimately change the behavior of less environmentally focused businesses). Here are a few resources for finding green products and services.

- The *Chinook Book* (www.chinookbok.net) is full of coupons for sustainable products and services from businesses in the Portland metro area. The publisher claims to use several screening criteria to weed out inappropriate businesses. The book is available at many stores and restaurants (especially businesses whose coupons are included in the book), and local schools and nonprofits also sell Chinook Books during fundraisers. The coupons are also available in a smartphone app.
- The *ReDirect Guide* (www.redirectguide.com), available for free at many libraries and businesses, is a directory of local businesses that are (or purport to be) sustainable or otherwise environmentally friendly.

A WORD ON GREENWASHING

Greenwashing is the unsavory but common practice of selling a product (or service, or building project, or corporate image) on the basis of purported "green" or "sustainable" characteristics when in fact those characteristics don't exist, have been misrepresented, or are outweighed by the product's negative environmental impacts. For example, while "certified organic" has a precise meaning, the words "green" and "natural" are extremely ambiguous in the product labeling context. A product made from the internal organs of polar bear cubs and baby manatees could be labeled "natural," although it probably wouldn't be a terrific choice from a conservation standpoint. It can be difficult for a consumer with good intentions to tell a truly sustainable product from a misleadingly labeled fraud—and that's just the way greenwashers like it.

While not everyone can become hyperinformed on the nuances of choosing products with their environmental impact in mind, a few helpful resources exist. The University of Oregon's www.greenwashingindex.com website has a goal of helping "consumers become more savvy about evaluating environmental marketing claims of advertisers." *Consumer Reports* maintains a website that assesses the environmental soundness of various products; visit **www.greenerchoices. org**. And of course, with a few exceptions (such as replacing inefficient, energy-hogging appliances), usually the greenest choice of all is to minimize your consumption and reuse what you already have.

FOOD

Most environmentally aware consumers know about the benefits of organic farming, but it is also a good idea to buy locally produced food when possible. Not only does supporting local farmers keep money circulating in the region, but it reduces the amount of greenhouse gases and other pollution associated with transporting the food from faraway fields. (Some foods that are grown in greenhouses, however, like out-of-season hothouse tomatoes, may have a bigger carbon footprint than tomatoes from California or Mexico.) Most local co-ops and natural food stores, and some supermarkets, identify the geographic origin of their produce. Farmers' markets generally sell locally grown produce; check the **Shopping for the Home** chapter for more information. *Edible Portland* (503-467-0806, www.edibleportland.com) is a quarterly publication covering local food issues.

When buying food in the store, in addition to organic labels look for certifications from **Salmon Safe** (www.salmonsafe.org), certifying that the source farm or vineyard uses watershed-friendly practices; the **Marine Stewardship Council** (www.msc.org), which certifies seafood as being from sustainable fisheries; and **Food Alliance** (www.foodalliance.org), which certifies farms and ranches for sustainable and humane practices.

Finally, consider reducing the amount of meat in your diet. (Livestock production is an extremely resource-intensive activity.) For information and moral support, contact **Northwest VEG** (503-746-8344, www.nwveg.org).

GREEN MONEY

You can use environmental criteria to decide not only where to spend your money but where to keep it. Some banks, including large national banks, are making efforts to become "greener" in their operations and lending practices. One bank that has gone further than most is **Beneficial State Bank** (888-326-2265, onepacificcoastbank.com), which focuses on environmentally sustainable community development and "triple bottom line" (i.e., including environmental sustainability) lending practices; although the bank is based in Oakland, California, it maintains an office in Portland (1101 SW Washington St, 503-916-1552). Be on the lookout for banks that offer incentives for specific eco-friendly transactions. For example, a few banks and credit unions, including **Unitus Community Credit Union** (www.unitusccu.com), offer reduced loan rates for the purchase of hybrid vehicles. Other banks and mortgage lenders may let you qualify for a larger home loan if you are buying a home with energy-efficient features that reduce your monthly outlay for utility costs. And **GreenStreet Lending**, a service of Umpqua Bank, offers loans for energy efficiency and renewable energy home and small business improvements (866-790-2121, www.umpquabank.com/personal-banking/greenstreet/).

Green investing is now well established, and many mutual funds claim to invest only in environmentally and/or socially responsible companies. Some of these funds, such as Portland-based **Portfolio 21** (877-351-4115, www.port-folio21.com), use environmental sustainability as one of its primary investing criteria. (Of course, you should still check out any fund to see if its fees, investment mix, and average returns are appropriate and acceptable for your situation.) For more information about green investing, visit **GreenMoneyJournal** (www.green-moneyjournal.com) or **The Progressive Investor** (www.sustainablebusiness.com/progressiveinvestor/).

GREENER TRANSPORTATION

Probably the single best transportation choice you can make is to live close to your place of work, or in a place where you have a public transit option to get to work. The **Transportation** chapter lists alternatives to travel by automobile; when using a car is necessary or desirable, combine errands, carpool when possible, and ask your employer about telecommuting options. The **Drive Less/Save More** website (www.drivelesssavemore.com) offers more ideas for reducing the amount you drive, explains why driving less is good for your pocketbook, and offers a handy driving cost calculator to hammer the point home.

If you need or want to drive, consider driving a more fuel-efficient vehicle. In addition to hybrids, which can at this point be considered mainstream, a new generation of fully electric cars is becoming available; the selection ranges from specialty fleet vehicles to mass production models like the new Nissan LEAF. If you have the money and/or skill, you can even convert an existing gasoline-powered vehicle to a fully electric car. (Of course, proving again that there is no environmental free lunch, electric car batteries raise a host of issues about production energy requirements, lifecycle impacts, toxicity, and mining.)

Currently, the most efficient mass production cars are gas-electric hybrids like the Toyota Prius or the Honda Insight. You'll have company, too: the Portland metropolitan area boasts the country's highest hybrid ownership rate. In Washington, certain alternative-fuel vehicles and hybrid cars are exempt from emissions testing, and most small hybrids and some alternative-fuel vehicles are exempt from state sales and use taxes. Most electric cars and plug-in hybrids are eligible for federal and Oregon tax credits.

Whatever kind of car you drive, make sure the car gets routine maintenance to ensure that the engine runs as efficiently as possible. The **Eco-Logical Business Program**, sponsored by several local governments, certifies automobile repair shops that take steps to minimize pollution; visit www.ecobiz.org for details or call 503-823-7807.

Finally, if you want to join an automobile club for roadside assistance and travel advice, consider **Better World Club** (866-238-1137, www.betterworldclub.com). Better World Club bills itself as the nation's only environmentally friendly auto club; they offer the usual menu of auto club services, along with discounts on hybrid rentals, bicycle roadside assistance, and a frequently hilarious electronic newsletter, *Kicking Asphalt*.

ALTERNATIVE FUELS

You can buy or modify cars to run on alternative fuels like pure ethanol or even natural gas, but by far the most popular alternative fuel in Portland is biodiesel. **Biodiesel** is essentially diesel fuel made from vegetable oil, and is usually sold blended with petroleum diesel fuel. The blend name designates the percentage of biodiesel: B100 is pure biodiesel, while B20 is 20% biodiesel and 80% petroleum diesel. You'll see "Powered by Biodiesel" stickers on everything from city trucks to TriMet buses to old Volvo station wagons. All diesel fuel sold within Portland city limits must contain a minimum blend of 5% biodiesel.

You can find current lists of stations that sell biodiesel or other alternative fuels at the U.S. Department of Energy's **Alternative Fuels Data Center** website (afdc. energy.gov/fuels/biodiesel-locations.html). Bear in mind that the use of biodiesel— particularly biodiesel blended with petro-diesel—is not without potential particulate pollution problems. If you already own a diesel-powered vehicle, bio-diesel is a great choice that reduces dependence on oil. However, unless you plan to run your car on B100 exclusively, you might think twice about buying a car just so you can fuel it with biodiesel. (New passenger car models with cleaner-burning diesel engines are now available, which could change the calculus.)

Also remember that, although biodiesel is made from vegetable oil, it is *not* the same as straight vegetable oil (SVO) fuel (a.k.a. "French fry car fuel"); most diesel engines can run on pure biodiesel or biodiesel blends—at most, you'll have to replace a hose or two—but SVO fuel requires substantial modifications to your car (including in most cases a second fuel tank).

If your home has oil heat, note that B20 biodiesel also works in most oil-fired home furnaces.

GREEN RESOURCES

The following are just a fraction of the resources on sustainability and environmental protection that are available in the region:

- **Ecotrust**, 721 NW 9th Ave, Suite 200, 503-227-6225, www.ecotrust.org; headquartered in the spiffy, eco-friendly Jean Vollum Natural Capital Center in the Pearl District, Ecotrust describes its mission as building "Salmon Nation." Its website offers lots of helpful information about the coastal eco-region from Alaska to California, along with links to pages about regional conservation issues.
- Almost everyone uses fossil fuels, whether indirectly or directly. Consider offsetting the resulting greenhouse gas emissions with **carbon offsets**. Carbon offsets fund projects that store carbon or reduce carbon emissions from other sources, such as tree planting projects, energy efficiency projects, and alter-

native energy investments. Although the practice is controversial and some observers have equated the practice with medieval indulgences, in theory, you can thus offset the carbon dioxide you generate. Offsets are available from sources like **My Climate** (www.myclimate.org), and **Terra Pass** (www.terrapass. com).

- The city of Portland's **Bureau of Planning and Sustainability**, 1900 SW 4th Ave, Suite 7100, 503-823-7700, www.portlandoregon.gov/bps/, provides information and assistance on topics ranging from green building and recycling to solar energy development. BPS's resources are useful for people who live outside the city of Portland, too.
- **Metro's** website (www.oregonmetro.gov) has a surprisingly helpful "Tools for Living" page with links to many good sources of information.
- The **Oregon Environmental Council**, 503-222-1963, www.oeconline.org, conducts outreach on a wide range of environmental topics that affect Oregonians.
- The **Regional Environmental Information Network** (RFIN), rein conservation registry.org, an online clearinghouse of environmental information, is part of the Metro regional government's Nature in Neighborhoods program.
- The website of the United States Department of Energy's **Office of Energy Efficiency and Renewable Energy** (www.eere.energy.gov) has some useful links and detailed (if not especially cutting-edge) information about renewable energy.
- The **Center for Earth Leadership**, 503-227-2807, www.earthleaders.org, offers classes and workshops on such topics as "How to Be an Agent of Change" for citizens who seek to play an effective role in creating a sustainable future.
- The **Northwest Earth Institute**, 503-227-2807, www.nwei.org, offers discussion courses, home eco-parties, and other programs dealing with environmental issues.
- **1000 Friends of Oregon**, 503-497-1000, www.friends.org, works on forest and land conservation and urban planning issues.

C HANCES ARE YOU'LL NEED TEMPORARY LODGINGS FOR AT LEAST A few nights at some point during your move to Portland, either during a house-hunting trip or while you're waiting for your lease to start or your home purchase to close. As a regional hub for business and tourism, Portland has a large selection of hotels and motels offering various levels of service, convenience, amenities, and cleanliness. If you need temporary lodgings for more than a week or so, an extended-stay hotel, sublet, or short-term lease might suit you better than a standard hotel or motel. (See **Extended-Stay Options,** below, for some suggestions.)

Note that the listings in this chapter are by no means comprehensive. For painfully complete listings, check the Yellow Pages under "Hotels and Other Accommodations." The **Portland Oregon Visitors Association (POVA)** (877-678-5263, www.travelportland.com) can provide a lengthy list of non-skanky hotels in the area.

RESERVATIONS AND DISCOUNTS

Lodging rates in Portland tend to be at their highest during the summer months and when big conventions hit town; at these peak times, you can usually find lower rates in outlying areas or at smaller downtown hotels.

If you plan to stay in a traditional hotel, there are several ways to save money off the "rack" or official rate. First, while last-minute bargains are not unknown, especially during winter, you'll generally get the best rates if you book well in advance of your visit. Second, always ask about discount offers—many aren't advertised and may change from day to day—and discounts for seniors, veterans, military personnel, and AAA members are common. Third, it's a good idea to check the hotel's website (if it has one), because some establishments offer Internet-only rates or special offers that might beat other available discounts.

Finally, check with an online reservation service; some have relationships with hotels and can offer lower rates than the hotels themselves. In addition to national companies like **Expedia.com**, **Orbitz.com**, **Hotels.com** (800-246-8357), **Priceline.com**, **Booking.com**, **Travelocity.com**, and **Quikbook** (800-789-9887, www.quikbook.com), the local tourism office, **POVA** (877-678-5263, www.travelportland.com), can book rooms by telephone or online, and sometimes offers discounts or packages at participating local hotels. If you know when you're coming but don't have any particular hotel in mind, sites such as **kayak.com** and **skyscanner.com** crawl various travel websites (including hotel chain websites) and show the lowest available rates for more than 200 Portland-area hotels.

Note that some reservation services charge cancellation fees or require payment in advance, and their discounts usually cannot be combined with promotions offered by hotels or membership organizations.

LODGINGS

LUXURY AND BOUTIQUE HOTELS

For a splurge, consider staying in one of Portland's downtown luxury or boutique hotels. Prices are high by Portland standards—rack rates typically start at $175 or so and climb skyward from there—but you get a lot more for your money than you would at a hotel in, say, Manhattan.

- **The Benson Hotel**, 309 SW Broadway, 503-228-2000, 888-716-6199, www.bensonhotel.com; the Benson is the kind of grand, traditional hotel that has dark paneled wood, marble floors, and giant crystal chandeliers in the lobby, with all the opulent comfort that implies.
- **Heathman Hotel**, 1001 SW Broadway, 503-241-4100, 800-551-0011, www.heathmanportland.com; this elegant and venerable luxury hotel is favored by authors on book tours and the occasional aging rock star, as well as less illustrious classes of well-heeled travelers. The hotel is adjacent to Portland's main performing arts complex, and offers, among other unusual amenities, a lending library of 2,000 books signed by authors who stayed at the hotel. Some of the rooms are surprisingly small.
- **Heathman Lodge**, 7801 NE Greenwood Dr, Vancouver, 360-254-3100, www.heathmanlodge.com; the Heathman's suburban sister hotel, just outside Vancouver, Washington, offers log-cabin luxury in a Northwest lodge-style building.
- **Hotel deLuxe,** 729 SW 15th Ave, 503-219-2094, www.hoteldeluxeportland.com; the decor has a "Golden Age of Hollywood" theme—to heighten the experience, you can stay in the top-of-the-line Marlene Dietrich Suite—but the amenities, including flat-screen televisions and iPod docks, are thoroughly modern. The hotel is on the periphery of downtown, convenient to the Pearl District. Some rooms are quite small.

- **Hotel Lucia**, 400 SW Broadway, 503-225-1717, 866-986-8086, www.hotellucia. com; this luxury boutique hotel manages to seamlessly combine a modern design aesthetic and hip vibe with traditional standards of comfort. Among the many nice touches is a pillow menu that allows you to order the kind and number of pillows you'd like for the night. Some rooms are a bit on the small side.
- **Hotel Modera**, 515 SW Clay St, 503-484-1084, 877-484-1084, www.hotelmodera. com, is a former Days Inn near Portland State University that has been stylishly remodeled in modernist style. The hotel courtyard features a "living wall," which is essentially a vertical green roof.
- **Hotel Monaco Portland,** 506 SW Washington St, 503-222-0001, 888-207-2201, www.monaco-portland.com; formerly the elegant Fifth Avenue Suites, in early 2007 the hotel became the *luxe* (and pet-friendly) Hotel Monaco Portland. Every room contains a stellar set of amenities, including a 32" plasma television and, on request, a complimentary loaner goldfish.
- **Hotel Rose,** 50 SW Morrison St, 503-221-0711, 866-866-7977, www. hotelroseportland.com; centrally located just across Naito Parkway from Waterfront Park, this formerly typical business hotel (in its incarnation as a Four Points by Sheraton) spent several years as the Hotel Fifty before morphing into its current incarnation as the Rose.
- **Hotel Vintage Plaza,** 422 SW Broadway, 503-228-1212, 800-263-2305, www. vintageplaza.com; you might surmise from its name that the Vintage Plaza has some kind of wine thing going on, and if you did you'd be right. The hotel hosts a wine hour each evening, and every room is dedicated to a local winery or vineyard.
- **Inn @ Northrup Station**, 2025 NW Northrup St, 503-224-0543, 800-224-1180, www.northrupstation.com; this small all-suite boutique hotel sits alongside the Portland Streetcar line in Northwest Portland. Filled with retro furnishings and bright colors, the Inn @ Northrup Station caters to a hip and evidently email-literate crowd. (This hotel also has among the lowest boutique hotel rates in the city.)
- **The Nines**, 525 SW Morrison St, 877-229-9995, www.thenines.com; occupying the top floors of what was once the historic Meier & Frank department store (now a remodeled and much smaller Macy's), this centrally located hotel is one of Portland's newest luxury offerings.
- **Paramount Hotel**, 808 SW Taylor St, 503-223-9900, www.portlandparamount. com; this 15-story boutique hotel is the Benson's younger and marginally hipper cousin. Guestrooms are generally spacious, with luxury baths; some have small balconies overlooking Director Park (more a public piazza than a greenspace).
- **RiverPlace Hotel**, 1510 SW Harbor Way, 503-228-3233, 888-869-3108, www. riverplacehotel.com; downtown's only truly riverfront hotel—a marina lies at its doorstep—the RiverPlace offers understated comfort and relative quiet.
- **River's Edge Hotel**, 0455 SW Hamilton Ct, 503-802-5800, 888-556-4402, www. riversedgehotel.com; located just south of downtown, on the west bank of the

Willamette River—on the river's edge, in fact — the River's Edge offers stylish, modern accommodation.

- **The Sentinel Hotel**, 614 SW 11th Ave, 503-224-3400, 800-554-3456, www. sentinelhotel.com; over a century old, this *grande dame* was for many years the Governor Hotel. It was recently renovated and re-branded, but still offers plush, traditional luxury. It stands on the streetcar line on the western fringe of downtown, not far from the Pearl District, so it makes a good base for car-free exploration.
- **Westin Portland**, 750 SW Alder St, 503-294-9000, 888-627-8401, www. westinportland.com; this centrally located hotel, while tailored to business travelers, offers more comforts and amenities than most chain hotels.

LARGE HOTELS

Most large hotels in Portland belong to big chains, and if they lack character they are at least predictable and generally clean. The available amenities are fairly standard—restaurants, room service, business centers, and often fitness centers. These hotels tend to focus on business travelers and conventioneers, and so the heaviest concentrations are in downtown Portland, in the Lloyd Center/Convention Center neighborhood, and near the airport. Rack rates are generally at least $140 a night, and sometimes much more. Many of these hotel chains also have facilities in the suburbs; check the Yellow Pages or the hotel's website for listings.

- **Century Hotel**, 8585 SW Tualatin-Sherwood Rd, Tualatin, 503-692-3600, 800-240-9494, www.thecenturyhotel.com
- **Courtyard by Marriott Beaverton**, 8500 SW Nimbus Dr, Beaverton, 503-641-3200, 800-321-2211, www.marriott.com/pdxcy
- **Courtyard by Marriott Downtown/Convention Center**, 435 NE Wasco St, 503-234-3200, 800-321-2211, www.marriott.com/pdxcl
- **Courtyard by Marriott Portland Airport**, 11550 NE Airport Way, 503-252-3200, 800-321-2211, www.marriott.com/pdxca
- **Courtyard by Marriott Portland City Center**, 550 SW Oak St, 503-505-5000, www.marriott.com/pdxpc
- **Courtyard by Marriott Portland North Harbour**, 1231 N Anchor Way, 503-735-1818, www.marriott.com/pdxnh
- **Courtyard by Marriott Portland Southeast**, 9300 SE Sunnybrook Blvd, Clackamas, 503-652-2900, 800-321-2211, www.courtyard.com/pdxck
- **Crowne Plaza Portland Downtown (Convention Center)**, 1441 NE 2nd Ave, 503-233-2401, www.cpportland.com
- **Crowne Plaza Portland Lake Oswego**, 14811 Kruse Oaks Blvd, Lake Oswego, 503-624-8400, www.cplakeoswego.com
- **DoubleTree by Hilton Hotel Portland**, 1000 NE Multnomah St, 503-281-6111, www.portlandlloydcenter.doubletree.com

- **Embassy Suites Portland Downtown**, 319 SW Pine St, 503-279-9000, www.embassyportland.com
- **Embassy Suites Hotel Portland Airport**, 7900 NE 82nd Ave, 503-460-3000, www.portlandairport.embassysuites.com
- **Embassy Suites Portland–Washington Square**, 9000 SW Washington Square Rd, Tigard, 503-644-4000, www.portlandembassysuites.com
- **Hilton Portland & Executive Tower**, 921 SW 6th Ave, 503-226-1611, www.portland.hilton.com
- **Holiday Inn Express Hotel & Suites–Jantzen Beach**, 2300 N Hayden Island Dr, 503-283-8000, 888-465-4329, www.ihg.com
- **Holiday Inn Express Hotel & Suites–Northwest Portland**, 2333 NW Vaughn St, 503-484-1100, 888-465-4329, www.hiexpress.com/portlandnwdtwn
- **Holiday Inn Portland Airport**, 8439 NE Columbia Blvd, 503-256-5000, 800-315-2621, www.holidayinn.com
- **Monarch Hotel & Conference Center**, 12566 SE 93rd Ave, 503-652-1515, 800-492-8700, www.monarchhotel.cc
- **Oxford Suites Portland—Jantzen Beach**, 12226 N Jantzen Dr, 503-283-3030, 800-548-7848, www.oxfordsuitesportland.com
- **Portland Marriott City Center**, 520 SW Broadway, 503-226-6300, 800-548-7848, www.marriottportland.com
- **Portland Marriott Downtown Waterfront**, 1401 SW Naito Pkwy, 503-226-7600, www.marriott.com/pdxor
- **Radisson Hotel Portland Airport**, 6233 NE 78th Ct, 503-251-2000, 800-967-9033, www.radisson.com/portlandor_airport
- **Red Lion Hotel on the River**, 909 N Hayden Island Dr, 503-283-4466, 800-733-5466, www.jantzenbeach.redlion.com
- **Red Lion Hotel on the Quay**, 100 Columbia St, Vancouver, 360-694-8341, 800-733-5466, www.redlion.com/our-hotels/Washington/Vancouver/
- **Sheraton Portland Airport Hotel**, 8235 NE Airport Way, 503-281-2500, 800-325-3535, www.sheratonportland.com
- **University Place Hotel and Conference Center–Portland State University**, 310 SW Lincoln St, 503-221-0140, 866-845-4647, www.uplacehotel.com

SMALL HOTELS

Portland has several small hotels that tend to attract tourists and couples rather than the business travelers, who stay in the big chain hotels. If you book ahead and ask about promotions, you might get into one of these establishments for as little as $70 a night, and even the premium rooms are less expensive than those at luxury hotels, although the service and atmosphere can be just as appealing.

- **Ace Hotel Portland**, 1022 SW Stark St, 503-228-2277, www.acehotel.com/Portland/; this Portland outpost of the small Ace hotel chain is another entrant into the hipness-trumps-elegance field.

- **Jupiter Hotel**, 800 E Burnside St, 503-230-9200, 877-800-0004, www.jupiterho-tel.com; a hip, retro, and often bustling ex-motel, the Jupiter Hotel is not the place to come for a quiet weekend. Look for their edgy ads in local weeklies.
- **Mark Spencer Hotel**, 409 SW 11th Ave, 503-224-3293, www.markspencer.com; favored by small tour groups and foreign visitors.
- The **McMenamins** brewpub empire (www.mcmenamins.com) includes several complexes that offer unique hotel accommodations. The **Kennedy School** (5736 NE 33rd Ave, 503-249-3983, 888-249-3983) in Northeast Portland was once an actual elementary school (some of the rooms still have chalkboards, and the hallway drinking fountains are at kid height); the **Edgefield** (2126 SW Halsey St, Troutdale, 503-669-8610, 800-669-8610) was the county poor farm; the **Grand Lodge** (3505 Pacific Ave, Forest Grove, 503-992-9533, 877-992-9533) used to be a Masonic lodge; and the tiny **White Eagle** (836 N Russell, 503-335-8900) started life as a Polish immigrants' social club. The **Crystal Hotel** on Burnside in downtown Portland (303 SW 12th Ave, 503-225-0047), adjacent to the Crystal Ballroom music venue, features a basement saltwater soaking pool.
- **Park Lane Suites & Inn**, 809 SW King Ave, 503-226-6288, 800-532-9543, www.parklanesuites.com; this hotel is close to Washington Park and Northwest Portland. All of its functional but comfortable studios and one- or two-bedroom suites have kitchens, making it a good choice for longer stays.

BUDGET HOTELS AND MOTELS

The Portland area has plenty of small hotels and motels. At these no-frills establishments, you can almost always get a room for less than $100, and occasionally for as little as $50. Many of the area's budget hotels represent such national chains as **Best Western** (800-780-7234, www.bestwestern.com), **Days Inn** (800-225-3297, www.daysinn.com**), **La Quinta** (800-753-3757, www.lq.com), **Motel 6** (800-4-MOTEL6, www.motel6.com), **Travelodge** (800-525-4055, www.travelodge.com), **Shilo Inns** (800-222-2244, www.shiloinns.com), and several others. Several chains, including Comfort Inn, Econo Lodge, and Quality Inn, are under the umbrella of **Choice Hotels International** (877-424-6423, www.choicehotels.com).

Although the chains predominate, Portland still has dozens of independent motels, both in the city itself and in many of the suburbs. A quick online search won't turn up some of these motels; look in the Yellow Pages under "Motels & Other Accommodation" and "Hotels & Other Accommodation" for complete listings. The greatest concentration of budget motels is found along Northeast and Southeast 82nd Avenue, especially at the northern end near the Airport. Other clusters of budget lodging exist along Southeast Powell Boulevard, Southwest Barbur Boulevard, and Highway 99 north of Vancouver, and at the southern end of downtown Portland, near Portland State University. Note that some of the cheapest motels, particularly those along parts of 82nd Avenue, are in high-crime areas and/or are frequently used for various illicit purposes. If one hotel or motel makes you uneasy, try another. You'll almost always be able to find an acceptable option in a decent neighborhood.

BED & BREAKFASTS AND GUESTHOUSES

If you're in the mood for quaint, consider a bed and breakfast ("B&B") or guesthouse. In Portland, most of these establishments are in residential areas outside the downtown core, so staying in one can be a good way to check out neighborhoods you're interested in. Keep in mind, however, that there's good quaint and bad quaint, and then there's just awful. Properties affiliated with an organization like the **Portland Metropolitan Innkeepers Association** (www.portlandinnkeepers.com) or the **Oregon Bed and Breakfast Guild** are usually good bets; call 800-944-6196 or visit www.obbg.org for information and reservations. Portland-area B&Bs and guesthouses include:

- **Bellaterra B&B**, 3935 SW Corbett Ave, 503-332-8125, www.bellaterrabnb.com
- **Bluebird Guesthouse**, 3517 SE Division St, 503-238-4333, 866-717-4333, www.bluebirdguesthouse.com
- **Briar Rose Inn**, 314 W 11th St, Vancouver, 360-694-5710, www.briarroseinn.com
- **Cornerstone Bed and Breakfast**, 17290 SW Alvord Lane, Beaverton, 503-747-2345, www.cornerstonebedandbreakfast.com
- **The Fulton House Bed & Breakfast**, 7006 SW Virginia Ave, 503-892-5781, www.thefultonhouse.com
- **Forest Springs Bed & Breakfast @ Historic Heiney House**, 3680 SW Towle Ave, Gresham, 503-674-8992, 877-674-9282, www.forestspring.com
- **Georgian House Bed & Breakfast**, 1828 NE Siskiyou St, 503-281-2250, 888-282-2250, www.thegeorgianhouse.com
- **Heron Haus Bed & Breakfast**, 2545 NW Westover Rd, 503-274-1846, www.heronhaus.com
- **Hostess House Bed and Breakfast**, 5758 NE Emerson St, 503-282-7892, 800-760-7799, www.hostesshouse.com
- **Lion and the Rose Victorian Bed & Breakfast Inn**, 1810 NE 15th Ave, 503-287-9245, 800-955-1647, www.lionrose.com
- **A Painted Lady Inn**, 1927 NE 16th Ave, 503-335-0070, www.apaintedladyinn.com
- **Portland International Guesthouse**, 2185 NW Flanders St, 503-224-0500, 877-228-0500, www.pdxguesthouse.com
- **Portland's White House**, 1914 NE 22nd Ave, 503-287-7131, 800-272-7131, www.portlandswhitehouse.com
- **Sandes of Time Bed and Breakfast**, 16022 SE River Rd, Milwaukie, 503-654-8813, www.sandesoftime.com

HOSTELS

Portland has two official **Hostelling International** youth hostels, both of which are well-located for the car-less.

- **Northwest Portland International Hostel and Guesthouse,** 425 NW 18th Ave, 503-241-2783, www.nwportlandhostel.com; close to the bustle of Northwest Portland and the Pearl District, this hostel is close-in without actually being downtown.
- **Portland Hostel Hawthorne District (Hostelling International)**, 3031 SE Hawthorne Blvd, 503-236-3380, 866-447-3031, www.portlandhostel.org; a converted house with an eco-roof and a huge front porch, this popular hostel is close to the shops, restaurants, and bars of the Hawthorne district.

Several cheap downtown hotels offer ostensible "hostel" rooms, but those establishments are best avoided by all but the truly desperate. If you don't mind being out of town and not having access to a kitchen, **McMenamins Edgefield**, in Troutdale, has some hostel-style dorm rooms. (See "Bed & Breakfasts and Guesthouses" above.)

EXTENDED-STAY OPTIONS

It could take you a few weeks or months to find a perfect (or at any rate a permanent) home. If you anticipate spending more than a week or two on your home search, one of the most convenient arrangements is an extended-stay hotel. These facilities, sometimes called corporate apartments, offer furnished suites with kitchens by the day, week, or month. Some extended-stay options in Portland include:

- **BridgeStreet Worldwide**, 800-278-7338, www.bridgestreet.com, operates three locations in the Pearl District, one location downtown, two locations in Gresham, and two locations in Washington County.
- **Extended Stay Hotels**, 800-804-3724, www.extendedstayamerica.com, has six locations in the metro area.
- **Larkspur Landing Hillsboro**, 3133 NE Shute Rd, Hillsboro, 503-681-2121, www.larkspurlanding.com/hotels/hillsboro/
- **Oakwood Worldwide**, 877-902-0832, www.oakwood.com, has nearly some three dozen furnished apartments lin and around Portland.
- **Park Lane Suites**, 809 SW King Ave, 503-226-6288, 800-532-9543, www.parklanesuites.com, offers an extended-stay discount.
- **Residence Inn by Marriott**, 888-236-2427, www.residenceinn.com, has eight locations in the greater Portland area.
- **Suite America**, 503-443-2033, 800-917-1092, www. suiteamerica.com, has furnished apartments in nearly 30 locations in and around Portland.

A potentially less expensive option is a sublet or short-term lease. In this type of arrangement, you rent or sublease all or part of a house, condo, or apartment for several weeks to several months while the owner or renter is away. Sublets aren't always furnished, and you would be very lucky to find one where the sublease term perfectly matches the dates for which you need lodgings, but when they work out subleases can be a great choice. To find sublets, look on **Craigslist** (portland.craigslist.org/sub/) or check out the classifieds in *Willamette Week*. Some rental property management companies and apartment complexes may offer short-term rentals, although such rentals are typically unfurnished. In 2014, the city of Portland legalized short-term and vacation rentals through **Airbnb** (www.airbnb.com), through which hundreds of Portland residents had already been offering rooms or houses on an unofficial (read: technically illegal) basis.

ONCE YOU'VE SETTLED IN TO PORTLAND, YOU'LL INEVITABLY WANT TO explore your surroundings. After all, you didn't move to one of the most beautiful regions in the world just so you could spend all your time in the city, did you? Within a few hours' drive (or in some cases, a bus, train, and/or ferry ride) you'll find volcanic peaks, raging rivers, dense forests, high desert plateaus, an atmospheric coastline, cosmopolitan cities, and some of the richest farmland in America. It really doesn't matter which direction you go; anywhere in the region, you're bound to encounter interesting destinations and some beautiful scenery.

For general Oregon travel information, suggested destinations, an accommodation guide, and much, much more, call **Travel Oregon** at 800-547-7842 or visit their comprehensive website at www.traveloregon.com. The **Washington State Tourism Office** (800-544-1800, www.experiencewa.com) is equally helpful; thankfully, it shelved its terrifying "Say WA" tourism campaign in 2006 in favor of "Experience Washington." The current slogan, evidently designed to minimize ambiguity, is "Washington. The State." For information on some of Oregon's natural areas, scan the **Greenspace** chapter of this book.

MOUNT HOOD AND THE NORTHERN OREGON CASCADES

Mount Hood, Portland's iconic backdrop (at least on a clear day), is the city's favorite year-round destination for outdoor recreation. While thousands of people summit the 11,240-foot glaciated peak every year—a feat that requires technical mountaineering skills and a fair amount of fortitude—the vast majority of visitors come to ski or snowboard, to hike, to mountain bike, or just to sightsee and enjoy the mountain air. The mountain's southwest slopes are only an hour from Portland.

The most direct route to the mountain is US Highway 26 from Gresham. (Unless you're coming from the southeast part of the metro area, it's usually fastest to take Interstate 84 east to Exit 16, then head south on NE 238th/242nd to Burnside, and take Burnside southeast to US 26.) Highway 26 climbs gently past ornamental plant nurseries, Christmas tree farms, and stands of dense forest, and through the towns of Sandy, Brightwood, Welches, Zigzag, and Rhododendron, until it reaches the outpost of **Government Camp** at 3500 feet. The main commercial center on the mountain, Government Camp offers ski rentals, grocery stores, a gas station, restaurants, a brewpub, and various overnight accommodation options. Government Camp is a good base for hiking and skiing—Mount Hood Skibowl is directly across the highway—but it's more of a convenient way station than a destination in itself, a recent condo boom notwithstanding.

From Government Camp, a six-mile road winds tortuously uphill to **Timberline Lodge** (800-547-1406, www.timberlinelodge.com) and its ski area (which is open almost all year). If the 1930s-vintage lodge looks familiar, you may have already seen it in the 1980 horror film *The Shining*. (Sweet dreams, kids.) The lodge's name is derived from its location at timberline on Mount Hood, at 6,600 feet above sea level; the slopes above are virtually devoid of trees, except for a few gnarled old specimens. On a clear day, it feels as if you could reach out and touch the summit of the mountain, although it's actually nearly a mile higher.

Back at Government Camp, US 26 continues east and south over two 4,000-foot passes toward dry Central Oregon (see below). A few miles east of Government Camp, State Highway 35 branches off and loops around the east side of Mount Hood and down the Hood River Valley (see below). A network of forest roads (many of them unpaved) lead to other destinations around Mount Hood, including picture-postcard-pretty **Lost Lake** (541-386-6366, www.lostlakeresort.org) on the mountain's north side; **Cooper Spur** on the east side, from where it is possible in late summer to hike to a promontory overlooking Eliot Glacier at an elevation of 8,700 feet; and the Salmon River, upstream from Welches, which flows out of the **Salmon-Huckleberry Wilderness**. An extensive zone surrounding Mount Hood's summit is also a designated wilderness area, as is the **Badger Creek Wilderness** east of the mountain and the newly created **Roaring River Wilderness** to the southwest.

Many of the forest trails around Mount Hood (including mountain bike trails and Nordic ski routes) depart directly from US 26 or Highway 35, but the ease of access from Portland ensures that these trails are crowded on good-weather weekends. The farther you get from the main highways, however, the fewer people you are likely to encounter; if you actually get out and hike more than a few miles it's possible to find solitude even in mid-summer. If you'd like to spend a bit more time on the mountain, there are plenty of inexpensive forest service campgrounds for tent or trailer camping; backpackers will find an abundance of backcountry campsites, especially in designated wilderness areas. For shelter under a roof, you can stay in one of several hotels, or rent a cabin in Government Camp or in one of the communities on the mountain's west side.

South of Mount Hood, the Cascade Mountains are a patchwork of clear cuts, stands of second-growth timber, and some small swaths of remnant old growth, primarily in roadless and wilderness areas. State Highway 224 winds from Estacada up the scenic valley of the Clackamas River; the river drainage harbors destinations like the **Bull of the Woods Wilderness** and Bagby Hot Springs (which for many years was plagued by frequent parking-lot break-ins, although the situation has improved in recent years). The adjacent **Opal Creek** area, east of Salem, harbors one of the finest remaining stands of old-growth forest in the state. The other main road to penetrate this region, State Highway 22, runs east from Salem past Detroit Lake, a reservoir that is a popular destination for boaters. Various byways and forest roads connect the two main roads and lead to out-of-the-way attractions like **Breitenbush Hot Springs** (503-854-3320, www.breitenbush.com) and **Olallie Lake**. At the crest of the range looms Oregon's second-highest peak, Mount Jefferson; the surrounding area, including such beauty spots as Jefferson Park (a lake-dotted meadow basin near timberline) and the curiously shaped peak of Three Fingered Jack, is part of the **Mount Jefferson Wilderness**, where motorized vehicles are prohibited.

Much of the Mount Hood region lies within Clackamas County; for trip ideas, contact the county tourism department, **Oregon's Mt. Hood Territory** (503-655-8490, 800-424-3002, www.mthoodterritory.com).

THE COLUMBIA RIVER GORGE AND THE HOOD RIVER VALLEY

Traffic permitting, you can drive east from downtown Portland on Interstate 84 and, within half an hour, find yourself amid the splendor of the **Columbia River Gorge**. Here, the Columbia River forces a passage westward through the Cascades, through a palisade of basalt cliffs that tower hundreds or thousands of feet above the river. The Gorge isn't wilderness—multiple dams shackle the Columbia, major highways and railroad tracks run along both shores, and several towns and small cities perch on the banks—but it is nonetheless a spectacular place.

Interstate 84 runs the length of the Gorge on the south side of the river, but by far the best sightseeing route is the Historic Columbia River Highway, which branches off from the interstate at Exit 17 in Troutdale and climbs through the town of Corbett to historic **Vista House** (www.vistahouse.com) at Crown Point, a promontory high above the river that offers a spectacular view eastward (upriver). From Crown Point, the highway descends through mossy forest, past several spectacular waterfalls, including two-stage, 620-foot **Multnomah Falls**, the state's biggest natural tourist draw. The area at the base of the falls can get very crowded on summer weekends, when tour buses disgorge their passengers to gawk at the spectacle, but the parking lot off the historic highway is often nearly deserted on winter weekdays. (A separate parking area, accessible from Interstate 84, attracts passing motorists all year.) A word of warning about parking near the waterfalls: these parking areas are notorious sites for car prowls (break-ins), so be sure to lock your car and keep all "attractive" possessions out of sight. Nearby **Oneonta Gorge** is a narrow, rock-bound chasm that leads to yet another waterfall. Many more waterfalls are accessible by trail only, as are the most spectacular views, which are available from Angel's Rest (a 4-mile roundtrip hike from the historic highway) and other similar clifftop perches on both sides of the Gorge.

Take a break from natural splendor at **Bonneville Dam** (541-374-8820, www. nwp.usace.army.mil/Locations/ColumbiaRiver/Bonneville.aspx) and admire the engineering feats that inspired Woody Guthrie. The dam's visitor center and fish ladder (with viewing window) are generally open daily from 9 a.m. to 5 p.m., and tours of the power plant are sometimes offered, but heightened security can cause closures on short notice; call or visit the website before scheduling a visit. Upstream of the dam, at the town of **Cascade Locks** (www.cascadelocks.net), the Bridge of the Gods leads to the Washington side of the Gorge. (The Pacific Crest Trail also crosses the river on this bridge.) Washington State Highway 14 runs along the north bank of the river for the length of the Gorge, and makes a good alternate or return route. The Washington side includes such attractions as **Beacon Rock State Park**, several hot springs resorts, and **Skamania Lodge** (509-427-7700, www.skamania.com), a resort outside Stevenson.

Continuing eastward on the Oregon side, as you approach **Hood River** (www.hoodriver.org) the climate quickly becomes noticeably drier, with oaks and ponderosa pines replacing the Douglas firs that cling to the mountainsides further west. Hood River, long a small regional commercial center and world-class windsurfing/kiteboarding destination, has recently boomed, and housing appreciation rates have been among the highest in the state. It's easy to see why—with Mount Hood to the south and the Columbia River and Mount Adams to the north, with abundant outdoor recreational opportunities, and with substantially less rain than Portland, it would be surprising if the place *didn't* boom. While not all locals are happy about Hood River's changing demographics, the change has led to the opening of several excellent (albeit spendy) restaurants in the historic, hilly downtown. At just over an hour from Portland, Hood River is a wonderful destination for a weekend getaway; try one of the many bed and breakfasts in town or across the Columbia in White Salmon, Washington.

From Hood River, you have a range of options for continuing your tour. You can turn south through the scenic **Hood River Valley**, a major fruit-growing region. The valley is especially beautiful in spring, when the apple, pear, and cherry orchards are in bloom (with a snow-covered Mount Hood looming picturesquely behind), and during the late summer and fall harvest, when fruit stands and pumpkin patches open for visitors. You can follow the so-called Fruit Loop (www.hoodriverfruitloop.com), and so start and end at Hood River, or continue up the valley on Highway 35, pass over the shoulder of Mount Hood, and return to Portland via US Highway 26. You can head north toward Mount Adams country and the hamlet of Trout Lake (see Washington State, below). Or you can continue eastward through the Gorge into an increasingly arid landscape.

If you choose to continue upstream along the Columbia from Hood River, you will pass scenic wonders like the Nature Conservancy's **Tom McCall Preserve**, which puts on a colorful show of wildflowers in April and May. At **The Dalles** (www.thedalleschamber.com), once a major stopover on the Oregon Trail, visit the **Columbia Gorge Discovery Center** (541-296-8600, www.gorgediscovery.org). About 24 miles east of The Dalles, on the Washington side, stands the peculiar, castle-like **Maryhill Museum of Art** (509-773-3733, www.maryhillmuseum.org). Built in the nineteen-teens by Quaker entrepreneur Sam Hill (who was *not* the basis for the expression, "What in the sam hill?"), the museum now houses an eclectic collection of European, American, and Native American art, including a major assemblage of Auguste Rodin sculptures and watercolors. Nearby, don't miss the full-size replica of Stonehenge, built on a bluff by Sam Hill as a memorial to soldiers who lost their lives in World War I. This part of the Gorge has a favorable climate for growing wine grapes, and a number of wineries have opened in recent years.

Much of the Gorge is protected within the **Columbia River Gorge National Scenic Area** (541-308-1700, www.fs.usda.gov/crgnsa). For general tourism information, contact the **Columbia River Gorge Visitors Association** (www.crgva.org).

THE OREGON COAST

Less than 90 minutes to the west of downtown Portland (as always, traffic permitting), the often fog-bound beaches and rugged headlands of Oregon's Pacific Ocean coastline beckon. The drive west on US 26 climbs over the low crest of the Coast Range—**Saddle Mountain State Natural Area** (www.oregonstateparks.org) encompasses the highest point in the northern Coast Range and makes a good detour on a clear day—and then leads through damp mossy valleys toward the sea. Eventually, Highway 26 dead-ends at US Highway 101, which runs the length of the Oregon Coast (and almost the entire length of the West Coast of the United States, in case you feel like heading to L.A.). Be aware that 101 is not a fast road; it has frequent hills, there are only two lanes for most of its length, and lumbering recreational vehicle traffic can be a nightmare during the summer. A scenic alternative to Route 26 is State Highway 6, which winds through the Tillamook State Forest to the bayside town of Tillamook (see below).

Seaside (www.seasideor.com), the first town to the north, has a bit of a carnival atmosphere, with a busy waterside promenade, several factory outlet stores, and plenty of saltwater taffy vendors. To the south, artsier **Cannon Beach** (www.cannonbeach.org) offers a long stretch of sand, with locally iconic Haystack Rock accessible at low tide. Between these two towns, scenic **Ecola State Park** (www.oregonstateparks.org) beckons visitors with isolated beaches, tidepools, and the rocky cliffs of Tillamook Head.

The short stretch of Highway 101 north of Seaside leads through the quiet, affluent resort town of Gearhart to **Fort Stevens State Park** (www.oregonstateparks.org) and its bike paths, crumbling military fortifications, swimmable lake, and excellent beach (complete with a small shipwreck) just south of the mouth of the Columbia River. Nearby **Fort Clatsop** (www.nps.gov/lewi/planyourvisit/fortclatsop.htm) marks the spot where Lewis and Clark passed the winter of 1805–06 (moaning all the while in their journals about the incessant rainfall). The city of **Astoria** (503-325-6311, 800-875-6807, www.oldoregon.com) lies just upriver from the mouth of the Columbia. This historic, quirky, and slightly gritty (yet generally attractive) waterfront town has a vibrant Scandinavian heritage—there are still Finnish saunas in Astoria—and a strong maritime flavor, as the exhibits in the **Columbia River Maritime Museum** (503-325-2323, www.crmm.org) attest. Victorian homes on steep hillsides are reminiscent of San Francisco homes (but with bigger lots and smaller price tags), and on (infrequent) clear days there is a magnificent view from the Astoria Column, perched on the city's highest hill. The city has seen a recent boom in good restaurants and boutique hotels.

From Astoria, you can loop back to Portland via Highway 30 along the Columbia River, or continue north over the Astoria-Megler Bridge to the beaches of the southern Washington coast. The community of **Long Beach** (360-642-2400, 800-451-2542, www.funbeach.com) is reputed to have the longest drivable beach in the world; this claim leaves unanswered the question of why you would want to drive 17 miles down a beach, avoiding volleyball players and giant chunks of driftwood, and hoping you don't get stuck in the sand with the tide advancing.

If, instead of heading north from Seaside, you choose to drive south from Cannon Beach, you'll pass through the small vacation communities of Arch Cape and Manzanita on your way to **Tillamook**, the state's cheese capital. The Tillamook Creamery (503-815-1300, 800-542-7290, www.tillamook.com), although not the blockbuster experience it once was, is still one of the most popular destinations on the coast, and the gift shop sells cheddar cheese curds. (It's not all about cheese though; you might want to visit the ice cream counter, the only location that stocks every flavor of Tillamook Ice Cream, and will even serve them all up to you at once in a multi-scoop bowl.) From Tillamook, take the **Three Capes Scenic Route** past Capes Meares, Lookout, and Kiwanda as an alternative to busy Highway 101.

Heading south, some consider bustling **Lincoln City** (www.oregoncoast.org) to be a great base for exploration, while others view it as an overbuilt tourist trap. The attractions in slightly more laid back **Newport** (www.discovernewport.com) include the historic bayfront, a working waterfront that boasts tacky souvenir parlors, sea lions lazing on the docks, and restaurants that have garnered rave reviews from the *New York Times*; charming Nye Beach; and the **Oregon Coast Aquarium** (541-867-3474, www.aquarium.org), one of the country's finest aquaria and famous as a former halfway house of sorts for the orca Keiko, a.k.a. Free Willy. South of Newport, the coast gets fewer visitors. You'll pass through rugged coastal scenery and often fog-bound towns like Waldport and Yachats on your way to Florence and the **Oregon Dunes National Recreation Area** (www.fs.usda.gov/recarea/siuslaw/recreation/recarea/?recid-42465), a 40-mile strip of sand dunes that in some places are more than 500 feet high; the dunes area also contains several swimmable freshwater lakes. Beyond **Coos Bay** and its large working harbor, the south coast includes towns such as Bandon (famous for its cheese, cranberries, and lightning-fast broadband network), Port Orford, Brookings (the so-called banana belt of Oregon, which typically has the state's mildest winter temperatures), and **Gold Beach** (800-525-2334, www.goldbeach.org), a good base for jet boat excursions up the Rogue River.

For more information on visiting the Oregon Coast, contact the **Oregon Coast Visitors Association** (541-574-2679, 888-628-2101, www.visittheoregoncoast. com). Dozens of the most scenic areas along the coast are part of the **Oregon State Parks** system (800-551-6949, www.oregonstateparks.org); while some state parks are little more than waysides open for day use only, others are fairly large and substantial parks with camping facilities, and sometimes yurts or cabins.

THE WILLAMETTE VALLEY AND OREGON'S WINE COUNTRY

The Willamette Valley stretches south from Portland for more than 100 miles. This broad valley is home to some of the nation's richest agricultural land, as well as the cities of Salem, Albany, **Corvallis** (541-757-1544, 800-334-8118, www.visitcorvallis. com), and **Eugene** (www.eugenecascadescoast.org, 541-484-5307, 800-547-5445). The latter two cities, home to Oregon State University and the University of Oregon, respectively, are both worthy stopovers, but the Willamette Valley generally lacks major tourist attractions. Its appeal lies primarily in its small towns and farm fields, some of which are full of unusual crops like peppermint and lavender, and its slower pace of life. To see the valley at its best, get off the main highways (Interstate 5 and highways 99E and 99W) and putter around the back roads; better still, tour the valley by bicycle. (Smell the mint, feel the burn.)

For wine lovers, the most compelling destinations in the Willamette Valley lie along its margins, on the low ranges of hills that rise from the flat valley floor. Here, on slopes that shed cold winter air and collect summer sunshine, grow the vineyards that supply the dozens of **wineries** in the six AVAs—American Viticultural Areas—in the Willamette Valley region. Oregon is globally famous for its pinot noirs, but it produces many other kinds of wines as well. The greatest concentration of wineries is in Yamhill County, especially around **Dundee**, less than an hour southeast of Portland. For more information about wines and wineries visit www. willamettewines.com or www.oregonwine.org.

One don't-miss destination, especially for waterfall lovers, is **Silver Falls State Park** (www.oregonstateparks.org) east of Salem. The park contains a canyon with no fewer than ten waterfalls, some of which are short walks from parking areas on the canyon rim; an 8.7-mile trail links the falls and actually passes through small rock amphitheaters behind four of them. Nearby, just south of Silverton, the **Oregon Garden** (503-874-8100, 877-674-2733, www.oregongarden.org) presents a wide range of specialty gardens, as well as the only Frank Lloyd Wright–designed house in Oregon.

For more ideas about Willamette Valley tour routes, contact the **Willamette Valley Visitors Association** (866-548-5018, www.oregonwinecountry.org).

CENTRAL OREGON

Fast-growing **Bend** (541-382-8048, 877-245-8484, www.visitbend.com) sprawls on the banks of the Deschutes River as it flows from forested highlands into the high desert. The hub of scenic central Oregon, Bend is a minimum three-hour drive from Portland via Mount Hood and Madras or Salem and Santiam Pass. Bend property values rose at one of the highest rates in the country during the mid-2000s real estate boom, and although some of the toniest eateries and shops did not survive the subsequent crash, the city still offers a wide range of restaurants and hotels, as well as the acclaimed **High Desert Museum** (541-382-4754, www.highdesertmuseum.org), three miles south of town. The real attraction of central Oregon, however, is the stunning landscape and the consequent recreational opportunities. The region immediately surrounding Bend is a semi-arid plateau of sagebrush, juniper, and ponderosa pine, but the volcanic peaks of the central Cascades rise just to the west, and scenic beauty can be found in every direction.

Mount Bachelor (800-829-2442, www.mtbachelor.com), only 20 miles away from Bend, is a major winter-sports destination, while one of the largest designated wilderness areas in the state, with more than 240 miles of hiking trails, encompasses the nearby **Three Sisters**. (South Sister, at 10,358 feet, is the third-highest mountain in the state; you don't need technical climbing skills to reach the top in late summer.) The McKenzie Pass Highway runs west from Sisters, a small, touristy town northwest of Bend, over a bleak, lava-strewn pass between Mount Washington and the Three Sisters, while the Cascade Lakes Highway, a National Scenic Byway, winds south from Mount Bachelor past a series of high mountain reservoirs (and abundant campsites).

North of Bend, past slightly lower and drier (but also fast-growing) Redmond is **Smith Rock State Park** (www.oregonstateparks.org), one of the premier rock climbing destinations in the country. Much of the land nearby is part of the **Crooked River National Grassland**. To the east, the relatively low, forested **Ochoco Mountains** are much less visited than the Cascades, and the range includes three small wilderness areas. South of Bend, the **Newberry National Volcanic Monument** (541-383-5700, www.fs.usda.gov/main/Deschutes/recarea/?recid=66159) includes lava tubes, cinder cones, and two beautiful, crystal-clear crater lakes set in a geologically active caldera. Practically anyplace in the region makes a great jumping-off point for backcountry trips.

For obvious reasons, central Oregon is a major outdoor sports center. Downhill and cross-country skiing and other winter sports bring crowds in the winter, while hiking and backpacking, mountain and road biking, rafting and other forms of boating, and golf are all popular pursuits during the summer and fall. Central Oregon has also become something of a hub for destination resorts; the two most venerable and best-known of these resorts are **Sunriver** (800-801-8765, www.sunriver-resort.com), about 15 miles south of Bend, and **Black Butte Ranch** (866-901-2961, www.blackbutteranch.com), off Highway 20 between Sisters and Santiam Pass. Closer to Portland, **Kah-Nee-Ta Resort and Spa** (800-554-4786, www.kahneeta.com) is located on the Warm Springs Indian Reservation. For more information on destinations in the region, contact the **Central Oregon Visitors Association** (800-800-8334, www.visitcentraloregon.com).

SOUTHERN OREGON

South of Eugene, the Willamette Valley peters out in a rugged jumble of forested mountains cleft by the valleys of the Umpqua and Rogue rivers and their various tributaries. Most southern Oregon cities, including Roseburg, Grants Pass, and Medford, huddle in the river valleys. **Roseburg** (541-672-9731, 800-444-9584, www.visitroseburg.com), although not particularly exciting, makes a good base for exploring the Umpqua Valley wine region (541-673-5323, www.umpquavalleywineries.org) and **Wildlife Safari** (541-679-6761, www.wildlifesafari.net), a drive-through wild animal park.

The Rogue River Valley in far southern Oregon, the site of Medford and Grants Pass, is a region of orchards, loggers, retirees, more wineries, and, surprisingly, smog. **Jacksonville** (www.jacksonvilleoregon.org), just west of Medford, is a well-preserved 19th-century gold-mining town, but the most popular "urban" destination in southern Oregon is **Ashland**. Home to the **Oregon Shakespeare Festival** (800-219-8161, www.osfashland.org), a nearly nine-month-long annual theatre series (and the attendant nice restaurants and hotels), as well as to large communities of environmentalists and California retirees, Ashland is an intriguing place to visit at any time of year. In winter, when the Shakespeare Festival is on hiatus, the **Mount Ashland Ski Area** (541-482-2897, www.mtashland.com) is a half-hour drive away.

Still more wineries nestle in the Applegate Valley, which winds through the botanically and geologically unique **Siskiyou Mountains**. Few roads pierce this rugged range (and none enter the large Kalmiopsis Wilderness), but US Highway 199 runs from Grants Pass toward the redwood country of northern California through the hippie-meets-logger community of Cave Junction (where there are still *more* wineries). A spur road leads to **Oregon Caves National Monument** (541-592-2100, www.nps.gov/orca), which centers on a marble cave system high in the Siskiyous.

The iconic natural attraction of southern Oregon, and arguably of the state as a whole, is **Crater Lake National Park** (541-594-3000, www.nps.gov/crla/). More than 1,900 feet deep and almost impossibly blue, Crater Lake fills the crater of ancient Mount Mazama, which erupted 7,700 years ago in a fashion that makes the 1980 Mt. St. Helens eruption look like a hiccup. Much of the park is inaccessible during the winter—the area averages some 44 *feet* of snow each year—but during the summer it's possible to drive around the lake, climb to the top of several neighboring peaks, or hike down to the water and take a boat to the mini-volcano of Wizard Island. Other regions of the Cascade spine north and south of the park are included within several wilderness areas, which receive far fewer visitors than the wilderness areas in the central and northern parts of the state. On the east side of the mountains, the city of **Klamath Falls** (www.discoverklamath.com) lies near broad, shallow Upper Klamath Lake, a major stopover point for migratory birds.

Information about southern Oregon destinations and accommodation options is available from the **Southern Oregon Visitors Association** (www. southernoregon.org).

EASTERN OREGON

Away from the Interstate 84 corridor (which follows the old route of the Oregon Trail), high, dry eastern Oregon receives comparatively few visitors. While it may not have many urban attractions—**Pendleton** (www.pendletonchamber.com), home of the annual Pendleton Round-up (www.pendletonroundup.com), being the main exception—this part of the state offers incredible scenery and wide-open spaces. Major mountain ranges—the Blue Mountains, the Strawberry Mountains, and the jagged, granitic Wallowas—thrust upward from the sagebrush and grassland, and offer outstanding and generally uncrowded recreational opportunities. The Wallowas in particular make an excellent hiking and backpacking destination; most of the range is protected within the vast **Eagle Cap Wilderness**, and more than 500 miles of trails link beautiful alpine lake basins. Non-hikers can enjoy the towns of Joseph and Enterprise, just north of glacial Wallowa Lake. Not far to the east, on the Oregon-Idaho border, is difficult-to-reach **Hells Canyon**, where the Snake River runs through North America's deepest river gorge.

The mountain-and-valley country of east-central Oregon includes the **John Day Fossil Beds National Monument** (541-987-2333, www.nps.gov/joda/); the monument has three separate units which protect not only abundant fossils but also the colorful Painted Hills. Remote southeastern Oregon has a host of adventurous destinations, including the canyons of the Owyhee River, Malheur and Harney lakes, and Hart Mountain Antelope Refuge, but the region's crown jewel is probably **Steens Mountain**. This fault-block mountain range rises fairly gradually from west to east; then, from the high point at nearly 10,000 feet, the east side plunges precipitously to the Alvord Desert, Oregon's driest spot, thousands of feet below. The mountain features aspen forests, cirque lakes, wildflower-dotted meadows, and bighorn sheep. A graded dirt road, passable by most passenger cars, runs from Frenchglen most of the way up the west side of the mountain (road open summer only).

The **Eastern Oregon Visitors Association** (541-574-2679, www.visiteasternoregon.com) is more than happy to suggest destinations and itineraries in this part of the state.

WASHINGTON STATE

Washington, like Oregon, is a topographically diverse state that encompasses coast, mountains, and semi-arid plateau, and has a correspondingly impressive range of getaway options.

One of the main attractions of southwestern Washington is clearly visible from Portland on a clear day. Mount St. Helens, which famously blew its top in May 1980, is now part of the **Mount St. Helens National Volcanic Monument** (360-449-7800, www.fs.usda.gov/mountsthelens). You can visit one of the two observatories that offer views of the crater (which contains a growing new lava dome), hike into the recovering blast zone, or make a long, ashy (or snowy) slog to the new summit at the crater rim (permit required). Ape Cave, on the south side of the mountain, is the longest lava tube in the Western Hemisphere; it's a great place to take kids. The next volcano to the east, **Mount Adams** (also visible from Portland), tops out at 12,276 feet and is thus more than 1,000 feet taller than Mount Hood. The area between the peaks is part of the **Gifford Pinchot National Forest** (360-891-5000, www.fs.usda.gov/gpnf/), which contains many wonderful (and, considering the proximity to Portland, often surprisingly uncrowded) hiking and backpacking options, including three wilderness areas; the lake-dotted Indian Heaven Wilderness is a particularly appealing destination (outside of peak mosquito season). The small community of **Trout Lake** makes a good base for exploring the Mount Adams region.

Moving north along the Cascades, **Mount Rainier National Park** (360-569-2211, www.nps.gov/mora) centers on the mountain of the same name, which at an elevation of 14,410 feet is the highest peak in the Pacific Northwest. In addition to the mountain itself and its many glaciers, the park offers alpine meadows, old-growth forest, and the 93-mile Wonderland Trail. Moving north along the spine of the Cascades, you can visit the Alpine Lakes Wilderness, Mount Baker and its adjacent wilderness and National Recreation Areas, and the rugged, glacier-clad peaks and steep-sided valleys of **North Cascades National Park** (360-854-7200, www.nps.gov/noca) on the Canadian border.

The bulk of Washington's population lives in the lowlands west of the Cascades along Puget Sound. Although cities like Olympia (the state capital), pleasant Bellingham, and gritty Tacoma are all worth a stop, the Big Kahuna of Washington cities is **Seattle**. Portlanders carry on a love-hate relationship with Seattle, 170 miles to the north. Despite legitimate gripes about Seattle's sprawl, traffic congestion, and high prices, Portlanders still flock to the city for its cultural attractions (which are arguably better and certainly more numerous than Portland's), its professional sports teams, and its matchless setting on the water between two mountain ranges (when you can see them). You can make a great weekend out of visiting Seattle's museums, sampling its cafés and restaurants, dodging airborne fish carcasses at Pike Place Market, and maybe even going to a Mariners or Seahawks game. Best of all, you can relax and go by train. For the official line on tourism in Seattle, contact the **Seattle Convention and Visitors Bureau** (866-732-2695, www.visitseattle.org).

The mountains visible across Puget Sound from Seattle are the Olympics, largely protected within **Olympic National Park** (360-565-3130, www.nps.gov/olym/). The park is incredibly diverse; besides the mountains, which are impressive enough, the park includes such attractions as the Hoh Rain Forest, the alpine meadows near Hurricane Ridge, and the longest stretch of wilderness coastline in the contiguous United States. Since 95% of the park is designated wilderness, the best way to explore its charms is on foot (with lots of time). Outside the park boundaries, overzealous forestry practices have compromised the Olympic Peninsula's tourism potential, but the region also includes interesting towns such as Port Angeles, Poulsbo, and charming, historic **Port Townsend** (www.enjoypt.com); soggy, unassuming Forks is the setting for the popular *Twilight* series, and as a result has become a tourist draw.

Puget Sound's islands offer fun maritime getaways, although they tend to be crowded with visitors from the Seattle area on summer and holiday weekends. Although largely rural, **Vashon Island** (206-463-6217, www.vashonchamber.com), southwest of Seattle, is home to many commuters to the city, who travel back and forth by ferry. Further north, the state's largest island, **Whidbey Island**, can be reached by ferry from either side of the Sound or by the bridge over Deception Pass; nearby **Camano Island** has bridge access only. Information about both destinations is available at www.whidbeycamanoislands.com.

At the northern end of the sound, the atmospheric **San Juan Islands** are accessible only by ferry (or air). It's best to give yourself at least a long weekend here; the wait for the ferry can take several hours, especially on summer weekends. Once you arrive, you'll find secluded beaches, charming towns, cozy coffee shops, and an abundance of quaint bed and breakfasts. Each of the three main islands—Lopez, Orcas, and San Juan—has a different character and is worth a visit; you can stay on all three islands over the course of a visit, or you could plan to use one as a base and take ferry rides to the others. If possible, bring or rent a bicycle or kayak and tour the islands that way. For more information, contact the **San Juan Islands Visitors Bureau** (888-468-3701, www.visitsanjuans.com). For details about ferry routes and schedules throughout the Puget Sound region, visit the **Washington State Ferries** website at www.wsdot.wa.gov/ferries/, or call their helpline at 888-808-7977 (206-464-6400 from outside Washington).

Eastern Washington, like eastern Oregon, is much drier than the western half of the state. The most popular draws are actually in the eastern Cascades or its fringes: **Lake Chelan**, the "Bavarian" village of **Leavenworth** (509-548-5807, www.leavenworth.org), and the cross-country skier's paradise of **Methow Valley**. Semi-arid eastern Washington contains some thriving cities, including Yakima, the Tri-Cities (Richland, Pasco, and Kennewick), and Spokane, along with vast fields of wheat; the major attractions, however, are the reservoirs along the Columbia River (including Lake Roosevelt, behind Grand Coulee Dam) and the mountain ranges of northeast Washington. In southeastern Washington, the area around **Walla Walla** (www.wallawalla.org) is a highly regarded wine-producing region; contact the **Walla Walla Valley Wine Alliance** (509-526-3117, www.wallawallawine.com) for details.

BRITISH COLUMBIA

Both cosmopolitan Vancouver and self-consciously anglophilic Victoria are popular getaways. **Vancouver**, which is accessible from Portland by car, train, bus, or nonstop flight, is a cosmopolitan port city with a spectacular setting, great shopping, and some of the best Asian restaurants on the West Coast. Thousand-acre Stanley Park, jutting out into Burrard Inlet not far from the central business district, is widely considered one of the most beautiful public parks in the world. For more information, contact **Tourism Vancouver** (www.tourismvancouver.com).

Victoria (www.tourismvictoria.com), near the southern tip of Vancouver Island, is a smaller and more laid-back destination that is sometimes called the most English city outside England. Apart from the double-decker buses and high tea at the Empress Hotel, Victoria has some beautiful gardens; the most famous of these, **Butchart Gardens** (866-652-4422, www.butchartgardens.com), was created out of a former quarry. Ships cruise directly to Victoria's Inner Harbour from downtown Seattle, Bellingham, and Port Angeles, while ferries from Anacortes, Washington, and the British Columbia mainland port of Tsawwassen go into Sidney or Swartz Bay, a few kilometers north of the city.

Beyond the province's big cities, major destinations in southwestern British Columbia include **Pacific Rim National Park** on the west coast of Vancouver Island; the **Gulf Islands**, the Canadian continuation of Washington's San Juan Islands, between Vancouver Island and the B.C. mainland; the world-class **Whistler Blackcomb** ski resort (www.whistlerblackcomb.com), host of most of the alpine events in the 2010 Winter Olympics; and the semi-arid, fruit-and-wine-producing **Okanogan Valley**.

FARTHER AFIELD

There are more than enough diversions in the Pacific Northwest to keep anyone busy for a lifetime. If you have a bad case of wanderlust (or sunshine lust), however, it's easy to venture farther afield. For one thing, long-distance driving is generally less stressful (or at least less crowded) here than in more heavily populated regions. In the Northeast, a drive from Boston to Washington, D.C., on Interstate 95 would pass through Providence, New York City, Newark, Philadelphia, Wilmington, and Baltimore (not to mention innumerable toll plazas); a drive of the same distance south from Portland on Interstate 5 wouldn't even get you to Sacramento.

A day's drive or less south from Portland could take you to the redwood forests of the northern California coast; 14,180-foot Mount Shasta or its nearby houseboat-infested reservoir, Lake Shasta; Lassen Volcanic National Park; the

Trinity Alps; Napa Valley or Sonoma; San Francisco; Lake Tahoe (or Reno, Nevada); or the California gold country. Heading east, you have access to most of Idaho (the scenic panhandle, rugged central Idaho, or Boise), as well as western Montana (including Glacier National Park and Missoula), the southern Canadian Rockies, and, if you have a really high tolerance for long-distance driving, Yellowstone National Park.

If you have the cash, and don't mind either the security hassles or the environmental impact of flying, Portland has nonstop flights to most major cities in the western United States. You can easily get away for a long weekend in Las Vegas, San Diego, Phoenix, or even Hawaii or Mexico.

PORTLAND'S EVENTS CALENDAR STARTS OFF SLOWLY IN THE DAMP, GRAY depths of winter, then builds to a crescendo in July, when the weather is reliably warm and dry. During the cooler, wetter months, most big events take place under cover; Portland is just not cold or snowy enough to support winter carnivals, and there is no ChillyDrizzleFest (yet). In contrast, summer celebrations tend to be outdoor affairs in parks and other open spaces. A sampling of Portland's more distinctive annual events is listed below.

Most Portland neighborhoods and suburban communities have one or more community festivals—street fairs, art festivals, intentionally cheesy historical celebrations, and the like—that are popular with local residents and make for fun, inexpensive outings.

JANUARY

- **Chocolate Fest**, 503-228-1367, www.chocolatefest.org; this benefit for the World Forestry Center takes place at the Convention Center.
- **Portland International Auto Show**, 503-233-5044, www.portlandautoshow. com; a celebration of all things automotive, the Portland International Auto Show fills the Oregon Convention Center with current-year car models and accessories, sneak peeks of forthcoming models, and a few concept cars that may never see production.
- **Portland Seafood & Wine Festival**, www.pdxseafoodnadwinefestival.com; held at the Oregon Convention Center in the middle of the Dungeness crab season, this festival indeed focuses on Oregon seafood and wine, which go together like a horse and carriage.
- **RiverCity Music Festival**, 503-282-0877, www.rivercitybluegrass.com; acoustic bluegrass rocks—well, reels, anyway—the Red Lion Hotel in Jantzen Beach for three days in January.

FEBRUARY

- **Portland Home & Garden Show**, 503-246-8291, www.otshows.com, is one of many home and garden–related trade shows held every year in Portland. The Home & Garden Show fills the Expo Center in North Portland with display gardens, art, and the booths of eager contractors. This event is usually held concurrently with the **Yard, Garden & Patio Show**, 360-210-5275, www.ygpshow.com, sponsored by the Oregon Association of Nurseries, at the Oregon Convention Center.
- **Portland International Film Festival**, 503-221-1156, www.nwfilm.org/festivals/piff; this two-week filmstravaganza is Oregon's biggest film festival. Now approaching 40 years old, PIFF typically screens over 100 films from more than two dozen countries, including some fresh-from-Sundance offerings.
- **Portland Jazz Festival,** www.pdxjazz.com/festival/; this multi-day festival, held at multiple venues in and around downtown Portland, features appearances by jazz artists of international renown, as well as dozens of free performances and educational events.

MARCH

- **Southeast Area ARTWalk**, www.seportlandartwalk.com; more than 100 artists in a large swath of inner Southeast Portland show their studios and their wares.
- **St. Patrick's Day**. Although it's no Boston, Portland celebrates St. Patrick's Day in style with a host of events scattered around the city. Fitness buffs can tackle the Shamrock Run (www.shamrockrunportland.com). The All-Ireland Cultural Society (www.oregonirishclub.org) hosts an annual family celebration at the Holy Rosary Church Hall (376 NE Clackamas St). As in other cities, bars and brewpubs all over town bedeck themselves in green and serve copious amounts of Harp and Guinness. Two downtown Irish-themed pubs throw the biggest bashes: **Paddy's** (65 SW Yamhill, 503-224-5626, www.paddys.com) sponsors St. Paddy's Blues & Brews, while **Kells Irish Restaurant & Pub** (112 SW 2nd Ave, 503-227-4057) hosts a massive three-day block party in heated tents (see www.kellsirishportland.com).

APRIL

- **82nd Avenue of Roses Parade**, www.rosefestival.org; the first sanctioned event of the Rose Festival season (see June), this small-town-worthy parade proceeds down part of 82nd Avenue, and is followed by a carnival and classic car show at Eastport Plaza.

- **Hood River Blossom Fest,** www.hoodriver.org; the Hood River Valley fills with fun events and the floral equivalent of leaf-peepers when the pear, cherry, and apple blossoms peak in the second half of April.
- The **Trillium Festival**, sponsored by Friends of Tryon Creek, 503-636-4398, www.tryonfriends.org, celebrates the emergence of spring in general, and the blooming of the native trillium in particular, at Tryon Creek State Natural Area in Southwest Portland. Festivities include a native plant sale.
- **Wooden Shoe Tulip Festival**, 503-634-2243, 800-711-2006, www.wooden-shoe.com/springshow.html; flower-lovers and Dutch-o-philes from all over Northwest Oregon converge on 40 acres of tulips near Woodburn from late March to early May.

MAY

- **Cinco de Mayo**, www.cincodemayo.org; Waterfront Park in downtown Portland hosts this annual celebration of Mexican food, entertainment, and *artesanía*, sponsored by the Portland Guadalajara Sister City Association.
- **Mother's Day Rhododendron Show**, Crystal Springs Rhododendron Garden, SE 28th Ave at Woodstock Blvd, 503-771-8386; Portland has an ideal climate for rhododendrons, and their blooms are usually at their most spectacular during this annual show.
- The **Portland Rose Festival** (see June) gets under way in May. The kickoff event is the **Rock 'n' Roll Half Marathon** (runrocknroll.competitor.com/portland) which zigs and zags its 13.1 miles through downtown Portland and the close-in eastside.

JUNE

- **Lake Oswego Festival of the Arts**, Lakewood Center for the Arts, 368 S State St, Lake Oswego, 503-635-3901, www.lakewood-center.org, is one of the largest art fairs in the region. In addition to an extensive art exhibition, a craft fair, and live entertainment, the festival usually highlights a specific art form or individual artist.
- **Portland Rose Festival**, 503-227-2681, www.rosefestival.org, is the biggest event on the Portland calendar. Seriously, some people in Portland live for this. The festival includes such diverse diversions as the Grand Floral Parade, the more lighthearted Starlight Parade, a raucous waterfront carnival, dragon boat races, fireworks, a children's parade, a rose show and competition, auto races, an arts festival, the crowning of the Rose Queen and her court, and the arrival of ships from the U.S. Coast Guard and the U.S. and Canadian navies. The Rose Festival is so big, so all-encompassing, and so long-lasting, that virtually no one dares to schedule any other events in Portland in June, except for the...

- **Portland Pride Festival & Parade**, 503-295-9788, www.pridenw.org; the Portland Pride march, festival, and parade are boisterous events held at Waterfront Park in mid-June, after the Rose Festival detritus has been removed. The parade route winds through downtown and ends in the Pearl District; participants range from local politicians to "dykes on bikes."
- **Tigard Festival of Balloons**, 503-612-8213, www.tigardballoon.org; if the Rose Festival has not exhausted your appetite for fun, skedaddle to the southwest suburb of Tigard for this festival of balloons—the big, hot air kind, not the kind that clowns twist into animal shapes.

JULY

- **Chamber Music Northwest Summer Festival**, 503-294-6400, www.cmnw.org, held on the Reed College and Portland State University campuses, is one of the largest chamber music festivals in the country; the festival program includes concerts, open rehearsals, and free lectures.
- **Concours d'Elegance Car Show**, 503-357-3006, 800-359-2310, www.forest-groveconcours.org, held on the Pacific University campus in Forest Grove, is the largest classic car show in the Pacific Northwest.
- **da Vinci Days**, 541-757-6363, www.davinci-days.org; science, technology, and weirdness intersect wonderfully in this annual celebration of creativity in Corvallis, about one and a half hours south of Portland. The kinetic sculpture race is a particular highlight.
- **Fourth of July Fireworks**. Fireworks shows take place in many locations around the metropolitan area, including over the Willamette River in downtown Portland, at Oaks Park, and at Fort Vancouver. (You may also find that neighborhood teenagers set off bottle rockets on an unofficial, and illegal, basis.)
- **Oregon Brewers Festival**, www.oregonbrewfest.com; a tradition among Portland beer aficionados, the Oregon Brewers Festival at Waterfront Park is one of the country's premier showcases of craft and micro brews. Admission is free, but tasting will cost you.
- **Oregon Country Fair**, 541-343-4298, www.oregoncountryfair.org; love it or hate it, Oregon Country Fair is unlike anything else anywhere in the world. Part Renaissance fair, part hippie revival, and part art-and-entertainment extravaganza, the Country Fair is more an experience than an event. It takes place over three days in Veneta, just outside Eugene, about two hours south of Portland. Look for cars around town that proudly display parking stickers from multiple years of the event.
- **Portland Scottish Highland Games**, 503-293-8501, www.phga.org, are a celebration of Scottish music, dancing, and such uniquely Celtic athletic contests as the Caber toss and the Scottish hammer throw. (Stay behind the safety nets.) Events usually take place at Mt. Hood Community College in Gresham.

- **Seattle to Portland Bicycle Classic**, 206-522-3222, www.cascade.org/ride-major-rides/group-health-stp; the Cascade Bicycle Club annual ride is one of the most anticipated long-distance cycling events in the country. Up to 10,000 participants from around the world cover the 200-odd miles between Seattle and Portland in one or two days.
- **Waterfront Blues Festival**, www.waterfrontbluesfest.com, held at Waterfront Park in downtown Portland in early July, bills itself as the largest blues festival west of the Mississippi. The event benefits the Oregon Food Bank and features multiple stages and big-name blues artists from around the country.

AUGUST

- **Bite of Oregon**, 503-248-0600, 800-452-6079, www.biteoforegon.com; no, it's not a mouthful of soil. A fundraiser for Special Olympics Oregon, the Bite of Oregon features food from dozens of local restaurants, Oregon wine and beer, an Iron Chef Oregon competition, and musical and comedy events on four different stages at Waterfront Park downtown.
- **Festa Italiana**, www.festa-italiana.org; the latter half of this week-long celebration of local Italian heritage and culture transforms Pioneer Courthouse Square into an ersatz Italian piazza, complete with food court, wine garden, strolling musicians, and a variety of entertainment and activities for the whole family.
- **Hood to Coast Relay**, 503-292-4626, www.hoodtocoast.com; thousands of runners take part every year in this event, which is exactly what its name implies: a relay race from Mount Hood to the Oregon Coast.
- **Mount Hood Jazz Festival**, 503-661-2700, www.mthoodjazz.com; the area's most venerable jazz festival features world-renowned headliners and lesser-known talents. Now more than three decades old, the festival takes place in Gresham. Posters from past festivals are local collectibles.
- **Portland Festival Symphony**, 503-481-1650, www.portlandfestivalsymphony.org; for over 30 years, the Portland Festival Symphony has presented free classical music concerts in Portland's city parks.
- **Providence Bridge Pedal**, 503-281-9198, www.bridgepedal.com, is your chance to ride your bike over all 10 of the city's Willamette River road bridges, including the Marquam (Interstate 5) and Fremont (Interstate 405) bridges. (The freeway bridges are closed to traffic in one direction, so you won't be dodging speeding semis.)
- **Street of Dreams**, 503-894-9596, www.streetofdreamspdx.com; every year, the Home Builders Association of Metropolitan Portland creates a showcase of luxury (i.e., ridiculously expensive) homes with unnecessarily complex rooflines. More than 100,000 people tour the homes to gawk at new innovations in high-end building trends.

- **Tualatin Crawfish Festival**, www.tualatincrawfishfestival.com; this family-friendly festival honors the crustaceans that lurk in the Tualatin River. The event features live entertainment, food and craft vendors, and of course copious crawfish consumption. (The crawfish actually come from Lake Billy Chinook in Central Oregon.)

SEPTEMBER

- **Art in the Pearl**, 503-722-9017, www.artinthepearl.com, takes place in the North Park Blocks over Labor Day weekend. In addition to art, the festivities include musical and theatrical performances, plenty of food, and hands-on activities for children and adults.
- **Cycle Oregon**, 503-287-0405, www.cycleoregon.com, is the highlight of the Oregon bicycle touring calendar. Each year, this week-long bike trek takes in a different scenic, rural, and (alas) hilly portion of the state; participants camp in small towns, which usually offer a hearty welcome.
- **Musicfest NW,** www.musicfestnw.com, features scores of mostly indie performers at Waterfront Park and other venues. Most acts are local, but some prominent national and international groups also make appearances.
- **Oktoberfest**. Most Portland area Oktoberfests actually take place in September, when the weather is more likely to be dry. The biggest such event is the family-oriented Mt. Angel Oktoberfest (855-899-6338, www.oktoberfest.org), held in the town of Mt. Angel, about 45 minutes south of Portland. Other Oktoberfest celebrations occur at Oaks Park in Southeast Portland, in St. Helens, and at brewpubs and German restaurants throughout the region.
- **Oregon State Fair**, 800-833-0011, www.oregonstatefair.org; while it's not really a match for the state fairs of the Midwest, Oregon's version, held at the state fairgrounds in Salem, features the same winning combination of agricultural displays, carnival rides, live entertainment, and deep-fried foods. It usually starts in late August and ends on Labor Day.
- **Polish Festival**, 503-281-7532, www.portlandpolonia.org/festival; billed as the largest Polish festival west of Chicago, this North Interstate Avenue classic includes Polish folk dancing, Polish beer, and food. Pierogi z kapusta and poppyseed cake, anyone?
- **Susan G. Komen Race for the Cure**, 503-552-9160, www.komenoregon.org; tens of thousands of people walk or run through downtown Portland each year in the Portland Race for the Cure, an event that raises funds for breast cancer research.
- **Time-Based Art Festival**, 503-242-1419, www.pica.org; the Portland Institute for Contemporary Art schedules 10 days of contemporary art from multiple genres—performance, music, visual arts, dance, and more—at a panoply of traditional and nontraditional venues.

OCTOBER

- **Greek Festival**, Holy Trinity Greek Orthodox Church, 3131 NE Glisan, 503-234-0468, www.goholytrinity.org/cGreekFest.html; a church in the Laurelhurst neighborhood throws this popular fundraiser every year. Look for very home-made Greek food, including scrumptious baklava and other pastries.
- **Howloween**, 503-226-1561, www.oregonzoo.org/Events/Howloween/index.htm; the Oregon Zoo gets spooky in late October. Activities include mildly scary storytelling and a kids' scavenger hunt, but the highlight is the opening event, where the zoo's elephants smash a giant pumpkin.
- **Pumpkin Patches and Corn Mazes.** Many Portland families make it an annual tradition to troop out to one of the many pumpkin patches outside Portland, pick a pumpkin or two from the fields, and even wander through a corn maze. Two of the most popular and well-established pumpkin patches are on Sauvie Island: The Pumpkin Patch, 503-621-7110, www.portlandmaze.com, and Sauvie Island Farms, 503-621-3988, www.sauvieislandfarms.com.
- **Portland Marathon**, 503-226-1111, www.portlandmarathon.org; the highlight of the Portland running calendar, the Portland Marathon's course takes in both sides of the Willamette River. Weather can be crisp and dry or completely sodden. The related festivities include a wheelchair competition, a 2-mile run for children, and a 10-kilometer fitness walk.
- **Portland Open Studios**, www.portlandopenstudios.com; during the second and third weekends of October many Portland artists—painters, sculptors, glassblowers, metalsmiths, potters, and more—open their studios to visitors.
- **Reel Music**, 503-221-1156, www.nwfilm.org/festivals/reelmusic/; one of several film festivals presented by the NW Film Center each year, the Reel Music festival focuses on music on film, but it is not just a theatrical clone of MTV.

NOVEMBER

- **Civil War.** No, not a re-enactment of the War Between the States, but the annual game between the University of Oregon and Oregon State University football teams (and associated tailgate parties), which takes place alternately in Eugene and Corvallis. Either way, if you're not going to the game, stay off Interstate 5 south of Portland on game day.
- **Columbia Gorge Model Railroad Show**, 2505 N Vancouver Ave, 503-28TRAIN, www.cgmrc.com; every November, the Columbia Gorge Model Railroad Club opens its clubhouse for public viewing of its enormous and incredibly detailed scale model of railroad operations in the Columbia Gorge.
- **Macy's Holiday Parade,** 503-223-0512. For years, the Meier & Frank Holiday Parade sent a meandering line of floats, marching bands, and costumed figures

(including Santa) through downtown Portland on the day after Thanksgiving. Following Macy's purchase of the Meier & Frank chain in 2006, the parade continues under a new name.

- **Wine Country Thanksgiving**, 503-646-2985, www.willamettewines.com/event/wine-country-thanksgiving; more than 100 wineries and tasting rooms, many otherwise closed to visitors, open to the public over Thanksgiving weekend for tastings, tours, and special events. (A similar event takes place during Memorial Day weekend.)
- **Wordstock**, www.wordstockfestival.com, is an annual literary event that features renowned and up-and-coming authors, writing workshops, and a children's festival.

DECEMBER

- **Festival of Lights at the Grotto**, NE 85th Ave at Sandy Blvd, 503-261-2400, www.thegrotto.org/Christmas/; the Grotto (formally the National Sanctuary of Our Sorrowful Mother) decorates its peaceful grounds in Northeast Portland with a walk-through display of more than 500,000 lights. Other attractions include nativity scenes, puppet shows, choral events, and a petting zoo.
- **Parade of Christmas Ships**, www.christmasships.org; two brightly lit flotillas ply the Willamette and Columbia rivers every night for two weeks in December. Riverside restaurants are frequently booked months in advance.
- **Peacock Lane,** one block east of SE 39th Ave between Stark St and Belmont St, www.peacocklane.net. In mid-December, this street of modest English-style homes becomes a wonderland of dazzling holiday decorations, many of which are quite elaborate and have been trotted out every holiday season for decades. It's best to walk down the street, both to avoid traffic snarls and to be better able to buy hot chocolate and other refreshments.
- The **Holiday Ale Festival**, www.holidayale.com, features winter ales and other holiday-themed brews. The event is held outdoors, at Pioneer Courthouse Square downtown (albeit under the shelter of a huge tent).
- **ZooLights**, 503-226-1561, www.oregonzoo.org/ZooLights; another bulb-related spectacle, the month-long ZooLights event sees the Oregon Zoo festooned with nearly a million lights. Light-peeping visitors are also treated to live performances and train rides.

THE VOLUME OF WRITING ABOUT THE PACIFIC NORTHWEST IN GENERAL, and Portland in particular, can be overwhelming, particularly if you walk into a place like the Pacific Northwest Room at Powell's Books, or even a branch library. This chapter lists only a few of the most useful and distinctive books about Portland and the region.

ARCHITECTURE AND URBAN PLANNING

Portland cries out for a comprehensive book about its historic and modern architecture. The following books are the best currently available choices.

- *An Architectural Guidebook to Portland* by Bart King
- *A Century of Portland Architecture* by Thomas Vaughn and George McMath, published in 1967, is out of print but worth seeking out for its detailed descriptions of the city's older buildings (many of which are still standing over 40 years later).
- *Classic Houses of Portland, Oregon, 1850-1950* by William J. Hawkins III and William Willingham
- *The Portland Bridge Book* by Sharon Wood Wortman and Ed Wortman is an engaging guide to—surprise!—Portland's bridges.

Urban planning may not be the sexiest topic around, but a grounding in the subject is essential to understanding Portland's development. Here are a few tomes to get you started:

- *City Limits: Walking Portland's Boundary* by David Oates describes the author's stroll along the entire urban growth boundary of the Portland metropolitan area.
- Portland State University professor of urban studies Carl Abbott has written several books about Portland urban life, history, and urban planning. Although an academic rather than a popular title, *Greater Portland: Urban Life and Landscape in the Pacific Northwest* ties together Portland's natural setting, culture,

and urban planning. Abbott's history of the city's planning and growth, *Portland: Planning, Politics, and Growth in a Twentieth-Century City*, is out of print but is available at most public libraries.

* *The Portland Edge: Challenges and Successes in Growing Communities*, edited by Connie P. Ozawa, is a compendium of essays about planning and its discontents.

FICTION

Lots of authors make their home in Portland—Ursula K. Le Guin, Chuck Palahniuk, Jean Auel, Phillip Margolin, Chelsea Cain, and Katherine Dunn are a few of the city's best known fiction writers—but not all of them use Portland as the setting for their stories. The majority of novels set in Portland seem to be mysteries and thrillers; the city's weather makes for great noirish, Raymond Chandleresque atmosphere. Novels and stories that are set in whole or in part in Portland include:

* Several of Beverly Cleary's children's stories, notably the *Ramona* books, which are set in Portland; Ramona Quimby (named after Portland's Quimby Street, just like Mayor Quimby of Springfield in *The Simpsons*) lives on Klickitat Street (an actual Northeast Portland thoroughfare).
* *Geek Love* by Katherine Dunn; narrated by an, um, hunchbacked albino dwarf, this truly disturbing novel is set partly in Portland.
* *The Lathe of Heaven* by Ursula K. Le Guin; this 1971 novel takes place in a post-apocalyptic (and yet not so—it's hard to explain) future Portland.
* Blake Nelson's *Paranoid Park* teen skate thriller was made into a movie in 2007 by local director Gus Van Sant.
* Chelsea Cain's series of best-selling thrillers (*HeartSick, Sweetheart, Evil at Heart*) featuring the intelligent, beautiful, irresistible female serial killer Gretchen Lowell, and the reporters and detectives who become entangled with her, takes place entirely in and around Portland, complete with recognizable locations at which bodies and body parts are discovered.

A recent anthology, *Reading Portland: The City in Prose*, edited by John Trombold and Peter Donahue, includes several short story selections about the Rose City. The *Portland Noir* anthology, edited by Kevin Sampsell, is a collection of noir-ish stories set in Portland. The many novels set elsewhere in Oregon include several Ken Kesey titles (such as *Sometimes a Great Notion* and *One Flew Over the Cuckoo's Nest*) and *Honey in the Horn* by H.L. Davis, a novel about homesteaders in Oregon in the first decade of the 20th century, which won the Pulitzer Prize for fiction in 1936.

GUIDEBOOKS

GENERAL

There are probably dozens of regional or city-specific tourist guidebooks that include Portland, from mainstream series like Fodor's and Frommer's to "backpacker" guides from Lonely Planet and Rough Guide. You probably won't need any of them. You're not a tourist; you live here now, or you're thinking about it, and the sort of necessarily shallow coverage and narrow advice that most guidebooks and travel articles provide—stay downtown, eat in the Pearl District, go to a food cart, stand in line at Voodoo for mediocre donuts, look at the quirky freaks!—is just not going to be useful. Here are a few guidebooks that may interest residents as well as visitors.

- The *Best Places* series of guidebooks (*Best Places Portland, Best Places Northwest*, etc.) is geared towards visitors, but the restaurant and leisure listings could be useful to newcomers.
- Kelly Melillo's *Best Places to Pee: A Guide to the Funky and Fabulous Bathrooms of Portland*, is much more illuminating than the title would suggest. And no, it's not part of the *Best Places* guidebook series.
- *Don't Jump! The Northwest Winter Blues Survival Guide*, by Seattle writers Traci Voget and Novella Carpenter, is a tongue-in-cheek guide to living with gray, rainy weather.
- For a unique and very alternative view of the city, try *Fugitives and Refugees: A Walk in Portland, Oregon* by Portland novelist Chuck Palahniuk (author of *Fight Club*, among other things).
- *Living With Earthquakes in the Pacific Northwest* by Robert S. Yeats
- *The Zinester's Guide to Portland: A Low/No Budget Guide to Visiting and Living in Portland, Oregon*, by Shawn Granton and Nate Beaty; although only a few years old, this book is somewhat dated—the scene waits for no hipster—but it will still be useful for certain demographics and not useful (but still amusing) to certain others.

OUTDOOR GUIDES

Visit your local bookstore and you'll find more hiking guides and other outdoor guidebooks to Oregon than you can shake a lightweight trekking pole at, not to mention field guides for everything from newts and ferns to whales and trees. Here are a few suggestions to get you started:

- **The Mountaineers Books** (www.mountaineersbooks.org), based in Seattle, publishes a slew of outdoor guides for Oregon and Southwest Washington, including guides to hiking, snowshoeing, cross-country skiing, bicycling, climbing, and boating. If you have a specialized interest, you'll want to check out their publications on the topic. The guidebooks with the broadest appeal include *The Waterfall Lover's Guide to the Pacific Northwest* by Gregory Plumb; *Best Short Hikes in Northwest Oregon* by Rhonda and George Ostertag; *100 Classic Hikes in Oregon* by Douglas Lorain; and *Best Hikes with Kids: Oregon* by Bonnie Henderson.

- Laura O. Foster's *Portland Hill Walks: Twenty Explorations in Parks and Neighborhoods, Portland City Walks: Twenty Explorations in and around Town,* and *The Portland Stairs Book,* along with *Walking Portland* by Becky Ohlsen, outline interesting walking tours around the city.
- Eugene-based explorer and prolific writer William L. Sullivan has authored many Oregon guidebooks, including the popular "100 Hikes" series; the Portland-area entry, *100 Hikes in Northwest Oregon and Southwest Washington*, now in its fourth edition, is possibly the best local hiking guide available. Other useful books include the *Atlas of Oregon Wilderness, Oregon Trips & Trails,* and *Hiking Oregon's History: The Stories Behind Historic Places You Can Walk To.*
- *Wild in the City: A Guide to Portland's Natural Areas,* edited by Mike Houck, the Audubon Society of Portland's urban naturalist, and travel writer M.J. Cody, exhaustively catalogues greenspaces in and near the metropolitan area; dozens of local writers and naturalists describe the landscape and natural history of these areas, and suggest walking, paddling, biking, and birdwatching tours.

REGIONAL HISTORY

Thousands of books, most now out of print, cover virtually every aspect you could imagine of Pacific Northwest history in general and Portland history in particular. If you're a history buff, a trip through the regional history section of your local public library, or a wander through the groaning aisles of used books at Powell's, will be a rewarding endeavor. The books below represent a small sample of what's available:

- *Fire at Eden's Gate: Tom McCall and the Oregon Story* by Brent Walth tells the story of Oregon's dynamic governor Tom McCall, who was largely responsible for many of the state's environmental innovations—the bottle bill, public ownership of the entire coastline, and statewide land use planning, among others—in the 1960s and 1970s. Read this and come away with the realization that they don't make 'em like they used to.
- *The Great Extravaganza: Portland and the Lewis and Clark Exposition* by Carl Abbott; that's "exposition," not "expedition"—the 1905 fair that marked the centennial of Lewis and Clark's expedition was a turning point in Portland's development.
- *Naked Against the Rain: The People of the Lower Columbia River 1770-1830* by Rick Rubin (out of print) tells the story of the native peoples of Northwest Oregon at the dawn of European settlement in the region.
- *Oregon 1859: A Snapshot in Time,* by Janice Marschner, describes each of Oregon's original counties in the year of statehood.

- *Oregon: This Storied Land* by William G. Robbins.
- *The Oregon Story: 1850-2000*, put together by the *Oregonian* newspaper, is a concise, accessible history of the state.
- *Portland: People, Politics and Power 1851-2001*, by Jewel Lansing, provides surprisingly juicy historical details about Portland's politics, personalities, and general development over the last 150 years.
- *Portland Then and Now* by Linda Dodds and Carolyn Buan is interesting mainly as a visual record of the city's evolution; the book juxtaposes old and new photos of various locations around Portland.
- *Sweet Cakes, Long Journey: The Chinatowns of Portland, Oregon* by Marie Rose Wang.
- *Timberline and a Century of Skiing on Mount Hood* by Jean Arthur.
- *Willamette Landings: Ghost Towns of the River* by Howard M. Coming describes the many riverboat landings along the river, and how every town vied to become the state's big metropolis.

REFERENCE BOOKS

- The *Atlas of Oregon*, issued by the University of Oregon Press, features nearly 300 pages of beautifully rendered, highly detailed maps dealing with virtually every aspect of the state's history, natural environment, and demographics, ranging from Native American language groups (circa 1850) to soil types, urban development patterns, and county-by-county voting results in every presidential election since 1928. If you get just one reference book about Oregon, this should be the one.
- Each year, the Oregon Secretary of State publishes the *Oregon Blue Book*, a compendium that's chock full o' facts and figures about state government.
- *The Oregon Almanac: Facts About Oregon* by Andrea Jarvela, as the title suggests, is an unofficial compendium of facts about the state.
- *Oregon Geographic Names* by Lewis McArthur describes the origins of thousands of Oregon place names, from Aaron Mercer Reservoir to Zwagg Island.

F OR HELP ON FINDING 800 NUMBERS, AND ESPECIALLY FOR TIPS ON HOW to reach an actual human being at hundreds of companies, go to **www. gethuman.com**.

- **211**, www.211info.org, Referral to Community Health and Social Services
- **411**, Telephone Directory Assistance (charge may apply)
- **511**, Road Conditions
- **711**, Telecommunications Relay Service
- **911**, Police, Fire, or Medical Emergencies

ANIMALS

See also "Veterinarians, Emergency Clinics" below.

- **Clackamas County Dog Services**, 503-655-8628, www.co.clackamas.or.us/dogs/
- **Clark County Community Development (Animals and Pets)**, 360-397-2488, www.clark.wa.gov/development/animals/index.html
- **Humane Society for Southwest Washington**, 360-693-4746, www.southwesthumane.org
- **Multnomah County Animal Services**, 503-988-7387, www.multcopets.org
- **Oregon Humane Society**, 503-285-7722, www.oregonhumane.com
- **Washington County Animal Services and Bonnie L. Hays Small Animal Shelter**, 503-846-7041, www.co.washington.or.us/hhs/AnimalServices/

AUTOMOBILES

- **Oregon Department of Environmental Quality Vehicle Inspection Program** (emissions testing), 503-229-5066, 877-476-0583, www.deq.state.or.us/aq/vip/
- **Oregon Driver and Motor Services Division**, 503-299-9999, www.oregon.gov/ODOT/DMV/

- **Washington Vehicle Emissions Check Program**, 253-395-1177, www.ecy.wa.gov/programs/air/cars/automotive_pages.htm
- **Washington Department of Licensing**, 360-902-3900, www.dol.wa.gov/driverslicense/

BIRTH AND DEATH CERTIFICATES

- **Oregon Center for Health Statistics**, 971-673-1190, www.oregon.gov/DHS/ph/chs/
- **Washington Center for Health Statistics**, 360-236-4300, www.doh.wa.gov/LicensesPermitsandCertificates/BirthDeathMarriageandDivorce/

CONSUMER PROTECTION AND SERVICES

- **Better Business Bureau**, 503-212-3022, www. bbb.org/alaskaoregonwesternwashington/
- **Federal Trade Commission**, 877-382-4357, www.ftc.gov
- **Identity Theft Resource Center**, 888-400-5530, www.idtheftcenter.org
- **Oregon Department of Justice, Office of the Attorney General**, 877-877-9392 (consumer hotline), www.doj.state.or.us/consumer
- **Oregon Insurance Division**, 503-947-7984, 888-877-4894, www.insurance.oregon.gov
- **Oregon Public Utility Commission**, 503-378-6600, 800-522-2404, www.puc.state.or.us
- **Oregon Construction Contractors Board**, 503-378-4621, www.hirealicensedcontractor.com
- **Washington Department of Labor and Industries**, 800-647-0982, secure.lni.wa.gov/verify/
- **Washington State Office of the Attorney General**, 800-551-4636, www.atg.wa.gov
- **Washington Utilities and Transportation Commission**, 888-333-9882, www.wutc.wa.gov

CREDIT BUREAUS

- **Equifax**, 800-685-1111, www.equifax.com
- **Experian**, 888-397-3742, www.experian.com
- **TransUnion**, 800-888-4213, www.transunion.com

CRISIS HOTLINES AND EMERGENCY SOCIAL SERVICES

It is always appropriate to call 911 and request police and/or emergency medical services if any person is in immediate danger of physical harm. In a non-emergency situation, dial **211** to be connected to community social services.

- **Aging & Disability Services 24-Hour Help Line**, 503-988-3646
- **AIDS/STD Hotline**, 503-223-2437, 800-777-2437
- **Alcohol and Drug Abuse HelpLine**, 800-923-HELP, 800-621-1646 (hotline)
- **Child Abuse Hotline**, 503-731-3100, 800-509-5439
- **Elder Abuse Hotline**, 503-945-5832. 800-232-3020
- **HopeLine** (suicide hotline), 800-SUICIDE
- **Mental Health Crisis Hotline**, 503-988-4888, 800-716-9769
- **National Domestic Violence Hotline**, 800-799-SAFE, www.ndvh.org
- **National Suicide Prevention Lifeline**, 800-273-TALK
- **Portland Women's Crisis Line**, 503-235-5333, www.pwcl.org
- **Problem Gambling Helpline**, 877-MYLIMIT
- **Teen Crisis and Counseling Line**, 877-553-TEEN
- **Sexual Assault Resource Center**, 503-640-5311, www.sarcoregon.org

DISABLED, SERVICES FOR

- **711**, Telecommunications Relay Service
- **Alliance of People with Disabilities** (Washington), 206-545-7055, www.disabilitypride.org
- **The Arc of Multnomah-Clackamas** (advocacy and support for the developmentally disabled), 503-223-7279, www.thearcmult.org
- **The Arc of Southwest Washington** (advocacy and support for the developmentally disabled), 360-254-1562, www.arcswwa.org
- **Disability Rights Oregon**, 503-243-2081, www.droregon.org
- **Independent Living Resources**, 503-232-7411, www.ilr.org
- **Oregon Department of Human Services, Division for Aging and People with Disabilities**, 503-945-5811, 800-282-8096, www.oregon.gov/DHS/spwpd
- **Ride Connection** (transportation services), 503-226-0700, www.rideconnection.org
- **Washington Aging and Long-Term Support Administration**, www.altsa.dshs.wa.gov

EMERGENCY

- **Fire, Police, Medical**, 911
- **Poison Control Center**, 800-222-1222

GARBAGE

See "Trash and Recycling" below

GOVERNMENT

PORTLAND
- **City Hall**, general information, 503-823-4000, www.portlandoregon.gov

- **City Ombudsman**, 503-823-0144
- **Mayor's Comment Line**, 503-823-4127
- **Office of Neighborhood Involvement**, 503-823-4519, www.portlandoregon.gov/oni/
- **Portland Maps**, www.portlandmaps.com

OTHER AREA CITIES

- **Banks**, 503-324-5112, www.cityofbanks.org
- **Battle Ground**, 360-342-5000, www.cityofbg.org
- **Beaverton**, 503-526-2222, www.beavertonoregon.gov
- **Camas**, 360-834-6864, www.cityofcamas.us
- **Canby**, 503-266-4021, www.ci.canby.or.us
- **Cornelius**, 503-357-9112, www.ci.cornelius.or.us
- **Damascus**, 503-658-8545, www.ci.damascus.or.us
- **Durham**, 503-639-6851, www.durham-oregon.us
- **Estacada**, 503-630-8270, www.cityofestacada.org
- **Fairview**, 503-665-7929, www.fairvieworegon.gov
- **Forest Grove**, 503-992-3207, www.ci.forest-grove.or.us
- **Gladstone**, 503-656-5225, www.ci.gladstone.or.us
- **Gresham**, 503-661-3000, www.greshamoregon.gov
- **Happy Valley**, 503-783-3800, www.ci.happy-valley.or.us
- **Hillsboro**, 503-681-6100, www.ci.hillsboro.or.us
- **King City**, 503-639-4082, www.ci.king-city.or.us
- **La Center**, 360-263-2782, www.ci.lacenter.wa.us
- **Lake Oswego**, 503-635-0270, www.ci.oswego.or.us
- **Maywood Park**, 503-255-9805, www.cityofmaywoodpark.com
- **Milwaukie**, 503-786-7555, www.milwaukieoregon.gov
- **Molalla**, 503-829-6855, www.cityofmolalla.com
- **Newberg**, 503-538-9421, www.newbergoregon.gov
- **North Plains**, 503-647-5555, www.cityofnp.org
- **Oregon City**, 503-657-0891, www.orcity.org
- **Ridgefield**, 360-887-3557, www.ci.ridgefield.wa.us
- **Sandy**, 503-668-5533, www.ci.sandy.or.us
- **Scappoose**, 503-543-7146, www.ci.scappoose.or.us
- **Sherwood**, 503-625-5522, www.sherwoodoregon.gov
- **St. Helens**, 503-397-6272, www.ci.st-helens.or.us
- **Tigard**, 503-639-4171, www.tigard-or.gov
- **Troutdale**, 503-665-5175, www.ci.troutdale.or.us
- **Tualatin**, 503-691-3061, www.tualatinoregon.gov
- **Vancouver**, 360-487-8600, www.cityofvancouver.us
- **Washougal**, 360-835-8501, www.cityofwashougal.us
- **West Linn**, 503-657-0331, www.westlinnoregon.gov
- **Wilsonville**, 503-682-1011, www.ci.wilsonville.or.us

- **Woodland**, 360-225-8281, www.ci.woodland.wa.us
- **Wood Village**, 503-667-6211, www.ci.wood-village.or.us

COUNTY AND REGIONAL GOVERNMENTS
- **Clackamas County**, 503-655-8656, www.clackamas.us
- **Clark County**, 360-397-2000, www.clark.wa.us
- **Columbia County**, 503-397-7210, www.co.columbia.or.us
- **Marion County,** 503-566-3916, www.co.marion.or.us
- **Multnomah County**, 503-823-4000, www.multco.us
- **Metro** (Regional Government), 503-797-1700, www.oregonmetro.gov
- **Washington County**, 503-846-8611, www.co.washington.or.us
- **Yamhill County,** 503-472-9371, www.co.yamhill.or.us

STATE GOVERNMENT
- **State of Oregon**, www.oregon.gov
- **State of Washington**, www.wa.gov

HOSPITALS

See **Health Care** section of **Helpful Services** chapter; see also Emergency Hospitals in Neighborhood Information listings.

HOUSING AND REAL ESTATE

- **Community Alliance of Tenants**, 503-460-9702, www.oregoncat.org
- **Craigslist**, www.portland.craigslist.org
- **Portland Housing Center**, 503-282-7744, www.portlandhousingcenter.org
- **RMLS** (multiple listing service), www.rmls.com
- **U.S. Department of Housing and Urban Development**, 202-708-1112, www.hud.gov

LEGAL REFERRALS

- **Legal Aid Services of Oregon**, www.oregonlawhelp.org
- **Oregon State Bar**, 503-684-3763, 800-452-7636, www.osbar.org
- **Clark County Bar Association Lawyer Referral Service**, 360-695-0599

LIBRARIES

- **Library Information Network of Clackamas County**, 503-723-4888, www.lincc.org
- **Fort Vancouver Regional District Library**, 360-906-5106, www.fvrl.org
- **Multnomah County Library**, 503-988-5402, www.multcolib.org
- **Washington County Cooperative Library Services**, 503-846-3222, www.wccls.org

NEWSPAPERS AND MAGAZINES

See **Getting Settled** chapter.

NUISANCES AND DISPUTES

- **Abandoned Auto Hotline** (City of Portland), 503-823-7309
- **Graffiti Abatement Hotline** (City of Portland), 503-823-4TAG
- **Liquor License Issues** (City of Portland), 503-823-4520
- **Noise Control Office** (City of Portland), 503-823-2663
- **Nuisance, Housing Code Violations** (City of Portland), 503-823-CODE
- **Resolutions Northwest** (mediation), 503-595-4890, www.resolutionsnorthwest.org

PARKS AND RECREATION

LOCAL AND REGIONAL
- **Battle Ground Parks and Recreation**, 360-342-5380
- **Camas Parks and Recreation**, 360-834-5307, www.cityofcamas.us/parks
- **Canby Parks & Recreation**, 503-266-9404
- **Clackamas County Parks Department**, 503-742-4414, www.clackamas.us/parks
- **Cornelius Parks Department**, 503-357-3011
- **Fairview Parks & Recreation, 503-665-9320**
- **Forest Grove Parks & Recreation**, 503-992-3237
- **Gresham Parks & Recreation**, 503-618-2235 www.greshamoregon.gov/play/
- **Hillsboro Parks & Recreation**, 503-681-6120
- **Lake Oswego Parks & Recreation**, 503-697-6500, www.ci.oswego.or.us/parksrec/
- **Metro Parks**, 503-797-1850, www.oregonmetro.gov/metro-parks-and-natural-areas
- **North Clackamas Parks & Recreation District**, 503-742-4348, www.ncprd.com
- **Oregon City Parks and Recreation**, 503-496-1201, www.orcity.org/parksandrecreation
- **Portland Parks and Recreation**, 503-823-PLAY, www.portlandparks.org
- **Sherwood Parks Department**, 503-625-5722, www.sherwoodoregon.gov/parksrec
- **Tigard Parks**, 503-718-2598, www.Tigard-or.gov
- **Troutdale Parks & Facilities,** 503-674-3300, www.ci.troutdale.or.us/parks-facilities/
- **Tualatin Parks and Recreation Division**, 503-691-3064, www.tualatinoregon.gov/recreation
- **Tualatin Hills Park and Recreation District**, 503-645-6433, www.thprd.org
- **Vancouver-Clark Parks**, 360-619-1111, www.cityofvancouver.us/parksrec
- **Washington County Parks**, 503-846-8881
- **Washougal Parks Department**, 360-835-2662
- **West Linn Parks & Recreation**, 503-557-4700, www.westlinnoregon.gov/parksrec/
- **Wilsonville Parks and Recreation**, 503-682-3727, www.wilsonvilleparksandrec.com

STATE

- **Oregon State Parks**, 800-551-6949, www.oregonstateparks.org
- **Washington State Parks**, 360-902-8844, www.parks.wa.gov

POLICE

- **Emergency**, 911

PORTLAND

- **Portland Police Bureau**, general, 503-823-0000; non-emergency police assistance, 503-823-3333; www.portlandpolice.com

SURROUNDING AREAS

- **Battle Ground Police Department**, 360-342-5200
- **Beaverton Police Department**, 503-526-2260, www.beavertonpolice.org
- **Camas Police Department**, 360 831 1151, www.cityofcamas.us/police
- **Canby Police Department**, 503-266-1104, www.canbypolice.com
- **Clackamas County Sheriff**, 503-785-5000, www.clackamas.us/sheriff/
- **Clark County Sheriff**, 360-397-2211, www. clark.wa.gov/sheriff/
- **Cornelius Police Department**, 503-359-1881
- **Fairview Police Department**, 503-674-6200
- **Forest Grove Police Department**, 503-629-0111
- **Gladstone Police Department**, 503-655-8211
- **Gresham Police Department**, 503-618-2318
- **Hillsboro Police Department**, 503-681-6190
- **King City Police Department**, 503-629-0111
- **La Center Police Department**, 360-263-2745
- **Lake Oswego Police Department**, 503-635-0238, www.ci.oswego.or.us/police
- **Milwaukie Police Department**, 503-786-7400
- **Multnomah County Sheriff**, 503-988-4300, www.mcso.us
- **North Plains Police Department**, 503-647-2604
- **Oregon City Police Department**, 503-657-4964, www.orcity.org/police
- **Oregon State Police**, 503-378-3720, www.oregon.gov/OSP/
- **Ridgefield Police Department**, 360-887-3556
- **Sandy Police Department**, 503-668-5566
- **Sherwood Police Department**, 503-625-5523, www.sherwoodoregon.gov/police
- **Tigard Police Department**, 503-629-0111
- **Troutdale Police Department**, 503-665-6129
- **Tualatin Police Department**, 503-629-0111, www.tualatinoregon.gov/police
- **Vancouver Police Department**, 360-487-7400, www.cityofvancouver.us/police.asp
- **Washington County Sheriff's Office**, 503-846-2700, www.co.washington.or.us/sheriff/
- **Washougal Police Department**, 360-835-8701
- **West Linn Police Department**, 503-635-0238, www.westlinnoregon.gov/police

RADIO/TV STATIONS

See **Getting Settled** chapter.

RECYCLING

See "Trash and Recycling" below.

RELOCATION

- **American Moving and Storage Association**, www.moving.org
- **Federal Motor Carrier Safety Administration**, 202-358-7028, 888-368-7238, www.protectyourmove.gov
- **MovingScam**, www.movingscam.com
- **Oregon Department of Transportation, Motor Carrier Transportation Division**, 503-378-5849, www.oregon.gov/ODOT/MCT/
- **Washington Utilities and Transportation Commission**, 360-664-1160, 888-333-9882, www.wutc.wa.gov

POST OFFICES

- **USPS**, 800-275-8777, www.usps.com

SCHOOLS

See **Childcare and Education** chapter.

SENIOR CITIZENS, SERVICES FOR

- **Meals-on-Wheels**, 503-736-6325 (Multnomah and Washington counties), 866-788-6325 (Clark County), www.mealsonwheelspeople.org
- **Metropolitan Family Service**, 503-232-0007, www.metfamily.org
- **Oregon Department of Human Services, Aging and People with Disabilities Division**, 503-945-5811, 800-282-8096, www.oregon.gov/DHS/spwpd
- **Southwest Washington Agency on Aging**, 888 637 6060, www.helpingelders.org

TAXES

FEDERAL
- **Internal Revenue Service**, 800-829-3676, tax help line 800-829-1040, www.irs.gov

STATE
- **Oregon Department of Revenue**, 503-378-4988, 800-356-4222, www.oregon.gov/DOR/
- **Washington Department of Revenue**, 800-647-7706, www.dor.wa.gov

COUNTY

- **Clackamas County Department of Assessment and Taxation**, 503-655-8671, www.clackamas.us/at/
- **Clark County Department of Assessment and GIS**, 360-397-2391, www.co.clark.wa.us/assessor/index.html
- **Multnomah County Division of Assessment and Taxation**, 503-988-3326, www.multcotax.org
- **Washington County Department of Assessment and Taxation**, 503-846-8741, www.co.washington.or.us/AssessmentTaxation/

TAXIS

- **Broadway Cab**, 503-333-3333, www.broadwaycab.com
- **Green Cab and Green Shuttle**, 503-234-1414, www.portlandgreencabtaxishuttle.com
- **Radio Cab**, 503-227-1212, www.radiocab.net
- **Union Cab**, 503-222-2222, www.unioncabpdx.com

TOURISM

- **Central Oregon Visitors Association**, 800-800-8334, www.visitcentraloregon.com
- **Columbia River Gorge Visitors Association**, www.crgva.org
- **Eastern Oregon Visitors Association**, 800-332-1843, www.visiteasternoregon.com
- **Oregon Coast Visitors Association**, 888-628-2101, www.visittheoregoncoast.com
- **Oregon's Mt. Hood Territory** (Clackamas County Tourism), 503-665-8490, 800-424-3002, www.mthoodterritory.com
- **Southern Oregon Visitors Association**, www.southernoregon.org
- **Travel Oregon**, 800-547-7842, www.traveloregon.com
- **Travel Portland**, 503-275-8355, 877-678-5263, www.travelportland.com
- **Washington State Tourism Office**, 800-544-1800, www.experiencewa.com
- **Willamette Valley Visitors Association**, 866-548-5018, www.oregonwinecountry.org

TRANSPORTATION

- **Oregon Department of Transportation**, 888-275-6368, www.oregon.gov/ODOT/
- **Portland International Airport**, 503-460-4234, 877-739-4636, www.pdx.com
- **Portland Bureau of Transportation**, 503-823-5185, www.portlandoregon.gov/transportation/
- **Washington Department of Transportation**, 360-705-7000, www.wsdot.wa.gov

ROAD CONDITIONS

- **Oregon Road Conditions**, 511 or 800-977-6368 (503-588-2941 outside Oregon), www.TripCheck.com

- **Washington Road Conditions**, 511 (800-695-7623 outside Washington), www.wsdot.wa.gov/traffic/

BICYCLING
- **Bicycle Transportation Alliance**, 503-226-0676,www.btaoregon.org
- **Shift**, www.shift2bikes.org

PUBLIC TRANSPORTATION
- **Columbia County Rider**, 503-366-0159, www.columbiacountyrider.com
- **C-TRAN**, 360-695-0123, www.c-tran.com
- **Canby Area Transit**, 503-266-4022
- **Sandy Area Metro**, 503-668-3466, www.ci.sandy.or.us/transit
- **South Clackamas Transportation District**, 503-632-7000, www.southclackamastransportation.com
- **South Metro Area Regional Transit (SMART)**, 503-682-7790, www.ridesmart.com
- **TriMet**, 503-238-RIDE, www.trimet.org
- **Yamhill County Transit Area**, 503-474-4910, www.yctransitarea.org

NATIONAL TRAIN AND BUS SERVICE
- **Amtrak**, 800-872-7245, www.amtrak.com
- **Bolt Bus**, 877-265-8277, www.boltbus.com
- **Greyhound**, 800-231-2222, www.greyhound.com

TRASH AND RECYCLING

- **Metro** (Oregon), 503-234-3000, www.oregonmetro.gov/hauler
- **Portland Bureau of Planning and Sustainability**, 503-823-7202, www.portlandonline.com/bps/recycle
- **Waste Connections Inc.** (Clark County), 360-892-5370, www.wcnorthwest.com

UTILITIES

- **Washington Utilities Underground Location Center** (buried utility locations in Washington), 800-424-5555, www.callbeforeyoudig.org/washington
- **Oregon Utility Notification Center** (buried utility locations in Oregon), 800-332-2344, www.digsafelyoregon.com

ELECTRICITY
- **Clark Public Utilities**, 360-992-3000, 800-562-1736, outages 360-992-8000, www.clarkpublicutilities.com
- **Pacific Power**, 888-221-7070, outages 877-LITESOUT, www.pacificpower.net
- **Portland General Electric**, 503-228-6322, 800-542-8818, outages 503-464-7777, www.portlandgeneral.com

NATURAL GAS
- **Northwest Natural**, 503-226-4211, 800-422-4012, gas leaks 800-882-3377, www.nwnatural.com

TELEPHONE
- **Do Not Call List**, 888-382-1222, www.donotcall.gov
- **CenturyLink**, 866-642-0444, 877-348-9007 (technical support)
- **Frontier Communications**, 800-921-8101, www.frontier.com
- **GetHuman**, www.gethuman.com, tips for reaching a live person at hundreds of companies, 800-475-7526, www.qwest.com

CABLE AND SATELLITE TELEVISION
- **Comcast**, 800-934-6489, www.comcast.com
- **DIRECTV**, 855-852-4388, www.directv.com
- **Dish Network**, 855-546-3408, www.dish.com

WATER
- **Portland Water Bureau**, 503-823-7770, www.portlandonline.com/water
- **Tualatin Valley Water District**, 503-642-1511, www.tvwd.org

VETERINARIANS, EMERGENCY CLINICS
- **Banfield, The Pet Hospital**, 866-894-7927, www.banfield.net
- **Columbia River Veterinary Specialists**, 360-694-3007, www.columbiarivervetspcialists.com
- **Dove Lewis** (emergency animal hospitals), 503-228-7281, www.dovelewis.org
- **Emergency Veterinary Clinic of Tualatin**, 503-691-7922, www.evcot.com
- **Northwest Veterinary Specialists**, 503-656-3999, www.northwestvetspecialists.com
- **Tanasbourne Veterinary Emergency**, 503 629 5800, www.tanasbourneveter.com

VOTING
- **Oregon Secretary of State, Elections Division**, 503-986-1518, 866-ORE-VOTE, oregonvotes.org
- **Washington Secretary of State**, 360-902-4180, 800-448-4881, vote.wa.gov

COUNTY ELECTIONS OFFICES
- **Clackamas County Clerk, Elections Division**, 503-655-8510, www.clackamas.us/elections
- **Clark County Elections Office**, 360-397-2345, www.clark.wa.gov/elections/
- **Multnomah County Elections Division**, 503-988-3720, www.mcelections.org
- **Washington County Elections Division**, 503-846-5800, www.co.washington.or.us/cgi/electhom/main.pl

WEATHER

- **National Weather Service**, Portland office, www.wrh.noaa.gov/pqr/
- **Oregon Department of Environmental Quality** (air pollution reports), www.deq.state.or.us/aqi/index.aspx

ZIP CODE INFORMATION

- **USPS**, 800-275-8777, www.usps.com

INDEX

BRYAN GEON moved to Portland for the first time in 1993 as a fresh-faced college grad. He left the area for law school and work, but Portland has always drawn him back, and he has spent over a decade relentlessly exploring and enjoying the city and its surroundings. He has lived in four of the city's five sections and in three different Oregon counties (although not simultaneously). As both a long-time resident and a serial newcomer, Bryan is well qualified to guide other newcomers to the region. He has traveled to all 50 states and more than 50 foreign countries, and he is happy to click his heels together and repeat at least three times that there is no place like Portland. When not practicing law or writing, he enjoys traipsing around the Northwest and spending time with his wife and two sons.

RAIL MAP - WEST

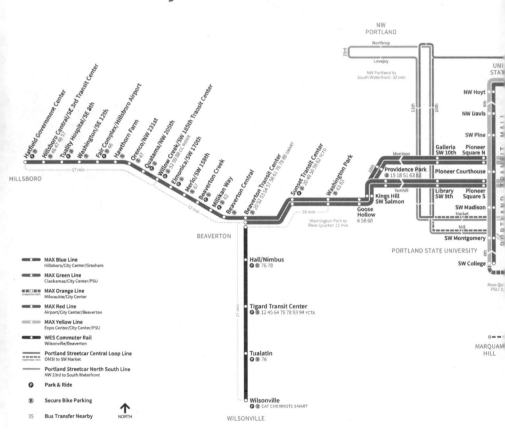

TRIⓂMET
Rail System

MAX Blue Line
Hillsboro/City Center/Gresham

MAX Green Line
Clackamas/City Center/PSU

MAX Orange Line
Milwaukie/City Center

MAX Red Line
Airport/City Center/Beaverton

MAX Yellow Line
Expo Center/City Center/PSU

WES Commuter Rail
Wilsonville/Beaverton

Portland Streetcar Central Loop Line
OMSI to SW Market

Portland Streetcar North South Line
NW 23rd to South Waterfront

Ⓟ **Park & Ride**

Ⓑ **Secure Bike Parking**

35 **Bus Transfer Nearby**

↑ NORTH

RAIL MAP - EAST

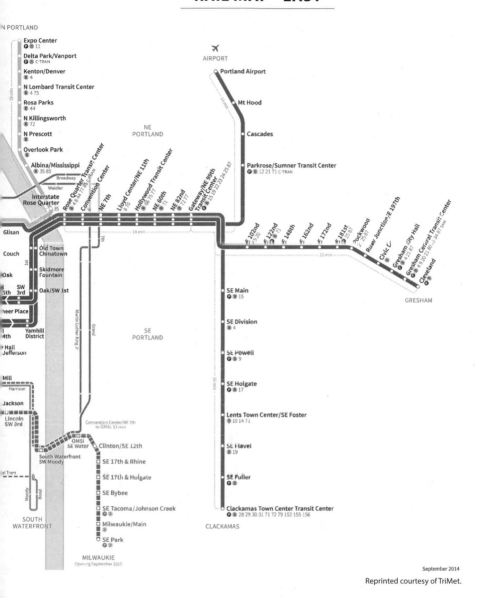

September 2014
Reprinted courtesy of TriMet.

TRIMET RAIL SYSTEM

READER RESPONSE

We would appreciate your comments regarding this second edition of the *Newcomer's Handbook® for Moving to and Living in Portland.* If you've found any mistakes or omissions or if you would just like to express your opinion about the guide, please let us know. We will consider any suggestions for possible inclusion in our next edition, and if we use your comments, we'll send you a free copy of our next edition. Please e-mail us at readerresponse@firstbooks.com, or mail or fax this response form to:

Reader Response Department
First Books
6750 SW Franklin, Suite A
Portland, OR 97223-2542
Fax: 503.968.6779

Comments: _____

_____

_____

_____

_____

_____

_____

_____

_____

Name: _____

Address: _____

_____

_____

Telephone: (   ) _____

Email: _____

6750 SW Franklin, Suite A
Portland, OR 97223-2542
USA
P: 503.968.6777
www.firstbooks.com

RELOCATION RESOURCES

Utilizing an innovative grid and "static" reusable adhesive sticker format, **Furniture Placement and Room Planning Guide...Moving Made Easy** provides a functional and practical solution to all your space planning and furniture placement needs.

MOVING WITH KIDS?

Look into *The Moving Book: A Kids' Survival Guide*. Divided into three sections (before, during, and after the move), it's a handbook, a journal, and a scrapbook all in one. Includes address book, colorful change-of-address cards, and a useful section for parents.

Children's Book of the Month Club "Featured Selection"; American Bookseller's "Pick of the List"; Winner of the Family Channel's "Seal of Quality" Award

And for your younger children, ease their transition with our brand-new title just for them, **Max's Moving Adventure: A Coloring Book for Kids on the Move.** A complete story book featuring activities as well as pictures that children can color; designed to help children cope with the stresses of small or large moves.

NEWCOMERSWEB.COM

Based on the award-winning *Newcomer's Handbooks*, **New-comersWeb.com** offers the highest quality neighborhood and community information in a one-of-a-kind searchable online database. The following areas are covered: Atlanta, Austin, Boston, Chicago, Dallas–Fort Worth, Houston, Los Angeles, Minneapolis–St. Paul, New York City, Portland (Oregon), San Francisco, Seattle, Washington DC, and the USA.

NEWCOMER'S HANDBOOKS®

Regularly revised and updated, these popular guides are now available for Atlanta, Boston, Chicago, China, Dallas–Ft. Worth, Houston, London, Los Angeles, Minneapolis–St. Paul, New York City, Portland, San Francisco Bay Area, Seattle, and Washington DC.

"Invaluable ...highly recommended" – *Library Journal*

If you're coming from another country, don't miss the *Newcomer's Handbook® for Moving to and Living in the USA* by Mike Livingston, termed "a fascinating book for newcomers and residents alike" by the *Chicago Tribune*.